SOURCEBOOK
of POETRY

Books by Al Bryant

Climbing the Heights
Day by Day with C. H. Spurgeon
New Every Morning
Revival Sermon Outlines
Sermon Outlines for Evangelistic Occasions
Sermon Outlines on Bible Characters (Old Testament)
Sermon Outlines on Bible Characters (New Testament)
Sermon Outlines on the Deeper Life
Sermon Outlines on Prayer
Sermon Outlines for Special Occasions
Sermon Outlines for Worship Occasions
Sourcebook of Poetry

SOURCEBOOK
of POETRY

Compiled by

Al Bryant

kregel PUBLICATIONS
Grand Rapids, MI 49501

Cover design: Alan G. Hartman

Library of Congress Cataloging-in-Publication Data
Sourcebook of poetry / compiled by Al Bryant.
    p.   cm.
   Originally published: Grand Rapids : Zondervan Pub. House, [© 1968].
   Includes bibliographical references and indexes.
   1. Poetry, I. Bryant, Al, 1926-
PN6101.B78   1992   808.81—dc 20   92-16102
                                               CIP
  ISBN 0-8254-2192-6 (pbk.)

1 2 3 4 5 6 printing / year 97 96 95 94 93 92

Printed in the United States of America

ACKNOWLEDGMENTS

The publisher wishes to express gratitude to the following who have granted permission for the privilege of including selections in this volume:

Abingdon Press for the "The Secret" and "Sheer Joy" from *Spiritual Hilltops*, by Ralph S. Cushman. Used by permission of Abingdon Press. Also for "I Love a Tree" and "Too Busy?" from *Hilltop Verses and Prayers* by Ralph S. Cushman. Copyright 1945 by Whitmore and Stone (Abingdon Press).

American Sunday School Union for "The Solitary Place" by Carlton Buck.

Bethany Press for "Light After Darkness" and "Grace to Share" by Carlton Buck.

Bobbs-Merrill Co. for "Faith" by James Whitcomb Riley from *The Biographical Edition of the Complete Works of James Whitcomb Riley*, copyright 1913 by James Whitcomb Riley, reprinted by permission of the publishers, The Bobbs-Merrill Company, Inc.

Carlton Buck for "Cheer the New Year," "Above Self," "Christ Supreme," "The Place of Prayer," "Work Motive," "Symphony of the Soul," "Take a Man," "Keep Looking Up," "Resolution," "Discovery," "Forward With Christ."

Century House Americana for "In the Garden of the Lord" by Helen Keller. Used by permission.

Christian Herald for "My Christ Was a Jew" by Virginia Auler. Copyright 1968 by *Christian Herald* and reprinted by permission.

Christianity Today for "Am I Running From You, Jesus?" by Warren Risch. Copyright 1967 by *Christianity Today*; reprinted by special permission.

E. Margaret Clarkson for "Prayer by the Open Book," "Adoration—*A Carol*," "By Faith," "Prayer to the Holy Spirit," "Song," Paradox," "To a Mute Musician," "He Knows," "This I know," "Unafraid," "The Homemaker."

Dohnavur Fellowship and the Society for the Promotion of Christian Knowledge for the following poems by Amy Carmichael: "Comforted," "Deliver Me," "The Last Defile," "Make Me Thy Mountaineer," "Love of God," "A Prayer," "I Promise Thee," "Fret Not Thyself," "Content With Thee," "Have We Not Seen Thy Shining Garment's Hem?" and "A Quiet Mind" from *Toward Jerusalem, Rose from Brier, Wings* and other books.

Helen Eberhard for "Lord, Give Me Life."

Evangelical Publishers for the following poems by Annie Johnson Flint: "The World's Bible," "Behold, I Come!," "The Threefold Work," "In Him," "But God," "He Giveth More," "Passing Through," "What God Hath Promised," "A Thanksgiving," "The Three Prayers," "My Prayer," "Trust," "One Day at a Time," "Why Should I Fear?," "The Red Sea Place in Your Life."

Mary Edith Halladay for "Friendships."

Harcourt, Brace & World, Inc. for a portion of the poem, "The Rock," by T. S. Eliot and for "The Faith of Abraham Lincoln" from *The War Years* by Carl Sandburg. Used by permission.

Harper & Row for the poem, "Because of Thy Great Bounty," by Grace Noll Crowell. From *Poems of Inspiration and Courage*, 1965. Copyright, 1936 by Harper & Brothers; renewed, 1964 by Grace Noll Crowell. Reprinted by permission of Harper & Row, Publishers, Incorporated.

Houghton Mifflin Co. for the following poems by Samuel Longfellow: "The Christian Life," "The Church Universal," "Summer Days Are Come Again." Also for "Work" by Angela Morgan.

Bob Jones, Jr. for the following poems: "Scarred, " "Learning," "Broken Things."

Jane W. Lauber for "Suffering."

Louis Paul Lehman, Jr. for the following poems: "When I Think of His Love," He Takes My Hand," "Dusk for Me."

Macmillan Co. for "L'Envoi" by Rudyard Kipling.

Virgil Markham for "If He Should Come," "Incarnation," "Guard at the Sepulcher," "Wind and Lyre," "Earth Is Enough," "A Prayer," "The Place of Peace," "The Man With the Hoe," by Edwin Markham. Reprinted by permission of Virgil Markham.

Phyllis Michael for the following poems: "God Keeps His Word," "A Little Child Shall Lead Them," "A Girl Is a Girl," "A Boy Is a Boy," "Merry Christmas," "God Knew," "We Thank Thee," "Feet of Clay," "Lord of All," "We," "Our Home," "He Cares," "All Nature Sings," "Prayer Is a Power," "It's Never Easy," "If You Believe," "God's Garden," "Rule On," "How Can I Doubt?" "God's Symphony," "Another New Year," "Until Eternity," "This Is Today," "Across the Great Divide," "Take Thou My Hand," "I Do Not Fear Tomorrow," "God's Gardener," and "God Is."

Moody Press for "Modern Miracle," by William Atherton and for the following poems by Martha Snell Nicholson: "To My Friend," "Until He Come," "My Lord," "A New Year's Blessing," "With Whom Is No Shadow of Turning," "In a Garden," "For the Blind," "If I But Read," "And His Name Shall be Called Wonderful," "The Cup," "Beauty for Ashes," "Looking Backward," "His Plan for Me."

Alice Hansche Mortenson for the following poems: "His Book," "Another Day," "Essence of Tomorrow," "The Beauty of Jesus in Me," "The Threads You Use," "Joy Is Built of Little Things," "Light for the North Room," "It's a Beautiful Day," "As I Go Down the Sunset Hill," "Spring Fever," "To This Lilac-Scented Room," "A Yellow Daffodil," "This Place He Gives," "I Needed the Quiet," "Go Tell Them That Jesus Is Living."

Miss Theo Oxenham for the following poems by John Oxenham: "Judgment Day," "Peter," "A Prayer for Peace," "Your Place," "No East or West," "Be With Me, Lord," "A Prayer," "We Thank Thee."

Oxford University Press for "I Love All Beauteous Things," by Robert Bridges. Reproduced from *The Shorter Poems by Robert Bridges* by permission of The Clarendon Press.

The Presbyterian Outlook for "Rise Up, O Men of God" by Wm. P. Merrill.

Rand McNally & Company for the following poems by Ella Wheeler Wilcox: "Love Thyself Last," "Optimism," "The Winds of Fate," "Faith," "Gethsemane," "Love Ship," "Lifters and Leaners."

Henry Regnery Company for "It Couldn't Be Done" and "The Laymen" by Edgar A. Guest.

Rodeheaver Company for "My God Is Near" by Carlton Buck.

Charles Scribner's Sons for the following: "Courage," "Death," "Companionship," "Not to Be Ministered To," "Be Strong," "Give Us This Day Our Daily Bread," "Speak Out," "This Is My Father's World" by Maltbie Babcock. For: "Jesus, Return," "Home," "Life," "Victoria," "Prayer," "Four Things," "Work," "Hymn of Labor," "Children in the Market Place," "One in Christ," "Peace Hymn of the Republic," "Night-Watch Prayer," "They Who Tred the Path of Labor," "Adoration" by Henry van Dyke. For: "A Ballad of Trees and the Master," and "Prayer at a Wedding" by Sidney Lanier.

Singspiration, Inc. for "Let Us Come Boldly" by E. Margaret Clarkson.

Oswald Smith for "The Saviour Can Solve Every Problem," "Take Thou, O Lord," "A Heart That Weeps," "He Must Do It," "God Is Near," "We Shall Meet Them," "The House of Many Mansions," "Blessed Saviour, Thou Art Mine," "The Master's Call," "In God We Trust," "A Prayer in the Night," "After," "O Lonely Heart," "God's Will," "Trust and Wait."

Joan Suisted for "Who—Me?"

Margaret Widdemer for "The Watcher" and "God and the Strong Ones."

Lon Woodrum for "Upon This Rock," "Transformation," "I Wasn't There," "To Make a Home," "The Harvest and the Tempest," "The Spirit," "The Prodigal," "He Sent Them Out," "Take My Heart," "Even in These Dying Leaves," "Know That I Am God."

The compiler has sought to locate and secure permission for the inclusion of all copyrighted material in this book. If any such acknowledgments have been inadvertently omitted, the compiler and publisher would appreciate receiving the information so that proper credit may be given in future editions.

A WORD FROM THE COMPILER

The purpose of this compilation is to offer the person who enjoys poetry a wide selection of poems from poets past and present in a readable arrangement. It is designed both for those who simply want to sit and bask in the beauty of good poetry, and those who in a public ministry find poems helpful in expressing and emphasizing their thoughts. The philosophy of selection used in this compilation might be summed up in the words of T. S. Eliot:*

"Why, I would ask, is most religious verse so bad and why does so little religious verse reach the highest levels of poetry? Largely, I think, because of a pious insincerity. The capacity for writing poetry is rare; the capacity for religious emotion of the first intensity is rare, and it is to be expected the existence of both capacities in the same individual should be rarer still. People who write devotional verse are usually writing as they *want* to feel, rather than as they do feel."

In selecting the works represented in this anthology, the compiler has attempted to choose with both his heart and his head. Some of the poems are not "great" in the classical sense of the word, but for this poetry-lover, at least, they have "heart-appeal"! Others in their provocative allusions to life have to be read and re-read until a warm glow begins to rise in the heart of the reader as he realizes that these poems are more than lofty phrases, but the authentic heart-cry of one who felt deeply the emotions of real life.

Every effort has been made to find and credit the sources of the poems in this collection. In the front of the book is an exhaustive Acknowledgments section. However, in the event any source has been overlooked or stated in error, the publishers will be happy to insert correction notices in future printings of the book. The collection is the compiler's and undoubtedly all will not agree with his choice in every instance, but it is hoped that the blessing of this anthology of poetry will far outweigh its shortcomings, and that speakers and all who love good poetry will find the reading of this book a heart-warming and meaningful experience.

AL BRYANT

* *After Strange Gods*

CONTENTS

His Plan for Me

When I stand at the judgment seat of Christ
  And He shows me His plan for me,
The plan of my life as it might have been
  Had He had His way, and I see.
How I blocked Him here, and I checked Him there,
  And I would not yield my will,
Will there be grief in my Saviour's eyes,
  Grief, though He loves me still?
He would have made me rich, and I stand there poor,
  Stripped of all but His grace,
While memory runs like a hunted thing
  Down the paths I cannot retrace.
Then my desolate heart will well-nigh break
  With the tears that I cannot shed;
I shall cover my face with my empty hands,
  I shall bow my uncrowned head.
Lord, of the years that are left me,
  I give them to Thy hand:
Take me and break me, mould me to
  The pattern Thou hast planned.

— *Martha Snell Nicholson*

WHAT THEN?

When the great busy plants of our cities
   Have turned out their last finished work;
When our merchants have sold their last order,
   And dismissed the last tired clerk;
When our banks have raked in their last dollar,
   And paid out their last dividend;
When the Judge of the earth shall say, "Closed for the night,"
   And calls for a balance — *what then?*

When the choir has sung its last anthem,
   And the preacher has made his last prayer;
When the people have heard the last sermon,
   And the sound has died out on the air;
When the Bible lies closed on the pulpit,
   And the pews are all emptied of men,
And each one stands facing his record,
   And the Books will be opened — *what then?*

When the actors have played their last drama,
   An the mimic has made his last fun;
When the film has flashed its last picture,
   And the billboards displayed their last run;
When the crowds seeking pleasure have vanished,
   And gone out in the darkness again;
When the trumpet of ages is sounded,
   And they stand up in judgment — *what then?*

When the bugle's call sinks into silence,
   And the long marching columns stand still;
When the captain repeats this last order,
   And they've captured the last fort and hill;
When the flag has been hauled from the masthead,
   And from far fields all men are called in;
When each man who rejected the Saviour
   Is asked for a reason — *what then?*

— *Author Unknown*

THE CRITIC

A little seed lay on the ground,
And soon began to sprout;
"Now, which of all the flowers around,"
It mused, "shall I come out?
The lily's face is fair and proud,
But just a trifle cold;
The rose, I think, is rather loud,
And then, its fashion's old.
The violet is all very well,
But not a flower I'd choose;
Nor yet the Canterbury bell —
I never cared for blues."
And so it criticized each flower,
This supercilious seed,
Until it woke one summer morn,
And found itself — a weed.

— *Author Unknown*

HAVE YOU FORGOTTEN GOD?

In the glare of earthly pleasure,
In the fight for earthly treasure,
'Mid your blessing without measure —
    Have you forgotten God?

While His daily grace receiving,
Are you still His Spirit grieving
By a heart that's unbelieving —
    Have you forgotten God?

While His bounty you're accepting,
Are you His commands neglecting
And His call to you rejecting —
    Have you forgotten God?

— *Author Unknown*

TO MY FRIEND

I spoke to you about your soul today.
Perhaps you wished that I would go away
And say no more and let you be. But, oh,
My cherished friend, if you could only know
The longing in my heart for you, the dread
Of looking forward, after you are dead,
Unto that certain day when you must stand
Before the throne of Christ! Works of your hand,
Fruits of your heart, will not avail, for He
Will ask you, "What did you do with Me?"
Dear friend of mine, there is no other way
Except through Him, whom you deny today.
How could I bear it, if in your despair
And bitter grief, you cried, "Did she not care
Enough for me to speak? to point the way?
To save me from this anguish and dismay?"
My heart is bleeding, thinking of your woe,
Your terror, and your helplessness and so
I spoke to you about your soul today.
I could not leave you, could not go away.

— *Martha Snell Nicholson*

THE OVER-CONFIDENT MAN

Believe as I believe, no more, no less;
That I am right, and no one else, confess;
Feel as I feel, think only as I think;
Eat what I eat, and drink but what I drink;
Look as I look, do always as I do;
And then, and only then, I'll fellowship with you.

That I am right, and always right, I know,
Because my own convictions tell me so;
And to be right is simply this — to be
Entirely and in all respects like me;
To deviate a hair's breadth, or begin
To question, or to doubt, or hesitate, is sin.

I reverence the Bible if it be
Translated first, and then explained by me;
By churchly laws and customs I abide
If they with my opinion coincide;
All creeds and doctrines I concede divine,
Excepting those, of course, which disagree with mine.

Let sink the drowning, if he will not swim
Upon the plank that I throw out to him;
Let starve the hungry, if he will not eat
My kind and quantity of bread and meat;
Let freeze the naked, if he will not be
Clothed in such garments as are made for me.

'Twere better that the sick should die than live
Unless they take the medicine I give;
'Twere better sinners perish than refuse
To be conformed to my peculiar views;
'Twere better that the world stand still, than move
In any other way than that which I approve.

— Author Unknown

ᘓ

KINDNESS

Be swift, dear heart, in saying
    The kindly word;
When ears are sealed thy passionate
      pleading
    Will not be heard.

Be swift, dear heart, in doing
    The gracious deed;
Lest soon, they whom thou hold
      dearest
    Be past thy need.

— Author Unknown

A Psalm of Life

Tell me not in mournful numbers,
"Life is but an empty dream!"
For the soul is dead that slumbers,
And things are not what they seem.

Life is real! Life is earnest
And the grave is not its goal;
"Dust thou art, to dust returnest,"
Was not written of the soul.

Not enjoyment, and not sorrow,
Is our destined end or way;
But to act, that each to-morrow
Finds us farther than to-day.

Art is long, and Time is fleeting,
And our hearts, tho' stout and brave,
Still, like muffled drums, are beating
Funeral marches to the grave.

In the world's broad field of battle,
In the bivouac of Life,
Be not like dumb, driven cattle!
Be a hero in the strife!

Trust no future, however pleasant!
Let the dead Past bury its dead!
Act, — act in the living Present!
Heart within and God o'erhead!

Lives of great men all remind us
We can make our lives sublime,
And, departing, leave behind us
Footprints on the sands of time;

Footprints, that perhaps another,
Sailing o'er life's solemn main,
A forlorn and shipwrecked brother,
Seeing, shall take heart again.

Let us, then, be up and doing,
With a heart for any fate;
Still achieving, still pursuing,
Learn to labor and to wait.

— *Henry Wadsworth Longfellow*

Consolation

The day is cold, and dark and dreary;
It rains, and the wind is never weary;
The vine still clings to the mouldering
    wall;
But at every gust the dead leaves fall,
    And the day is dark and dreary.

My life is cold and dark, and dreary;
It rains, and the wind is never weary;
My thoughts still cling to the moulder-
    ing Past,
But the hopes of youth fall thick in the
    blast,
    And the days are dark and dreary.

Be still, sad heart! and cease repining;
Behind the clouds is the sun still shin-
    ing;
Thy fate is the common fate of all,
Into each life some rain must fall,
    Some days must be dark and dreary.

— *Henry Wadsworth Longfellow*

ᢍᣅ

The Watchful Servant

Ye servants of the Lord,
Each in his office wait,
Observant of His Heavenly Word,
And watchful at His gate.

Let all your lamps be bright,
And trim the golden flame;
Gird up your loins, as in His sight,
For awful is His Name.

Watch: 'tis your Lord's command,
And while we speak He's near;
Mark the first signal of His hand,
And ready all appear.

Oh, happy servant he,
In such a posture found!
He shall his Lord with rapture see,
And be with honor crowned.

— *Philip Doddridge*

DAILY STRENGTH

"As thy day thy strength shall be!"
This should be enough for thee;
He who knows thy frame will spare
Burdens more than thou canst bear.

When thy days are veiled in night,
Christ shall give thee heavenly light;
Seem they wearisome and long,
Yet in Him thou shalt be strong.

Cold and wintry though they prove,
Thine the sunshine of His love;
Or with fervid heat oppressed,
In His shadow thou shalt rest.

When thy days on earth are past,
Christ shall call thee home at last,
His redeeming love to praise,
Who hath strengthened all thy days.

— *Frances Ridley Havergal*

SHADOWS

The sun burns bright in the azure sky
And sheds its glory from heaven to earth,
It gilds with lustre the clouds on high
And quickens the trees into life's new birth;
Wherever it shines, above or below,
Both light and life from its radiance flow.

But beneath the clouds the thick shadows lie,
And deep is the shade 'neath the leaves of green,
For the light that is bright in the upper sky
Is turned to dark where things lie between;
And so the light which God's eyes doth scan
Is deepest dark to the eyes of man.

Yet the shadows are good as the light is good,
For each comes forth from the heavenly will,
And light and dark have for ever stood
For the love of God which His ways fulfil;
And blest is the man who deems dark and light
As wholly and changelessly good and right.

No clouds or trees ever alter the light,
However deep their dark shadows are,
Yea, the dark of their shadows makes more bright
The light which comes from the light afar; —
And oh, how cool are the shadows sweet
When the soul is aflame with the noon-tide heat!

— *Henry W. Frost*

If I Had Known

I might have said a word of cheer
  Before I let him go.
His wistful eyes — they haunt me yet!
  But how could I foreknow
That slighted chance would be the last
  To me in mercy given?
Remorseful yearnings cannot send
  That word from earth to heaven.

I might have looked the love I felt;
  My brother had sore need
Of that for which, all shy and proud,
  He had not speech to plead.
But self is near, and self is strong,
  And I was blind that day!
He sought within my careless eyes
  And went athirst away.

O smile and clasp and word withheld!
  O brother-heart, now stilled!
Dear life, forever out of reach,
  I might have warmed and filled.
Talents misused and treasures lost
  O'er which I mourn in vain,
A waste as barren to my tears,
  As desert sands to rain!

Ah, friends! whose eyes today may hold
  Converse with living eyes,
Whose touch or tone or smile may thrill
  Sad souls with sweet surprise;
Be instant, like your Lord, with love
  And constant as His grace,
With dew and light and manna fall —
  The night comes on apace.

— *Mary Virginia Terhune*

Love Thyself Last

Love thyself last; look near, behold thy duty
  To those who walk beside thee down life's road;
Make glad their days by little acts of beauty,
  And help them bear the burden of earth's load.

Love thyself last; look far and find the stranger
  Who staggers 'neath his sin and his despair;
Go, lend a hand and lead him out of danger
  To heights where he may see the world is fair.

Love thyself last; the vastnesses above thee
  Are filled with spirit forces, strong and pure;
And fervently these faithful friends shall love thee,
  Keep thy watch over others and endure.

Love thyself last; and thou shalt grow in spirit
  To see, to hear, to know and understand;
The message of the stars, lo, thou shalt hear it,
  And all God's joys shall be at thy command.

— *Ella Wheeler Wilcox*

BUILDING THE BRIDGE FOR HIM

An old man, traveling a lone highway,
Came at the evening cold and gray,
To a chasm deep and wide.

The old man crossed in the twilight dim,
For the sullen stream held no fears for him,
But he turned when he reached the other side,
And builded a bridge to span the tide.

"Old man," cried a fellow pilgrim near,
"You are wasting your strength with building here;
Your journey will end with the ending day,
And you never again will pass this way.

"You have crossed the chasm deep and wide.
Why build you a bridge at eventide?"
And the builder raised his old gray head:
"Good friend, on the path I have come," he said,
"There followeth after me today
A youth whose feet will pass this way.

"This stream, which has been as naught to me,
To that fair-haired boy may a pitfall be;
He, too, must cross in the twilight dim —
Good friend, I am building this bridge for him."

— W. A. Dromgoole

TOMORROW

Lord, what am I, that, with unceasing care,
Thou didst seek after me, that thou didst wait,
Wet with unhealthy dews, before my gate,
And pass the gloomy nights of winter there?
O strange delusion, that I did not greet
Thy blest approach, and oh, to heaven how lost,
If my ingratitude's unkindly frost
Has chilled the bleeding wounds upon thy feet,
How oft my guardian angel gently cried,
"Soul, from thy casement look and thou shalt see
How he persists to knock and wait for thee!"
And oh! how often to that voice of sorrow,
"Tomorrow we will open," I replied,
And when the morrow came I answered still, "Tomorrow."

— Lope de Vega

"Where There's Drink"

Write it on the schoolhouse door,
Write it on the office floor,
Write it once, and write it o'er,
Write it, and then underscore —
  "Where there's drink there's danger!"

Write it on the common way,
Write it where the children play,
Write it where a man breaks the sod,
Write it in the name of God —
  "Where there's drink there's danger!"

Write it high, write it low,
Write it quick, write it slow,
Write it here, write it there,
Write it yonder, everywhere —
  "Where there's drink there's danger!"

                    — *Author Unknown*

From The Ballad of Reading Gaol

I know not whether Laws be right,
  Or whether Laws be wrong;
All that we know who lie in jail
  Is that the wall is strong;
And that each day is like a year,
  A year whose days are long.

But this I know, that every Law
  That men have made for Man,
Since first Man took his brother's life,
  And this sad world began,
But straws the wheat and saves the
    chaff
  With a most evil fan.

This too I know — and wise it were
  If each could know the same —
That every prison that men build
  Is built with bricks of shame,
And bound with bars lest Christ
    should see
  How men their brothers maim.

                    — *Oscar Wilde*

Noah's Carpenters

Many hundred years ago
  They ventured to remark
That Noah had some carpenters
  To help him build the Ark.
But sad to say on that last day
  When Noah entered in,
Those carpenters were left outside
  And perished in their sin.

How sad to think they may have
    helped
  To build the Ark so great,
Yet still they heeded not God's Word
  And awful was their fate.
Today the same sad fate exists
  Among the sons of men,
They helped to build the so-called
    Church
  Who are not born again.

They stay behind for sacrament,
  They work, they sing, they pray;
Yet never have accepted Christ,
  The Life, the Truth, the Way.
Another judgment day will come,
  As sure as came the flood,
And only those will be secure
  Who shelter 'neath Christ's Blood.

                    — *Author Unknown*

Contentment

Oh, what a happy soul am I!
Although I cannot see,
I am resolved that in this world
Contented I will be.

How many blessings I enjoy,
That other people don't!
To weep and sigh because I'm blind
I cannot and I won't.

                    — *Fanny J. Crosby*

Trust God

How gentle God's commands!
How kind His precepts are!
Come, cast your burdens on the Lord,
And trust His constant care.

Beneath His watchful eye
His saints securely dwell;
That hand which bears all nature up
Shall guard His children well.

Why should this anxious load
Press down your weary mind?
Haste to your heavenly Father's throne,
And sweet refreshment find.

His goodness stands approved,
Unchanged from day to day:
I'll drop my burden at His feet,
And bear a song away.

— *Philip Doddridge*

Kindness

Do you wish the world were better?
Let me tell you what to do:
Set a watch upon your actions,
Keep them always straight and true.
Rid your minds of selfish motives.
Let your thought be clean and high;
You can make a little Eden
Of the sphere you occupy.

Do you wish the world were happy?
Then remember, day by day,
Just to scatter seeds of kindness
As you pass along the way;
For the pleasures of the many
May be ofttimes traced to one,
As the hand that plants the acorn
Shelters armies from the sun.

— *Author Unknown*

The Tongue

"The boneless tongue, so small and weak,
Can crush and kill," declared the Greek.
"The tongue destroys a greater horde,"
The Turk asserts, "than does the sword."
The Persian proverb wisely saith,
"A lengthy tongue — an early death."
Or sometimes takes this form instead:
"Don't let your tongue cut off your head."
"The tongue can speak a word whose speed,"
Says the Chinese, "outstrips the steed."
While Arab sage doth this impart:
"The tongue's great storehouse is the heart."
From Hebrew wit the maxim sprung,
"Though feet should slip, ne'er let the tongue."
The sacred writer crowns the whole,
"Who keeps his tongue doth keep his soul."

— *Philip Burrows Strong*

COMMITMENT

Commit thou all thy griefs
And ways into His hands,
To His sure trust and tender care
Who earth and heaven commands;

Who points the clouds their course,
Whom winds and seas obey,
He shall direct thy wandering feet,
He shall prepare thy way.

No profit canst thou gain
By self-consuming care;
To Him commend thy cause; His ear
Attends the softest prayer.

Thy everlasting truth,
Father, Thy ceaseless love,
Sees all Thy children's wants, and
    knows
What best for each will prove.

Thou everywhere hast sway,
And all things serve Thy might;
Thy every act pure blessing is,
Thy path unsullied light.

— *Paul Gerhardt*
Translated by John Wesley

SACRIFICE

Summer lilies, sweet and rare,
How they perfume all the air,
White as pure, and pure as white,
Blooming through the day and night;
Lo, they stand in garden bed
Midst tall roses, crimson red.

Tell me, lilies, are you white
Since the roses weep at night,
Letting fall their tears of blood
Round your roots, a crimson flood;
Are you sweet and are you pure
Since their weeping doth endure?

Weep, red roses, weep and weep,
Through the nights your vigils keep,
If your watching, weeping long
Will the sweet and pure prolong;
Red for white and white for red —
This is as the Master said.

Roses red and lilies white,
Thro' the day and thro' the night,
Blooming ever side by side,
One by the other beautified;
White from red — the red the sign
Of that death which was divine!

—*Henry W. Frost*

❧

COURAGE

Be strong!
We are not here to play, to dream, to drift.
We have hard work to do, and loads to lift.
Shun not the struggle — face it; 'tis God's gift.

Be strong!
Say not the days are evil. Who's to blame?
And fold the hand and acquiesce — oh, shame!
Stand up, speak out, and bravely, in God's name.

Be strong!
It matters not how deep intrenched the wrong,
How hard the battle goes, the day how long;
Faint not — fight on! To-morrow comes the song.
—*Malthie D. Babcock*

Rise!

Christian, rise, and act thy creed,
Let thy prayer be in thy deed;
Seek the right, perform the true,
Raise thy work and life anew.

Hearts around thee sink with care;
Thou canst help their load to bear,
Thou canst bring inspiring light,
Arm their faltering wills to fight.

Let thine alms be hope and joy,
And thy worship God's employ;
Give Him thanks in humble zeal,
Learning all His will to feel.

Come then, Law divine, and reign,
Freest faith assailed in vain,
Perfect love bereft of fear,
Born in heaven and radiant here.

— *F. A. Rollo Russell*

Misunderstanding

I said in haste, The sun shines not to-day!
For I had gazed at the great, vaulted sky
Where God had set the lights to cheer the eye
And had seen naught but clouds, hence I did say
The light had failed; — yet back of cloudy lining
The sun, through all the day, was brightly shining!

I said in haste, God loves me not to-day!
For I had prayed that all my life might be
Hedged fast about, and so from sorrow free;
Hence, when dark sorrow came, I shrank away
And thought God's love had ceased; — yet Love's denying
Costs more than granting, when sad souls are crying!

— *Henry W. Frost*

Manhattan

Here in the furnace City, in the humid air they faint,
　　God's pallid poor, His people, with scarcely space for breath;
So foul their teeming houses, so full of shame and taint,
　　They cannot crowd within them for the frightful fear of Death.

Yet somewhere, Lord, Thine open seas are singing with the rain,
　　And somewhere underneath Thy stars the cool waves crash and beat;
Why is it here, and only here, are huddled Death and Pain,
　　And here the form of Horror stalks, a menace in the street!

The burning flagstones gleam like glass at morning and at noon,
　　The giant walls shut out the breeze — if any breeze should blow;
And high above the smothering town at midnight hangs the moon,
　　A red medallion in the sky, a monster cameo.

— *Charles Hanson Towne*

THE BOOK OF BOOKS

Within this ample volume lies
The mystery of mysteries.
Happiest they of human race
To whom their God has given grace
To read, to fear, to hope, to pray,
To lift the latch, to force the way;
But better had they ne'er been born
That read to doubt, or read to scorn.

— *Sir Walter Scott*

THE BOOK OF GOD

Thy thoughts are here, my God,
    Expressed in words divine,
The utterance of heavenly lips
    In every sacred line.

Across the ages they
    Have reached us from afar,
Than the bright gold more golden
        they,
    Purer than purest star.

More durable they stand
    Than the eternal hills;
Far sweeter and more musical
    Than music of earth's rills.

Fairer in their fair hues
    Than the fresh flowers of earth,
More fragrant than the fragrant climes
    Where odors have their birth.

Each word of thine a gem
    From the celestial mines,
A sunbeam from that holy heaven
    Where holy sunlight shines.

Thine, thine, this book, though given
    In man's poor human speech,
Telling of things unseen, unheard,
    Beyond all human reach.

No strength it craves or needs
    From this world's wisdom vain;
No filling up from human wells,
    Or sublunary rain.

No light from sons of time,
    Nor brilliance from its gold;
It sparkles with its own glad light,
    As in the ages old.

A thousand hammers keen,
    With fiery force and strain,
Brought down on it in rage and hate,
    Have struck this gem in vain.

Against this sea-wept rock
    Ten thousand storms their will
Of foam and rage have wildly spent;
    It lifts its calm face still.

It standeth and will stand,
    Without or change or age,
The word of majesty and light,
    The church's heritage.

— *Horatius Bonar*

A BIT OF THE BOOK

A bit of the Book in the morning,
    To order my onward way.
A bit of the Book in the evening,
    To hallow the end of the day.

— *Margaret E. Sangster*

20

HIS BOOK

If I should live a thousand years
And search it every day,
The precious Word of God would still
Shed light upon my way.

Exhaustless store of treasured gems
Within this Book I hold;
And as I read, it comes alive
New treasures to unfold.

The Author is my dearest Friend,
So we oft commune awhile —
Sweet foretaste of the joy to come
Beyond that farthest mile.

Should every other earthly thing
Be severed from my grasp,
I pray that I may every hold
My Bible till the last.

But should the printed page dissolve,
Or failing sight grow dim,
Remembering, I'll oft repeat
Sweet promises from Him.

And when someday He calls me home
And I at last can look
Upon His face, I'll want to kneel
And thank Him for — His Book!

— *Alice Hansche Mortenson*

ADAM'S COMPLAINT

"The Lord my Maker, forming me of clay,
By his own breath the breath of life conveyed;
O'er all the bright new world he gave me sway, —
A little lower than the angels made.
But Satan, using for his guile
The crafty serpent's cruel wile,
Deceived me by the tree;
And severed me from God and grace,
And wrought me death, and all my race,
As long as time shall be.
O Lover of the sons of men,
Forgive, and call me back again!

"In that same hour I lost the glorious stole
Of innocence, that God's own hands had made;
And now, the tempter poisoning all my soul,
I sit in fig-leaves and in skins arrayed;
I sit condemned, distressed, forsaken;
Must till the ground, whence I was taken,
By labor's daily sweat.
But thou, that shalt hereafter come,
The offspring of a virgin womb,
Have pity on me yet!
Oh, turn on me those gracious eyes,
And call me back to Paradise!

"O glorious Paradise! O lovely clime!
O God-built mansions! Joy of every saint!
Happy remembrance to all coming time!
Whisper, with all thy leaves, in cadence faint,
One prayer to him who made them all,
One prayer for Adam in his fall!—
That he, who formed thy gates of yore,
Would bid those gates unfold once more
That I had closed by sin:
And let me taste that holy tree
That giveth immortality
To them that dwell therein!
Or have I fallen so far from grace
That mercy hath for me no place?"

Adam sat right against the eastern gate,
By many a storm of sad remembrance tost:
"O me! so ruined by the serpent's hate!
O me! so glorious once, and now so lost!
So mad that bitter lot to choose!
Beguiled of all I had to lose!
Must I then, gladness of my eyes,—
Must I then leave thee, Paradise,
And as an exile go?
And must I never cease to grieve
How once my God, at cool of eve,
Came down to walk below?
O Merciful! on thee I call:
O Pitiful! forgive my fall!"

— Theophanes
Translated by John Mason Neale

ᢙᣝ

THE BIBLE

Lamp of our feet, whereby we trace
    Our path when wont to stray;
Steam from the fount of heavenly
        grace,
    Brook by the traveler's way;

Bread of our souls, whereon we feed,
    True manna from on high,
Our guide and chart, wherein we read
    Of realms beyond the sky;

Word of the everlasting God,
    Will of His glorious Son;
Without Thee how could earth be trod,
    Or heaven itself be won?

Lord, grant us all aright to learn
    The wisdom it imparts;
And to its heavenly teaching turn,
    With simple, childlike hearts.

— Bernard Barton

SWEET OLD CHAPTERS

Whenever the heart is aching
  And the days are thick with care;
Whenever the worry and trouble
  Seem more than my soul can bear;
Whenever it's dark and dreary,
  And the way seems rough before,
Turn to one of the sweet old chapters
  Where the dew and the sun are
    sweet,
And the blossoms of peace and comfort
  Seem springing around the feet.

Whenever the bitter battle
  Is more than I've strength to fight,
Oh, one of the sweet old chapters
  Will soon give back my might;
And I'll rise and lift the banner,
  And go forth brave again
For my part in the daily struggle
  Of men in a world of men.
One of the sweet old chapters,
  Read it, and feel its gleam,
As you bask in its tender beauty
And walk in its lovely dream.

Never a downcast spirit
  That cannot rise and go
When the words of a sweet old chapter
  From the Holy Scriptures flow;
And the glory of God's great Heaven,
  And the streets of the Heavenly
    way,
Stretch forth thro' the dreary shadows
  That cloaked you and kept you gray.
The voice of a tender message,
  The word of a higher trust,
How the sound of a sweet old chapter
  Can lift us from the dust.

Whenever the feet are aching
  That have marched their many
    miles,
Thro' the light of a sweet old chapter
  A valley of beauty smiles;
And the flowers are blooming gaily,
And the birds sing in the trees,
And you walk in the peaceful pastures
  With the green grass to your knees.
The sunshine follows the shadows,
  And the sweet hills lift their crest,
And each word of the sweet old chap-
    ter
  Is a sound that lulls to rest.

I feel the touch of that healing,
  That boon and that gift of love,
When I read in a sweet old chapter
  Of the mansions that shine above;
And my shoulders rise from their bur-
    den
  And my heart forgets its care,
For the dews of God are about me,
  And the sweet and pleasant air.
The words of a sweet old chapter,
  Ah, wonderful cure are they,
For the pain of the weary spirit
  And the cares that infest the day!

— Baltimore Sun

ﻌ

LORD, KEEP US STEADFAST IN THY WORD

Lord, keep us steadfast in Thy Word;
Curb those who fain by craft or sword
Would wrest the Kingdom from Thy
    Son;
And set at naught all He hath done.

Lord Jesus Christ, Thy power make
    known,
For Thou art Lord of lords alone;
Defend Thy Christendom, that we
May evermore sing praise to Thee.

O Comforter of priceless worth,
Send peace and unity on earth;
Support us in our final strife,
And lead us out of death to life.

— Martin Luther

THE BIBLE

Study it carefully,
Think of it prayerfully,
Till in thy heart its precepts dwell.
Slight not its history,
Ponder its mystery;
None can e'er prize it too fondly or
well.

Accept the glad tidings,
The warnings and chidings
Found in this volume of heavenly lore.
With faith that's unfailing
And love all-prevailing,
Trust in its promises of life evermore.

May this message of love
From the Father above
Unto all nations and kindreds be
given;
Till the ransomed shall raise
Joyous anthems of praise,
Hallelujahs in earth and in heaven.

— *Author Unknown*

THE SACRED PAGE

Upon the Gospel's sacred page
The gathered beams of ages shine;
And, as it hastens, every age
But makes its brightness more
divine.

On mightier wing, in loftier flight,
From year to year does knowledge
soar;
And, as it soars, the Gospel light
Becomes effulgent more and more.

More glorious still, as centuries roll,
New regions blest, new powers un-
furled,
Expanding with the expanding soul,
Its radiance shall o'erflow the world:

Flow to restore, but not destroy;
As when the cloudless lamp of day
Pours out its floods of light and joy,
And sweeps the lingering mists
away.

— *John Bowring*

THE WONDERFUL WORD

Oh, wonderful, wonderful Word of the Lord!
True wisdom its pages unfold,
And though we may read them a thousand times o'er
They never, no never, grow old!
Each line has a treasure, each promise a pearl,
That all if they will may secure;
And we know that when time and the world pass away
God's Word shall forever endure.

Oh, wonderful, wonderful Word of the Lord!
Our only salvation is there;
It carries conviction down deep in the heart,
And shows us ourselves as we are.
It tells of a Saviour, and points to the Cross,
Where pardon we now may secure;
And we know that when time and the world pass away
God's Word shall forever endure.

— *John Newton*

My Old Bible

Though the cover is worn,
And the pages are torn,
And though places bear traces of tears,
Yet more precious than gold
Is this Book worn and old,
That can shatter and scatter my fears.

This old Book is my guide,
'Tis a friend by my side,
It will lighten and brighten my way;
And each promise I find
Soothes and gladdens the mind,
As I read it and heed it each day.

To this Book I will cling,
Of its worth I will sing,
Tho' great losses and crosses be mine;
For I cannot despair,
Though surrounded by care,
While possessing this blessing divine.

— *Author Unknown*

ᕗ

Holy Bible, Book Divine

Holy Bible, book divine,
Precious treasure, thou art mine;
Mine to tell me whence I came,
Mine to teach me what I am.

Mine to chide me when I rove,
Mine to show a Saviour's love;
Mine art thou to guide my feet,
Mine to judge, condemn, acquit.

Mine to comfort in distress,
If the Holy Spirit bless;
Mine to show by living faith
Man can triumph over death.

Mine to tell of joys to come,
And the rebel sinner's doom;
Holy Bible, book divine,
Precious treasure, thou art mine.

— *John Burton*

My Bible and I

We've traveled together
My Bible and I,
Through all kinds of weather,
With smile and with sigh.
And all through the darkness
Of error and wrong,
I've found it a solace,
A prayer, and a song.
So now shall they part us,
My Bible and I?
Shall isms or schisms,
Or critics who try?
Ah, no, through life's journey,
Until my last sigh,
We'll travel together,
My Bible and I!

— *Author Unknown*

ᕗ

O Blessed Word

Eternal life God's Word proclaims
To lost and dying men;
By it alone we know the Lord
Unseen by mortal ken.

God's grace is in His Holy Word;
We need it every day;
In all our conflicts this the sword
Our every foe to slay.

By this same Word we know our work,
And how it should be done;
How we should live, and how through
grace
The promised crown is won.

O blessed Word, O gracious Word,
We love it more and more;
O may it be our strength and sword,
Till earthly strife is o'er.

— *Author Unknown*

MY BIBLE AND I

I have a companion of infinite worth;
We travel together through this dreary earth.
  From pilgrimage here to a home in the sky.
  We're traveling together, my Bible and I.

I have a companion, a wonderful guide!
A solace and comfort whatever betide;
  A friend never failing when others pass by —
  Oh, blessed communion — my Bible and I!

I have a companion, 'tis God's Holy Word,
Revealing from heaven the mind of my Lord;
  My rock and my refuge when danger is nigh —
  We've blessings eternal, my Bible and I.

I have a companion, a heavenly light,
A pillar by day and a fire by night;
  A lamp from the cradle until I shall die —
  What blessed communion — my Bible and I!

I have a companion, a dear faithful friend,
A union of blessing that never shall end,
  Till Jesus returns with His saints from on high,
  We'll travel together, my Bible and I!

O light of my pathway! Thou lamp to my feet!
O manna from heaven! So precious and sweet.
  For thee do I live, and for thee would I die,
  Forever and ever, my Bible and I.

                              — M. H. Knobloch

THE OLD, OLD BIBLE

I opened the old, old Bible
  And looked at a page of Psalms;
Till the wintry sea of my trouble,
  Was soothed as by summer calms.

For the words that have helped so
    many,
  And that ages have made more dear,
Seemed new in their power to comfort,
  And they brought me their word of
    cheer.

  — Marianne Farmingham

THE BIBLE

We search the world for truth. We
    cull
The good, the true, the beautiful,
From graven stone and written scroll,
And all old flower fields of the soul;
And, weary seekers of the best,
We come back laden from our quest,
To find that all the sages said
Is in the Book our mothers read.

  — John Greenleaf Whittier

THY WORD

Thy Word is like a garden, Lord,
  With flowers bright and fair;
And every one who seeks may pluck
  A lovely cluster there.
Thy Word is like a deep, deep mine;
  And jewels rich and rare
Are hidden in the mighty depths
  For every searcher there.

Thy Word is like a starry host,
  A thousand rays of light
Are seen to guide the traveler,
  And make his pathway bright.
Thy Word is like an armory,
  Where soldiers may repair,
And find for life's long battle-day
  All needful weapons there.

Oh, may I love Thy precious Word;
  May I explore the mine;
May I its fragrant flowers glean;
  May light upon me shine.
Oh, may I find my armor there;
  Thy Word my trusty sword,
I'll learn to fight with every foe
  The battle of the Lord.

— *Author Unknown*

"THE WORLD'S BIBLE"

Christ has no hands but our hands
  To do His work today;
He has no feet but our feet
  To lead men in His way;
He has no tongue but our tongue
  To tell men how He died;
He has no help but our help
  To bring them to His side.

We are the only Bible
  The careless world will read;
We are the sinners' gospel,
  We are the scoffer's creed;
We are the Lord's last message,
  Given in deed and word;
What if the type is crooked?
  What if the print is blurred?

What if our hands are busy
  With other work than His?
What if our feet are walking
  Where sin's allurement is?
What if our tongues are speaking
  Of things His lips would spurn?
How can we hope to help Him
  And hasten His return?

— *Annie Johnson Flint*

GOD'S WORD

I paused last eve beside the blacksmith's door,
  And heard the anvil ring, the vesper's chime,
And looking in I saw upon the floor
  Old hammers, worn with beating years of time.
"How many anvils have you had?" said I,
  "To wear and batter all these hammers so?"
"Just one," he answered. Then with twinkling eye:
  "The anvil wears the hammers out, you know."
And so, I thought, the anvil of God's Word
  For ages skeptics' blows have beat upon,
But though the noise of falling blows was heard
  The anvil is unchanged; the hammers gone.

— *John Clifford*

From THE ROCK

In the land of lobelias and tennis flannels
Where My Word is unspoken,
The rabbit shall burrow and the thorn revisit,
The nettle shall flourish on the gravel court,
And the wind shall say: "Here were decent godless people:
Their only monument the asphalt road
And a thousand lost golf balls."

—T. S. *Eliot*

DWELL IN THE DEPTHS

How fast they fly — these passing years,
With all their joys, and pains, and tears;
How much these years are like the sea,
Now calm, now rough, now rollingly —
    With ebb and flood each day.

There is, beneath what seems to be
Naught but a troubled, restless sea,
An undisturbed and peaceful calm,
So quiet, and so different from
    The surface which we see.

Beneath the surface of all time
There is a purpose, vast, sublime;
A purpose unperturbed, and still,
Unchanged as God's own sovereign will,
    By time's vicissitudes.

In part that purpose we may know,
But not thro' man's vain tho't or show;
The things from mortal eyes concealed
Are unto ransomed souls revealed,
    Through God's eternal Word.

God's Word is deeper than the sea,
And broad as all eternity;
And there may we time's meaning know,
But only as we dare to go
    Into the depths with God.

— J. E. *Dean*

THE HOLY BOOK

I want the proved certainties
    To soothe the soul's deep cries;
And not man's vain philosophies
    Based only on surmise.

I want a book that is inspired
    In which to posit faith;
And not some multilated scroll,
    Or literary wraith.

I want the calm assurance of
    A voice beyond this dust,
A voice from out eternity
    In which to place my trust.

For when I come, at eventide
    To Jordan's swollen stream,
I want the tested verities,
    And not some mystic dream.

This mortal life is far too brief,
    Eternity too vast,
To follow human sophistries
    And lose the soul at last.

Then give me back the Holy Book
    By inspiration penned;
I'm through with fabled falsities,
    And allegoric trend.

— M. D. *Clayburn*

THY WORD

The heav'ns declare Thy glory, Lord,
In ev'ry star Thy wisdom shines;
But when our eyes behold Thy Word,
We read Thy Name in fairer lines.

The rolling sun, the changing light,
And nights and days, Thy pow'r confess;
But the blest volume Thou didst write,
Reveals Thy justice and Thy grace.

Sun, moon, and stars convey Thy praise
Round the whole earth, and never stand;
So, when Thy truth began its race,
It touch'd and glanc'd on ev'ry land.

Nor shall Thy spreading Gospel rest,
Till thro' the world Thy truth has run;
Till Christ has all the nations blest
That see the light or feel the sun.

Great Sun of Righteousness, arise;
Bless the dark world with heavenly light;
The Gospel makes the simple wise;
Thy laws are pure, Thy judgments right.

Thy noblest wonders here we view,
In souls renewed and sins forgiven;
Lord, cleanse our sins, our souls renew,
And make Thy Word our guide to heaven.

— *Isaac Watts*

THE BIBLE

When I am tired, the Bible is my bed;
    Or in the dark, the Bible is my light.
When I am hungry, it is the vital bread;
    Or fearful, it is armor for the fight.
When I am sick, 'tis healing medicine;
Or lonely, thronging friends I find therein.

If I would work, the Bible is my tool;
    Or play, it is a harp of happy sound.
If I am ignorant, it is my school;
    If I am sinking, it is solid ground.
If I am cold, the Bible is my fire;
And wings, if boldly I aspire.

Should I be lost, the Bible is my guide;
    Or naked, it is raiment, rich and warm.
Am I imprisoned, it is ranges wide;
    Or tempest-tossed, a shelter from the storm.
Would I adventure, 'tis a gallant sea;
Or would I rest, it is a flowery lea.

Does gloom oppress? The Bible is a sun.
Or ugliness? It is a garden fair.

— *Author Unknown*

IN THE GARDEN OF THE LORD

The word of God came unto me,
Sitting alone among the multitudes;
And my blind eyes were touched with light.
And there was laid upon my lips a flame of fire.

I laugh and shout for life is good,
Though my feet are set in silent ways.
In merry mood I leave the crowd
To walk in my garden. Ever as I walk
I gather fruits and flowers in my hands.
And with joyful heart I bless the sun
That kindles all the place with radiant life.

I run with playful winds that blow the scent
Of rose and jasmine in eddying whirls.
At last I come where tall lilies grow,
Lifting their faces like white saints to God.
While the lilies pray, I kneel upon the ground;
I have strayed into the holy temple of the Lord.

— *Helen Keller*

∽

MIRIAM'S SONG

Sound the loud timbrel o'er Egypt's dark sea!
Jehovah has triumphed, — his people are free.
Sing, — for the pride of the tyrant is broken,
   His chariots, his horsemen, all splendid and brave, —
How vain was their boast; for the Lord has but spoken,
   And chariots and horsemen are sunk in the wave.
Sound the loud timbrel o'er Egypt's dark sea!
Jehovah has triumphed, — his people are free.

Praise to the Conqueror, praise to the Lord!
His word was our arrow, his breath was our sword.
Who shall return to tell Egypt the story
   Of those she sent forth in the hour of her pride?
For the Lord hath looked out from his pillar of glory,
   And all her brave thousands are dashed in the tide.
Sound the loud timbrel o'er Egypt's dark sea!
Jehovah has triumphed, — his people are free!

— *Thomas Moore*

WRESTLING JACOB

Come, O thou Traveller unknown,
  Whom still I hold, but cannot see!
My company before is gone,
  And I am left alone with thee;
With thee all night I mean to stay,
And wrestle till the break of day.

I need not tell thee who I am,
  My misery or sin declare.
Thyself hast called me by my name:
  Look on thy hands, and read it there.
But who, I ask thee, who art thou?
Tell me thy name, and tell me now.

In vain thou strugglest to get free;
  I never will unloose my hold.
Art thou the Man that died for me?
  The secret of thy love unfold:
Wrestling, I will not let thee go,
Till I thy name, thy nature know.

Wilt thou not yet to me reveal
  Thy new, unutterable name?
Tell me, I still beseech thee, tell;
  To know it now resolved I am:
Wrestling, I will not let thee go,
Till I thy name, thy nature know.

'Tis all in vain to hold thy tongue,
  Or touch the hollow of my thigh:
Though every sinew be unstrung,
  Out of my arms thou shalt not fly;
Wrestling, I will not let thee go,
Till I thy name, thy nature know.

What though my shrinking flesh com-
    plain,
  And murmur to contend so long?
I rise superior to my pain:
  When I am weak, then I am strong:
And when my all of strength shall fail,
I shall with the God-man prevail.

My strength is gone, my nature dies;
  I sink beneath thy weighty hand;
Faint to revive, and fall to rise:

I fall, and yet by faith I stand.
I stand, and will not let thee go,
Till I thy name, thy nature know.

Yield to me now, for I am weak,
  But confident in self-despair;
Speak to my heart, in blessings speak;
  Be conquered by my instant prayer:
Speak, or thou never hence shalt move,
And tell me if thy name is Love.

'Tis Love! 'tis Love! thou diedst for me;
  I hear thy whisper in my heart.
The morning breaks, the shadows flee;
  Pure, universal Love thou art:
To me, to all, thy bowels move;
Thy nature and thy name is Love.

I know thee, Saviour, who thou art,
  Jesus, the feeble sinner's Friend;
Nor wilt thou with the night depart,
  But stay and love me to the end:
Thy mercies never shall remove;
Thy nature and thy name is Love.

The Sun of Righteousness on me
  Hath rose with healing in his wings;
Withered my nature's strength; from
    thee
  My soul its life and succor brings.
My help is all laid up above:
Thy nature and thy name is Love.

Contented now, upon my thigh
  I halt, till life's short journey end;
All helplessness, all weakness, I
  On thee alone for strength depend;
Nor have I power from thee to move:
Thy nature and thy name is Love.

Lame as I am, I take the prey;
  Hell, earth, and sin, with ease o'er-
    come;
I leap for joy, pursue my way,
  And as a bounding hart fly home,
Through all eternity to prove
Thy nature and thy name is Love.

             — *Charles Wesley*

It Means Just What It Says

There are some who believe the Bible,
  And some who believe a part;
Some who trust with a reservation,
  And some with all the heart.
But I know that its every promise
  Is firm and true always;
It is tried as the precious silver,
  And it means just what it says.

It assures me of salvation
  Thro' Jesus' precious Blood,
For the souls that will trust His mercy,
  And yield themselves to God.
And I claim for myself the promise
  And just begin to praise,
For it says I am saved by trusting,
  And I trust just as it says.

And it tells me there is cleansing,
  From every secret sin,
And a great and full salvation
  To keep the heart within;
And I take Him in His fullness,
  With all His glorious grace,
For He says it is mine for taking,
  And I take just what He says.

And it tells me He will heal me,
  And hear my feeblest cry,
And that all His royal bounty,
  Will all my need supply.
And I seem to know no better,
  Than to trust Him all my ways,
For He says I must trust Him fully,
  And I trust just as He says.

Let me hearken to all His precepts,
  And instantly obey;
Let me run to perform His bidding,
  Whatever He may say.
Let me cherish His least command-
    ment,
  And walk in all His ways;
Let me always obey my Master
  And do just what He says.

It is strange we trust each other,
  And only doubt our Lord;
We will take the words of mortals
  And yet distrust His Word;
But oh, what a light and glory,
  Would shine o'er all our days,
If we always would remember
  He means just what He says.

— *Author Unknown*

Moses —
No Man Knoweth His Sepulchre

When he, who, from the scourge of
    wrong
  Aroused the Hebrew tribes to fly,
Saw the fair region, promised long,
  And bowed him on the hills to die;

God made his grave, to men unknown,
  Where Moab's rocks a vale infold,
And laid the aged seer alone
  To slumber while the world grows
    old.

Thus still, whene'er the good and just
  Close the dim eye on life and pain,
Heaven watches o'er their sleeping
    dust
  Till the pure spirit comes again.

Tho' nameless, trampled, and forgot,
  His servant's humble ashes lie,
Yet God has marked and sealed the
    spot,
  To call its inmate to the sky.

— *William Cullen Bryant*

BELSHAZZAR

Midnight came slowly sweeping on;
In silent rest lay Babylon.

But in the royal castle high
Red torches gleam and courtiers cry.

Belshazzar there in kingly hall
Is holding kingly festival.

The vassals sat in glittering line,
And emptied the goblets with glowing wine.

The goblets rattle, the choruses swell,
And it pleased the stiff-necked monarch well.

In the monarch's cheeks a wild fire glowed,
And the wine awoke his daring mood.

And, onward still by his madness spurred,
He blasphemes the Lord with a sinful word;

And he brazenly boasts, blaspheming wild,
While the servile courtiers cheered and smiled.

Quick the king spoke, while his proud glance burned,
Quickly the servant went and returned.

He bore on his head the vessels of gold,
Of Jehovah's temple the plunder bold.

With daring hand, in his frenzy grim,
The king seized a beaker and filled to the brim,

And drained to the dregs the sacred cup,
And foaming he cried, as he drank it up,

"Jehovah, eternal scorn I own
To thee. I am monarch of Babylon."

Scarce had the terrible blasphemy rolled
From his lips, ere the monarch at heart was cold.

The yelling laughter was hushed, and all
Was still as death in the royal hall.

And see! and see! on the white wall high
The form of a hand went slowly by,

And wrote, — and wrote, on the broad wall white,
Letters of fire, and vanished in night.

Pale as death, with a steady stare,
And with trembling knees, the king sat there;

The horde of slaves sat shuddering chill;
No word they spoke, but were deathlike still.

The Magicians came, but of them all,
None could read the flame-script on the wall.

But that same night, in all his pride,
By the hands of his servants Belshazzar died.

— *Heinrich Heine*

THE BIBLE

The charter of all true liberty.
The forerunner of civilization.
The moulder of institutions and governments.
The fashioner of law.
The secret of national progress.
The guide of history.
The ornament and mainspring of literature.
The friend of science.
The inspiration of philosophies.
The textbook of ethics.
The light of intellect.
The answer to the deepest human heart hungerings.
The soul of all strong heart life.
The illuminator of darkness.
The foe of superstition.
The enemy of oppression.
The uprooter of sin.
The regulator of all high and worthy standards.
The comfort in sorrow.
The strength in weakness.
The pathway in perplexity.
The escape from temptation.
The steadier in the day of power.
The embodiment of all lofty ideals.
The begetter of life.
The promise of the future.
The star of death's night.
The revealer of God.
The guide and hope and inspiration of man.

— *Bishop Anderson*

One of the Sweet Old Chapters

One of the sweet old chapters,
    After a day like this —
The day brought tears and troubles,
    The evening brings no kiss,
Nor rest in the arms I long for,—
    Rest and refuge and home;
Grieved and lonely and weary,
    Unto the Book I come.

One of the sweet old chapters,
    That always will avail,
So full of heavenly comfort,
    When earthly comforts fail,
A sweet and blessed message
    From God to His children dear,
So rich in precious promises,
    So full of love and cheer.

One of the sweet old chapters,
    When comes the lonely night,
When all things earthly fail us;
    And tears have dimmed our sight,
This only can relieve us,
    A message from above,
Then we can rest so sweetly,
    In faith, and hope, and love.

                — *Author Unknown*

The Bible

A better love than mine
    This holy volume gives;
It shows no shadow of decline,
    And when I die it lives.

This book binds man and wife
    In closer love and fears;
And all the ties that bless our life
    It hallows and endears.

                — *N. Frothingham*

God's Unchanging Word

For feelings come and feelings go,
And feelings are deceiving;
My warrant is the word of God,
Naught else is worth believing.
Though all my heart should feel condemned
For want of some sweet token,
There is One greater than my heart
Whose word cannot be broken.
I'll trust in God's unchanging word
Till soul and body sever;
For, though all things shall pass away,
His word shall stand forever.

                — *Martin Luther*

Upon Thy Word

Upon Thy Word I rest
    Each pilgrim day;
This golden staff is best
    For all the way.
What Jesus Christ hath spoken
Cannot be broken!

Upon Thy Word I rest,
    So strong, so sure!
So full of comfort blest,
    So sweet, so pure!
The charter of salvation,
Faith's broad foundation.

Upon Thy Word I stand,
    That cannot die;
Christ seals it in my hand,
    He cannot lie!
Thy Word that faileth never,
Abideth ever.

                — *Frances Ridley Havergal*

THE SIFTING OF PETER
A Folk Song

In St. Luke's Gospel we are told
How Peter in the days of old
    Was sifted;
And now, though ages intervene,
Sin is the same, while time and scene
    Are shifted.

Satan desires us, great and small,
As wheat, to sift us, and we all
    Are tempted;
Not one, however rich or great,
Is by his station or estate
    Exempted.

No house so safely guarded is
But he, by some device of his,
    Can enter;
No heart hath armor so complete
But he can pierce with arrows fleet
    Its centre.

For all at last the cock will crow
Who hear the warning voice, but go
    Unheeding,

Till thrice and more they have denied
The Man of Sorrows, crucified
    And bleeding.

One look of that pale suffering face
Will make us feel the deep disgrace
    Of weakness;
We shall be sifted till the strength
Of self-conceit be changed at length
    To meekness.

Wounds of the soul, though healed,
        will ache;
The reddening scars remain, and make
    Confession;
Lost innocence returns no more;
We are not what we were before
    Transgression.

But noble souls, thro' dust and heat,
Rise from disaster and defeat
    The stronger,
And conscious still of the divine
Within them, lie on earth supine
    No longer.

— *Henry Wadsworth Longfellow*

THE BIBLE

The Book of books, holy, sublime and true,
    Spirit-inspired in every thought and word,
    Revealing God, and Christ as Saviour-Lord,
Teacher of all that men should be and do;
A heavenly light within earth's midnight gloom,
    A quickening life amidst death's dread decay,
    A steadfast hand, pointing the upward way,
A voice of triumph o'er the grave and tomb:

Here is a peace which sets the spirit free,
    Here is a love which casts out every fear,
    Here is a hope which gives the life good cheer
And here are visions of the world to be;
Here then I rest; — and thus I ever may,
E'en when this earth and heaven have passed away!

— *Henry W. Frost*

WHEN I READ THE BIBLE THROUGH

I supposed I knew my Bible,
    Reading piecemeal, hit and miss,
Now a bit of John or Matthew,
    Now a snatch of Genesis,
Certain chapters of Isaiah,
    Certain Psalms (the twenty-third);
Twelfth of Romans, First of Proverbs—
    Yes, I thought I knew the Word;
But I found that thorough reading
    Was a different thing to do,
And the way was unfamiliar
    When I read the Bible through.

Oh, the massive, mighty volume!
    Oh, the treasures manifold!
Oh, the beauty and the wisdom
    And the grace it proved to hold!
As the story of the Hebrews
    Swept in majesty along,
As it leaped in waves prophetic,
    As it burst to sacred song,
As it gleamed with Christly omens,
    The Old Testament was new,
Strong with cumulative power,
    When I read the Bible through.

Ah! imperial Jeremiah,
    With his keen, coruscant mind;
And the blunt old Nehemiah,
    And Ezekiel refined!
Newly came the Minor Prophets,
    Each with his distinctive robe;
Newly came the song idyllic,
    And the tragedy of Job;
Deuteronomy, the regal,
    To a towering mountain grew,
With its comrade peaks around it —
    When I read the Bible through.

What a radiant procession
    As the pages rise and fall,
James the sturdy, John the tender —
    Oh, the myriad-minded Paul!
Vast apocalyptic glories
    Wheel and thunder, flash and flame,

While the church triumphant raises
    One incomparable name.
Ah, the story of the Saviour
    Never glows supremely true
Till you read it whole and swiftly,
    Till you read the Bible through.

You who like to play at Bible,
    Dip and dabble, here and there,
Just before you kneel, aweary,
    And yawn thro' a hurried prayer;
You who treat the Crown of Writings
    As you treat no other book —
Just a paragraph disjointed,
    Just a crude, impatient look —
Try a worthier procedure,
    Try a broad and steady view;
You will kneel in very rapture
    When you read the Bible through.

                                                        — *Amos R. Wells*

ᢙᣆ

THE QUIET HOUR

In the stillness of the quiet hour
When I pause a while to rest,
I read about God's promises
From the book I love the best.

It tells me of His wondrous love
And of His tender care,
He fills my soul with blessing
As I linger with Him there.

He whispers softly do not fear,
Though the billows round me roll,
I have found in Him a hiding place
The anchor of my soul.

In the stillness of the quiet hour,
I can feel the tempest cease
When I read about God's promises
And Jesus whispers peace.

                                            — *Harvey E. Haver*

DESTRUCTION OF SENNACHERIB

The Assyrian came down like the wolf on the fold,
And his cohorts were gleaming in purple and gold;
And the sheen of their spears was like stars on the sea,
When the blue wave rolls nightly on deep Galilee.

Like the leaves of the forest when Summer is green,
That host with their banners at sunset were seen:
Like the leaves of the forest when Autumn hath blown,
That host on the morrow lay wither'd and strown.

For the Angel of Death spread his wings on the blast,
And breathed in the face of the foe as he pass'd;
And the eyes of the sleepers wax'd deadly and chill,
And their hearts but once heaved, and forever grew still!

And there lay the steed with his nostrils all wide,
But through it there roll'd not the breath of his pride;
And the foam of his gasping lay white on the turf,
And cold as the spray of the rock-beating surf.

And there lay the rider distorted and pale,
With the dew on his brow, and the rust on his mail:
And the tents were all silent, the banners alone,
The lances unlifted, the trumpet unblown.

And the widows of Ashur are loud in their wail
And the idols are broke in the temple of Baal;
And the might of the Gentile, unsmote by the sword,
Hath melted like snow in the glance of the Lord!

— Lord Byron

ॐ

IN EARTHEN VESSELS

The dear Lord's best interpreters
　　Are humble human souls;
The gospel of a life like His
　　Is more than books or scrolls.

From scheme and creed the light
　　　　goes out,
　　The saintly fact survives;
The blessed Master none can doubt,
　　Revealed in holy lives.

— John Greenleaf Whittier

LIGHT AND GLORY OF THE WORLD

The Spirit breathes upon the Word,
　　And brings the truth to sight;
Precepts and promises afford
　　A sanctifying sight.

A glory gilds the sacred page,
　　Majestic like the sun;
It gives a light to ev'ry age,
　　It gives, but borrows none.

— William Cowper

FIRST BIBLE

A little boy's first Bible
Is the greatest thrill he's known
There's a sweet, unique excitement
In a Bible all his own!
And yet my heart is smitten
As this touching sight I see —
Has his reverence for that Bible
Depended much on me?
As I see him with his Bible,
I bow my head and pray —
May he always love that Bible
The way he does today.
Then I hear a voice within me
Speak in solemn words and true;
How he cherishes that Bible
Will depend a lot on you!
I love my Bible better
Since I've seen the beaming joy
This wonderful possession
Has afforded to my boy.
May I seek to give mine daily
A devotion he can see,
For the love he bears his Bible
Will depend a lot on me.

— *United Presbyterian*

MY MOTHER'S BIBLE

This book is all that's left me now,—
  Tears will unbidden start,—
With faltering lip and throbbing brow
  I press it to my heart.
For many generations past
  Here is our family tree:
My mother's hands this Bible clasped,
  She, dying, gave it me.

Ah! well do I remember those
  Whose names these records bear;
Who round the hearthstone used to
    close,
  After the evening prayer,

And speak of what these pages said
  In tones my heart would thrill!
Though they are with the silent dead,
  Here are they living still!

My father read this holy book
  To brothers, sisters, dear;
How calm was my poor mother's look,
  Who loved God's word to hear!
Her angel face, — I see it yet!
  What thronging memories come!
Again that little group is met
  Within the halls of home!

Thou truest friend man ever knew,
  Thy constancy I've tried;
When all were false, I found thee true,
  My counsellor and guide.
The mines of earth no treasures give
  That could this volume buy;
In teaching me the way to live,
  It taught me how to die!

— *George P. Morris*

OUR GUIDING LIGHT

If we could plunge to the depths of
    truth
  And grasp the whole rich story,
Our souls would rise to Paradise
  Enraptured by its glory.

What boundless wealth lies in this
    Book
  Peculiar as a treasure.
Its brilliant rays shine on our ways
  Availing without measure.

Oh, Word divine! Oh, Book sublime!
  Oh, Wisdom so transcending!
We look to Thee, we cling to Thee,
  For guiding light unending.

— *S. F. Logsdon*

O WORD OF GOD, INCARNATE

O Word of God Incarnate,
O Wisdom from on high,
O Truth unchanged, unchanging,
O Light of our dark sky;
We praise Thee for the radiance
That from the hallowed page,
A lantern to our footsteps,
Shines on from age to age.

The Church from her dear Master
Received the gift divine,
And still that light she lifteth
O'er all the earth to shine.
It is the golden casket
Where gems of truth are stored;
It is the heav'n-drawn picture
Of Christ the living Word.

It floateth like a banner
Before God's host unfurled;
It shineth like a beacon
Above the darkling world;
It is the chart and compass
That o'er life's surging sea,
'Mid mists and rocks and quicksands
Still guides, O Christ, to Thee.

— *William W. How*

GOD'S TREASURE

There is a Treasure,
Rich beyond measure,
    Offered to mortals today;
Some folk despise it,
Some criticize it,
    Some would explain it away.

Some never read it,
Some never heed it,
    Some say "It's long had its day";
Some people prize it,
And he who tries it
    Finds it his comfort and stay.

God gave this Treasure,
Rich beyond measure,
    His Word, we call it today.
Let us believe it,
Gladly receive it,
    Read, mark, and learn to obey.

                    —*A. M. N.*

THE BIBLE

Contains:
Best Loved Words
of the Best Loved Book in all the World.
Most Precious Thoughts
ever told in human language.
Sweetest Story ever heard by mortal ears.
God's Own Words.   Wonderful Words.
Beautiful Words.   Sublime Words.
Glorious Words.   Heavenly Words.
Words of Power.   Words of Life.
Timeless, Eternal Words.
Words that Shall Never Die.
Words we Read, and Re-Read.

                    — *H. H. Halley*

THE SACRED BOOK

I love the sacred Book of God,
    No other can its place supply;
It points me to the saints' abode,
    And bids me from destruction fly.

Sweet Book! In thee my eyes discern
    The image of my absent Lord;
From thy instructive page I learn
    The joys His presence will afford.

But while I'm here thou shalt supply
    His place, and tell me of His love;
I'll read with faith's discerning eye,
    And thus partake of joys above.

                    — *Thomas Kelly*

God Speaks Through the Bible

God, in the Gospel of His Son,
Makes His eternal counsels known;
Where love in all its glory shines,
And truth is drawn in fairest lines.

Here sinners of a humble frame
May taste His grace, and learn His
Name;
May read, in characters of blood,
The wisdom, pow'r and grace of God.

The pris'ner here may break his chains;
The weary rest from all his pains;
The captive feel his bondage cease;
The mourner find the way of peace.

Here faith reveals to mortal eyes
A brighter world beyond the skies;
Here shines the light which guides our
way
From earth to realms of endless day.

O grant us grace, Almighty Lord,
To read and mark Thy holy Word;
Its truths with meekness to receive,
And by its holy precepts live.

— *Thomas Cotterill*

Prayer by the Open Book

Lord Jesus, show Thyself to me
Within Thy Book divine,
That I may know and worship Thee,
And draw my life from Thine.
Be Thou the Light of every page,
The Life in every word;
Thro' pen of saint and seer and sage
Reveal Thyself, O Lord!

Lord Jesus, show Thyself to me
In very truth and deed;
Help me to find, O Christ, in Thee,
More than my deepest need.

Show me my worthless self, O Lord,
And Thine amazing grace;
Help me to know the price outpoured
That I might see God's face!

Lord Jesus, show Thyself to me,
And help me make Thee mine,
That I may walk by faith with Thee
And prove each word of Thine!
Fulfill Thy promises to me;
Help me Thy power to claim
Till all my life transformed shall be
Through Thy redeeming Name!

— *E. Margaret Clarkson*

The Word of God

The Word of God which ne'er shall
cease,
Proclaims free pardon, grace and peace,
Salvation shows in Christ alone,
The perfect will of God makes known.

This holy Word exposes sin,
Convinces us that we're unclean,
Points out the wretched, ruined state
Of all mankind, both small and great.

It then reveals God's boundless grace,
Which justifies our sinful race,
And gives eternal life to all
Who will accept the gospel call.

It gently heals the broken heart,
And heavenly riches doth impart,
Unfolds redemption's wondrous plan,
Thro' Christ's atoning death for man.

O God, in Whom our trust we place,
We thank Thee for Thy Word of
grace;
Help us its precepts to obey,
Till we shall live in endless day.

— *John Huss*

IF I BUT READ

The Lord I love went on ahead
To make a home for me. He said
He would come back again, and He—
Oh, gracious love — He wrote to me!
He knew I was so weak and blind
And foolish that I could not find
The road alone. He told me things
That all earth's wise men, and its kings,
Have never guessed, yet I foreknow
If I but read His Word. And, oh,
Such depths of love on every sheet!
My soul is trembling at His feet.
What would He think of me
If when I saw Him I should say;
"I was too busy every day
To read what Thou didst write to me;
I really hadn't time for Thee!"

— *Martha Snell Nicholson*

HIS WORD IS POWERFUL

His Word is like fire consuming,
   His Word is a hammer to break;
His Word is a sword with two edges.
   His Word like a lamp you can take.

His Word is against the false prophets,
   His Word is opposed to all sin;
His Word will endure forever,
   His Word will the victory win.

His Word is both written and living,
   His Word will outlive sword and
      pen;
His Word is His eternal edict,
   His Word: — it is yea and amen.

— *H. H. Savage*

THE BOOK

The books men write are but a fragrance blown
   From transient blossoms crushed by human hands;
But high above them all, splendid and alone,
   Staunch as a tree, there is a Book that stands

Unmoved by storms, unchallenged by decay;
   The winds of criticism would profane
Its sacred pages, but the Truth, the Way,
   The Life are in it — and they beat in vain.

O traveler from this to yonder world,
   Pause in the shade of God's magnificent,
Eternal Word — that tree whose roots are curled
   About our human need. When strength is spent,
Stretch out beneath some great, far-reaching limb
   Of promise, and find rest and peace in Him.

— *Helen Frazee-Bower*

SYMPHONY OF THE SOUL *(Psalm 23)*

He leads His own beside and in and through,
Restores the soul and comforts with the rod;
He makes the valley but an avenue
Through which the soul companions with its God.
The table of necessities is spread,
And all is well despite the enemy;
The cup is full, there is no need, instead,
His goodness follows to eternity.

This melody of Heaven reaches me
And teaches me that God is good, and though
The darkened shadows fall, the harmony
Of love divine supports me where I go.
The Shepherd Psalm is both a guide and goal,
Symphonic movements in the human soul. — *Carlton Buck*

WHERE WERE YOU?

"I came to your church last Sunday,
  I walked up and down the aisle,
I noticed your seat was vacant,"
  Said the Master, with kindly smile.

"Yes, I was at home," I answered,
  "Some folks from up Salem way
Drove down for a week-end visit,
  So we stayed in the house all day."

Or, "I had an awful headache,"
  "I had a roast in the pan,"
Or, "We overslept this morning,
  But I go whenever I can."

The Master gazed at me sadly,
  As He was about to speak,
"My child," He replied, "Are there not
  Six other days in the week?"

I saw I had grieved my Master,
  As slowly He turned away,

And I vowed He'd not find me absent
  Again on His holy day!
            — *Author Unknown*

BE TRUE THYSELF

Thou must be true thyself
  If thou the truth wouldst teach;
Thy soul must overflow if thou
  Another's soul wouldst reach,
It needs the overflow of heart
  To give the lips full speech.

Think truly, and thy thoughts
  Shall the world's famine feed;
Speak truly, and each word of thine
  Shall be a fruitful seed;
Live truly, and thy life shall be
  A great and noble creed.
            — *Horatius Bonar*

YOUTH AND TRUTH

I saw a youth go forth one day
Who met with Truth along the way;
Said Truth to youth, "Come, go with
    me,
I'll make you noble as can be;
I'll lead you far from ev'ry wrong,
And build you up and make you strong
For God and His eternal cause,
And keep you true to nature's laws."

Said youth to Truth, "I'll go with you
And trust your strength to take me
    through
This world of sin, with ev'ry test,
Because I want to do my best
To live for God and all that's right,
And be a burning, shining light,
So when my race on earth is run
I'll hear my Master say, 'Well done.'"

I saw the youth begin to climb,
And rise in life to things sublime;
His aims were high, his purpose good;
He used his time as each one should;
He formed no habits bad or vile,
Tho' others said, "He's out of style";
He proved himself a noble youth
As on and on he followed Truth.

He lived a life upright and clean,
And shunned the low, and vile, and
    mean;
He didn't steal, he didn't lie,
Nor serve the devil on the sly;
His face was bright, his eyes were clear,
As on he journeyed year by year
Along the road that leads to God,
Which blessed, saintly men have trod.

In after years I saw this youth,
Whose strength and leader still was
    Truth,
Come up to grand and hoary age,
Like some blest patriarch or sage;
And looking back across the past,
He said, "I'm nearing home at last";
Then soon he went to meet his Lord,
And to receive his rich reward.

Although he didn't reach a throne
And cause a monument of stone
To be erected to his name
To long perpetuate his fame,
His sons and daughters call him great,
And strive his good to emulate,
While hundreds live for God today
Because he led them in this way.

— *Walter E. Isenhour*

GIVE US MEN!

God give us men. The time demands
Strong minds, great hearts,
    True faith and willing hands;
Men whom the lust of office does not kill;
    Men whom the spoils of office cannot buy;
Men who possess opinions and a will;
    Men who have honor; men who will not lie;
Men who can stand before a demagogue
    And condemn his treacherous flatteries without winking;
Tall men, sun-crowned who live above the fog
    In public duty and in private thinking.

— *John G. Holland*

If Jesus Came to Your House

If Jesus came to your house to spend a day or two,
If He came unexpectedly, I wonder what you'd do.
Oh, I know you'd give your nicest room to such an honored Guest,
And all the food you'd serve to Him would be the very best —
And you would keep assuring Him you're glad to have Him there,
That serving Him in your home is joy beyond compare!
But when you saw Him coming, would you meet Him at the door,
With arms outstretched in welcome to your Heavenly Visitor?
Or would you have to change your clothes before you let Him in,
Or hide some magazines and put the Bible where they'd been?
Would you turn off the radio and hope He hadn't heard —
And wish you hadn't uttered that last, loud, hasty word?
Would you hide your worldly music and put some hymn books out?
Could you let Jesus walk right in, or would you rush about?
And I wonder — if the Saviour spent a day or two with you —
Would you go right on doing the things you always do?
Would you keep right on saying the things you always say?
Would life for you continue as it does from day to day?
Would your family conversation keep up its usual pace?
And would you find it hard each meal to say a table grace?
Would you sing the songs you always sing and read the books you read,
And let Him know the things on which your mind and spirit feed?
Would you take Jesus with you everywhere you'd planned to go,
Or would you, maybe, change your plans for just a day or so?
Would you be glad to have Him meet your very closest friends,
Or would you hope they'd stay away until His visit ends?
Would you be glad to have Him stay forever on and on,
Or would you sigh with great relief when He at last was gone?
It might be interesting to know the things that you would do
If Jesus came in person to spend some time with you.

— *Author Unknown*

Happiness

Life's happiness is woven
  Of very simple things —
A room all bright with sunshine,
  The flash of redstarts' wings;
The tranquil hush of twilight hours,
Winter's snow and summer showers;
Country gardens gay with flowers
  And a heart that sings.

It greets us in the shining eyes
  Of little ones at play,
And meets us in some unexpected
  Kindness every day.
It lives in friendships that abide,
Thoughts that reach out far and wide
Grateful prayers at eventide,
  And love along the way.

— *Anna E. Wimmer*

No Time

I knelt to pray, but not for long,
  I had too much to do,
Must hurry off and get to work,
  For bills would soon be due.

And so I said, a hurried prayer,
  Jumped up from off my knees;
My Christian duty now was done,
  My soul could be at ease.

All through the day I had no time
  To speak a word of cheer,
No time to speak of Christ to friends—
  They'd laugh at me, I feared.

No time, no time, too much to do—
  That was my constant cry;
No time to give to those in need—
  At last 'twas time to die.

And when before the Lord I came,
  I stood with downcast eyes,
Within His hands He held a Book,
  It was the "Book of Life."

God looked into His Book and said,
  "Your name I cannot find,
I once was going to write it down,
  But never found the time."

                    — *Author Unknown*

Watching

Shall He come — and find me watch-
      ing,
  As the watchers watch for morn,
As the hour of midnight passes,
  And the coming day is born?

Shall He come — and find me waiting,
  With my loins well girt about,
Staff in hand — the more to welcome—
  Waiting without fear or doubt?

Shall He come—and find me standing,
  From the worldling's joys apart,
Outside all its mirth and folly,
  With a true and loyal heart?

Shall He come — and find me faithful
  To His parting words to me:
"If I go, a place preparing,
  I will quickly come for thee"?

Shall He come—and find me working,
  In His vanguard full of love,
Laboring only till the glory
  Breaks upon me from above?

Jesus, let me thus be waiting,
  Full of love and hope and zeal,
Let Thy coming to my spirit;
  Be a hope divine and real.

                    — *Author Unknown*

Lead Me to Calvary

King of my life, I crown Thee now,
  Thine shall the glory be;
Lest I forget Thy thorn-crowned brow,
  Lead me to Calvary.

Show me the tomb where Thou wast
      laid,
  Tenderly mourned and wept;
Angels in robes of light arrayed
  Guarded Thee whilst Thou slept.

Let me like Mary, thro' the gloom,
  Come with a gift to Thee;
Show to me now the empty tomb,
  Lead me to Calvary.

May I be willing, Lord, to bear
  Daily my cross for Thee;
Even Thy cup of grief to share,
  Thou hast borne all for me.

                    — *Jennie Evelyn Hussey*

ONWARD

Soldier of the cross, arise!
Lo! your leader from the skies
Waves before you glory's prize,
    The prize of victory.
Seize your armor, gird it on;
Fight until the battle's won;
Soon the conflict will be done,
    Then struggle manfully.

Jesus conquered when He fell,
Met and vanquished earth and hell;
Now He leads you on to swell
    The triumphs of His Cross.
Though your enemies appear,
Who will doubt, or who can fear?
God, our strengthened shield is near;
    We cannot lose our cause.

Onward, then, ye hosts of God!
Jesus points the victor's rod,
Follow where your leader trod;
    You soon shall see His face.
Soon, your enemies all slain,
Crowns of glory you shall gain;
Soon you'll join that glorious train,
    Who shout their Saviour's praise.

— *Early Methodist Hymnal*

WHO — ME?

"Go ye"
Who — ME?
But, Lord, how could I go?
Dost Thou not know
I have so much to do
For me — and You?
And when my future is secure
You may be very sure
That I shall give quite readily,
But go,—and now? No, Lord, not me.

"Pray ye"
Who — ME?
To really yearn and pray

And every day?
But, Lord, those days are past
For modern life is fast
I haven't even time to go
Just once a week, although I know
The older folk pray faithfully,
But pray, — and now? No, Lord, not
    me.

But say,
On that great day
When in eternity
The Blessed Trinity
Took counsel for a plan
To rescue fallen man,
And He Who orders earth and sky
Said *He* would die,
Oh busy soul, where would *you* be
If He
Had said
Who — ME?

— *Joan Suisted*

DO YOUR BEST

When the days are dark and dreary,
And the heart is sad and weary,
Look to Him, keep sweet and cheery.
    Do your best!

Be the duties great or small,
Though you falter, often fall,
He will hear when e'er you call.
    Do your best!

Give a loving word of cheer;
Bear your burdens, never fear,
He will strengthen. He is near.
    Do your best!

Look to Him in all you do,
For some work He's planned for you,
And be faithful, loyal, true.
    Do your best!

— *Author Unknown*

EARLY SUMMER THOUGHT

God gives so much of beauty
  No day is common fare.
If we but took the time to look,
  Some loveliness is there.

Regret not Spring's departure,
  June dawns with clover field.
Along each way, through every day
  Some beauty is revealed.

—*Marie J. Post*

ᴏᴧᴏ

THE SPIRIT OF VICTORY

We all were lonely and bereft
Who in that upper room had met,
We were obeying what He said,
When He was risen from the dead.
We knelt and wept and suffered there
Whilst James or John would offer
    prayer.

It came so swift—a mighty wind
Blew out our lamps, and there defined
A radiance blazed on every face,
And each to each we seemed to trace
A Deity that filled the place.

We who were cowards now were kings;
We who were dumb had words with
    wings,
A mighty impulse swept us there
To hasten forth and to declare
What we had seen and known of Him
To all men to earth's farthest rim,
That they might see Him face to face
And know His love and saving grace.

Great Spirit, God, the One in Three,
Christ's Church is dead apart from
    Thee,
Breathe on us Pentecostal power
That we may triumph in this hour.

—*William H. Hudnut, Sr.*

IF THE LORD SHOULD COME

If the Lord should come in the morn-
    ing
  As I go about my work,
The little things and the quiet things
  That a servant cannot shirk,
Though nobody ever sees them,
  And only the dear Lord cares
That they always are done in the light
    of the sun,
  Would He take me unawares?

If the Lord came hither at evening,
  In the fragrant dew and dusk,
When the world drops off its mantle
  Of daylight like a husk,
And flowers in wonderful beauty
  And we fold our hands and rest,
Would His touch of my hand, His low
    command,
  Bring me unhoped-for zest?

Why do I ask and question?
  He is ever coming to me,
Morning and noon and evening,
  If I have but eyes to see.
And the daily load grows lighter,
  The daily cares grow sweet,
For the Master is near, the Master is
    here,
  I have only to sit at His feet.

—*J. R. Miller*

ᴏᴧᴏ

JUDGMENT DAY

Every day is Judgment Day,
  Count on no to-morrow.
He who will not, when he may,
Act to-day, to-day, to-day,
  Doth but borrow
    Sorrow.

—*John Oxenham*

TRUTH NEVER DIES

Truth never dies. The ages come and go;
  The mountains wear away; the seas retire;
Destruction lays earth's mighty cities low;
  And empires, states, and dynasties expire;
But caught and handed onward by the wise,
  Truth never dies.

Though unreceived and scoffed at through the years;
  Though made the butt of ridicule and jest;
Though held aloft for mockery and jeers,
  Denied by those of transient power possessed,
Insulted by the insolence of lies,
  Truth never dies.

Truth answers not; it does not take offense:
  But with mighty silence bides its time.
As some great cliff that braves the elements,
  And lifts through all the storms its head sublime,
So truth, unmoved, it puny foes defies,
  And never dies.

—*Author Unknown*

"WHO IS ON THE LORD'S SIDE?"

Who is on the Lord's side?
  Who will bid the world good-by?
Who will stand forth bravely,
  Saying, "Master, here am I?"

Who will offer service,
  Join the ranks of marching host?
Who will take all orders
  From the precious Holy Ghost?

Who will give God glory,
  Take the hidden, humble place?
Who will wield God's weapon
  Of redeeming love and grace?

Who is on the Lord's side?
  Who will lift the banner high?
Hear the call that's sounding!
  Answer, comrade, "Here am I"!

—*Grace B. Renfrow*

UPSTREAM

The easy roads are crowded, and
  The level roads are jammed.
The pleasant little rivers
  With the drifting folks are crammed.
But off yonder where it's rocky,
  Where you get the better view,
You will find the ranks are thinning,
  And the travelers are few.

Where the going's smooth and pleasant
  You will always find the throng,
For the many — more's the pity —
  Seem to like to drift along.
But the steeps that call for courage
  And the task that's hard to do
In the end results in glory
  For the never wavering few!

—*Author Unknown*

A Single Stitch

One stitch dropped as the weaver drove
  His nimble shuttle to and fro,
In and out, beneath, above,
  Till the pattern seemed to bud and grow
As if the fairies had helping been;
One small stitch which could scarce be seen,
But the one stitch dropped pulled the next stitch out,
And a weak place grew in the fabric stout;
And the perfect pattern was marred for aye
By the one small stitch that was dropped that day.

One small life in God's great plan,
  How futile it seems as the ages roll,
Do what it may or strive how it can
  To alter the sweep of the infinite whole!
A single stitch in an endless web,
A drop in the ocean's flood and ebb!
But the pattern is rent where the stitch is lost,
Or marred where the tangled threads have crossed;
And each life that fails of its true intent
Mars the perfect plan that its Master meant.

                   — *Susan Coolidge*

Scarred

The shame He suffered left its brand
In gaping wound in either hand;
Sin's penalty He deigned to meet
Has torn and scarred His blessed feet;
The condemnation by Him borne
Marred His brow with print of thorn.
Trespass and guilt for which He died
Have marked Him with a riven side.

Mine was the shame, the penalty:
The sin was mine; it was for me
He felt the nails, the thorns, the spear.
For love of me the scars appear
In hands and feet and side and brow.
Beholding them I can but bow
Myself a living sacrifice
To Him who paid so dear a price.

         — *Bob Jones, Jr.*

A Little Word

A little word in kindness spoken,
  A motion or a tear,
Has often healed the heart that's
    broken!
  And made a friend sincere.

A word—a look—has crushed to earth,
  Full many a budding flower,
Which had a smile but owned its birth,
  Would bless life's darkest hour.

Then deem it not an idle thing,
  A pleasant word to speak;
The face you wear, the thoughts you
    bring,
  A heart may heal or break.

         — *Author Unknown*

UNTIL HE COMES

Keep Thou me ever hungry, Lord,
Until I famish for Thy Word —
Thy Word, which is my meat, my
    bread,
Thy Word, which feeds whenever
    read.

Keep Thou me ever thirsty, Lord,
Stay not Thy hand till Thou hast
    poured
Thy living water in my cup
Which I am humbly holding up.

Keep me dissatisfied, dear Lord;
Use Thou Thy Spirit's shining sword
To pierce my foolish self-esteem
And rouse me from my empty dream.

Keep me awake, that I may hear
Thy bugles calling, loud and clear.
Stir Thou my slugglish soul to fight
For Thee beneath Thy banner bright.

Yea, this my prayer, that I may be
Hungry and thirsty, Lord, for Thee,
Dissatisfied with self, awake!
And this I ask for Jesus' sake.

— *Martha Snell Nicholson*

OTHERS

Lord, help me live from day to day
    In such a self-forgetful way,
That even when I kneel to pray
    My prayers will be for others.

Help me in all the work I do
    To ever be sincere and true,
And know that all I do for You
    Must needs be done for others.

Let self be crucified and slain
    And buried deep, and all in vain
May efforts be to rise again,
    Unless to live for others.

And when my work on earth is done
    And my new work in heaven begun,
May I forget the crown I've won
    While thinking still of others.

Others, Lord, yes, others,
    Let this my motto be;
Help me to live for others
    That I may live like Thee.

— *C. D. Meigs*

PROVE THE DOCTRINE

So let our lips and lives express
The holy Gospel we profess,
So let our words and virtues shine
To prove the doctrine all divine.

— *Author Unknown*

O MASTER,
LET ME WALK WITH THEE

O Master, let me walk with Thee
In lowly paths of service free;
Tell me Thy secret! help me bear
The strain of toil, the fret of care.

Help me the slow of heart to move
By some clear, winning word of love;
Teach me the wayward feet to stay,
And guide them in the homeward way.

Teach me Thy patience; still with
    Thee
In closer, dearer company,
In work that keeps faith sweet and
    strong,
In trust that triumphs over wrong.

In hope that sends a shining ray
Far down the future's broad'ning way;
In peace that only Thou canst give,
With Thee, O Master, let me live.

— *Washington Gladden*

THINK IT OVER

I'll go where You want me to go, dear Lord;
    Real service is what I desire;
I'll say what You want me to say, dear Lord —
    But don't ask me to sing in the choir.

I'll say what You want me to say, dear Lord;
    I like to see things come to pass;
But don't ask me to teach girls and boys, dear Lord —
    I'd rather just stay in my class.

I'll do what You want me to do, dear Lord;
    I yearn for the Kingdom to thrive;
I'll give You my nickels and dimes, dear Lord —
    But please don't ask me to tithe.

I'll go where You want me to go, dear Lord;
    I'll say what You want me to say;
I'm busy just now with myself, dear Lord —
    I'll help You some other day.

— *Author Unknown*

PASS IT ON

Have you had a kindness shown?
    Pass it on.
'Twas not given for thee alone,
    Pass it on.
Let it travel down the years,
Let it wipe another's tears,
'Till in Heav'n the deed appears —
    Pass it on.

Did you hear the loving word?
    Pass it on —
Like the singing of a bird?
    Pass it on.
Let its music live and grow,
Let it cheer another's woe;
You have reaped what others sow —
    Pass it on.

'Twas the sunshine of a smile —
    Pass it on.
Staying but a little while!
    Pass it on.
April beam a little thing,

Still it wakes the flowers of spring,
Makes the silent birds to sing —
    Pass it on.

Have you found the heavenly light?
    Pass it on.
Souls are groping in the night,
    Daylight gone —
Hold thy lighted lamp on high,
Be a star in someone's sky,
He may live who else would die —
    Pass it on.

Be not selfish in thy greed,
    Pass it on.
Look upon thy brother's need,
    Pass it on.
Live for self, you live in vain;
Live for Christ, you live again;
Live for Him, with Him you reign —
    Pass it on.

— *Henry Burton*

SAIL ON!

Behind him lay the gray Azores,
    Behind the gates of Hercules;
Before him not the ghost of shores,
    Before him only shoreless seas.
The good Mate said: "Now we must pray,
    For lo! the very stars are gone.
Brave Admiral, speak, what shall I say?"
    "Why, say, 'Sail on! sail on! sail on!'"

"My men grow mutinous day by day;
    My men grow ghastly wan and weak!"
The stout Mate thought of home; a spray
    Of salt wave washed his swarthy cheek.
"What shall I say, brave Admiral, say,
    If we sight naught but seas at dawn?"
"Why, you shall say at break of day,
    'Sail on! sail on! sail on! and on!'"

They sailed. They sailed. Then spake the Mate:
    "This mad sea shows its teeth tonight.
He curls his lip, he lies in wait,
    With lifted teeth, as if to bite!
Brave Admiral, say but one good word;
    What shall we do when hope is gone?"
The words leapt like a leaping sword:
    "Sail on! sail on! sail on! and on!"

Then, pale and worn, he kept his deck
    And peered through darkness. Ah! that night
Of all dark nights! And then a speck —
    A light! A light! A light! A light!
It grew, a starlit flag unfurled!
    It grew to be Time's burst of dawn.
He gained a world; he gave that world
    Its grandest lesson: "On! sail on!"

                      — *Joaquin Miller*

I SHALL NOT PASS THIS WAY AGAIN

Through this toilsome world, alas!
Once and only once I pass;
If a kindness I may show,
If a good deed I may do
To a suffering fellow man,
Let me do it while I can.
No delay, for it is plain
I shall not pass this way again.

                      — *Author Unknown*

SAVED, BUT—

I am saved, but is self buried?
 Is my one, my only aim,
Just to honor Christ my Saviour,
 Just to glorify His Name?

I am saved, but is my home life
 What the Lord would have it be?
Is it seen in every action,
 Jesus has control of me?

I am saved, but am I doing,
 Everything that I can do,
That the dying souls around me,
 May be brought to Jesus, too?

I am saved, but could I gladly,
 Lord, leave all and follow Thee;
If Thou callest can I answer,
 Here am I, send me, send me?

— *Author Unknown*

AWAKE, MY SOUL

Awake, my soul; stretch every nerve,
 And press with vigor on:
A heavenly race demands thy zeal,
 And an immortal crown.

A cloud of witnesses around
 Hold thee in full survey;
Forget the steps already trod,
 And onward urge thy way.

'Tis God's all-animating voice
 That calls thee from on high;
'Tis His own hand presents the prize
 To thine aspiring eye,—

That prize, with peerless glories bright,
 Which shall new luster boast
When victors' wreaths and monarchs'
  gems
 Shall blend in common dust.

— *Philip Doddridge*

ശു

THE DAY BEFORE

Some time some ordinary day will come,
A busy day, like this, filled to the brim
With ordinary tasks — perhaps so full
That we have little care or thought for Him.

And there will be no hint from silent skies,
No sign, no clash of cymbals, roll of drums —
And yet that ordinary day will be
The very day before our Lord returns!

The day before we lay our burdens down,
And learn instead the strange feel of a crown!
The day before all grieving will be past,
And all our tears be wiped away at last!

O child of God, awake and work and pray!
That ordinary day might be — today!
Make ready all thine house — tomorrow's sun
May dawn upon the Kingdom of God's Son.

— *Author Unknown*

FIRST THINGS FIRST

No time, no time for study,
  To meditate and pray —
And yet much time for *"doing"*
  In a fleshly, worldly way.

No time for things Eternal
  But much for things of earth,
The things important set aside
  For things of little worth.

Some things, 'tis true, are needful
  But first things must come first;
And what displaces God's own Word
  Of God it shall be cursed.

— *M. E. H.*

WATCH AND PRAY

Christian, seek not yet repose,
  Cast thy dreams of ease away;
Thou art in the midst of foes;
  Watch and pray.

Gird thy heavenly armor on,
  Wear it ever night and day;
Near thee lurks the evil one;
  Watch and pray.

Hear the victors who o'ercame;
  Still they watch each warrior's way;
All with one deep voice exclaim,
  "Watch and pray."

— *Charlotte Elliott*

ETERNITY

He who bends to himself a Joy
Doth the wingèd life destroy;
But he who kisses the Joy as it flies
Lives in Eternity's sunrise.

— *William Blake*

SLAVES

They are slaves who fear to speak
For the fallen and the weak;
They are slaves who will not choose
Hatred, scoffing and abuse,
Rather than in silence shrink
From the truth they needs must think;
They are slaves who dare not be
In the right with two or three.

— *James Russell Lowell*

JUST FOR TODAY

Lord, for tomorrow and its needs
  I do not pray;
Keep me, my God, from stain of sin,
  Just for today.

Let me both diligently work
  And duly pray;
Let me be kind in word and deed
  Just for today.

Let me be slow to do my will,
  Prompt to obey;
Help me to overcome my flesh
  Just for today.

Let me no wrong or idle word
  Unthinking say:
Set thou a seal upon my lips
  Just for today.

Let me in season, Lord, be grave,
  In season gay;
Let me be faithful to Thy grace
  Just for today.

So for tomorrow and its needs
  I do not pray;
But keep me, guide me, love me, Lord,
  Just for today.

— *Sybil F. Partridge*

FESTAL SONG

Rise up, O men of God!
  Have done with lesser things,
Give heart, and soul, and mind, and
      strength
  To serve the King of Kings.

Rise up, O men of God!
  His kingdom tarries long,
Bring in the day of brotherhood
  And end the night of wrong.

Lift high the cross of Christ!
  Tread where His feet have trod;
As brothers of the Son of Man,
  Rise up, O men of God!
              — William Pierson Merrill

ɔᴎ

LEND A HAND

I am only one,
But still I am one.
I cannot do everything,
But still I can do something;
And because I cannot do everything
I will not refuse to do the something
      that I can do.
              — Edward Everett Hale

ɔᴎ

GOD KEEPS HIS WORD

The Lord above has kept you safe
  Yes, all throughout the night;
Why, then, should you awake to fear
  The things beyond your sight?

Has He not promised to be near?
  Has He not kept His word?
Why, then, should you awake to fear
  Things all unseen, unheard?

Just place your all in His dear hands
  And rest assured this day
God loves you, loves you very much,
  He'll keep you ALL the way.
              — Phyllis C. Michael

ARE ALL THE CHILDREN IN?

I think ofttimes as the night draws nigh
  Of an old house on the hill,
Of a yard all wide and blossom-starred
  Where the children played at will.
And when the night at last came down,
  Hushing the merry din,
Mother would look around and ask,
  "Are all the children in?"

'Tis many and many a year since then,
  And the old house on the hill
No longer echoes to childish feet,
  And the yard is still, so still.
But I see it all, as the shadows creep,
  And tho' many the years have been
Since then, I can hear mother ask,
  "Are all the children in?"

I wonder if when the shadows fall
  On the last short, earthly day,
When we say good-bye to the world
      outside,
  All tired with our childish play,
When we step out into the Other Land
  Where mother so long has been,
Will we hear her ask, just as of old,
  "Are all the children in?"

              — Author Unknown

ɔᴎ

"YOU TOLD ME OF JESUS"

When the voice of the Master is call-
      ing
  And the gates into Heaven unfold,
And the saints of all ages are gathering
  And are thronging the city of gold;
How my heart shall o'erflow with the
      rapture
  If a brother shall greet me and say,
"You pointed my footsteps to Heaven.
  You told me of Jesus the Way."

              — Author Unknown

CALL BACK

If you have gone a little way ahead of me, call back;
It will cheer my heart and help my feet along the stony track.
And, if the light of my faith is dim, because the oil is low,
You will guide my lagging steps as wearily I go.
Call back and tell me He went with you into the storm.
Call back and say He kept you when the forest's roots were torn,
And that, when the heavens thundered and the earthquake shook the hill,
He bore you up and held you where the very air was still.

Friend of mine, call back and tell me, for I cannot see your face;
They say it glows with triumph and your feet bound in the race.
But there are mists between us, and my spirit eyes are dim,
And I cannot see the glory, though I long for word of Him.
But if you'll say He heard you when your prayer was but a cry,
And if you'll say He saw you through the night's sin-darkened sky;
If you have gone a little way ahead, friend of mine, call back;
It will cheer my heart and help my feet along the stony track.

— *Author Unknown*

∽

FILL ME NOW

Hover o'er me, Holy Spirit,
  Bathe my trembling heart and brow;
Fill me with Thy hallowed presence,
  Come, O come and fill me now.

Thou canst fill me, gracious Spirit,
  Though I cannot tell Thee how;
But I need Thee, greatly need Thee,
  Come, O come and fill me now.

I am weakness, full of weakness,
  At Thy sacred feet I bow;
Blest, divine, eternal Spirit,
  Fill with pow'r, and fill me now.

Cleanse and comfort, bless and save
    me,
  Bathe, O bathe my heart and brow;
Thou art comforting and saving,
  Thou art sweetly filling now.

— *E. R. Stokes*

A LAST PRAYER

Father, I scarcely dare to pray,
  So clear I see, now it is done,
That I have wasted half my day,
  And left my work but just begun;

So clear I see that things I thought
  Were right or harmless were a sin;
So clear I see that I have sought
  Unconscious, selfish aims to win;

So clear I see that I have hurt
  The soul I might have helped to
    save;
That I have slothful been, inert,
  Deaf to the calls thy leaders gave.

In outskirts of thy kingdom vast,
  Father, the humblest spot give me;
Set me the lowliest task thou hast,
  Let me repentant work for thee.

— *Helen Hunt Jackson*

THE HOUND OF HEAVEN

I fled Him, down the nights and down the days;
    I fled Him, down the arches of the years;
I fled Him, down the labyrinthine ways
    Of my own mind; and in the mist of tears
I hid from Him, and under running laughter.
        Up vistaed hopes, I sped;
        And shot, precipitated,
Adown Titanic glooms of chasmed fears,
    From those strong Feet that followed, followed after.
        But with unhurrying chase,
        And unperturbed pace,
    Deliberate speed, majestic instancy,
        They beat — and a Voice beat
        More instant than the Feet —
    "All things betray thee, who betrayest Me."

        I pleaded, outlaw-wise,
By many a hearted casement, curtained red,
    Trellised with intertwining charities;
(For, though I knew His love Who followèd,
        Yet was I sore adread
Lest, having Him, I must have naught beside.)
But, if one little casement parted wide,
    The gust of His approach would clash it to.
    Fear wist not to evade as Love wist to pursue.
Across the margent of the world I fled,
    And troubled the gold gateways of the stars,
    Smiting for shelter on their clangèd bars;
        Fretted to dulcet jars
And silvern chatter the pale ports o' the moon.
I said to dawn: Be sudden; to eve: Be soon —
    With thy young skyey blossoms heap me over
        From this tremendous Lover!
Float thy vague veil about me, lest He see!
    I tempted all His servitors, but to find
My own betrayal in their constancy,
In faith to Him their fickleness to me,
    Their traitorous trueness, and their loyal deceit.
To all swift things for swiftness did I sue;
    Clung to the whistling mane of every wind.
        But whether they swept, smoothly fleet,
    The long savannahs of the blue;
        Or whether, Thunder-driven,
    They clanged His chariot 'thwart a heaven,

Plashy with flying lightnings round the spurn o' their feet:—
Fear wist not to evade as Love wist to pursue.
Still with unhurrying chase,
And unperturbèd pace,
Deliberate speed, majestic constancy,
Came on the following Feet,
And a Voice above their beat—
"Naught shelters thee, who wilt not shelter Me."
I sought no more that after which I strayed
In the face of man or maid;
But still within the little children's eyes
Seems something, something that replies,
They at least are for me, surely for me!
I turned me to them very wistfully;
But just as their young eyes grew sudden fair
With dawning answers there,
Their angel plucked them from me by the hair.
"Come then, ye other children, Nature's—share
With me" (said I) "your delicate fellowship;
Let me greet you lip to lip,
Let me twine with you caresses,
Wantoning
With our Lady-Mother's vagrant tresses.
Banqueting
With her in her wind-walled palace,
Underneath her azured dais,
Quaffing, as your taintless way is,
From a chalice
Lucent-weeping out of the dayspring."
So it was done:
I in their delicate fellowship was one—
Drew the bolt of Nature's secrecies;
I knew all the swift importings
On the wilful face of skies;
I knew how the clouds arise,
Spumèd of the wild sea-snortings;
All that's born or dies
Rose and drooped with; made them shapers
Of mine own moods, or wailful or divine—
With them joyed and was bereaven.
I was heavy with the even,
When she lit her glimmering tapers
Round the day's dead sanctities
I laughed in the morning's eyes.
I triumphed and I saddened with all weather,

Heaven and I wept together,
And its sweet tears were salt with mortal mine;
Against the red throb of its sunset-heart
        I laid my own to beat
        And share commingling heat;
But not by that, by that, was eased my human smart.
In vain my tears were wet on Heaven's gray cheek.
For ah! we know not what each other says,
        These things and I; in sound I speak —
Their sound is but their stir, they speak by silences.
Nature, poor stepdame, cannot slake my drouth;
        Let her, if she would owe me,
Drop yon blue bosom-veil of sky, and show me
        The breasts o' her tenderness:
Never did any milk of hers once bless
        My thirsting mouth.
Nigh and nigh draws the chase,
        With unperturbèd pace,
    Deliberate speed, majestic instancy,
        And past those noisèd Feet
        A Voice comes yet more fleet —
"Lo! naught contents thee, who content'st not Me."
Naked I wait Thy love's uplifted stroke!
My harness piece by piece Thou hast hewn from me,
        And smitten me to my knee;
        I am defenseless utterly.
        I slept, methinks, and woke,
And, slowly gazing, find me stripped in sleep.
In the rash lustihead of my young powers,
        I shook the pillaring hours
And pulled my life upon me; grimed with smears,
I stand amid the dust o' the mounded years —
My mangled youth lies dead beneath the heap.
My days have crackled and gone up in smoke,
Have puffed and burst as sun-starts on a stream.
        Yea, faileth now even dream
The dreamer, and the lute the lutanist;
Even the linkèd fantasies, in whose blossomy twist
I swung the earth a trinket at my wrist,
Are yielding; cords of all too weak account
For earth, with heavy griefs so overplussed,
        Ah! is Thy love indeed
A weed, albeit an amaranthine weed,
Suffering no flowers except its own to mount?
        Ah! must —

Designer infinite! —
Ah! must Thou char the wood ere Thou canst limn with it?
My freshness spent its wavering shower i' the dust;
And now my heart is as a broken fount,
Wherein tear-dripping stagnate, split down ever
From the dank thoughts that shiver
Upon the sightful branches of my mind.
Such is; what is to be?
The pulp so bitter, how shall taste the rind?
I dimly guess what Time in mists confounds;
Yet ever and anon a trumpet sounds
From the hid battlements of Eternity:
Those shaken mists a space unsettle, then
Round the half-glimpsèd turrets slowly wash again;
But not ere him who summoneth
I first have seen, enwound
With glooming robes purpureal, cypress-crowned;
His name I know, and what his trumpet saith.
Whether man's heart or life it be which yields
Thee harvest, must Thy harvest fields
Be dunged with rotten death?

Now of that long pursuit
Comes on at hand the bruit;
That Voice is round me like a bursting sea:
"And is thy earth so marred,
Shattered in shard on shard?
Lo, all things fly thee, for thou fliest Me!
Strange, piteous, futile thing!
Wherefore should any set thee love apart?
Seeing none but I makes much of naught"
(He said),
"And human love needs human meriting:
How hast thou merited —
Of all man's clotted clay the dingiest clot?
Alack, thou knowest not
How little worthy of any love thou art!
Whom wilt thou find to love ignoble thee,
Save Me, save only Me?
All which I took from thee I did but take,
Not for thy harms,
But just thou might'st seek it in My arms,
All which thy child's mistake
Fancies as lost, I have stored for thee at home:
Rise, clasp My hand, and come!"

Halts by me that footfall:
Is my gloom, after all,
Shade of His hand, outstretched caressingly?
"Ah, fondest, blindest, weakest,
I am He Whom thou seekest!
Thou dravest love from thee, who dravest Me."

— *Francis Thompson*

ॐ

THE GOD OF ONE MORE CHANCE

A man named Peter stumbled bad,
Lost all the love he ever had.
Fouled his own soul's divinest spring,
Cursed, swore, and all that sort of
    thing.
He got another chance, and then
He reached the goal of God-like men!

A boy goes wrong, the same as he
Who fed swine in the far country;
He seems beyond the utmost reach
Of hearts that pray, of lips that preach;
Give him another chance, and see
How beautiful his life may be.

Paul cast the young man, Mark, aside,
But Barnabas his metal tried,
Called out his courage, roused his vim,
And made a splendid man of him.
Then Paul, near death, longed for one
    glance
At Mark, who had another chance.

King David, one dark day, fell down,
Lost every jewel from his crown;
He had another chance and found
His kingly self redeemed, recrowned.
Now lonely souls and countless
    throngs
Are lifted by his deathless songs!

Far-fallen souls, arise! Advance!
Ours is the God of one more chance!

— *Author Unknown*

THE LOST CHORD

Seated one day at the organ,
    I was weary and ill at ease,
And my fingers wandered idly
    Over the noisy keys.

I do not know what I was playing,
    Or what I was dreaming then;
But I struck one chord of music,
    Like the sound of a great Amen!

It flooded the crimson twilight,
    Like the close of an angel's psalm,
And it lay on my fevered spirit
    With a touch of infinite calm.

It quieted pain and sorrow,
    Like love overcoming strife;
It seemed the harmonious echo
    From our discordant life.

It linked all perplexed meanings
    Into one perfect peace,
And trembled away into silence
    As if it were loth to cease.

I have sought, but I seek it vainly,
    That one lost chord divine,
That came from the soul of the organ,
    An entered into mine.

It may be that death's bright angel
    Will speak in that chord again;
It may be that only in heaven
    I shall hear that grand Amen.

— *Adelaide Anne Procter*

RESOLUTION

I've reached the point of no return,
 My hands are on the plow;
I've seen His face, my heart did burn,
 I'd never go back now.

For once a man has seen the Lord,
 Has watched Him point the way,
Has known the joy His ways afford
 He can no longer stay.

I've reached the point of no return,
 The old allures grow dim,
The way of sin I gladly spurn,
 I'm going on with Him.

 — *Carlton Buck*

∞

WHO FOLLOWS IN HIS TRAIN?

The Son of God goes forth to war,
 A kingly crown to gain;
His blood-red banner streams afar;
 Who follows in his train?
Who best can drink his cup of woe,
 Triumphant over pain,
Who patient bears his cross below:
 He follows in his train!

That martyr first, whose eagle eye
 Could pierce beyond the grave;
Who saw his master in the sky,
 And called on him to save;
Like him with pardon on his tongue,
 In midst of mortal pain,
He prayed for those that did the
 wrong;
 Who follows in his train?

A glorious band, the chosen few,
 On whom the Spirit came;
Twelve valiant saints their hope they
 knew,
 And mocked the cross and flame;
They met the tyrant's brandished steel,
 The lion's gory mane,

They bowed their necks the death to
 feel!
 Who follows in their train?

A noble army, men and boys,
 The matron and the maid,
Around the Saviour's throne rejoice,
 In robes of light arrayed.
They climbed the steep ascent of
 heaven,
 Through peril, toil, and pain;
Oh God, to us may grace be given
 To follow in their train!

 — *Reginald Heber*

∞

LIGHT AFTER DARKNESS

Light after darkness,
 Gain after loss,
Strength after weakness,
 Crown after cross,
Sweet after bitter,
 Song after fears,
Home after wandering,
 Praise after tears.

Sheaves after sowing,
 Sun after rain,
Light after mystery,
 Peace after pain,
Joy after sorrow,
 Calm after blast,
Rest after weariness,
 Sweet rest at last.

Near after distant,
 Gleam after gloom,
Love after loneliness,
 Life after tomb;
After long agony,
 Rapture of bliss;
Right was the pathway
 Leading to this!

 — *Author Unknown*

My Daily Creed

Let me be a little kinder,
Let me be a little blinder
To the faults of those about me;
Let me praise a little more;
Let me be, when I am weary,
Just a little bit more cheery;
Let me serve a little better
Those that I am striving for.

Let me be a little braver
When temptation bids me waver;
Let me strive a little harder
To be all that I should be;
Let me be a little meeker
With the brother that is weaker;
Let me think more of my neighbor
And a little less of me.

— *Author Unknown*

Happiness

Happiness is like a crystal,
Fair and exquisite and clear,
Broken in a million pieces,
Shattered, scattered far and near.
Now and then along life's pathway,
Lo! some shining fragments fall;
But there are so many pieces,
No one ever finds them all.

You may find a bit of beauty,
Or an honest share of wealth,
While another just beside you
Gathers honor, love or health.
Vain to choose or grasp unduly,
Broken is the perfect ball;
And there are so many pieces,
No one ever finds them all.

Yet the wise as on they journey
Treasure every fragment clear,
Fit them as they may together,
Imaging the shattered sphere,
Learning ever to be thankful,
Though their share of it is small;
For it has so many pieces
No one ever finds them all.

— *Author Unknown*

Ahead

Those who win are those who try;
Not the kind who alibi!
Start, and never let it die —
    Keep going!

Life will never bring success
To the man who's motionless;
Crowns are made for those who press—
    Keep moving!

Do you want to gain the prize?
All those castles realize?
There's no limit but the skies —
    Keep climbing!

Those who've won are round about;
When you score you'll hear them
        shout!
Let no foe your courage flout —
    Keep fighting!

Sure! It's worth it when you stand
With that chosen, faithful band
Who inherit Canaan land —
    Keep striving!

Guess there won't be much to do
When you're dead, and buried too:
Now's the time to see it through —
    Keep driving!

On to vict'ry! Never quit!
Heroes make a drive for it!
Here's life! Use it every bit —
    Keep living!

— *Author Unknown*

THE MAN WITH THE HOE

Bowed by the weight of centuries he leans
Upon his hoe and gazes on the ground,
The emptiness of ages in his face,
And on his back the burden of the world.
Who made him dead to rapture and despair,
A thing that grieves not and that never hopes,
Stolid and stunned, a brother to the ox?
Who loosened and let down this brutal jaw?
Whose was the hand that slanted back this brow?
Whose breath blew out the light within this brain?

Is this the Thing the Lord God made and gave
To have dominion over sea and land;
To trace the stars and search the heavens for power;
To feel the passion of Eternity?
Is this the Dream He dreamed who shaped the suns
And pillared the blue firmament with light?
Down all the stretch of Hell to its last gulf
There is no shape more terrible than this —
More tongued with censure of the world's blind greed —
More filled with signs and portents for the soul —
More fraught with menace to the universe.

What gulfs between him and the seraphim!
Slave of the wheel of labor, what to him
Are Plato and the swing of Pleiades?
What the long reaches of the peaks of song,
The rift of dawn, the reddening of the rose?
Through this dread shape the suffering ages look;
Time's tragedy is in that aching stoop;
Through this dread shape humanity betrayed,
Plundered, profaned and disinherited,
Cries protest to the Judges of the World,
A protest that is also prophecy.

O masters, lords and rulers in all lands,
Is this the handiwork you give to God,
This monstrous thing distorted and soul-quenched?
How will you ever straighten up this shape;
Touch it again with immortality;
Give back the upward looking and the light;
Rebuild in it the music and the dream;
Make right the immemorial infamies,
Perfidious wrongs, immedicable woes?

O masters, lords and rulers in all lands,
How will the Future reckon with this Man?
How answer his brute question in that hour
When whirlwinds of rebellion shake the world?
How will it be with kingdoms and with kings —
With those who shaped him to the thing he is —
When this dumb Terror shall reply to God,
After the silence of the centuries?

— Edwin Markham

ᔆᖆᓀ

PIED BEAUTY

Glory be to God for dappled things —
   For skies of couple-colour as a brinded cow;
     For rose-moles all in stipple upon trout that swim;
Fresh-firecoal chestnut-falls; finches' wings;
   Landscape plotted and pieced — fold, fallow, and plough;
     And all trades, their gear and tackle and trim.

All things counter, original, spare, strange;
   Whatever is fickle, freckled (who knows how?)
     With swift, slow; sweet, sour; adazzle, dim;
He fathers-forth whose beauty is past change:
     Praise him.

— Gerard Manley Hopkins

ᔆᖆᓀ

SPRING

Nothing is so beautiful as spring —
   When weeds, in wheels, shoot long and lovely and lush;
   Thrush's eggs look little low heavens, and thrush
Through the echoing timber does so rinse and wring
The ear, it strikes like lightnings to hear him sing;
   The glassy peartree leaves and blooms, they brush
   The descending blue; that blue is all in a rush
With richness; the racing lambs too have fair their fling.

What is all this juice and all this joy?
   A strain of the earth's sweet being in the beginning
In Eden garden. — Have, get, before it cloy,
   Before it cloud, Christ, lord, and sour with sinning,
Innocent mind and Mayday in girl and boy,
   Most, O maid's child, thy choice and worthy the winning.

— Gerard Manley Hopkins

LOOK!

Say not the struggle naught availeth,
  The labor and the wounds are vain,
The enemy faints not, nor faileth,
  And as things have been they remain.

If hopes were dupes, fears may be liars;
  It may be in yon smoke concealed,
Your comrades chase e'en now the fliers,
  And, but for you, possess the field.

For while the tired waves, vainly breaking,
  Seem here no painful inch to gain,
Far back, through creeks and inlets making,
  Comes silent, flooding in, the main.

And not by eastern windows only,
  When daylight comes, comes in the light;
In front, the sun climbs slow, how slowly,
  But westward, look, the land is bright.

—Arthur Hugh Clough

OPTIMISM

Talk happiness. The world is sad enough
Without your woes. No path is wholly rough;
Look for the places that are smooth and clear,
And speak of those, to rest the weary ear
Of Earth, so hurt by one continuous strain
Of human discontent and grief and pain.

Talk faith. The world is better off without
Your uttered ignorance and morbid doubt.
If you have faith in God, or man, or self,
Say so. If not, push back upon the shelf
Of silence all your thoughts, till faith shall come;
No one will grieve because your lips are dumb.

Talk health. The dreary, never-changing tale
Of mortal maladies is worn and stale.
You cannot charm, or interest, or please
By harping on that minor chord, disease.
Say you are well, or all is well with you,
And God shall hear your words and make them true.

—Ella Wheeler Wilcox

ON THE SUMMIT

The path was steep and snowy — the way was hard and cold,
The wind rushed fiercely at us like a wolf upon the fold;
And we bit our lips and struggled in the terror of the blast,
And we blessed our staffs and wondered if the storm would soon be past.
Sometimes our feet slipped backward on the crusty ice and snow,
Sometimes we stumbled, helpless, for the way was hard to go;
Sometimes we fell, and falling, we were sorry we had tried
To reach the mountain's summit, and the hope within us died.

The path was steep and snowy — the way was hard and cold,
But we struggled ever forward, half afraid — no longer bold;
And with dogged perseverance, we pushed up the hidden trail,
And we seemed but children playing with the elements — too frail
To live long in the displeasure of the wind and hail and sleet,
And the snowy down-like blanket seemed a mammoth winding sheet —
And we almost started homeward with a weary broken sigh,
But we flinched and struggled forward 'neath the scorn that cleft the sky.

The path was steep and snowy — the way was hard and cold,
But at last we reached the summit, and it glittered with the gold
Of the sun that had been shining, with a perfect, glowing light
From behind the heavy storm clouds that had turned the day to night.
And standing on the summit, we looked down and tried to pray,
For we wished to thank the Father who had kept us on our way;
For the snow and sleet and windstorm were but trifles in the past,
And they made the sunshine brighter when we reached the top at last.

— Margaret E. Sangster, Jr.

GIVING

See the rivers flowing downward to the sea,
Pouring all their treasures bountiful and free;
Yet, to help their giving, hidden streams arise,
Or, if need be, showers feed them from the skies.
Watch the princely flowers their rich fragrance spread;
Load the air with perfume from their beauty shed.
Still their lavish spending leaves them not in dearth,
With fresh life replenished from their mother earth.
So the more thou spendest from thy little store,
With a double bounty, God will give thee more.

— Adelaide Anne Procter

Open the Door

Open the door, let in the air;
The winds are sweet, and the flowers are fair;
Joy is abroad in the world today;
If our door is wide, it may come in this way.
Open the door!

Open the door, let in the sun;
It hath a smile for every one;
It hath made the raindrops gold and gems;
It may change our tears to diadems.
Open the door!

Open the door of the soul; let in
Strong, pure thoughts which shall banish sin.
They will grow and bloom with a grace divine,
And their fruit shall be sweeter than that of the vine.
Open the door!

Open the door to the heart; let in
Sympathy sweet for stranger and kin;
It will make the halls of the heart so fair
That angels may enter unaware.
Open the door!

— *Author Unknown*

For Inspiration

The Prayers I make will then be sweet indeed,
    If Thou the spirit give by which I pray;
    My unassisted heart is barren clay,
Which of its native self can nothing feed;
Of good and pious works Thou art the seed
    Which quickens where Thou say'st it may;
    Unless Thou show us then Thine own true way,
No man can find it! Father, Thou must lead!
Do Thou, then, breathe those thoughts into my mind
    By which such virtue may in me be bred
    That in Thy holy footsteps I may tread;
The fetters of my tongue do Thou unbind,
    That I may have the power to sing of Thee
    And sound Thy praises everlastingly.

— *Michelangelo Buonarroti*

BUILDERS

We would be building; temples still undone
  O'er crumbling walls their crosses scarcely lift
Waiting till love can raise the broken stone,
  And hearts creative bridge the human rift;
We would be building, Master, let Thy plan
  Reveal the life that God would give to man.

Teach us to build; upon the solid rock
  We set the dream that hardens into deed,
Ribbed with the steel that time and change doth mock,
  Th' unfailing purpose of our noblest creed;
Teach us to build; O Master, lend us sight
  To see the towers gleaming in the light.

O keep us building, Master; may our hands
  Ne'er falter when the dream is in our hearts,
When to our ears there come divine commands
  And all the pride of sinful will departs;
We build with Thee, O grant enduring worth
  Until the heav'nly Kingdom comes on earth.

— *Purd E. Deitz*

∿

From ESSAY ON MAN

Know then thy selfe, presume not God to scan;
The proper study of Mankind is Man.
Plac'd on this isthmus of a middle state,
A Being darkly wise, and rudely great:
With too much knowledge for the Sceptic side,
With too much weakness for the Stoic's pride,
He hangs between; in doubt to act, or rest;
In doubt to deem himself a God, or Beast;
In doubt his Mind or Body to prefer;
Born but to die, and reas'ning but to err,
Alike in ignorance, his reason such,
Whether he thinks too little, or too much:
Chaos of Thought and Passion, all confus'd;
Still by himself abus'd, or disabus'd;
Created half to rise and half to fall;
Great lord of all things, yet a prey to all;
Sole judge of Truth, in endless Error hurl'd;
The glory, jest and riddle of the world.

— *Alexander Pope*

CHRISTIAN PARADOX

It is in loving — not in being loved,—
The heart is blest;
It is in giving — not in seeking gifts,—
We find our quest.

If thou art hungry, lacking heavenly food,—
Give hope and cheer.
If thou art sad and wouldst be comforted,—
Stay sorrow's tear.

Whatever be thy longing and thy need,—
That do thou give;
So shall thy soul be fed, and thou indeed,
Shalt truly live.
— *Author Unknown*

SAILING

My soul is sailing through the sea
But the past is heavy and hindereth me.
My soul is sailing through the sea
The past hath crusted cumbrous shells
That hold the flesh of cold sea-mells
About my soul.
The huge waves wash, the high waves roll,
Each barnacle clingeth and worketh dole
And hindereth me from sailing!

Old past let go and drop i' the sea
Till fathomless waters cover thee!
For I am living but thou art dead;
Thou drawest back, I strive ahead
The day to find.
Thy shells unbind! Night comes behind,
I needs must hurry with the wind
And trim me best for sailing.
— *Sidney Lanier*

THE DOOMED MAN

There is a time, we know not when,
A point we know not where,
That marks the destiny of men,
For glory or despair.

There is a line, by us unseen,
That crosses every path;
The hidden boundary between
God's patience and His wrath.

— *Joseph Addison Alexander*

SPRING AND FALL
To a Young Child

Margaret, are you grieving
Over Goldengrove unleaving?
Leaves, like the things of man, you
With your fresh thoughts care for,
    can you?
Ah, as the heart grows older
It will come to such sights colder
By and by, not spare a sigh
Though worlds of wanwood leafmeal
    lie;
And yet you will weep and know why.
Now no matter, child, the name:
Sorrow's springs are the same.
Nor mouth had, no nor mind, ex-
    pressed
What heart heard of, ghost guessed:
It is the blight man was born for,
It is Margaret you mourn for.

— *Gerard Manley Hopkins*

ANOTHER DAY

Another day lies just before me —
    Another day in which to live;
Another day to meet the challenge
    To work and pray and love — and
        give!

Another day to read the Bible,
    Another day to meet the test,
Another day of prayerful choosing
    Between the better and the best!

Another day to follow Jesus,
    Another day to trust and wait.
Another day of pressing forward
    T'ward the prize at Heaven's gate!

Another day to be a witness —
    Oh, what a privilege is mine!
Another day — life's candle burning;
    Another day to let it shine!

— *Alice Hansche Mortenson*

SPRING UP, O WELL!

We sing the song that Israel sang in the desert long ago:
Spring up, O well; spring up, O well; let the living waters flow.

Spring up, O well of blessing, spring in our midst today,
    For thirsty souls are longing to drink abundantly;
Come from the hidden fountains, come in a brimming flood,
    Refresh us in the desert, thou precious gift of God.

Spring up, O well of blessing, we cry to Thee today;
    Break forth in mighty torrent as now we sing and pray.
The souls that round us perish — the old, the young, the strong —
    To Thee, by right and ransom, the Lord of hosts, belong.

Spring up, O well of blessing, we sing to Thee today.
    The "princes" and the "nobles" Thy great command obey
In toiling and in labour amid the burning sand.
    Spring up, flow forth, and gladden the whole expectant band.

— *Author Unknown*

To Any Daddy

There are little eyes upon you, and they're watching night and day;
There are little ears that quickly take in every word you say;
There are little hands all eager to do everything you do,
And a little boy who's dreaming of the day he'll be like you.
You're the little fellow's idol, you're the wisest of the wise;
In his little mind about you no suspicions ever rise;
He believes in you devoutly, holds that all you say and do
He will say and do in your way when he's grown up like you.
There's a wide-eyed little fellow who believes you're always right,
And his ears are always open and he watches day and night,
You are setting an example every day in all you do,
For the little boy who's waiting to grow up to be like you.

—Author Unknown

The Winds of Fate

One ship drives east and another drives
    west
  With the selfsame winds that blow.
    'Tis the set of the sails
    And not the gales
  Which tells us the way to go.

Like the winds of the sea are the ways
    of fate,
  As we voyage along through life:
    'Tis the set of a soul
    That decides its goal,
  And not the calm or the strife.

—Ella Wheeler Wilcox

Compensation

Is thy cruse of comfort failing?
  Rise and share it with another,
And through all the years of famine
  It shall serve thee and thy brother.
Love Divine will fill thy storehouse,
  Or thy handful still renew;
Scanty fare for one will often
  Make a royal feast for two.

For the heart grows rich in giving,
  All its wealth is living grain;
Seeds which mildew in the garner,
  Scattered, fill with gold the plain,
Is thy burden hard and heavy?
  Do thy steps drag wearily?
Help to bear thy brother's burden,
  God will bear both it and thee.

—Mrs. Rundle Charles

Blessed Are the Eyes That See

Blessed are the eyes that see
  The things that you have seen,
Blessed are the feet that walk
  The ways where you have been.

Blessed are the eyes that see
  The agony of God,
Blessed are the feet that tread
  The paths His feet have trod.

Blessed are the souls that solve
  The paradox of pain,
And find the path that, piercing it,
  Leads through to peace again.

—G. A. Studdert-Kennedy

FRIENDLY OBSTACLES

For every hill I've had to climb,
For every stone that bruised my feet,
For all the blood and sweat and grime,
For blinding storms and burning heat,
My heart sings but a grateful song —
These were the things that made me
    strong!

For all the heartaches and the tears,
For all the anguish and the pain,
For gloomy days and fruitless years,
And for the hopes that lived in vain,
I do give thanks: for now I know
These were the things that helped me
    grow.

'Tis not the softer things of life
Which stimulate man's will to strive,
But bleak adversity and strife
Do most to keep man's will alive.
O'er rose-strewn paths the weaklings
    creep,
But brave hearts dare to climb the
    steep!

— *Author Unknown*

TAKE THE SUPREME CLIMB!

Jesus lead me up the mountain,
    Where the whitest robes are seen,
Where the saints can see the fountain,
    Where the pure are keeping clean.

Higher up, where light increases,
    Rich above all earthly good,
Where the life of sinning ceases,
    Where the Spirit comes in floods.

Lead me higher, nothing dreading,
    In the race to never stop;
In thy footsteps keep me treading,
    Give me grace to reach the top.

— *Author Unknown*

ODE TO LIFE

Life! I know not what thou art,
But know that thou and I must part;
And when, or how, or where we met,
I own to me's a secret yet.

Life! we've been long together
Through pleasant and through cloudy
    weather;
'Tis hard to part when friends are
    dear,—
Perhaps 'twill cost a sigh, a tear;
—Then steal away, give little warning,
    Choose thine own time,
Say not Good Night, — but in some
    brighter clime
    Bid me Good Morning.

— *Anna Letitia Barbauld*

THERE ALWAYS WILL BE GOD

They cannot shell His temple,
    Nor dynamite His throne;
They cannot bomb His city,
    Nor rob Him of His own.

They cannot take Him captive,
    Nor strike Him deaf and blind,
Nor starve Him to surrender,
    Nor make Him change His mind.

They cannot cause Him panic,
    Nor cut off His supplies;
They cannot take His kingdom,
    Nor hurt Him with their lies.

Though all the world be shattered,
    His truth remains the same,
His righteous laws still potent,
    And "Father" still His name.

Though we face war and struggle
    And feel their goal and rod,
We know above confusion
    There always will be God.

— *A. L. Murray*

The Heart of a Child

The heart of a child is a scroll,
  A page that is lovely and white;
And to it as fleeting years roll,
  Come hands with a story to write.
Be ever so careful, O hand;
  Write thou with a sanctified pen;
Thy story shall live in the land
  For years in the doings of men.
It shall echo in circles of light,
  Or lead to the death of a soul.
Give here but a message of right,
  For the heart of a child is a scroll.

I thought, perhaps he'd make a saint,
  And bless the nation and the earth,
If kept from sins that blight and taint,
  And held to things of greatest worth.

I knew this little bed contained
  A mighty force for right or wrong,
And prayed that he be saved and
    trained,
  And lead to God a blessed throng.

—Author Unknown

—Walter E. Isenhour

Beside a Baby's Bed

I stood beside a baby's bed,
  And looked into his lovely face,
And wondered what should lie ahead
  For him along life's future race.

He looked so innocent and pure
  To be in such a fallen world,
With many evils to allure
  Where Satan's banners fly unfurled.

I knew he'd need much earnest prayer
  Across the weeks and months and
    years,
A mother's love and tender care
  To save him from remorseful tears.

The world, I knew, would tempt him
    sore
  To waste his talents and his time,
And turn from Jesus, more and more,
  And from the life that is sublime.

A Little Child Shall Lead Them

"A little child shall lead them"—
How often this is true!
Many times he's discovered oases
In deserts where nothing grew.

"A little child shall lead them"—
Will soon and unprompted forgive,
Forget every wrong that's been done
    him;
Then laugh, and love, and live.

"A little child shall lead them"—
When he climbs up on your knee
And whispers softly, "I love you,"
His words are honest and free.

"A little child shall lead them"—
My little tyke home in bed—
(Folks say that he looks just like me)
He'll keep my feet straight ahead.

—Phyllis C. Michael

75

FOR THE YOUNGEST

Gentle Jesus, meek, and mild,
Look upon a little child;
Pity my simplicity,
Suffer me to come to thee.

Fain I would to thee be brought;
Dearest God, forbid it not:
Give me, dearest God, a place
In the kingdom of thy grace.

Put thy hands upon my head,
Let me in thine arms be stayed;
Let me lean upon thy breast,
Lull me, lull me, Lord, to rest.

Hold me fast in thy embrace,
Let me see thy smiling face.
Give me, Lord, thy blessing give;
Pray for me, and I shall live.

I shall live the simple life,
Free from sin's uneasy strife,
Sweetly ignorant of ill,
Innocent and happy still.

Oh that I may never know
What the wicked people do!
Sin is contrary to thee,
Sin is the forbidden tree.

Keep me from the great offence,
Guard my helpless innocence;
Hide me, from all evil hide,
Self and stubbornness and pride.

Lamb of God, I look to thee;
Thou shalt my Example be;
Thou art gentle, meek, and mild.
Thou wast once a little child.

Fain I would be as thou art;
Give me thy obedient heart.
Thou art pitiful and kind;
Let me have thy loving mind.

Meek and lowly may I be;
Thou art all humility.
Let me to my betters bow;
Subject to thy parents thou.

Let me above all fulfil
God my heavenly Father's will;
Never his good Spirit grieve,
Only to his glory live.

Thou didst live to God alone,
Thou didst never seek thine own;
Thou thyself didst never please,
God was all thy happiness.

Loving Jesu, gentle Lamb,
In thy gracious hands I am.
Make me, Saviour, what thou art,
Live thyself within my heart.

I shall then show forth thy praise,
Serve thee all my happy days:
Then the world shall always see
Christ, the holy child, in me.

— *Charles Wesley*

∽

A CHILD'S THOUGHT OF GOD

They say that God lives very high!
    But if you look above the pines,
You cannot see our God. And why?

And if you dig down in the mines,
    You never see him in the gold,
Tho' from him all that's glory shines.

God is so good, he wears a fold
    Of heaven and earth across his face:
Like secrets kept, for love, untold.

But still I feel that his embrace
    Slides down by thrills, through all
            things made,
Thro' sight and sound of every place:

As if my tender mother laid
    On my shut lids her kisses' pressure,
Half waking me at night, and said,
    "Who kissed you through the dark,
            dear guesser?"

— *Elizabeth Barrett Browning*

THE DEAR LITTLE ARMS

I think sometimes of the dear little arms
    That used to entwine around my neck,
And the old quaint saying that always charms,
    "I love you a bushel and a peck."
I think of the hug and the sweet, sweet kiss
    Of my darling little girls and boys;
The laughs and the smiles no father would miss
    As they played with their dolls and their toys.

And I think of the crib in which they slept
    When they were infants and tiny tots;
And when they were sick how we prayed and wept
    And felt of their pulse and watched them lots;
And when they smiled after the fever cooled
    And the doctor said, "They'll soon be well,"
How we thanked our God in Heaven who ruled
    In a way that words never can tell.

I think of the days when they played about
    And made their cakes and little mud pies;
How they darted in and they darted out
    Sometimes with their frets and childish cries;
How the girls "kept house" and the boys rode sticks
    And thought the world is a place of glee;
A place for frolic and a place for "tricks,"
    Where tests and trials never could be.

I think of the little moss beds they made
    And laid their dollies in them to sleep;
How the boys went out like men on parade,
    Or to see how high each one could leap;
And I think how they knelt in the pale, dim light
    When their many hours of play were through,
And said their prayers and a sweet "Good night,
    I love you Mamma and Daddy too."

I think of the days when they left for school,
    How I longed and yearned for their return;
I think of their books on a chair or stool
    And the early lessons each would learn;
I think of their games and little playmates,
    The balls they tossed, the marbles they rolled;
I think how they ran through the doors and gates
    In summer's heat or in winter's cold.

But the years have come and the years have gone
 And the sweet little ones are away;
No longer they play in the woods and lawn,
 Nor run and romp through the livelong day;
But I sometimes long for those dear little arms
 To again entwine around my neck,
And hear the quaint saying that always charms,
 "I love you a bushel and a peck."

—Walter E. Isenhour

ক৺৯

"ONE OF THE LEAST OF THESE"

I hurried down a busy street
 To church one Sunday morn;
I saw a ragged little boy,
 Who stood there all forlorn.

As I passed by, his pleading eyes
 Just seemed to fairly shout,
"Open your heart and take me in" —
 Instead I pushed him out.

In church that morn I also heard
 My Saviour say to me,
"Open your heart and take Me in."
 So I took Him in, you see.

Then, while the door was open wide,
 I found to my surprise,
My Saviour brought along with Him
 The boy with pleading eyes.

— Lois Duffield

ক৺৯

BABY

Where did you come from, baby dear?
Out of the everywhere into here.

Where did you get those eyes so blue?
Out of the sky as I came through.

What makes the light in them sparkle
 and spin?
Some of the starry spikes left in.

Where did you get that little tear?
I found it waiting when I got here.

What makes your forehead so smooth
 and high?
A soft hand stroked it as I went by.

What makes your cheek like a warm
 white rose?
I saw something better than any one
 knows.

Whence that three-cornered smile of
 bliss?
Three angels gave me at once a kiss.

Where did you get this pearly ear?
God spoke, and it came out to hear.

Where did you get those arms and
 hands?
Love made itself into bonds and bands.

Feet, when did you come, you darling
 things?
From the same box as the cherubs'
 wings.

How did they all just come to be you?
God thought about me, and so I grew.

But how did you come to us, you dear?
God thought about you, and so I am
 here.

— George Macdonald

THE NEW NAME

A little boy, well known to me,
  Sat reading in a Book;
And childlike sweet simplicity
  Beamed in his earnest look:
He read of warriors, shepherds, kings,
  Of little children, too;
And grand and noble were the things
  That passed before his view.

One day of Samuel he read
  That holy Book within;
When suddenly he raised his head,
  And thus he did begin:
"Oh, Mother, call me Samuel,
  And then I shall be good."
But Mother knew, and knew quite
    well,
  How much he understood.

Yet, willing to indulge his whim,
  She readily complied,
To take this way of teaching him
  God's grace must be supplied.
So Willie ceased to be his name
  As he was known before,
And Samuel at once became
  The title that he bore.

For twenty days the sky was clear,
  And everything went well;
But one dark day a storm drew near,
  And down his castle fell.
"How now, my boy?" his mother said,
  "So soon to come to shame?
Where have thy pleasing visions fled,
  And where thy nice new name?"

Then she endeavored earnestly
  This lesson to impart,
That if he would be holy, he
  Must have a change of heart:
That from the heart our actions flow,
  By nature full of sin;
That all who wish true joy to know
  Must know a change within.

Some years have passed away since he
  Sat reading in that Book;
But still a calm sincerity
  Beams in his earnest look:
And now he loves to tell this tale,
  (Quite true in every part),
That change of name has no avail
  Without a change of heart.

— *The Christian*

TOO LITTLE CHILDREN

Said a precious little laddie,
  To his father one bright day,
"May I give myself to Jesus,
  Let Him wash my sins away?"

"Oh, my son, but you're too little,
  Wait until you older grow,
Bigger folk, 'tis true, do need Him,
  But little folk are safe you know."

Said the father to his laddie
  As a storm was coming on,
"Are the sheep safely sheltered,
  Safe within the fold, my son?"

"All the big ones are, my father,
  But the lambs, I let them go,
For I didn't think it mattered,
  Little ones are safe, you know."

Oh, my brother! Oh, my sister!
  Have you too made that mistake?
Little hearts that now are yielding
  May be hardened then — too late.

E'er the evil days come nigh them,
  "Let the children come to Me,
And forbid them not," said Jesus,
  "For such shall My Kingdom be."

— *Author Unknown*

A Girl Is a Girl

A girl is a girl so frilly and sweet
You'd just like to hug her the moment you meet.

She's little pink ruffles and nylon and lace;
She's an innocent look on a little pink face;

She's dozens of dollies of ev'ry known size —
This cute little angel with stars in her eyes;

She's little toy dishes and parties and teas —
A princess at heart, you can say what you please;

She's all kinds of ribbons and buttons and bows,
A pleasure to have as any one knows.

She's little play houses and red rocking chairs,
Soft pinked eye bunnies and brown teddy bears;

She's the pictures she colored and wants you to see,
This wee little pixie who climbs on your knee;

She's roses and sunshine, yes, she's all that —
Wearing pink gloves and a little pink hat;

In Mother's lace curtain this miniature bride
Is really quite charming it can't be denied.

She's an artist, a teacher, a nurse all in white,
Yet the mother of four from morning till night;

She's perfume and powder and all pretty things
Like bracelets and beads and play diamond rings;

She's ice cream and candy and pink birthday cake
She's also the cookies she helped Mother bake;

She's the one perfect nuisance to each little boy
But she's Daddy's own sweetheart, his pride and his joy;

She can pout, she can stomp, she can tease, she can cry,
But still she's his pet, the very apple of his eye.

She's kittens and everything cuddly and nice —
Ah, sure 'n' she's a bit of God's own paradise.

—*Phyllis C. Michael*

A Boy Is a Boy

A boy is a boy — an integral part
Of all that pulls and tugs at your heart.
He's all kinds of trains and new windup toys,
He's fish hooks and kites, he's mischief and noise;
He's no stranger to drums and bugles and such,
And all straggly dogs he loves very much.
He's the master of bikes and of baseball gloves;
He's brown sparkling eyes that ev'ryone loves.
He's a partner of penknives and little toy guns;
He's dozens of cookies and hot dogs and buns.

He's a fireman, a cowboy, a pilot, a cop —
His hands and his feet, well they just never stop.
He's all kinds of scooters, airplanes and balls;
He loves to wear T-shirts and old overalls.
He's covered with mud from his head to his toes
And where he finds trouble nobody knows.
Yet a boy is a boy — an integral part
Of all that pulls and tugs at your heart.

— *Phyllis C. Michael*

Child's Evening Hymn

Now the day is over,
   Night is drawing nigh,
Shadows of the evening
   Steal across the sky.

Now the darkness gathers,
   Stars begin to peep,
Birds and beasts and flowers
   Soon will be asleep.

Jesus, give the weary
   Calm and sweet repose,
With thy tenderest blessing
   May our eyelids close.

Grant to little children
   Visions bright of thee,
Guard the sailors tossing
   On the deep blue sea.

Comfort every sufferer
   Watching late in pain,
Those who plan some evil
   From their sin restrain.

Through the long night-watches
   May thine angels spread
Their white wings above me,
   Watching round my bed.

When the morning wakens,
   Then may I arise
Pure and fresh and sinless
   In thy holy eyes.

Glory to the Father,
   Glory to the Son,
And to thee, blest Spirit,
   Whilst all ages run. Amen.

— *Sabine Baring-Gould*

WHO WANTS THE BOYS AND GIRLS?

God wants the boys, the merry, merry
    boys,
The noisy boys, the funny boys,
  The thoughtless boys;
God wants the boys with all their joys
That He as gold may make them pure,
And teach them trials to endure,
    His heroes brave
      He'd have them be.
    Fighting for truth
     And purity,
  GOD WANTS THE BOYS!

God wants the happy-hearted girls,
The loving girls, the best of girls,
  The worst of girls;
God wants to make the girls His pearls,
And so reflect His holy face,
And bring to mind His wondrous
    grace,
    That beautiful
      The world may be,
    And filled with love
     And purity.
  GOD WANTS THE GIRLS!

                          — *Author Unknown*

"OF SUCH IS THE KINGDOM OF GOD"

I think when I read that sweet story of old,
  When Jesus was here among men,
How he called little children as lambs to his fold;
  I should like to have been with them then.

I wish that his hands had been placed on my head,
  That his arm had been thrown around me,
And that I might have seen his kind look when he said,
  "Let the little ones come unto me."

Yet still to his footstool in prayer I may go,
  And ask for a share in his love;
And if I thus earnestly seek him below,
  I shall see him and hear him above,

In that beautiful place he has gone to prepare
  For all who are washed and forgiven;
And many dear children shall be with him there,
  For of such is the kingdom of heaven.

But thousands and thousands who wander and fall
  Never heard of that heavenly home;
I wish they could know there is room for them all,
  And Jesus has bid them to come.

I long for the joy of that glorious time,
  The sweetest, the brightest, the best;
When the dear little children of every clime
  Shall crowd to his arms and be blest!
               — *Mrs. Jemima (Thompson) Luke*

HAND IN HAND, A CHILD AND I

Dear Lord, I do not ask
  That Thou shouldst give me some high work of Thine,
Some noble calling or some wondrous task;
  Give me a little hand to hold in mine;
Give me a little child to point the way
  Over the strange sweet path that leads to Thee;
Give me a little voice to teach to pray;
  Give me two shining eyes Thy face to see.
The only crown I ask, dear Lord, to wear
  Is this — that I may teach a little child.
I do not ask that I should ever stand
  Among the wise, the worthy, or the great;
I only ask that softly, hand in hand,
  A child and I may enter at Thy gate.

                     — *Author Unknown*

THE CHRISTIAN CAMP

The hill was cool and silent,
No moon was in the sky;
The stars shone forth in beauty
And in brilliance there on high;
They sparkled in their laughter,
They twinkled with delight;
God had hung His perfect diamonds
In the sky to give us light.

A little child was running
O'er the fields, so glad and free,
Her shrill and childish laughter
Filled all the world with glee;
Her little feet were dancing;
Her eyes were sparkling, too,
God's sweetest, choicest diamonds
Shone in those eyes of blue.

God is gathering up His diamonds
From every age and clime;
The big ones and the small ones,
The dull, and those who shine.
Those are His precious jewels,
These are His own delight;
He shapes them with His loving hand,
Till each is sparkling bright.

He is touching each with beauty
Grinding off the earthly clay;
He is polishing His diamonds
To shine with Him for aye.

         — *Artemisia E. Strout*

MODERN MIRACLE

A little boy once long ago,
At even, ere the sun sank low,
Freely offered his meager food,
Which Thou didst take and bless and
    break,
And with it fed the multitude.

Dear Lord, with like simplicity
I bring and give my life to Thee
To bless and break as seems most good;
Then of it take, for Thy dear sake,
And use — to feed the multitude.

         — *William Atherton*

THERE SHALL BE WARS

My son knelt down beside his bed and prayed a small boy's prayer:
"Dear Lord, bless Mommy. Find my ball; I've hunted everywhere.
Help Daddy in his work, and help my Sis at school, and then
Help me when I grow up to be 4-F. Amen."

I, listening, smiled. And then the truth of what he prayed gripped me.
In his whole life there's been no peace nor hope of peace. And he
Has prayed as best he knows. Why should he pray that wars should cease
When all his life there's been no time of peace?

"There is a peace," I told my son, "that you can know for life.
The peace of God will bring you through the times of war and strife.
No need to fear, for God is here. Just lean on Him and know
God's peace within your heart; and where you go, He'll go."

— Anna Williams

᧳

THE SOUL OF A CHILD

The soul of a child is the loveliest flower
    That grows in the Garden of God;
Its climb is from weakness to knowledge and power,
    To the sky from the clay and the clod.

To beauty and sweetness its grows under care,
    Neglected, 'tis ragged and wild.
'Tis a plant that is tender but wondrously rare,
    The sweet, wistful soul of a child.

Be tender, O gardener, and give it its share
    Of moisture, of warmth and of light,
And let it not lack for thy painstaking care
    To protect it from frost and from blight.

A glad day will come when its bloom shall unfold,
    It will seem that an angel has smiled.
Reflecting its beauty and sweetness untold,
    In the sensitive heart of a child.

— Author Unknown

᧳

A Song of Hope

Children of yesterday,
Heirs of tomorrow,
What are you weaving?
Labor and sorrow?
Look to your loom again,
Faster and faster
Fly the great shuttles
Prepared by the Master.
Life's in the loom!
Room for it --
Room!

Children of yesterday,
Heirs of tomorrow,
Lighten the labor
And sweeten the sorrow.
Now, while the shuttles fly
Faster and faster,
Up and be at it,
At work with the Master.
He stands at your loom;
Room for Him --
Room!

Children of yesterday,
Heirs of tomorrow,
Look at your fabric
Of labor and sorrow.
Seamy and dark
With despair and disaster,
Turn it, and --lo!
The design of the Master!
The Lord's at the loom;
Room for Him --
Room!

— Mary A. Lathbury

Poor and Wealthy Children

The children in a Christian home
Are rich beyond compare;
They learn to read the Word of God
And speak His name in prayer.
Saved parents try to lead the child
Along the heavenward way,
To trust the Christ of Calvary
And walk with Him each day.

But when the parents know not God,
How poor the children are.
Great wealth of store without the
    Christ
Leaves children very poor,
With parents without peace or rest,
No Christ with power to save,
No wealth they will not have to leave,
No hope beyond the grave.

May God in mercy grant to us
A home where He has sway,
Where peace and joy from heaven
    above
Abide from day to day;
Where Bible reading is the rule
And fellowship is sweet
Because the members of our home
All worship at His feet.

— Edward L. Crane

I GREET THEE . . .

I greet Thee, who my sure Redeemer art,
  My only Trust and Savior of my heart,
Who pain didst undergo for my poor sake;
  I pray Thee from our hearts all cares to take.

Thou art the King of mercy and of grace,
  Reigning omnipotent in every place:
So come, O King, and our whole being sway;
  Shine on us with the light of Thy pure day.

Thou art the life, by which alone we live,
  And all our substance and our strength receive;
Sustain us by Thy faith and by Thy power,
  And give us strength in every trying hour.

Thou hast the true and perfect gentleness,
  No harshness hast Thou and no bitterness:
O grant to us the grace we find in Thee,
  That we may dwell in perfect unity.

Our hope is in no other save in Thee;
  Our faith is built upon Thy promise free;
Lord, give us peace, and make us calm and sure,
  That in Thy strength we evermore endure.

— *John Calvin*

THROUGH HIS NAME

I look at the sun, and I think of the power
  And majesty of God;
I look on the earth where the flowers bloom,
  And I think of the path he trod.
I look at the trees, and think of the wood
  Which made his cross of shame;
Then I look in my heart, and see my sin,
  And believing, I've life through his name.

— *Author Unknown*

THE HEALER

So stood of old the holy Christ
　Amidst the suffering throng;
With whom his slightest touch sufficed
　To make the weakest strong.

That healing gift he lends to them
　Who use it in his name;
The power that filled his garment's
　hem
Is evermore the same.

The paths of pain are thine. Go forth
　With patience, trust, and hope;
The sufferings of a sin-sick earth
　Shall give thee ample scope.

So shalt thou be with power endued
　From him who went about
The Syrian hillsides doing good,
　And casting demons out.

That Good Physician liveth yet
　Thy friend and guide to be;
The Healer by Gennesaret
　Shall walk the rounds with thee.

— *John Greenleaf Whittier*

ᔣ

THE FACE OF CHRIST

What can strip the seeming glory
　From the idols of the earth?
Not a sense of right and duty,
　But a sight of peerless worth.
'Tis the look that melted Peter,
　'Tis the face that Stephen saw,
'Tis the heart that wept with Mary
　Can alone from idols draw.
Draw, and win, and fill completely,
　Till the cup o'erflows its brim.
What have we to do with idols
　Since we've companied with Him?

—*J. Stuart Holden*

THE WOUNDS OF JESUS

His Hands were pierced, the Hands
　that made
The mountain range and everglade;
That washed the stains of sin away
And changed earth's darkness into day.

His Feet were pierced, the Feet that
　trod
The farthest shining star of God;
And left their imprint deep and clear
On every winding pathway here.

His Heart was pierced, the Heart that
　burned
To comfort every heart that yearned!
And from it came a cleansing flood,
The river of redeeming Blood.

His Hands and Feet and Heart, all
　three
Were pierced for me on Calvary,
And here and now, to Him I bring
My hands, feet, heart, an offering.

— *Cecil J. Allen*

ᔣ

EYES UP!

Center well upon His promise,
Let the world jet on its way,
For our land lies just before us
And the parapet of day.

We will rise to heaven's highland,
And we'll learn the answers, too,
Of the trials that have bothered
And the thorn we have passed thro'.

Eyes up, then, to face His morning,
Eternity beyond the known,
To the time of dreamed fulfillment...
He is coming for His own!

— *Mary Gustafson*

AM I RUNNING FROM YOU, JESUS?

Lord, I told them things they wanted to hear,
Safe things to say to college students:
That Birchites and fundamentalists are bad;
That sex is good;
The Establishment is the cause of everyone's trouble;
The answer to the "root causes" of the world's problems
Is to overthrow institutions;
And all it takes for people to do the good
Is for them to know they should.

Lord, I didn't tell them what they didn't want to hear:
That the trouble with the world isn't simply
With oppressive structures and citizens of status quo;
The trouble with life is us;
That somehow although we know we shouldn't be the way we are,
We still are,
And without your help we don't really have the strength
To be any different;
That Jesus Christ was something more
Than a social revolutionary;
Somehow his life, death, and resurrection speaks
Directly to our plight of fear, weakness, and selfishness.

Lord, I told them what they wanted to hear,
And not what they needed to hear,
Because I wanted them —
I needed them —
To "dig" me.

Am I running from You, Jesus?

— *Warren Risch*

ოფ

CHRIST HONORED, LOVED, EXALTED

Not I but Christ be honored, loved, exalted.
Not I but Christ be seen, be known, be heard.
Not I but Christ in every look and action,
Not I but Christ, no idle word e'er falling.
Christ, only Christ, no self important bearing.
Christ, only Christ, no trace of "I" be found.

— *Author Unknown*

THE TOUCH DIVINE

In the beauty of the morning;
In the glory of the noon;
In the glory of the evening;
By the silv'ry light of moon;
Stands a Presence ever near us;
Reaches forth a hand Divine;
And the touch, the touch of Jesus,
Yearns to thrill your heart and mine.

In the house when duties press us;
In the days of stress and strain;
When temptation's hosts beset us;
Thro' long hours of grief and pain
Still that Presence hovers o'er us;
Still that hand is stretched to heal;
And the touch, the touch of Jesus,
Bears the soul through woe to weal.

In the days when joys uplift us,
With a gladness none can tell;
When hope sings her grateful praises;
When faith trusts that all is well;
Then the touch, the touch of Jesus,
Tunes our lips to joyous lays,
As we sing the love that keeps us
"Simply trusting" all our days.

Oh, that wondrous touch of Jesus!
How it soothes us! how it thrills!
How from countless ills it frees us!
How our heart with rapture thrills!
Holy Presence, hover near us!
Touch Divine, upon us fall!
Till from earth Thy touch releases,
At Thy word and at Thy call.

— *Jennie Wilson-Howell*

ᢙ

KNOWN OF HIM

"Mary!" just one word;
'Twas all He need employ
To turn a woman's sorrowing heart
Into a well of joy.

She thought He was the gardener;
"Master!" she answered now.
His voice, her name — it was enough
She asked not, "Is it Thou?"

In my great hour of trial
The Saviour oft appears;
He makes no long, impressive speech
To scatter all my fears.

He gently speaks my name,
Enough! What need I more,
Than to be known and loved of Him
Whom Heaven and earth adore?

Men know not Jesus lives,
In unbelief they dwell;
And as to Mary then, so now,
He bids us, "Go — and tell."

— *Barbara Cornet Ryberg*

ᢙ

MY MASTER'S FACE

No pictured likeness of my Lord have
I;
He carved no record of his ministry
On wood or stone.
He left no sculptured tomb nor parch-
ment dim,
But trusted for all memory of him
Men's hearts alone.
Who sees the face but sees in part;
who reads
The spirit which it hides, sees all; he
needs
No more. Thy grace —
Thy life in my life, Lord, give Thou
to me;
And then, in truth, I may forever see
My Master's face!

— *William Hurd Hilmer*

CROWNED OR CRUCIFIED

I stood alone at the bar of God
  In the hush of the twilight dim,
And faced the question that pierced my heart:
  "What will you do with Him?
Crown'd or crucified? Which shall it be?"
  No other choice was offered to me.

I look'd on the face so marr'd with tears
  That were shed in His agony;
The look in His kind eyes broke my heart,
  'Twas so full of love for me.
"The Crown or the Cross," it seem'd to say;
  "For or against Me choose thou today!"

He held out His loving hands to me,
  While He pleadingly said, "Obey!
Make Me thy choice, for I love thee so,"
  And I could not say Him nay.
Crown'd, not crucified; this must it be!
  No other way was open to me.

I knelt in tears at the feet of Christ,
  In the hush of the twilight dim,
And all that I was or hoped or sought,
  I surrendered unto Him.
Crown'd, not crucified! My heart shall know
  No king but Christ, who loveth me so!

                    — *Author Unknown*

ഹ

THE HOPE OF THE COMING OF THE LORD

A lamp in the night, a song in time of sorrow;
A great glad hope which faith can ever borrow
To gild the passing day with the glory of the morrow,
Is the hope of the Coming of the Lord!

A star in the sky, a beacon bright to guide us,
An anchor sure to hold when storms betide us,
A refuge for the soul where in quiet we may hide us,
Is the hope of the Coming of the Lord!

A word from One to all our hearts the dearest,
A parting word to make Him aye the nearest,
Of all His precious words, the sweetest, brightest, clearest,
Is the hope of the Coming of the Lord!
                    — *Major Whittle*

EMMAUS

His eyes had altered since he'd looked on death
And the mysterious secret death disclosed.
His voice had changed after that last hard breath;
Its tones were in a different key transposed.
Nothing he spoke of made the two suspect
They walked with one they loved along the way,
But it was late, the supper table decked,
And they must urge the stranger to stay.
Something about the way he held the bread
Made them remember someone's outstretched palm
That once poured healing on the nearly dead,
And on the raging sea spilled a great calm.
Sudden, amazed that such a joy could be,
They knew his hands, and saw that it was he.

— *Edith Lovejoy Pierce*

ᏮᏛ

THE UNCHANGING ONE

Through the yesterday of ages,
Jesus, Thou art still the same;
Thro' our own life's checkered pages,
Still the one, dear, changeless Name!
Well may we in Thee confide,
Faithful Saviour, proved and "tried."

Gazing down the far forever,
Brighter glows the one sweet Name;
Steadfast radiance, paling never!
Jesus, Jesus! Still the same
Evermore Thou shalt endure,
Our own Saviour, strong and "sure."

— *Frances Ridley Havergal*

ᏮᏛ

THOU HAST PUT ALL THINGS UNDER HIS FEET

O North, with all thy vales of green!
O South, with all thy palms!
From peopled towns and fields between
Uplift the voice of psalms.

Raise, ancient East, the anthem high,
And let the youthful West reply.

Lo! in the clouds of heaven appears
God's well-beloved Son;
He brings a train of brighter years;
His kingdom is begun.
He comes a guilty world to bless
With mercy, truth, and righteousness.

O Father! haste the promised hour,
When at his feet shall lie
All rule, authority, and power,
Beneath the ample sky:
When he shall reign from pole to pole,
The Lord of every human soul:

When all shall heed the words he said,
Amid their daily cares,
And, by the loving life he led,
Shall strive to pattern theirs;
And he, who conquered Death, shall win
The mightier conquest over sin.

— *William Cullen Bryant*

TILL HE COME

In the busy street,
  In the crowded mart,
If a friend you meet,
  If a friend depart,
Take the sweet remembrance ever,
Nothing from the Lord can sever.

In the pilgrim way
  Where the thorns grow fast,
When the summer day,
  Turns to winter's blast,
Lean upon the Lord who leadeth,
He the Priest who intercedeth.

In the courts of love
  Where the holy tread,
Sunshine from above
  Streaming o'er your head,
Raise your voice the Saviour praising,
Sweetly sing His grace amazing.

In the upper room
  Where the Lord saith, "Peace,"
Victor o'er the tomb
  Bondmen to release,
Theme of Heavenly contemplation,
Spirit-taught your adoration.

Let your words be few,
  Let your heart be pure,
What is pure and true
  Can alone endure.
In His presence lowly bowing,
Naught of sin nor self allowing.

Till the Master come
  In the golden dawn,
Think that there are some
  Who in darkness mourn.
Go then to these lost ones straying;
And the Saviour's call obeying,
Bid them come without delaying.
                              —L. R.

LORD, IS IT I?

A crown of thorns
  And a purple robe —
Somebody fashioned them both;
  Somebody platted the bloody crown,
  Somebody fitted the gaudy gown —
Somebody fashioned them both.

A crown of thorns
  And a purple robe —
And was it so long ago
  They made that vesture our Saviour wore,
  And wove that crown that He meekly bore?
And was it so long ago?

A crown of thorns
  And a purple robe —
I read the words with a sigh:
  But when I remember my own misdeeds
  My soul awakes, and my conscience pleads,
And I say to myself, "Is it I?"
                    — *John Philo Trowbridge*

REMEMBER

He who is the Bread of Life, began His ministry hungering.
He who is the Water of Life, ended His ministry thirsting.
He who was weary, is our true rest.
He who paid tribute, is the King of Kings.
He prayed, yet hears our prayers.
He wept, but dries our tears.
He was sold for thirty pieces of silver, yet redeemed us.
He was led as a lamb to the slaughter, but is the Good Shepherd.
He died and gave His life, and by dying destroyed death
    for all who believe.

— Author Unknown

∽

VIGIL IN GETHSEMANE

I think we were the only ones who slept
The hour by, while waiting for Him there —
The olive trees seemed whispering in prayer,
And dew fell soft as if the Garden wept.

Beneath the Mount of Olivet, the rim
Of city lights was spread as at our feet;
Above, the stars moved slowly on their beat
As if they longed to keep a tryst with Him.

Below us, in their dens, the watchers stood
With robes drawn close about them, undefiled;
And, hovering near, the hosts of Satan smiled
And jeered their soundless jeers, in brotherhood.

Beyond, one came his way with eager breath
And every nerve held taut at sight and sound —
That one whose eyes would never more be found
In sleep, except it be the sleep of death . . .

We heard our Master's agonizing cry
Within the Garden, and in sorrow's dread
That holy place of prayer became our bed,
While all the world and heaven itself stood by . . .

This be our shame — that we who loved Him most
Could not have watched one hour with Him, nor fear
To drain the cup and see the cross appear:
His faithful numbered with the watching host.

— Ruth Margaret Gibbs

A THOUGHT

He who died on Calvary,
Died to ransom you and me.

On the cross He bowed His head,
In the grave He made His bed.

Ever since, the lilies bloom
Round the portal of the tomb.

Ever since, o'er all our loss
Shines the glory of the cross.

— *Margaret E. Sangster*

THE WALK TO EMMAUS

It happened, on a solemn eventide,
Soon after He that was our surety died,
Two bosom friends, each pensively inclined,
The scene of all those sorrows left behind,
Sought their own village, busied, as they went,
In musings worthy of the great event:
They spake of Him they loved, of Him whose life,
Though blameless, had incurred perpetual strife,
Whose deeds had left, in spite of hostile arts,
A deep memorial graven on their hearts.
The recollection, like a vein of ore,
The farther traced, enriched them still the more;
They thought Him, and they justly thought Him, one
Sent to do more than He appeared t'have done;
To exalt a people, and to place them high
Above all else, and wondered He should die.
Ere yet they brought their journey to an end,
A Stranger joined them, courteous as a friend,
And asked them, with a kind engaging air,
What their affliction was, and begged a share.
Informed, He gathered up the broken thread,
And, truth and wisdom gracing all He said,
Explained, illustrated, and searched so well
The tender theme on which they chose to dwell,
That reaching home, "The night," they said, "is near,
We must not now be parted, sojourn here."
The new acquaintance soon became a guest,
And, made so welcome at their simple feast,
He blessed the bread, but vanished at the word,
And left them both exclaiming, " 'Twas the Lord!
Did not our hearts feel all He deigned to say,
Did they not burn within us by the way?"

— *William Cowper*

THE CHURCH'S ONE FOUNDATION

The Church's one foundation
  Is Jesus Christ her Lord;
She is from every nation
  By water and the word:
From heaven he came and sought her
  To be his holy bride;
With his own blood he bought her,
  And for her life he died.

Elect from every nation,
  Yet one o'er all the earth,
Her charter of salvation,
  One Lord, one faith, one birth;
One holy Name she blesses,
  Partakes one holy food,
And to one hope she presses,
  With every grace endued.

The Church shall never perish!
  The dear Lord to defend,
To guide, sustain, and cherish,
  Is with her to the end:
Though there be those who hate her,
  And false sons in her pale,
Against her foe or traitor
  She ever shall prevail.

Though with a scornful wonder,
  Men see her sore opprest,
By schisms rent asunder,
  By heresies distrest;
Yet saints their watch are keeping,
  Their cry goes up, "How long?"
And soon the night of weeping
  Shall be the morn of song.

'Mid toil and tribulation,
  And tumult of her war,
She waits the consummation
  Of peace forevermore;
Till with the vision glorious
  Her longing eyes are blest,
And the great Church victorious
  Shall be the Church at rest;

With all her sons and daughters,
  Who, by the Master's hand,
Led through the deathly waters,
  Repose in Eden land.
Yet she on earth hath union
  With God the Three in One,
And mystic sweet communion
  With those whose rest is won.

O happy ones and holy!
  Lord, give us grace that we,
Like them, the meek and lowly,
  On high may dwell with thee.
There, past the border-mountains,
  Where in sweet vales the bride
With thee by living fountains
  Forever shall abide. Amen.

— *Samuel John Stone*

❧

THE TRUE LIGHT

Christ, whose glory fills the skies,
  Christ, the true, the only Light,
Sun of righteousness, arise,
  Triumph o'er the shades of night;
Dayspring from on high, be near,
Daystar, in my heart appear.

Dark and cheerless is the morn,
  Unaccompanied by Thee;
Joyless is the day's return.
  Till Thy mercy's beams I see;
Till Thy inward life impart,
Glad my eyes, and warm my heart.

Visit then this soul of mine;
  Pierce the gloom of sin and grief;
Fill me, Radiance Divine,
  Scatter all my unbelief;
More and more Thyself display,
Shining to the perfect day.

— *Charles Wesley*

Happy Day

Oh, happy day, that fixed my choice
On thee, my Saviour and my God!
Well may this glowing heart rejoice,
And tells its raptures all abroad.

Oh, happy bond, that seals my vows
To him who merits all my love!
Let cheerful anthems fill his house,
While to that sacred shrine I move.

'Tis done, the great transaction's done;
I am my Lord's, and he is mine;
He drew me, and I followed on,
Charmed to confess the voice divine.

Now rest, my long-divided heart!
Fixed on this blissful centre, rest;
Oh, who with earth would grudge to
part,
When called with angels to be blest?

High Heaven, that heard the solemn
vow,
That vow renewed shall daily hear,
Till in life's latest hour I bow,
And bless in death a bond so dear.

— *Philip Doddridge*

Lovest Thou Me? Feed My Lambs

Do not I love thee, O my Lord?
Behold my heart and see;
And turn each cursed idol out
That dares to rival thee.

Do not I love thee from my soul?
Then let me nothing love:
Dead be my heart to every joy,
When Jesus cannot move.

Is not thy name melodious still
To mine attentive ear?
Doth not each pulse with pleasure
bound
My Saviour's voice to hear?

Hast thou a lamb in all thy flock,
I would disdain to feed?
Hast thou a foe, before whose face
I fear thy cause to plead?

Would not my ardent spirit vie,
With angels round the throne,
To execute thy sacred will,
And make thy glory known?

Would not my heart pour forth its
blood
In honor of thy name?
And challenge the cold hand of death
To damp the immortal flame?

Thou know'st I love thee, dearest Lord;
But oh, I long to soar
Far from the sphere of mortal joys,
And learn to love thee more!

— *Philip Doddridge*

Thoughts of Him

I love to dwell upon the thought
That Jesus cares for me;
It matters not what life may bring —
He loves me tenderly!

I may not see the path ahead
Or find my way with ease,
But Jesus leads me by the hand —
He knows the way — He sees!

The very thought of Jesus makes
My shadows disappear,
And when I come to Him in prayer
He draws so very near!

When I am thinking thoughts of Him
Earth's cares and troubles cease.
And o'er my soul there gently rolls
A sweet and precious peace!

— *Georgia Adams*

THE DAYSMAN

Well named "A Man of Sorrow,"
For so indeed He was.
"No sorrow like His sorrow,"
Hated, without a cause.
The Source of untold goodness,
Come down from heaven above;
Yields to our scorn and rudeness,
In condescending love.

They named Him "Friend of Sinners."
This thrills my soul to praise.
All heavenward path beginners,
Their hallelujahs raise.
Only the sick and weakly
Need the physician's care.
The Friend of Sinners, meekly
Submits their sins to bear.

Misnamed a malefactor!
No evil did He do.
He was a benefactor!
And died for me and you.
In grace to bring us blessing,
He took our load of guilt:
Met God, our sins confessing,
For us, His blood was spilt.

Paul names Him Mediator.
Job's Daysman now is found.
A Man, tho' our Creator,
Upon God's Throne sits crowned.
As God, God's rights maintaining
From that bright throne on high.
As Man, our new place gaining,
Blest with Himself, so nigh.

His sorrows now are over,
But Friend of Sinners still.
His thoughts of kindness hover
Round those who served Him ill.
And still His meditation
Can *free you from the thrall*
Of Satan's devastation.
He gave Himself, . . . for all.

— *William J. Barnes*

"TILL HE COME!"

"Till He come!" Oh, let the words
Linger on the trembling chords;
Let the little while between
In their golden light be seen;
Let us think how Heaven and Home
Lie beyond that "Till He come!"

Clouds and conflicts round us press;
Would we have one sorrow less?
All the sharpness of the Cross,
All that tells the world is loss —
Death, and darkness, and the tomb—
Only whisper, "Till He come!"

See, the feast of love is spread,
Drink the wine and break the bread—
Sweet memorials — till the Lord
Call us round His Heavenly board;
Some from earth, from glory some,
Severed only "Till He come!"

— *Bishop of Exeter*

THE CHRIST OF TODAY

Not only on Judean hills,
Where He in distant ages trod,
Are seen the footprints of the Christ,
The gentle Messenger of God;
For in the midst He walks today,
In busy marts, in quiet ways,
And speaks to every soul that hears
And fills each waiting heart with
praise.

Not only by blue Galilee
Did He the leper cleanse, the dead
Raise unto life, and on all hearts
That mourned His matchless glory
shed;
Today He speaks, in homes of men,
To heal each spirit sick with sin,
And at the door of every life
He stands and seeks to enter in.

— *Thomas Curtis Clark*

THEY WATCHED HIM THERE

"And sitting down they watched Him there";
His blood-stained face, disheveled hair,
His flesh torn from the nails by body's weight,
The writhing agony of such a fate,
The spear wound in His side, the gaze of pain.
His agony — the grace of God made plain.

One day I climbed that hill so bare
And kneeling down, I watched Him there.
My sin upon His shoulders heavily laid;
My punishment and ransom price He paid;
With tears of gratitude and heart bowed low
I cried, "O Christ, how could You love me so?"

And this the lesson that my heart has learned
That often I must watch Him — hated, spurned.
They who would live the life of Christ below
Must often up the hill to Calvary go.

— *Shirley Elizabeth Reitz*

IN TEMPTATION

Jesu, lover of my soul,
  Let me to thy bosom fly,
While the nearer waters roll,
  While the tempest still is high;
Hide me, O my Saviour, hide,
  Till the storm of life be past;
Safe into the haven guide;
  Oh, receive my soul at last!

Other refuge have I none;
  Hangs my helpless soul on thee;
Leave, ah, leave me not alone,
  Still support and comfort me!
All my trust on thee is stayed,
  All my help from thee I bring;
Cover my defenseless head
  With the shadow of thy wing!

Wilt thou not regard my call?
  Wilt thou not accept my prayer?
Lo! I sink, I faint, I fall!
  Lo! on thee I cast my care!

Reach me out thy gracious hand!
  While I of thy strength receive,
Hoping against hope I stand,
  Dying, and behold I live!

Thou, O Christ, art all I want;
  More than all in thee I find:
Raise the fallen, cheer the faint,
  Heal the sick, and lead the blind!
Just and holy is thy name;
  I am all unrighteousness;
False and full of sin I am,
  Thou art full of truth and grace.

Plenteous grace with thee is found,
  Grace to cover all my sin;
Let the healing streams abound;
  Make and keep me pure within!
Thou of life the fountain art;
  Freely let me take of thee;
Spring thou up within my heart!
  Rise to all eternity!

— *Charles Wesley*

SAVIOUR

Saviour, Thou art always near me
  Near amidst each trial, each care,
Saviour, Thou dost ever hear me
  When I go to Thee in prayer.
Oh, I pray that Thou may keep me
  In the center of Thy will,
That Thy grace will ever find me
  Loving, hoping, trusting, still.

Saviour, Thou dost never fail me,
  In temptation, in despair,
When the storms of life assail me
  Thou dost hear and answer prayer.
Saviour, Thou who died for me
  Gave so much, Thy life, Thy all;
Help me to obedient be
  Ready, willing, at Thy call.

Saviour, Thou dost give such peace,
  That our fears do flee.
Thou hast given from sin release,
  All the glory, praise to Thee!
Saviour, oh, I pray, tonight,
  That Thou'lt keep me day by day
Walking daily in the light
  That Thou shedst along my way.

— *Author Unknown*

MY CHRIST

My Christ was a Jew.
Whether His eyes were brown
  or blue,
His hair auburn
  or black,
I do not know
Nor care.

But this I know:
He was not the drunk in the gutter,
  but seeing him there
  Christ knelt in the filth.

With tender care He
  lifted the broken life
  with healing in His words
  and in His hands.
He would never just pass by.
Nor may I.

He walked with tired feet
Through littered city streets;
  strong, corded muscles
  tested the dusty robe.
Those powerful hands
  had hewn trees;
Those broad shoulders
  had carried with ease
  the cumbersome, wooden load.

But I walk with well-shod feet
By those lonely in the street.
  I sit with cushioned seat
  meeting cushioned seat,
  riding with haughty soul
  in arrogance and pride.
I know He watches me
  with anguish in His heart,
  disappointment in His eyes,
Because this, too, I know:
  It was for them He died.

My Christ is God's Son.
God's will was His own
  and was perfectly obeyed.
He is relevant to this very hour.
It is I who am compelled to change!
  I must be like Him
  if He would speak and serve
  through me
  with power
  today.
There is no other way.

— *Virginia Auler*

In Sweet Communion

May the grace of Christ our Saviour,
   And the Father's boundless love,
With the Holy Spirit's favor,
   Rest upon us from above.

Thus may we abide in union
   With each other and the Lord,
And possess in sweet communion
   Joys which earth cannot afford.

— *John Newton*

When Will He Come?

Perhaps he will come at the dawning
   Of a beautiful summer day,
When the birds and flowers are awakening
   To welcome the sun's first ray.
And the Eastern sky will brighten
   With the light of the dawn's caress,
And herald the swift arising
   Of the "Sun of Righteousness."

Perhaps he will come at evening,
   When, weary of toil and care,
We rest and watch as the darkness
   Creeps o'er the landscape fair,
And behold the stars in their beauty
   Shine forth from their depths afar
But their radiance dims in the glory
   Of the "Bright and Morning Star."

And perhaps he will come at midnight
   When earth and its dwellers sleep.
When over the mountains and valleys
   Broods a silence vast and deep,
And the trump of the great archangel
   Shall awaken the slumbers there.
And his saints will be caught up together
   To meet the Lord in the air.

But whether at dawn or evening,
   At midnight or sultry noon,
And whether awake or sleeping,
   And the time be distant or soon;
May I live so that I shall be ready
   With joy my Saviour to meet,
And feel no harm at his coming,
   But hasten his heralds to greet.

— *Author Unknown*

PEACE

Is this the grace of God, this strange sweet calm?
The weary day is at its zenith still,
Yet 'tis as if beside some cool, clear rill,
    Through shadowy stillness rose an evening psalm,
And all the noise of life were hushed away,
And tranquil gladness reigned with gently soothing sway.

It was not so just now. I turned aside
With aching head, and heart most sorely bowed;
Around me cares and griefs in crushing crowd,
    While inly rose the sense, in swelling tide,
Of weakness, insufficiency, and sin,
And fear, and gloom, and doubt in mighty flood rolled in.

That rushing flood I had no power to meet,
Nor power to flee: my present, future, past,
Myself, my sorrow, and my sin I cast
    In utter helplessness at Jesu's feet:
Then bent me to the storm, if such his will.
He saw the winds and waves, and whispered,
        "Peace, be still!"

And there was calm! O Saviour, I have proved
That thou to help and save art really near:
How else this quiet rest from grief and fear
    And all distress? The cross is not removed,
I must go forth to bear it as before,
But, leaning on thine arm, I dread its weight no more.

Is it indeed thy peace? I have not tried
To analyze my faith, dissect my trust,
Or measure if belief be full and just,
    And therefore claim thy peace. But thou hast died,
I know that this is true, and true for me,
And, knowing it, I come, and cast my all on thee.

It is not that I feel less weak, but thou
Wilt be my strength; it is not that I see
Less sin, but more of pardoning love with thee,
    And all-sufficient grace. Enough! and now
All fluttering thought is stilled, I only rest,
And feel that thou art near, and know that I am blest.

                            — *Frances Ridley Havergal*

As He Walked With Us

Calm, strong, and gentle Man of Galilee,
Whose heart by every human woe is stirred;
By whom are plaintive cries of creatures heard;
Whose eye escapes no tracery of tree,
Or modest wayside flower; alert to see
The fantasy of cloud, the flight of bird;
Whose ear can catch the faintest note and word
Of wind and stream, and distant Western sea;
When I am treading on the open space,
Or threading slowly through the crowded marts.
Skilled Craftsman of the woods and market-place,
Companion to all life and human hearts,
I crave, Thou unseen, understanding Guide,
To find Thee, silent, walking by my side.

— Harry Webb Farrington

ᔕ

Forward With Christ

Forward with Christ comes the challenge today,
Forward with Christ, forward with Christ!
He marks the path and will lead all the way
Forward, then forward with Christ.

God ever lives and His truth marches on,
Forward with Christ, forward with Christ!
Darkness may threaten but His is the dawn,
Let us go forward with Christ.

Taking His message of love as we go
Forward with Christ, forward with Christ!
Into a world wrapped in sorrow and woe,
We must go forward with Christ.

Forward with Christ, forward with Christ!
Trust Him to lead though the path may be dim;
Following on into the dawn —
Forward then follow on with Him.

—Carlton Buck

Christ

THIRTY PIECES OF SILVER

Thirty pieces of silver
  For the Lord of life they gave;
Thirty pieces of silver —
  Only the price of a slave!
But it was the priestly value
  Of the Holy One of God;
They weighed it out in the temple,
  The price of the Saviour's blood.

Thirty pieces of silver
  Laid in Iscariot's hand;
Thirty pieces of silver
  And the aid of an armed band,
Like a lamb that is led to the slaughter
  Brought the humbled Son of God
At midnight from the garden,
  Where His sweat had been like
    blood.

Thirty pieces of silver
  Burns on the traitor's brain;
Thirty pieces of silver!
  O it is hellish gain!
"I have sinned and betrayed the guilt-
    less!"
He cried, with a fevered breath;
And he cast them down in the temple
  And rushed to a madman's death.

Thirty pieces of silver
  Lay in the House of God;
Thirty pieces of silver
  But O 'twas the price of blood!
And so for a place to bury
  The strangers in they gave
The price of their own Messiah.
  Who lay in a borrowed grave.

It may not be for silver,
  It may not be for gold,
But still by tens of thousands
  Is this precious Saviour sold,
Sold for a godless friendship,
  Sold for a selfish aim,
Sold for a fleeting trifle,

  Sold for an empty name,
Sold in the mart of Science,
  Sold in the seat of Power,
Sold at the shrine of Fortune,
  Sold in Pleasure's bower,
Sold where the awful bargain
  None but God's eye can see!
Ponder, my soul the question:
  Shall He be sold by thee?
Sold! O God, what a moment!
  Stifled is conscience' voice!
Sold! And a weeping angel
  Records the fatal choice!
Sold! But the price of the Saviour
  To a living coal shall turn,
With the pangs of Remorse forever
  Deep in the soul to burn.

          —Wm. Blane

TRIUMPH OF HIS GRACE

O, for a thousand tongues to sing
  My dear Redeemer's praise!
The glories of my God and King,
  The triumphs of His grace!

My gracious Master and my God!
  Assist me to proclaim,
To spread thro' all the earth abroad,
  The honors of Thy name.

Jesus — the name that calms my fears,
  That bids my sorrows cease;
'Tis music to my ravished ears;
  'Tis life, and health, and peace.

He breaks the power of canceled sin,
  He sets the prisoner free;
His blood can make the foulest clean;
  His blood availed for me.

        — Charles Wesley

SALUTATION TO JESUS CHRIST

I greet thee, my Redeemer sure,
  I trust in none but thee,
Thou who hast borne such toil and
    shame
And suffering for me;
Our hearts from cares and cravings vain
And foolish fears set free.

Thou art the King compassionate,
  Thou reignest everywhere,
Almighty Lord, reign thou in us,
  Rule all we have and are:
Enlighten us and raise to heaven,
  Amid thy glories there.

Thou art the life by which we live;
  Our stay and strength's in thee;
Uphold us so in face of death;
  What time soe'er it be,
That we may meet it with strong heart,
  And may die peacefully.

The true and perfect gentleness
  We find in thee alone;
Make us to know thy loveliness,
  Teach us to love thee known;
Grant us sweet fellowship with thee,
  And all who are thine own.

Our hope is in none else but thee;
  Faith holds thy promise fast;
Be pleased, Lord, to strengthen us,
  Whom thou redeemèd hast,
To bear all troubles patiently,
  And overcome at last.

Children of Eve, and heirs of ill,
  To thee thy banished cry;
To thee in sorrow's vale we bring
  Our sighs and misery;
We take the sinners' place, and plead:
  Lord, save us, or we die.

Look, thou, our Daysman and High
    Priest,
  Upon our low estate;

Make us to see God's face in peace
  Through thee, our Advocate;
With thee, our Saviour, may our feet
  Enter at heaven's gate.

Lord Jesus Christ of holy souls,
  The Bridegroom sweet and true,
Meet thou the rage of Antichrist,
  Break thou his nets in two;
Grant us thy Spirit's help, thy will
  In very deed to do.
                                    — John Calvin

ം

I LOVE TO HEAR THE STORY

I love to hear the story
Which angel voices tell,
How once the King of glory
Came down on earth to dwell.
I am both weak and sinful,
But this I surely know,
The Lord came down to save me,
Because He loved me so.

I'm glad my blessed Savior
Was once a child like me,
To show how pure and holy
His little ones should be;
And if I try to follow
His footsteps here below,
He never will forget me,
Because He loves me so.

To sing His love and mercy
My sweetest songs I'll raise;
And though I cannot see Him,
I know He hears my praise;
For He has kindly promised
That even I may go
To sing among His angels
Because He loves me so.

                          — Emily Huntington Miller

GOOD FRIDAY

Am I a stone, and not a sheep,
   That I can stand, O Christ, beneath Thy cross,
   To number drop by drop Thy Blood's slow loss,
And yet not weep?

Not so those women loved
   Who with exceeding grief lamented Thee;
   Not so fallen Peter weeping bitterly;
Not so the thief was moved;

Not so the Sun and Moon
   Which hid their faces in a starless sky.
   A horror of great darkness at broad noon —
I, only I.

Yet give not o'er
   But seek Thy sheep, true Shepherd of the flock;
   Greater than Moses, turn and look once more
And smite a rock.

                — *Christina Rossetti*

IN CHRIST ALONE

Oh, futile search of earth which ends in sorrow,
   In Christ alone is happiness unfeigned,
Thy shallow depths reveal a broken cistern,
   Thy songs are fleeting; yea, thy boasts are vain.
In Christ alone is cleansing for the guilty,
   The knowledge sin is gone, the heart is pure,
The shield of faith with which to face the battle,
   The armor for the soul, a peace secure,
In Christ alone is manna for the hungry,
   The well-of-water springing up within,
The Friend who sticketh closer than a brother,
   He conquers death! He gives release from sin!
In Christ alone is love that knows no parting,
   A joy that brings no sorrow in its wake,
He goes before; He knows the path we travel,
   Tho' night be deep, this Christ doth not forsake.
In Christ alone the earth shall find its answer,
   A refuge from its doubts, its fears, its strife;
This God-revealed-in-flesh, this precious Saviour,
   Forever is *the Way . . . the Truth . . . the Life!*
                —*Connie Calenberg*

THE MYSTERY OF LIFE IN CHRIST

I walk along the crowded streets, and mark
    The eager, anxious faces;
Wondering what this man seeks, what that heart craves,
    In earthly places.

Do I want anything that they are wanting?
    Is each of them my brother?
Could we hold fellowship, speak heart to heart,
    Each to the other?

Nay, but I know not! only this I know,
    That sometimes merely crossing
Another's path, where life's tumultuous waves
    Are ever tossing,

He, as he passes, whispers in mine ear
    One magic sentence only,
And in the awful loneliness of crowds
    I am not lonely.

Ah, what a life is theirs who live in Christ;
    How vast the mystery!
Reaching in height to heaven, and in its depth
    The unfathomed sea!

                —*Elizabeth Payson Prentiss*

THE MASTER'S CALL

Rise, said the Master, come unto the feast.
She heard the call, and rose with willing feet;
But thinking it not otherwise than meet
For such a bidding to put on her best,
She is gone from us for a few short hours
Into her bridal closet, there to wait
For the unfolding of the palace-gate,
That gives her entrance to the blissful bowers.
We have not seen her yet, though we have been
Full often to her chamber-door, and oft
Have listened underneath the postern green,
And laid fresh flowers, and whispered short and soft;
But she hath made no answer; and the day
From the clear west is fading fast away.

                — *Henry Alford*

NOT ASHAMED OF CHRIST

Jesus! and shall it ever be,
A mortal man ashamed of thee?
Ashamed of thee, whom angels praise,
Whose glories shine thro' endless days!

Ashamed of Jesus! sooner far
Let evening blush to own a star;
He sheds the beams of light divine
O'er this benighted soul of mine.

Ashamed of Jesus! just as soon
Let midnight be ashamed of noon;
'Tis midnight with my soul, till he,
Bright Morning Star, bid darkness flee.

Ashamed of Jesus! that dear Friend
On whom my hopes of heaven depend!
No: when I blush, be this my shame,
That I no more revere his name.

Ashamed of Jesus! yes, I may,
When I've no guilt to wash away,
No tear to wipe, no good to crave,
No fears to quell, no soul to save.

Till then, — nor is my boasting vain, —
Till then, I boast a Saviour slain:
And oh, may this my glory be,
That Christ is not ashamed of me!

— Joseph Grigg

THE FOUNTAIN OPENED

There is a fountain filled with blood,
  Drawn from Emmanuel's veins;
And sinners plunged beneath that
    flood,
  Lose all their guilty stains.

The dying thief rejoiced to see
  That fountain in his day;
And there have I, as vile as he,
  Washed all my sins away.

Dear dying Lamb! thy precious blood
  Shall never lose its power,
Till all the ransomed church of God
  Be saved to sin no more.

E'er since, by faith, I saw the stream
  Thy flowing wounds supply,
Redeeming love has been my theme,
  And shall be till I die.

Then in a nobler, sweeter song,
  I'll sing thy power to save;
When this poor lisping, stammering
    tongue
  Lies silent in the grave.

Lord, I believe thou hast prepared
  (Unworthy though I be)
For me a blood-bought free reward,
  A golden harp for me:

'Tis strung and tuned for endless years,
  And formed by power divine;
To sound in God the Father's ears
  No other name but thine.

— William Cowper

HIM EVERMORE I BEHOLD

Him evermore I behold
Walking in Galilee,
Through the cornfield's waving gold,
In hamlet or grassy wold,
By the shores of the Beautiful Sea.
He toucheth the sightless eyes;
Before Him the demons flee;
To the dead He sayeth: Arise!
To the living: Follow me!
And that voice still soundeth on
From the centuries that are gone,
To the centuries that shall be!

— Henry Wadsworth Longfellow

LOOKING UNTO JESUS

Thou, who didst stoop below
To drain the cup of woe,
Wearing the form of frail mortality;
Thy blessed labors done,
Thy crown of victory won,
Hast passed from earth, passed to thy home on high.

Our eyes behold thee not,
Yet hast thou not forgot
Those who have placed their hope, their trust, in thee;
Before thy Father's face
Thou hast prepared a place,
That where thou art, there they may also be.

It was no path of flowers,
Which, through this world of ours,
Beloved of the Father, thou didst tread;
And shall we in dismay
Shrink from the narrow way,
When clouds and darkness are around it spread?

O thou, who are our life
Be with us through the strife;
Thy holy head by earth's fierce storms was bowed;
Raise thou our eyes above,
To see a Father's love
Beam like the bow of promise through the cloud.

And, oh, if thoughts of gloom
Should hover o'er the tomb,
That light of love our guiding star shall be;
Our spirits shall not dread
The shadowy way to tread,
Friend, Guardian, Saviour, which doth lead to thee.

—*Sarah Elizabeth Miles*

ॐ

BREAD OF THE WORLD

Bread of the world in mercy broken,
Wine of the soul in mercy shed,
By whom the words of life were
    spoken,
And in whose death our sins are dead.

Look on the heart by sorrow broken,
Look on the tears by sinners shed;
And be Thy feast to us the token
That by Thy grace our souls are fed.

— *Reginald Heber*

HE IS MY REFUGE

The Lord is my Refuge
My Haven from storm,
My Strength in all weakness,
My Peace in alarm,
My Joy in all sorrow,
My Hope in despair,
My Courage in conquest,
My Helper in prayer.

The Lord is my Fortress,
To Him I can go
When all others fail me,
And waters o'erflow.
The Lord is my Buckler
He's strong to defend,
My Rock of salvation,
My Hope to the end.

So what though the mountains
Be moved to the sea,
Or the heavens above
Should cease there to be;
Or friends may forsake me,
And Satan my foe,
Be strong to uproot me;
He's with me I know!

— *Author Unknown*

∽

CHRIST THE CORNER STONE

Christ is our corner-stone,
On him alone we build;
With his true saints alone
The courts of heaven are filled:
On his great love
Our hopes we place
Of present grace
And joys above.

Oh, then with hymns of praise
These hallowed courts shall ring;
Our voices we will raise,
The Three in One to sing;

And thus proclaim
In joyful song
Both loud and long
That glorious name.

Here, gracious God, do thou
Forevermore draw nigh;
Accept each faithful vow,
And mark each suppliant sigh;
In copious shower
On all who pray
Each holy day
Thy blessings pour!

Here may we gain from Heaven
The grace which we implore;
And may that grace, once given,
Be with us evermore,
Until that day
When all the blest
To endless rest
Are called away!

— *Translated from an unknown author of*
about the eighth century by John Chandler

∽

THE STRANGER

A Stranger came to Bethlehem,
With great gifts in His hands.
But many people only saw
A babe in swaddling bands.
A Stranger lived in Nazareth,
And in His heart was Truth.
But many thought Him Joseph's son,
An ordinary youth.
A Stranger taught in Galilee,
With wisdom from on high.
To many He was just a man,
And so they passed Him by.
That Stranger walks the world today,
In hearts that have received
The Son of God. No Stranger, He,
To those who have believed!

— *Helen Frazee-Bower*

JESU! THE VERY THOUGHT OF THEE

Jesu, the very thought of thee
　　With sweetness fills my breast;
But sweeter far thy face to see,
　　And in thy presence rest.

Nor voice can sing, nor heart can
　　　frame,
　　Nor can the memory find,
A sweeter sound than thy blest name,
　　O Saviour of mankind!

O hope of every contrite heart,
　　O joy of all the meek,
To those who fall, how kind thou art!
　　How good to those who seek!

But what to those who find? ah! this
　　Nor tongue nor pen can show:
The love of Jesus, what it is,
　　None but his loved ones know.

Jesu! our only joy be thou,
　　As thou our prize wilt be;
Jesu! be thou our glory now,
　　And through eternity.

O Jesu! King most wonderful!
　　Thou Conqueror renowned!
Thou sweetness most ineffable,
　　In whom all joys are found!

When once thou visitest the heart,
　　Then truth begins to shine;
Then earthly vanities depart;
　　Then kindles love divine.

O Jesu! light of all below!
　　Thou fount of life and fire!
Surpassing all the joys we know,
　　All that we can desire:

May every heart confess thy name,
　　And ever thee adore;
And seeking thee, itself inflame
　　To seek thee more and more.

Thee may our tongues forever bless
Thee may we love alone;

And ever in our lives express
　　The image of thine own.

O Jesu! thou the beauty art
　　Of angel worlds above;
Thy name is music to the heart,
　　Enchanting it with love.

Celestial sweetness unalloyed!
　　Who eat thee hunger still;
Who drink of thee still feel a void,
　　Which naught but thou can fill.

O my sweet Jesu! hear the sighs
　　Which unto thee I send;
To thee mine inmost spirit cries,
　　My being's hope and end!

Stay with us, Lord, and with thy light
　　Illume the soul's abyss;
Scatter the darkness of our night,
　　And fill the world with bliss.

O Jesu! spotless Virgin flower!
　　Our life and joy! to thee
Be praise, beatitude, and power,
　　Through all eternity!

　　　　　　　— Bernard of Clairvaux
　　　　　　Translated by Edward Caswall

თ

FORGIVENESS

When at Thy footstool, Lord, I bend,
　　And plead with Thee for mercy
　　　there,
Think of the sinner's dying Friend,
　　And for His sake receive my prayer!
Oh, think not of my shame and guilt,
　　My thousand stains of deepest dye!
Think of the blood which Jesus spilt,
　　And let that blood my pardon buy!

　　　　　　　— Henry Francis Lyte

Now I Have Found a Friend

Now I have found a friend,
  Jesus is mine;
His love shall never end,
  Jesus is mine.
Though earthly joys decrease,
Though earthly friendships cease,
Now I have lasting peace;
  Jesus is mine.

Though I grow poor and old,
  Jesus is mine;
Though I grow faint and cold,
  Jesus is mine.
He shall my wants supply,
His precious blood is nigh,
Nought can my hope destroy;
  Jesus is mine.

— *Henry Hope*

Emmanuel's Land

Come, we who love the Lord,
  And let our joys be known;
Join in a song of sweet accord,
  And thus surround the throne.

The sorrows of the mind
  Be banished from this place!
Religion never was designed
  To make our pleasures less.

Let those refuse to sing
  Who never knew our God;
But servants of the heavenly King
  Should speak their joys abroad.

The God that rules on high,
  And thunders when he please,
That rides upon the stormy sky,
  And manages the seas;

This awesome God is ours,
  Our Father and our love;
He shall send down his heavenly
      powers
  To carry us above.

There we shall see his face,
  And never, never sin;
And from the rivers of his grace
  Drink endless pleasures in.

Yea, and before we rise
  To that immortal state,
The thoughts of such amazing bliss
  Should constant joys create.

The men of grace have found
  Glory begun below;
Celestial fruits, on earthly ground,
  From faith and hope may grow.

The hill of Zion yields
  A thousand sacred sweets
Before we reach the heavenly fields,
  Or walk the golden streets.

Then let our songs abound,
  And every tear be dry;
We're marching through Emmanuel's
      ground
  To fairer worlds on high.

— *Isaac Watts*

Wedding

Since Jesus freely did appear,
  To grace a marriage feast,
O Lord, we ask thy presence here,
  To make a wedding guest.

Upon the bridal pair look down,
  Who now have plighted hands;
Their union with thy favour crown,
  And bless their nuptial bands.

With gifts of grace their hearts endow,
  Of all rich dowries best;
Their substance bless, and peace be-
      stow
  To sweeten all the rest.

— *Author Unknown*

His Birth

The sky can still remember
  The earliest Christmas morn,
When in the cold December
  The Saviour Christ was born.
No star unfolds its glory,
  No trumpet wind is blown,
But tells the Christmas story
  In music of its own.

O never failing splendor!
  O never silent song!
Still keep the green earth tender,
  Still keep the gray earth strong,
Still keep the brave earth dreaming
  Of deeds that shall be done,
While children's lives come streaming
  Like sunbeams from the sun.

O angels sweet and splendid,
  Throng in our hearts and sing
The wonders which attended
  The coming of the King;
Till we too, boldly pressing
  Where once the shepherds trod,
Climb Bethlehem's Hill of Blessing,
  And find the Son of God.

— *Phillips Brooks*

ℴ

Watchman, Tell Us of the Night

Watchman, tell us of the night,
  What its signs of promise are!
Traveller, o'er yon mountain's height
  See that glory-beaming star!
Watchman, does its beauteous ray
  Aught of joy or hope foretell?
Traveller, yes; it brings the day,
  Promised day of Israel.

Watchman, tell us of the night;
  Higher yet that star ascends!
Traveller, blessedness and light,
  Peace and truth, its course portends!
Watchman, will its beams alone
  Gild the spot that gave them birth?
Traveller, ages are its own;
  See, it bursts o'er all the earth.

Watchman, tell us of the night,
  For the morning seems to dawn!
Traveller, darkness takes its flight,
  Doubt and terror are withdrawn.
Watchman, let thy wanderings cease;
  Hie thee to thy quiet home:
Traveller, lo, the Prince of peace,
  Lo, the Son of God is come!

— *John Bowring*

ℴ

He Is Near!

I know not in what watch He comes
  Or at what hour He may appear,
Whether at midnight or at morn,
  Or in what season of the year;
  I only know that He is near.

The centuries have gone and come,
  Dark centuries of absence drear;
I dare not chide the long delay,
  Nor ask when I His voice shall hear;
  I only know that He is near.

I do not think it can be long
  Till in His glory He appear;
And yet I dare not name the day,
  Nor fix the solemn Advent year;
  I only know that He is near.

— *Horatius Bonar*

A Friend That Sticketh Closer Than a Brother

One there is above all others,
  Well deserves the name of Friend!
His is love beyond a brother's,
  Costly, free, and knows no end:
They who once his kindness prove,
Find it everlasting love!

Which of all our friends, to save us,
  Could or would have shed their
    blood?
But our Jesus died to have us
Reconciled in him to God.
This was boundless love indeed!
Jesus is a friend in need.

Men, when raised to lofty stations,
  Often know their friends no more;
Slight and scorn their poor relations,
  Though they valued them before:
But our Saviour always owns
Those whom he redeemed with groans.

When he lived on earth abased,
  Friend of sinners was his name;
Now above all glory raised,
  He rejoices in the same:
Still he calls them brethren, friends,
And to all their wants attends.

Could we bear from one another
  What he daily bears from us?
Yet this glorious Friend and Brother
  Loves us though we treat him thus:
Though for good we render ill,
He accounts us brethren still.

Oh, for grace our hearts to soften!
  Teach us, Lord, at length to love;
We, alas! forget too often
  What a Friend we have above.
But when home our souls are brought,
We will love thee as we ought.

— *John Newton*

Praise to Jesus

All praise to Jesus' hallowed name,
Who of virgin pure became
True man for us! The angels sing,
As glad news to earth they bring,
  Hallelujah!

The everlasting Father's Son
For a manger leaves his throne;
The mighty God, the eternal Good,
Hath clothed himself in flesh and
  blood.
  Hallelujah!

He whom the world could not inwrap
Yonder lies in Mary's lap;
He is become an infant small,
Who by his might upholdeth all.
  Hallelujah!

The eternal Light, come down from
  heaven,
Hath to us new sunshine given;
It shineth in the midst of night,
And maketh us the sons of light.
  Hallelujah!

The Father's Son, God ever blest,
In the world became a guest;
He leads us from this vale of tears,
And makes us in his kingdom heirs.
  Hallelujah!

He came to earth so mean and poor,
Man to pity and restore,
And make us rich in heaven above,
Equal with angels through his love.
  Hallelujah!

All this he did to show his grace
To our poor and sinful race;
For this let Christendom adore
And praise his name forevermore.
  Hallelujah!

— *Martin Luther*

CHRIST IN THE TEMPEST

Fierce was the wild billow;
  Dark was the night;
Oars labored heavily;
  Foam glimmered white;
Mariners trembled;
  Peril was nigh;
Then said the God of God,
  "Peace, It is I!"

Ridge of the mountain-wave,
  Lower thy crest!
Wail of Euroclydon,
  Be thou at rest!
Peril can none be,
  Sorrow must fly,
Where saith the Light of light,
  "Peace! It is I!"

Jesu, Deliverer!
  Come thou to me:
Soothe thou my voyaging
  Over life's sea!
Thou, when the storm of death
  Roars, sweeping by,
Whisper, O Truth of truth!
  "Peace! It is I!"
                    — St. Anatolius

❧

THE EFFORT

Approach, my soul, the mercy-seat,
  Where Jesus answers prayer;
There humbly fall before his feet,
  For none can perish there.

Thy promise is my only plea,
  With this I venture nigh;
Thou callest burdened souls to thee,
  And such, O Lord, am I.

Bowed down beneath a load of sin,
  By Satan sorely pressed;
By war without, and fears within,
  I come to thee for rest.

Be thou my shield and hiding-place!
  That, sheltered near thy side,
I may my fierce accuser face,
  And tell him thou hast died.

O wondrous love! to bleed and die,
  To bear the cross and shame,
That guilty sinners, such as I,
  Might plead thy gracious name.

"Poor tempest-tossed soul, be still,
  My promised grace receive":
'Tis Jesus speaks — I must, I will,
  I can, I do believe.
                    — John Newton

❧

JESUS SHALL REIGN

Jesus shall reign where'er the sun
Does his successive journeys run;
His kingdom spread from shore to
      shore,
Till moons shall wax and wane no
      more.

From north to south the princes meet
To pay their homage at His feet;
While western empires own their
      Lord,
And savage tribes attend His word.

To Him shall endless prayers be made,
And endless praises crown His head;
His name like sweet perfume shall rise
With every morning sacrifice.

People and realms of every tongue
Dwell on His love with sweetest song;
And infant voices shall proclaim
Their early blessings on His name.

Let every creature rise and bring
Peculiar honors to our King;
Angels descend with songs again,
And earth repeat the loud Amen.
                    — Isaac Watts

He Is the Truth

Long ages past in Caiaphas' Court
  Where they my precious Lord did try,
His words were branded blasphemy,
  His life as one of villainy;
The verdict came from chieftains high:
  "This evil Man must surely die!"

His words? They were eternal truth!
  'Twas said, "Ne'er man spake such as He!"
But to the unrepentant heart
  They stabbed as like a piercing dart;
In blinding rage these could not see
  That they were slaying Deity!

Who were these foes so false and cruel —
  The lowly heathen and the base?
Nay, leaders, by themselves so styled
  As righteous servants, undefiled;
To please Jehovah, full of grace,
  They smote upon Christ's blessed face!

My soul is burdened to reflect:
  Famed teachers of the Word were they;
How was it that they could not tell
  That He was their Emmanuel?
Because they pride and power would sway,
  They shouted long, "Away! Away!"

He is the Truth, His ways are meek;
  He teaches that all self must die;
Today, as then, they'll not believe;
  With outward show their souls deceive;
The lowly Cross they yet defy,
  Yes, Jesus' foes believe a lie!

O Christ, I plead Thy mercy great
  For those who wrest against the light;
Though oft with swelling words they call,
  "Lord, Lord!" they know Thee not at all;
Oh, may they yet with hearts contrite
  Receive all truth e'er comes the night!

—Ilse L. Schlaitzer

THE STRANGER AND HIS FRIEND

A poor wayfaring Man of grief
  Hath often crossed me on my way,
Who sued so humbly for relief,
  That I could never answer, Nay.
I had not power to ask his name,
Whither he went, or whence he came,
Yet there was something in his eye
That won my love, I knew not why.

Once, when my scanty meal was
    spread,
  He entered,—not a word he spake,—
Just perishing for want of bread;
  I gave him all; he blessed it, brake,
And ate,—but gave me part again:
Mine was an angel's portion then;
For while I fed with eager haste.
That crust was manna to my taste.

I spied him where a fountain burst
  Clear from the rock; his strength
    was gone;
The heedless water mocked his thirst,
  He heard it, saw it hurrying on:
I ran to raise the sufferer up;
Thrice from the stream he drained my
    cup,
Dipt, and returned it running o'er;
I drank, and never thirsted more.

'Twas night; the floods were out; it
    blew
  A winter hurricane aloof;
I heard his voice abroad, and flew
  To bid him welcome to my roof;
I warmed, I clothed, I cheered my
    guest,
Laid him on my own couch to rest;
Then made the hearth my bed, and
    seemed
In Eden's garden while I dreamed.

Stript, wounded, beaten, nigh to death,
  I found him by the highway side;
I roused his pulse, brought back his
    breath,

Revived his spirit, and supplied
Wine, oil, refreshment; he was healed:
I had myself a wound concealed;
But from that hour forgot the smart,
And peace bound up my broken heart.

In prison I saw him next, condemned
  To meet a traitor's death at morn;
The tide of lying tongues I stemmed,
  And honored him midst shame and
    scorn;
My friendship's utmost zeal to try,
He asked if I for him would die?
The flesh was weak, my blood ran chill,
But the free spirit cried, "I will."

Then in a moment to my view
  The Stranger darted from disguise;
The tokens in his hands I knew,
  My Saviour stood before mine eyes!
He spake; and my poor name he
    named:
"Of me thou hast not been ashamed;
These deeds shall thy memorial be;
Fear not, thou didst them unto me."

         — *James Montgomery*

ॐ

OUR CHRIST

I know not how that Bethlehem's Babe
  Could in the God-head be;
I only know the Manger Child
  Has brought God's life to me.

I know not how that Calvary's cross
  A world from sin could free:
I only know its matchless love
  Has brought God's love to me.

I know not how that Joseph's tomb
  Could solve death's mystery:
I only know a living Christ,
  Our immortality.

         — *Harry Webb Farrington*

REALITY

Reality, reality.
Lord Jesus Christ Thou art to me!
From the spectral mist and the driving clouds,
From the shifting shadows and phantom crowds
From unreal words and unreal lives,
Where truth with falsehood feebly strives;
From the passings away, the chance and change,
Flickerings, vanishings, swift and strange,
    I turn to my glorious rest in Thee,
    Who art the grand Reality!

Reality in greatest need,
Lord Jesus Christ Thou art indeed!
Is the pilot real who alone can guide
The drifting ship o'er the midnight tide?
Is the life-boat real, as it nears the wreck,
And the saved ones leap from the parting deck?
Is the haven real, where the barque may flee
From the autumn gales of the wild north sea?
    Reality indeed art Thou,
    My pilot, life-boat, haven now.

Reality, reality,
In the brightest days art Thou to me!
Thou art the sunshine of my mirth,
Thou art the heaven above my earth,
The spring of love of all my heart,
And the fountain of my song Thou art;
For dearer than the dearest now,
And better than the best art Thou,
    Beloved Lord, in whom I see
    Joy-giving, glad Reality.

Reality, reality,
Lord Jesus Thou hast been to me,
When I thought the dream of life was past
And "the Master's home-call" come at last;
When I thought I had only to wait
A little while at the Golden Gate,—
Only another day or two,
Till Thou Thyself shouldst bear me through;
    How real Thy presence was to me!
    How precious Thy Reality!

Reality, reality,
Lord Jesus Christ Thou art to me;
Thy name is sweeter than songs of old,
Thy words are better than "most fine gold,"
Thy deeds are greater than hero-glory,
Thy life is grander than poet story;
But Thou, Thyself for aye the same
Art more than words and life and name!
Thyself Thou hast revealed to me,
In glorious reality.

Reality, reality,
Lord Jesus Christ is crowned in Thee,
In Thee is every type fulfilled,
In Thee is every yearning stilled
For perfect beauty, truth and love:
For Thou art always far above
The grandest glimpse of our Ideal,
Yet more and more we know Thee real,
And marvel more and more to see
Thine infinite Reality.

Reality, reality,
Lord Jesus Christ Thou art to me!
My glorious King, my Lord, my God,
Life is too short for half the laud,
For half the debt of praise I owe,
For this blest knowledge that "I know
The reality of Jesus Christ,"—
Unmeasured blessing, gift unpriced!
Will I not praise Thee when I see
In the long noon of Eternity
Unveiled, Thy "bright reality"?

— *Frances Ridley Havergal*

His Hands

The hands of Christ
Seem very frail
For they were broken
By a nail.

But only they
Reach heaven at last
Whom these frail, broken
Hands hold fast.

— *John Richard Moreland*

MAJESTIC SWEETNESS

To Christ, the Lord, let every tongue
  Its noblest tribute bring:
When he's the subject of the song,
  Who can refuse to sing!

Survey the beauties of his face,
  And on his glories dwell;
Think of the wonders of his grace,
  And all his triumphs tell.

Majestic sweetness sits enthroned
  Upon his awesome brow;
His head with radiant glories crowned,
  His lips with grace o'erflow.

No mortal can with him compare,
  Among the sons of men:
Fairer he is than all the fair
  That fill the heavenly train.

He saw me plunged in deep distress,
  He flew to my relief;
For me he bore the shameful cross,
  And carried all my grief.

His hand a thousand blessings pours
  Upon my guilty head;
His presence gilds my darkest hours,
  And guards my sleeping bed.

To him I owe my life and breath,
  And all the joys I have:
He makes me triumph over death,
  And saves me from the grave.

To heaven, the place of his abode,
  He brings my weary feet;
Shows me the glories of my God,
  And makes my joys complete.

Since from his bounty I receive
  Such proofs of love divine,
Had I a thousand hearts to give,
  Lord, they should all be thine!

— *Samuel Stennett*

THE LAMB

Little lamb who made thee?
Dost thou know who made thee,
Gave thee life and bid thee feed
By the stream and o'er the mead;
Gave thee clothing of delight,
Softest clothing, woolly, bright;
Gave thee such a tender voice?
Making all the vales rejoice?
Little lamb who made thee?
Dost thou know who made thee?

Little lamb, I'll tell thee,
Little lamb, I'll tell thee.
He is callèd by thy name,
For He calls Himself a Lamb:
He is meek and He is mild,
He became a little child.
I a child and thou a lamb,
We are callèd by His name.
Little lamb, God bless thee,
Little lamb, God bless thee.

— *William Blake*

ॐ

COMFORTED

A great wind blowing, raging sea,
And rowers toiling wearily,
Far from the land where they would
  be.

And then One coming, drawing nigh;
They care not now for starless sky.
The Light of life says *It is I.*

They care not now for toil of oar,
For lo, the ship is at the shore,
And their Beloved they adore.

Lord of the Lake of Galilee,
Who long ago walked on the sea,
My heart is comforted in Thee.

— *Amy Carmichael*

NOTHING THE BLOOD CANNOT COVER

There is nothing the Blood cannot cover,
  Tho' sin is as black as can be.
You heart may be darker than midnight,
  But grace is abounding for thee.
Your life may be cursed by its shadow,
  And hope has all vanished from view,
But there's nothing the Blood cannot cover,
  Since Jesus has shed it for you.

There is nothing the Blood cannot cover,
  Since Jesus has died for us all.
No nation or tongue is excluded,
  For all are condemned by the Fall.
On Calv'ry He cried, "It is finished;
  Forgive them, O Father, I pray."
There is nothing the Blood cannot cover,
  That was not atoned for that day.

Come now to the fountain of cleansing,
  Plunge deep in its lifegiving flow.
His mercy and grace are sufficient,
  His pardon He longs to bestow.
Say not, "I'm too vile and unworthy,"
  That fact will not sinners debar,
For there's nothing the Blood cannot cover
  If you'll come to Him just as you are.

So come while His love and His mercy
  Is freely extended to you.
Be wise to your need of salvation,
  And do what you know you should do.
Heed now His sweet call to repentance,
  And walk in the Blood-sprinkled way,
For there's nothing the Blood cannot cover,
  If you will but trust Him today.

                       — F. E. Robinson

EXCELLENCY OF CHRIST

He is a path, if any be misled;
  He is a robe, if any naked be;
If any chance to hunger, he is bread;
  If any be a bondman he is free;
  If any be but weak, how strong is he!
To dead men life he is, to sick men
    health;
To blind men sight, and to the needy
    wealth;
A pleasure without loss, a treasure
    without stealth.

  — *Giles Fletcher*

ᕦᕤ

JESUS, THOU JOY OF LOVING HEARTS

Jesus, thou joy of loving hearts,
  Thou Fount of life, thou Light of
    men,
From the best bliss that earth imparts,
  We turn unfilled to thee again.

Thy truth unchanged hath ever stood;
  Thou savest those that on thee call;
To them that seek thee, thou art good,
  To them that find thee, All in all.

We taste thee, O thou living Bread,
  And long to feast upon thee still;
We drink of thee, the Fountain-head,
  And thirst, our souls from thee to fill.

Our restless spirits yearn for thee,
  Where'er our changeful lot is cast;
Glad, when thy gracious smile we see,
  Blest, when our faith can hold thee
    fast.

O Jesus, ever with us stay;
  Make all our moments calm and
    bright;
Chase the dark night of sin away;
  Shed o'er the world thy holy light.

  — *Bernard of Clairvaux*

MY COMPANION

He walks beside me every day,
He guides me in the things I say,
He stands beside me when I pray,
  He's all the world to me.

I feel His footsteps leading mine,
I hear His voice speak words divine,
His touch weaves all my life's design,
  His wondrous face I see.

I never knew a Friend so true;
He's made my skies a clearer blue,
He's let the light of heaven shine thro',
  He even died for me!

His blood washed all my sins away,
He'll keep me in the narrow way,
This Saviour who still lives today,
  The Christ of Calvary.

  — *Joyce Ramage*

ᕦᕤ

BLESS THE BLESSED MORN

Lo, God, our God, has come!
  To us a Child is born,
  To us a Son is given;
  Bless, bless the blessed morn,
O happy, lowly, lofty birth,
Now God, our God, has come to earth.
Rejoice, our God has come!
  In love and lowliness.
The Son of God has come,
  The sons of men to bless.
God with us now descend to dwell,
God in our flesh, Immanuel.
Praise ye the Word made flesh!
  True God, true man is He.
Praise ye the Christ of God!
  To Him all glory be.
Praise ye the Lamb that once was slain,
Praise ye the King that comes to reign.

  — *Horatius Bonar*

THE SAVIOUR CAN SOLVE EVERY PROBLEM

The Saviour can lift every burden,
  The heavy as well as the light;
His strength is made perfect in weakness,
  In Him there is power and might.

The Saviour can bear every sorrow,
  In Him there is comfort and rest;
No matter how great the affliction,
  He only permits what is best.

The Saviour can strengthen the weary,
  His grace is sufficient for all;
He knows every step of the pathway,
  And listens to hear when we call.

The Saviour can break sin's dominion,
  The victory He won long ago;
In Him there is freedom from bondage,
  He's able to conquer the foe.

The Saviour can satisfy fully
  The heart that the world cannot fill;
His presence will sanctify wholly
  The soul that is yielded and still.

The Saviour can solve every problem,
  The tangles of life can undo;
There is nothing too hard for Jesus,
  There is nothing that He cannot do.

            — *Oswald J. Smith*

ᐁ

JUST AS I AM

Just as I am — without one plea
But that thy blood was shed for me,
And that thou bid'st me come to thee—
  O Lamb of God, I come!

Just as I am — and waiting not
To rid my soul of one dark blot,
To thee, whose blood can cleanse each spot —
  O Lamb of God, I come!

Just as I am — though tossed about,
With many a conflict, many a doubt,
Fightings and fears within, without —
  O Lamb of God, I come!

Just as I am — poor, wretched, blind;
Sight, riches, healing of the mind,
Yea, all I need, in thee to find —
  O Lamb of God, I come!

Just as I am — thou wilt receive,
Wilt welcome, pardon, cleanse, relieve,
Because thy promise I believe —
  O Lamb of God, I come!

Just as I am — thy love unknown
Has broken every barrier down;
Now to be thine, yea, thine alone —
  O Lamb of God, I come!

Just as I am — of that free love,
The breadth, length, depth, and
    height to prove,
Here for a season, then above —
  O Lamb of God, I come!

            — *Charlotte Elliott*

ᐁ

THE BREAD OF THE SACRAMENT

Be thoughtful when you touch the
    bread,
Let it not lie unwanted, uncared for.

So often bread is taken for granted,
Yet there is so much of beauty in
    bread —
Beauty of the sun and the soil,
Beauty of human toil.
Winds and rains have caressed it,
Christ, Himself, blessed it.

Be prayerful when you touch the
    bread.
It is a symbol of His body,
Broken for you.

            — *Author Unknown*

And His Name Shall Be Called Wonderful

"His name shall be Wonderful." This Babe for whom,
Even in village inn, there was no room?

The lowing of cattle was His lullaby,
Though caroling angels were thronging the sky.

"His name shall be Wonderful." This little Lad,
Living so simply, and so plainly clad?

"His name shall be Wonderful." This Carpenter,
Know from His childhood by each villager?

"His name shall be Wonderful." Spat upon, shamed,
Tortured and crucified — how is He named?

Wonderful, Counsellor, Mighty God,
He who one dark day Golgotha's road did trod?

His name *shall* be Wonderful — Jesus, God's Son!
God's Word has promised, and it shall be done!

Not meek and lowly, despised among men,
This same Lord Jesus is coming again!

With clouds and great glory, to reign here below,
And all men shall praise Him, and each knee shall bow.

From ocean to ocean His name shall be heard,
Wonderful name of our wonderful Lord!

— *Martha Snell Nicholson*

It Is I, Be Not Afraid

When the storm was fiercely raging
  On the Lake of Galilee,
And their helpless bark was tossing
  On the wild, tempestuous sea,
Walking on the raging waters
  In a robe of light arrayed,
Jesus came, oh, hear Him calling —
  "It is I, be not afraid!"

When the storms of life are raging,
  And the night is long and drear,
When our strength is spent with toil-
    ing,
  And our spirit sinks with fear,

Oft again we see Him coming,
  Swiftly hast-ning to our aid;
Often still we hear Him calling —
  "It it I, be not afraid!"

When the night of death shall lower,
  And the Jordan's surges roll,
When the hour and power of darkness
  Overwhelm the sinking soul,
Then above the raging billows,
  And night's deepest, darkest shade,
We shall hear Him calling to us —
  "It is I, be not afraid!"

— *A. B. Simpson*

LOOKING TO JESUS

My faith looks up to thee,
Thou Lamb of Calvary,
  Saviour divine!
Now hear me while I pray,
Take all my guilt away,
Oh, let me, from this day,
  Be wholly thine!

May thy rich grace impart
Strength to my fainting heart,
  My zeal inspire;
As thou hast died for me,
Oh! may my love to thee
Pure, warm, and changeless be,
  A living fire!

While life's dark maze I tread
And griefs around me spread,
  Be thou my Guide;
Bid darkness turn to day,
Wipe sorrow's tears away,
Nor let me ever stray
  From thee aside.

When ends life's transient dream,
When death's cold, sullen stream
  Shall o'er me roll;
Blest Saviour, then, in love,
Fear and distrust remove;
Oh, bear me safe above,
  A ransomed soul.

— *Ray Palmer*

LET US SEE JESUS

We would see Jesus — for the shadows lengthen
  Across the little landscape of our life;
We would see Jesus — our weak faith to strengthen
  For the last weariness, the final strife.

We would see Jesus — for life's hand hath rested
  With its dark touch on weary heart and brow;
And though our souls have many billows breasted,
  Others are rising in the distance now.

We would see Jesus — the great Rock-foundation
  Whereon our feet were set through sovereign grace;
Nor life nor death, with all their agitation,
  Can thence remove us, if we see His face.

We would see Jesus — other lights are paling,
  Which for long years we have rejoiced to see;
The blessings of our pilgrimage are failing:
  We would not mourn them, for we go to Thee.

We would see Jesus — this is all we're needing;
  Strength, joy and willingness come with the sight;
We would see Jesus — dying, risen, pleading —
  Then welcome day, and farewell mortal night!

— *Anna B. Warner*

THE GOOD SHEPHERD

Saviour! like a shepherd lead us;
  Much we need thy tender care;
In thy pleasant pastures feed us,
  For our use thy folds prepare:
    Blessed Jesus!
  Thou hast bought us, thine we are.

We are thine; do thou befriend us,
  Be the guardian of our way;
Keep thy flock, from sin defend us,
  Seek us when we go astray:
    Blessed Jesus!
  Hear young children when they
    pray.

Thou hast promised to receive us,
  Poor and sinful though we be;
Thou hast mercy to relieve us,
  Grace to cleanse, and power to free.
    Blessed Jesus!
  Let us early turn to thee.

Early let us seek thy favor,
  Early let us do thy will;
Holy Lord, our only Saviour!
  With thy grace our bosom fill:
    Blessed Jesus!
  Thou has loved us, love us still.

— *Dorothy Ann Thrupp*

ROCK OF AGES

Rock of Ages, cleft for me,
Let me hide myself in thee!
Let the water and the blood,
From thy riven side which flowed,
Be of sin the double cure,
Cleanse me from its guilt and power.

Not the labors of my hands
Can fulfill thy law's demands;
Could my zeal no respite know,
Could my tears forever flow,
Thou must save, and thou alone.
All for sin could not atone;

Nothing in my hand I bring;
Simply to thy cross I cling;
Naked, come to thee for dress;
Helpless, look to thee for grace;
Foul, I to the fountain fly;
Wash me, Saviour, or I die!

While I draw this fleeting breath,
When my eye-strings break in death,—
When I soar through tracts unknown;
See thee on thy judgment-throne; —
Rock of Ages, cleft for me,
Let me hide myself in thee!

— *Augustus Montague Toplady*

WIDE OPEN ARE THY LOVING HANDS

Wide open are Thy loving hands
  To pay with more than gold
The awful debt of guilty men,
  Forever and of old.

Ah, let me grasp those pierced hands,
  That we may never part,
And let the power of their blood
  Sustain my fainting heart.

Wide open are Thy saving arms,
  A fallen world t'embrace;
To take to love and endless rest
  Our whole forsaken race.

Lord, I am helpless, sad, and poor,
  But boundless is Thy grace;
Give me the soul-transforming joy
  For which I seek Thy face.

Draw all my mind, my soul, and heart
  Up to Thy throne on high,
And let Thy sacred cross exalt
  My spirit to the sky.

To these, Thy mighty, faithful hands,
  My spirit I resign;
In life, I live alone to Thee,
  In death, alone am Thine.

— *Bernard of Clairvaux*

Go Tell Them That Jesus Is Living

A light on the dark horizon,
  Shining with luminous ray,
Banishes fear and sorrow,
  For Christ is risen today!

O sing it to those who sorrow,
  The message is clear and sweet,
"He is the Resurrection,"
  Go tell it to those who weep.

Go tell them that Jesus is living,
  He's living just as He said,
And some day He's coming in glory,
  Coming to quicken the dead.

Then all the pain and the suffering
  That now His beloved ones feel,
Will pass, for "There is no sorrow
  On earth that heaven can't heal!"

So tell them that Jesus is living,
  That He will illumine the way
Over the troublesome waters,
  For Christ is risen today!

Alice Hansche Mortenson

ꭥ

More Love to Christ

More love to thee, O Christ!
  More love to thee!
Hear thou the prayer I make,
  On bended knee;
This is my earnest plea,—
More love, O Christ! to thee,
  More love to thee!

Once earthly joy I craved,
  Sought peace and rest;
Now thee alone I seek,
  Give what is best:
This all my prayer shall be,—
More love, O Christ! to thee,
  More love to thee!

Let sorrow do its work,
  Send grief and pain;
Sweet are thy messengers,
  Sweet their refrain,
When they can sing with me,—
More love, O Christ! to thee,
  More love to thee!

Then shall my latest breath
  Whisper thy praise;
This be the parting cry
  My heart shall raise,—
This still its prayer shall be,—
More love, O Christ! to thee,
  More love to thee!

— *Elizabeth Payson Prentiss*

ꭥ

My Need

I thought I needed many things
  Along life's toilsome way,
When days were long and heavy cares
  Left scarcely time to pray.

I thought I needed many things
  For those I held most dear,
When they were sad and longed for
    rest
  Or change of portion here.

When it was Thee I needed, Lord,
  To satisfy my heart,
To fill my days with rest and peace,
  And every grace impart.

And those I loved, but needed Thee,
  Not change of scene or place,
But faith, just now, thro' sun or shade
  Thy loving hand to trace.

Just Thee alone, my blessed Lord,
  For every time and place;
Just Thee alone — until we all
  Shall see Thee face to face.

— *Grace E. Troy*

ABIDE WITH ME

Abide with me! Fast falls the eventide;
The darkness deepens: Lord, with me abide!
When other helpers fail, and comforts flee,
Help of the helpless, oh, abide with me!

Swift to its close ebbs out life's little day;
Earth's joys grow dim; it's glories pass away:
Change and decay in all around I see;
O thou, who changest not, abide with me!

Not a brief glance I beg, a passing word,
But as thou dwell'st with thy disciples, Lord,
Familiar, condescending, patient, free,—
Come, not to sojourn, but 'bide, with me!

Come not in terrors, as the King of kings;
But kind and good, with healing in thy wings:
Tears for all woes, a heart for every plea.
Come, Friend of sinners, and thus 'bide with me!

Thou on my head in early youth didst smile,
And, though rebellious and perverse meanwhile,
Thou hast not left me, oft as I left thee.
On to the close, O Lord, abide with me!

I need thy presence every passing hour.
What but thy grace can foil the Tempter's power?
Who like thyself my guide and stay can be?
Through cloud and sunshine, oh, abide with me!

I fear no foe with thee at hand to bless:
Ills have no weight, and tears no bitterness.
Where is death's sting, where, grave, thy victory?
I triumph still, if thou abide with me.

Hold thou thy cross before my closing eyes;
Shine through the gloom, and point me to the skies:
Heaven's morning breaks, and earth's vain shadows flee.
In life and death, O Lord, abide with me!

— Henry Francis Lyte

THE NAME OF JESUS

How sweet the name of Jesus sounds
  In a believer's ear!
It soothes his sorrows, heals his wounds,
  And drives away his fear.

It makes the wounded spirit whole,
  And calms the troubled breast;
'Tis manna to the hungry soul,
  And to the weary, rest.

Dear name! the rock on which I build,
  My shield and hiding-place;
My never-failing treasury, filled
  With boundless stores of grace.

By thee my prayers acceptance gain,
  Although with sin defiled;
Satan accuses me in vain,
  And I am owned a child.

Jesus, my Shepherd, Husband, Friend,
  My Prophet, Priest, and King,
My Lord, my Life, my Way, my End,
  Accept the praise I bring.

Weak is the effort of my heart,
  And cold my warmest thought;
But when I see thee as thou art,
  I'll praise thee as I ought.

Till then, I would thy love proclaim
  With every fleeting breath;
And may the music of thy name
  Refresh my soul in death!

— *John Newton*

ᢵᢆᢙ

From THE EVERLASTING MERCY

O Christ who holds the open gate,
O Christ who drives the furrow
    straight,
O Christ, the plough, O Christ, the
    laughter
Of holy white birds flying after,
Lo, all my heart's field red and torn,

And Thou wilt bring young green
    corn,
The young green corn divinely spring-
    ing,
The young green corn forever singing;
And when the field is fresh and fair
Thy blessed feet shall glitter there.
And we will walk the weeded field,
And tell the golden harvest's yield,
The corn that makes the holy bread
By which the soul of man is fed,
The holy bread, the food unpriced,
Thy everlasting mercy, Christ.

— *John Masefield*

ᢵᢆᢙ

THE KING SHALL COME

The King shall come when morning
    dawns,
  And light triumphant breaks;
When beauty gilds the eastern hills,
  And life to joy awakes.

Not as of old a little child
  To bear, and fight, and die,
But crowned with glory like the sun
  That lights the morning sky.

O brighter than the rising morn
  When He, victorious, rose,
And left the lonesome place of death,
  Despite the rage of foes —

O brighter than the glorious morn
  Shall this fair morning be,
When Christ, our King, in beauty
    comes,
  And we His face shall see!

The King shall come when morning
    dawns,
  And light and beauty brings:
Hail, Christ, the Lord! Thy people
    pray,
  "Come quickly, King of kings."

— *Greek Hymn*

THE SEARCH

I went to seek for Christ,
And Nature seemed so fair
That first the woods and fields my youth enticed,
And I was sure to find him there:
The temple I forsook,
And to the solitude
Allegiance paid; but Winter came and shook
The crown and purple from my wood;
His snows, like desert sands, with scornful drift,
Besieged the columned aisle and palace-gate;
My Thebes, cut deep with many a solemn rift,
But epitaphed her own sepulchred state:
Then I remembered whom I went to seek,
And blessed blunt Winter for his counsel bleak.

Back to the world I turned,
For Christ, I said, is King;
So the cramped alley and the hut I spurned,
As far beneath his sojourning:
'Mid power and wealth I sought,
But found no trace of him,
And all the costly offerings I had brought
With sudden rust and mould grew dim:
I found his tomb, indeed, where, by their laws,
All must on stated days themselves imprison,
Mocking with bread a dead creed's grinning jaws,
Witless how long the life had thence arisen;
Due sacrifice to this they set apart,
Prizing it more than Christ's own living heart.

So from my feet the dust
Of the proud World I shook;
Then came dear Love and shared with me his crust,
And half my sorrow's burden took.
After the World's soft bed,
Its rich and dainty fare,
Like down seemed Love's coarse pillow to my head
His cheap food seemed as manna rare;
Fresh-trodden prints of bare and bleeding feet,
Turned to the heedless city whence I came,
Hard by I saw, and springs of worship sweet
Gushed from my cleft heart smitten by the same;
Love looked me in the face and spake no words,
But straight I knew those footprints were the Lord's.

I followed where they led
And in a hovel rude,
With naught to fence the weather from his head,
The King I sought for meekly stood;
A naked, hungry child
Clung round his gracious knee,
And a poor hunted slave looked up and smiled
To bless the smile that set him free;
New miracles I saw this presence do,—
No more I knew the hovel bare and poor,
The gathered chips into a woodpile grew,
The broken morsel swelled to goodly store;
I knelt and wept: my Christ no more I seek,
His throne is with the outcast and the weak.

— *James Russell Lowell*

ⷮ

"My Beloved Is Mine, and I Am His"

Long did I toil, and knew no earthly rest;
Far did I rove, and found no certain home;
At last I sought them in His sheltering breast,
Who opes His arms, and bids the weary come:
With Him I found a home, a rest-divine;
And I since then am His, and He is mine.

The good I have is from His stores supplied;
The ill is only what He deems the best;
With Him as Friend I'm rich, with nought beside,
And poor without Him, though of all possest:
Changes may come — I take, or I resign,
Content while I am His, while He is mine.

Whate'er may change, in Him no change is seen;
A glorious Sun, that wanes not, nor declines;
Above the clouds and storms He walks serene,
And on His people's inward darkness shines:
All may depart — I fret not nor repine,
While I my Saviour's am, while He is mine.

While here, alas! I know but half His love,
But half discern Him, and but half adore;
But when I meet Him in the realms above,
I hope to love Him better, praise Him more,
And feel, and tell, amid the choir divine,
How fully I am His, and He is mine.

— *John Quarles*

AMID THE DIN OF EARTHLY STRIFE

Amid the din of earthly strife,
    Amid the busy crowd,
The whispers of eternal life
    Are lost in clamors loud;
When lo! I find a healing balm,
    The world grows dim to me;
My spirit rests in sudden calm
    With Him of Galilee.

I linger near Him in the throng,
    And listen to His voice;
I feel my weary soul grow strong,
    My saddened heart rejoice.
Amid the storms that darkly frown
    I hear His call to me,
And lay my heavy burden down
    With Him of Galilee.

    — *Henry Warburton Hawkes*

THERE IS A NAME I LOVE TO HEAR

There is a name I love to hear,
    I love to speak its worth;
It sounds like music in mine ear,
    The sweetest name on earth.

It tells me of a Saviour's love
    Who died to set me free;
It tells me of His precious blood,
    The sinner's perfect plea.

It tells me of a Father's smile,
    Beaming upon His child;
It cheers me thro' this "little while,"
    Through desert, waste, and wild.

It bids my trembling heart rejoice,
    It dries each rising tear,
It tells me, in "a still small voice,"
    To trust and never fear.

Jesus! the name I love so well,
    The name I love to hear!
No saint on earth its worth can tell,
    No heart conceive how dear.

This name shall shed its fragrance still
    Along this thorny road,
Shall sweetly smooth the rugged hill
    That leads me up to God.

And there with all the blood-bought throng,
    From sin and sorrow free,
I'll sing the new eternal song
    Of Jesus' love to me.

    — *Frederick Whitfield*

JESUS, RETURN

Return, dear Lord, to those who look
    With eager eyes that yearn
For Thee among the garden flowers;
After the dark and lonely hours,
    As morning light return.

Return to those who wander far,
    With lamps that dimly burn,
Along the troubled road of thought,
Where doubt and conflict come unsought,—
    With inward joy return.

Return to those on whom the yoke
    Of life is hard and stern;
Renew the hope within their breast,
Draw them to Thee and give them rest:
    O Friend of Man, return.

Return to this war-weary world,
    And help us all to learn
Thy secret of victorious life,
The love that triumphs over strife,—
    O Prince of Peace, return.

Jesus, we ask not now that day
    When all men shall discern
Thy coming with the angelic host;
Today, to all who need Thee most,
    In silent ways, return!

    — *Henry van Dyke*

An Hour With Thee

Lord, what a change within us one short hour
  Spent in Thy presence will avail to make!
  What heavy burdens from our bosoms take!
  What parched grounds refresh as with a shower!
We kneel, and all around us seems to lower;
  We rise, and all, the distant and the near,
  Stands forth in sunny outline, brave and clear;
  We kneel, how weak; we rise, how full of power!
Why, therefore, should we do ourselves this wrong,
  Or others — that we are not always strong —
That we are sometimes overborne with care —
  That we should ever weak or heartless be,
Anxious or troubled — when with us is prayer,
  And joy and strength and courage are with Thee?

— *Richard Chenevix Trench*

From In Memoriam

Ring out, wild bells, to the wild sky,
  The flying cloud, the frosty light:
  The year is dying in the night;
Ring out, wild bells, and let him die.

Ring out a slowly dying cause,
  And ancient forms of party strife;
  Ring in the nobler modes of life,
With sweeter manners, purer laws.

Ring out false pride in place and blood,
  The civic slander and the spite;
  Ring in the love of truth and right,
Ring in the common love of good.

Ring out old shapes of foul disease;
  Ring out the narrowing lust of gold;
  Ring out the thousand wars of old,
Ring in the thousand years of peace.

Ring in the valiant man and free,
  The larger heart, the kindlier hand;
  Ring out the darkness of the land,
Ring in the Christ that is to be.

— *Alfred, Lord Tennyson*

For Me

Amid a rabble cry,
Under an Eastern sky,
A Man went forth to die
  For me!

Thorn-crowned His blessed head,
Blood-stained His every tread,
Cross-laden on He sped,
  For me!

Pierced through His hands and feet,
Three hours o'er Him did beat
Fierce rays of noontide heat,
  For me!

Thus wert Thou made all mine.
Lord, make me wholly Thine,
Give grace and strength divine
  To me!

In thought and word and deed,
Thy will to do; oh! lead my feet
E'en though they bleed
  To Thee.

— *Author Unknown*

MY LORD

I cannot see
Why men should turn from Thee,
My Lord, my Lord.

If they could only guess
Thy matchless loveliness,
The beauty of Thy face,
The richness of Thy grace
My Lord, my Lord.

If they could only see
Thee on the cruel tree.
Nor pain nor death was stayed
Till all our debt was paid,
My Lord, my Lord.

If they could only know
That heart which loves them so,
Their only thought would be
How they might come to Thee,
My Lord, my Lord.

— *Martha Snell Nicholson*

ɔᴥ

FAIREST LORD JESUS

Fairest Lord Jesus,
  Ruler of all nature,
O thou of God and man the Son;
  Thee will I cherish, thee will I
    honour,
Thou, my soul's glory, joy, and crown.

Fair are the meadows,
  Fairer still the woodlands,
Robed in the blooming garb of spring:
  Jesus is fairer, Jesus is purer,
Who makes the woeful heart to sing.

Fair is the sunshine,
  Fairer still the moonlight,
And all the twinkling, starry host:
  Jesus shines brighter, Jesus shines
    purer,
Than all the angels heaven can boast.

— *Author Unknown*

ɔᴥ

REDEMPTION

A Mother and her Child;
  A wondrous Boy,
A dead man raised to life;
A few poor fishermen,
  An Upper Room,
A feast, a garden, and a judgment hall.

A crown of thorns, a scourge,
  A bitter Cross;
A great stone rolled away
  And tears;
A springtime morning
And an empty tomb;
A Feast, a Blessing and a Risen Christ.

— *Mary Winter Ware*

ɔᴥ

WISHING

I'd like to view the whole wide earth
And all the things within it,
I'd like to know its richest worth
And then have power to win it;
  I'll tell you what I'd do with everything;—
  I'd give it all to Jesus Christ, my King!

— *Henry W. Frost*

THE CONCLUSION

When first I heard of Jesus,
    It seemed some mystic tale,
A root of barren dryness,
    No fragrance could exhale;
But as I came to know Him,
    His precious name grew sweet,
And, like a perfumed rainbow,
    Love arched the mercy seat.

At first, I saw no beauty,
    No captivating spell;
Felt no divine emotion
    In my cold bosom swell;
But when, through beams of glory,
    God shone in Jesus' face,
All other objects tarnished
    Before His matchless grace.

I read that He was wounded,
    And bruised upon the tree,
Yet felt no thrilling wonder,
    As though He died for *me*.
But since, oh since, I know it,
    And saw Him bear my load,
I cannot cease from praising
    My great redeeming God.

O Rose of rarest odor!
    O Lily white and pure!
O chiefest of ten thousand,
    Whose glory must endure!
The more I see Thy beauty,
    The more I know Thy grace,
The more I long unhindered
    To gaze upon Thy face.

— *Author Unknown*

OUR MASTER

Immortal Love, forever full,
    Forever flowing free,
Forever shared, forever whole,
    A never-ebbing sea!

Our outward lips confess the name
    All other names above;
Love only knoweth whence it came,
    And comprehendeth love.

We may not climb the heavenly steeps
    To bring the Lord Christ down:
In vain we search the lowest deeps,
    For Him no depths can drown.

But warm, sweet, tender, even yet
    A present help is He;
And faith has still its Olivet,
    And love its Galilee.

The healing of His seamless dress
    Is by our beds of pain;
We touch Him in life's throng and
        press,
    And we are whole again.

Through Him the first fond prayers
        are said
    Our lips of childhood frame,
The last low whispers of our dead
    Are burdened with His name.

O Lord and Master of us all!
    Whate'er our name or sign,
We own Thy sway, we hear Thy call,
    We test our lives by Thine.

— *John Greenleaf Whittier*

St. Thomas the Apostle

We were not by when Jesus came,
        But round us, far and near,
We see His trophies, and His name
        In choral echoes hear.
In a fair ground our lot is cast,
As in the solemn week that past,
While some might doubt, but all adored,
Ere the whole widowed Church had seen her risen Lord.

Slowly, as then, His bounteous hand
        The golden chain unwinds,
Drawing to Heaven with gentlest band
        Wise hearts and loving minds.
Love sought Him first; at dawn of morn
From her sad couch she sprang forlorn,
She sought to weep with Thee alone,
And saw Thine open grave, and knew that Thou wert gone.

Reason and Faith at once set out
        To search the Saviour's tomb;
Faith faster runs, but waits without,
        As fearing to presume
Till Reason enters in, and trace
Christ's relics round the holy place —
"Here lay His limbs, and here His sacred head:
And who was by, to make His new-forsaken bed?"

Both wonder, one believes — but while
        They muse on all at home,
No thought can tender Love beguile
        From Jesus' grave to roam.
Weeping she stays till He appear —
Her witness first the Church must hear —
All joy to souls that can rejoice
With her at earliest call of His dear gracious voice.

Joy too to those who love to talk
        In secret how He died,
Though with sealed eyes, awhile they walk,
        Nor see Him at their side;
Most like the faithful pair are they,
Who once to Emmaus took their way,
Half darkling, till their Master shed
His glory on their souls, made known in breaking bread.

Thus, ever brighter and more bright,
　On those He came to save
The Lord of new-created light
　Dawned gradual from the grave:
Till passed the inquiring daylight hour,
And with closed door in silent bower
The Church in anxious musing sate,
As one who for redemption still had long to wait.

— *John Keble*

༄

CHRIST IN THE STREET

He came to earth one blue-skied day —
　He walked with world-men down the street:
The people stared in a wide-eyed way,
　Noting his wounded hands and feet.

Then they whispered and hurried by:
　Some of them mockingly jibed and smiled
When he stopped where buildings towered high
　To stroke the head of a ragged child.

"Out of the way," the world-men cried;
　"Hurry along," called one in blue:
"You look like a man we crucified,
　"But no . . . Oh, no . . . it was not you!"

"Have you the price of board and bed?"
　They hurled at him as nightfall neared,
And when he shook his thorn-scourged head
　The mob pressed close and laughed and jeered.

"Have you a house of bricks?" they called,
　"Or a chariot which runs alone —
A vault for silver, steeled and walled
　With blocks of mighty granite stone?"

"Have you some other earth-made thing —
　A purse of coins or flying plane?
You who have called yourself a king —
　You must have prospered through your reign."

The night closed in — none gave a crust:
　I heard the wan Christ groan and say:
"Better my dark tomb in the dust
　Than the world today . . . than men today."

— *Jay G. Sigmund*

THE GREATEST EVENT

I gaze into the heavens
And into my view
Swim millions of stars.

They have existed since
Time Eternal,
And have seen all of the
Sorrows and joys,
Laughter and heartaches,
That the universe has known
Since the long ago.

Arcturus saw Joseph sold into Egypt,
And Moses bringing the Ten Com-
mandments
Down from Sinai.

Orion saw Socrates
Drink the poison hemlock
With a smile that shines through the
ages.

Pegasus took note of Caesar
Crossing the Rubicon,
And Jupiter looked on while
Luther and Zwingli and Hus
Fought for religious freedom.

At last Pleiades saw Hitler and Musso-
lini
Try to tramp out the sparks of
Freedom that remained in the world.

Yes, the stars
Have discerned many things —
But sober history
Is not all they have surveyed.

They have seen heroes and heroines,
Cowards and traitors.

They have laughed with the mother
As she watches her baby
Take his first steps,
And they have wept with the same
mother

As she learns of her son's death in
battle.

They have seen the first robin
Wing his way northward
To bring the glorious springtime
To hearts burdened with winter.

They have also seen men despair
And give up their lives as hopeless,
Because they did not know God.

These stars have seen many things —
From the earth's beginning until now
They have viewed its progress,
And many times its degradation.
But, the stars remain silent!

They do not
Speak in earthly tones.
They cannot let us know all they
Would like to tell.
But if they could —

If each star had its chance to
Relate to the world the

Greatest event that it ever looked on —
Had its chance to say,
"This, O mortal man,
Is the greatest event
That ever took place on earth —"
Each would tell the same story.

What would the stars say?
That Jesus the Christ,
The Saviour of all men
Gave His life on a felon's cross,
A ransom for many.

That God so loved the world
That He gave
His only begotten Son,
That whosoever believeth in Him
Should not perish,
But have everlasting life!

— *Author Unknown*

If Christ Were Here To-night

If Christ were here to-night, and saw me tired,
    And half afraid another step to take,
I think He'd know the thing my heart desired,
    And ease that heart of all its throbbing ache.

If Christ were here in this dull room of mine,
    That gathers up so many shadows dim,
I am quite sure its narrow space would shine,
    And kindle into glory around Him.

If Christ were here, I might not pray so long;
    My prayer would have such little way to go;
'Twould break into a burst of happy song,
    So would my joy and gladness overflow.

If Christ were here to-night, I'd touch the hem
    Of His fair, seamless robe, and stand complete
In wholeness and in whiteness; I, who stem
    Such waves of pain, to kneel at His dear feet.

If Christ were here to-night, I'd tell Him all
    The load I carry for the ones I love —
The blinded ones, who grope and faint and fall,
    Following false guides, nor seeking Christ above.

If Christ were here! Ah, faithless soul and weak,
    Is not the Master ever close to thee?
Deaf is thine ear, that canst not hear Him speak;
    Dim is thine eye, His face that cannot see.

Thy Christ is here, and never far away;
    He entered with thee when thou camest in;
His strength was thine through all the busy day;
    He knew thy need, He kept thee pure from sin.

Thy blessèd Christ is in thy little room,
    Nay more, the Christ Himself is in thy heart;
Fear not, the dawn will scatter darkest gloom,
    And heaven will be of thy rich life a part.

— *Margaret E. Sangster*

INDIFFERENCE

When Jesus came to Golgotha they hanged Him on a tree,
They drave great nails through hands and feet, and made a Calvary;
They crowned Him with a crown of thorns, red were His wounds and deep,
For those were crude and cruel days, the human flesh was cheap.

When Jesus came to Birmingham, they simply passed Him by,
They never hurt a hair of Him, they only let Him die;
For men had grown more tender, and they would not give Him pain,
They only just passed down the street, and left Him in the rain.

Still Jesus cried, "Forgive them, for they know not what they do,"
And still it rained the winter rain that drenched Him through and through;
The crowds went home and left the streets without a soul to see,
And Jesus crouched against a wall and cried for Calvary.

         — G. A. Studdert-Kennedy

THE COMING OF HIS FEET

In the crimson of the morning, in the whiteness of the noon,
    In the amber glory of the day's retreat,
In the midnight, robed in darkness, or the gleaming of the moon,
    I listen for the coming of His feet.

I have heard His weary footsteps on the sands of Galilee
    On the temple's marble pavement, on the street,
Worn with weight of sorrow, faltering up the slopes of Calvary,
    The sorrow of the coming of His feet.

Down the minster-aisles of splendor, from between the cherubim,
    Through the wondering throng, with motion strong and fleet,
Sounds His victor tread, approaching with a music far and dim,
    The music of the coming of His feet.

Sandled not with sheen of silver, girdled not with woven gold,
    Weighted not with shimmering gems and odors sweet,
But white-winged and shod with glory in the Tabor light of old —
    The glory of the coming of His feet.

He is coming, oh my spirit! with His everlasting peace,
    With His blessedness, immortal and complete;
He is coming, oh, my spirit, and His coming brings release,
    I listen for the coming of His feet.

         — Author Unknown

THREE CROSSES

Three crosses on a lonely hill,
  A thief on either side,
And, in between, the Son of God . . .
  How wide the gulf — how wide!

Yet one thief spanned it with the
    words,
  "O Lord, remember me";
The other scoffed and turned aside
  To lost eternity.

Forsaken is the hilltop now,
  And all the crosses gone,
But in believing hearts of men
  The center cross lives on.

And still, as when these sentinels
  First met earth's wondering view,
The presence of the Lord divides —
  Upon which side are you?

— *Helen Frazee-Bower*

THE CUP

"There is a way I cannot take;
There is a cup I cannot drink,
There is a cross I cannot bear;
There is a fear from which I shrink."

Throughout the long years of my life
These are the words I used to say;
But time, like a relentless tide,
Bore me, unwilling, to a day. . . .

I drank the cup, I took the way,
I bore the cross, I looked upon
The face of him I loved so well,
Scarcely believing he was gone.

And then I found my tender Lord
Had gone before me and prepared
All things for me. I did not drink
The bitter cup alone; He shared

Its every drop with me, and in
Its dregs I found a sweetness rare;
And when I lifted up my cross,
His arms were ever there to bear

The heavy end. I did not walk
My lonely way alone; His feet
Kept pace with my worn, weary ones;
And His companionship was sweet.

And when I thought upon the face
Of him whom they called dead, be-
    hold:
I saw him waiting there for me,
Alive, more precious than of old!

— *Martha Snell Nicholson*

JESUS, THY LIFE IS MINE!

Jesus, Thy life is mine!
  Dwell evermore in me;
  And let me see
That nothing can untwine
  Thy life from mine.

Thy life in me be shown!
  Lord, I would henceforth seek
  To think and speak
Thy thoughts, Thy words alone,
  No more my own.

Thy fullest gift, O Lord,
  Now at Thy word I claim,
  Through Thy dear Name,
And touch the rapturous chord
  Of praise forth-poured.

Jesus, my life is Thine,
  And evermore shall be
  Hidden in Thee!
For nothing can untwine
  Thy life from mine.

— *Frances Ridley Havergal*

THE LOOK

The Saviour looked on Peter. Ay, no word,
No gesture of reproach; the Heavens serene
Though heavy with armed justice, did not lean
Their thunders that way: the forsaken Lord
Looked only, on the traitor. None record
What that look was, none guess; for those who have seen
Wronged lovers loving through a death-pang keen,
Or pale-cheeked martyrs smiling to a sword,
Have missed Jehovah at the judgment-call.
And Peter, from the height of blasphemy —
"I never knew this man" — did quail and fall
As knowing straight *that God;* and turnèd free
And went out speechless from the face of all,
And filled the silence, weeping bitterly.

— Elizabeth Barrett Browning

THE YOUNG MAN OF NAZARETH

The young man out of Nazareth
Was good to see —
I felt a breath
Awaken, dew-fresh, like a breeze
Astir among the olive trees,
The grace of youth flowered in His
    speech —
Into my heart. I followed His
Brave, eager words with a strange
    reach,
Half-wondering why, until the rim
Of the gray mountain ridge was white
With stars —
    Men told strange tales of sight
Come to a beggar, one born blind —
I do not know. Some say they find
Those still who think it was a king
They killed. And never anything
Has brought such quiet to my bed
As thinking of the things He said:
A kingdom simple as a child —
Its king a servant —
    Though He smiled

A lion looked out of His eye.
His brave, young heart brake like a cry.
If time came back, and He as then,
I could but follow Him again.

— Author Unknown

THE HUNGRY

Whom does He love the most —
    The poor, the sick, the blind,
The rich, the maimed, the host
    Unknowingly unkind?

The ones who strive, and fail;
    The ones who have, and lose;
The ones who will not quail
    Nor martyrdom refuse?

The wind went sobbing low
    To His great Heart and cried;
"Dear God, they need you so —
    Who die unsatisfied."

— Caroline Giltinan

Himself He Could Not Save

In vision now I seem to see
  Mount Calvary dark and lone:
And Christ, my Saviour, on the tree,
  In agony unknown.
I see the angry, jeering throng,
  I hear them mock and rave,
"Others He saved, but see Him there—
  Himself He cannot save!"

Ah Lord, how true, how true indeed!
  If Thou wouldst set me free
From the eternal curse of sin,
  Its awful penalty,
Thyself Thou couldst not save; alas,
  The bitter cup of woe,
Must needs be drained unto the dregs,
  And Thou through death must go.

I see Thee hanging on that Cross,
  And low my heart is laid,
To think my sin helped nail Thee
    there;
  My ransom there was paid.
From heaven's throne to Calvary's tree,
  One purpose led Thee on —

To bear the sin of all the world
  Since e'er it was begun.
" 'Tis finished!" was Thy glorious cry,
  While earth was wrapped in gloom;
The temple veil was rent in twain,
  And death had met its doom.
'Tis finished, yea 'tis finished, Lord!
  Eternal life is mine
Because to Calv'ry Thou didst go
  In sacrifice sublime.

Unto a dying, sin-cursed world
  New life that day He gave,
And saving others on the tree,
  Himself He could not save.
He yielded up His life, but lo,
  Death could not hold Him prey.
He burst apart its cruel bands,
  And rose to reign for aye.
The Lord of life and light, He rose,
  Eternal life to give
To all who by dark Calvary's way
  Will come to Him and live.

                — *Avis B. Christiansen*

The Meaning of the Look

I think that look of Christ might seem to say —
"Thou Peter! art thou then a common stone
Which I at last must break my heart upon,
For all God's charge to his high angels may
Guard my foot better? Did I yesterday
Wash *thy* feet, my beloved, that they should run
Quick to deny me 'neath the morning sun?
And do thy kisses, like the rest, betray?
The cock crows coldly. — Go, and manifest
A late contrition, but no bootless fear!
For when thy final need is dreariest,
Thou shalt not be denied, as I am here;
My voice to God and angels shall attest,
Because I know this man, let him be clear."

                — *Elizabeth Barrett Browning*

WHERE CROSS THE CROWDED WAYS OF LIFE

Where cross the crowded ways of life,
  Where sound the cries of race and clan,
Above the noise of selfish strife,
  We hear Thy voice, O Son of man!

In haunts of wretchedness and need,
  On shadowed thresholds dark with fears,
From paths where hide the lures of greed,
  We catch the vision of Thy tears.

From tender childhood's helplessness,
  From woman's grief, man's burdened toil,
From famished souls, from sorrow's stress,
  Thy heart has never known recoil.

The cup of water given for Thee
  Still holds the freshness of Thy grace;
Yet long these multitudes to see
  The sweet compassion of Thy face.

O Master, from the mountain side,
  Make haste to heal these hearts of pain;
Among these restless throngs abide,
  Oh tread the city's streets again.

Till sons of men shall learn Thy love,
  And follow where Thy feet have trod;
Till glorious from Thy heaven above,
  Shall come the City of our God.

— *Frank Mason North*

MINE WERE THE STREETS OF NAZARETH

When I am tempted to repine
That such a lowly lot is mine,
There comes to me a voice which saith
"Mine were the streets of Nazareth."

So mean, so common and confined,
And He the Monarch of mankind!
Yet patiently He traveleth
Those narrow streets of Nazareth.

It may be I shall never rise
To place or fame beneath the skies —
But walk in straitened ways till death,
Narrow as streets of Nazareth.

But if through honor's arch I tread
And there forget to bend my head,
Ah! let me hear the voice which saith,
"Mine were the streets of Nazareth."

— *Nettie Rooker*

It May Be

It may be in the evening,—
    When the work of the day is done,
And you have time to sit in the twilight
    And watch the sinking sun.
While the long bright day dies slowly
    Over the sea —
And the hour grows quiet and holy
    With thoughts of Me;—
While you hear the village children
    Passing along the street,
Among those thronging footsteps
    May come the sound of My feet:
Therefore I tell you: Watch!
    By the light of the evening star,
When the room is growing dusky
    As the clouds afar;
Let the door be on the latch
    In your home.
For it may be through the gloaming
    I Will Come!

It may be in the morning,
    When the sun is bright and strong,
And the dew is glittering sharply
    Over the little lawn;
When the waves are laughing loudly
    Along the shore,
And the little birds are singing sweetly
    About the door;
With the long day's work before you,
    You rise up with the sun,
And the neighbors come and talk a
    little
Of all that must be done;
But remember that I may be the next
    To come in at the door,
To call you from all your busy work
    For evermore;
As you work your heart must watch,
    For the door is on the latch
        In your room;
And it may be in the morning
    I Will Come!

So I am watching quietly,
    Every day;
Whenever the sun shines brightly,
    I rise and say, —
"Surely it is the shining of His face!"
And look unto the gates of His high
    place
    Beyond the sea;
For I know He is coming shortly
    To summon me;
And when a shadow falls across the
    window
    Of my room,
Where I am working my appointed
    task,
I lift my head to watch the door, and
    ask
    If He is come;
And the angel answers sweetly
    In my home,
"Only a few more shadows,
    And He Will Come!"
                    — Author Unknown

His Return

He is coming! He is coming!
    We can almost hear the sound
Of His footsteps at the threshold,
    And our hearts with gladness bound.
All around us men are seeking,
    Turning blind eyes to the light,
Longing, fearing, not yet daring
    To escape from sin's dark night,
Yet the message is so simple,
    "I will surely come again."
'Tis the glad news of the Gospel,
    Ringing sweetly thro' earth's pain.
When He comes may I be ready,
    Watching, praying, working still,
Though He tarry, may I daily
    Learn more perfectly His will.
                    — D. N. R.

He Expecteth

He expecteth, He expecteth! Down the stream of time
Still the words come softly ringing like a chime.
Ofttimes faint, now waxing louder, as the hour draws near
When the King in all His glory shall appear.

He is waiting with long patience for His crowning day,
For that Kingdom which shall never pass away,
And till every tribe and nation bow before His throne,
He expecteth loyal service from His own.

He expecteth — but He heareth still the bitter cry
From earth's millions, "Come and help us for we die."
He expecteth — doth He see us busy here and there,
Heedless of those pleading accents of despair?

Shall we — dare we disappoint Him? Brethren let us rise!
He who died for us is watching from the skies;
Watching till His royal banner floateth far and wide,
Till He seeth of His travail satisfied!

— *Alice J. Janurin*

His Coming

Wide-flung, the rosy banners of the dawn
    Blazon the eastern sky,
A whisp'ring zephyr stirs the breathless trees
    And passes by.

Etched 'gainst the changing pageant
    Clear stand the sombre pines.
While all the low horizon, deeply gold,
    With splendor shines.

Wrapt in a fragrant stillness now the earth
    Holds up her dew-washed face,
Waiting the daily miracle of God,
    His act of Grace.

Then, in my list'ning heart, a still small voice,
    These words I hear Him say:
"Whose coming is as certain as the dawn,
    Perhaps today."

— *Ivy M. Fordham*

NONE BUT HE

None other Lamb! none other name!
  None other hope in heaven, or earth, or sea!
None other hiding-place for sin and shame!
  None beside Thee!

My faith burns low; my hope burns low;
  Only my soul's deep need comes out in me
By the deep thunder of its want and woe,
  Calls out to Thee.

Lord, Thou art life though I be dead!
  Love's Flame art Thou, however cold I be!
Nor heavens have I, nor place to lay my head,
  Nor home, but Thee.

                              — *Christina Rossetti*

WHAT CHRIST IS TO US

The Shield from every dart;
The Balm for every smart;
The Sharer of each load;
Companion on the road.

The Door into the fold;
The Anchor that will hold;
The Shepherd of the sheep;
The Guardian of my sleep.

The Friend with Whom I talk;
The Way by which I walk;
The Light to show the way;
The Strength for every day.

The Source of my delight;
The Song to cheer the night;
The Thought that fills my mind;
The Best of All to find — is Jesus!

                              — *Author Unknown*

NO EAST OR WEST

In Christ there is no East or West,
  In Him no South or North,
But one great-Fellowship of Love
  Throughout the whole wide earth.

In Him shall true hearts everywhere
  Their high communion find.
His service is the golden cord
  Close-binding all mankind.

Join hands then, Brothers of the Faith,
  Whate'er your race may be!—
Who serves my Father as a son
  Is surely kin to me.

In Christ now meet both East and
    West,
  In Him meet South and North,
All Christly souls are one in Him,
  Throughout the whole wide earth.

                              — *John Oxenham*

A LIGHT UPON THE MOUNTAINS

There's a light upon the mountains,
  And the day is at the spring,
When our eyes shall see the beauty
  And the glory of the King:
Weary was our heart with waiting,
  And the night-watch seemed so long,
But His triumph-day is breaking,
  And we hail it with a song.

In the fading of the starlight
  We may see the coming morn;
And the lights of men are paling
  In the splendors of the dawn;
For the eastern skies are glowing
  As with light of hidden fire,
And the hearts of men are stirring
  With the throbs of deep desire.

There's a hush of expectation
  And a quiet in the air,
And the breath of God is moving
  In the fervent breath of prayer;
For the suffering, dying Jesus
  Is the Christ upon the throne,
And the travail of our spirit
  Is the travail of His own.

He is breaking down the barriers,
  He is casting up the way;
He is calling for His angels
  To build up the gates of day:
But His angels here are human,
  Not the shining hosts above;
For the drum-beats of His army
  Are the heart-beats of our love.

Hark! we hear a distant music,
  And it comes with fuller swell;
'Tis the triumph-song of Jesus,
  Of our King, Immanuel!
Go ye forth with joy to meet Him!
  And, my soul, be swift to bring
All thy sweetest and thy dearest
  For the triumph of our King!

— *Henry Burton*

JESUS

Jesus, these eyes have never seen
  That radiant form of Thine;
The veil of sense hangs dark between
  Thy blessed face and mine.

I see Thee not, I hear Thee not,
  Yet art Thou oft with me;
And earth hath ne'er so dear a spot
  As where I meet with Thee.

Like some bright dream that comes un-
    sought
  When slumbers o'er me roll,
Thine image ever fills my thought
  And charms my ravished soul.

Yet though I have not seen, and still
  Must rest in faith alone,
I love Thee, dearest Lord, and will,
  Unseen but not unknown.

— *Hymns of Consecration*

'TIS FINISHED!

" 'Tis finished!" so the Saviour cried,
And meekly bowed His head and
    died;
'Tis finished! yes, the race is run,
The battle fought, the victory won.

'Tis finished! all that heaven foretold
By prophets in the days of old,
And truths are opened to our view
That kings and prophets never knew.

'Tis finished! Son of God, Thy power
Hath triumphed in this awful hour,
And yet our eyes with sorrow see
That life to us was death to Thee.

'Tis finished! let the joyful sound
Be heard thro' all the nations round;
'Tis finished! let the triumph rise
And swell the chorus of the skies!

— *Samuel Stennett*

A VISION OF ETERNITY

Give me, O Lord, a vision of eternity,
　　For life, with all its petty care and fears,
So blinds my eyes that oft I fail to see
　　The greatness of Thy love beyond my tears.

Give me a glimpse of glory, lest today
　　The burdens of this sphere of time and space
So crush me, that I faint beside the way,
　　Unmindful of Thine all-sufficient grace.

Forever and forever, Lord, with Thee!
　　Ah then, how trifling all life's cares will seem!
One breath of air celestial, pure, and free
　　And all the past will vanish as a dream.

So help me live, dear Saviour, day by day,
　　As one who waits the coming of the dawn;
Whole glory now doth shed a blessed ray
　　Upon my path, and helps me to fight on.

— Avis B. Christiansen

HEART WISH

That I may know, yet more and more,
The love of God, whom I adore,
That I may be, increasingly,
The man that He would have me be,
That, loved and kept, I may find grace
To serve before Him, face to face,
And that, at last, my great reward
May be the "Well done!" of my Lord;
This is my wish; — may all beside
Be on yon cross, and crucified!

— Henry W. Frost

LONGING

If I could look across the waste
Of life's long, barren, wintry miles,
And see Christ's sun-lit, radiant face
And one of His most radiant smiles,
In spite of miles and snow and ice
All life would be a Paradise!

— Henry W. Frost

AND JESUS WEPT

Bright were the mornings first im-
　　pearl'd
　　O'er earth, and sea, and air;
The birthdays of a rifing world —
　　For power divine was there.

But fairer shone the tears of Christ
　　For Lazarus, o'er his grave;
Since love divine bedew'd the sod
　　Of one He sought to save.

Sweet drops of grace, the pledges given
　　Of Mercy's mighty plan —
That He, who was the Prince of
　　heaven,
　　Had pity upon man!

Let us Thy dear example, Lord,
　　Fix'd in our memories keep —
That we, obedient to Thy word,
　　May weep with those that weep.

— Brydges

THE SAVIOUR COMES

Hark, the glad sound! the Saviour
  comes,
  The Saviour promised long;
Let every heart prepare a throne,
  And every voice a song.

He comes, the prisoner to release,
  In Satan's bondage held;
The gates of brass before Him burst,
  The iron fetters yield.

He comes, the broken heart to bind,
  The wounded soul to cure,
And, with the treasures of His grace,
  To enrich the humble poor.

Our glad hosannas, Prince of Peace,
  Thy welcome shall proclaim;
And heaven's eternal arches ring
  With Thy beloved name.

— *Philip Doddridge*

THE HELPER

When, wounded sore, the stricken
  heart
  Lies bleeding and unbound,
One only hand — a piercèd hand —
  Can salve the sinner's wound.

When sorrow swells the laden breast,
  And tears of anguish flow,
One only heart — a broken heart —
  Can feel the sinner's woe.

When penitence has wept in vain
  Over some dark, foul spot,
One only stream — a stream of blood —
  Can wash away the blot.

Lift up Thy bleeding hand, O Lord;
  Unseal that cleansing tide;
We have no shelter from our sin
  But in Thy wounded side.

— *Cecil Frances Alexander*

LEARNING

Wisdom of God, we would by Thee be taught;
Control our minds, direct our ev'ry thought;
Knowledge alone life's problems cannot meet;
We learn to live while sitting at Thy feet.

Light of the world, illumine us we pray;
Our souls are dark without Thy kindling ray,
Torches unlighted, of all rad'ance bare.
Touch them to flame, and burn in glory there!

Incarnate Truth, help us Thy truth to learn,
Prone to embrace the falsehood we would spurn,
Groping in error's maze for verity;
Thou art the Truth we need to make us free.

Unfailing love, we are so cold in heart,
To us Thy passion for the lost impart;
Give us Thy vision of the need of men;
All learning will be used in service then.

— *Bob Jones, Jr.*

CHILD

The young child, Christ, is straight and wise
And asks questions of the old men, questions
Found under running water for all children,
And found under shadows thrown on still waters
By tall trees looking downwards, old and gnarled,
Found to the eyes of children alone, untold,
Singing a low song in the loneliness.
And the young child, Christ, goes asking,
And the old men answer nothing, and only know love
For the young child, Christ, straight and wise.

— *Carl Sandburg*

IF HE SHOULD COME

If Jesus should tramp the streets tonight,
    Storm-beaten and hungry for bread,
Seeking a room and a candle light
    And a clean though humble bed,
Who would welcome the Workman in,
    Though He came with panting breath,
His hands all bruised and His garments thin —
    This Workman from Nazareth?

Would rich folk hurry to bind His bruise
    And shelter His stricken form?
Would they take God in with His muddy shoes
    Out of the pitiless storm?
Are they not too busy wreathing their flowers
    Or heaping their golden store —
Too busy chasing the bubble hours
    For the poor man's God at the door?

And if He should come where churchmen bow,
    Forgetting the greater sin,
Would He pause with a light on His wounded brow,
    Would He turn and enter in?
And what would He think of their creeds so dim,
    Of their weak, uplifted hands,
Of their selfish prayers going up to Him
    Out of a thousand lands?

— *Edwin Markham*

HYMN OF LABOR

Jesus, Thou divine Companion,
 By Thy lowly human birth
Thou hast come to join the workers,
 Burden-bearers of the earth.
Thou, the Carpenter of Naz'reth,
 Toiling for Thy daily food,
By Thy patience and Thy courage,
 Thou hast taught us toil is good.

They who tread the path of labor
 Follow where Thy feet have trod;
They who work without complaining
 Do the holy will of God.
Thou, the peace that passeth knowl-
 edge,
 Dwellest in the daily strife;
Thou, the Bread of heaven, art broken
 In the sacrament of life.

Every task, however simple,
 Sets the soul that does it free;
Every deed of love and kindness
 Done to man is done to Thee.
Jesus, Thou divine Companion,
 Help us all to work our best;
Bless us in our daily labor,
 Lead us to our Sabbath rest.
 — *Henry van Dyke*

༈

THE LIVING JESUS

Jesus, Thou Living Bread,
 Ground in the mills of death,
Let me by Thee be fed;
 Thy servant hungereth.

Jesus, Thou Choicest Vine,
 Nailed to the Cross of woe,
Now let Thy life Divine
 Into my being flow.

Strength for the coming day
 Thy Body doth impart,
Thy Blood doth cleanse away
 The sins that stain my heart.

Let not my heart be cold,
 Nor doubt when faith doth prove
That in my hand I hold
 Thy Sacrament of love.

Jesus, be not a guest
 That tarrieth but a day;
Come to my longing breast,
 Come, and for ever stay.
 — *R. F. Pechey*

༈

TELL ME ABOUT THE MASTER!

Tell me about the Master!
 I am weary and worn tonight.
The day lies behind me in shadow,
 And only the evening is light.
Light with a radiant glory
 That lingers about the west,
My poor heart is aweary, aweary,
 And longs like a child for rest.

Tell me about the Master!
 Of the wrong He freely forgave,
Of His love and tender compassion,
 Of His love that is mighty to save.
For my heart is aweary, aweary,
 Of His woes and temptations of life,
Of the error that stalks in the noonday,
 Of falsehoods and malice and strife.

Yet, I know that whatever of sorrow,
 Or pain or temptation befall,
The Infinite Master has suffered,
 And knoweth and pitieth all.
So tell me the old, old story
 That falls on each wound like a
 balm,
And my heart that was burdened and
 broken
 Shall grow patient, and calm, and
 strong.
 — *Author Unknown*

THE MORNING COMETH!

A shout!
A trumpet note!
A Glorious Presence in the azure sky!
A gasp,
A thrill of joy,
And we are with Him in the twinkling of an eye!

A glance,
An upward look,
Caught up to be with Christ forevermore!
The dead alive!
The living glorified!
Fulfilled are all His promises that came before!

His face!
His joy supreme
Our souls find rapture only at His feet!
Blameless!
Without a spot!
We enter into heaven's joy complete!

Strike harps,
Oh, sound His praise . . .
We know Him as we never knew before!
God's love!
God's matchless grace!
'Twill take eternity to tell while we adore!

—Anne Catherine White

∽

"WHOSE I AM"

Jesus, Master, whose I am,
   Purchased Thine alone to be,
By Thy blood, O spotless Lamb,
   Shed so willingly for me;
Let my heart be all Thine own,
Let me live to Thee alone.

Other lords have long held sway;
   Now, Thy name alone to bear,
Thy dear voice alone obey,
Is my daily, hourly prayer.
Whom have I in heaven by Thee?
Nothing else my joy can be.

Jesus, Master! I am Thine;
   Keep me faithful, keep me near,
Let Thy presence in me shine
   All my homeward way to cheer.
Jesus! at Thy feet I fall,
Oh, be Thou my All-in-all.

— Frances Ridley Havergal

'TIS MIDNIGHT; AND ON OLIVE'S BROW

'Tis midnight; and on Olive's brow
  The star is dimmed that lately shone:
'Tis midnight; in the garden now
  The suffering Saviour prays alone.

'Tis midnight; and from all removed,
  The Saviour wrestles lone with fears;
E'en that disciple whom He loved
  Heeds not his Master's grief and tears.

'Tis midnight; and for others' guilt
  The Man of Sorrows weeps in blood;
Yet He that hath in anguish knelt
  Is not forsaken by His God.

'Tis midnight; and from heavenly plains
  Is borne the song that angels know;
Unheard by mortals are the strains
  That sweetly soothe the Saviour's woe.

— *William B. Tappan*

RENUNCIATION

He might have built a palace at a word,
Who sometimes had not where to lay His head;
Time was when He had nourished crowds with bread;
Would not one meal unto Himself afford.
Twelve legions girded with angelic sword
Were at His beck — the scorned and buffeted!
He healed another's scratch: His own side bled,
Side, feet, and hands, with cruel piercings gored.
Oh, wonderful the wonders left undone!
And scarce less wonderful than those He wrought!
Oh, self-restraint, passing all human thought,
To have all power and He as having none!
Oh, self-denying love, which felt alone
For needs of others, never for its own.

— *Richard Chenevix Trench*

CONSIDER WELL

Consider well that both by night and day
While we busily provide and care
For our disport, our revel and our play,
For pleasant melody and dainty fare,
Death stealeth on full slily; unaware
He lieth at hand and shall us all surprise,
We wot not when nor where nor in what wise.

When fierce temptations threat thy soul with loss
Think on His Passion and the bitter pain,
Think on the mortal anguish of the Cross,
Think on Christ's blood let out at every vein,
Think of His precious heart all rent in twain;
For thy redemption think all this was wrought,
Nor be that lost which He so dearly bought.

— *Sir Thomas More*

JESUS AND ALEXANDER

Jesus and Alexander died at thirty-three;
One lived and died for self; one died for you and me.
The Greek died on a throne; the Jew died on a cross;
One's life a triumph seemed; the other but a loss.
One led vast armies forth; the other walked alone;
One shed a whole world's blood; the other gave His own.
One won the world in life and lost it all in death.
The other lost His life to win the whole world's faith.

Jesus and Alexander died at thirty-three;
One died in Babylon; and one on Calvary.
One gained all for self; and one Himself He gave;
One conquered every throne; the other every grave.
The one made himself God; The God made Himself less;
The one lived but to blast; the other but to bless!
When died the Greek, forever fell his throne of swords;
But Jesus died to live forever Lord of lords.

Jesus and Alexander died at thirty-three.
The Greek made all men slaves; the Jew made all men free.
One built a throne on blood; the other built on love,
The one was born of earth; the other from above;
One won all this earth, to lose all earth and heaven.
The other gave up all, that all to Him be given.
The Greek forever died; the Jew forever lives;
He loses all who get, and wins all things who gives.

— *Author Unknown*

THE DIVINE

Behold the blind their sight receive;
Behold the dead awake and live;
The dumb speak wonders, and the
lame
Leap like the hart, and bless His
Name.

Thus doth th' eternal Spirit own
And seal the mission of the Son;
The Father vindicates His cause
While He hangs bleeding on the cross.

He dies; the heavens in mourning
stood;
He rises, and appears a God;
Behold the Lord ascending high,
No more to bleed, no more to die.
Hence and forever from my heart
I bid my doubts and fears depart,
And to those hands my soul resign
Which bear credentials so divine.

— Isaac Watts

ꙮ

JESUS CHRIST THE LORD

A thousand years have come and gone,
And near a thousand more,
Since happier light from heaven shone
Than ever shone before:
And in the hearts of old and young
A joy most joyful stirred,
That sent such news from tongue.to
tongue
As ears had never heard.

Then angels on their starry way
Felt bliss unfelt before,
For news that men should be as they,
To darkened earth they bore;

So toiling men and spirits bright
A first communion had,
And in meek mercy's rising light
Were each exceeding glad.

And we are glad, and we will sing,
As in the days of yore;
Come all, and hearts made ready bring,
To welcome back once more
The day when first on wintry earth
A summer change began,
And, dawning in a lowly birth,
Up rose the Light of man.

For trouble such as men must bear
From childhood to fourscore,
He shared with us, that we might
share
His joy for evermore;
And twice a thousand years of grief,
Of conflict, and of sin,
May tell how large the harvest sheaf
His patient love shall win.

— Thomas Toke Lynch

ꙮ

DEAR MASTER, IN WHOSE LIFE I SEE

Dear Master, in whose life I see
All that I would, but fail, to be,
Let thy clear light forever shine,
To shame and guide this life of mine.

Though what I dream and what I do
In all my days are often two,
Help me, oppressed by things undone,
O thou whose deeds and dreams were
one.

— John Hunter

ANOTHER CHRISTMAS

Again they peal, the wistful Yuletide chimes,
Amid the jarring clang of changing times;
The angel songs float down through history —
God born as Man! — time's super-mystery!
Sad marvel: millions hear without surprise
The biggest news which ever clove the skies!

Again they play, the children with their toys,
Gay parties draw the older girls and boys;
Regathered families hail the festive day,
And jovial revellers their gifts display:
How strange! — how almost inconceivable,
So few receive Heaven's "Gift Unspeakable"!

Yet none the less, as carol strains resound,
Adoring hearts will everywhere be found;
The throne-room of the soul they will prepare,
To give the Saviour-King new welcome there:
And He will see, and say, with gentle smile,
"The nails and thorny-crown were all worthwhile."

— *J. Sidlow Baxter*

"AS YE DO IT UNTO THESE"

In little faces pinched with cold and hunger
    Look, lest ye miss Him! In the wistful eyes,
And on the mouths unfed by mother kisses,
    Marred, bruised, and stained His precious image lies!
And when ye find Him in the midnight wild,
    Even in the likeness of an outcast child,
O wise men, own your King!
    Before His cradle bring
You gold to raise and bless,
    Your myrrh of tenderness,
For, "As ye do it unto these," said He,
    "Ye do it unto Me."

— *Author Unknown*

156

ALL MY HEART THIS NIGHT

All my heart this night rejoices,
As I hear,
Far and near,
Sweetest angel voices:
"Christ is born" their choirs are sing-
    ing,
Till the air,
Everywhere,
Now with joy is ringing.

Hark! a voice from yonder manger,
Soft and sweet,
Doth entreat,
"Flee from woe and danger;
Brethren come; from all that grieves
    you
You are freed;
All you need
I will surely give you."

Come, then, let us hasten yonder;
Here let all,
Great and small,
Love Him who with love is yearning;
Hail the Star
That from far
Bright with hope is burning.

Thee, dear Lord, with heed I'll cherish,
Live to Thee,
and with Thee
Dying, shall not perish,
But shall dwell with Thee forever
Far on high
in the joy
That can alter never.

— *Paul Gerhardt*

THE THREE CHILDREN

There's a beautiful legend, that's never been told,
It may have been known to the wise men of old —
How three little children came early at dawn,
With hearts that were sad, to where Jesus was born.
One could not see, one was too lame to play;
While the other, a mute, not a word could he say.

Yet led by His star, they came there to peep
At the little Lord Jesus, with eyes closed in sleep.
But how could the Christ child, so lovely and fair,
Not waken and smile when He heard their glad prayer,

Of hope at His coming, of faith in His birth,
Of praise at His bringing God's peace to the earth.
And then as the light softly came through the door,
The lad that was lame stood up right once more;
The boy that was mute started sweetly to sing,
While the child that was blind looked with joy on the King!

— *Charles W. H. Bancroft*

A Christmas Carol

The shepherds went their hasty way,
  And found the lowly stable-shed
Where the virgin-mother lay:
  And now they checked their eager tread,
For to the babe, that at her bosom clung,
A mother's song the virgin-mother sung.

They told her how a glorious light,
  Streaming from a heavenly throng,
Around them shone, suspending night;
  While sweeter than a mother's song,
Blessed angels heralded the Saviour's birth,
Glory to God on high! and peace on earth.

She listened to the tale divine,
  And closer still the babe she pressed;
And while she cried, "The babe is mine!"
  The milk rushed faster to her breast:
Joy rose within her, like a summer's morn:
Peace, peace on earth! the Prince of peace is born.

Thou mother of the Prince of peace,
  Poor, simple, and of low estate;
That strife should vanish, battle cease,
  Oh! why should this thy soul elate?
Sweet music's loudest note, the poet's story,
Didst thou ne'er love to hear of fame and glory?

And is not War a youthful king,
  A stately hero clad in mail?
Beneath his footsteps laurels spring;
  Him earth's majestic monarchs hail!
Their friend, their playmate! and his bold bright eye
Compels the maiden's love-confessing sigh.

"Tell this in some more courtly scene,
  To maids and youths in robes of state!
I am a woman poor and mean,
  And therefore is my soul elate.
War is a ruffian, all with guilt defiled,
That from the aged father tears his child!

"A murderous fiend, by fiends adored,
  He kills the sire and starves the son,
The husband kills, and from her board

Steals all his widow's toil had won;
Plunders God's world of beauty; rends away
All safety from the night, all comfort from the day.

"Then wisely is my soul elate,
That strife should vanish, battle cease;
I'm poor, and of a low estate,
The mother of the Prince of peace!
Joy rises in me, like a summer's morn;
Peace, peace on earth! the Prince of peace is born!"

— *Samuel Taylor Coleridge*

ᔕᔓ

BETHLEHEM'S BABE

I know that Christ died long ago
Upon a cruel tree,
That for my sin and sinful woe
He suffered there for me;
But oh, tonight, my Man of men
Is a wee Babe in Bethlehem.

He is not risen to heaven's throne,
The only deified;
He is not reigning o'er His own,
The greatly glorified;
He is the One who, from above,
Is mothered by the Virgin's love.

He is not far away from me,
The Christ whom men adore;
He is not in eternity,
The King whom men implore;
He lies within a manger rude
And 'round Him stand the shepherds
crude.

O little, feeble, smiling Babe,
To Thee I bow the knee;
I worship where Thou hast been laid
And fondly bend o'er Thee;
At other time, I'll praise Thy might —
But Thou art just my Babe tonight!

— *Henry W. Frost*

A CHRISTMAS HYMN

Behold in swaddling clothes a Child
Within a manger gently sleeps,
While close beside a mother mild,
In awe her vigil keeps.

Above the hills the angels sing
To shepherds watching in the field:
"In Bethlehem is born a King,
To you is Christ revealed.

A Savior is this tiny One,
The promised Lord, Immanuel.
All glory be to God the Son
Who came on earth to dwell."

The Christmas season comes again.
Let all the earth with one accord
Rejoice that God has given to men
A Savior, Christ the Lord.

Sing loud His praise in all the land!
Lift up your voices joyfully!
Ring out, ye bells, on every hand
Majestic melody!

"Peace on the earth, good will to men."
Let that our Christmas anthem be,
For Christ is born in Bethlehem —
Salvation full and free.

— *Harry Baker*

WONDER

Shall I tell you what I saw?
Camels tethered at the door . . .
Costly gifts upon the floor . . .
Kings a-kneeling in the straw,
Lost in wonder, pale with awe,
While a Child, smiled!

— *Dawn Finlay*

∽

THE GLORY OF CHRISTMAS

When first man's heart was overcast
  By sin's benighting gloom;
When fear and anguish first had
    flashed
  Its death-appalling doom;

When from God's presence man had
    fled,
  To hide his guilt and shame,
That caused him first God's face to
    dread
  And tremble at His name;

'Twas then a wondrous scheme began,
  The task of love divine,
To woo man to Himself again,
  His lost estate to find.

"Did He succeed?" I hear some say.
  "Was 'balm in Gilead' found
To heal our hurt, and ope the way?
  Has One so great been found?"

He triumphs! Angels shout from
    heaven;
  Yon virgin bears a Son!
By Him the power of sin is riven;
  By Him the victory's won.

We worship at Thy feet, O Christ;
  Thy name we do adore.
With Thee we'll keep a holy tryst,
  And love Thee more and more!

— *V. P. Drake*

SAID THE INNKEEPER

I cannot take these poor;
They do not pay;
They brand the house, they bring dis-
    grace;
I had to send that pair away . . .
And yet there was a strange look on
    her face,
This girl who kept her eyes upon the
    floor,
So strange I stopped a space
Before I sent them from the door.

What could I do?
A man must make a living while he
    may,
And trade is trade, and money, too,
And sentiment is not, I say.

And yet this girl was strangely fair:
She shivered in the doorway there,
And once she raised her eyes to mine...
I bowed; I would have knelt, I swear,
But at the table some poor lout
Made cry for wine
And broke the spell . . .
I saw the poorness of the pair
And put them out.
And I did well.
Two merchants took the great room
    overhead.
It is my principle: I buy and sell
And give my pity to the dead.

And yet this girl, this girl . . .
I turned her from my door,
But she looked back with kindly eyes
And fairer than before,
And went away
As if she walked with emperors
And was a queen, and all the world
    was hers!

What could I say?
A man must make his living while he
    may.

— *Myles Connolly*

In the Bleak Midwinter

In the bleak midwinter,
Frosty wind made moan,
Earth stood hard as iron,
Water like a stone;
Snow had fallen, snow on snow,
Snow on snow,
In the bleak midwinter,
Long ago.

Our God, heaven cannot hold him,
Nor earth sustain;
Heaven and earth shall flee away,
When he comes to reign;
In the bleak midwinter
A stable place sufficed
The Lord God almighty,
Jesus Christ.

Angels and archangels
May have gathered there,
Cherubim and seraphim
Thronged the air;
But his mother only,
In her maiden bliss,
Worshipped the beloved
With a kiss.

What can I give him,
Poor as I am?
If I were a shepherd,
I would bring a lamb;
If I were a wise man,
I would do my part;
Yet what I can give him —
Give my heart.

— *Christina Rossetti*

Brightest and Best of the Sons of the Morning

Brightest and best of the sons of the morning,
Dawn on our darkness and lend us thine aid,
Star of the east, the horizon adorning,
Guide where our infant Redeemer is laid.

Say, shall we yield Him, in costly devotion,
Odors of Edom and offerings divine,
Gems of the mountain and pearls of the ocean,
Myrrh from the forest, or gold from the mine?

Vainly we offer each ample oblation,
Vainly with gifts would His favor secure;
Richer by far is the heart's adoration,
Dearer to God are the prayers of the poor.

Cold on His cradle the dew drops are shining,
Low lies His head with the beasts of the stall;
Angels adore Him in slumber reclining,
Maker and Monarch and Saviour of all.

— *Reginald Heber*

A Christmas Hymn

Calm on the listening ear of night
  Come heaven's melodious strains,
Where wild Judea stretches far
  Her silver-mantled plains.

Celestial choirs from courts above
  Shed sacred glories there;
And angels, with their sparkling lyres,
  Make music on the air.

The answering hills of Palestine
  Send back a glad reply,
And greet from all their holy heights
  The Dayspring from on high.

O'er the blue depths of Galilee
  There comes a holier calm;
And Sharon waves in solemn praise
  Her silent groves of palm.

"Glory to God!" the sounding skies
  Loud with their anthems ring;
"Peace on the earth—good-will to men
  From Heaven's Eternal King."

Light on thy hills, Jerusalem!
  The Savior now is born!
More bright on Bethlehem's joyous
    plains
Breaks the first Christmas morn;

And brighter on Moriah's brow,
  Crowned with her temple spires,
Which first proclaim the newborn
    light,
  Clothed with its orient fires.

This day shall Christian tongues be
    mute,
  And Christian hearts be cold?
O catch the anthem that from heaven
  O'er Judah's mountains rolled!
When nightly burst from seraph harps
  The high and solemn lay,—
"Glory to God; on earth be peace;
  Salvation comes to-day!"
       — Edmund Hamilton Sears

Shall I Be Silent?

The shepherds sing; and shall I silent
    be?
  My God, no hymn for thee?
My soul's a shepherd, too; a flock it
    feeds
  Of thoughts and words and deeds:
The pasture is thy Word; the streams
    thy grace,
  Enriching all the place.
       —George Herbert

Let Us Keep Christmas

Whatever else be lost among the years,
Let us keep Christmas still a shining
    thing:
Whatever doubts assail us, or what
    fears,
Let us hold close one day, remember-
    ing
Its poignant meaning for the hearts of
    men.
Let us get back our childlike faith
    again.
       —Grace Noll Crowell

What Makes Christmas?

"What is Christmas?"
I asked my soul,
And this answer
Came back to me:
"It is the
Glory of heaven come down
In the hearts of humanity —
Come in the spirit and heart of a Child,
And it matters not what we share
At Christmas; it is not Christmas at all
Unless the Christ Child be there."

       — Author Unknown

GOD REST YE, MERRY GENTLEMEN

God rest ye, merry gentlemen; let nothing you dismay,
For Jesus Christ, our Saviour, was born on Christmas-day.
The dawn rose red o'er Bethlehem, the stars shone thro' the gray,
When Jesus Christ, our Saviour, was born on Christmas-day.

God rest ye, little children; let nothing you affright,
For Jesus Christ, our Saviour, was born this happy night;
Along the hills of Galilee the white flocks sleeping lay,
When Christ, the child of Nazareth, was born on Christmas-day.

God rest ye, all good Christians; upon this blessed morn
The Lord of all good Christians was of a woman born:
Now all your sorrows he doth heal, your sins he takes away;
For Jesus Christ, our Saviour, was born on Christmas-day.

— *Dinah Maria Mulock*

STARS

Come out in the night when darkness has fallen,
    Fallen a cloak on the shoulders of earth;
Away from the glaring, bright lights of the city,
    Away from confusion and singing and mirth.

Out under the stars, when the moon is not shining,
    And no cloud obscures the great milky way;
Look well at the heavens, the work of his fingers,
    And ponder the wonders unseen in the day.

He made the stars; man's mind cannot fathom
    The placing of each in immeasurable space;
Each one in its orbit; no nearer, no further;
    He spake and each one was there in its place.

One night long ago, "the stars in their courses"
    Were carrying out their Maker's great plan;
One gem of the heavens was brilliant in beauty,
    A message of hope and fulfillment to man.

The God of eternity moved in his wisdom;
    A star in the east, when the long day was done,
Followed the bidding of its great Creator,
    And guided the wise men to his beloved Son.

— *Martha Hird*

A Visit to Bethlehem in Spirit

The scene around me disappears,
    And, borne to ancient regions,
While time recalls the flight of years,
    I see angelic legions
Descending in an orb of light:
Amidst the dark and silent night
    I hear celestial voices.

"Tidings, glad tidings from above
    To every age and nation!
Tidings, glad tidings! God is love,
    To man he sends salvation!
His Son beloved, his only Son,
The work of mercy hath begun;
    Give to his name the glory!"

Through David's city I am led;
    Here all around are sleeping;
A light directs to yon poor shed;
    There lonely watch is keeping:
I enter; ah, what glories shine!
Is this Immanuel's earthly shrine,
    Messiah's infant temple?

It is, it is; and I adore
    This Stranger meek and lowly,
As saints and angels bow before
    The throne of God thrice holy!
Faith through the veil of flesh can see
The face of thy divinity,
    My Lord, my God, my Saviour!

— James Montgomery

ᘏᕬ

Bells Across the Snow

O Christmas, merry Christmas,
    Is it really come again,
With its memories and greetings,
    With its joy and with its pain!
There's a minor in the carol
    And a shadow in the light,
And a spray of cypress twining
    With the holly wreath tonight.

And the hush is never broken
    By laughter light and low,
As we listen in the starlight
    To the "bells across the snow."

O Christmas, merry Christmas,
    'Tis not so very long
Since others voices blended
    With the carol and the song!
If we could but hear them singing,
    As they are singing now,
If we could but see the radiance
    Of the crown on each dear brow,
There would be no sigh to smother,
    No hidden tear to flow,
As we listen in the starlight
    To the "bells across the snow."

O Christmas, merry Christmas,
    This never more can be;
We cannot bring again the days
    Of our unshadowed glee,
But Christmas, happy Christmas,
    Sweet herald of good will,
With holy songs of glory
    Brings holy gladness still.
For peace and hope may brighten,
    And patient love may glow,
As we listen in the starlight
    To the "bells across the snow."

— Frances Ridley Havergal

ᘏᕬ

The Hand That Held It

He held the lamp of Truth that day
So low that none could miss the way;
And yet so high to bring in sight
That picture fair — the World's Great
        Light —
That gazing up (the lamp between)
The hand that held it scarce was seen.

— W. G. Elmslie

THE NATIVITY

This is the month, and this the happy morn,
  Wherein the Son of Heaven's Eternal King,
Of wedded maid and virgin mother born,
  Our great redemption from above did bring;
  For so the holy sages once did sing,
That he our daily forfeit should release,
And with his Father work us a perpetual peace.

That glorious form, that light unsufferable,
  And that far-beaming blaze of majesty,
Wherewith he wont at Heaven's high council-table
  To sit the midst of Trinal Unity,
  He laid aside, and here with us to be,
Forsook the courts of everlasting day,
And chose with us a darksome house of mortal clay.

Say, heavenly Muse, shall not thy sacred vein
  Afford a present to the Infant-God?
Hast thou no verse, no hymn, or solemn strain,
  To welcome him to this his new abode,
  Now while the heaven, by the sun's team untrod,
Hath took no print of the approaching light,
And all the spangled host keep watch in squadrons bright?

See, how from far, upon the eastern road,
  The star-led wizards haste with odors sweet;
Oh, run, prevent them with thy humble ode,
  And lay it lowly at his blessed feet;
  Have thou the honor first thy Lord to greet,
And join thy voice unto the angel-choir,
From out his secret altar touch'd with hallow'd fire.

— John Milton

THE HOLY STAR

As shadows cast by cloud and sun
  Flit o'er the summer grass,
So, in thy sight, Almighty One,
  Earth's generations pass.

And while the years, an endless host,
  Come pressing swiftly on,
The brightest names that earth can
    boast
Just glisten and are gone.

Yet doth the Star of Bethlehem shed
  A lustre pure and sweet,
And still it leads, as once it led,
  To the Messiah's feet.

O Father, may that holy star
  Grow every year more bright,
And send its glorious beams afar
  To fill the world with light.

—William Cullen Bryant

A Bed in My Heart

Ah, dearest Jesus, holy Child,
Make Thee a bed, soft, undefiled,
  Within my heart, that it may be
  A quiet chamber kept for Thee.
My heart for very joy doth leap,
My lips no more can silence keep.
  I too must sing, with joyful tongue,
  That sweetest ancient cradle song,
Glory to God in highest Heaven,
Who unto man His Son hath given,
  While angels sing with pious mirth,
  A glad New Year to all the earth.

— *Martin Luther*

The Angels' Song

It came upon the midnight clear,
  That glorious song of old,
From angels bending near the earth
  To touch their harps of gold:
"Peace to the earth, good-will to men
  From heaven's all-gracious King!"
The world in solemn stillness lay
  To hear the angels sing.

Still thro' the cloven skies they come,
  With peaceful wings unfurled;
And still their heavenly music floats
  O'er all the weary world:
Above its sad and lowly plains
  They bend on hov'ring wing,
And ever o'er its Babel sounds
  The blessed angels sing.

Yet with the woes of sin and strife
  The world has suffered long;
Beneath the angel-strain have rolled
  Two thousand years of wrong;
And man at war with man, hears not
  The love-song which they bring:
Oh! hush the noise, ye men of strife,
  And hear the angels sing!

And ye, beneath life's crushing load
  Whose forms are bending low;
Who toil along the climbing way
  With painful steps and slow,—
Look now! for glad and golden hours
  Come swiftly on the wing;
Oh! rest beside the weary road,
  And hear the angels sing.

For lo! the days are hastening on,
  By prophet-bards foretold,
When with the ever-circling years
  Comes round the age of gold;
When Peace shall over all the earth
  Its ancient splendors flung,
And the whole world send back the
    song
  Which now the angels sing.

— *Edmund Hamilton Sears*

The Oxen

Christmas Eve, and twelve of the
    clock.
  "Now they are all on their knees,"
An elder said as we sat in a flock
  By the embers in hearthside ease.

We pictured the meek mild creatures
    where
  They dwelt in their strawy pen,
Nor did occur to one of us there
  To doubt they were kneeling then.

So fair a fancy few would weave
  In these years! Yet, I feel,
If some one said on Christmas Eve,
  "Come; see the oxen kneel

"In the lonely barton by yonder coomb
  Our childhood used to know,"
I should go with him in the gloom,
  Hoping it might be so.

— *Thomas Hardy*

EVERYWHERE, EVERYWHERE, CHRISTMAS TONIGHT

Everywhere, everywhere, Christmas tonight!
Christmas in lands of the fir tree and pine,
Christmas in lands of the palm tree and vine,
Christmas where snows peaks stand solemn and white,
Christmas where cornfields lie sunny and bright,
Everywhere, everywhere, Christmas tonight!

For the Christ Child who comes is the Master of all,
No palace too great and no cottage too small;
The angels who welcome Him sing from the height,
"In the city of David, a King in his might."
Everywhere, everywhere, Christmas tonight!

Then let every heart keep its Christmas within,
Christ's pity for sorrow, Christ's hatred for sin,
Christ's care for the weakest, Christ's courage for right,
Christ's dread of the darkness, Christ's love for the light,
Everywhere, everywhere, Christmas tonight!

— Phillips Brooks

CHRISTMAS BELLS

I heard the bells on Christmas Day
Their old, familiar carols play,
    And wild and sweet
    The words repeat
Of peace on earth, good-will to men!

And tho't how, as the day had come,
The belfries of all Christendom
    Had rolled along
    The unbroken song
Of peace on earth, good-will to men!

Till, ringing, singing on its way,
The world revolved from night to day,
    A voice, a chime,
    A chant sublime
Of peace on earth, good-will to men!

Then from each black, accursed mouth
The cannon thundered in the South,
    And with the sound
    The carols drowned
Of peace on earth, good-will to men!

It was as if an earthquake rent
The hearth-stones of a continent,
    And made forlorn
    The households born
Of peace on earth, good-will to men!

And in despair I bowed my head;
"There is no peace on earth," I said;
    "For hate is strong,
    And mocks the song
Of peace on earth, good-will to men!"

Then pealed the bells more loud and
    deep:
"God is not dead; nor doth he sleep!
    The Wrong shall fail,
    The Right prevail,
With peace on earth, good-will to
    men!"

— Henry Wadsworth Longfellow

INCARNATION

He has come! the skies are telling;
He has quit the glorious dwelling;
And first the tidings came to us, the humble shepherd folk.
He has come to field and manger,
And no more is God a Stranger:
He comes as Common Man at home with cart and crooked yoke.

As the shade of a cool cedar
To a traveller in gray Kedar
Will be the Kingdom of His love, the Kingdom without end.
Tongues and ages may disclaim Him,
Yet the Heaven of heavens will name Him
Lord of peoples, Light of nations, elder Brother, tender Friend.

— *Edwin Markham*

LO, HE COMES!

Lo, he comes! let all adore him!
  'Tis the God of grace and truth!
Go! prepare the way before him,
  Make the rugged places smooth!
Lo, he comes, the mighty Lord!
Great his work, and his reward.

Let the valleys all be raised;
  Go, and make the crooked straight;
Let the mountains be abased;
  Let all nature change its state;
Through the desert mark a road,
Make a highway for our God.

Through the desert God is going,
  Through the desert waste and wild,
Where no goodly plant is growing,
  Where no verdure ever smiled;
But the desert shall be glad,
And with verdure soon be clad.

Where the thorn and brier flourished,
  Trees shall there be seen to grow,
Planted by the Lord and nourished,
  Stately, fair, and fruitful too;
They shall rise on every side,
They shall spread their branches wide.

From the hills and lofty mountains
  Rivers shall be seen to flow;
There the Lord will open fountains,
  Thence supply the plains below;
As he passes, every land
Shall confess his powerful hand.

— *Thomas Kelly*

THE ETERNAL LIGHT

The star that guided the wise men
Has long since faded and gone,
But the light from that first Christmas
Keeps shining on and on.

It doesn't shine in the heavens
Like the wise men's star of old,
But it shines in the hearts of the people
Wherever the Gospel is told.

And it will keep on shining
When the sun and moon are gone,
For in God's great forever
It will keep shining on and on.

— *William C. Fisher*

THERE'S A SONG IN THE AIR!

There's a song in the air!
There's a star in the sky!
There's a mother's deep prayer
And a baby's low cry;
And the star rains its fire while the beautiful sing,
For the manger of Bethlehem cradles a king!

There's a tumult of joy
O'er the wonderful birth,
For the Virgin's sweet boy
Is the Lord of the earth.
Ay, the star rains its fire, and the beautiful sing,
For the manger of Bethlehem cradles a king!

In the light of that star
Lie the ages impearled;
And that song from afar
Has swept over the world:
Every hearth is aflame, and the beautiful sing,
In the homes of the nations, that Jesus is king!

We rejoice in the light,
And we echo the song
That comes down thro' the night
From the heavenly throng.
Ay, we shout to the lovely evangel they bring,
And we greet in his cradle our Saviour and King!

— *Josiah Gilbert Holland*

THE NATIVITY

A God in heaven above,
With heart of infinite love;
A virgin on earth, all mild,
And near to her heart a child.

A stable bedecked with snow;
A stall with a manger low;
The manger soft with new hay
In which the little child lay.

Above, an angelic choir,
Whose voices can never tire,
Their hearts and their lips beguiled,
Sing to the praise of the child.

Around, the baby divine
The wondering sheep and kine,
And shepherds bending the knee
In worshipful ecstasy.

The mother worships her Lord,
His being and form adored;—
And I before Him would bring
My heart as an offering.

— *Henry W. Frost*

SONG OF THE ANGELS

While shepherds watched their flocks
    by night,
All seated on the ground;
The angel of the Lord came down,
    And glory shone around.
"Fear not," said he,—for mighty dread
    Had seized their troubled mind,—
"Glad tidings of great joy I bring
    To you and all mankind.

"To you, in David's town this day,
    Is born of David's line
The Saviour, who is Christ the Lord,
    And this shall be the sign:
"The heavenly babe you there shall
    find
    To human view displayed
All meanly wrapped in swathing-
    bands,
    And in a manger laid."

Thus spake the seraph, and forthwith
    Appeared a shining throng
Of angels, praising God, who thus
    Addressed their joyful song:
"All glory be to God on high,
    And to the earth be peace;
Good-will henceforth from heaven to
    men
    Begin, and never cease!"
               — *Nahum Tate*

THE WHOLE YEAR CHRISTMAS

Oh, could we keep the Christmas
    thrill,
The goad of gladness and good-will,
The lift of laughter and the touch
Of kindled hands that utter much,
Not once a year, but all the time,
The melody of hearts in chime,
The impulse beautiful and kind,

Of soul to soul and mind to mind
That swings the world
And brings the word
On one great day of all the year
Close to God's treasure house of
    cheer . . .
Oh, could we keep the Christmas feast,
Even when goods and gold are least;
Here, 'mid our common, daily scenes,
Could we but live what Christmas
    means,
Not one day, but for every day
The miracle of wholesome play,
The spirit sweet, gift-giving, young,
From deepest wells of feeling sprung...

What a different world this world
    would be!
For we would see as children see,
If only a magic way were found
To make us children the whole year
    round!
               — *Angela Morgan*

MERRY CHRISTMAS

Merry Christmas to you, the young and the gay;
God guard you and guide you in His perfect way!

Merry Christmas to you, the lonely and sad;
Remember Christ came to make all people glad.

Merry Christmas to you, the ones we hold dear;
God bless you and keep you and stay very near!

Merry Christmas to you, our neighbors and friends,
As wider and wider this circle extends.

Merry Christmas to you, the stranger within;
May true understanding and friendship begin!

Merry Christmas to you! Merry Christmas tonight,
And deep in each heart may the Star still shine bright!

Merry Christmas to you, *every*one *every*where;
Peace on earth and good will — this be our prayer!

— *Phyllis C. Michael*

As With Gladness Men of Old

As with gladness men of old
Did the guiding star behold;
As with joy they hailed its light,
Leading onward, beaming bright;
So, most gracious Lord, may we
Evermore be led to thee.

As with joyful steps they sped
To that lowly manger-bed
There to bend the knee before
Him whom heaven and earth adore;
So may we with willing feet
Ever seek Thy mercy seat.

As they offered gifts most rare,
At that manger rude and bare,
So may we with holy joy,
Pure and free from sin's alloy,
All our costliest treasures bring,
Christ, to Thee, our heavenly King.

Holy Jesus, every day
Keep us in the narrow way;
And, when earthly things are past,
Bring our ransomed souls at last,
Where they need no star to guide,
Where no clouds Thy glory hide.

— *William Chatterton Dix*

Adoration — *A Carol*

The carol of the angels
  Is heard no more today,
The chorus of the heavenly hosts
Long since has died away.
Their anthem swells no longer,
  Their hallelujah-hymn
No more shall rend the midnight skies
O'er sleeping Bethlehem!

Long years have passed since Judah
  Resounded to the song
Poured forth upon the silent night
  By the angelic throng;
And yet the joyous anthem
  That flooded Judah's air
Is swelling in this heart of mine,
  And rings and echoes there!

They sang the Saviour's praises,
  And glorious was the song
Poured forth by countless heavenly
    hosts
  Who knew no sin or wrong;
But e'en that holy anthem
  With my song cannot vie,
For never angels knew such joy
  In Jesus Christ as I!

A carol such as angels
  Can never learn to sing,
A carol ever glorious,
  A carol to my King,
To Him whose love redeemed me,
  The Christ of Calvary,
Shall ring within this heart of mine
  Throughout eternity!

— *E. Margaret Clarkson*

ANOTHER NEW YEAR

Another New Year and what shall I make it?
　God gave it to me alone;
Shall I search for earth's cheer, her sparkle, and take it—
　No bread for my soul but a stone?

Another New Year and what shall I gather?
　Earth's tinsel, her rabble, her show?
Another New Year and what would I rather —
　A flash or a deep inner glow?

A year full of getting or a year full of giving
　The best that I have to give?
A year full of fretting or a year full of living
　The way God wants me to live?

Another New Year and what shall I make it?
　God gave me the right to choose;
Another New Year, God helping, I'll take it
　And give it to Him to use.
　　　　　　　　　　—*Phyllis C. Michael*

ANOTHER YEAR

Another year is dawning!
　Dear Master, let it be
In working or in waiting
　Another year with Thee.

Another year of leaning
　Upon Thy loving breast,
Of ever-deepening trustfulness,
　Of quiet, happy rest.

Another year of mercies,
　Of faithfulness and grace;
Another year of gladness
　In the shining of Thy face.

Another year of progress;
　Another year of praise;
Another year of proving
　Thy presence "all the days."

Another year of service,
　Of witness for Thy love;
Another year of training
　For holier work above.

Another year is dawning!
　Dear Master, let it be
On earth, or else in Heaven,
　Another year for Thee!
　　　　　　　　　　—*Frances Ridley Havergal*

A PRAYER FOR THE NEW YEAR

Lord, I would ask for a holy year,
    Spent in Thy perfect will:
Help me to walk in Thy very steps;
Help me to please Thee still.

Lord, I would ask for a busy year,
    Filled up with service true;
Doing with all Thy Spirit's might;
All that I find to do.

Lord, I would ask for a dying world;
    Stretch forth Thy mighty hand,
Scatter Thy Word—Thy power display
This year in every land.

Lord, I would ask for a year of hope,
    Looking for Thee to come,
And hastening on that year of years
That brings us Christ and Home.
                    — *A. B. Simpson*

GOD KNOWS

And I said to the man
Who stood at the gate of the year:
"Give me a light that I may tread
Safely into the unknown."
And he replied:
"Go out into the darkness
And put your hand
Into the hand of God.
That shall be to you
Better than light
And safer than a known way."
So I went forth,
And finding the Hand of God,
Trod gladly into the night.
And He led me towards the hills
And the breaking of day
In the lone East.
                    — *Minnie Louise Haskins*

THE NEW YEAR

The New Year is an open door
    Through which we each must go;
The opportunities it holds,
    Are still for us to know.

There will be chances to do good,
    To help our fellow man;
Let's use each moment that it brings
The very best we can.

There will be countless golden hours,
    God gives them to us free;
Time is the greatest of all gifts
He gives to you and me.

The New Year is an open door:
    It will swing open wide;
We must resolve to give our best
Before we step inside.

The New Year is a priceless gift,
    So let us use it well;
The tears and happiness it holds,
    The next twelve months will tell.

                    — *Raymond Orner*

THE NEW LEAF

He came to my desk with quivering
    lip;
The lesson was done.
"Have you a new leaf for me, dear
    Teacher?
I have spoiled this one!"
I took his leaf, all soiled and blotted,
And gave him a new one, all un-
    spotted,
Then into his tired heart I smiled:
"Do better now, my child."

I went to the throne with trembling
    heart;
The year was done.
"Have you a new year for me, dear
    Master?
I have spoiled this one!"
He took my year, all soiled and blotted,
And gave me a new one, all unspotted,
Then into my tired heart He smiled:
"Do better now, my child!"

                    — *Author Unknown*

THE NEW YEAR

Upon the threshold of the year we stand,
    Holding Thy Hand;
The year holds mysteries and vague surprise
    To meet our eyes;
What will its passing moments bring,
    To weep, or sing?

We fear to take one step without Thy care
    And presence there;
But all is clear to Thine all-seeing gaze,
    Counting the days
From dawn of time, till ages cease to be —
    Eternity!

Upon the threshold of the year we stand,
    Holding Thy Hand;
Thou wilt walk step by step along the 'way
    With us each day;
So whether joy or woe shall come this year,
    We shall not fear!

— Homera Homer-Dixon

NEW YEAR THOUGHTS

The New Year, untried, is before me, I know not what it may bring,
But my Father in Heaven has bidden me trust Him for everything,
And when sorest oppressed or dismayed, in His arms closer to cling.

If He calls me to walk in the shadow, He's sure to be at my side;
If tempests and storms overtake me, safe under His wings I may hide;
If temptations lurk in my pathway, a way of escape He'll provide.

If sorrow's full cup He present me, and bid me its bitterness drink,
Though my heart at the trial may tremble, my spirit falter and shrink,
Yet Jesus, whose own cup was bitter, will strengthen my weakness I think.

Perhaps in the shadowy future, new brightness my glad eyes shall see,
And joys of most wonderful sweetness, right in my pathway may be;
And blessings I scarcely dare hope for, God may be keeping for me.

And so thro' the months which are coming, each step of the way I may tread,
Knowing that if I look upward, by a strong, loving hand I'll be led,
And be daily from evil defended, by Him who died, yes, for me.

— N. M. B.

A New Year Wish

What shall I wish thee this new year—
Health, wealth, prosperity, good cheer,
All sunshine — not a cloud or tear?
    Nay! only this:

That God may lead thee His own way,
That He may choose thy path each
    day,
That thou mayest feel Him near alway,
    For this is bliss.

I dare not ask aught else for thee,
How could I tell what best would be?
But God the end of all can see —
    His will is best.

To know He rules—come loss or gain,
Sorrow or gladness, sun or rain;
To know He loves — in ease or pain,
    Is perfect rest.

    — *Mary J. Lewis*

A New Year's Message

Sickened with slaughter and weary of
    war,
Torn by bereavement and pain,
Daily our eyes are searching the skies
For signs of His coming again.
Longing, we pray at dawning of day,
"Lord, wilt Thou come before noon,"
Imploring Him yet in the fading sun-
    set,

"O, blessed Lord Jesus, come soon!"
Precious the word the ear of faith
    heard;
"Lo, I come quickly, My Bride.
This longing of thine is not greater
    than Mine
To have thee at last by My side!"

    —*Martha Snell Nicholson*

New Year

Dear Master, for this coming year
    Just one request I bring:
I do not pray for happiness,
    Or any earthly thing —
I do not ask to understand
    The way Thou leadest me,
But this I ask: Teach me to do
    The thing that pleaseth Thee.

I want to know Thy guiding voice,
    To walk with Thee each day.
Dear Master, make me swift to hear
    And ready to obey.
And thus the year I now begin
    A happy year will be —
If I am seeking just to do
    The thing that pleaseth Thee.

    — *Author Unknown*

An Opening Prayer

Father, lest I stumble in the new year,
Give me courage, give me strength, for
    every day;
Give me wisdom for tasks before me,
Give me hope when clouds are gray.
Give me love in greatest measure;
Love that is likened unto Thee;
A love that was great enough to send
An only Son to Calvary!
Give me tolerance of all evil,
As Thou hast always had;
Strength to leave the ninety and nine,
And go for the wayward lad.
And on thoughts that are not kind,
Lord, forgive my wilful way;
Teach me not to judge another,
Since I too so often stray!

    —*Author Unknown*

GOD'S WILL

I asked the New Year for some motto sweet,
Some rule of life by which to guide my feet,
I asked and paused; it answered soft and low,
  "God's will to *know*."

Will knowledge then suffice? New Year, I cried,
But ere the question into silence died
The answer came, "No, this remember too,
  God's will to *do*."

Once more I asked, is there still more to tell?
And once again the answer sweetly fell;
"Yes, this one thing all other things above,
  God's will to *love*."

— *Author Unknown*

MY ONLY PLEA

Just one thing, O Master, I ask today,
Now that the old year has passed away
And a promising new year, thro' grace
  of Thine,
With all the dreams of youth is mine—
Just one thing I ask as I onward go,

That I'll walk with Thee—not too fast,
  nor slow;
Just one thing I ask and nothing more,
Not to linger behind, nor run before.
O Master! This is my only plea —
Take hold of my life and pilot me.

— *Walter J. Kuhn*

CROWN THE YEAR

Crown the year with Thy goodness,
  Lord!
  And make every hour a gem
  In living diadem,
    That sparkles to Thy praise.

Crown the year with Thy grace, O
  Lord!
  Be Thy fresh anointing shed
  On Thy waiting servant's head,
    Who treads Thy royal ways.

Crown the year with Thy glory, Lord!
  Let the brightness and the glow
  Of its heavenly overflow
    Crown Thy beloved's days!

— *Frances Ridley Havergal*

CHEER THE NEW YEAR

Cheer the New Year
Heavy with treasure.
Take it and make it
To fullest of measure.

Use, don't abuse
Each hour and each minute,
For time is sublime
When love is put in it;

Nor fear the New Year
By shapeless forebodings,
With night time, no-light time
And sharp, painful goadings.

God's care is out there
Beneath and descending;
His love from above
Brings blessings unending.

— *Carlton Buck*

MOTHERS

MOTHERS — AND OTHERS

Others weary of the noise,
Mothers play with girls and boys.

Others work with patient will,
Mothers labor later still.

Other's love is more or less,
Mothers love with steadiness.

Others pardon, hating yet;
Mothers pardon and forget.

Others keep the ancient score,
Mothers never shut the door.

Others grow incredulous,
Mothers still believe in us.

Others throw their faith away,
Mothers pray, and pray, and pray.
— *Amos R. Wells*

HER MOTHER

Sometimes, I wonder if my life
Has really been worth-while;
I wonder if I've done my best
In meeting every trial.

I've never done a single thing
To glorify my name.
I've never carved the slightest niche
In any hall of fame.

And yet, somehow, I know I've been
What God would have me be;
For He has shown with one great gift
That He approves of me.

It was just a little bundle placed
By angels at my side.
A little bit of heaven sent
For me to love and guide.

I showered it with kindness, and
I nurtured it with truth;
I thrilled at every movement,
Every cry, and each new tooth.

One day, I sent her off to school
A time of jubilation;
And soon, I made a dress for her
To wear at graduation.

Today, she reaches womanhood,
The fairest bloom on earth.
I could have done no greater thing
Than give my daughter birth!
— *Worral G. Sonastine*

MOTHER

You painted no Madonnas
On chapel walls in Rome,
But with a touch diviner
You lived one in your home.

You wrote no lofty poems
That critics counted art,
But with a nobler vision
You lived them in your heart.

You carved no shapeless marble
To some high soul design,
But with a finer sculpture
You shaped this soul of mine.

You built no great cathedrals
That centuries applaud,
But with a grace exquisite
Your life cathedraled God.

Had I the gift of Raphael
Or Michelangelo,
Oh, what a rare Madonna
My mother's life would show.
— *Thomas W. Fessenden*

MY MOTHER

She carried me under her heart;
Loved me before I was born;
Took God's hand in hers and walked through the Valley of Shadows
    that I might live;
Bathed me when I was helpless;
Clothed me when I was naked;
Gave me warm milk from her own body when I was hungry;
Rocked me to sleep when I was weary;
Pillowed me on pillows softer than down, and sang to me in the voice
    of an Angel;
Held my hand when I learned to walk;
Suffered with my sorrow;
Laughed with my joy;
Glowed with my triumph; and while I knelt at her side, she taught
    my lips to pray.
Through all the days of my youth she gave strength for my weakness,
    courage for my despair, and hope to fill my hopeless heart;
Was loyal when others failed;
Was true when tried by fire;
Was my friend when other friends were gone;
Prayed for me through all the days, when flooded with sunshine
    or saddened by shadows;
Loved me when I was unlovely, and led me into man's estate to walk
    triumphant on the King's Highway and play a manly part.
Though we lay down our lives for her we can never pay the debt
    we owe to a Christian mother.

— Author Unknown

ᴕ

MOTHER

If I could take the beauty of the orchid,
    And mix it with the sweetness of the rose;
The purity and whiteness of the lily,
    Combine it with the sweetest thing that grows;
If I could capture some of the sunshine's brightness,
    And mix it with the dignity of trees;
If I could claim that strange and ancient power
    That bids men tarry by the seas;
If I could catch a strain of children's laughter,
    And quiet it with earnest, tender tears;
And put that mixture here beside me,
    It couldn't be as sweet as Mother dear.

— Author Unknown

THE OTHER MOTHER

When Jesus hung upon the tree,
He looked to John entreatingly,
    Said, "Son, behold your Mother."
John harkened to his Lord's request,
And to his home and to his breast,
    He took his Other Mother.

But other Mothers since that day,
Whose blessed sons have gone away,
    Concern our Elder Brother;
And on this holy Mother's Day
    To you, to me, does He not say,
    "My son, behold your Mother?"

The Other Mother, left alone,
No child, no husband, of her own,
    As truly is our Mother
As Mary there to John could be
When Jesus spoke on Calvary
    And said, "Behold your Mother."

The mothers dear whose sons passed on
Are mothers still to everyone
    Who hears his Elder Brother.
And how on this glad Mother's Day
Can we show love a better way
    Than help an Other Mother?

                    — *F. M. Roger*

A MOTHER SINGS

I wish I had a golden voice
To sing my Maker's praise;
With perfect tone and time and pitch
My voice I'd ever raise.

But as I scrub my floor today
My heart is full of love
And thanks for home; so I will lift
My tuneless hymn above.

And while I sing, my little girl
Will crow with rapt delight;

She thinks her mother's voice is like
An angel in its flight.

Perhaps my Maker listens, too,
With those same ears of love;
And just the tones I mean to sing
Reach to His Throne above.

                    — *Lois Duffield*

TO "HIS" MOTHER

"Mother-in-law" they say, and yet —
Somehow I simply can't forget
'Twas you who watched his baby ways,
Who taught him his first hymn of
            praise,
Who smiled on him with loving pride
When first he toddled by your side;
And as I think of this today,
I think that I'd much rather say —
    Just Mother.

"Mother-in-law," but oh, 'twas you
Who taught him to be kind and true;
When he was tired, almost asleep,
'Twas in your arms he used to creep;
And when he hurt his tiny knee
'Twas you who kissed it tenderly
When he was sad you cheered him,
            too,
And so I'd rather speak of you —
    As Mother.

"Mother-in-law," they say, and yet
Somehow I never shall forget
How very much I'll always owe
To you who taught him how to grow.
You trained your son to look above,
You made of him the man I love,
And so I think of that today,
And then with thankful heart I say —
    Dear Mother.

                    — *Minnie Price*

My Mother

There is a loved one, far away,
Who taught my heart, first, how to
    pray;
Who sent me off with blessing rare
My weil and woe to ever share.
    She is my Mother.

There is a cherished hope that lies
Beyond the tears that dim her eyes,
That some day soon, I'll find a way
To come back home, always to stay
    With Mother.

As life is ebbing fast away,
And she grows weaker day by day,
I long to take her hand in mine,
To kiss her cheek, and, somehow find
    Sweet words to say to Mother.

I can't forget there'll come a day,
When friends will lay her form away,
And hidden under flowers rare —
'Twill be too late that day, to care
    For Mother.

I'll take the time and write today —
'Twill cheer her on her lonely way —
I'll assure her that I love her still,
For she loves me, and always will,
    My Mother.
                        — J. F. Cuthriell

God Knew

God knew we'd need—a guiding hand,
A loving heart to understand
When all the world was strange and
    new,
For babies don't know what to do.
    That's why He made — mothers!

God knew we'd need — a lullaby,
A soothing voice if we should cry,
Two list'ning ears if we should wake,
A kiss to heal each childish ache;

God knew we'd need—a gentle touch,
Much more than a friend's, yes, twice
    as much
To make and keep us ever strong
When we were tempted to do wrong.

God knew we'd need — a place to rest,
The solace of a mother's breast,
The hope that she alone can give,
Her blessing ev'ry hour we live;
God knew we'd need—a mother's smile,
Two eyes to guard us all the while,
Two arms to comfort and to care,
A love that no one else could share.

God knew we'd need—her help to walk,
Her words to teach us how to talk,
Her faith to follow day and night,
Her prayers to give us — second sight;
God knew we'd need—her patient way,
Her loyalty day after day;
God knew we'd need—her love to teach
The human things His hands can't
    reach.
    That's why He made — mothers!
                        — Phyllis C. Michael

Mother Love

Love of our mothers living yet,
In cradle song and bedtime prayer,
In nursery rhyme and fireside lore,
Thy presence still pervades the air;
Love of our mothers, priceless gift,
Our grateful hearts thy praise uplift.

Love of our mothers, tender love,
The fount of childhood's trust and
    grace,
Oh, may thy consecration prove
The wellspring of a nobler race;
Love of our mothers, priceless gift,
Our grateful hearts thy praise uplift.
                        — Author Unknown

A CHRISTIAN MOTHER

She tells her child to have no fear;
She comforts and is always near;
She seems to drive away all pain;
She teaches truth — from lies refrain;
She's kind and good and knows what's
    best;
She does her household chores with
    zest.

She'll help you, when you are in
    doubt;
She'll make a way, you will find out;
She brightens life, when things seem
    rough;
She cheers you, when the going's
    tough;
She teaches you there's One on High
Who'll keep you, if you just draw
    nigh.

She makes all sadness fly away;
She tells you how to live and pray.
May our lives be to this dear one
A blessing rich for all she's done!
This one, to whom we give our love
Is "Mother" sent from God above.

— *Phyllis E. Parlett*

MOTHER LOVE

If I were hanged on the highest hill,
    Mother o' mine, O mother o' mine!
I know whose love would follow me
    still,
    Mother o' mine, O mother o' mine!

If I were drowned in the deepest sea,
    Mother o' mine, O mother o' mine!
I know whose tears would come down
    to me,
    Mother o' mine, O mother o' mine.

— *Rudyard Kipling*

A PRAYER FOR MOTHER

God help us all to do our part,
    Each day to start anew,
To lend a helping hand and heart,
    And make our prayers come true.

God help each one of us to see
    Just what our mothers need,
For if we know, then we can make
    Them very glad indeed.

Make each of us a ray of light
    A sunbeam on its way,
Help us to make the days all bright
    And each a Mother's Day.

— *Author Unknown*

A MOTHER

God sought to give the sweetest thing
    In His almighty power
To earth; and deeply pondering
    What it should be, one hour
In fondest joy and love of heart
    Outweighing every other,
He moved the gates of heaven apart
    And gave to earth a mother.

— *Author Unknown*

OLD MOTHERS

I love old mothers — mothers with white hair,
And kindly eyes, and lips grown softly sweet
With murmured blessings over sleeping babes.
There is a something in their quiet grace
That speaks the calm of Sabbath afternoons;
A knowledge in their deep, unfaltering eyes,
That far outreaches all philosophy.
Time with caressing touch, about them weaves
The silver-threaded fairy-shawl of age,
While all the echoes of forgotten songs
Seem joined to lend a sweetness to their speech.
Old mothers! — as they pass, one sees again
Old garden-walks, old roses and old loves.

— Charles S. Ross

FATHERS

FATHER's DAY (— *So He Says*)

Once there was a boy who never
　Tore his clothes — or hardly ever,
Never made his sister mad,
　Was not whipped for being bad,
Was not scolded by his ma,
　Was not frowned at by his pa,
Always fit for folks to see,
　Always good as good could be.

This good little boy from Heaven,
　So I'm told, was only seven,
Yet he never shed real tears
　When his mother scrubbed his ears.
And at times when he was dressed
　For a party, in his best,
He was careful of his shirt,
　Not to get it smeared with dirt.

Used to study late at night,
　Learning how to read and write.
When he played a baseball game,
　Right away he always came
When his mother called him in,
　And he never made a din,
But as quiet as a mouse
　When they had guests in the house.

Liked to wash his hands and face,
　Like to work around the place,
Never, when he'd tire of play,
　Left his wagon in the way
Or his bat and ball around —
　Put 'em where they could be found.
And that good boy married ma
　And today he is my pa!

—Author Unknown

A FATHER'S PLACE

It is a father's place
    To be concerned about his own,
His household's faith in God;
    The love of Christ enthrone.

A father e'er should be
    Responsible, the head
Of all his house; feed them
    The Word, the Living Bread.

By him his children should
    Be led to worship God,
Through Christ; as in Him paths
    Of righteousness are trod.

It is a father's place
    (Today and every day)
To read the Word in circle sweet,
    And lead and guide and pray.

Will you be one of those
    To take his proper place?
To sit at meat with grateful heart,
    His table, in Christ, grace?

Oh, Christian fathers! Hear
    God's Word! His voice obey!
And, thereby, teach your families
    To love and trust and pray.

— *Eva Gray*

THE KIND OF DAD I'D BUY

If I went shopping for a dad,
    Here is what I'd buy:
One who would always stop
    To answer a little boy's "why?"
One who would always speak kindly
    To a little girl or boy,
One who would give to others
    A bit of sunshine and joy.
I'd pick a dad that followed

The Bible's Golden Rule,
    And one who went regularly
To Church and Sunday School.
I'd buy the very finest dad
    To place on our family tree,
And then I'd try to live like him
    So he would be proud of me.

— *Helen Kitchell Evans*

THANKSGIVING

GRATITUDE

I thank You for these gifts, dear God,
    Upon Thanksgiving Day —
For love and laughter and the faith
    That makes me kneel to pray.

For life that lends me happiness,
    And sleep that gives me rest,

These are the gifts that keep my heart
    Serene within my breast.

Love, laughter, faith and life and sleep,
    We owe them, every one —
They carry us along the road
    That leads from sun to sun.

— *Margaret E. Sangster*

We Plow the Fields

We plow the fields, and scatter
  The good seed on the land,
But it is fed and watered
  By God's almighty hand;
He sends the snow in winter,
  The warmth to swell the grain,
The breezes and the sunshine,
  And soft, refreshing rain.

He only is the Maker
  Of all things near and far;
He paints the wayside flower,
  He lights the evening star;
The winds and waves obey Him,
  By Him the birds are fed;
Much more, to us, His children,
  He gives our daily bread.

We thank Thee, then, O Father,
  For all things bright and good,
The seedtime and the harvest,
  Our life, our health, our food:
No gifts have we to offer
  For all Thy love imparts.
But that which Thou desirest,
  Our humble, thankful hearts.

All good gifts around us
  Are sent from Heav'n above;
Then thank the Lord, oh, thank the
    Lord
  For all His love.
  — *Translated by Jane M. Campbell*

Thanksgiving

O precious Father, as we bow
  Before Thy throne today —
We count the many blessings
  Thou hast shower'd upon our way.

The comfort of our humble homes,
  Our health and happiness,
The strength provided for each day
  To meet the strain and stress.

We thank Thee for Thy precious Son
  Who brought salvation free,
And for this mighty land of ours —
  A land of liberty!

So, Lord, help us to give Thee thanks
  For all that we hold dear —
Not only on Thanksgiving Day
  But each day of the year!
  — *Author Unknown*

The Lord's Day

Sweet day of Christ, earth's perfect peace,
  Blest token of the yonder life;
  From thy bright light, man's sinful strife
Flees far and bids earth's darkness cease.

Calm of the soul, storm-tossed and driven
  Through days of doubt and dark despair;
  Sweet promise that the nearing There
Will bring the rest of sins forgiven.

Then peace, my soul; thy turmoil still;
  Put far away the troubled mind;
  In this day's holy quiet find
The joy which heaven will fulfill!
  — *Henry W. Frost*

THANK THEE

An easy thing, O power Divine,
To thank Thee for these gifts of Thine!
For summer's sunshine, winter's snow,
For hearts that kindle, thoughts that glow;
But when shall I attain to this:
To thank Thee for the things I miss?

For all young fancy's early gleams,
The dreamed-of joys that still are dreams,
Hopes unfulfilled, and pleasures known
Through others' fortunes, not my own,
And blessings seen that are not given,
And ne'er will be — this side of heaven.

Had I, too, shared the joys I see,
Would there have been a heaven for me?
Could I have felt Thy presence near
Had I possessed what I held dear?
My deepest fortune, highest bliss,
Have grown, perchance, from things I miss.

Sometimes there comes an hour of calm;
Grief turns to blessing, pain to balm;
A Power that works above my will
Still leads me onward, upward still;
And then my heart attains to this:
To thank Thee for the things I miss.

— *Thomas Wentworth Higginson*

ɔɾɔ

A GOOD THANKSGIVING

Said old gentleman Gay on a Thanksgiving Day:
"If you want a good time, then give something away."
So he sent a fat turkey to shoemaker Price,
And the shoemaker said: "What a big bird! How nice!
With such a good dinner before me I ought
To give Widow Lee the small chicken I bought."
"This fine chicken, oh, see!" said the sweet Widow Lee,
"And the kindness that sent it how precious to me!
I'll give washwoman Biddy my big pumpkin pie."
"And, oh, sure," Biddy said, "'tis the queen o' all pies!
Just to look at its yellow face gladdens my eyes!

Now it's my turn, I think, and a sweet ginger cake
For the motherless Finnigan children I'll bake."
Cried the Finnigan children, Rose, Denny and Hugh:
"It smells sweet of spice, and we'll carry a slice
To little lame Jake, who has nothing that's nice."
"Oh, I thank you and thank you!" said little lame Jake;
"What a bootiful, bootiful, bootiful cake!
And oh, such a big slice! I'll save all the crumbs,
And give them to each little sparrow that comes."
And the sparrows, they twittered, as if they would say,
Like old gentleman Gay: "On a Thanksgiving Day,
If you want a good time, then give something away."

— *Author Unknown*

ᔆ

We Thank Thee

For all the beauty of the world, dear Lord,
    For skies of blue above,
And for the harvest round about our feet
    That shows Thy perfect love,
        We thank Thee.

For pleasant sleep wherein each tiny care
    Is somehow put aside,
For each new dawn that lets us wake refreshed
    To blessings yet untried,
        We thank Thee.

For days of warm spring rain and summer sun,
    For fall and winter chill,
For bringing us safe through another year
    With strength to do Thy will,
        We thank Thee.

For home and fam'ly ties of love within,
    For friendships just begun,
For all the tender mercy, Lord,
    You grant to everyone,
        We thank Thee.

For freedom's torch held high as in the past,
    For constant hope in youth,
For blessings seen and those we cannot see,
    We thank Thee, Lord, in truth,
        We thank Thee.

— *Phyllis C. Michael*

THE HOUSE OF GOD

Lord of the worlds above,
  How pleasant and how fair
The dwellings of thy love,
  Thine earthly temples, are!
    To thine abode
    My heart aspires,
    With warm desires
    To see my God.

The sparrow for her young
  With pleasure seeks a nest,
And wandering swallows long
  To find their wonted rest!
    My spirit faints
    With equal zeal,
    To rise and dwell
    Among thy saints.

O happy souls, who pray
  Where God appoints to hear!
O happy men, who pay
  Their constant service there!
    They praise thee still;
    And happy they,
    Who love the way
    To Zion's hill.

They go from strength to strength,
  Through this dark vale of tears;
Till each arrives at length,
  Till each in heaven appears.
    O glorious seat,
    When God, our King,
    Shall thither bring
    Our willing feet!

To spend one sacred day
  Where God and saints abide,
Affords diviner joy
  Than thousand days beside:

Where God resorts,
  I love it more
    To keep the door,
    Than shine in courts.

God is our sun and shield,
  Our light and our defence;
With gifts his hands are filled,
  We draw our blessings thence.
    He shall bestow,
    On Jacob's race,
    Peculiar grace,
    And glory too.

The Lord his people loves;
  His hand no good withholds
From those his heart approves,
  From pure and pious souls.
    Thrice happy he,
    O God of hosts,
    Whose spirit trusts
    Alone in thee.
                    — Isaac Watts

CHURCHES

Beautiful is the large church,
With stately arch and steeple;
Neighborly is the small church,
With groups of friendly people;
Reverent is the old church,
With centuries of grace;
And a wooden church or a stone
    church
Can hold an altar place.
And whether it be a rich church
Or a poor church anywhere,
Truly it is a great church
If God is worshiped there.
                    — Author Unknown

THE BONES GO TO CHURCH

Quite often wishbones go to church
　And do a lot of wishing,
But if a headache's coming on,
　They spend the day a-fishing.

My, how they wish the church would
　　grow;
　More go to Sunday School;
The choir greater interest show;
　A good sermon were the rule.

Then there are the jawbones
　Who always have their say;
They scold, advise, and criticize,
　And drive the folks away.

They forget it takes a Samson
　Who knows how to wield this bone,
And without just such an expert,
　The jawbones should stay at home.

But, oh, those faithful backbones —
　They really do the work;
Pick up the load and carry on;
　Not one is known to shirk.

They go to church on Sunday morn
　To swing doors open wide,
And then shake hands with all the
　　bones
　To welcome them inside!

　　　　— Florence Dolby Wolfe

A NEW ENGLAND CHURCH

The white church on the hill
　Looks over the little bay —
A beautiful thing on the hill
　When the mist is gray;
When the hill looks old, and the air
　　turns cold
　With the dying day!

The white church on the hill —
　A Greek in a Puritan town —
Was built on the brow of the hill
　For John Wesley's God's renown,
And a conscience old set a steeple cold
　On its Grecian crown.

In a storm of faith on the hill
　Hands raised it over the bay.
When the night is clear on the hill,
　It stands up strong and gray;
But its door is old, and the tower points
　　cold
　To the Milky Way.

The white church on the hill
　Looks lonely over the town.
Dim to them under the hill
　Is its God's renown,
And its Bible old, and its creed grown
　　cold,
　And the letters brown.

　　　　— Wilton Agnew Barrett

CLUTTERED TEMPLES

When thou goest into thy church,
Let vain or busy thoughts have there no part;
Bring not thy plow, thy plots, thy pleasures thither.
Christ purged His Temple, so must thou thy heart.
All worldly thoughts are but thieves met together
To cozen thee. Look to thy actions well:
For churches either are our Heaven or hell.

　　　　— George Herbert

Is This Your Church?

A room of quiet, a temple of peace;
The home of faith — where doubtings cease.
A house of comfort, where hope is given;
A source of strength to make earth Heaven;
A shrine of worship, a place to pray —
I found all this in my church today.

— *Pulpit Digest*

ᚙ

Love to the Church

I love thy kingdom, Lord,
  The house of thine abode,
The church our blest Redeemer saved
  With his own precious blood.

I love thy church, O God:
  Her walls before thee stand,
Dear as the apple of thine eye,
  And graven on thy hand.

If e'er to bless thy sons
  My voice or hands deny,
These hands let useful skill forsake,
  This voice in silence die.

For her my tears shall fall,
  For her my prayers ascend;
To her my cares and toils be given,
  Till toils and cares shall end.

Beyond my highest joy
  I prize her heavenly ways,
Her sweet communion, solemn vows,
  Her hymns of love and praise.

Jesus, thou friend divine,
  Our Saviour and our King,
Thy hand from every snare and foe
  Shall great deliverance bring?

Sure as thy truth shall last,
  To Zion shall be given
The brighest glories earth can yield,
  And brighter bliss of heaven.

— *Timothy Dwight*

The Church Universal

One holy Church of God appears
  Through every age and race
Unwasted by the lapse of years,
  Unchanged by changing place.

From oldest time, on farthest shores,
  Beneath the pine or palm,
One Unseen Presence she adores,
  With silence or with psalm.

Her priests are all God's faithful sons
  To serve the world raised up;
The pure in heart her baptized ones;
  Love, her communion-cup.

The truth is her prophetic gift,
  The soul her sacred page;
And feet on mercy's errands swift
  Do make her pilgrimage.

O living Church! thine errand speed,
  Fulfill thy task sublime;
With bread of life earth's hunger feed,
  Redeem the evil time!

— *Samuel Longfellow*

ᚙ

Dedication

We dedicate a church today.
Lord Christ, I pray
Within the sound of its great bell
There is no mother who must hold
Her baby close against the cold —
So only have we served Thee well.

— *Author Unknown*

UPON THIS ROCK

Upon this rock Christ built His
    Church:
The human consciousness
That He is God come in the flesh
But true Man nonetheless!

Against this mystery the gates
    Of hell shall not prevail
The Church is His; and it shall
        stand
    When kings and kingdoms fail.

Though many faults the Church may
    have,
    And wounded though she be;
His love for her will hold her as
    His love at Calvary.

A thousand foes shall whelm her not,
    And hell shall break her never!
While Christ shall live the Church
    shall live;
    And Christ shall live forever!

— *Lon Woodrum*

ᐅᐊ

DELIGHT IN GOD'S HOUSE

Sweet is the solemn voice that calls
    The Christian to the house of prayer;
I love to stand within its walls,
    For thou, O Lord, art present there.

I love to tread the hallowed courts,
    Where two or three for worship
        meet;
For thither Christ himself resorts,
    And makes the little band complete.

'Tis sweet to raise the common song,
    To join in holy praise and love;
And imitate the blessed throng
    That mingle hearts and songs above.

Within these walls may peace abound,
    May all our hearts in one agree!
Where brethren meet, where Christ is
    found,
    May peace and concord ever be!

— *Henry Francis Lyte*

ᐅᐊ

GIVE A MESSAGE, PULPIT!

Give us a message, pulpit,
out of some awesome desire;
keep it simple, but oh,
touch it somehow with fire!
Speak of the dust-things, pulpit,
for out of the dust came man;
but speak not of dust alone —
show us our souls, if you can!
Break, if need be, our hearts,
draw, if you must, our blood;
but give us a message, pulpit,
show us some vision from God!

— *Lon Woodrum*

TOGETHER, LORD —

Together, Lord, we seek Thy will.
We bow before Thee — yielded, still,
We come today, as oft before,
And with each coming love Thee more.

Assembled, Lord, to hear Thy Word,
May Thy Truth by each heart be
    heard;
Then, strengthened by Thy touch to-
    day,
May we more truly walk Thy way.

— *Veda Group*

A House Not Made With Hands

O where are kings and empires now,
 Of old that went and came?
But, Lord, Thy church is praying yet,
 A thousand years the same.

We mark her goodly battlements,
 And her foundations strong;
We hear within the solemn voice
 Of her unending song.

Unshaken as eternal hills,
 Immovable she stands,
A mountain that shall fill the earth,
 A house not made with hands.

— *A. Cleveland Coxe*

ᐛ

The Place of Prayer

Jesus, where'er thy people meet,
There they behold thy mercy-seat;
Where'er they seek thee, thou art
 found,
And every place is hallowed ground.

For thou, within no walls confined,
Inhabitest the humble mind;
Such ever bring thee where they come,
And going, take thee to their home.

Dear Shepherd of thy chosen few,
Thy former mercies here renew;
Here too our waiting hearts proclaim
The sweetness of thy saving name.

Here may we prove the power of
 prayer,
To strengthen faith and sweeten care,
To teach or faint desires to rise,
And bring all heaven before our eyes.

Behold, at thy commanding word
We stretch the curtain and the cord;
Come thou, and fill this wider space,
And bless us with a large increase.

Lord, we are few, but thou art near;
Nor short thine arm, nor deaf thine
 ear;
Oh, rend the heavens, come quickly
 down,
And make a thousand hearts thine
 own!

— *William Cowper*

ᐛ

Prayer on Entering Church

Heat and burden of the day
Help us, Lord, to put away.
Let no crowding, fretting cares
Keep earth-bound our spirit's prayers.
Carping criticism take
From our hearts for Jesus' sake.

— *Author Unknown*

ᐛ

Prayer

In this hour of worship
 Grant Thy presence, Lord!
Here, the world forgotten,
 Feed us on Thy Word.
From our sins and sorrows
 Here we seek release;
Of Thy love persuaded,
 Find the path of peace.

— *Author Unknown*

✻ CONSECRATION ✻

THE TOUCH OF HIS HAND

In the still air the music lies unheard;
  In the rough marble, beauty hides unseen:
To wake the music and the beauty, needs
  The master's touch, the sculptor's chisel keen.

Great Master, touch us with Thy skillful hand;
  Let not the music that is in us die!
Great Sculptor, hew and polish us; nor let,
  Hidden and lost, Thy form within us lie!

Spare not the stroke! Do with us as Thou wilt!
  Let there be naught unfinished, broken, marred;
Complete Thy purpose, that we may become
  Thy perfect image, O our God and Lord!

— *Horatius Bonar*

CONSECRATION

When the dawn at last is breaking
  And the light of day is near —
Then, O Lord, wilt Thou but touch
    me
  With Thy pierced hand so dear.
Wilt Thou help me to see clearly
  My great need of Thee this day;
Cause this eager heart to trust Thee—
  May I early kneel to pray
Asking that Thy Holy Spirit
  By my guide throughout this day;
Helping me to seek the lost ones
  In my work and in my play.
At the close of day, Lord, grant me
  Sweet repose in Thee, at last;
Knowing well, Thou wilt be with me
  Till the storms of life are past.

— *Loma Ried Lauden*

HUMAN PENS

Fleeting life is a human pen,
  To post the passing hour.
May we write again and again,
  Words of truth and power.
Jesus writes with His hand divine,
  And guides His pens each day;
Oh, may the Lord inspire each line,
  And all we do and say.

Let me be a willing pen,
  Used by His hand divine.
Write with my life, dear Lord, to men,
  To wisely spend their time.
Use my life as a human pen,
  And write of lasting good.
You may have all the glory then,
  Your pen wrote what Ye would.

— *Stanley Elster Wilkin*

Dwell in Stillness

Christ never asks of us such busy labor
   As leaves no time for resting at His feet;
The waiting attitude of expectation
   He ofttimes counts a service most complete.

He sometimes wants our ear — our rapt attention —
   That He some sweetest secret may impart;
'Tis always in the time of deepest silence
   That heart finds deepest fellowship with heart.

We sometimes wonder why our Lord doth place us
   Within a sphere so narrow, so obscure,
That nothing we call work can find an entrance;
   There's only room to suffer — to endure!

Well, God loves patience! Souls that dwell in stillness,
   Doing the little things, or resting quiet,
May just as perfectly fulfill their mission,
   Be just as useful in the Father's sight,

As they who grapple with some giant evil,
   Clearing a path that every eye may see!
Our Saviour cares for cheerful acquiescence,
   Rather than for a busy ministry.

And yet He does love service, where 'tis given
   By grateful love that clothes itself in deed;
But work that's done beneath the scourge of duty
   Be sure to such He gives but little heed.

Then seek to please Him, whatsoe'er He bids thee
   Whether to do, to suffer, to lie still!
'Twill matter little by what path He led us,
   If in it all we sought to do His will.

            — *Author Unknown*

The Preacher's Prayer

If thou wouldst have me speak, Lord, give me speech.
So many cries are uttered nowadays,
That scarce a song, however clear and true,
Will thread the jostling tumult safe, and reach
The ears of men buz-filled with poor denays:
Barb thou my words with light, make my song new,
And men will hear, or when I sing or preach.

            — *George Macdonald*

MAKE ME AVAILABLE

Lord, make me available today
To hear Thy voice, and do Thy will;
And cheerfully my own small place to
    fill.
Let me Thy clear reflection be,
So those I meet may see in me
Thy goodness and serenity;
Yet give me strength withal
    And courage to endure.
                    — *Florence Duncan Long*

SELF-EXAMINATION

Before Communion —
What strange perplexities arise,
What anxious fears and jealousies,
What crowds in doubtful light appear,
How few, alas, approved and clear!

And what am I? — My soul awake,
And an impartial survey take;
Does no dark sign, no ground of fear,
In practice or in heart appear?

What image does my spirit bear?
Is Jesus formed, and living there?
Say, do His lineaments divine
In thought, and word, and action
    shine?

Searcher of hearts, O! search me still;
The secrets of my soul reveal;
My fears remove; let me appear
To God and my own conscience clear.

May I, consistent with Thy word,
Approach Thy table, O my Lord?
May I among Thy saints appear?
Shall I a welcome guest be there?

Have I the wedding garment on?
Or do I naked, stand alone?
O! quicken, clothe and feed my soul;
Forgive my sins, and make me whole.
                    —*Author Unknown*

LIVE FOR SOMETHING

Live for something, have a purpose,
    And that purpose keep in view;
Drifting like a helmless vessel,
    Thou canst ne'er to life be true.
Half the wrecks that strew life's ocean,
    If some star had been their guide
Might have now been riding safely.
    But they drifted with the tide.

Live for something, and live earnest,
    Though the work may humble be,
By the world of men unnoticed,
    Known alone to God and thee.
Every act has priceless value
    To the architect of fate;
'Tis the spirit of thy doing
    That alone will make it great.

Live for something — God and angels
    Are thy watchers in the strife,
And above the smoke and conflict
    Gleams the victor's crown of life.
Live for something; God has given
    Freely of His stores Divine;
Richest gifts of earth and Heaven,
    If thou willest, may be thine.
                    — *Robert Whitaker*

THIS DAY THAT'S MINE

Give me strength, Lord, just for today
    To do my every task.
Strength and courage to do Thy will
    Is all that I can ask.

The fleeting moment is all I claim,
    Only today is mine;
Moment by moment it comes to me —
    Tomorrow, Lord, is thine.

Graciously grant me anew, I pray
    Thy great grace divine,
To comfort, bless and lead me through
    This day that's mine.
                    — *Theresa Gamble Head*

THE SOUL'S RESPONSE

He said: "Wilt thou go with Me
   Where shadows eclipse the light?"
And she answered: "My Lord, I will follow Thee
   Far under the stars of night."
But He said: "No starlight pierces the gloom
   Of the valley thy feet must tread;
But it leads thee on to a cross and tomb —"
   "But I go with Thee," she said . . .

"Count the cost — canst thou pay the price —
   Be as the dumb thing led;
Laid on an altar of sacrifice?"
   "Bind me there, my Lord," she said.

"Bind, that I may not fail —
   Or hold with Thy wounded hand;
For I fear the knife and the piercing nail,
   And I shrink from the burning brand.
Yet whither Thou goest I will go,
   Though the way be lone and dread —"
His voice was tender, and sweet, and low,
   "Thou shalt go with Me," He said.

And none knew the anguish sore
   Or the night of the way she came;
Alone, alone with the cross she bore,
   Alone in her grief and shame.
Brought to the altar of sacrifice,
   There as a dumb thing slain:
Was the guerdon more than the bitter price?
   Was it worth the loss and pain?

Ask the seed corn, when the grain
   Ripples its ripened gold;
Ask the sower when, after toil and pain,
   He garners the hundredfold.
He said (and His voice was glad and sweet):
   "Was it worth the cost, My own?"
And she answered, low at His pierced feet,
   "I found at the end of the pathway lone
Not death, but life on a throne!"

           — Annie Clarke

PRAYER FOR PEACE

Lord, make me an instrument of Your
    peace!
Where there is hatred—let me sow love
Where there is injury — pardon
Where there is doubt — faith
Where there is despair — hope
Where there is darkness — light
Where there is sadness — joy
O Divine Master, grant that I may not
    so much seek
To be consoled — as to console
To be understood — as to understand
To be loved — as to love for
It is in giving — that we receive;
It is in pardoning — that we are par-
    doned;
And it is in dying — that we are born
    to eternal life.
                    — St. Francis of Assisi

ονο

REFLECTED GLORY

The moon looked down on its double,
    In the placid lake below;
Its light reflected the glory
    Of the sun's God-given glow.

It sailed aloft in the heaven,
    'Twas the pride of all the sky
'Mid bright-eyed stars that kept twin-
        kling,
    While lazy clouds passed by.

I watched in wonder, then softly
    Came a voice distinct and low,
"The hand that formed me is mighty,
    And guides me well, I know."

Tirelessly through the long nights
    On my journey hour by hour,
I travel o'er the same course
    Propelled by God's great power.

With smiling face, though the storm
        clouds
    And the darkness hide from view,
I glorify my Creator
    And ever carry through.

With contrite heart I prayed humbly,
    "Help me, Lord, to shine for Thee,
And steadfast keep on my giv'n course
    May Thy beauty be seen in me."

                    — Fannie Brown

ονο

A DEDICATION

Oh, Lord, I present myself to Thee;
My Will,
My Time,
My Talents,
My Tongue,
My Property,
My Reputation,
My Entire Being,
To be — and to do —
Anything Thou requirest of me.
    Now,
As I have given myself to Thee —
I am no longer my own — but all the
        Lord's.
    I believe
That Thou wilt accept the offering I
        bring;
    I trust Thee
To work in me all the good pleasure of
        Thy will.
    I am willing,
To receive what Thou givest,
To lack what Thou witholdest,
To relinquish what Thou takest,
To surrender what Thou claimest,
To suffer what Thou ordainest,
To do what Thou commandest,
To wait — 'til Thou sayest, "Go."

                    — Author Unknown

AN INTERCESSOR

Make me an intercessor,
  One who can really pray,
One of "the Lord's remembrancers"
  By night as well as day.

Make me an intercessor,
  Thro' whom the Spirit can plead,
For the sin and sorrow on every side
  Of this world in darkness and need.

Make me an intercessor,
  In spirit-touch with Thee,
And given the Heavenly vision,
  Pray through to victory.

Make me an intercessor,
  Teach me how to prevail,
To stand my ground and still pray on,
  Though powers of hell assail.

Make me an intercessor,
  Till pleading at Thy throne,
The sins and sorrows of other lives
  Become as my very own.

Make me an intercessor,
  Sharing Thy death and life,
In prayer claiming for others
  Victory in the strife.

Make me an intercessor,
  Such as Thou dost require,
Who will understand and enter
  Into Thy heart's desire.

Make me an intercessor,
  Willing for deeper death,
Emptied, broken, then made anew,
  And filled with living breath.

Make me an intercessor,
  Reveal this mighty thing,
The wondrous possibility
  Of praying back my King.

Make me an intercessor,
  Hidden — unknown — set apart,
Thought little of by those around,
  But satisfying Thine heart.

— *Frances Ridley Havergal*

༄

WHAT ARE YOU BUILDING?

"What are you doing, friend?" I asked of one;
  And he, while spreading on the mortar thick,
Eyed me with a look of mild surprise
  And answered simply, "I am laying brick."

Another one I watched, and questioned him,
  "What is this that you do with tireless speed?"
His skillful hands worked on without a pause,
  "I have a wife and little ones to feed."

Then to a third my query still I brought.
  With trowel poised, he slowly raised his head,
A glorious vision shining in his eyes.
  "I'm building a cathedral, sir," he said.

— *Helen W. Richardson*

Two Ways of Giving

"If I could find a dollar,"
　Said little Tommy Gill,
"A-layin' in a pig's track,
　Or rollin' up a hill,
I'd send it to the heathen
　As fast as it could go,
For they are needin' money,—
　My teacher told me so."

"I can give a penny now,"
　Said little Willie Pool,
"And that will buy a paper
　To start a Sunday School.
I'd better give a penny,
　And give it right away,
Than wait to find a dollar,
　To give another day."

So Willie gave his penny,
　A wish gave Tommy Gill;
Now which saw his dollar first
　Go rollin' up the hill?

　　　　　— *Author Unknown*

The Chimes

I climbed the winding stairway
　That led to the belfry tower,
As the sinking sun in the westward
　Heralded twilight's hour.
For methought that surely the music
　Would be clearer and sweeter there
Than when thro' the din of the city
　It seemed to float from afar.

But, lo, as I reached the belfry
　No sound of music was there —
But a noisy jar and discord
　Painfully filled the air.
Only a brazen clangor
　Fell harshly on my ear;
And I missed the mellow chiming
　Which everyone else could hear.

The ringer stood at the keyboard,
　Far down beneath the chimes,
And patiently struck the noisy keys,
　As he had uncounted times.
He only knew his duty,
　And he did it with patient care,
But he did not hear the music
　That everyone else could hear.

So we from our quiet watchtower
　May be sending a sweet refrain,
And gladdening the lives of the lowly,
　Though we hear not a single strain.
Our lives may seem but a discord
　(Though we do the best we can),
But others will hear the music
　If we carry out God's plan.

　　　　　— *Author Unknown*

Grace to Do Without

My heart rejoices in God's will,
　'Tis ever best — I do not doubt;
He may not give me what I ask,
　But gives me grace to do without.

I blindly ask for what I crave,
　With haughty heart and will so
　　　stout;
He oft denies me what I seek,
　But gives me grace to do without.

He makes me love the way He leads,
　And every fear is put to rout;
When, with my fondest wish denied,
　He gives me grace to do without.

O blessed, hallowed will of God,
　To it I bow with heart devout;
I will abide in all God's will,
　His will is best, I do not doubt;
He may not give me what I ask,
　But gives me grace to do without.

　　　　　—*Author Unknown*

MORNING CHALLENGE

The fingers of the sunrise
  Beckon at the sill,
Urging me to waken
  To do the Father's will;

To walk this day with Jesus,
  Led by the Spirit's power,
And wisely spend the currency
  Of every priceless hour.

— *Charles E. Bayley*

WHAT CAN HE DO WITH YOU?

If God can make of an ugly seed,
  With a bit of earth and air
And dew and rain, sunshine and shade,
  A flower so wondrous fair,
What can He make of a soul like you,
  With the Bible and faith and prayer
And the Holy Spirit, if you do His will
  And trust His love and care?

— *Author Unknown*

TEACHING, I AM TAUGHT

I heard the Father say, "Go teach,"
  And marveled at His call;
"I cannot others teach," said I,
  "For I am least of all."

"Tho' thou be least," the Father said,
  "Yet I have need of thee;
Where thou art weak, I am full strong,
  Thou canst do all through Me."

And since I've yielded to His call,
  Whene'er His help I've sought,
His Spirit fills my every need
  And, teaching, I am taught.

— *Hazel M. Lindsey*

AN APT PRAYER

Lord, make me a man.
Give me the strength to stand for the
  right.
When other folks have left the fight,
Give me the courage of a man
Who knows that, if he wills, he can.
Teach me to see in every face
The good, the kind and not the base.

Make me sincere in word and deed;
Blot out from me all sham and greed;
Help me to guard my troubled soul
By constant, active self-control.
Clean up my thought, my speech, my
  play,
Lord, keep me pure from day to day —
Make me a man.

— *A. F. Thomas*

DELIVER ME

From prayer that asks that I may be
Sheltered from winds that beat on
  Thee,
From fearing when I should aspire,
From faltering when I should climb
  higher,
From silken self, O Captain, free
Thy soldier who would follow Thee.

From subtle love of softening things,
From easy choices, weakenings
(Not thus are spirits fortified,
Not this way went the Crucified),
From all that dims Thy Calvary,
O Lamb of God, deliver me.

Give me the love that leads the way,
The faith that nothing can dismay,
The hope no disappointments tire,
The passion that will burn like fire;
Let me not sink to be a clod;
Make me Thy fuel, Flame of God.

— *Amy Carmichael*

WALK QUIETLY

Walk quietly —
And know that He is God.
When the dawn on winged steed, comes riding high,
To blazon painted banners on the morning sky,
And the Holy Spirit seemeth nigh —
Walk quietly.

Walk quietly —
And know that He is God.
When the blaring trumpets roar a thrilling beat
Life is lived in storm and strife and noonday heat —
With the mighty tread of tramping feet
Walk quietly.

Walk quietly —
When evening shadows lie against the hill —
In the hush of twilight, when the world is still.
And the balm of peace soothes every ill —
Walk quietly.

Walk quietly —
And know that He is God.
Let your life be governed by His guiding hand
E'en though it varies from the way you planned,
Bow your head in sweet submission and
Walk quietly.

— Author Unknown

A NARROW WINDOW

A narrow window may let in the light,
A tiny star dispel the gloom of night,
A little deed a mighty wrong set right.

A rose, abloom, may make a desert fair,
A single cloud may darken all the air,
A spark may kindle ruin and despair.

A smile, and there may be an end to
    strife;
A look of love, and Hate may sheathe
    the knife;
A word—ah, it may be the word of life!

— Florence Earle Coates

THE SHEPHERD BOY'S SONG

He that is down needs fear no fall,
    He that is low, no pride;
He that is humble ever shall
    Have God to be his guide.

I am content with what I have,
    Little be it, or much:
And, Lord, contentment still I crave,
    Because Thou savest such.

Fulness to such a burden is
    That go on pilgrimage;
Here little, and hereafter bliss,
    Is best from age to age.

— John Bunyan

TALK WITH US, LORD

Talk with us, Lord, Thyself reveal,
  While here o'er earth we move;
Speak to our hearts, and let us feel
  The kindling of Thy love.

With Thee conversing, we forget
  All time, and toil, and care;
Labor is rest, and pain is sweet,
  If Thou, my God, art here.

Here then, my God, vouchsafe to stay,
  And bid my heart rejoice;
My rebounding heart shall own Thy
    sway
  And echo to Thy voice.

Thou callest me to seek Thy face;—
  'Tis all I wish to seek;
To attend the whispers of Thy grace,
  And hear Thee only speak.

Let this my every hour employ,
  Till I Thy glory see;
Enter into My Master's joy.
  And find my Heaven in Thee.

—*Charles Wesley*

ⱷ

GOD MUST BE LIKE THAT

As he taught and healed the multi-
    tudes,
  Or fed them by the sea,
As he prayed upon a mountain
  Overlooking Galilee,
As he stilled the raging tempest,
  As he made the waves obey,
There was something in his majesty
  That made the people say,
    "God must be like that."

As he blessed the little children,
  Cheered the aged and depressed,
As he healed the broken-hearted
  And relieved the sore-distressed,

As he taught men to be neighbors,
  As he taught men how to pray,
There was something in his winsome-
    ness
  That made the people say,
    "God must be like that."

O Christ, who healed the lepers
  With a power from God above,
Cleanse thou my heart from secret sin
  And fill it full of love —
Love that will manifest itself
  In likeness unto thee,
For something in thy godliness
  Has gripped the soul of me —
    And I would be like that.

—*Kenneth W. Sollitt*

ⱷ

GOD'S BEST

God has His best thing for the few
  That dare to stand the test;
God has His second choice for those
  Who will not have His best.

It is not always open ill
  That risks the Promised Rest;
The better, often, is the foe
  That keeps us from the best.

Some seek the highest choice,
  But, when by trials pressed
They shrink, they yield, they shun the
    cross
  And so they lose the best.

Give me, O Lord, Thy highest choice;
  Let others take the rest.
Their good things have no charm for
    me,
  I want Thy very best.

I want, in this short life of mine,
  As much as can be pressed
Of service true for God and man:
  Make me to be Thy best.

—*A. B. Simpson*

HIS STRENGTH

And, as the path of duty is made plain,
May grace be given that I may walk therein,
Not like the hireling, for his selfish gain,
With backward glances and reluctant tread,
Making a merit of his coward dread —
    But, cheerful, in the light around me thrown,
    Walking as one to pleasant service led;
    Doing God's will as if it were my own
Yet trusting not in mine, but in His strength alone!

— *John Greenleaf Whittier*

CHRIST SUPREME

Christ supreme in all of life,
This is my soul's ambition;
Praise His name, He's always the
        same,
I bow in humble contrition.

Christ supreme in everything,
Giver of life eternal;
He is King, His praises I sing,
Claiming His blessings supernal.

Yielded to the Christ supreme,
Filled with the Holy Spirit;
"Go ye" then, is His blest command,
Challenging all who will hear it.

Wean me from earth's allure,
Take, bless and make me pure,
Reign Thou, O Christ, supreme in me;
I yielded my all to Thee.

— *Carlton Buck*

ABOVE SELF

Lift me above myself, I pray,
That I may walk with Thee today;
Out of my smallness into Thy great,
Away from jealousy, greed and hate,
Above the fog and din of things,
Up where the song of victory sings.

And not alone would I walk there,
For others I would lift in prayer;
That thro' this day the selfish masks
May all be stripped from daily tasks,
That fellow-workers, too, may see
And want to walk this day with Thee.

— *Carlton Buck*

UNTIL ETERNITY

It's not my role to ask today
    Why life seems all in vain;
It is but mine to walk by faith
    With God through sun or rain.

It's not my task to choose life's span —
    But then it's better so;
For God can see beyond today
    Things I can't see or know.

It's not my place to question now
    Why I am asked to trust;
It's simply mine to try to do
    The things I know I must.

It's mine to live within God's plan
    Whatever it may be;
It's mine to walk by faith with Him
    Until Eternity.

— *Phyllis C. Michael*

LORD, SPEAK TO ME

Lord, speak to me, that I may speak,
In living echoes of Thy tone;
As Thou hast sought, so let me seek
Thy erring children, lost and lone.

O lead me, Lord, that I may lead
The wand'ring and the wav'ring feet;
O feed me, Lord, that I may feed
Thy hung'ring ones with manna
sweet.

O strengthen me, that while I stand
Firm on the Rock, and strong in
Thee,
I may stretch out a loving hand
To wrestlers with the troubled sea.

O teach me, Lord, that I may teach
The precious things Thou dost impart;

And wing my words, that they may
reach
The hidden depth of many a heart.

O give Thine own sweet rest to me,
That I may speak with soothing
power
A word in season, as from Thee,
To weary ones in needful hour.

O fill me with Thy fullness, Lord,
Until my very heart o'erflow
In kindling thought and glowing word
Thy love to tell, Thy praise to show.

O use me, Lord — use even me,
Just as Thou wilt, and when and
where,
Until Thy blessed face I see,
Thy rest, Thy joy, Thy glory share.

— Frances Ridley Havergal

TAKE THOU, O LORD

Take Thou my voice, O Lord, I give it gladly,
Let it proclaim to all the world Thy love;
Take Thou my tongue and may it glorify Thee,
Until at last I sing Thy praise above.

Take Thou my hands and let them do Thy bidding,
Use them, dear Lord, to work for Thee alone;
Take Thou my feet, and train them for Thy service,
May they be swift to make Thy message known.

Take Thou my heart and consecrate it wholly,
May it be true no matter what betide;
Take Thou my life, it must be Thine forever
For I would turn away from all beside.

Take Thou my love, O Lord, and consecrate it,
Burn out the dross and make it all Thine own;
Save me from self and all of earth's ambitions
Till self has died and Thou dost reign alone.

— Oswald J. Smith

JESUS HIMSELF

I do not ask Thee, Lord, for outward sign,
　For portents in the earth or flaming sky;
It is enough to know that Thou art mine,
　And not far off, but intimately nigh.

No burning bush I need to speak Thy name,
　Or call me forward to the newer task;
Give me a burning heart, with love aflame,
　Which sees Thee everywhere, is all I ask.

No pillar-cloud I seek to mark my way
　Through all the windings of the trackless years;
Thou art my Guide, by night as well as day,
　To choose my path, and hush my foolish fears.

I do not look for fiery cloven tongues,
　To tell for me the pentecostal hour;
The Father's promise for all time belongs
　To him who seeks the Spirit's quickening power.

I do not ask for voices from the sky;
　The thunder-peal I might not understand;
But let me hear Thy whisper, "It is I!
　Fear not the darkness, child, but take My hand!"

What can I ask but Thine own Self, dear Lord?
　Omniscience and omnipotence are Thine.
Let but my will with Thy sweet will accord,
　And all Thou hast, and all Thou art is mine!

— Henry Burton

O JESUS, I HAVE PROMISED

O Jesus, I have promised
To serve Thee to the end;
Be Thou forever near me,
My Master and my Friend:
I shall not fear the battle
If Thou art by my side,
Nor wander from the pathway
If Thou wilt be my Guide.

O let me feel Thee near me,
The world is ever near;
I see the sights that dazzle,
The tempting sounds I hear:
My foes are ever near me,
Around me and within;
But, Jesus, draw Thou nearer,
And shield my soul from sin.

O Jesus, Thou hast promised
To all who follow Thee
That where Thou art in glory
There shall Thy servant be;
And, Jesus, I have promised
To serve Thee to the end;
O give me grace to follow
My Master and my Friend.

— John E. Bode

ALONE WITH GOD

Into my closet fleeing, as the dove
    Doth homeward flee,
I haste away to ponder o'er Thy love
    Alone with Thee!

In the dim wood, by human ear un-
    heard,
    Joyous and free,
Lord! I adore Thee, feasting on Thy
    Word
    Alone with Thee!

Amid the busy city, thronged and gay,
    But One I see,
Tasting sweet peace, as unobserved I
    pray
    Alone with Thee!

O happy life! Life hid with Christ in
    God!
    So making me,
At home and by the wayside and
    abroad,
    Alone with Thee!
    — *Elizabeth Payson Prentiss*

I WAS A WANDERING SHEEP

I was a wand'ring sheep,
I did not love the fold,
I did not love my Shepherd's voice
I would not be controlled:
I was a wayward child,
I did not love my home,
I did not love my Father's voice,
I loved afar to roam.

The Shepherd sought His sheep
The Father sought His child
He followed me o'er vale and hill,
O'er deserts waste and wild:
He found me nigh to death,
Famished, and faint, and lone;
He bound me with the bands of love,
He saved the wandr'ing one.

Jesus my Shepherd is;
'Twas He that loved my soul,
'Twas He that washed me in His
    blood,
'Twas He that made me whole:
'Twas He that sought the lost,
That found the wand'ring sheep;
'Twas He that bro't me to the fold,
'Tis He that still doth keep.

No more a wand'ring sheep,
I love to be controlled,
I love my tender Shepherd's voice,
I love the peaceful fold;
No more a wayward child,
I seek no more to roam;
I love my heav'nly Father's voice,
I love, I love His home!
    — *Horatius Bonar*

A HEART THAT WEEPS

Oh for a heart that weeps o'er souls,
    Weeps with a love in anguish born!
Oh for a broken, contrite heart,
    A heart for sinners rent and torn!

Oh for the pangs of Calv'ry's death,
    In fellowship with Thee, my Lord!
Oh for the death that lives in life,
    And bleeds for those who spurn
    Thy Word!

Naught have I sought of blessing,
    Lord,
    Save that which brings lost souls to
    Thee;
All else is vain, nor dare I boast —
    This, Lord, I crave, be this my plea.

Have Thou Thy way whate'er the cost,
    In death I live, in life I die;
Thy way, not mine, dear Lord, I pray,
    Souls, precious souls, my ceaseless
    cry.
    — *Oswald J. Smith*

To Glorify My God

To glorify my God — no lesser aim
My God-given life and power shall henceforth claim;
My body, soul, and spirit, Lord, are Thine;
The joy to give them back to Thee be mine.

His Father's glory Jesus ever sought;
To do His work and will His only thought;
About His Father's business He must be;
Lord, may that business be as much to me.

How best can I my Father glorify?
Nought can be added to His Majesty;
But I can let His glory through me shine
And shed on all around His light Divine.

And like the legend that they tell of one
Who thought to build a temple to the sun,
And reared the chiseled stone and burnished gold,
But still the splendid walls were dark and cold,

Until another architect appeared;
A temple of transparent glass he reared;
And lo, the sun came down his work to own,
And with his glory through the temple shone.

So let my soul be flooded with Thy light;
So let my heart be opened to Thy sight;
So glorify Thyself, O Lord, in me,
Till all my being answers, Lord, to Thee.

— *A. B. Simpson*

Teach Me to Live

Teach me to live! 'Tis easier far to die —
    Gently and silently to pass away —
On earth's long night to close the heavy eye,
    And waken in the glorious realms of day.
Teach me that harder lesson — how to live
    To serve Thee in the darkest paths of life.
Arm me for conflict, now fresh vigor give,
    And make me more than conqu'ror in the strife.

— *Author Unknown*

THE GOSPEL ACCORDING TO YOU

There's a sweet old story translated for men,
   But writ in the long, long ago—
The Gospel according to Mark, Luke, and John—
   Of Christ and His mission below.

You are writing a gospel, a chapter each day,
   By deeds that you do, by words that you say.
Men read what you write, whether faithless or true.
   Say, what is the gospel according to you?

Men read and admire the gospel of Christ,
   With its love so unfailing and true;
But what do they say, and what do they think
   Of the gospel according to you?

'Tis a wonderful story, that gospel of love,
   As it shines in the Christ-life divine,
And oh, that its truth might be told again
   In the story of your life and mine!

Unselfish mirrors in every scene,
   Love blossoms on every sod,
And back from its vision the heart comes to tell
   The wonderful goodness of God.

You are writing each day a letter to men;
   Take care that the writing is true.
'Tis the only gospel some men will read,
   That gospel according to you.
                              —*Author Unknown*

CHRIST, MY LIFE

Lord, let me see Thy glory,
   That like Thee I may grow;
Transformed to Thy blest image,
   While I am here below!

Like Thee, alone, blest Saviour,
   'Tis my desire to be;
To share Thy joys and sorrows,
   United now to Thee.

No strength have I to follow
   Thy holy pathway, Lord,
Except Thy hand uphold me,
   According to Thy word.

O Lord, be this my portion:
   To show Thy glory forth,
And in Thy love abiding
   To tread Thy path on earth;

Mere earthly fame despising,
   Thine own reproach to bear,
Till, at Thy bright appearing,
   Thy triumph I shall share!
                              —*Margaret J. Lucas*

ABIDING

I have learned the wondrous secret
  Of abiding in the Lord;
I have found the strength and sweet-
      ness
  Of confiding in His Word.
I have tasted life's pure fountain,
  I am trusting in His blood;
I have lost my self in Jesus,
  I am sinking into God.

I am crucified with Jesus,
  And He lives and dwells with me;
I have ceased from all my struggling.
  'Tis no longer I but He.
All my will is yielded to Him,
  And His Spirit reigns within;
And His precious blood each moment,
  Keeps me cleansed and free from sin.

For my words, I take His wisdom;
  For my work, His Spirit's power,
For my ways, His ceaseless Presence
  Guides and guards me every hour.
Of my heart, He is the Portion,
  Of my joy, the boundless Spring;
Saviour, Sanctifier, Healer,
  Glorious Lord, and coming King!

                        — A. B. Simpson

MY LORD KNOWS BEST FOR ME

My part is not to choose the way,
  But walk with Him, my Guide;
Although the road may rugged be
  He's ever by my side.

Sometimes He leads me thro' the deep,
  Sometimes my way He shrouds
With darkness and with dangers, and
  Sometimes with low'ring clouds.

Sometimes in deepest mystery
  My life seems prone to be:

I cannot understand, but He,
  My Lord, knows best for me.

Within the water's brink may I
  (With confidence, ahead)
Walk as the Israelites of old,
  With faith and onward tread.

O, may my will to follow as
  He leadeth me, be e'er
My heart's desire toward Him, my
      Lord,
  My victory, my prayer!
                        — Eva Gray

MORE HOLINESS

More holiness give me;
  More striving within,
More patience in suffering,
  More sorrow for sin.
More faith in my Saviour,
  More sense of His care,
More joy in His service,
  More purpose in prayer.

More gratitude give me,
  More trust in the Lord,
More pride in His glory,
  More hope in His Word.
More tears for His sorrows,
  More pain at His grief,
More meekness in trial,
  More praise for relief.

More purity give me,
  More strength to o'ercome,
More freedom from earth-stains,
  More longings for home;
More fit for the kingdom,
  More used I would be,
More blessed and holy —
  More, Saviour, like Thee.
                        — Philip Paul Bliss

TEACH ME, O LORD

Teach me, O Lord, Thy love to know,
  With all my powers of mind and
    thought;
The utmost consecration show
  Of all this being Thou hast bought.

To do Thy will, most Merciful,
  I seek Thy guidance day by day;
To bear the trials that befall,
  I would for constant courage pray.

Teach me to love Thy children, Lord,
  Redeemed by Thy most precious
    Blood;
And may my love, on them outpoured,
  Be pure and true, like Thine, O
    God!

  —Grand Duke Constantine of Russia

CHRIST'S BONDSERVANT

Make me a captive, Lord,
  And then I shall be free;
Force me to render up my sword,
  And I shall conqueror be.
I sink in life's alarms
  When by myself I stand;
Imprison me within Thine arms,
  And strong shall be my hand.

My heart is weak and poor
  Until it master find;
It has no spring of action sure —
  It varies with the wind;
It cannot freely move
  Till Thou hast wrought its chain;
Enslave it with Thy matchless love,
  And deathless it shall reign.

My will is not my own
  Till Thou hast made it Thine;
If it would reach a monarch's throne
  It must its crown resign:
It only stands unbent
  Amid the clashing strife,
When on Thy bosom it has lent
  And found in Thee its life.

  —George Matheson

A PILGRIM'S SONG

He who would valiant be
  'Gainst all disaster,
Let him with constancy
  Follow the Master.
There's no discouragement
Shall make him once relent,
His first avow'd intent
  To be a pilgrim.

Who so beset him round
  With dismal stories,
Do but themselves confound,
  His strength the more is;
No lion can him fright,
He'll with a giant fight;
But he will have a right
  To be a pilgrim.

Since, Lord, Thou dost defend
  Him with Thy Spirit,
He knows he, at the end,
  Shall life inherit.
Then fancies fly away,
He'll fear not what men say —
He'll labour night and day
  To be a pilgrim.

  — John Bunyan (ADAPTED)

BEHOLD, I COME!

"Behold, I come," His voice is calling
    Above the conflicts of the world,
Above the crash of high thrones falling
    And earthly empires downward hurled;
Above the tramp of armies treading,
    The bugles' blare, the cannon's roar,
Above the flames of strife, still spreading
    As host on host goes forth to war.

"Behold, I come," His voice is crying,
    Above the voices of the earth,
Above the shouting and the sighing,
    Above the moaning and the mirth;
Above the mandates of the monarchs,
    The impious prayers their lips have said,
Above the mourning of the mothers,
    Above the children's cries for bread.

"Behold, I come"; ye people, hear Him,
    The day of man is well-nigh spent;
Above your heads the skies will darken,
    Beneath your feet the rocks be rent,
Your swords and spears shall yet be shattered;
    Your kingdoms all be overthrown;
Your power and pride like dust be scattered,
    Like chaff before the whirlwind blown.

"Behold, I come"; ye nations, hearken:
    While yet His words rebuke and warn,
Lest at His coming ye shall fear Him,
    Lest when ye see Him, ye shall mourn;
Seek ye His face while yet He's pleading,
    The Christ who on the cross has died,
While yet His wounds are interceding
    To turn the wrath of God aside.

"Behold, I come"; the darkness lightens
    Above all sorrow and all fear;
Beyond the clouds the Daystar brightens,
    And our deliverance is near;
The groaning earth awaits the hour
    When all the wrongs of time are past,
And clothed with glory and with power,
    The King of kings shall reign at last.

— Annie Johnson Flint

THE IMAGE OF GOD

Father of eternal grace,
  Glorify Thyself in me;
Sweetly beaming in my face
  May the world Thine image see.

Happy only in Thy love,
  Poor, unfriended, or unknown;
Fix my thought on things above;
  Stay my heart on Thee alone.

To Thy gracious will resign'd —
  All Thy will by me be done;
Give me, Lord, the perfect mind
  Of Thy well-beloved Son.

Counting gain and glory loss,
  May I tread the path He trod;
Die with Jesus on the Cross,
  Rise with Him to live with God.

— *Charles Wesley*

ɔ↩

BEAUTY FOR ASHES

I do not ask for golden mists,
Nor rosy paths to tread,
Nor even that the least small flower
May bloom above my head;

Nor wealth nor fame, nor ease nor love
Find place in these my prayers,
Nor brightening of the sober robe
My spent soul ever wears.

I only pray that Thou wilt take
My pain and grief and fear,
And to Thy glory will transmute
My every pang and tear;

I only plead that Thou wilt *use*
This broken life of mine,
And for my dust and ashes give
The beauty that is Thine!

— *Martha Snell Nicholson*

DISCIPLINE

A block of marble caught the glance
  Of Buonarotti's eyes,
Which brightened in their solemn
      deeps
  Like meteor-lighted skies.

And one who stood beside him listened,
  Smiling as he heard;
For "I will make an angel of it,"
  Was the sculptor's word.

And soon mallet and chisel sharp
  The stubborn block assailed,
And blow by blow, and pang by pang,
  The prisoner unveiled.

A brow was lifted high and pure,
  The wakening eyes outshone,
And as the master sharply wrought,
  A smile broke through the stone!

Beneath the chisel's edge the hair
  Escaped in floating rings;
And plume by plume was slowly freed
  The sweep of half-furled wings.

The stately bust and graceful limbs
  Their marble fetters shed,
And where the shapeless block had
      been,
  An angel stood instead!

O blows that smite! O hurts that pierce
  This shrinking heart of mine!
What are ye but the Master's tools
  Forming a work divine?

O hope that crumbles to my feet,
  O joy that mocks and flies,
What are ye but the clogs that bind
  My spirit from the skies?

Sculptor of souls! I lift to Thee
  Encumbered heart and hands;
Spare not the chisel, set me free,
  However dear the bands.

— *Author Unknown*

GIVE ME THY HEART

With echoing steps the worshippers
  Departed one by one;
The organ's pealing voice was stilled,
  The vesper hymn was done;
The shadows fell from roof and arch,
  Dim was the incensed air,
One lamp alone, with trembling ray,
  Told of the Presence there!

In the dark church she knelt alone;
  Her tears were falling fast;
"Help, Lord," she cried, "the shades of
    death
  Upon my soul are cast!
Have I not shunned the path of sin,
  And chosen the better part?"—
What voice came thro' the sacred air?—
  "My child, give me thy heart!"

"Have I not laid before thy shrine
  My wealth, O Lord?" she cried;
"Have I kept aught of gems or gold,
  To minister to pride?
Have I not bade youth's joys retire,
  And vain delights depart?"—
But sad and tender was the voice,—
  "My child, give me thy heart!"

"Have I not, Lord, gone day by day
  Where thy poor children dwell;
And carried help, and gold, and food?
  O Lord, thou knowest it well!
From many a house, from many a soul,
  My hand bids care depart":—
More sad, more tender was the voice,—
  "My child, give me thy heart!"

"Have I not worn my strength away
  With fast and penance sore?
Have I not watched and wept?" she
    cried;
  "Did thy dear saints do more?
Have I not gained thy grace, O Lord,
  And won in heaven my part?"—
It echoed louder in her soul,—
  "My child, give me thy heart!"

"For I have loved thee with a love
  No mortal heart can show;
A love so deep, my saints in heaven
  Its depths can never know:
When pierced and wounded on the
    cross,
  Man's sin and doom were mine,
I loved thee with undying love,
  Immortal and divine!

"I loved thee ere the skies were spread;
  My soul bears all thy pains;
To gain thy love my sacred heart
  In earthly shrines remains:
Vain are thy offerings, vain thy sighs,
  Without one gift divine;
Give it, my child, thy heart to me,
  And it shall rest in mine!"

In awe she listened, and the shade
  Passed from her soul away;
In low and trembling voice she cried,—
  "Lord, help me to obey!
Break thou the chains of earth, O Lord,
  That bind and hold my heart;
Let it be thine, and thine alone,
  Let none with thee have part.

"Send down, O Lord, thy sacred fire!
  Consume and cleanse the sin
That lingers still within its depths:
  Let heavenly love begin.
That sacred flame thy saints have
    known,
  Kindle, O Lord, in me,
Thou above all the rest forever,
  And all the rest in thee."

The blessing fell upon her soul;
  Her angel by her side
Knew that the hour of peace was come;
  Her soul was purified:
The shadows fell from roof and arch,
  Dim was the incensed air,—
But peace went with her as she left
  The sacred Presence there!

— *Adelaide Anne Procter*

FULL-HEARTED MEN!

Give me full-hearted men, who love their Lord,
　　With a sparkle and flash in their eye,
Who are ready to fight, to work, to win,
　　Who are ready to do, or to die.

Give me men who are clean in their words and thoughts,
　　Who can wrestle and labor in prayer;
For the world is dark and sin-sick and sad,
　　And there are heavy loads to bear.

Men full of grace and the Holy Ghost
　　Are the men we must have today;
Full-hearted, strong-hearted, cross-bearing men,
　　Who will valiantly lead the way!

　　　　　　　　　　　　　— Paul Martin

THE POTTER'S HAND

To the Potter's house I went down one day,
And watched him while moulding the vessels of clay;
And many a wonderful lesson I drew,
As I noted the process the clay went through:
Trampled and broken, downtrodden and rolled,
To render more plastic and fit for the mold.
How like the clay that is human, I thought,
When in Heavenly hands to perfection brought;
For self must be cast as the dust at His feet,
Before it is ready, for service made meet.
And pride must be broken, and self-will lost,
All laid on the altar, whatever the cost.

But lo! by and by, a delicate vase
Of wonderful beauty and exquisite grace.
Was it once the vile clay? Ah, yes; yet how strange,
The Potter has wrought so marvelous a change!
Not a trace of the earth, nor mark of the clay,
The fires of the furnace have burned them away.
Wondrous skill of the Potter — the praise is His due —
In whose hands to perfection and beauty it grew;
Thus with souls lying still, content in God's hand,
That do not His power of working withstand,
They are moulded and fitted, a treasure to hold;
Vile clay now transformed into purest of gold.

　　　　　　　　　　　　　— M. F. Clarkson

THE PRIEST OF CHRIST

Give me the priest these graces shall possess;
Of an ambassador the just address,
A Father's tenderness, a Shepherd's care,
A Leader's courage, which the cross can bear,
A Ruler's arm, a Watchman's wakeful eye,
A Pilot's skill, the helm in storms to ply,
A Fisher's patience, and a Labourer's toil,
A Guide's dexterity to disembroil,
A Prophet's inspiration from above,
A Teacher's knowledge, and a Saviour's love.
Give me a priest, a light upon a hill,
Whose rays his whole circumference can fill,
In God's own Word and Sacred Learning verse,
Deep in the study of the heart immersed,
Who in such souls can the disease descry,
And wisely fair restoratives supply.

— *Thomas Ken*

ᴄᴛᴐ

WHATE'ER GOD WILL

Whate'er God will, let that be done;
  His will is ever wisest:
His grace will all thy hope outrun,
  Who to that faith arisest.
    The gracious Lord
    Will help afford;
  He chastens with forbearing:
    Who God believes
    And to him cleaves,
  Shall not be left despairing.

My God is my sure confidence,
  My light and my existence;
His counsel is beyond my sense
  But stirs no weak resistance.
    His word declares
    The very hairs
  Upon my head are numbered.
    His mercy large
    Holds me in charge,
  With care that never slumbered.

— *Albrecht of Brandenburg*

THE CHOICE

There is an altar and a throne
Within my ransomed heart.
If Christ as Lord shall reign therein,
Then self must have no part.

The choice is mine — oh, may I lay
Self on the altar, Lord, today!
'Tis mine to choose if self shall die
And never rise again;
'Tis mine to yield the throne to Christ
And bid Him rule and reign.

Lord Jesus, Thee as king I own,
Thine, Thine shall ever be the throne!

Accounted dead indeed to sin
Through Christ who died for me,
The life I live I owe to Him
For all eternity.

I choose the altar — He alone
Shall evermore possess the throne!

— *Avis B. Christiansen*

CHOOSE THOU FOR ME

I dare not choose my lot,
  I would not if I might,
Choose Thou for me, my God,
  So shall I walk aright.

The kingdom that I seek
  Is Thine; so let the way
That leads to it be Thine,
  Else surely I might stray.

Take Thou my cup, and it
  With joy or sorrow fill,
As best to Thee may seem,
  Choose Thou my good and ill.

Choose Thou for me my friends,
  My sickness or my health,
Choose Thou my cares for me,
  My poverty or wealth.

Not mine — not mine the choice,
  In things both great and small,
Be Thou my Guide, my Strength,
  My Wisdom and my All.

— *Horatius Bonar*

DECISION

I said — "Let me walk in the fields."
  He said — "No, walk in the town."
I said — "There are no flowers there."
  He said—"No flowers, but a crown."
I said — "But the skies are dark;
  There is nothing but noise and din."
And He wept as He sent me back —
  "There is more," He said; "there is
      sin."

I said — "I shall miss the light
  And friends will miss me, they say."
He answered, "Choose to-night
  If I am to miss you, or they."
I pleaded for time to be given.
  He said — "Is it hard to decide?
It will not be hard in Heaven
  To have followed the steps of your
      guide."
Then into His hand went mine,
  And into my heart came He,
And I walk in a light Divine
  The path I had feared to see.

— *George Macdonald*

చెం

HIS WILL BE DONE

"His will be done," we say with sighs and trembling,
  Expecting trial, bitter loss and tears;
And then how doth He answer us with blessings
  In sweet rebuking of our faithless fears.

God's will is peace and plenty and the power
  To be and have the best that He can give,
A mind to serve Him and a heart to love Him,
  The faith to die with, and the strength to live.

It means for us all good, all grace, all glory,
  His kingdom coming and on earth begun.
Why should we fear to say: "His will — His righteous,
  His tender, loving, joyous will — be done?"

— *Lucy M. Waelty*

BEFORE THY THRONE

Before Thy throne, O God, we kneel;
Give us a conscience quick to feel,
A ready mind to understand
The meaning of Thy chastening hand;
Whate'er the pain and shame may be,
Bring us, O Father, nearer Thee.

Search out our hearts and make us
    true,
Wishful to give to all their due;
From love of pleasure, lust of gold,
From sins which make the heart grow
    cold,
Wean us and train us with Thy rod;
Teach us to know our faults, O God.

For sins of heedless word and deed,
For pride ambitious to succeed;
For crafty trade and subtle snare
To catch the simple unaware;
For lives bereft of purpose high,
Forgive, forgive, O Lord, we cry.

Let the fierce fires, which burn and try,
Our inmost spirits purify:
Consume the ill; purge out the shame;
O God! be with us in the flame;
A newborn people may we rise,
More pure, more true, more nobly wise.

— *William Boyd Carpenter*

THE TWO PATHWAYS

Two pathways lay before me —
The one was smooth and wide;
Gay was the song and laughter
I heard on every side.

The other path was narrow,
And dark and steep and lone,
Beset by many a danger,
And foes unseen, unknown.

The broad way was inviting —
The narrow way was grim,
But 'twas this path my Saviour
Called me to walk with Him.

And ne'er have I regretted
The choice I made one day,
To travel with my Saviour
The steep and narrow way.

His precious love grows sweeter
As darker grows the night,
For 'mid the deep'ning shadows
I lean upon His might.

Oh what has earth to offer,
That ever could compare
With fellowship so blessed
As that with Christ I share!

— *Avis B. Christiansen*

ATTRACTION

Be Thou my Object, Lord, this day,
Controlling all I do or say;
That thro' this mortal frame of mine,
Thy blessed traits may ever shine!

Oh! fill me, Lord, with Thy deep love,
Attract my mind to things above;
That I a pilgrim here may be,
And truly serve and follow Thee!

— *M. W. Biggs*

CHRIST'S CALL

Have you heard the voice of Jesus
    Whisper — "I have chosen you"?
Does He tell you in communion
    What He wishes you to do?
Are you in the inner circle?
    Have you heard the Master's call?
Have you given your heart to Jesus?
    Is He now your All in All?

— *Author Unknown*

MADE PERFECT THROUGH SUFFERING

I bless Thee, Lord, for sorrows sent
  To break my dream of human power;
For now, my shallow cistern spent,
  I find Thy founts, and thirst no more.

I take Thy hand, and fears grow still;
  Behold Thy face, and doubts remove;
Who would not yield his wavering will
  To perfect Truth and boundless Love?

That Love this restless soul doth teach
  The strength of Thine eternal calm;
And tune its sad but broken speech
  To join on earth the angel's psalm.

Oh, be it patient in Thy hands,
  And drawn, through each mysterious hour,
To service of Thy pure commands,
  The narrow way of Love and Power.

— *Samuel Johnson*

ༀ

BREATHE ON ME

Breathe on me, Breath of God,
  Fill me with life anew,
That I may love what thou dost love,
  And do what thou wouldst do.

Breathe on me, Breath of God,
  Until my heart is pure,
Until with thee I will one will,
  To do or to endure.

Breathe on me, Breath of God,
  Till I am wholly thine;
Till all this earthly part of me
  Glows with thy fire divine.

Breathe on me, Breath of God,
  So shall I never die,
But live with thee the perfect life
  Of thine eternity.

— *Edwin Hatch*

A PRAYER FOR FORGIVENESS

Jesus, let Thy pitying eye
  Call back a wandering sheep;
False to Thee, like Peter, I
  Would fain, like Peter weep.
Let me be by grace restored;
  On me be all long-suffering shown;
Turn, and look upon me, Lord,
  And break my heart of stone.

Look, as when Thy languid eye
  Was closed that we might live;
"Father," at the point to die
  My Saviour prayed, "Forgive!"
Surely, with that dying word,
  He turns, and looks, and cries, " 'Tis
    done."
O my bleeding, loving Lord,
  Thou break'st my heart of stone!

— *Charles Wesley*

CONFLICT AND VICTORY

What now, my Soul, and hast thou sinned again,
    Thou deeply sinful, desperately wicked Soul?
Wilt thou of sinning never have an end?
    Wilt never let thy Maker make thee whole?
Thou seemest bound by strong iniquity,
When thou should'st be, once and for ever, free!

O Soul, wilt thou forever follow on,
    Like hound upon the scent, hard after sin?
Like a wild beast, art thou insatiate?
    Like a foul demon, hast thou hell within?
Ah, once I thought that thou might'st changèd be;
But thou dost sin, and sin continually!

And yet, O sinful Soul, thou knowest well,
    That I have struggled hard against thy reign;
As often as I've sinned, I have resolved,
    That thou should'st never rule o'er me again;
Alas, deceitful Soul, I did not see,
That, spite of struggle, thou could'st master me!

What can I do, my Soul? Thou art myself;
    I cannot 'scape thy presence, nor thy power;
Turn where I will, I feel thy close embrace;
    Thou pressest hard upon me, hour by hour;—
Oh, that a Master Man might rise in me;
Then, I should be the man I long to be!

What now, my Soul! What does this quiet mean,
    This deep, abiding peace I find within?
Surely, thou hast not changed, since flesh is flesh,
    And well I know that thou art full of sin;
And yet, a new, strange calm has come to me;
A calm like that of high eternity!

Oh, Soul, art thou again deceiving me?
    Is this some subtle, more mysterious way
Than thou hast erstwhile taken? Shall I wake,
    To find my footsteps, as of old, astray?
It cannot be, for heaven has come to me,
With all its peace, and power, and victory!

Temptations press me sore; and yet I stand,
    Upheld, unmoved, abiding in my rest;
Like lifted rock, amidst the surging sea,

Remaining firm, though often tempest prest:
This is not chance; nor I; O Christ, 'tis Thou;
I worship Thee, and at Thy feet I bow.

My prayer is answered, O my sinning Soul,
For thou art conquered by a Conqueror;
Thy Master thou hast met, and He doth reign;
I am set free by a Deliverer;
The Man, Christ Jesus, hath arisen in me,
That I may be the man I long to be!

— *Henry W. Frost*

ᕯᕯᕯ

FOLLOWING

How shall I follow Him I serve?
How shall I copy Him I love?
Nor from those blessed footsteps
swerve,
Which lead me to His seat above?

Lord, should my path through suffer-
ing lie,
Forbid it I should e'er repine;
Still let me turn to Calvary,
Nor heed my griefs, remembering
Thine.

O let me think how Thou didst leave
Untasted every pure delight,
To fast, to faint, to watch, to grieve,
The toilsome day, the homeless
night:—

To faint, to grieve, to die for me!
Thou camest not Thyself to please:
And, dear as earthly comforts be,
Shall I not love Thee more than
these?

Yes! I would count them all but loss,
To gain the notice of Thine eye:
Flesh shrinks and trembles at the cross,
But Thou canst give the victory.

— *Joseph Conder*

A PRAYER

My Redeemer and my Lord,
I beseech Thee, I entreat Thee,
Guide me in each act and word,
That hereafter I may meet Thee,
Watching, waiting, hoping, yearning,
With my lamp well trimmed and
burning,
Interceding with these bleeding
wounds
Upon Thy hands and side,
For all who have lived and erred,
Thou hast suffered,
Thou hast died,
Scourged and mocked and crucified,
And in the grave hast Thou been
buried.

If my feeble prayer can reach Thee,
Oh, my Saviour, I beseech Thee,
Even as Thou hast died for me,
More sincerely
Let me follow where Thou leadest,
Let me, bleeding as Thou bleedest,
Die if dying I may give
Life to one who asks to live,
And more nearly,
Dying thus, resemble Thee.

— *Henry Wadsworth Longfellow*

MY DESIRE

I want a principle within,
  Of jealous, godly fear;
A sensibility of sin,
  A pain to feel it near:
I want the first approach to feel
  Of pride, or fond desire;
To catch the wandering of my will,
  And quench the kindling fire.

From Thee that I no more may part
  No more Thy goodness grieve,
The filial awe, the fleshly heart,
  The tender conscience, give.
Quick as the apple of an eye,
  O God, my conscience make!
Awake my soul when sin is nigh,
  And keep it still awake.

If to the right or left I stray,
  That moment, Lord, reprove;
And let me weep my life away
  For having grieved Thy love.
O may the least omission pain
  My well-instructed soul,
And drive me to the blood again
  Which makes the wounded whole!

— *Charles Wesley*

THE RIDICULOUS OPTIMIST

There was once a man who smiled
  Because the day was bright,
  Because he slept at night,
  Because God gave him sight
To gaze upon his child;
  Because his little one,
  Could leap and laugh and run;
  Because the distant sun
Smiled on the earth he smiled.

He smiled because the sky
  Was high above his head,
  Because the rose was red,
  Because the past was dead!

He never wondered why
  The Lord had blundered so
  That all things have to go
  The wrong way, here below
The over-arching sky.

He toiled, and still was glad
  Because the air was free,
  Because he loved, and she
  That claimed his love and he
Shared all the joys they had!
  Because the grasses grew,
  Because the sweet winds blew,
  Because that he could hew
And hammer, he was glad.

Because he lived he smiled,
  And did not look ahead
  With bitterness or dread,
  But nightly sought his bed
As calmly as a child.
  And people called him mad
  For being always glad
  With such things as he had,
And shook their heads and smiled.

— *Samuel Ellsworth Kiser*

THY WILL BE DONE!

My God, my Father, while I stray
Far from my home, on life's rough way,
O teach me from my heart to say,
  "Thy will be done!"

Though dark my path, and sad my lot,
Let me be still and murmur not,
But breathe the prayer divinely taught,
  "Thy will be done!"

Renew my will from day to day;
Blend it with Thine, and take away
All that now makes it hard to say,
  "Thy will be done!"

— *Charlotte Elliott*

FORGIVE ME

Forgive me, Lord, for careless words
  When hungry souls are near;
Words that are not of Faith and Love,
  Heavy with care and fear;

Forgive me for the words withheld,
  For words that might have won
A soul from darkened paths and sin
  To follow Thy dear Son.

Words are such mighty things, dear
    Lord,
  May I so yielded be
That Christ, who spake as never man,
  May ever speak through me.

— *Author Unknown*

A PLEA

O Thou, to whose all searching sight
The darkness shineth as the light,
Search, prove my heart, it pants for
    Thee;
O burst these bonds, and set it free!

Saviour, where'er Thy steps I see,
Dauntless, untired, I follow Thee;
O let Thy hand support me still,
And lead me to Thy holy hill.

If rough and thorny be the way,
My strength proportion to my day;
Till toil and grief and pain shall cease,
Where all is calm and joy and peace.

— *Nikolaus L. von Zinzendorf*

I MET THE MASTER

I had walked life's way with an easy tread,
Had followed where comforts and pleasures led,
Until one day in a quiet place
I met the Master face to face.

With station and rank and wealth for my goal,
Much thought for my body but none for my soul,
I had entered to win in life's mad race,
When I met the Master face to face.

I met Him and knew Him and blushed to see
That His eyes full of sorrow were fixed on me,
And I faltered and fell at His feet that day
While my castles melted and vanished away.

Melted and vanished, and in their place,
Naught else did I see but the Master's face;
And I cried aloud, "Oh, make me meet
To follow the steps of Thy wounded feet."

My thought is now for the souls of men;
I have lost my life to find it again,
E'er since one day in a quiet place
I met the Master face to face.

— *Author Unknown*

ADORATION

I love my God, but with no love of mine,
　For I have none to give;
I love Thee, Lord, but all the love is Thine
　For by Thy love I live.
I am as nothing, and rejoice to be
Emptied and lost and swallowed up in Thee.

Thou, Lord, alone art all Thy children need,
　And there is none beside;
From Thee the streams of blessedness proceed,
　In Thee the blest abide —
Fountain of life and all-abounding grace,
Our source, our center, and our dwelling place.

　　　　　　　　　　　— *Madame Guyon*

THE THREEFOLD WORK

Three things the Master hath to do,
　And we who serve Him here below
And long to see His Kingdom come,
　May pray or give or go.

He needs them all — the open hand,
　The willing feet, the asking heart —
To work together and to weave
　The threefold cord that shall not
　　part.

Nor shall the giver count his gift
　As greater than the worker's need,
Nor he in turn his service boast
　Above the prayers that voice his
　　need.

Not all can go, nor all can give
　To arm the other for the fray;
But young or old or rich or poor,
　Or strong or weak — we all can pray.

Pray that the full hands open wide
　To speed the message on its way,
That those who hear the call may go
　And pray — that other hearts may
　　pray.

　　　　　　　— *Annie Johnson Flint*

CONSECRATION

My Jesus, as Thou wilt!
　O may Thy will be mine;
Into Thy hand of love
　I would my all resign.
Through sorrow, or through joy,
　Conduct me as Thine own;
And help me still to say,
　My Lord, Thy will be done.

My Jesus, as Thou wilt;
　Though seen through many a tear,
Let not my star of hope
　Grow dim or disappear.
Since Thou on earth has wept
　And sorrowed oft alone,
If I must weep with Thee,
　My Lord, Thy will be done.

My Jesus, as Thou wilt!
　All shall be well for me;
Each changing future scene
　I gladly trust with Thee.
Straight to my home above
　I travel calmly on,
And sing, in life or death,
　My Lord, Thy will be done.

　　　　　　　— *Benjamin Schmolck*

HAVE THINE OWN WAY, LORD!

Have Thine own way, Lord!
  Have Thine own way!
Thou art the Potter;
  I am the clay.
Mold me and make me
  After Thy will,
While I am waiting,
  Yielded and still.

Have Thine own way, Lord!
  Have Thine own way!
Search me and try me,
  Master, today!
Whiter than snow, Lord,
  Wash me just now,
As in Thy presence
  Humbly I bow.

Have Thine own way, Lord!
  Have Thine own way!
Wounded and weary,
  Help me, I pray!
Power — all power —
  Surely is Thine!
Touch me and heal me,
  Saviour divine!

Have Thine own way, Lord!
  Have Thine own way!
Hold o'er my being
  Absolute sway!
Fill with Thy Spirit
  Till all shall see
Christ only, always,
  Living in me!

    — Adelaide A. Pollard

A MOMENT IN THE MORNING

A moment in the morning, ere the cares of the day begin,
Ere the heart's wide door is open for the world to enter in,
Ah, then, alone with Jesus, in the silence of the morn,
In heavenly sweet communion, let your duty-day be born.
In the quietude that blesses with a prelude of repose
Let your soul be smoothed and softened, as the dew revives the rose.

A moment in the morning take your Bible in your hand,
And catch a glimpse of glory from the peaceful promised land:
It will linger still before you when you seek the busy mart,
And like flowers of hope will blossom into beauty in your heart.
The precious words, like jewels, will glisten all the day
With a rare effulgent glory that will brighten all the way;
When comes a sore temptation, and your feet are near a snare,
You may count them like a rosary and make each one a prayer.

A moment in the morning — a moment, if no more —
Is better than an hour when the trying day is o'er.
'Tis the gentle dew from heaven, the manna for the day;
If you fail to gather early — alas! it melts away.
So, in the blush of morning, take the offered hand of love,
And walk in heaven's pathway and the peacefulness thereof.

    — Arthur Lewis Tubbs

LORD, CARRY ME

Lord, carry me. — "Nay, but I grant thee strength
To walk and work thy way to heaven at length."

Lord, why then am I weak? — "Because I give
Power to the weak, and bid the dying live."

Lord, I am tired. — "He hath not much desired
The goal, who at the starting-point is tired."

Lord, dost Thou know? — "I know what is in man;
What the flesh can, and what the spirit can."

Lord, dost Thou care? — "Yes, for thy gain or loss
So much I cared, it brought me to the cross."

Lord, I believe; help Thou mine unbelief.
"Good is the word; but rise, for life is brief.
The follower is not greater than the Chief:
Follow thou Me along My way of grief."
— *Christina G. Rossetti*

THE RICH YOUNG RULER

We are not told his name — this "rich young ruler"
    Who sought the Lord that day;
We only know that he had great possessions
    And that — he went away.

He went away; he kept his earthly treasure
    But oh, at what a cost!
Afraid to take the cross and lose his riches —
    And God and Heaven were lost.

So for the tinsel bonds that held and drew him
    What honor he let slip —
Comrade of John and Paul and friend of Jesus —
    What glorious fellowship!

For they who left their all to follow Jesus
    Have found a deathless fame,
On his immortal scroll of saints and martyrs
    God wrote each shining name.

We should have read his there — the rich young ruler —
    If he had stayed that day;
Nameless — though Jesus loved him — ever nameless
    Because — he went away.
— *Author Unknown*

GO TO DARK GETHSEMANE

Go to dark Gethsemane,
   Ye that feel the tempter's power;
Your Redeemer's conflict see;
   Watch with Him one bitter hour;
Turn not from His griefs away;
Learn of Jesus Christ to pray.

See Him at the judgment hall,
   Beaten, bound, reviled, arraigned;
See Him meekly bearing all;
   Love to man His soul sustained;
Shun not suffering, shame or loss;
Learn of Christ to bear the cross.

Calvary's mournful mountain climb;
   There adoring at His feet,
Mark that miracle of time,
   God's own sacrifice complete:
"It is finished!" hear Him cry;
Learn of Jesus Christ to die.

— *James Montgomery*

∞

YIELDED TO HIM

I would be yielded to Jesus,
   Lost in His infinite love,
Striving to please Him forever,
   Laying my treasures above.

I would be yielded to Jesus,
   Filled with His Spirit Divine,
Following close in His footsteps,
   Knowing His hand over mine.

I would be yielded to Jesus,
   Cleansed in His life-giving flood,
Finding His perfect salvation,
   Trusting alone in His Blood.

I would be yielded to Jesus,
   Looking for Him to appear,
Dying to sin and temptation,
   Finding Him wondrously near.

I would be yielded to Jesus,
   Bearing His banner on high,
Ready to live for His glory,
   Equally ready to die!

I would be yielded to Jesus —
   Completely, forever, His own!
Living my life for His Glory,
   Yielded to Jesus alone.

— *Connie Calenberg*

∞

DELAY

I loved Thee late
   Too late I loved Thee, Lord,
Yet not so late
   But Thou dost still afford
The proof that Thou wilt bear
   With winning art,
One sinner more
   Upon Thy loving heart.
And may I prove,
   When all my warfare's past,
Though late I loved Thee,
   I loved Thee to the last.

— *St. Augustine*

∞

A YIELDED INSTRUMENT

Oh to be used of Jesus,
   A tool in His mighty hand,
Ready for instant service,
   Waiting for His command,
Oh to be used of Jesus,
   A vessel emptied and clean
Reserved for the promised blessing
   Poured forth by His hand unseen.
Oh to be used of Jesus,
   A mirror polished and bright,
With which to reflect His glory
   In a world of sorrow and night.

— *Avis B. Christiansen*

THE LIVING SERMON

I'd rather see a sermon than hear one any day,
I'd rather one would walk with me than merely tell the way;
The eye's a better pupil and more willing than the ear,
Fine counsel is confusing, but example's always clear;
The best of all the preachers are the men who live their creeds,
For to see good put in action is what everybody needs.

I soon can learn to do it, if you'll let me see it done,
I can watch your hands in action, your tongue too fast may run;
The lectures you deliver may be very wise and true,
But I'd rather get my lessons by observing what you do;
I may not understand the high advice you give,
But there's no misunderstanding how you act and how you live.

— *Author Unknown*

THE PREACHER'S WIFE

You may think it quite an easy task,
    And just a pleasant life;
But really it takes a lot of grace
    To be a preacher's wife.
She's supposed to be a paragon
    Without a fault in view,
A saint when in the parsonage
    As well as in the pew.

Her home must be a small hotel
    For folks that chance to roam,
And yet have peace and harmony —
    The perfect preacher's home!
Whenever groups are called to meet,
    Her presence must be there,
And yet the members all agree
    She should live a life of prayer.

Though hearing people's burdens,
    Their grief both night and day,
She's supposed to spread but sunshine
    To those along the way.
She must lend a sympathetic ear
    To every tale of woe,
And then forget about it,
    Lest it to others go.

Her children must be models rare
    Of quietness and poise,
But still stay on the level
    With other girls and boys.
You may think it quite an easy task,
    And just a pleasant life,
But really it takes a lot of grace
    To be a preacher's wife!

— *Author Unknown*

WELCOME TO MY HEART

O Saviour, welcome to my heart;
    Possess Thy humble throne;
Bid every rival, Lord, depart,
    And reign, O Christ, alone.

The world and Satan I forsake;
    To Thee I all resign;
My longing heart, O Saviour, take,
    And fill with love divine.

O may I never turn aside,
    Nor from Thy bosom flee;
Let nothing here my heart divide,
    I give it all to Thee.

— *Author Unknown*

BROKEN THINGS

Five broken loaves beside the sea and thousands fed,
As Thy hand, Lord, in breaking, blessed the bread.
Men would the throng in emptiness have sent away
Whose need was met with broken bread that day.

A broken vase of priceless worth rich fragrance shed
In ointment poured in worship on Thy head.
A lovely thing all shattered thus — *What waste,* they thought.
But Mary's deed of love Thy blessing brought.

A broken form upon the cross and souls set free.
Thy anguish there has paid the penalty —
Sin's awful price in riven flesh and pain and blood —
Redemption's cost, the broken Lamb of God.

Oh, break my life if it must be
No longer mine, I give it Thee.
Oh, break my will; the off'ring take.
For blessing comes when Thou dost break.

— *Bob Jones, Jr.*

ᐁ

CONSECRATION

A man I know has made an altar
Of his factory bench.
And one has turned the counter in his store
Into a place of sacrifice and holy ministry.
Another still has changed his office desk
Into a pulpit desk, from which to speak and write,
Transforming commonplace affairs
Into the business of the King.
A Martha in our midst has made
Her kitchen table a communion table.
A postman makes his daily round
A walk in the temple of God. . . .

To all of these each daily happening
Has come to be a whisper from the lips of God,
Each separate task a listening post,
And every common circumstance
A wayside shrine.

— *Edgar Tramp*

DEDICATION

Thou, whose unmeasured temple
 stands,
 Built over earth and sea,
Accept the walls that human hands
 Have raised, O God, to Thee!

Lord, from Thine inmost glory send,
 Within these courts to bide,
The peace that dwelleth without end
 Serenely by Thy side!

May erring minds that worship here
 Be taught the better way;
And they who mourn, and they who
 fear,
 Be strengthened as they pray.

May faith grow firm, and love grow
 warm,
 And pure devotion rise,
While round these hallowed walls the
 storm
 Of earthborn passion dies.

— *William Cullen Bryant*

PETER

Peter, outworn
And menaced by the sword,
Shook off the dust of Rome;
And, as he fled,
Met one with eager face,
Hastening cityward,
And, to his vast amaze,
It was the Lord.

"Lord, whither goest Thou?"
He cried, importunate;
And Christ replied,
 "Peter I suffer loss,
 I go to take thy place,
 To bear thy cross."

Then Peter bowed his head,
Discomforted;
Then at the Master's feet,
Found grace complete,
And courage, and new faith,
And turned, with Him
To death.

— *John Oxenham*

GIVE ME HARD TASKS

Give me the hard tasks, with strength that shall not fail;
 Conflict, with courage that shall never die!
Better the hill-path, climbing toward the sky,
 Than languid air and smooth sward of the vale!

Better to dare the wild wrath of the gale
 Than with furled sails in port forever lie!
Give me hard tasks, with strength that shall not fail;
 Conflict with courage that shall never die!

Not for a light load fitting shoulders frail,
 Not for an unearned victory I sigh;
Strong is the struggle that wins triumph high,
 Not without loss the hero shall prevail;
Give me hard tasks, with strength that shall not fail!

— *Author Unknown*

WHOLLY THE LORD'S

My whole tho' broken heart, O Lord,
  From henceforth shall be Thine;
And here I do my vow record —
  This hand, these words are mine;
All that I have, without reserve,
  I offer here to Thee;
Thy will and honor all shall serve
  That Thou bestow'st on me.

All that exceptions save I lose;
  All that I lose I save;
The treasures of Thy love I choose,
  And Thou art all I crave.
My God, Thou hast my heart and
    hand;
  I all to thee resign;
I'll ever to this covenant stand,
  Though flesh hereat repine.

I know that Thou wast willing first,
  And then drew my consent;
Having thus loved me at the worst
  Thou wilt not now repent.
Now I have quit all self-pretense,
  Take charge of what's thine own:
My life, my health, and my defense,
  Now lie on Thee alone.

— *Richard Baxter*

I WOULD BE A CHANNEL

Oh, I would be a channel, Lord,
  Deep-cleft and wide for thee,
That all the blessings thou dost send
  Might find a way through me.
My feet to do thy errands, Lord,
  My hands to serve thee well,
My heart to beat in tune with thine,
  My lips thy love to tell.

I would not be a vessel, Lord.
  No longer dare I pray
That thou wouldst fill me to the brim
  And keep me day by day;

Not even that I overflow
  And reach those close around,
But break me somewhere, Lord, and let
  Thy blessings onward bound.

Yes, I would be a channel, Lord,
  With naught to call my own,
For children, houses, gold and land
  Are chattels thou dost loan.
If thou shouldst give them me, I dare
  Not clasp them to my breast,
But ever let them onward flow;
  Thus, only, I am blessed.

Oh, I would be a channel, Lord,
  Where living waters flow,
For on the banks of such a stream
  The sweetest flowers grow.
I'm least of those who love thee, Lord,
  Yet used I long to be;
Then break my selfish will and let
  Thy blessings flow through me.

— *Myra Brooks Welch*

THY WILL

O Lord, fulfill Thy will,
Be the days few or many, good or ill:
Prolong them, to suffice
For offering up ourselves Thy sacrifice;
Shorten them if Thou wilt,
To make in righteousness an end of
    guilt.
Yea, they will not be long
To souls who learn to sing a patient
    song:
Yea, short they will not be
To souls on tiptoe to flee home to Thee.
O Lord, fulfill Thy will,
Make Thy will ours, and keep us pa-
    tient still,
Be the days few or many, good or ill.

— *Christina G. Rossetti*

YIELDED

Time was, I shrank from what was
        right,
    From fear of what was wrong;
I would not brave the sacred fight,
    Because the foe was strong.

But now I cast that finer sense
    And sorer shame aside;
Such dread of sin was indolence,
    Such aim at heaven was pride.

So when my Saviour calls, I rise
    And calmly do my best;
Leaving to Him, with silent eyes
    Of hope and fear, the rest.

I step, I mount where He has led;
    Men count my haltings o'er:
I know them; yet though self I dread,
    I love His precept more.

                — *John Henry Newman*

ॐ

SEARCHER OF HEARTS

Searcher of Hearts! — from mine erase
    All thoughts that should not be,
And in its deep recesses trace
    My gratitude to Thee!

Hearer of Prayer! — oh, guide aright
    Each word and deed of mine;
Life's battle teach me how to fight,
    And be the victory Thine.

Giver of All! — for every good
    In the Redeemer came —
For raiment, shelter and for food,
    I thank Thee in His Name.

Father and Son and Holy Ghost!
    Thou glorious Three in One!
Thou knowest best what I need most,
    And let Thy will be done.

                — *George Pope Morris*

LIFE

Life is a burden; bear it.
Life is a duty; dare it.
Life is a thorn crown; wear it.
Though it break your heart in twain,
Though the burden crush you down,
Close your lips and hide the pain;
First the cross and then the crown.
                — *Author Unknown*
ॐ

SURRENDER

Father, I know that all my life
    Is portioned out for me;
The changes that are sure to come
    I do not fear to see;
I ask Thee for a present mind
    Intent on pleasing Thee.

I ask Thee for a thoughtful love,
    Through constant watching wise,
To meet the glad with joyful smiles,
    And wipe the weeping eyes;
A heart at leisure from itself,
    To soothe and sympathize.

I ask Thee for the daily strength,
    To none that asked denied,
A mind to blend with outward life
    While keeping at Thy side;
Content to fill a little space,
    If Thou be glorified.

And if some things I do not ask
    Among my blessings be,
I'd have my spirit filled the more
    With grateful love to Thee;
More careful, not to serve Thee much,
    But please Thee perfectly.

In service which Thy love appoints
    There are no bonds for me;
My secret heart is taught the truth
    That makes Thy children free:
A life of self-renouncing love
    Is one of liberty.
                — *Anna L. Waring*

SURRENDER

It is Thy right to choose, my blessèd Lord;
  All that I have is Thine, and Thine alone;
Whatever Thou wilt ask, at Thy dear word,
  That will I give, to be indeed Thine own.

If Thou would'st take from out my weary life
  Something on which I lean for peace and rest,
Accept it, Lord; my heart will know no strife;
  I leave with Thee to judge the right and best.

Or, if Thou think'st my joys too much of earth,
  And Thou would'st have them found more oft in heaven;
Take from me, Lord, pleasures of lesser worth,
  And to my soul let holier joys be given.

And if, perchance, some precious gift of Thine,
  Needs to be lifted from my clinging love,
Take even this, and fix this heart of mine
  For e'er and only on Thyself above!

Ah, Lord, I trust Thee! Thou wilt never take
  Aught from my life but what my life should give;
Choose what Thou wilt; that choice I too will make,
  And in my death to self learn how to live.

—*Henry W. Frost*

✑

THE LANGUAGE JESUS SPOKE

I want to know the language Jesus spoke,
  Pure words, uncritical and ever kind;
At Jesus' voice the sleeping dead awoke,
  The sick were healed, and sight came to the blind.

I'd rather know the language of my King,
  Than perfectly to speak my native tongue,
I'd rather, by my words, glad tidings bring,
  Than win the applause and fame on fields far-flung.

Oh, Master, let me daily with Thee walk,
  The secret of Thy words to me confide;
Then let the world be conscious when I talk
  That I received instruction at Thy side.

—*Author Unknown*

DISAPPOINTMENT—HIS APPOINTMENT

"Disappointment — His *appointment*,"
    Change one letter, then I see
That the thwarting of my purpose
    Is God's better choice for me.
His appointment must be blessing,
    Tho' it may come in disguise,
For the end from the beginning
    Open to His wisdom lies.

"Disappointment — His *appointment*,"
    Whose? The Lord, who loves me
        best,
Understands and knows me fully,
    Who my faith and love would test;
For, like loving earthly parent,
    He rejoices when He knows
That His child accepts, *unquestioned*,
    All that from His wisdom flows.

"Disappointment — His *appointment*,"
    "No good thing will He withhold,"
From denials oft we gather
    Treasures of His love untold.
Well He knows each broken purpose
    Leads to fuller, deeper trust,
And the end of all His dealings
    Proves our God is wise and just.

"Disappointment — His *appointment*,"
    Lord, I take it, then, as such.
Like the clay in hands of potter,
    Yielding wholly to Thy touch.
All my life's plan is Thy moulding,
    Not one single choice be mine;
Let me answer, unrepining —
    Father, "Not my will, but Thine."

                        — *Edith Lillian Young*

FOLLOWING

O Jesus, do Thou lead me
    By Thy good hand of love,
Through life's long, toilsome journey
    To Thy blest home above;

Dark is the way and dreary,
    My heart is full of fear,
But I shall never falter
    If only Thou art near.

Choose Thou my path, O Jesus,
    If smooth or wholly rough;
To walk in Thy dear footsteps
    Will ever be enough;
My strength will be in seeing
    Thyself, my Lord and Friend;
With Thee beside, before me,
    I'll follow to the end.

And when the journey's over
    And heaven is reached at last,
O Jesus, grant restoring
    From all the weary past;
Through ages long unfolding,
    Amidst the holy blest,
May I find in Thy presence
    Eternal peace and rest.

Then shall I know Thy guidance
    Through life's bewildering maze;
Then shall I know Thy purpose
    Of dark and suffering days;
And then shall I adore Thee,
    With all the saints above,
And praise Thee, blessèd Jesus,
    Thou God of changeless love.

                        — *Henry W. Frost*

TRUE WISDOM

True wisdom is in leaning
    On Jesus Christ, our Lord;
True wisdom is in trusting
    His own life-giving word;
True wisdom is in living
    Near Jesus every day;
True wisdom is in walking
    Where He shall lead the way.

                        — *Author Unknown*

PRESSURE

Pressed out of measure and pressed to all length;
Pressed so intensely it seems, beyond strength;
Pressed in the body and pressed in the soul,
Pressed in the mind till the dark surges roll.
Pressure by foes, and a pressure from friends.
Pressure on pressure, till life nearly ends.

Pressed into knowing no helper but God;
Pressed into loving the staff and the rod.
Pressed into liberty where nothing clings;
Pressed into faith for impossible things.
Pressed into living a life in the Lord,
Pressed into living a Christ-life outpoured.

— *Author Unknown*

THE OLD LAMP

A lamp once hung in an ancient town
  At the corner of a street
Where the wind was keen and the
    way was dark
And the rain would often beat;
And all night long its light would
    shine
  To guide the travelers' feet.

The lamp was plain, and rough and
    old
  As it weathered the storm alone;
And it wasn't a thing of beauty
  That a man would care to own;
But no one thought what the lantern
    was —
  'Twas the light that within it shone.

That lamp is the frame of a human
    heart
Who seeks, tho' it's worn and tried,
To shine for God, and to show the
    Road
  To souls who have gone aside!
You are the lantern—a thing of naught;
  But Christ is the Light inside!

— *Author Unknown*

CAPTURED

Hast thou heard Him, seen Him,
    known Him,
  Is not thine a captured heart?
Chief among ten thousands own Him,
  Joyful choose the better part.

What has stripped the seeming beauty
  From the idols of the earth?
Not a sense of right or duty,
  But the sight of peerless worth.

Not the crushing of those idols,
  With its bitter void and smart;
But the beaming of His beauty,
  The unveiling of His heart!

'Tis that look that melted Peter,
  'Tis that Face that Stephen saw,
'Tis that Heart that wept with Mary
  Can alone from idols draw.

Draw and win and fill completely,
  Till the cup o'erflow the brim;
What have we to do with idols
  Who have companied with Him?

— *Author Unknown*

COME, SAVIOUR!

Come, Saviour, Jesus from above!
  Assist me with Thy heavenly grace,
Empty my heart of earthly love,
  And for Thyself prepare the place.

O let Thy sacred presence fill,
  And set my longing spirit free!
Which pants to have no other will,
  But day and night to feast on Thee.

While in this region here below,
  No other good will I pursue:
I'll bid this world of noise and show,
  With all its glittering snares, adieu!

That path with humble speed I'll seek,
  In which my Saviour's footsteps
    shine;
Nor will I hear, nor will I speak,
  Of any other love but Thine.

Henceforth may no profane delight
  Divide this consecrated soul;
Possess it, Thou who hast the right,
  As Lord and Master of the whole.

                  — *Antoinette Bourignon*

👁️

LORD, SHOW ME

Lord, show me the thing that stands in
    the way,
  The stone that is under the wheel,
Reveal the idol to be cast down,
  Lord, hear me as I kneel.

And, Lord, if I have not the strength
    to cut off
  The part that offendeth me,
Nor have I the courage to overthrow
  The thing I love more than Thee:

Oh, cripple the limb with a touch of
    Thy hand!
  To bear it give me grace,
And when I awake tomorrow morn
  May the idol be on its face.

But more than this I would ask, O
    Lord,
  Grind it to powder fine,
Then fill up my heart with Thy won-
    drous love,
  Making my face to shine.

                  — *Author Unknown*

👁️

THE HEAVENLY VISION

'Twas on the Isle of Patmos,
  Forsaken and alone,
That John beheld Heav'n's open door,
  And God's eternal throne.

The rocky cliffs about him,
  The chains that bound him there
Could not restrain his spirit's flight,
  Or dim that vision fair.

How oft has God in mercy,
  In times of dire distress,
Revealed to us some precious truth
  Our lonely hearts to bless!

The hour of deepest darkness
  Was oft the open door
To hidden heights and depths of love
  Unknown to us before.

Lord, help us follow gladly
  The pathway Thou dost show,
That as we yield our lives to Thee
  Thy fulness we may know.

                  — *Avis B. Christiansen*

The Last Hour

If I were told that I must die to-morrow,
    That the next sun
Which sinks should bear me past all fear and sorrow
    For any one,
All the fight fought, all the short journey through,
    What should I do?

I do not think that I should shrink or falter,
    But just go on,
Doing my work, nor change, nor seek to alter
    Aught that is gone;
But rise and move, and love and smile and pray
    For one more day.

And lying down at night for a last sleeping,
    Say in that ear
Which hearkens ever: "Lord, within thy keeping,
    How should I fear?
And when to-morrow brings thee nearer still,
    Do thou thy will."

I might not sleep for awe; but peaceful, tender,
    My soul would lie
All night long; and when the morning splendor
    Flushed o'er the sky,
I think that I could smile, — could calmly say,
    "It is his day."

But if a wondrous hand from the blue yonder
    Held out a scroll,
On which my life was writ, and I with wonder
    Beheld unroll
To a long century's end its mystic clew,
    What should I do?

What *could* I do, O blessed Guide and Master,
    Other than this:
Still to go on as now, not slower, faster,
    Nor fear to miss
The road, although so very long it be,
    While led by thee?

Step after step, feeling thee close beside me,
        Although unseen,
Thro' thorns, thro' flowers, whether the tempest hide thee,
        Or heavens serene,
Assured thy faithfulness cannot betray,
        Thy love decay.

I may not know, my God, no hand revealeth
        Thy counsels wise;
Along the path a deepening shadow stealeth,
        No voice replies
To all my questioning thought, the time to tell,
        And it is well.

Let me keep on, abiding and unfearing
        Thy will always,
Through a long century's ripening fruition,
        Or a short day's;
Thou canst not come too soon; and I can wait,
        If thou come late.

                        — *Susan Coolidge*

∾

A Few More Years Shall Roll

A few more years shall roll,
A few more seasons come,
And we shall be with those that rest
Asleep within the tomb.
Then, O my Lord, prepare
My soul for that great day;
Oh, wash me in thy precious blood,
And take my sins away.

A few more suns shall set
O'er these dark hills of time,
And we shall be where suns are not,
A far serener clime:
Then, O my Lord, prepare
My soul for that blest day;
Oh, wash me in thy precious blood,
And take my sins away.

A few more storms shall beat
On this wild rocky shore,
And we shall be where tempests cease,
And surges swell no more:

Then, O my Lord, prepare
My soul for that calm day;
Oh, wash me in thy precious blood,
And take my sins away.

A few more struggles here,
A few more partings o'er,
A few more toils, a few more tears,
And we shall weep no more:
Then, O my Lord, prepare
My soul for that bright day;
Oh, wash me in thy precious blood,
And take my sins away.

'Tis but a little while
And he shall come again,
Who died that we might live, who lives
That we with him may reign:
Then, O my Lord, prepare
My soul for that glad day;
Oh, wash me in thy precious blood,
And take my sins away. Amen.

                        — *Horatius Bonar*

THE SLEEP

Of all the thoughts of God that are
Borne inward unto souls afar,
Along the Psalmist's music deep,
Now tell me if that any is,
For gift or grace, surpassing this —
"He giveth *His* belovèd sleep"?

What would we give to our beloved?
The hero's heart, to be unmoved,
The poet's star-tuned harp, to sweep,
The patriot's voice, to teach and rouse,
The monarch's crown, to light the
brows? —
"He giveth *His* belovèd sleep."

What do we give to our beloved?
A little faith all undisproved,
A little dust to overweep,
And bitter memories to make
The whole earth blasted for our sake.
"He giveth *His* belovèd sleep."

"Sleep soft, beloved!" we sometimes
say,
But have no tune to charm away
Sad dreams that thro' the eyelids creep;
But never doleful dream again
Shall break the happy slumber when
"He giveth *His* belovèd sleep."

O earth, so full of dreary noises!
O men, with wailing in your voices!
O delvèd gold, the wailers heap!
O strife, O curse, that o'er it fall!
God strikes a silence through you all,
And "giveth *His* belovèd sleep."

His dews drop mutely on the hill,
His cloud above it saileth still,
Though on its slope men sow and reap.
More softly than the dew is shed,
Or cloud is floated overhead,
"He giveth *His* belovèd sleep."

For me, my heart that erst did go
Most like a tired child at a show,

That sees through tears the mummers
leap,
Would now its wearied vision close,
Would childlike on *His* love repose,
Who "giveth *His* belovèd sleep!"

And, friends, dear friends, — when it
shall be
That this low breath is gone from me,
And round my bier ye come to weep,
Let one, most loving of you all,
Say, "Not a tear must o'er her fall —
'He giveth *His* belovèd sleep.'"

— *Elizabeth Barrett Browning*

ETERNITY

Has it ever occurred to you that the word "eternity" is found only once in the Bible? Isaiah 57:15. Yet it is a word so often used by Christians everywhere.

How long sometimes a day appears,
And weeks, how long are they?
They move as if the months and years
Would never pass away;
But months and years are passing by,
And soon must all be gone,
Day by day as the moments fly,
Eternity comes on,
All these must have an end,
Eternity has none.
It will always have as long to run,
As when it first begun.

Eternity is unoriginated, beginningless, endless, measureless, imperishable, indescribable and boundless.

To think when heaven and earth are
fled,
And times and seasons o'er
When all that can die, shall be dead;
That I shall die no more;
Oh, what shall then my portion be,
Where shall I spend eternity?

— *Author Unknown*

BLESSED ARE THEY THAT MOURN

Oh, deem not they are blest alone
　Whose lives a peaceful tenor keep;
The Power who pities man, has shown
　A blessing for the eyes that weep.

The light of smiles shall fill again
　The lids that overflow with tears;
And weary hours of woe and pain
　Are promises of happier years.

There is a day of sunny rest
　For every dark and troubled night;
And grief may bide an evening guest,
　But joy shall come with early light.

And thou, who o'er thy friend's low
　　bier
Dost shed the bitter drops like rain,
Hope that a brighter, happier sphere
　Will give him to thy arms again.

Nor let the good man's trust depart,
　Tho' life its common gifts deny,—
Tho' with a pierced and bleeding heart,
　And spurned of men, he goes to die.

For God hath marked each sorrowing
　　day
And numbered every secret tear,
And heaven's long age of bliss shall
　　pay
For all his children suffer here.

　　　　— *William Cullen Bryant*

&

THE DAY IS DONE

The day is done, and the darkness
　Falls from the wings of Night,
As a feather is wafted downward
　From an eagle in his flight.

I see the light of the village
　Gleam thro' the rain and the mist,
And a feeling of sadness comes o'er me
　That my soul cannot resist.

A feeling of sadness and longing,
　That is not akin to pain,
And resembles sorrow only
　As the mist resembles the rain.

Come, read to me some poem,
　Some simple and heartfelt lay,
That shall soothe this restless feeling,
　And banish the thoughts of day.

Such songs have power to quiet
　The restless pulse of care,
And come like the benediction
　That follows after prayer.

Then read from the treasured volume
　The poem of thy choice,
And lend to the rhyme of the poet
　The beauty of thy voice.

And the night shall be filled with
　　music,
　And the cares, that infest the day,
Shall fold their tents, like the Arabs,
　And as silently steal away.
　　　　— *Henry Wadsworth Longfellow*
&

"ONE LITTLE ROSE . . ."

I would rather have one little rose
　From the garden of a friend,
Than to have the choicest flowers
　When my stay on earth must end.
I would rather have a pleasant word
　In kindness said to me
Than flattery when my heart is still
　And this life has ceased to be.
I would rather have a loving smile
　From friends I know are true
Than tears shed around my casket
　When this world I bid adieu.
Bring me all the flowers today,
　Whether pink or white, or red.
I'd rather have one blossom now
　Than a truck load when I'm dead.
　　　　— *Author Unknown*

I Would Not Live Alway

I would not live alway — live alway below!
Oh no, I'll not linger when bidden to go:
The days of our pilgrimage granted us here
Are enough for life's woes, full enough for its cheer:
Would I shrink from the path which the prophets of God,
Apostles, and martyrs, so joyfully trod?
Like a spirit unblest, o'er the earth would I roam,
While brethren and friends are all hastening home?

I would not live alway — I ask not to stay
Where storm after storm rises dark o'er the way;
Where seeking for rest we but hover around,
Like the patriarch's bird, and no resting is found;
Where Hope, when she paints her gay bow in the air,
Leaves its brilliance to fade in the night of despair,
And Joy's fleeting angel ne'er sheds a glad ray,
Save the gleam of the plumage that bears him away.

I would not live alway — thus fettered by sin,
Temptation without and corruption within;
In a moment of strength if I sever the chain,
Scarce the victory is mine, ere I'm captive again;
E'en the rapture of pardon is mingled with fears,
And the cup of thanksgiving with penitent tears:
The festival trump calls for jubilant songs,
But my spirit her own *miserere* prolongs.

I would not live alway — no, welcome the tomb!
Since Jesus hath lain there, I dread not its gloom;
Where he deigned to sleep, I'll too bow my head,
All peaceful to slumber on that hallowed bed.
Then the glorious daybreak, to follow that night,
The orient gleam of the angels of light,
With their clarion call for the sleepers to rise
And chant forth their matins, away to the skies.

Who, who would live alway — away from his God,
Away from yon heaven, that blissful abode
Where the rivers of pleasure flow o'er the bright plains,
And the noontide of glory eternally reigns;
Where the saints of all ages in harmony meet,
Their Saviour and brethren transported to greet,
While the songs of salvation exultingly roll,
And the smile of the Lord is the feast of the soul?

That heavenly music! what is it I hear?
The notes of the harpers ring sweet in mine ear!
And see, soft unfolding those portals of gold,
The King all arrayed in his beauty behold!
Oh give me, oh give me the wings of a dove,
To adore him, be near him, enrapt with his love;
I but wait for the summons, I list for the word —
Alleluia — Amen — evermore with the Lord.

— *William August Muhlenberg*

ⱷ

Up-Hill

Does the road wind up-hill all the way?
    Yes, to the very end.
Will the day's journey take the whole long day?
    From morn to night, my friend.

But is there for the night a resting-place?
    A roof for when the slow dark hours begin.
May not the darkness hide it from my face?
    You cannot miss that inn.

Shall I meet other wayfarers at night?
    Those who have gone before.
Then must I knock, or call when just in sight?
    They will not keep you standing at the door.

Shall I find comfort, travel-sore and weak?
    Of labor you shall find the sum.
Will there be beds for me and all who seek?
    Yea, beds for all who come.

— *Christina Rossetti*

ⱷ

From Thanatopsis

So live, that when thy summons comes to join
The innumerable caravan, which moves
To that mysterious realm, where each shall take
His chamber in the silent halls of death,
Thou go not, like the quarry-slave at night,
Scourged to his dungeon, but, sustained and soothed
By an unfaltering trust, approach thy grave,
Like one who wraps the drapery of his couch
About him, and lies down to pleasant dreams.

— *William Cullen Bryant*

No, No, It Is Not Dying

No, no, it is not dying
  To go unto our God,
This gloomy earth forsaking,
Our journey homeward taking
  Along the starry road.

No, no, it's not dying
  To hear this gracious word,
"Receive a Father's blessing,
Forevermore possessing
  The favor of thy Lord."

No, no, it is not dying
  The Shepherd's voice to know;
His sheep he ever leadeth,
His peaceful flock he feedeth,
  Where living pastures grow.

No, no, it is not dying
  To wear a lordly crown;
Among God's people dwelling,
The glorious triumph swelling
  Of him whose sway we own.

O no, this is not dying,
  Thou Saviour of mankind!
There, streams of love are flowing,
No hindrance ever knowing;
  Here, drops alone we find.

     — *César Malan*

What Is Death?

What is death? Oh, what is death?
  'Tis the snapping of the chain —
    'Tis the breaking of the bowl —
  'Tis relief from ev'ry pain —
    'Tis freedom to the soul —
'Tis the setting of the sun
  To rise again tomorrow,
A brighter course to run,
  Nor sink again to sorrow.
Such is death! Yes, such is death!

What is death? Oh! what is death?
  'Tis slumber to the weary —
  'Tis rest to the forlorn —
  'Tis shelter to the dreary —
  'Tis peace amid the storm —
  'Tis the entrance to our home —
'Tis the passage to that God
Who bids His children come,
  When their weary course is trod.
Such is death! Yes, such is death!

     — *Author Unknown*

"Tired"

"Tired!" Oh yes! so tired, dear.
  The day has been very long;
But shadowy gloaming draweth near.
  'Tis time for the even song,
I'm ready to go to rest at last,
  Ready to say "Good night":
The sunset glory darkens fast,
  To-morrow will bring me light.

It has seemed so long since morning-
    tide,
  And I have been left so lone,
Young smiling faces thronged my side,
  When the early sunlight shone;
But they grew tired long ago,
  And I saw them sink to rest,
With folded hands and brows of snow,
  On the green earth's mother-breast.

Sing once again, "Abide with me,"
  That sweetest evening hymn;
And now "Good night!" I cannot see,
  The light has grown so dim;
"Tired!" Ah, yes, so tired, dear,
  I shall soundly sleep to-night,
With never a dream, and never a fear
  To wake in the morning light.

     — *Helen Burnside*

DROPPING DOWN THE RIVER

Dropping down the troubled river,
  To the tranquil, tranquil shore;
Dropping down the misty river,
Time's willow-shaded river,
  To the spring-embossed shore;
Where the sweet light shineth ever,
And the sun goes down no more;
  O wondrous, wondrous shore!

Dropping down the winding river,
  To the wide and welcome sea;
Dropping down the narrow river,
Man's weary, wayward river,
  To the blue and ample sea;
Where no tempest wrecketh ever,
Where the sky is fair and free;
  O joyous, joyous sea!

Dropping down the noisy river,
  To our peaceful, peaceful home;
Dropping down the turbid river,
Earth's bustling, crowded river,
  To our gentle, gentle home:
Where the rough roar riseth never,
And the vexings cannot come,
  O loved and longed-for home!

Dropping down the eddying river,
  With a Helmsman true and tried;
Dropping down the perilous river,
Mortality's dark river,
  With a sure and heavenly Guide;
Even him, who to deliver
My soul from death hath died;
  O Helmsman true and tried!

Dropping down the rapid river,
  To the dear and deathless land;
Dropping down the well-known river,
Life's swollen and rushing river,
  To the resurrection-land;
Where the living live forever,
And the dead have joined the band,
In that fair and blessed land!

— *Horatius Bonar*

IN SORROW

Gently, Lord, oh, gently lead us,
  Pilgrims in this vale of tears,
Through the trials yet decreed us,
  Till our last great change appears.
When temptation's darts assail us,
  When in devious paths we stray,
Let thy goodness never fail us,
  Lead us in thy perfect way.

In the hour of pain and anguish,
  In the hour when death draws near,
Suffer not our hearts to languish,
  Suffer not our souls to fear;
And, when mortal life is ended,
  Bid us in thine arms to rest,
Till, by angel bands attended,
  We awake among the blest.

— *Thomas Hastings*

THE DYING CHRISTIAN TO HIS SOUL

Vital spark of heavenly flame,
Quit, oh, quit this mortal frame.
Trembling, hoping, lingering, flying,
Oh the pain, the bliss of dying!
Cease, fond nature, cease thy strife,
And let me languish into life!

Hark! they whisper; angels say,—
"Sister spirit, come away!"
What is this absorbs me quite,
Steals my senses, shuts my sight,—
Drowns my spirit, draws my breath?
Tell me, my soul, can this be death?

The world recedes; it disappears!
Heaven opens on my eyes! my ears
  With sounds seraphic ring!
Lend, lend your wings! I mount! I fly!
O grave! where is thy victory?
  O death! where is thy sting?

— *Alexander Pope*

AFRAID? OF WHAT?

Afraid? Of what?
To feel the spirit's glad release?
To pass from pain to perfect peace,
The strife and strain of life to cease?
Afraid — of that?

Afraid? Of what?
Afraid to see the Saviour's face,
To hear His welcome, and to trace
The glory gleam from wounds of grace?
Afraid — of that?

Afraid? Of what?
A flash, a crash, a piercèd heart;
Darkness, light, O Heaven's art;
A wound of His a counterpart:
Afraid — of that?

Afraid? Of what?
To enter into Heaven's rest,
And yet to serve the Master blest,
From service good to service best?
Afraid — of that?

Afraid? Of what?
To do by death what life could not —
Baptize with blood a stony plot,
Till souls shall blossom from the spot?
Afraid — of that?

— *E. H. Hamilton*

WHY SHOULD WE WEEP?

Why should we weep for those who
   sleep?
Our God doth comfort give;
Above the night, in realms of light
Our dead in Christ still live:
Our God is God not of the dead
   Who cease to see and know,
He is the God of saints who live
   Where joys forever flow.

Our dead are blest, from toil they rest,
   Beyond all pain and care;
No tear, no sigh, no wailing cry
   Can touch their spirits there:
In safe retreat, in joy replete,
   They dwell in peace at home;
They always wait, at heaven's gate,
   The hour that we shall come.

Our Lord hath said, "I'll bring your
   dead
When I come down the skies";
Then, from the gloom, of dismal tomb,
   Their bodies shall arise:
Up in the air, some place up there
   We'll all be gathered home;
With Christ to dwell, where all is well,
   Where death can never come.

— *R. E. Neighbour*

CAN THIS BE DEATH?

Can this be death —
   To be released from fear and sorrow,
      From sickness, weariness and pain?
   To be removed from sin's enslavement,
      From Satan's influence and domain?

Can this be death —
   To be set free from my sin nature,
      From evil bent to do the wrong?
   To be set free from inclinations
      That would rob me of my song?

Can this be death —
  To be presented in His presence,
  The One who loves me evermore?
To be accepted in the fullness
  Of Christ whom I adore?

Can this be death —
  To be escorted by the angels
  To my home prepared above?
To be established in the dwelling
  That is furnished by His love?

Can this be death —
  To know complete fulfillment
  As I look upon His face?
To feast upon the glories
  And the riches of His grace?

No, this is *life* —
  With all that it can offer,
  It is joy that overflows!
It is peace that knows no measure,
  It is vict'ry o'er my foes!

— *Martin Wedge*

There Is No Death

There is a plan far greater than the plan you know;
  There is a landscape broader than the one you see;
  There is a haven where storm-tossed souls may go;
  You call it death — we, immortality.

You call it death, this seeming endless sleep;
  We call it birth, the soul at last set free;
  'Tis hampered not by time or space — you weep;
  Why weep at death? 'Tis immortality.

Farewell, dear voyager, 'twill not be long;
  Your work is done, now may peace rest with thee;
Your kindly thoughts and deeds — they will live on;
  This is not death — 'tis immortality.

Farewell, dear voyager, the river winds and turns;
  The cadence of your song wafts near to me;
And now you know the thing that all men learn:
  There is no death — there's immortality.

— *Author Unknown*

PROSPICE

Fear death? — to feel the fog in my throat,
　The mist in my face,
When the snows begin, and the blasts denote
　I am nearing the place,
The power of the night, the press of the storm,
　The post of the foe;
Where he stands, the Arch Fear in a visible form,
　Yet the strong man must go:
For the journey is done and the summit attained,
　And the barriers fall,
Though a battle's to fight ere the guerdon be gained,
　The reward of it all.
I was ever a fighter, so — one fight more,
　The best and the last!
I would hate that death bandaged my eyes, and forbore,
　And bade me creep past.
No! let me taste the whole of it, fare like my peers
　The heroes of old,
Bear the brunt in a minute pay glad life's arrears
　Of pain, darkness and cold.
For sudden the worst turns the best to the brave,
　The black minute's at end,
And the elements' rage, the fiend-voices that rave,
　Shall dwindle, shall blend,
Shall change, shall become first a peace, then a joy,
　Then a light, then thy breast,
O thou soul of my soul! I shall clasp thee again,
　And with God be the rest.

— Robert Browning

WEARY IN WELL-DOING

I would have gone; God bade me stay:
　I would have worked; God bade me
　　rest.
He broke my will from day to day,
　He read my yearnings unexpressed,
　　And said them nay.

Now I would stay; God bids me go:
　Now I would rest; God bids me
　　work.
He breaks my heart, tossed to and fro,

My soul is wrung with doubts that
　　lurk
　And vex it so.

I go, Lord, where thou sendest me;
　Day after day I plod and moil:
But, Christ, my God, when will it be
　That I may let alone my toil,
　　And rest in thee?

— Christina Rossetti

What Then?

After the joys of earth,
After the songs of mirth,
After the hours of light,
After its dreams so bright —
    What then?

Only an empty name,
Only a weary frame,
Only a conscious smart,
Only an aching heart.

After this empty name,
After this weary frame,
After this conscious smart,
After this aching heart —
    What then?

Only a sad farewell,
To a world loved too well,
After this silent bed
With the forgotten dead —
    What then?

Oh, then the judgment throne!
Oh, then the last hope gone!
Then all the woes that dwell
In an eternal hell.

After the Christian's tears,
After his fights and fears,
After his weary cross,
"All things below but loss" —
    What then?

Oh, then a holy calm,
Resting on Jesus' arm,
Oh, then a deeper love
For the pure home above.

After this holy calm,
Resting on Jesus arm,
After this deepened love
For the pure home above —
    What then?

Oh, then hard work for Him
Immortal souls to win;

Then Jesus' presence near,
Death's darkest hour to cheer —
    What then?

And then the work is done,
When the last soul is won,
When Jesus' love and power,
Have cheered the dying hour —
    What then?

Oh, then the crown is given!
Oh, then the rest in Heaven:
Then endless life in endless day,
While sin and death have passed away.

      — Author Unknown

ॐ

What Is Death?

It is not death to die —
    To leave this weary road,
And, 'mid the brotherhood on high,
    To be at home with God.

It is not death to close
    The eye long dimmed by tears,
And wake in glorious repose
    To spend eternal years.

It is not death to bear
    The wrench that sets us free
From dungeon chain, to breathe the air
    Of boundless liberty.

It is not death to fling
    Aside this sinful dust,
And rise on strong exulting wing
    To live among the just.

Jesus, thou Prince of life,
    Thy chosen cannot die!
Like thee they conquer in the strife
    To reign with thee on high.

      — César Malan

A World Without Pain

Man is prone to hope and pray
That God will take all pain away
And bring to him a blest relief
From ills that mar a perfect peace.

Freed from suffering evermore
He feels his spirit then could soar
Unhampered, toward his highest goal
With satisfaction for his soul.

Suppose a world devoid of pain!
Could tender pity ever reign?
Would man grow in grace and power
To endure well his trying hour?

Suppose a sky that's always blue!
Would there be a rainbow hue,
And valiant smiles in spite of loss,
Or victory after Calvary's cross?

— *Emily May Young*

Lord, Dismiss Us

Lord, dismiss us with thy blessing,
  Fill our hearts with joy and peace;
Let us each, thy love possessing,
    Triumph in redeeming grace:
      Oh, refresh us!
Travelling through this wilderness.

Thanks we give, and adoration,
  For thy gospel's joyful sound;
May the fruits of thy salvation
  In our hearts and lives abound:
    Ever faithful
To the truth may we be found!

So, whene'er the signal's given
  Us from earth to call away;
Borne on angels' wings to heaven,
  Glad the summons to obey,
    May we ever
Rise, and reign in endless day!

— *John Fawcett* or *Walter Shirley*

How Blest the Righteous

How blest the righteous when he dies!
When sinks a weary soul to rest,
How mildly beam the closing eyes,
How gently heaves th' expiring breast!

So fades a summer cloud away;
So sinks the gale when storms are o'er;
So gently shuts the eye of day;
So dies a wave along the shore.

A holy quiet reigns around,
A calm which life nor death destroys;
And naught disturbs that peace pro-
    found
Which his unfettered soul enjoys.

Life's labor done, as sinks the clay,
Light from its load the spirit flies,
While heaven and earth combine to
    say,
"How blest the righteous when he
    dies!"

— *Anna Letitia Barbauld*

Three Characteristic Epitaphs

Atheist

I was not, and I was conceived;
I lived, and did a little work;
I am not, and I grieve not.

Pantheist

O drop of spray cast from the Infinite,
I hung an instant there, and threw my
    ray
To make the rainbow. A microcosm I,
Reflecting all. Then back I fell again:
And tho' I perished not, I was no more.

Christian

God willed: I was. What He had
    planned I wrought,
That done, He called, and now I dwell
  with Him.

— *Author Unknown*

EVENING HYMN

Interval of grateful shade,
Welcome to my weary head!
Welcome slumbers to mine eyes,
Tired with glaring vanities!
My great Master still allows
Needful periods of repose:
By my Heavenly Father blest,
Thus I give my power to rest;
Heavenly Father, gracious name!
Night and day his love the same;
Far be each suspicious thought,
Every anxious care forgot;
Thou, my ever-bounteous God,
Crownest my days with various good:
Thy kind eye, that cannot sleep
These defenceless hours shall keep;
Blest vicissitude to me!
Day and night I'm still with thee.

What though downy slumbers flee,
Strangers to my couch and me?
Sleepless well I know to rest,
Lodged within my Father's breast.
While the empress of the night
Scatters mild her silver light;
While the vivid planets stray
Various through their mystic way;
While the stars unnumbered roll
Round the ever-constant pole;
Far above these spangled skies,
All my soul to God shall rise;
Midst the silence of the night
Mingling with those angels bright,
Whose harmonious voices raise
Ceaseless love and ceaseless praise:
Through the throng his gentle ear
Shall my tuneless accents hear:
From on high doth he impart
Secret comfort to my heart.
He in these serenest hours
Guides my intellectual powers,
And his spirit doth diffuse,
Sweeter far than midnight dews;
Lifting all my thoughts above,

On the wings of faith and love.
Blest alternative to me,
Thus to sleep, or wake, with thee!

What if death my sleep invade?
Should I be of death afraid?
Whilst encircled by thine arm,
Death may strike, but cannot harm.
What if beams of opening day
Shine around my breathless clay?
Brighter visions from on high
Shall regale my mental eye;
Tender friends awhile may mourn
Me from their embraces torn;
Dearer, better friends I have
In the realms beyond the grave.
See the guardian angels nigh
Wait to waft my soul on high!
See the golden gates displayed!
See the crown to grace my head!
See a flood of sacred light,
Which no more shall yield to night.
Transitory world, farewell!
Jesus calls, with him to dwell.
With thy heavenly presence blest,
Death is life, and labor rest.
Welcome sleep or death to me,
Still secure, for still with thee.

— *Philip Doddridge*

ᘒ

THE CONCLUSION

Even such is time, that takes in trust
    Our youth, our joys, our all we have,
And pays us but with earth and dust;
    Who in the dark and silent grave,
When we have wander'd all our ways,
Shuts up the story of our days:
But from this earth, this grave, this
        dust,
My God shall raise me up, I trust.

— *Sir Walter Raleigh*

DECLINING DAYS

Why do I sigh to find
Life's evening shadows gathering round my way?
The keen eye dimming, and the buoyant mind
  Unhinging day by day?

Is it the natural dread
Of that stern lot, which all who live must see?
The worm, the clay, the dark and narrow bed,—
  Have these such awe for me?

Can I not summon pride
To fold my decent mantle round my breast,
And lay me down, at nature's eventide,
  Calm to my dreamless rest?

As nears my soul the verge
Of this dim continent of woe and crime,
Shrinks she to hear eternity's long surge
  Break on the shores of time?

Asks she how she shall fare
When conscience stands before the Judge's throne,
And gives her record in, and all shall there
  Know as they all are known?

A solemn scene and time,—
And well may nature quail to feel them near,—
But grace in feeble breasts can work sublime,
  And faith o'ermaster fear.

Hark! from that throne comes down
A voice which strength to sinking souls can give:
That voice all judgment's thunders cannot drown;
  "Believe," it cries, "and live!"

Weak, sinful as I am,
That still small voice forbids me to despond;
Faith clings for refuge to the bleeding Lamb,
  Nor dreads the gloom beyond.

'Tis not then earth's delights
From which my spirit feels so loath to part;
Nor the dim future's solemn sounds or sights
  That press so on my heart.

No! 'tis the thought that I —
My lamp so low, my sun so nearly set,

Have lived so useless, so unmissed should die:
    'Tis this I now regret.

I would not be the wave
That swells and ripples up to yonder shore;
That drives impulsive on, the wild wind's slave,
    And breaks, and is no more!

I would not be the breeze,
That murmurs by me in its viewless play,
Bends the light grass, and flutters in the trees,
    And sighs and flits away.

No! not like wave or wind
Be my career across the earthly scene;
To come and go, and leave no trace behind
    To say that I have been.

I want not vulgar fame,—
I seek not to survive in brass or stone;
Hearts may not kindle when they hear my name,
    Nor tears my value own.

But might I leave behind
Some blessing for my fellows, some fair trust
To guide, to cheer, to elevate my kind
    When I was in the dust!

Within my narrow bed
Might I not wholly mute or useless be;
But hope that they, who trampled o'er my head,
    Drew still some good from me!

Might my poor lyre but give
Some simple strain, some spirit-moving lay;
Some sparklet of the soul, that still might live
    When I was passed to clay!

Might verse of mine inspire
One virtuous aim, one high resolve impart;
Light in one drooping soul a hallowed fire,
    Or bind one broken heart!

Death would be sweeter then,
More calm my slumber 'neath the silent sod;
Might I thus live to bless my fellow-men,
    Or glorify my God!

Why do we ever lose,
As judgment ripens, our diviner powers?

Why do we only learn our gifts to use
When they no more are ours?

O thou! whose touch can lend
Life to the dead, thy quickening grace supply,
And grant me, swanlike, my last breath to spend
In song that may not die!

— Henry Francis Lyte

ᐬᑌᕆ

WHEN ALL IS DONE

When all is done, and my last word is said,
And ye who loved me murmur, "He is dead,"
Let no one weep for fear that I should know,
And sorrow too that ye should sorrow so.

When all is done and in the oozing clay,
Ye lay this cast-off hull of mine away,
Pray not for me, for, after long despair,
The quiet of the grave will be a prayer.

For I have suffered loss and grievous pain,
The hurts of hatred and the world's disdain,
And wounds so deep that love, well-tried and pure,
Had not the pow'r to ease them or to cure.

When all is done, say not my day is o'er,
And that thro' night I seek a dimmer shore:
Say rather that my morn has just begun,—
I greet the dawn and not a setting sun,
When all is done.

— Paul Laurence Dunbar

ᐬᑌᕆ

From RESIGNATION

There is no Death. What seems so is transition;
This life of mortal breath
Is but the suburb of the life elysian,
Whose portal we call Death.

She is not dead,— the child of our affection,—
But gone unto that school
Where she no longer needs our poor protection,
And Christ Himself doth rule.

— Henry Wadsworth Longfellow

GROW OLD ALONG WITH ME

Grow old along with me!
The best is yet to be,
The last of life, for which the first was
    made:
Our times are in His hand
Who saith, "A whole I planned,
Youth shows but half; trust God:
See all, nor be afraid!"

Not for such hopes and fears
Annulling youth's brief years,
Do I demonstrate: folly wide the mark!
Rather I prize the doubt
Low kinds exist without,
Finished and finite clods, untroubled
    by a spark.

Then, welcome each rebuff
That turns earth's smoothness rough,
Each sting that bids nor sit nor stand
    but go!

Be our joys three-parts pain!
Strive, and hold cheap the strain;
Learn, nor account the pang; dare,
    never grudge the throe!

For thence — a paradox
Which comforts while it mocks —
Shall life succeed in that it seems to
    fail:
What I aspired to be,
And was not, comforts me;
A brute I might have been, but would
    not sink i' the scale.

As it was better, youth
Should strive, through acts uncouth,
Toward making, than repose on aught
    found made:
So, better, age, exempt
From strife, should know, than tempt
Further. Thou waitedest age: wait
    death nor be afraid!

— *Robert Browning*

∾

DEATH BE NOT PROUD

Death be not proud, though some have called thee
Mighty and dreadful, for, thou art not soe,
For, those, whom thou think'st, thou dost overthrow,
Die not, poore death, nor yet canst thou kill mee;
From rest and sleepe, which but thy pictures bee,
Much pleasure, then from thee, much more must flow,
And soonest our best men with thee do goe,
Rest of their bones, and soules deliverie.
Thou art slave to Fate, Chance, kings, and desperate men,
And doth with poyson, warre, and sicknesse dwell
And poppie, or charmes can make us sleepe as well,
And better then thy stroake; why swell'st thou then?
One short sleepe past, wee wake eternally,
And death shall be no more, death, thou shalt die.

— *John Donne*

He Will Give Them Back

We are quite sure
That He will give them back — bright, pure and beautiful.
We know He will but keep
Our own and His, until we fall asleep.
He does not mean,— though Heaven be fair,—
To change the spirits entering there,
That they should soon forget
Our upraised eyes and wet.

He will not take
The spirits which He gave, and make
The glorified so new
That they are lost to me and you.
I just begin to think about the gladness and the day,
When they shall tell us all about the way
That they have learned to go —
Heaven's pathway show.

My lost, my own and I
Shall have so much to see together by and by,
I do believe that just the same sweet face,
But glorified, is waiting in the place
Where we shall meet, if only I
Am counted worthy in that by and by.
I do believe that God will give a sweet surprise
To tear-stained, saddened eyes.

God never made
Spirit for spirit, answering shade to shade,
And meant to break the quivering threads between;
When we shall wake,
I am quite sure we will be very glad
That for a little while we were so sad.

— *Author Unknown*

❧

In Him

"We dwell in Him," — oh, everlasting Home,
   Imperishable House not made with hands!
When all the world has melted as a dream,
   Eternal in the heav'ns this dwelling stands.

— *Annie Johnson Flint*

MAN'S LIFE

The sun arises from its ocean bed
    All clothed with crimson light, a radiant morn,
Flashing through air to earth its glory-red,
    It wakens men to greet the day, new-born;—
From off yon hearth, from newly kindled fire,
The flames leap upward, and the sparks mount higher.

The sun is west'ring, and is sinking low
    Behind the sea's horizon, far away,
Now night has fallen, and the night-winds blow,
    Moaning the death-song of departed day;—
Upon the hearth grey ashes lie about;
The last spark's vanished, and the fire is out!

— *Henry W. Frost*

SLEEPY HOLLOW

No abbey's gloom, nor dark cathedral stoops,
    No winding torches paint the midnight air;
Here the green pines delight, the aspen droops
    Along the modest pathway, and those fair
Pale asters of the season spread their plumes
    Around this field, fit garden for our tombs.

And shalt thou pause to hear some funeral bell
    Slow stealing o'er thy heart in this calm place,
Not with a throb of pain, a feverish knell,
    But in its kind and supplicating grace,
It says, Go, pilgrim, on thy march, be more
    Friend to the friendless than thou wast before;

Learn from the loved one's rest serenity:
    To-morrow that soft bell for thee shall sound,
And thou repose beneath the whispering tree,
    One tribute more to this submissive ground;—
Prison thy soul from malice, bar out pride,
    Nor these pale flowers nor this still field deride:

Rather to those ascents of being turn
    Where a ne'er-setting sun illumes the year
Eternal, and the incessant watch-fires burn
    Of unspent holiness and goodness clear,—
Forget man's littleness, deserve the best,
    God's mercy in thy thought and life confest.

— *William Ellery Channing*

THE TENANT

This body is my house, it is not I;
Here I sojourn till, in some far sky,
I lease a fairer dwelling, built to last
Till all the carpentry of time is past.
When from my high place, viewing this lone star,
What shall I care where these poor timbers are?
What though the crumbling walls turn dust and loam —
I shall have left them for a larger home.
What though the rafters break, the stanchions rot,
When earth hath dwindled to a glimmering spot,
When thou, clay cottage, fallest, I'll immerse
My long cramped spirit in the universe;
Through uncomputed silences of space
I shall yearn upward to the leaning Face.
The ancient heavens will roll aside for me
As Moses monarched the dividing sea.
This body is my house — it is not I;
Triumphant in this faith I live and die.

— *Lawrence Knowles*

WAITING

I see the light
Of the city bright,
And the walls which the saints enfold;
I hear the song
Of the countless throng
Who walk on the streets of gold;
And I long to be
By the crystal sea,
In the life which will never grow old.

I hear the chime
Of the bells of Time;
Which tell of the passing day;
And I think of the hour
When, by angel power,
My soul will be carried away,
To the upper home,
No longer to roam,
But in glory for ever to stay.

I long to be
Eternally free
From the sinning which holds me here;
To walk in white
With garments of light,
In the love which casteth out fear;
To see the face
Of the God of grace
And His rapturous welcome to hear.

And so I wait
Outside of the gate
Of the city all pure and fair,
Till I shall arise
To the mansioned skies,
To be for evermore where
The Lamb is the light
Of the city bright,
And of those who His glory will share.

— *Henry W. Frost*

DEATH

Death?—
Christ said not death;
He called it sleep;
A vast awaking,
A new day breaking,
A bright way taking,
With visions deep.

Tears?—
Christ said not tears;
He said, "Weep not!"
The body dying;
The still form lying;
Then soul upflying,
And grief forgot.

Loss?—
Christ said not loss;
He spoke of gain,
In light diurnal,
In worlds all vernal,
In joy eternal,
With no more pain.

End?—
Christ said not end;
He promised life;
The last word spoken,
A parting token,
Sweet love unbroken,
And ended strife.

Dust?—
Christ said not dust;
He called it this —
A tender yearning,
A quick upturning,
A Face discerning
And endless bliss.

— *Henry W. Frost*

MORTAL AND IMMORTAL

I stand between the Future and the Past,—
   That which has been and that which is to be;—
A feeble ray from the Eternal cast;
   A scanty rill, that seeks a shoreless sea;
A living soul, treading this earthly sod;
A finite being, yet a child of God!

A body crumbling to the dust away;
   A spirit panting for eternal peace;
A heavenly kingdom in a frame of clay;
   An infant-angel fluttering for release;
An erring man, whose race has just begun;
A pilgrim, journeying on from sun to sun!

Creature of clay, yet heir of future life;
   Dweller upon a world I shall outlive;
Soldier of Christ, battling midst earthly strife,
   Yet hoping, by that strength which God may give,
To burst the doors of death, and glorying rise
Triumphant from the grave, to tread the skies!

— *Robert Cassie Waterston*

Rest

[The following lines were found under the pillow of a soldier lying dead in a hospital near Port Royal, South Carolina.]

I lay me down to sleep, with little thought or care,
Whether waking find me here, or there.

A bowing, burdened head, that only asks to rest,
Unquestioning, upon a loving breast.

My good right hand forgets its cunning now;
To march the weary march I know not how.

I am not eager, bold, nor strong — all that is past,
I'm ready now to die, at last, at last.

My half day's work is done, and this is all my part:
I give a patient God my patient heart,

And grasp His banner still, though all its blue be dim;
These stripes, no less than stars, lead after Him.

∞

In Memoriam

Ah, no; he is not dead; he only sleeps;
Christ said it long ago, that death is sleep,
To that poor woman, full of doubts and fears,
Who mournful wept beside her brother's grave;
Yea, He who spoke truth said, to that sad heart,
"Thy brother, Lazarus, shall rise again";
And we believe it, both for him and us.
Dost call it death when at the eventide
Some one lies down and folds his weary hands,
To rest all still throughout the shadowy night,
And then awakes to greet the radiant morn,
And go, in strength, into the brightening day?
No, no; that closing of the tired eyes,
That folding on the breast of toil-stained hands,
That lying still in rest, all this is sleep:
Ah, surely then, and surely far, far more,
When some poor, weary, fainting, pilgrim-saint,
Lies down in slumber's deep and blest repose,
His life deep hid within the life of God!
If this were death, would there have been
This calm, glad waiting for the darkening hour?
And would there, even yet, lingeringly,

Upon the upturned face, the peaceful smile?
What if the eyes ope not to waiting gaze
Or breath no longer greets the listening ear;
It only means that sleep is very deep,
Too deep for mortal eyes to see the Life
That circles it around and holds it safe:
Ah, no, the light of life has not gone out,
For God's good gift was that of endless life;
Christ promised it, and this too, we believe.
We say it then, triumphant over death,
"He is not dead; he but takes rest in sleep!"
For this we surely know, he will awake,
And rise renewed, all strong and beautiful,
And serve as ne'er before, in glorious day,
Alive with God and Christ, for evermore!
Then sleep, belovèd one, till morning light;
Sleep deep, sleep sweet, thy weary labor past;
Christ watches over thee, and He will keep
That which thou gavest Him, all trustingly.
And so we lay thy weary body down,
On flower-decked bed of earth, till night is past,
In blessèd, ardent hope that very soon
The day-spring from on high will visit us,
And thou, with us, will rise to greet the day,
And be with Christ, thy Life, to sleep no more!

— Henry W. Frost

ᥴᥣᥩ

IMMORTALITY

What matters it to us who are immortal
Which side of the grave we stand on, when we know
That what the world calls death is but the portal
Leading to life again? 'Tis but to go
Across the gurgling river in the dark
Hanging on God; and but a moment so
Till we are over, and we disembark
And enter life afresh. 'Tis basely wrong
We should so meanly understrike the mark
As measures life by years; and all along
Busy ourselves arranging little schemes
That death will dash to pieces, when we might
Be building, far above those earthly dreams,
Houses that stand forever in God's sight.

— Author Unknown

DEATH'S SUMMONS

Adieu, farewell, earth's bliss,
This world uncertain is:
Fond are life's lustful joys,
Death proves them all but toys.
None from his darts can fly:
I am sick, I must die.
Lord, have mercy on us!

Rich men, trust not in wealth,
Gold cannot buy you health;
Physic himself must fade;
All things to end are made;
The plague full swift goes by:
I am sick, I must die.
Lord, have mercy on us!

Beauty is but a flower,
Which wrinkles will devour:
Brightness falls from the air;
Queens have died young and fair;
Dust hath closed Helen's eye:
I am sick, I must die.
Lord, have mercy on us!

Strength stoops unto the grave;
Worms feed on Hector brave;
Swords may not fight with fate;
Earth still holds ope her gate;
Come, come, the bells do cry.
I am sick, I must die.
Lord, have mercy on me!

Wit with his wantonness,
Tasteth death's bitterness;
Hell's executioner
Hath no ears for to hear
What vain art can reply;
I am sick, I must die:
Lord, have mercy on us!

Haste therefore each degree
To welcome destiny!
Heaven is our heritage,
Earth but a player's stage;
Mount we unto the sky:
I am sick, I must die.
Lord, have mercy on us!

— Thomas Nash

COMPENSATION

The year is slowly, sadly dying —
    Let it die!
Dead leaves on withered flowers are lying —
    Let them lie!
Were there no autumn, there would be no spring,
And hearts 'midst springtime joys would never sing!

My life is surely, sadly ending —
    Let it end!
Its way toward death is swiftly tending —
    Let it tend!
Should earth not cease, then heav'n would not begin,
And heaven's eternal joys I ne'er should win!

— Henry W. Frost

RESURRECTION

(Written after seeing a butterfly in a garden.)

And so thou hast burst forth from place of death,
  With slender body and with radiant wing,
Wast thou made suddenly by God's sweet breath,
  Enshrouded as thou wast, thou beauteous thing!
    Out of dark nothingness,
    This shadowy world to bless,
    With seven-hued colors bright
    Like ray of glory-light?
Who could have thought on yesterday,
When thou didst lie like sodden clay,
  That, in thy wrapped-up, dark cocoon,
  There should have happened, and so soon,
  This miracle of life and light?
As well imagine darksome night
    Could suddenly be day!—
    What, goest thou away,
      And higher up,
      From buttercup,
  To white rose on the lifted stem?
  Thou lookest like a flashing gem
Held fast at snow-white throat; only thy wings
Do pulsate in the very joy of things,
And show thou art not dead, as once before,
E'er God had opened wide the fast-closed door
Which held thy radiance in — thou wondrous thing,
Thou restless insect with the quivering wing!—
    What, art thou not content
    With thine environment?
    Must leave the snow-white rose
    To be the joy of those
      Who, by their birth,
      Love lower earth?
    Dost fly to higher trees
    Where hum the busy bees,
    Seeking their honeyed dower
    From newly bloss'ming flower?
    There, weary insect, take thy rest,
    And dip thy dark-hued, breathing breast
In the bright calyx where the fruit will be
When the same Hand hath wrought that fashioned thee;
    Now, thou dost glow with light;
    No one could think that night

Once wrapped thee round
As one close-bound;
Thou dost with sunlight gleam
As if thou wert its beam,
Thyself the very light;—
What now? Another flight,
Still higher up? Wilt mount so high
That thou wilt touch the azure sky?
Where art thou now?—I only see
A faint-winged, throbbing flash of thee,
As thou art merged in seven-fold ray
Of the fair gleaming, glittering day;—
Ah, thou art wholly gone;
Thou didst to heaven belong,
God made thee for the skies,
So thou didst heavenward rise:
Good-bye,
Bright butterfly!
I too, a worm, shall turn to clay;
But I shall follow thee one day,
Thou happy thing,
Thou radiant insect with the outspread wing!

— Henry W. Frost

DEATH

Why be afraid of death, as though your life were breath?
Death but anoints your eyes with clay. O glad surprise!

Why should ye be forlorn? Death only husks the corn.
Why should you fear to meet the thresher of the wheat?

Is sleep a thing to dread? Yet sleeping you are dead
Till you awake and rise, here, or beyond the skies.

Why should it be a wrench to leave your wooden bench!
Why not, with happy shout, run home when school is out!

The dear ones left behind? Oh, foolish one and blind!
A day and you will meet—a night and you will greet.

This is the death of death, to breathe away a breath
And know the end of strife, and taste the deathless life,

And joy without a fear, and smile without a tear;
And work, nor care to rest, and find the last the best.

— Maltbie D. Babcock

After the Storm

A night without of wind and rain,
And a night in my soul of grief and
    pain.

A night without of darkness and gloom,
And a night in my soul because of a
    tomb.

A lonely tomb on the hillside made,
Under the oak tree's sheltering shade.

A lowly grave where a loved one lies,
With the shadow of death on brow
    and eyes;

And a pallor that only comes when life
Is ended, with all of mortal strife.

With folded hands and a quiet breast:
Dear hands that never before knew
    rest!

And close sealed lips that never again,
Will make the way of life so plain

To faltering feet; nor will I prove
The sweetness of all their words of love.

What wonder if anguish fills my breast,
That sadden my days and break my
    rest!

What wonder if life and its pleasures
    seem
But a fitful glow, and a fading dream!

                    — *Annie Howe Thomson*

Why Should I Fear?

Why should I fear the darkest hour,
Or tremble at the tempter's power?
Jesus vouchsafes to be my tower.

Tho' hot the fight, why quit the field,
Why must I either flee or yield,
Since Jesus is my mighty shield?

When creature comforts fade and die,
Worldlings may weep, but why should
    I?
Jesus still lives, and still is nigh.

Tho' all the flocks and herds were dead,
My soul a famine need not dread,
For Jesus is my living bread.

I know not what may soon betide,
Or how my wants shall be supplied;
But Jesus knows, and will provide.

Tho' sin would fill me with distress,
The throne of grace I dare address,
For Jesus is my righteousness.

Though faint my prayers, and cold my
    love,
My steadfast hope shall not remove,
While Jesus intercedes above.

Against me earth and hell combine,
But on my side is power divine:
Jesus is all, and he is mine.

                    — *John Newton*

Death Is Only a Door

Death is only an old door,
    Set in a garden wall,
On gentle hinges it gives at dusk
    When the thrushes call.

Along the lintel are green leaves,
    Beyond the light lies still,
Very willing and weary feet
    Go over that sill.

There is nothing to trouble any heart,
    Nothing to hurt at all.
Death is only a quiet door,
    In an old wall.

                    — *Nancy Byrd Turner*

'TIS IMMORTALITY

There is a plan far greater than the plan you know;
There is a landscape broader than the one you see;
There is a haven where storm-tossed souls may go.
You call it death — we, immortality!

You call it death, this seeming endless sleep.
We call it birth, the soul at last set free.
'Tis hampered not by time or space — you weep.
Why weep at death? 'Tis immortality!

Farewell, dear voyageur; 'twill not be long.
Your work is done — now may peace rest with thee.
Your kindly thoughts and deeds, they will live on.
This is not death — 'tis immortality!

Farewell, dear voyageur. The river winds and turns.
The cadence of your song wafts near me.
And now you know the thing that all men learn:
There is no death — there's immortality.

— *Author Unknown*

∽

THE LONG LAST MILE

Carry me over the long last mile,
    Man of Nazareth, Christ for me!
Weary I wait by Death's dark stile,
In the wild and the waste, where the winds blow free,
And the shades and sorrows come out of my past,
    Look keen through my heart,
    And will not depart,
Now that my poor world has come to its last!

Lord, is it long that my spirit must wait?
    Man of Nazareth, Christ for me!
Deep is the stream, and the night is late,
And grief blinds my soul that I cannot see,
    Speak to me out of the silences, Lord,
      That my spirit may know
      As forward I go,
Thy pierced hands are lifting me over the ford!

— *L. Maclean Watt* from THE TRYST

HOME-BOUND

'Tis a long, long way to my waiting home,
And the roadway is rough and steep,
And few are the smiles in the weary miles
While there's many a chance to weep;
But on at the end of the long, rough way
There's a door which is opened wide,
And the day will come, at some set of sun,
When I'll enter to there abide.

'Tis a desolate road I am travelling on,
For the crowd does not pass this way,
And the heart oft longs for the heartening songs
Of those who make holiday;
But, on beyond, in the home on the hill,
There are faces I love more dear,
So I take my way, through the long-drawn day,
To its welcome and holier cheer.

The daylight fades as I journey along
And shadows are deepening around,
And I sometimes fear as the night draws near
For pitfalls and dangers abound;
But this is my joy along the hard way,
Whatever the shadows portend,
The darker the night, the brighter the light
In my home at my journey's end.

So then I'll go on with never a pause,
Whatever my sorrows may be,
Yea, nothing shall stay my journeying way
Till the distant portal I see;
And when I shall stand 'neath its shelter, at last,
At rest in my blessèd abode,
I'll praise, without end, my heavenly Friend
For the home at the end of the road!

— Henry W. Frost

ᭅ

THE EVERLASTING MEMORIAL

Up and away, like the dew of the morning,
Soaring from earth to its home in the sun;
So let me steal away, gently and lovingly,
Only remembered by what I have done.

My name, and my place, and my tomb all forgotten,
    The brief race of time well and patiently run,
So let me pass away, peacefully, silently,
    Only remembered by what I have done.

Gladly away from this toil would I hasten,
    Up to the crown that for me has been won;
Unthought of by man in rewards or in praises,—
    Only remembered by what I have done.

Up and away, like the odors of sunset,
    That sweeten the twilight as darkness comes on;
So be my life, — a thing felt but not noticed,
    And I but remembered by what I have done.

Yes, like the fragrance that wanders in freshness,
    When the flowers that it came from are closed up and gone,—
So would I be to this world's weary dwellers,
    Only remembered by what I have done.

Needs there be praise of the love-written record,
    The name and the epitaph graved on the stone?
The things we have lived for, — let them be our story,
    We, our selves, but remembered by what we have done.

I need not be missed, if my life has been bearing,
    (As its summer and autumn moved silently on)
The bloom, and the fruit, and the seed of its season;
    I shall still be remembered by what I have done.

I need not be missed, if another succeed me,
    To reap down those fields which in spring I have sown;
He who plowed and who sowed is not missed by the reaper.
    He is only remembered by what he has done.

Not myself, but the truth that in life I have spoken,
    Not myself, but the seed that in life I have sown,
Shall pass on to ages, — all about me forgotten,
    Save the truth I have spoken, the things I have done.

So let my living be, so be my dying;
    So let my name lie, unblazoned, unknown;
Unpraised and unmissed, I shall still be remembered;
    Yes, — but remembered by what I have done.

                           — *Horatius Bonar*

THE LAST INVOCATION

At the last, tenderly,
From the walls of the powerful fortress'd house,
From the clasp of the knitted locks, from the keep of the
    well-closed doors,
Let me be wafted.

Let me glide noiselessly forth;
With the key of softness unlock the locks — with a whisper,
Set ope the doors O soul.
Tenderly — be not impatient,
(Strong is your hold O mortal flesh,
Strong is your hold O love).

— Walt Whitman

WAITING YONDER

They are not dead, those loved ones who have passed
    Beyond our vision for a little while,
They have but reached the Light while we still grope
    In darkness where we cannot see them smile.

But smile they do, and love us, and do not
    Forget, nor ever go so far away
But that their hands still clasp our hands and hold
    Us safe from falling when we fain would stray.

They are not dead. Theirs is the fuller life,
    Theirs is the victory, the joy, the gain;
For us is still the waiting and the strife,
    For us the loneliness, for us the pain.

Then let us gird us once again with hope,
    And give them smile for smile the while we wait;
And loving, serving, when Our Father calls,
    We'll go to find our dear ones wait us at the gate.

— H. A. C.

THE VOYAGE

All I shall ask, at last, when I put forth to sea,
Is that a Pilot, good and true, will sail with me:
If his hand holds the helm and his eye scans the foam,
In spite of wave and tempest, I shall sail straight home.

— Henry W. Frost

THE GLOAMING

(Written on reaching seventy years of age.)
A few hours since, the radiant sun was standing
High in the heaven, firm-fixed in deepest blue,
Sending its beams in infinite expanding
Where clouds lay white and great winged eagles flew.

Its rays fell on the earth where flowers were blooming,
Where birds were mating on the leafy limbs,
Where flocks, by streams, were tender grass consuming,
Where shepherds thrilled the air with praiseful hymns.

I thought the day would never know declining;
All was bright light, and all was vibrant life;
My joy rose up to heav'n, where light was shining,
And hope displaced all fear of coming strife.

But suddenly long shadows fell a-slanting
Upon the path which tiring feet betrod,
And I began to pray for gracious granting
Of strength which only could be found in God.

At this, I saw that the bright sun was sinking
Tow'rd the far hills where night's deep darkness lies,
And I, who had been brave, fell all a-shrinking
From the dark valley where the daylight dies.

When lo, 'midst shades, appeared the evening gloaming,
All red and golden in the western sky;
At which, like a lone bird in happy homing,
I hastened on with thoughts fast fixed on high.

For I was sure if God makes evening golden,
So that the path shines as the perfect day,
He would, in spite of fears, my soul embolden
To walk with Him to end of the long way.

So now I fear not what the eve is bringing
Of lessening light, and shadows' darkening shade;
Through twilight's gloaming I shall go a-singing
Into the glory which God's hand has made.

— *Henry W. Frost*

EARTH-BOUND

I cannot rise
To wished-for place within the skies,
But I am left to stand
Upon this clod-heaped land,
Pressed down with burd'ning discon-
    tent
Because of earth's environment,
Destined to die and sleep
Beneath the sod, so deep
That soon the earth will hold
Myself turned into mold;
Taken from dust I must
Return, at last, to dust.
The eagle cleaves the topmost sky,
The gull spreads forth his wings on
    high,
E'en tiny insects mount on strong,
    swift wings
And look down, from their height, on
    earthly things;
Yet I, a man
But can
Walk heavy-footed on this lower earth
Longing and waiting for a higher birth:

If I had wings
Like the sweet lark that sings,
And as he sings, soars out of sight,
I should take flight

And rise into the heavenly blue;
This I should do
Because I long
To learn the heavenly song
Which those can never know
Who grovel here below;
Yet here on earth I walk
To envy e'en some carrion hawk,
A common thing,
And yet on wing,
With wings outspread
Above my head!

Oh, to cast off this heavy weight
Which keeps me in this lower state;
Oh, for strong power to rise and rise
To longed-for place in upper skies!
Hark to the birds on high
Which heavenward fly;
Hark to the glad, pulsating song
Which they in upper skies prolong;
But I can never with them sing
Since I am not on wing;
I can but moan and wait,
    Disconsolate:—
And lo, the turtle-dove moans with me
    from his nest;
Had I but wings I too should fly away
    and be at rest!

— *Henry W. Frost*

Easter

Last Easter when my voice was lifted up
    To sing the praises of my Risen Lord,
I had not tasted sorrow's bitter cup;
    The music held for me no minor chord.
This Eastertide my stricken heart sends up
    The strains I lift in accents clear and strong,
For I have drained the dregs of sorrow's cup
    And learned the meaning of the Easter song.
I know the sweetness of the minor chord,
    The glory of the major full and clear;
I know the power of the Risen Lord —
    He lives, and they shall live whom I hold dear.
And though I cannot help the tears that flow,
    And though my heart is sad as heart can be,
I sing the Easter song because I know
    The blessed Easter message is for me.

                         — *Zula Evelyn Coon*

Easter Prayer

Oh, let me know
The power of Thy resurrection!
Oh, let me show
Thy risen life in clear reflection!
Oh, let me soar
Where Thou, my Saviour Christ, art
    gone before!
In mind and heart
Let me dwell always, only, where
    Thou art.

Oh, let me give
Out of the gifts Thou freely givest;
Oh, let me live
With life abundantly because Thou
    livest;

Oh, make me shine
In darkest places, for Thy light is mine;
Oh, let me be
A faithful witness for Thy truth and
    Thee.

Oh, let me show
The strong reality of gospel story;
Oh, let me go
From strength to strength, from glory
    unto glory;
Oh, let me sing
For very joy, because Thou art my
    King;
Oh, let me praise
Thy love and faithfulness through all
    my days.

            — *Frances Ridley Havergal*

CALVARY

O Cross on which my Saviour died,
With wounded hands and feet and
    side,
Within thy shadow I would hide;
O Calvary, blest Calvary!

Before thine awful mystery
I pour my soul's great agony;
O God of pity, look on me;
O Calvary, blest Calvary!

I would not flee thy dreadful pain,
Prostrate before thee I remain;
O God of love, turn loss to gain;
O Calvary, blest Calvary!

I kiss thy Victim's wounds of woe,
I bathe me in their crimson flow;
O Christ, Thy healing power bestow;
O Calvary, blest Calvary!

May I arise on the last day,
All cleansed and pure, in bright array,
The Cross my righteousness for aye;
O Calvary, blest Calvary!

— *Henry W. Frost*

∾

LOOKING AT THE CROSS

In evil long I took delight,
    Unawed by shame or fear,
Till a new object struck my sight,
    And stopped my wild career.
I saw one hanging on a tree,
    In agonies and blood,
Who fixed his languid eyes on me,
    As near his cross I stood.

Sure, never till my latest breath
    Can I forget that look;
It seemed to charge me with his death,
    Though not a word he spoke.

My conscience felt and owned the
    guilt,
    And plunged me in despair;
I saw my sins his blood had spilt,
    And helped to nail him there.

Alas! I knew not what I did:
    But now my tears are vain;
Where shall my trembling soul be hid?
    For I the Lord have slain.
A second look he gave, which said,
    "I freely all forgive;
This blood is for thy ransom paid,
    I die that thou mayst live."

Thus while his death my sin displays
    In all its blackest hue;
Such is the mystery of grace,
    It seals my pardon too.
With pleasing grief and mournful joy
    My spirit now is filled,
That I should such a life destroy,
    Yet live by him I killed.

— *John Newton*

∾

EASTER

Jesus Christ to-day is risen,
    And o'er Death triumphant reigns;
He has burst the grave's strong prison,
    Leading Sin herself in chains.
        Kyrie eleison.

For our sins the sinless Saviour
    Bare the heavy wrath of God;
Reconciling us, that favor
    Might be shown us thro' his blood.
        Kyrie eleison.

In his hands he hath forever
    Mercy, life and sin, and death;
Christ his people can deliver,
    All who come to him in faith.
        Kyrie eleison.

— *Martin Luther* from *John Huss*

HOPE

He died!
And with Him perished all that men hold dear;
Hope lay beside Him in the sepulcher,
Love grew corse cold, and all things beautiful beside,
Died, when He died!

He rose!
And with Him hope arose, and life and light.
Men said, "Not Christ, but Death, died yesternight."
And joy and truth and all things virtuous
Rose, when He rose.

— *Author Unknown*

THE RESURRECTION

The day of resurrection,
Earth, tell it out abroad;
The passover of gladness,
The passover of God.
From death to life eternal,
From this world to the sky,
Our Christ hath brought us over
With hymns of victory.

Our hearts be pure from evil,
That we may see aright
The Lord in rays eternal
Of resurrection-light;
And, listening to His accents,
May hear, so calm and plain,
His own, "All Hail!" and, hearing,
May raise the victor-strain.

Now let the heavens be joyful,
Let earth her song begin;
Let the round world keep triumph,
And all that is therein;

Invisible and visible,
Their notes let all thing blend;
For Christ the Lord hath risen,
Our joy that hath no end.

— *St. John of Damascus*

HOW EXCELLENT IS THY NAME!
— *Psalm 8*

How excellent, O Lord, Thy Name
Is in the earth, for Thou
Hast set Thy glory far above
The heavens. Even now
When I consider these, Thy works;
The heavens, moon and stars,
I bow in adoration, as
I see no thing that mars
Thy handiwork. In beauty lies
Its great, majestic birth;
How excellent Thy Name is, Lord!
Thy Name in all the earth.

— *Eva Gray*

The Easter Glory

'Twas in the grey and dawning light
Two women came with hearts of grief
To shed a tear, to sob, or, as a woman, just to weep
For Him, their hope, unjustly slain.

An angel clothed in light sat by the door
Upon a stone just rolled away.
Majestically he raised his hand! "He is not here!
He is risen! Look, see the place where once He lay.
No more is numbered among the slain;
Seek not the living here among the dead."

Amazed, o'erwhelmed, they ran to tell
This great event to His disciples and the world —
These tidings great — this gospel for all —
"Christ is risen!" All other christs live but to die,
And are forgot, and stay among the dead,
But this Christ lives, Amen, for evermore.

Awake, O Earth, and hear this living Word,
Of Christ arisen from the dead;
And may thou in thy blinding sin
Run headlong, breaking onto Him
Upon some long and hard Damascus Road,
And there be thus enacted once again
A second resurrection — that of thy soul,
Out from among the dead,
To everlasting light and life.

— A. J. Beattie

An Easter Prayer

God's blessing rest upon you
   This happy Easter Day,
God make His joy to shine
   As sunlight on your way;
God fill your heart with song
   So glad it will not cease;
God bless you every day
   With love and joy and peace.

— Author Unknown

My Easter Prayer

May you walk a little surer
   On the path that lies before,
May you see a little clearer
   May you trust a little more.
May you come a little closer
   To the Lord of Love Divine,
That your heart may sing for gladness,
   Is this Easter prayer of mine.

— Author Unknown

EASTER DAY

The Lord is risen;—
I must arise
And seek His face
In upper skies;
I will not turn
To cross or grave,
He lives above
Who died to save.

The crocus flower
In garden bed
Has lifted up
Its spotless head;
It raised its face
Toward gleaming sun
Before the day
Had well begun.

The song-birds flit
From hedge to trees
To fill with song
The morning's breeze;
Hark, to the burst
Of sweet accord
As they unite
To praise earth's Lord;

And borne on air,
In rythmic time,
There sounds the beat
Of tuneful chime,
As pealing bells
In steeple high
Ring, "Christ is risen,"
To earth and sky.

Then rise, my soul,
Seek Christ above,
The Lord of light
And life and love;
The cross is past,
No more death's pain,
Christ lives for e'er,
For e'er to reign!

— *Henry W. Frost*

WHEN I SURVEY THE WONDROUS CROSS

When I survey the wondrous cross
    On which the Prince of Glory died,
My richest gain I count but loss,
    And pour contempt on all my pride.

Forbid it, Lord, that I should boast,
    Save in the death of Christ, my God:
All the vain things that charm me most,
    I sacrifice them to his blood.

See, from his head, his hands, his feet,
    Sorrow and love flow mingled down:
Did e'er such love and sorrow meet,
    Or thorns compose so rich a crown?

His dying crimson, like a robe,
    Spreads o'er his body on the tree:
Then am I dead to all the globe,
    And all the globe is dead to me.

Were the whole realm of nature mine,
    That were a present far too small:
Love so amazing, so divine,
    Demands my soul, my life, my all.

— *Isaac Watts*

NOW MAY HE WHO FROM THE DEAD

Now may he who from the dead
    Brought the Shepherd of the sheep,
Jesus Christ, our King and Head,
    All our souls in safety keep.

May he teach us to fulfil
    What is pleasing in his sight;
Perfect us in all his will,
    And preserve us day and night!

To that dear Redeemer's praise,
    Who the covenant sealed with
        blood,
Let our hearts and voices raise
    Loud thanksgivings to our God.

— *John Newton*

ANGELS, ROLL THE ROCK AWAY!

Angels, roll the rock away;
Death, yield up the mighty prey!
See! the Saviour quits the tomb,
Glowing with immortal bloom.
　　Hallelujah! hallelujah!
Christ the Lord is risen to-day.

Shout, ye seraphs! angels, raise
Your eternal song of praise!
Let the earth's remotest bound
Echo to the blissful sound!
　　Hallelujah! hallelujah!
Christ the Lord is risen to-day.

Holy Father, holy Son,
Holy Spirit, Three in One,
Glory as of old to thee,
Now and evermore, shall be!
　　Hallelujah! hallelujah!
Christ the Lord is risen to-day.

— *Thomas Scott*

FOR EASTER DAY

Christ the Lord is risen to-day,
Sons of men and angels say:
Raise your joys and triumphs high,
Sing, ye heavens, and earth reply.

Love's redeeming work is done,
Fought the fight, the battle won:
Lo! our Sun's eclipse is o'er:
Lo! he sets in blood no more.

Vain the stone, the watch, the seal;
Christ hath burst the gates of hell!
Death in vain forbids him rise;
Christ hath opened paradise!

Lives again our glorious King!
Where, O Death, is now thy sting?
Once he died, our souls to save:
Where's thy victory, boasting Grave?

Soar we now where Christ hath led,
Following our exalted head:

Made like him, like him we rise,
Ours the cross, the grave, the skies!

What though once we perished all,
Partners in our parents' fall?
Second life we all receive,
In our heavenly Adam live.

Risen with him, we upward move;
Still we seek the things above;
Still pursue, and kiss the Son
Seated on his Father's throne.

Scarce on earth a thought bestow,
Dead to all we leave below;
Heaven our aim, and loved abode,
Hid our life with Christ in God:

Hid, till Christ our Life appear
Glorious in his members here;
Joined to him, we then shall shine,
All immortal, all divine.

Hail the Lord of earth and heaven!
Praise to thee by both be given!
Thee we greet triumphant now!
Hail, the Resurrection thou!

King of glory, Soul of bliss!
Everlasting life is this:
Thee to know, thy power to prove,
Thus to sing, and thus to love!

— *Charles Wesley*

AN EASTER SONG

A song of sunshine through the rain,
Of Spring across the snow;
A balm to heal the hurts of pain,
A peace surpassing woe.
Lift up your heads, ye sorrowing ones,
And be ye glad at heart,
For Calvary and Easter Day,
Earth's saddest day and gladdest day,
Were just three days apart!

— *Susan Coolidge*

EASTER MORNING

Tomb, thou shalt not hold Him longer;
Death is strong, but life is stronger;
Stronger than the dark, the light;
Stronger than the wrong, the right;
Faith and hope triumphant say,
"Christ will rise on Easter day!"

While the patient earth lies waking
Till the morning shall be breaking,
Shuddering 'neath the burden dread
Of her Master, cold and dead,
Hark! she hears the angels say,
"Christ will rise on Easter day!"

And when sunrise smites the mountains,
Pouring light from heavenly fountains,
Then the earth blooms out to greet
Once again the blessed feet;
And her countless voices say:
"Christ has risen on Easter day!"

— *Phillips Brooks*

RESURRECTION

Except
A grain of wheat
Shall fall and die
Alone,
It cannot bring to life
The blade, the ear,
And full, ripe, glowing grain;

But if it die,
Abundant fruit
Shall bless the earth.

A soul
That hoards its life
For selfish ends
Will be a barren field
That lifts but empty hands
To God at last.

— *Esther H. Turner*

A BALLAD OF TREES AND THE MASTER

Into the woods my Master went,
Clean forspent, forspent.
Into the woods my Master came,
Forspent with love and shame.
But the olives they were not blind to
    Him;
The little gray leaves were kind to
    Him;
The thorn-tree had a mind to Him
When into the woods He came.

Out of the woods my Master went,
And He was well content.
Out of the woods my Master came,
Content with death and shame.
When Death and Shame would woo
    Him last,
From under the trees they draw Him
    last:
'Twas on a tree they slew Him — last
When out of the woods He came.

— *Sidney Lanier*

HE LIVES

I know that my Redeemer lives;
What joy the blest assurance gives!
He lives, He lives, who once was dead;
He lives, my everlasting Head!

He lives, to bless me with His love;
He lives, to plead for me above;
He lives, my hungry soul to feed;
He lives, to help in time of need.

He lives, to grant me daily breath;
He lives, and I shall conquer death;
He lives, my mansion to prepare;
He lives, to bring me safely there.

He lives, all glory to His Name;
He lives, my Saviour, still the same;
What joy the blest assurance gives,
I know that my Redeemer lives!

— *Samuel Medley*

ASPIRATIONS

Oh, teach me, thou forest, to testify glad,
    As in autumn the gloom of thy yellowing leaf,
That my spring cometh back after winter the sad,
    That my tree gleameth green after mournfulness brief.
The roots of my tree stand strong, deep, and divine
In eternity's summer; oh, why then repine?

Bird of passage, thou frail little thing, oh, teach me
    To fly with bold wing and with spirit as bold,
To lands undiscovered far over the sea.
    When all here is stormy and cloudy and cold,
Throw wide open its gates, a sweet paradise there;
Let me haste to its sunshine, its odorous air.

Oh, teach me, oh, teach me, thou butterfly bright.
    To shatter the chrysalis dungeon and chain,
Which rob me of freedom, of joy, and of light:
    I grovel, a worm, in this desert of pain;
But soon, ah! sublimely transfigured, I fly,
With wings valiant, of purple and gold, in the sky.

From thy throne in the clouds, thou, Lord, smilest to me.
    My Christ, my loved Jesus, thou mighty to save,
Oh, help me to conquer all sorrow, like thee.
    Hope's green banner, Redeemer, victorious wave;
How bitter thy cross amid Calvary's gloom!
Thy triumph how wondrous, how grand, o'er the tomb!

— *Adam G. Oehlenschlaeger*

და

MY RISEN LORD

My risen Lord, I feel thy strong protection;
I see thee stand among the graves today;
I am the Way, the Life, the Resurrection,
        I hear thee say,
And all the burdens I have carried sadly
Grow light as blossoms on an April day;
My cross becomes a staff, I journey gladly
        This Easter day.

— *Author Unknown*

If Easter Be Not True

If Easter be not true,
Then all the lilies low must lie;
The Flanders poppies fade and die;
The spring must lose her fairest bloom,
For Christ were still within the tomb—
If Easter be not true.

If Easter be not true,
Then faith must mount on broken
    wing;
Then hope no more immortal spring;
Then love must lose her mighty urge;
Life prove a phantom, death a dirge—
If Easter be not true.

If Easter be not true,
'Twere foolishness the cross to bear;
He died in vain who suffered there;
What matter though we laugh or cry,
Be good or evil, live or die,
If Easter be not true?

If Easter be not true —
But it is true, and Christ is risen!
And mortal spirit from its prison
Of sin and death with Him may rise!
Worth-while the struggle, sure the
    prize,
Since Easter, aye, is true!

— *Henry H. Barstow*

Hope of Our Hearts

Hope of our hearts, O Lord! appear:
    Thou glorious Star of day,
Shine forth, and chase the dreary
    night,
    With all our fears, away!

Strangers on earth, we wait for Thee:
    Oh! leave the Father's throne;
Come with the shout of victory, Lord,
    And claim us for Thine own!

Oh! bid the bright archangel now
    The trump of God prepare,
To call Thy saints — the quick, the
    dead —
    To meet Thee in the air.

No resting-place we seek on earth,
    No loveliness we see;
Our eye is on the royal crown
    Prepared for us and Thee.

But, dearest Lord, however bright
    That crown of joy above,
What is it to the brighter hope
    Of dwelling in Thy love?

What to the joy — the deeper joy,
    Unmingled, pure, and free —
Of union with our Living Head,
    Of fellowship with Thee?

This joy e'en now on earth is ours:
    But only, Lord, above,
Our hearts, without a pang, shall know
    The fullness of Thy love.

There, near Thy heart, upon the
    throne,
    Thy ransomed bride shall see
What grace was in the bleeding Lamb
    Who died to make her free.

— *Sir Edward Denny*

The Lord of Life Is Risen

The Lord of life is risen!
Sing, Easter heralds, sing!
He burst his rocky prison:
Wide let the triumph ring!
Tell how the graves are quaking,
The saints their fetters breaking:
Sing, heralds! Jesus lives!

— *Johann Peter Lange*

Behold Your King!

Behold your King! Though the moonlight steals
  Through the silvery shade of the olive-tree,
No star-gemmed sceptre or crown it reveals
  In the solemn shades of Gethsemane;
    Only a form of prostrate grief,
    Fallen, crushed, like a broken leaf.
  Oh, think of this sorrow, that we may know
  The depth of love in the depth of woe!

Behold your King! Is it nothing to you,
  That the crimson tokens of agony
From the kingly brow must fall like dew,
  Through the shuddering shades of Gethsemane?
    Jesus himself, the Prince of life,
    Bows in mysterious mortal strife.
  Oh, think of this sorrow, that we may know
  The unknown love in the unknown woe!

Behold your King, with his sorrow crowned!
  Alone, alone in the valley is he!
The shadows of death are gathering round,
  And the Cross must follow Gethsemane.
    Darker and darker the gloom must fall,
    Filled is the cup,— he must drink it all!
  Oh, think of his sorrow, that we may know
  His wondrous love in his wondrous woe!

— Frances Ridley Havergal

ᏯᎥᎨ

Passion Hymn

O sacred Head, surrounded
  By crown of piercing thorn!
O bleeding Head, so wounded,
  Reviled, and put to scorn!
Death's pallid hue comes o'er thee,
  The glow of life decays,
Yet angel-hosts adore thee,
  And tremble as they gaze.

I see thy strength and vigor
  All fading in the strife,
And death with cruel rigor
  Bereaving thee of life;

O agony and dying!
  O love to sinners free!
Jesu, all grace supplying,
  Oh, turn thy face on me.

In this thy bitter passion,
  Good Shepherd, think of me,
With thy most sweet compassion,
  Unworthy though I be:
Beneath thy cross abiding,
  Forever would I rest;
In thy dear love confiding,
  And with thy presence blest.

— Bernard of Clairvaux

AN EASTER PRAYER

Lord, now that spring is in the world,
 And every tulip is a cup
Filled with the wine of thy great love,
 Lift thou me up.

Raise thou my heart as flowers arise
 To greet the glory of thy day,
With soul as clean as lilies are,
 And white as they.

Let me not fear the darkness now,
 Since Life and Light break through
 thy tomb;
Teach me that doubts no more oppress,
 No more consume.

Show me that thou art April, Lord,
 And thou the flowers and the grass;
Then, when awake the soft spring
 winds,
 I'll hear thee pass!

— *Charles Hanson Towne*

I HAD A PART

Throughout His sojourn here below,
 Integrally, I had a part
In all His sufferings and His woe —
 I helped to break the Saviour's heart.

My thoughtless spirit closed a door
 In rustic Bethlehem one night;
What shame, the Saviour to ignore,
 The Heav'nly Stranger thus to slight!

My heavy eyes, no doubt He saw,
 As His disciples fell asleep;
Alas, unmindful of the awe,
 My vigil, lo, I failed to keep.

The dawning light my shadow cast
 In Pilate's crowded judgment hall;
"For or against," a question vast,
 With strident voice, was asked of all.

My voice gave volume to the cry
 Which rang, "Away with Him,
 away!"
I cried with others, "Crucify!"
 The multitude I helped to sway.

The nails which pierced the Saviour's
 hands,
 Were sharpened by my sins, I know;
Yea, I assisted Romans bands,
 My sins gave force to every blow.

He wore a crown whose every thorn
 Was pointed by my sin and shame;
The thirst endured, the bitter scorn,
 This guilt I dare not to disclaim.

The gloom surrounding Christ that day
 Was deepened by my blinded sight;
The levity, its rank display,
 With it my guilty soul indict.

I thrust the spear which rent His side,
 I caused His holy Blood to flow;
I heard the Saviour as He cried,
 "Forgive!" unmindful of His woe.

The load of sin which broke the heart
 Of Christ upon the cruel Tree,
Alas, 'twas mine, a major part,
 He took my place to set me free.

— *David F. Nygren*

MY EASTER WISH

May the glad dawn,
Of Easter morn
 Bring joy to thee.

May the calm eve
Of Easter leave
 A peace divine with thee.

May Easter night,
On thine heart write,
 O Christ, I live for Thee

— *Author Unknown*

EASTER

O soul of mine, awake, awake,
Slumber no more, for Christ's dear sake,
Behold, the glorious light doth break
 Of a new Easter day!

Come forth; — but not with fear and dread,
The darkness of the night has fled;
Seek not the Living 'midst the dead,
 On this glad Easter day!

Bring not the spices, sweet and rare,
Behold the grave — Christ is not there,
He has arisen, fresh and fair,
 Like this bright Easter day!

Nay, linger not beside the tomb;
Christ rose from out the morning's womb
To scatter Death's o'ershadowing gloom;
 Now shines the Easter day!

Yea, shine, bright sun; blow, balmy breeze;
Spring flowers and shrubs and buds on trees;
Sure token of Christ's power are these
 On this, His Easter day!

Hark, 'tis the Christ who to thee cries,
He calls thee to the radiant skies;
O heart of mine, arise, arise
 To heaven's sweet Easter day!

Glad Easter day, so fair and bright,
So full of glory and of might;
O Christ, Thou art its life and light;—
 Hail, blessed Easter day!
     — *Henry W. Frost*

∽

TRANSFORMATION

The cross was such an ugly thing!—
A shape to make the heart afraid;
A beam of death for lawless men,
A gibbett for the renegade.

The cross is such a lovely thing!—
The lamp in night where people grope;
The emblem of eternal life;

The symbol of eternal hope;
The subject of a thousand songs;
The sign of truth and liberty.

The cross was such an ugly thing
Until it went to Calvary.

     — *Lon Woodrum*

THE CROSS

In the cross of Christ I glory,
  Towering o'er the wrecks of time;
All the light of sacred story
  Gathers round its head sublime.

When the woes of life o'ertake me,
  Hopes deceive, and fears annoy,
Never shall the Cross forsake me;
  Lo, it glows with peace and joy.

When the sun of bliss is beaming
  Light and love upon my way,
From the Cross the radiance streaming
  Adds more lustre to the day.

Bane and blessing, pain and pleasure,
  By the Cross are sanctified;
Peace is there that knows no measure,
  Joys that through all time abide.

In the Cross of Christ I glory,
  Towering o'er the wrecks of time;
All the light of sacred story
  Gathers round its head sublime.

— John Bowring

Ↄ

I GAVE MY LIFE FOR THEE

I gave my life for thee,
  My precious blood I shed,
That thou mightst ransomed be,
  And quickened from the dead.
I gave my life for thee;
What hast thou given for me?

I spent long years for thee
  In weariness and woe,
That an eternity
  Of joy thou mightest know.
I spent long years for thee;
Hast thou spent *one* for me?

My Father's home of light,
  My rainbow-circled throne,
I left, for earthly night,
  For wanderings sad and lone.
I left it all for thee;
Hast thou left aught for me?

I suffered much for thee,
  More than thy tongue may tell,
Of bitterest agony,
  To rescue thee from hell.
I suffered much for thee;
What canst thou bear for me?

And I have brought to thee,
  Down from my home above,
Salvation full and free,
  My pardon and my love.
Great gifts I brought to thee;
What hast thou brought to me?

Oh, let thy life be given,
  Thy years for him be spent,
World-fetters all be riven,
  And joy with suffering blent;
I gave myself for thee:
Give thou thyself to me!

— Frances Ridley Havergal

Ↄ

AN EASTER PRAYER

O Crucified Son of God, I pray
All hate and evil in me slay.
That I may live with spirit free
Not unto self, but unto Thee.

Risen, living, triumphant Lord,
Breathe in my soul Thy living word,
That risen, I may walk with Thee,
Within appointed paths for me.

Ascended now upon Thy throne
Thou wilt not leave us here alone.
Holy Spirit, walk by our side
And bless us on this Eastertide.

— Chester M. Davis

WHAT DOES EASTER MEAN TO YOU?

What does Easter mean to you?
Stately church with cushioned pew?
Where, Lenten season gone at last
And days of self-denial past,
Richly-clad, devoted throngs
Of worshipers unite in songs
Of praise in lily-scented air?
Is this what makes your Easter fair?

Does it mean the end of winter's reign,
Bright skies and welcome warmth
     again,
Singing of birds, budding of trees,
Sweet spring odors on the breeze
From daffodil and crocus bed
And balsam branches overhead?
Sad is the world and cold and gray
If this is all of Easter Day.

But if this blessed season brings,
A firmer faith in holy things;
Assurance of a living Lord;
A strengthening of the tender chord
Of love that binds us to the life to
     come
Where loved ones 'wait us in the
     heavenly home,
No pain or loss can e'er efface the bliss,
Dear friend of Easter, when it means
     all this.
                    — May Ricker Conrad

THE CROSS

The Cross is such a simple thing,
Yet of it men may talk and sing.

It is a ladder to the skies,
On which a mounting soul may rise.

It is a sign-board on the road,
To cheer man with his weary load.

It is a key that fits the door
To joyousness for evermore.

It signals to the human race
That God in mercy offers grace.

To some it is a stumbling block
That causes men to curse and mock;

To others who their sins bemoan
It can become a stepping stone.

To voyagers its sturdy form
Becomes an anchor in the storm.

A hammer, it has won renown
By battering old oppressions down.

Gripped by still others as a sword,
It has won battles for the Lord.

Dragged as a plowshare thro' the heart,
New furrows cause the grain to start.

It is a tree upon a hill,
Whose fruit the hungry heart can fill.

It is a window for the soul;
'Tis medicine to make one whole.

The Cross is such a simple thing,
And yet it touches everything.

We cannot feel that such a sign
Is other than a power divine.

It is a beacon ever lit
By One identified with it.
                    — Charles N. Pace

LIGHT AFTER DARKNESS

Dark was the night when Jesus suf-
     fered,
Dark was the night when Jesus died;
Dark was the night when sin was can-
     celed
By our Saviour crucified.

Bright was the dawn that Easter morn-
     ing,
Bright was the path the Saviour trod;
Bright is the everlasting glory
Of the conquering Son of God.
                    — Carlton Buck

GUARD AT THE SEPULCHER

I was a Roman soldier in my prime;
Now age is on me, and the yoke of time.
I saw your Risen Christ, for I am he
Who reached the hyssop to Him on the tree,
And I am one of two who watched beside
The sepulcher of Him we crucified.

All that last night I watched with sleepless eyes;
Great stars arose and crept across the skies.
The world was all too still for mortal rest,
For pitiless thoughts were busy in the breast.
The night was long, so long it seemed at last
I had grown old and a long life had passed.
Far off, the hills of Moab, touched with light,
Were swimming in the hallow of the night.
I saw Jerusalem all wrapped in cloud,
Stretched like a dead thing folded in a shroud.

Once in the pauses of our whispered talk
I heard a something on the garden walk.
Perhaps it was a crisp leaf lightly stirred —
Perhaps the dream-note of a waking bird.
Then suddenly an angel, burning white,
Came down with earthquake in the breaking light,
And rolled the great stone from the sepulcher,
Mixing the morning with a scent of myrrh.
And lo, the Dead had risen with the day:
The Man of Mystery had gone His way!

Years have I wandered, carrying my shame;
Now let the tooth of time eat out my name.
For we, who all the wonder might have told,
Kept silence, for our mouths were stopt with gold.

— *Edwin Markham*

Faith to Understand

I came to God in prayer, I asked for health,
For the joy of walking with a free and easy stride.
The answer, when it came, was, "Nay, child, I must break your pride.
Only through affliction can your soul be purified."
Now I come to God in prayer, and ask for strength to bear my cross,
And for faith to see the hidden blessing in my loss.
And while my lips do tremble and the tears do flow,
I ask for faith to know and grace to see
That 'twas Thy kindly wisdom took this joy from me.
And in my weakness I tremblingly ask, "Why, why, dear God, is it so?"
And in the stillness of the morning I hear a whisper,
"Trust, trust, Child, and some day thou shalt know."

— Philora Hintz

ᴄᴡᴏ

At Rest

The day is past and all the light has fled;
Where shall I lay at rest my weary head?
Upon my soul falls down the dreadful night,
And in the dark I see no welcoming light.

Fearful I stand, not daring to go on;
Strengthless I wait, my hope and courage gone;
I reach forth trembling hands, with pleading cry:—
"O God, show mercy, or I fall and die!"

But not a voice is heard through midnight gloom,
No form draws near to save from threatening doom;
At last, I sink in dark despair, alone,
The earth my bed, my pillow flinty stone;

But in the dark my heart is strangely blest;
Yea, in the gloom my soul obtains its rest;
For, spite of night, I find that God on high
Is near the anguished soul, where'er it lie!

—Henry W. Frost

284

FAITH

What if I say,
"The Bible is God's Holy Word,
Complete, inspired, without a flaw,"
But let its pages stay
Unread from day to day,
And fail to learn there from God's law;
What if I go not there to seek
The truth of which I glibly speak,
For guidance on this earthly way;
Does it matter what I say?

What if I say
That Jesus Christ is Lord divine;
Yet fellow-pilgrims can behold
Naught of the Master's love in me,
No grace of kindly sympathy?
If I am of the Shepherd's fold,
Then shall I know the Shepherd's
        voice
And gladly make His way my choice.
We are saved by faith, yet faith is one
With life, like daylight and the sun.
Unless they flower in our deeds,
Dead, empty husks are all the creeds.
To call Christ, Lord, but strive not to
        obey,
Belies the homage that with words I
        pay.

— *Maud Frazer Jackson*

ᐁ

OVERNIGHT, A ROSE

That overnight a rose could come
    I one time did believe,
For when the fairies live with one,
    They wilfully deceive.
But now I know this perfect thing
    Under the frozen sod
In cold and storm grew patiently
    Obedient to God.
My wonder grows since knowledge
        came
    Old fancies to dismiss:

And courage comes. Was not the rose
    A winter doing this?
Nor did it know, the weary while,
    What color and perfume
With this completed loveliness
    Lay in that earthy tomb.
So maybe I, who cannot see
    What God wills not to show,
May, some day, bear a rose for Him
    It took my life to grow.

— *Caroline Giltinan*

ᐁ

A NAME IN THE SAND

Alone I walked the ocean strand,
A pearly shell was in my hand;
I stooped, and wrote upon the sand
    My name, the year, the day.
As onward from the spot I passed,
One lingering look behind I cast,—
A wave came rolling high and fast,
    And washed my lines away.

And so, methought, 'twill shortly be
With every mark on earth from me;
A wave of dark oblivion's sea
    Will sweep across the place
Where I have trod the sandy shore
Of time, and been, to be no more;
Of me, my frame, the name I bore,
    To leave no track nor trace;

And yet, with Him who counts the
        sands,
And holds the waters in his hands,
I know a lasting record stands
    Inscribed against my name,
Of all this mortal part has wrought,
Of all this thinking soul has thought,
And from these fleeting moments
        caught
    For glory or for shame!

—*Hannah Flagg Gould*

A LITTLE BIRD I AM

A little bird I am,
  Shut in from fields of air,
And in my cage I sit and sing,
  To him who placed me there;
Well pleased a prisoner to be,
Because, my God, it pleases thee!

Naught have I else to do,
  I sing the whole day long;
And he whom I most love to please
  Doth listen to my song;
He caught and bound my wandering
    wing,
And still he bends to hear me sing.

Thou hast an ear to hear,
  A heart to love and bless;
And tho' my notes were e'er so rude,
  Thou wouldst not hear the less;
Because thou knowest as they fall,
That love, sweet love, inspires them all.

My cage confines me round,
  Abroad I cannot fly;
But though my wing is closely bound,
  My heart's at liberty;
My prison walls cannot control
The flight, the freedom of the soul.

Oh, it is good to soar,
  These bolts and bars above,
To him whose purpose I adore,
  Whose providence I love;
And in thy mighty will to find
The joy, the freedom of the mind.

— *Madame Guyon*

oๆ

THE CRY OF FAITH

Ten leprous men, condemned to die
Thro' endless nights and lonely days,
"Unclean, unclean," forlornly cry
To warn unwary passers by
  Along the desert ways.

But laws gave way to faith's decree
When Jesus chanced to pass that way.
Ten men, as one, on bended knee
For mercy made an earnest plea
  And health was theirs that day.

O weary world, so sick within,
When will you learn in faith to pray?
Their leprosy but types your sin,
And if new life you would begin,
  Seek Christ without delay.

Who knows his sin and heeds not holy
    will,
Who trusts in men for life, is dying
    still!
Most blessed is he whose spirit thrills
With such a faith as cures a thousand
    ills!

— *M. Allen Gibson*

oๆ

FAITH

Faith looks across the storm —
  It does not doubt
Or stop to look at clouds
  And things without.

Faith does not question why
  When all his ways
Are hard to understand,
  But trusts and prays.

It seeks the greatest gift
  And asks not sight;
It does not need to see —
  He is its light.

Above the tempest's roar
  It hears his voice;
And, with its hands in his,
  Faith can rejoice.

It fears no cloud, or wind
  That it can bring;
Faith looks across the storm
  And still can sing.

— *Author Unknown*

He Must Do It

When I do it, faith is lacking,
    And ambition takes me through;
I promote it for my glory,
    By myself His work I do.
If He does it, I am nothing,
    Just a channel, nothing more,
He the Worker, I the agent,
    This I covet and implore.
He must do it, oh, to let Him!
    If I'm yielded to His will
Whether then success or failure,
All is well, and naught is ill.

—*Oswald J. Smith*

Guidance

There's a tender hand that guides me
    When I cannot see the way;
There's a loving arm that hides me
    From the storms that rise each day.
There's a gentle voice that cheers me
    When the path ahead grows dim;
There's a ready ear that hears me
    Every time I cry to Him.
'Tis my Lord, my blessed Saviour!
    He it is who walks with me.
I shall dwell with Him forever,
    Now and through eternity!

—*Avis B. Christiansen*

It Couldn't Be Done

Somebody said that it couldn't be done,
    But he with a chuckle replied
That "Maybe it couldn't," but he would be one
    Who wouldn't say so till he tried.
So he buckled right in with the trace of a grin
    On his face. If he worried he hid it.
He started to sing as he tackled the thing
    That couldn't be done, and he did it.

Somebody scoffed: "Oh, you'll never do that;
    At least no one ever has done it";
But he took off his coat and he took off his hat,
    And the first thing we knew he'd begun it.
With a lift of his chin and a bit of a grin,
    Without any doubting or quiddit,
He started to sing as he tackled the thing
    That couldn't be done, and he did it.

There are thousands to tell you it can't be done.
    There are thousands to prophesy failure;
There are thousands to point out to you one by one,
    The dangers that wait to assail you.
But just buckle in, with a bit of a grin,
    Just take off your coat and go to it;
Just start to sing as you tackle the thing
    That "cannot be done," and you'll do it.

—*Edgar A. Guest*

God's Bank Ain't Busted Yet!

The bank had closed; my earthly store had vanished from my hand;
I felt that there was no sadder one than I in all the land.
My washerwoman, too, had lost her little mite with mine,
And she was singing as she hung the clothes upon the line.
"How can you be so gay?" I asked; "Your loss don't you regret?"
"Yes, ma'am, but what's the use to fret? God's bank ain't busted yet!"

I felt my burden lighter grow; her faith I seemed to share;
In prayer I went to God's great throne and laid my troubles there.
The sun burst from behind the clouds, in golden splendor set;
I thank God for her simple words: "God's bank ain't busted yet!"

And now I draw rich dividends, more than my hands can hold
Of faith and love and hope and trust and peace of mind untold.
I thank the Giver of it all, but still I can't forget
My washerwoman's simple words: "God's bank ain't busted yet!"

Oh, weary ones upon life's road, when everything seems drear,
And losses loom on every hand, and skies seem not to clear;
Throw back your shoulders, lift your head, and cease to chafe and fret.
Your dividend will be declared: "God's bank ain't busted yet!"

— Alice P. Moss

Faith

Faith is not in understanding;
Faith is yielding to God's will,
Resting on His Word of Promise
In assurance calm and still.

Faith is waiting for the answer
Though no hopeful ray is giv'n,
Knowing that the final outcome
Now is clearly seen in Heav'n.

Faith is looking through the shadows
To the dawn of endless day,
Singing thro' the gath'ring darkness,
"Christ will lead me all the way!"

Faith is looking unto Jesus,
Trusting where it cannot see.
Faith is resting on His Promise —
Faith is glorious victory!

— Avis B. Christiansen

Rejoicing in Hope

Lift up your hearts to things above,
  Ye followers of the Lamb,
And join with us to praise His love,
  And glorify His name.

To Jesus' name give thanks and sing,
  Whose mercies never end:
Rejoice! rejoice! the Lord is King;
  The King is now our friend!

We for His sake count all things loss;
  On earthly good look down;
And joyfully sustain the cross,
  Till we receive the crown.

O let us stir each other up,
  Our faith by works to approve,
By holy, purifying hope,
  And the sweet task of love.

— Charles Wesley

FAITH'S EXPULSIVE POWER

Faith came singing into my room,
  And other guests took flight;
Fear and Anxiety, Grief and Gloom
  Sped out into the night;
I wondered that such peace could be,
But Faith said gently, "Don't you see?
They really cannot live with me."

— *Elizabeth Cheney*

ono

THE EYE OF FAITH

I do not ask for earthly store
  Beyond a day's supply;
I only covet more and more
  The clear and single eye.
To see my duty face to face,
And trust the Lord for daily grace.

Whate'er the crosses mine shall be,
  I will not dare to shun;
I only ask to live for Thee,
  And that Thy will be done.
Thy will, O Lord, be mine each day,
While passing on my homeward way.

And when at last my labor o'er,
  I cross the narrow sea,
Grant, Lord, that on the other shore
  My soul may dwell with Thee.
And learn what here I cannot know:
Why Thou hast ever loved me so.

— *J. J. Maxfield*

ono

FAITH

The sea was breaking at my feet,
  And looking out across the tide,
Where placid waves and heaven
      meet,
  I thought me of the Other Side.

For on the beach on which I stood
  Were wastes of sand, and wash, and
      roar,
Low clouds, and gloom, and solitude,
  And wrecks, and ruins — nothing
      more.

"O tell me if beyond the sea
  A heavenly port there is!" I cried,
And back the echoes laughingly
  "There is! there is!" replied.

— *James Whitcomb Riley*

ono

SONG OF FAITH

The lilied fields behold;
  What king in his array
Of purple pall and cloth of gold
  Shines gorgeously as they?
Their pomp, however gay,
  Is brief, alas! as bright;
It lives but for a summer's day,
  And withers in a night.

If God so clothe the soil,
  And glorify the dust,
Why should the slave of daily toil
  His providence distrust?
Will he, whose love has nursed
  The sparrow's brood, do less
For those who seek his kingdom first,
  And with it righteousness?

The birds fly forth at will;
  They neither plough nor sow:
Yet theirs the sheaves that crown the
      hill,
  Or glad the vale below.
While through the realms of air
  He guides their trackless way,
Will man, in faithlessness, despair?
  Is he worth less than they?

— *William Croswell*

LEAVE IT WITH HIM

Yes, leave it with Him; the lilies all do,
  And they grow;
They grow in the rain, and they grow in the dew —
  Yes, they grow;
They grow in the darkness, all hid in the night,
They grow in the sunshine, revealed by the light —
  Still they grow.

They ask not your planting, they need not your care
  As they grow.
Dropped down in the valley, the field — anywhere —
  Yet, they grow.
They grow in their beauty, arrayed in pure white;
They grow, clothed in glory, by heaven's own light —
  Sweetly they grow.

The grasses are clothed and the ravens are fed
  From His store;
But you who are loved and guarded and led,
  How much more
Will He clothe you, and feed you, and give you His care!
Then, leave it with Him; he has, everywhere,
  Ample store.

Yes, leave it with Him; 'tis more dear to His heart,
  You will know,
Than the lilies that bloom or the flowers that start
  'Neath the snow.
Whatever you need, if you ask it in prayer,
You can leave it with Him, for you are His care —
  You, you know.
          — *Author Unknown*

MY CREED

I would be true, for there are those who trust me;
I would be pure, for there are those who care;
I would be strong, for there is much to suffer;
I would be brave, for there is much to dare.

I would be friend of all, — the foe, the friendless;
I would be giving, and forget the gift;
I would be humble, for I know my weakness;
I would look up—and laugh—and love—and lift.

         — *Howard Arnold Walter*

BLIND

"Show me your God!" the doubter
   cries.
I point him out the smiling skies;
I show him all the woodland greens;
I show him peaceful sylvan scenes;
I show him winter snows and frost;
I show him waters tempest-tossed;
I show him hills rock-ribbed and
   strong;
I bid him hear the thrush's song;
I show him flowers in the close—
The lily, violet and rose;
I show him rivers, babbling streams;
I show him youthful hopes and
   dreams;
I show him stars, the moon, the sun;
I show him deeds of kindness done;
I show him joy, I show him care,
And still he holds his doubting air,
And faithless goes his way, for he
Is blind of soul, and cannot see!

     — *John Kendrick Bangs*

ST. AUGUSTINE, BISHOP OF HIPPO

What though the shades of night
Gather in darkness round thy closing
   eye:
   Thy Lord will give thee light
   No more to die.

The voice of Monica
Calls thee from Paradise—"Augustine,
   come:
   Lo! at the gates of day
   Thy destined home."

What though the tempest roar
In fury round thy Church's tottering
   wall!
   From the eternal shore
   Her voice doth call.

The Master Architect
Will shield against the advancing gates
   of hell
   The Church of his elect
   He loves so well.

He died to lay that stone
Elect and precious, bathed in his life-
   blood,
   That it may stand alone
   Against the flood.

In waves the quicksands swim:
Fear not the Syrtes' shift, the tempest
   shock:
   Thy faith is built on him
   Who is the Rock.

     — *Gerard Moultrie*

POSSESSION

Heaven above is softer blue
   Earth beneath is sweeter green.
Something lives in every hue,
   Christless eyes have never seen.
Birds with gladder songs o'erflow,
   Flowers with deeper beauty shine
Since I know as now I know
   I am His and He is mine.

     — *Wade Robinson*

FAITH

God knows, not I, the reason why
   His winds of storm drive through
     my door;
I am content to live or die
   Just knowing this, nor knowing
     more.
My Father's hand appointing me
My days and ways, so I am free.

     —*Margaret E. Sangster*

He Can

Canst thou take the barren soil
And with all thy pains and toil
    Make lilies blow?
Thou canst not. O helpless man,
Have faith in God — He can.

Canst thou paint the clouds at eve?
And all the sunset colors weave
    Into the sky?
Thou canst not. O powerless man,
Have faith in God — He can.

Canst thou still thy troubled heart
And make all cares and doubts depart
    From out thy soul?
Thou canst not. O faithless man,
Have faith in God — He can.

— Author Unknown

ოა

The Pearl of Great Price

Came a merchantman of yore,
Seeking goodly pearls to store;
One he found, and straightway sold
All he had, that one to hold.

But another merchant came,
Seeking pearls he knew by name,—
Seeking, gave his all for me;
Bought his treasure on the tree.

Seek I many pearls to own,
These for crown and those for throne?
All I have I sell, to buy
One I find so fair to eye.

This the pearl all price above,
And I know who calls it love:
Faith and hope, bright gems they shine,
But the pearl is love divine.

I, too, now for Jesus Christ,
Look within for pearls unpriced;
Hid in heart and stored in mind,
But the merchantman must find.

Down beneath strong passion's tide,
Down where weeds of sin-growth hide;
Scarce discerned from what is base,
Yet how sweet the hidden grace.

Seeking many, finding one,
Find all, thus lacking none,
Hold I each possession vain,
If I only this may gain.

Toiling on in life's swift whirl,
If I find this goodly pearl,
Till time's merchant own at last,
Heart, not hand, must hold it fast.

— William Chatterton Dix

ოა

But God

I know not, but God knows;
    Oh, blessed rest from fear!
All my unfolding days
    To Him are plain and clear.
Each anxious, puzzled "why?"
    From doubt or dread that grows,
Finds answer in this thought:
    I know not, but He knows.

I cannot, but God can;
    Oh, balm for all my care!
The burden that I drop
    His hand will lift and bear.
Though eagle pinions tire,
    I walk where once I ran,
This is my strength to know
    I cannot, but He can.

I see not, but God sees;
    Oh, all sufficient light!
My dark and hidden way
    To Him is always bright.
My strained and peering eyes
    May close in restful ease,
And I in peace may sleep;
    I see not, but He sees.

— Annie Johnson Flint

FAITH

I will not doubt, though all my ships at sea
Come drifting home with broken masts and sails;
I shall believe the Hand which never fails,
From seeming evil worketh good to me;
  And, though I weep because those sails are battered,
  Still will I cry, while my best hopes lie shattered,
     "I will trust in Thee."

I will not doubt, though all my prayers return
Unanswered from the still, white realm above;
I shall believe it is an all-wise Love
Which has refused those things for which I yearn;
  And though, at times, I can not keep from grieving,
  Yet the pure ardor of my fixed believing
     Undimmed shall burn.

I will not doubt, though sorrows fall like rain,
And troubles swarm like bees about a hive;
I shall believe the heights for which I strive
Are only reached by anguish and by pain;
  And, though I groan and tremble with my crosses,
  I yet shall see, through my severest losses,
     The greater gain.

I will not doubt; well anchored in the faith,
Like some stanch ship, my soul braves every gale,
So strong its courage that it will not fail
To breast the mighty, unknown sea of death.
  Oh, may I cry when body parts with spirit,
  "I do not doubt," so listening worlds may hear it
     With my last breath.
              — *Ella Wheeler Wilcox*

ᘏᕬ

A PARABLE FROM LIEBIG

The church bells were ringing, the Devil sat singing
On the stump of a rotting old tree;
"Oh, faith, it grows cold, and the creeds they grow old,
And the world is nigh ready for me."

The bells went on ringing, a spirit came singing,
And smiled as he crumbled the tree;
"Yon wood does but perish new seedlings to cherish,
And the world is too live yet for thee."
              — *Charles Kingsley*

THE FAITH OF ABRAHAM LINCOLN

I believe the will of God prevails;
Without Him all human reliance is vain;
Without the assistance of that Divine Being I cannot succeed;
With that assistance I cannot fail.

I believe I am a humble instrument in the hands of our
        Heavenly Father;
I desire that all my works and acts be according to His will;
And that it may be so I give thanks to the Almighty and seek His aid.

— Abraham Lincoln
(formulated by Carl Sandburg from Lincoln's own words; from *The War Years*)

WHY DIDST THOU DOUBT?

When all the haunting shadows of the night
Come thronging round me with a sudden sweep,
Whispering and echoing the fears I keep
By faith and hope and prayer, hidden from sight;

When white-lipped doubt suggests that my delight
Is a delusion, and my faith a leap
Into the dark, and that the years will reap
In pain and trouble what has seemed so right:

And when the floods encompass me about,
And the sweet vision of my Lord doth fade
In the blind darkness, and the words He said
Seem lost; I feel once more His hand stretched out;

Once more He speaks, "'Tis I, be not afraid;
O thou of little faith, why didst thou doubt?"

— Lucy Guiness Kumm

FAITH

Only believe! How sweet that tender message
    While roundabout the night grows dark and drear.
Only believe! It is the voice of Jesus
    That gently calls in accents soft and clear.
Only believe! Fear not the tempest's raging.
    Only believe! The darkness fadeth fast.
Only believe! Oh grip the Rock of Ages!
    Only believe! The day will dawn at last.

— Avis B. Christiansen

FAITH

Faith is a living power from heaven
That grasps the promise God hath
      given,
A trust that cannot be o'erthrown,
Fixed heartily on Christ alone.

Faith finds in Christ whate'er we need
To save or strengthen us indeed;
Receive the grace He sends us down,
And makes us share His cross and
      crown.

Faith in the conscience worketh peace
And bids the mourner's weeping cease;
By faith the children's place we claim,
And give all honor to one Name.

Faith feels the Spirit's kindling breath
In love and hope that conquer death;
Faith worketh hourly joy in God,
And trusts and blesses e'en the rod.

We thank Thee, then, O God of
      heaven,
That Thou to us this faith hast given
In Jesus Christ Thy Son, who is
Our only fount and source of bliss.

— *Petrus Herbert*

∽

ESSENCE OF TOMORROW

I feel the far-off cry of spring
Borne on the air today,
Though winds of February's sting
Hint not the least of May.
There's something deep within me lies,
A steadfast faith that knows
A thing of beauty never dies,
And there beneath the snows
Of winter's icy hand there's life —
And so the unborn flowers
Lend sweetness to my heart today,
And spring to winter hours.
And so it is when chilling blast

Of sorrows pierce the soul,
And anguished heart cries out "Alas!
I'll never more be whole,"
That faith within, though challenged
      now,
Will rise to meet the test,
And as we walk with God, somehow,
There'll still be hope and zest
To live for Him and work for Him;
For now — by faith — we feel
An essence of the ecstasy
That Heaven will reveal!

— *Alice Hansche Mortenson*

∽

GOD KNOWS

We ask and are answered not,
And so we say, God has forgot,
Or else, there is no God.

      The years
Roll back and thro' a mist of tears,
I see a child turn from her play,
And seek with eager feet, the way
That led her to her father's knee.

"If God is wise and kind," said she,
"Why did He let my roses die?"
A moment's pause, a smile, a sigh,
And then, "I do not know, my dear,
Some questions are not answered here."

"But is it wrong to ask?" "Not so,
My child; that we should seek to know
Proves right to know, beyond a doubt;
And some day we shall yet find out
Why roses die."

      And then I wait,
Sure of my answer, soon or late;
Secure that love doth hold for me
The key to life's great mystery;
And oh, so glad to leave it there,
Though my dead roses were so fair.

— *Author Unknown*

TRY THE UPLOOK

When the outlook is dark, try the uplook.
  These words hold a message of cheer;
Be glad while repeating them over,
  And smile when the shadows appear.
Above and beyond stands the Master;
  He sees what we do for His sake.
He never will fail nor forsake us;
  He knoweth the way that we take.

When the outlook is dark, try the uplook.
  The uplook of faith and good cheer;
The love of the Father surrounds us,
  He knows when the shadows are near.
Be brave, then, and keep the eyes lifted,
  And smile on the dreariest day.
His smile will glow in the darkness;
  His light will illumine the way.

— Author Unknown

WOMAN

Not she with traitorous kiss her Savior stung,
Not she denied him with unholy tongue;
She, while apostles shrank, could dangers brave,
Last at the cross and earliest at the grave.

— E. S. Barret

LORD, GIVE ME FAITH

Lord, give me faith! — to live from day to day,
With tranquil heart to do my simple part,
And, with my hand in Thine, just go Thy way.

Lord, give me faith — to trust, if not to know;
With quiet mind in all things Thee to find,
And child-like, go where Thou wouldst have me go.

Lord, give me faith! — to leave it all to Thee,
The future is Thy gift, I would not lift
The veil Thy love has hung 'twixt it and me.

— J. O.

"More Than They All"

"Two mites" — a simple little farthing,
    It was so small!
And yet — she might e'en then have
        halved it.
    It was her all.
One mite for God, and one she needed,
    Of wealth so small?
No; trusting to the God of widows,
    She gave her all.
And so, in sight of Him who "saw" it,
    It was not small,
For He who watched "how" it was
        given—said,
    "More than they all."
                — *L. M. Warner*

ono

Perseverance

Say, the man's not a man
    Who can quit when he can;
Who will cast down the load
    In the heat of the road
And not share in the sweat of the fray.
No! — the man is a man
    Who will stay!

There are cowards who fight
    When the going is right;
But the cause is forgot
    When the battle is hot —
And the foe takes the spoils of the day.
But the man is a man
    Who will stay!

Many soldiers have fought
    Where their efforts found naught
But the smile of the brave
    O'er the sod of their grave:
All their trophies were taken away —
Yet the man is a man
    Who will stay!

So let others disdain
    All the torture and pain
That must come with the fight

Against forces of night:
All our loss He will richly repay!
He loves men — stubborn men —
    Who will stay!

And when God meets His men
    At the roll call in Heav'n
And the crown and the throne
    Shall belong to His own,
Then with glory and grace He will say,
"You are mine! You are men
    Who will stay!"
                — *Author Unknown*

ono

Overheard in an Orchard

Said the Robin to the Sparrow:
    "I should really like to know
Why these anxious human beings
    Rush about and worry so."

Said the Sparrow to the Robin:
    "Friend, I think that it must be
That they have no heavenly Father
    Such as cares for you and me."

                — *Elizabeth Cheney*

ono

O for a Faith That Will Not Shrink

O for a faith that will not shrink,
    Though pressed by every foe,
That will not tremble on the brink
    Of any earthly woe!

That will not murmur nor complain
    Beneath the chastening rod,
But, in the hour of grief or pain,
    Will lean upon its God;

A faith that shines more bright and
        clear
    When tempests rage without;
That when in danger knows no fear,
    In darkness feels no doubt.

                — *William H. Bathurst*

THE RIFT

There was a rift tonight;
I saw a grey cloud break and let the light
Shine through — a ray of hope to all the earth;
Long had I waited here; I found it hard to say,
"The clouds will drift apart, the darkness melt away
Before the radiance of the night's new birth."

That promised glow to guide a wayward one;
At last, after long hours of doubt and fear,
Came light again and life, and sweet security,
As though a hidden ray from God's eternity
Peeped out, that I might look and see it there.

So, if I can but wait,
I know that God will send it, soon or late —
This break within my life's grey cloud; His gift
To me, one star of perfect love to shine and show
That they who walk by faith are told the way to go,
And after storm will come the blessed rift.

— *Ruth Margaret Gibbs*

THE ONE WHO PLANS

Often darkness fills the pathway of the pilgrim's onward track,
And we shrink from going forward — trembling, feel like going back:
But the Lord, Who plans so wisely, leads us on both day and night,
Till at last, in silent wonder, we rejoice in Wisdom's light.

Though the tunnel may be tedious thro' the narrow, darkened way,
Yet it amply serves its purpose — soon it brings the light of day:
And the way so greatly dreaded, as we backward take a glance,
Shows the skill of careful planning: never the result of chance!

Is your present path a tunnel, does the darkness bring you fear?
To the upright, oh, remember, He doth cause a light to cheer.
Press on bravely, resting calmly, though a way you dimly see,
Till, at length, so safely guided, you emerge triumphantly.

Trust the Engineer Eternal, surely all His works are right,
Though we cannot always trace them, faith will turn at last to sight:
Then no more the deepening shadows of the dark and dismal way,
There for ever in clear sunlight, we'll enjoy "the perfect day."

— *Author Unknown*

By Faith

By faith and not by sight,
  Saviour, I walk with Thee;
Lead Thou my feet aright;
  Choose Thou the path for me.

Choose Thou the path for me;
  I would not if I could;
For only Thou canst see
  My highest, heavenly good.

My highest, heavenly good.
  Lies in Thy will alone,
Designed and understood
  By Love upon His Throne.

By Love upon His Throne
  My life is planned aright;
Secure in Christ alone
  I walk by faith, not sight.

— *E. Margaret Clarkson*

Feet of clay! Feet of clay!
Man has but feet of clay —
A heart of gold and love untold
But hands and feet of clay.

I've learned that I must keep my eyes
Turned always toward the Lord
If I would find the perfect path
That leads to sweet accord.

For only God has perfect love,
The same both night and day —
A heart divine, not gold like mine,
Nor hands and feet of clay.

— *Phyllis C. Michael*

Feet of Clay

Feet of clay! Feet of clay!
Man has but feet of clay —
A heart of gold and love untold
But hands and feet of clay.

I took my eyes from God one day
And looked to man alone —
A certain man, a Christian man
Like one you may have known.

This man was faithful, kind and good
As good as he could be;
But as I looked I saw he, too,
Had feet like you and me.

We May Not Understand

We may not understand nor know
  Just how the giant oak-trees throw
Their spreading branches wide,
  Nor how upon the mountain-side
The dainty wild-flowers grow.

We may not understand nor see
  Into the depth and mystery
Of suffering and tears;
  Yet, thro' the stress of patient years
The flowers of sympathy

Spring up and scatter everywhere
  Their perfume on the fragrant air:
But lo! the seed must die,
  If it would bloom and multiply
And ripened fruitage bear.

— *Thomas Kimber*

HITHERTO

We have come very safely — hitherto;
And sometimes seas were calm, and skies were blue;
Sometimes the wild waves rose — the tempests roared;
But never barque went down with Christ on board.

And so it shall be to the very end —
Through ebb or flow, the one unchanging Friend,
Ruling the waves which sink at His command,
Holding them in the hollow of His hand.

A lonely track perchance, a darkened sky,
A mist of tears, and only God knows why —
Is He not worth our trust the voyage through,
He who has never failed us — hitherto?

Here all things pass, but Heaven keeps them fair;
The partings here — the joyous meetings there —
God's waves and winds drive onward to that rest;
Tossed home, as children to a Father's breast.

There comes an hour, when, every tempest o'er,
The harbour lights are reached, the golden shore:
Never, oh never more to fret or fear —
Christ, give us faith to praise Thee even here!

— *Mary Gorges*

MY CREED

That God doth live, enthroned in heaven above,
    Existing in three persons, and yet One,
    The everlasting Father, Spirit, Son,
Whom I may worship and forever love;
That Jesus died for me on Calvary's tree,
    And then ascended to His Father's throne,
    Thenceforth for e'er to intercede for me
    Until He comes to gather home His own:
That God hath sent the Holy Spirit down,
    To keep, to guide, to sanctify, to bless,
So I may wear, at last, a victor's crown
    And reign with Christ, who will my name confess:
This — 'spite of sin and failure's shadowing grief —
This I believe; Lord, help mine unbelief!

— *Henry W. Frost*

"Can God?"

"Can God?" the subtle Tempter breathes within,
   When all seems lost, excepting sure defeat,
"Can God roll back the raging seas of sin?"
   "Can God?" the fainting heart doth quick repeat.

"God can!" in trumpet tones rings faith's glad cry,
   And, David-like, it fears no giant foe,
For faith dwells on the Mount; serene, and high,
   While unbelief's dark clouds roll far below.

"God can!" His Saints of old did ever give
   Their fullest confirmation o'er and o'er,
And He Who made the long-dead bones to live,
   E'en now can bring the dead to life once more.

"God can!" Then let us fear not, but arise!
   Our motto be this word that He doth give,
If we have faith, before our wondering eyes
   A mighty army shall arise and live!

—*J. A. R.*

God Knoweth

I know not what awaits me,
   God kindly veils mine eyes,
And o'er each step of my onward way
   He makes new scenes to rise;
And every joy he sends me, comes
   A sweet and glad surprise.

Where he may lead I'll follow,
   My trust in Him repose;
And every hour in perfect peace
   I'll sing, He knows, He knows.

One step I see before me,
   'Tis all I need to see,
The light of heaven more brightly
         shines,
   When earth's illusions flee;

And sweetly through the silence, came
   His loving "Follow Me."

O blissful lack of wisdom,
   'Tis blessed not to know;
He holds me with His own right hand,
   And will not let me go,
And lulls my troubled soul to rest
   In Him who loves me so.

So on I go not knowing,
   I would not if I might;
I'd rather walk in the dark with God
   Than go alone in the light;
I'd rather walk by faith with Him
   Than go alone by sight.

—*Mary G. Brainard* and *P. P. Bliss*

BLESSED

Blessed is he whose faith is not offended,
    When all around his way
The power of God is working out deliverance
    For others day by day;

Though in some prison drear his own soul languish,
    Till life itself be spent,
Yet still can trust his Father's love and purpose,
    And rest therein content.

Blessed is he who, through long years of suffering,
    Cut off from active toil,
Still shares by prayer and praise the work of others,
    And thus "divides the spoil."

Blessed art thou, O child of God, who sufferest,
    And canst not understand
The reason for thy pain, yet gladly leavest
    Thy life in His blest Hand.

Yea, blessed art thou whose faith is "not offended"
    By trials unexplained,
By mysteries unsolved, past understanding,
    Until the goal is gained.

                 — *Freda Hanbury Allen*

GOD MAKES A PATH

God makes a path, provides a guide,
    And feeds a wilderness;
His glorious name, while breath re-
    mains,
    O that I may confess.

Lost many a time, I have had no guide,
    No house but a hollow tree!
In stormy winter night no fire,
    No food, no company;

In Him I found a house, a bed,
    A table, company;
No cup so bitter but's made sweet,
    Where God shall sweetening be.

         — *Roger Williams*

FEELING, FAITH AND FACT

Three men were walking on a wall,
Feeling, Faith and Fact,
When Feeling got an awful fall,
And Faith was taken back.
So close was Faith to Feeling,
He stumbled and fell too,
But Fact remained,
And pulled Faith back
And Faith brought Feeling too.

         — *Author Unknown*

My Friend

The Christian, like his Lord of old,
Must look for foes and trials here;
Yet may the weakest saint be bold,
With such a friend as Jesus near.

The lion's roar need not alarm,
O Lord, the feeblest of thy sheep;
Nor can the fiercest monster harm,
While thou art nigh to watch and keep.

Therefore I will thy foes defy,
And own thee as my God, my friend;
No fear shall make me e'er deny
The God on whom my hopes depend.

— *Author Unknown*

ᖇᖇ

To Know All Is to Forgive All

If I knew you and you knew me —
If both of us could clearly see,
And with an inner sight divine
The meaning of your heart and mine,
I'm sure that we would differ less
And clasp our hands in friendliness;
Our thoughts would pleasantly agree
If I knew you and you knew me.

If I knew you and you knew me,
As each one knows his own self, we
Could look each other in the face
And see therein a truer grace.
Life has so many hidden woes,
So many thorns for every rose;
The "why" of things our hearts would
     see,
If I knew you, and you knew me.

— *Nixon Waterman*

Pass It On

Love demands the loving deed,
     Pass it on!
Look upon your brother's need —
     Pass it on!
Live for self, you live in vain;
Live for Christ, with Him you reign —
     Pass it on!

— *Author Unknown*

ᖇᖇ

Transforming Friendship

Have you and I today
Stood silent, as with Christ, apart from
     joy or fray
Of life, to see by faith His face;
To look, if but a moment, at its grace,
And grow, by brief companionship,
     more true,
More nerved to lead, to dare, to do
For Him at any cost? Have we today
Found time, in tho't, our hand to lay
In His and thus compare
His will with ours, and wear
The impress of His wish? Be sure
Such contact will endure
Throughout the day; will help us walk
     erect
Through storm and flood; detect
Within the hidden life sin's dross, its
     stain;
Revive a tho't of love for Him again;
Steady the steps which waver; help us
     see
The footpath meant for you and me.

— *Author Unknown*

303

THE HOUSE BY THE SIDE OF THE ROAD

There are hermit souls that live withdrawn
    In the peace of their self-content;
There are souls, like stars, that dwell apart
    In a fellowless firmament;
There are pioneer souls that blaze their paths
    Where highways never ran —
But let me live by the side of the road
    And be a friend to man.

Let me live in a house by the side of the road,
    Where the race of men go by —
The men who are good and the men who are bad,
    As good and as bad as I.
I would not sit in the scorner's seat,
    Or hurl the cynic's ban —
Let me live in a house by the side of the road,
    And be a friend to man.

I see from my house by the side of the road,
    By the side of the highway of life,
The men who press with the ardor of hope
    The men who are faint with the strife.
But I turn not away from their smiles nor their tears —
    Both parts of an infinite plan —
Let me live in a house by the side of the road
    And be a friend to man.

I know there are brook-gladdened meadows ahead
    And mountains of wearisome height;
And the road passes on through the long afternoon
    And stretches away to the night.
But I still rejoice when the travelers rejoice,
    And weep with the strangers that moan,
Nor live in my house by the side of the road
    Like a man who dwells alone.

Let me live in my house by the side of the road
    Where the race of men go by —
They are good, they are bad, they are weak, they are strong,
    Wise, foolish — so am I.
Then why should I sit in the scorner's seat
    Or hurl the cynic's ban?
Let me live in my house by the side of the road
    And be a friend to man.

                    — *Sam Walter Foss*

THE PRECIOUS FRIEND

I have a Friend so precious,
  So very dear to me!
He loves me with such tender love,
  He loves so faithfully,
I could not live apart from Him,
  I love to feel Him nigh;
And so we dwell together,
  My Lord and I.

Sometimes I'm faint and weary;
  He knows that I am weak,
And as He bids me lean on Him,
  His help I gladly seek;
He leads me in the paths of light,
  Beneath a sunny sky;
And so we walk together,
  My Lord and I.

He knows how much I love Him.
  He knows I love Him well;
But with what love He loveth me,
  My tongue can never tell;
It is an everlasting love,
  An ever rich supply;
And so we love each other,
  My Lord and I.

> Sung in the rocks and caves of France
> during the persecution of the Hugue-
> nots, three hundred years ago.

MY NEIGHBOR

My Neighbor, who is he?
Who lives next door to me —
The man I daily meet,
Out on the crowded street?

The man to whom I talk,
With whom I daily walk;
Who smiles across the fence,
Nor lacks good common sense?

The man afar from me,
In his great need of me,
May be the nearest me,
And so my neighbor be.

My neighbor, who is he?
Mayhap who most needs me,
Whose want lays hold of me,
He must my neighbor be.

— *E. A. Repass*

FRIENDSHIPS

This life is like a garden place.
  Our friendships are the flowers,
The perfumes of the blossoms fair
  Are friendship's pleasant hours.
Some friendships flower much too fast,
  And fading, quickly die,
While others are like posies sweet
  That flower perennially.

— *Mary Edith Halladay*

IN GRATITUDE FOR FRIENDS

I thank You, God in Heaven, for
    friends.
When morning wakes, when daytime
    ends,
  I have the consciousness
Of loving hands that touch my own,
Of tender glance and gentle tone,
  Of thoughts that cheer and bless!

If sorrow comes to me I know
That friends will walk the way I go,
  And, as the shadows fall,
I know that I will raise my eyes
And see — ah, hope that never dies! —
  The dearest Friend of All.

— *Margaret E. Sangster*

FRIENDSHIP

To have a friend who follows all my thought
    As it may vagrant roam from earth to heaven,
    Who there will hold it fast until its leaven
Be purged away, by purer word in-wrought;
To have him understand when words have failed
    To make my better, nobler meaning plain;
    Who, when I'm silent, will his words restrain
And show by look that silence hath availed;

To know that he, if others adulate,
    Will dare to warn of pride's presumptuous sin;
    That he will speak of love, when others hate,
That he, to his strong self, my soul may win;
    Such friendship do I crave, till life shall end;
    And such I have — in Jesus Christ, my Friend!

                                    — *Henry W. Frost*

LITTLE BLACK DOG

I wonder if Christ had a little black dog
    All curly and woolly like mine;
With two silky ears, and a nose round and wet
    And eyes brown and tender that shine.

I am sure, if He had, that the little black friend
    Knew right from the first He was God;
That he needed no proofs that Christ was divine,
    But just worshiped the ground that He trod.

I'm afraid that He hadn't, because I have read
    How He prayed in the garden, alone!
For all of His friends and disciples had fled —
    Even Peter, the one called "a stone."

And, oh, I am sure that the little black dog
    With a heart so tender and warm
Would never have left Him to suffer alone,
    But creeping right under His arm

Would have licked those dear fingers in agony clasped
    And counting all favors but loss;
When they took Him away, would have trotted behind,
    And followed Him clear to the Cross!

                                    — *Author Unknown*

*   GOD   *

The Riddle of the World

The riddle of the world is understood
Only by him who feels that God is good;
As only he can feel who makes his love
The ladder of his faith, and climbs above
On the rounds of his best instincts; draws no line
Between mere human goodness and divine.
But judging God by what in him is best,
With a child's trust leans on a Father's breast.

— John Greenleaf Whittier

Omnipresent

I found God in the dawning
   In the crimson flight of night,
In the notes of the birds at matins,
   In the sun-burst glory light.

I found Him in a garden,
   In the dew-drenched columbine,
In the shy and modest clinging
   Of the morning-glory vine.

I found Him in the patches
   Of the white clouds floating high,
That touched with animation
   The majestic vault of sky.

I found Him in a roadway,
   Through a quiet countryside,
And on a lake at sunset,
   Where the golden ripples ride.

At last in purple twilight
   In the cooling, fragrant air,
I heard God's presence whisper —
   I knew that He was there.

— Frank G. Weaver

O God of the Impossible

O God of the impossible!
   Since all things are to Thee
But soil in which Omnipotence
   Can work almightily,

Each trial may to us become
   The means that will display
How o'er what seems impossible
   Our God hath perfect sway!

The very storms that beat upon
   Our little barque so frail,
But manifest thy power to quell
   All forces that assail.

The things that are to us too hard,
   The foes that are too strong,
Are just the very ones that may
   Awake a triumph song.

O God of the impossible,
   When we no hope can see,
Grant us the faith that still believes
   All possible to Thee!

— J. H. S.

My Rendezvous With God

I have a rendezvous with God,
  Where spirit doth with spirit meet;
Where He enfolds me in His love,
  While I anoint His blessed feet:
I have a rendezvous with God —
  Detain me not from its retreat.

For there He clasps me by the hand,
  And there I see Him face to face;
I tell Him all my vexing cares,
  He whispers of sufficient grace;
I have a rendezvous with God,
  A holy, happy meeting-place;
No earthly thing dare enter there
  To mar the fellowship we share.

The turmoil of the daily life,
  The burdens of the mind and heart,
Cannot dismay, must not distract
  My soul from meeting God apart!
For I've a rendezvous with God,
  And well I know that at that hour,
Abounding grace, more faith, new
      power
  For all these needs He doth impart.

World-vision of His harvest field,
  Supernal strength, its work to do,
In that blest hour with God alone
  Within my heart He doth renew:
With Christ's constraining love for
      souls
  With joy the labor to imbue.

Lord, keep me to this love-tryst true —
Let me not fail our rendezvous!

                    —Anne M. Waite

O God, I Need Thee!

O God, I need Thee!
When morning crowds the night away
And the tasks of waking seize my mind,
I need Thy Poise,

O God, I need Thee!
When clashes come with those
Who walk the way with me,
I need Thy smile.

O God, I need Thee!
When the path to take before me lies,
I see it — courage flees —
I need Thy Faith.

O God, I need Thee!
When the day's work is done,
Tired, discouraged, wasted;
I need Thy Rest.

                    — Author Unknown

The Secret

I met God in the morning
  When my day was at its best,
And His presence came like sunrise,
  Like a glory in my breast.

All day long the Presence lingered,
  All day long He stayed with me,
And we sailed in perfect calmness
  O'er a very troubled sea.

Other ships were blown and battered,
  Other ships were sore distressed,
But the winds that seemed to drive
      them
  Brought to us a peace and rest.

Then I thought of other mornings,
  With a keen remorse of mind,
When I too had loosed the moorings,
  With the Presence left behind.

So I think I know the secret,
  Learned from many a troubled way:
You must seek Him in the morning
  If you want Him through the day!

                    — Ralph Spaulding Cushman

ALONE WITH HIM

Alone, dear Lord, in solitude serene,
Thy servant Moses was constrained to go,
Into the silent desert with the sheep;
The silvery stars his lovely vigil know.

And Paul, the fiery warrior, zealous, bold
In desert places, 'neath Arabian skies,
Learned God's own lessons, harkened to His voice,
Grew calm, resourceful, humble, meek and wise.

Alone, dear Lord, I fear to be alone;
My heart demands the blest companionship
Of those that love Thee; friendships nectar sweet,
With those beloved, I evermore would sip.

But in the desert, Moses, David, Paul,
Were not alone, afar from love or care:
They companied with heav'nly visitors,
They knew no loneliness, for Thou wert there.

— Alice E. Sherwood

COME, NOW!

Come, now, you most careful layers of T-squares,
  You tedious extractors of square roots and cube roots,
You stooping squinters through microscopes,
  You merciless probers and meticulous dissectors,
You would-be plotters of the curves of life,
  Mathematically sure or else unbelieving;
You scorners of all but what mechanics
  Can drearily prove: I challenge you,
Even in your pride, even in your own citadel,
  Using those very instruments in which alone
You have such almighty faith,
  Draw for me now the design, the plan
Of the universe; tell me how this earth, a star, is hung,
  Diurnally turning for the refreshment of darkness and dew;
With your unfailing knowledge instruct me now
  Who sensitively fringed the retiring gentian's beauty;
Or with your calipers, infallibly certain, bound for me
  The mystic wild parabola of love.

— Archibald Rutledge

God, Thou Hast Made the World Beautiful

God — Thou hast made the world so beautiful!
A flock of birds on pinions fleet and strong,
Then — though it were not yet enough to soar —
    Gave to them song.
God — Thou hast made the world so beautiful;
A bower of June roses gay abloom,
Then — though it were not yet enough to grow —
    Gave them perfume.
God — Thou hast made the world so beautiful;
A million beings, soul their priceless gem,
Then — though it were not yet enough to live —
    Gave love to them.

                — *Theodosia Pearce*

Vespers

God, that madest Earth and Heaven,
    Darkness and light,
Who the day for toil hast given,
    For rest the night,
May thine angel guards defend us,
Slumber sweet thy mercy send us,
Holy dreams and hopes attend us.
    This livelong night.

            — *Reginald Heber*

God's Autographs

I stood upon a hill one night
And saw the great Creator write
His autograph across the sky
In lightning strokes, and there was I
To witness this magnificent
Tumultuous, divine event!

I stood one morning by a stream
When night was fading to a dream,
The fields were bright as fields may be
At spring, in golden mystery
Of buttercups — then God came on
And wrote his autograph in dawn.

One afternoon long years ago,
Where glacial tides did ebb and flow,
I found a cliff which God had smitten;
I scanned its breast, where he had
    written
With some great glacier for a pen
His signature for time and men.

One night I stood and watched the
    stars;
The Milky Way and ranging Mars,
Where God in letters tipped with fire
The story of his tall desire
Had writ in rhyme and signed his
    name
A stellar signature of flame.

Creation's dawn was deep in night,
When suddenly: "Let there be light!"
Awakened grass, and flower, and tree,
Chaotic skies, the earth, and sea;
Then, to complete creation's span
In his own image, God made man,
And signed his name, with stroke most
    sure —
Man is God's greatest signature!

           — *William L. Stidger*

God Is Near

'Mid the darkest scenes of life
   God is near!
In the turmoil and the strife
   God is near!
When the angry waves roll high
And the clouds obscure the sky,
Through the storm there comes a cry:
   God is near!

Though the dearest friend depart
   God is near!
He can heal the broken heart,
   God is near!
Do the tears fall thick and fast
As you ponder o'er the past?
There is One whose love will last,
   God is near!

In the midst of deepest grief
   God is near!
He alone can bring relief,
   God is near!
When the hand of death so cold
Snatches loved ones from the fold,
And you suffer grief untold,
   God is near!

Go and tell it far and wide:
   God is near!
Dry the tears on every side;
   God is near!
Take it to the darkest soul,
Let the message onward roll;
Hark! the bells of Heaven toll!
   God is near!

                —*Oswald J. Smith*

Broken Hearts

With His healing hand on a broken heart,
   And the other on a star,
Our wonderful God views the miles apart,
   And they seem not very far.

O it makes us cry—then laugh—then sing,
   Tho' 'tis all beyond our ken;
He bindeth up wounds on that poor crushed thing,
   And He makes it whole again.

Was there something shone from that healed new heart
   Made the Psalmist think of stars—
That bright as the sun or the lightnings' dart,
   Sped away past earthly bars?

In a low place sobbing by death's lone cart,
   Then a flight on whirlwind's cars;
One verse is about a poor broken heart,
   And the next among the stars.

There is hope and help for our sighs and tears,
   For the wound that stings and smarts;
Our God is at home with the rolling spheres,
   And at home with broken hearts.

                —*M. P. Ferguson*

See God in Everything

"Give me a new idea," I said,
While musing on a sleepless bed;
"A new idea that'll bring to earth
A balm for souls of priceless worth;
That'll give men tho'ts of things above,
And teach them how to serve and love,
That'll banish every selfish thought,
And rid men of the sins they've
    fought."

The new tho't came, just how, I'll tell:
'Twas when on bended knee I fell,
And sought from HIM who knows full
    well
The way our sorrow to expel.
SEE GOD IN ALL THINGS, great and
    small,
And give HIM praise whate'er befall,
In life or death, in pain or woe,
See God, and overcome thy foe.

I saw HIM in the morning light,
HE made the day shine clear and
    bright;
I saw HIM in the noontide hour,
And gained from HIM refreshing
    shower.
At eventide, when worn and sad,
HE gave me help, and made me glad.
At midnight, when on tosssing bed
My weary soul to sleep HE led.

I saw HIM when great losses came,
And found HE loved me just the same.
When heavy loads I had to bear,
I found HE lightened every care.
By sickness, sorrow, sore distress,
HE calmed my mind and gave me rest.
HE's filled my heart with gladsome
    praise
Since I gave HIM the upward gaze.

'Twas new to me, yet old to some,
This thought that to me has become
A revelation of the way

We all should live throughout the day;
For as each day unfolds its light,
We'll walk by faith and not by sight.
Life will, indeed, a blessing bring,
If we SEE GOD IN EVERYTHING.

                            — A. E. Finn

The World Can Neither Give Nor Take

The world can neither give nor take,
    Nor can it comprehend,
That peace of God, which Christ hath
    bought,
    That peace which knows no end.

The burning bush was not consumed
    Whilst God remained there;
The three, when Jesus made the
    fourth,
    Found fire as soft as air.

God's furnace doth in Zion stand;
    But Zion's God sits by,
As the refiner views his gold
    With an observant eye.

His thoughts are high, His love is wise,
    His wounds a cure intend;
And, tho' He doth not always smile,
    He loves unto the end.

His love is constant as the sun,
    Though clouds come oft between;
And, could my faith but pierce these
    clouds,
    It might be always seen.

Yet I shall ever, ever sing,
    And Thou forever shine;
I have Thine own dear pledge for this;
    Lord, Thou art ever mine.

            — Selina, Countess of Huntingdon

Hymn of the Waldenses

Hear, Father, hear thy faint afflicted flock
Cry to thee, from the desert and the rock;
While those, who seek to slay thy children hold
Blasphemous worship under roofs of gold;
And the broad goodly lands, with pleasant airs
That nurse the grape and wave the grain, are theirs.

Yet better were this mountain wilderness,
And this wild life of danger and distress,—
Watching by night and perilous flight by day,
And meeting in the depths of earth to pray,
Better, far better, than to kneel with them,
And pay the impious rite thy laws condemn.

Thou, Lord, dost hold the thunder; the firm land
Tosses in billows when it feels thy hand;
Thou dashest nation against nation, then
Stillest the angry world to peace again.
Oh, touch their stony hearts who hunt thy sons,—
The murderers of our wives and little ones.

Yet, mighty God, yet shall thy frown look forth
Unveiled, and terribly shall shake the earth.
Then the fool power of priestly sin and all
Its long upheld idolatries shall fall.
Thou shalt raise up the trampled and oppressed,
And thy delivered saints shall dwell in rest.

—*Willam Cullen Bryant*

He Giveth More

He giveth more grace when the burden grows greater,
    He sendeth more strength when the labors increase;
To added affliction He addeth mercy,
    To multiplied trials, His multiplied peace.

When we have exhausted our store of endurance,
    When our strength has failed ere the day is half done,
When we reach the end of our hoarded resources,
    Our Father's full giving is only begun.

His love has no limit, His grace has no measure,
    His power no boundary known unto men;
For out of His infinite riches in Jesus
    He giveth and giveth and giveth again.

—*Annie Johnson Flint*

OMNIPOTENCE

He telleth the stars in their number,
  And calleth each star by its name.
The hours run their course through
    the ages
  Forever and ever the same.
The tides time their rising and falling
  Today in their rhythm of old.
The sun knoweth the time of his set-
    ting
  And sinks to his cloud-bed of gold.

He hollowed the cup for the oceans,
  And stilleth its storms at His will,
While the waves that sweep over its
    bosom
  Rise but His command to fulfill.
He scattereth the hoarfrost like ashes,
  Saith, "Be thou on the ground," to
    the snow.
He maketh the storm clouds His
    chariot
  As on the swift wind wings they go.

Great is our Lord; of great power.
  All things are upheld by His hand.
The universe moves at His bidding,
  Or is stilled at His slightest com-
    mand.
Yet more than these marvels tran-
    scendent
  This wonder of wonders I see —
That the God of such infinite greatness
  Should care for the sparrows — and
    me.

                — Mabel Brown Denison

                   ❧

THE CLOCK OF GOD

The clock of God ticks surely on,
  From dawn to night, from night to
    dawn.
It ceases not as ages go,
  And never varies, fast or slow.

It keeps time while the world endure
For Him whose purposes are sure,
  Whose careful plans will come to
    flower,
Full and complete, when strikes the
    hour.

The clock of God has tolled the day
Of nations that have passed away,
And tolls the judgment now as then
On evil deeds and evil men.
It points the moment of release,
Of fear and hope, of strife and peace;
And promises with steady pace
The coming kingdom of His grace.

                — Clarence Edwin Flynn

                   ❧

GOD HAS TIME

God has time to watch the star fade
  And the sun grow dim and cold,
See the endless ages enter
  And the centuries unfold.

God has time to watch the redwood
  Grow to full maturity,
And to note the ceaseless minutes
  Nibbling at eternity.

God has time to shape the sunbeams
  And the slanting, silvery rain,
Color every flower that groweth
  And to count the amber grain.

God has time to note the falling
  Of a sparrow to the ground,
And rejoice with all His angels
  When a lost sheep has been found.

And when life's short race is finished,
  And we face the setting sun,
He'll have time to smile upon us
  And to greet us, one by one!

                — Ruth M. Williams

THE BLIND CHILD

I know what Mother's face is like,
  Although I cannot see;
It's like the music of a bell;
It's like the roses I can smell —
  Yes, these it's like to me.

I know what Father's face is like;
  I'm sure I know it all;
It's like his whistle on the air;
It's like his arms which take such care
  And never let me fall.

And I can tell what God is like —
  The God whom no one sees.
He's everything my parents seem;
He's fairer than my fondest dream,
  And greater than all these.

— *Author Unknown*

WALKING WITH GOD

To walk with God, O fellowship divine!
Man's highest state on earth — Lord, be it mine!
With Thee, may I a close communion hold;
To Thee, the deep recesses of my heart unfold:

Yet, tell Thee all — each weary care and grief
Into Thy bosom pour — till there I find relief.
O let me walk with thee, Thou Mighty One;
Lean on Thine arm, and trust Thy love alone;

With Thee hold converse sweet where'er I go;
Thy smile of love my highest bliss below!
With Thee transact life's business — doing all
With single aim for Thee — as Thou dost call:

My every comfort at Thy hand receive,
My every talent to Thy glory give;
Thy counsel seek in every trying hour,
In all my weakness trust Thy mighty power.

Oh, may this high companionship be mine,
And all my life by its reflection shine,
My great, my wise, my never-failing Friend,
Whose love no change can know, nor turn, nor end!

My Saviour-God! who gavest Thy life for me,
Let nothing come between my heart and Thee!
From Thee no thought, no secret, would I keep,
But on Thy breast my tears of anguish weep.

My every wound to Thee I take to heal,
For Thou art touched with every pang I feel.
O Friend of friends — the faithful, true and tried, —
In Thee, and Thee alone, I now confide.

— *C. H. I.*

GOD'S GIFT

As solid as it is, yet gold may fail,
    And leave us empty-handed in our need.
Pride's bastions fall before a taloned gale;
    Grief cuts our hearts as sickles fell a reed.
Our bodies can become as helpless things,
    Our eyes unseeing stare into the sun,
Pain give to us her hourly christenings,
    And all of joy seem over with and done.

But God is still at work upon the earth,
    Still calling forth the light from out the dark;
Let him who doubts watch miracles of brith;
    Watch life's quick flame leap from a tiny spark.
And God still holds this gift for mortal men:
    The strength through faith for them to start again.

— *Enola Chamberlin*

THE DIVINE IMAGE

To Mercy, Pity, Peace, and Love
All pray in their distress;
And to these virtues of delight
Return their thankfulness.

For Mercy, Pity, Peace and Love
Is God, our Father dear,
And Mercy, Pity, Peace and Love
Is Man, his child and care.

For Mercy has a human heart,
Pity a human face,
And Love, the human form divine,
And Peace, the human dress.

Then every man, of every clime,
That prays in this distress,
Prays to the human form divine,
Love, Mercy, Pity, Peace.

And all must love the human form,
In heaven, Turk, or Jew;
Where Mercy, Love, and Pity dwell
There God is dwelling too.

— *William Blake*

I SAW GOD WASH THE WORLD

I saw God wash the world last night
    With His sweet showers on high,
And then, when morning came, I saw
    Him hang it out to dry.

He washed each tiny blade of grass
    And every trembling tree;
He flung His showers against the hill,
    And swept the billowing sea.

The white rose is a cleaner white,
    The red rose is more red,
Since God washed every fragrant face
    And put them all to bed.

There's not a bird, there's not a bee
    That wings along the way
But is a cleaner bird and bee
    Than it was yesterday.

I saw God wash the world last night.
    Ah, would He had washed me
As clean of all my dust and dirt
    As that old white birch tree.

— *William L. Stidger*

From THE ETERNAL GOODNESS

I see the wrong that round me lies,
  I feel the guilt within;
I hear, with groan and travail-cries,
  The world confess its sin.

Yet, in the maddening maze of things,
  And tossed by storm and flood,
To one fixed trust my spirit clings:
  I know that God is good!

— *John Greenleaf Whittier*

ROCKED IN THE CRADLE OF THE DEEP

Rocked in the cradle of the deep
I lay me down in peace to sleep;
Secure I rest upon the wave,
For thou, O Lord, hast power to save.
I know thou wilt not slight my call,
For thou dost mark the sparrow's fall;
And calm and peaceful shall I sleep,
Rocked in the cradle of the deep.

When in the dead of night I lie
And gaze upon the trackless sky,
The star-bespangled heavenly scroll,
The boundless waters as they roll,—
I feel thy wondrous power to save
From perils of the stormy wave:
Rocked in the cradle of the deep
I calmly rest and soundly sleep.

And such the trust that still were mine,
Though stormy winds swept o'er the
    brine,
Or though the tempest's fiery breath
Roused me from sleep to wreck and
    death.
In ocean cave still safe with Thee
The gem of immortality!
And calm and peaceful shall I sleep
Rocked in the cradle of the deep.

— *Emma Willard*

NOW I SEE

"Now I see!" But not the parting
  Of the melting earth and sky,
Not a vision dread and startling,
  Forcing one despairing cry.
But I see the solemn saying,
  All have sinned and all must die,
Holy precepts disobeying,
  Guilty all the world must lie.
Bending, silenced, to the dust,
Now I see that God is just.

"Now I see!" But not the glory,
  Not the face of Him I love,
Not the full and burning story
  Of the mysteries above.
But I see what God hath spoken,
  How His well-beloved Son
Kept the laws which man hath broken,
  Died for sins which man hath done;
Dying, rising, throned above!
"Now I see" that God is love.

— *Frances Ridley Havergal*

I FOUND GOD

Sophisticated, worldly-wise,
I searched for God and found Him not,
Until one day, the world forgot,
I found Him in my baby's eyes.

—*Mary Afton Thacker*

THE ANCIENT THOUGHT

The round moon hangs like a yellow
    lantern in the trees
That lie like lace against the sky,
Oh, still the night! Oh, hushed the
    breeze —
  Surely God is nigh.

— *Watson Kerr*

GOD'S GRANDEUR

The world is charged with the grandeur of God.
It will flame out, like shining from shook foil;
It gathers to a greatness, like the ooze of oil
Crushed. Why do men then now not reck his rod?
Generations have trod, have trod, have trod;
And all is seared with trade; bleared, smeared with toil;
And wears man's smudge and shares man's smell: the soil
Is bare now, nor can foot feel, being shod.

And for all this, nature is never spent;
There lives the dearest freshness deep down things;
And though the last lights off the black West went
Oh, morning, at the brown brink eastward, springs —
Because the Holy Ghost over the bent
World broods with warm breast and with ah! bright wings.

— Gerald Manley Hopkins

ᨏᨏᨏ

THE WORLD

I saw Eternity the other night,
Like a great ring of pure and endless light,
All calm, as it was bright;
And round beneath it, Time in hours, days, years,
Driven by the spheres
Like a vast shadow moved; in which the world
And all her train were hurled.
The doting lover in his quaintest strain
Did there complain;
Near him, his lute, his fancy, and his flights,
Wit's sour delights,
With gloves, and knots, the silly snares of pleasure,
Yet his dear treasure,
All scattered lay, while he his eyes did pour
Upon a flower.

The darksome statesman, hung with weights and woe
Like a thick midnight-fog, moved there so slow,
He did not stay, nor go;
Condemning thoughts — like sad eclipses — scowl
Upon his soul,
And clouds of crying witnesses without
Pursu'd him with one shout.

Yet digg'd the mole, and lest his ways be found,
Worked under ground,
Where he did clutch his prey; (But one did see
That policy);
Churches and altars fed him; perjuries
Were gnats and flies;
It rained about him blood and tears; but he
Drank them as free.

The fearful miser on a heap of rust
Sat pining all his life there, did scarce trust
His own hands with the dust,
Yet would not place one piece above, but lives
In fear of thieves.
Thousands there were as frantic as himself
And hugged each one his pelf.
The downright epicure placed heaven in sense
And scorn'd pretence,
While others, slipp'd into a wide excess,
Said little less;
The weaker sort, slight trivial wares enslave,
Who think them brave;
And poor, despisèd Truth sat counting by
Their victory.

Yet some, who all this while did weep and sing,
And sing, and weep, soared up into the Ring;
But most would use no wing.
O fools (said I) thus to prefer dark night
Before true light!
To live in grots and caves, and hate the day
Because it shows the way,
The way, which from this dead and dark abode
Leads up to God,
A way where you might tread the sun, and be
More bright than he.
But as I did their madness so discuss,
One whisper'd thus,
"This Ring the Bridegroom did for none provide,
But for his bride."

— Henry Vaughan

⌇

LIGHT SHINING OUT OF DARKNESS

God moves in a mysterious way,
  His wonders to perform;
He plants his footsteps in the sea,
  And rides upon the storm.

Deep in unfathomable mines
  Of never failing skill,
He treasures up his bright designs,
  And works his sovereign will.

Ye fearful saints, fresh courage take;
  The clouds ye so much dread
Are big with mercy, and shall break
  In blessings on your head.

Judge not the Lord by feeble sense,
  But trust him for his grace;
Behind a frowning providence,
  He hides a smiling face.

His purposes will ripen fast,
  Unfolding every hour:
The bud may have a bitter taste,
  But sweet will be the flower.

Blind unbelief is sure to err,
  And scan his work in vain;
God is his own interpreter,
  And he will make it plain.

— *William Cowper*

THE MANUSCRIPTS OF GOD

And nature, the old nurse, took
  The child upon her knee,
Saying, "Here is a story book
  My father hath writ for thee.
Come, wander with me," she said,
  "In regions yet untrod
And read what is still unread
  In the manuscripts of God."

— *Henry Wadsworth Longfellow*

MAN'S HAND — AND GOD'S

Once I heard a prima donna sing,
  And marveled at such art;
But today an oriole's fluted note
  Lights a candle in my heart.

One day I walked thro' a lovely place
  Where wonderful paintings hung,
But I climbed this ridge just now and
    looked
  At the hills God's hand has flung.

I stood last year where I could see
  A city, magnificent — grand;
But I glance just now where the sunset
    clouds
  Are by an Artist's hand.

Today I might have viewed a work
  Of engineering skill;
But I caught the heavenly scent of
    plums
  Blooming upon this hill.

— *Mae Traller*

LORD OF ALL

Along the rims of outer space
  God moves as here on earth;
His love creates, His hand provides
  Each thing of noble worth.

Where'er worlds are or soon shall be
  Each thing shall sing God's praise
For He by whom each dawn is made
  Shall rule o'er all our days.

No heart too small, no world too wide
  To feel the Master's touch;
Dear Lord of all, we give Thee thanks
  For Thou hast sent so much.

O keep us, Lord, and help us live
  Within these worlds of Thine
With hearts that look to Thee for grace
  To grow in Light divine.

— *Phyllis C. Michael*

GOD IS OUR REFUGE
(Psalm 46)

God is our refuge, our strong tow'r,
Securing by His mighty pow'r,
When dangers threaten to devour.

Thus arm'd no fears shall chill our
blood,
Tho' earth no longer steadfast stood,
And shook her hills into the flood;

Although the troubled ocean rise
In foaming billows to the skies,
And mountains shake with horrid
noise.

Clear streams purl from a crystal
spring,
Which gladness to God's city bring,
The mansion of th' Eternal King;

He in her centre takes His place,
What foe can her fair tow'rs deface,
Protected by His early grace?

Tumultuary nations rose,
And armèd troops our walls enclose,
But His fear'd Voice unnerv'd our
foes.

The Lord of Hosts is on our side,
The God by Jacob magnified,
Our Strength, on Whom we have re-
lied.

Come, see the wonders He hath
wrought;
Who hath to desolation brought
Those kingdoms which our ruin
sought.

He makes destructive war surcease,
The earth, deflower'd of her increase,
Restores with universal peace.

He breaks their bows, unarms their
quivers,
The bloody spear in pieces shivers,
Their chariots to the flame delivers.

Forbear, and know that I, the Lord,
Will by all nations be ador'd,
Prais'd with unanimous accord.

The Lord of Hosts is on our side,
The God by Jacob magnified,
Our Strength on Whom we have re-
lied.

— George Sandys

O LITTLE SELF

O little self, within whose smallness lies
All that man was, and is, and will become,
Atom unseen that comprehends the skies
And tells the tracks by which the planets roam;
That, without moving, knows the joys of wings,
The tiger's strength, the eagle's secrecy,
And in the hovel can consort with kings,
Or clothe a God with his own mystery.
O with what darkness do we cloak thy light,
What dusty folly gather thee for food,
Thou who alone art knowledge and delight,
The heavenly bread, the beautiful, the good.
O living self, O God, O morning star,
Give us thy light, forgive us what we are.

— John Masefield

SOMETIME

Sometime, when all life's lessons have been learned,
    And sun and stars forevermore have set,
The things which our weak judgment here had spurned,
    The things o'er which we grieved with lashes wet,
Will flash before us out of life's dark night,
    As stars shine most in deeper tints of blue;
And we shall see how all God's plans were right,
    And how what seemed reproof was love most true.

And we shall see how, while we frown and sigh,
    God's plans go on as best for you and me;
How, when we called, he heeded not our cry,
    Because his wisdom to the end could see.
And even as prudent parents disallow
    Too much of sweet to craving babyhood,
So God, perhaps, is keeping from us now
    Life's sweetest things, because it seemeth good.

And if, sometimes, commingled with life's wine,
    We find the wormwood and rebel and shrink,
Be sure a wiser hand than yours or mine
    Pours out this portion for our lips to drink.
And if some friend we love is lying low,
    Where human kisses cannot reach his face,
Oh, do not blame the loving Father so.
    But wear your sorrow with obedient grace.

And you shall shortly know that lengthened breath
    Is not the sweetest gift God sends his friend,
And that, sometimes, the sable pall of death
    Conceals the fairest boon his love can send.
If we could push ajar the gates of life,
    And stand within and all God's working see,
We could interpret all this doubt and strife,
    And for each mystery could find a key!

But not to-day. Then be content, poor heart!
    God's plans, like lilies, pure and white, unfold;
We must not tear the close-shut leaves apart,
    Time will reveal the calyxes of gold.
And if, through patient toil, we reach the land
    Where tired feet, with sandals loose, may rest,
When we shall clearly know and understand —
    I think that we will say, "God knew the best!"

                                        — *May Riley Smith*

GOD'S PRESENCE

But God is never so far off
As even to be near
He is within; our spirit is
The home He holds most dear.

To think of Him as by our side
Is almost as untrue
As to remove His throne beyond
Those skies of starry blue.

So all the while I thought myself
Homeless, forlorn, and weary.
Missing my joy, I walked the earth,
Myself God's sanctuary.

I come to Thee once more, my God!
No longer will I roam;
For I have sought the wide world thro'
And never found a home.

Though bright and many are the spots
Where I have built a nest —
Yet in the brightest still I pined
For more abiding rest.

For Thou hast made this wondrous
soul
All for Thyself alone;
Ah! send Thy sweet transforming grace
To make it more Thine own.

— *Frederick William Faber*

ᕯᕮᕲ

RECESSIONAL

God of our fathers, known of old —
Lord of our far-flung battle-line —
Beneath whose awful Hand we hold
Dominion over palm and pine —
Lord God of Hosts, be with us yet,
Let we forget, lest we forget!

The tumult and the shouting dies —
The captains and the kings depart —
Still stands Thine ancient sacrifice,
An humble and a contrite heart.
Lord God of Hosts, be with us yet,
Lest we forget, lest we forget!

Far-call'd out navies melt away —
On dune and headland sinks the
fire —
Lo, all our pomp of yesterday
Is one with Nineveh and Tyre!
Judge of the Nations, spare us yet,
Lest we forget, lest we forget!

If, drunk with sight of power, we loose
Wild tongues that have not Thee in
awe —
Such boasting as the Gentiles use
Or lesser breeds without the Law —
Lord God of Hosts, be with us yet,
Lest we forget, lest we forget!

For heathen heart that puts her trust
In reeking tube and iron shard —
All valiant dust that builds on dust,
And guarding calls not Thee to
guard —
For frantic boast and foolish word,
Thy Mercy on Thy People, Lord!

— *Rudyard Kipling*

ᕯᕮᕲ

DISCOVERY

Scientific proof of how I know
That God concerns Himself with me?
Can finite eye glimpse heaven's glow?
Is there a light for man to see?
Can I be certain of the way?
May I know truth in essence pure?
Does God reveal Himself today?
Do love, and truth, and man endure?

By tube or scale, I cannot place
My faith in laboratory test
To prove God's loving, proffered care,
But in His Word, I see His face
And hear His voice; and what is best,
My soul responds to find Him there.

— *Carlton Buck*

ALL THINGS BRIGHT AND BEAUTIFUL

All things bright and beautiful,
    All creatures great and small,
All things wise and wonderful,
    The Lord God made them all.

Each little flower that opens,
    Each little bird that sings,
He made their glowing colours,
    He made their tiny wings.

The purple-headed mountain,
    The river running by,
The sunset, and the morning
    That brightens up the sky,

The cold wind in the winter,
    The pleasant summer sun,
The ripe fruits in the garden,
    He made them every one.

The tall trees in the greenwood,
    The meadows where we play,
The rushes by the water,
    We gather every day.

He gave us eyes to see them,
    And lips that we might tell
How great is God Almighty,
    Who has made all things well.

— *Cecil Frances Alexander*

LUTHER'S HYMN

A mighty fortress is our God,
    A bulwark never failing;
Our helper he amid the flood
    Of mortal ills prevailing.
        For still our ancient foe
        Doth seek to work us woe;
        His craft and power are great,
        And, armed with cruel hate,
        On earth is not his equal.

Did we in our own strength confide,
    Our striving would be losing,—
Were not the right man on our side,
    The man of God's own choosing.
        Dost ask who that may be?
        Christ Jesus, it is he,
        Lord Sabaoth his name,
        From age to age the same,
        And he must win the battle.

And tho' this world, with devils filled,
    Should threaten to undo us,
We will not fear, for God hath willed
    His truth to triumph through us.
        The Prince of Darkness grim,
        We tremble not for him,
        His rage we can endure,
        For lo! his doom is sure,
        One little word shall fell him.

That word above all earthly powers,
    No thanks to them, abideth;
The spirit and the gifts are ours
    Through Him who with us sideth.
        Let goods and kindred go,
        This mortal life also:
        The body they may kill,
        God's truth abideth still,
        His kingdom is forever.

— *Martin Luther*
Translated by Frederic Henry Hedge

"GIVE US THIS DAY OUR DAILY BREAD"

Back of the loaf is the snowy flour,
    And back of the flour the mill,
And back of the mill is the wheat and
        the shower,
    And the sun and the Father's will.

— *Maltbie D. Babcock*

He Leadeth Me

In "green pastures"? Not always; sometimes He
Who knowest best, in kindness leadeth me
In weary ways, where heavy shadows be.
Out of the sunshine, warm and soft and bright,
Out of the sunshine into darkest night,
I oft would faint with sorrows and affright,
Only for this: I know He holds my hand;
So, whether led in green or desert land,
I trust, although I may not understand.
Beside "still waters"? No, not always so;
Ofttimes the heavy tempests 'round me blow,
And o'er my soul the waves and billows go.
But when the storms beat loudest, and I cry
Aloud for help, the Master standeth by,
And whispers to my soul, "Lo, it is I."
Above the tempest wild I hear Him say:
"Beyond this darkness lies the perfect day;
In every path of thine I lead the way."
So whether on the hill-tops high and fair
I dwell, or in the sunless valleys where
The shadows lie, what matter? He is there.
And more than this; where'er the pathway lead,
He gives to me no helpless, broken reed,
But His own hand, sufficient for my need.

— Henry H. Barry

ᏳᎸ

Jehovah Tsidkenu — *The Lord Our Righteousness*

I once was a stranger to grace and to God,
I knew not my danger, and felt not my load;
Though friends spoke in rapture of Christ on the tree,
Jehovah Tsidkenu was nothing to me.

I oft read with pleasure, to soothe or engage,
Isaiah's wild measure and John's simple page;
But e'en when they pictured the blood-sprinkled tree,
Jehovah Tsidkenu seemed nothing to me.

Like tears from the daughters of Zion that roll,
I wept when the waters went over His soul;
Yet thought not that my sins had nailed to the tree
Jehovah Tsidkenu — 'twas nothing to me.

When free grace awoke me, by light from on high,
Then legal fears shook me, I trembled to die;
No refuge, no safety in self could I see —
Jehovah Tsidkenu my Saviour must be.

My terrors all vanished before the sweet name;
My guilty fears banished, with boldness I came
To drink at the fountain, life-giving and free —
Jehovah Tsidkenu is all things to me.

Jehovah Tsidkenu! my treasure and boast,
Jehovah Tsidkenu! I ne'er can be lost;
In Thee I shall conquer by flood and by field —
My cable, my anchor, my breastplate and shield!

Even treading the valley, the shadow of death,
This watchword shall rally my faltering breath;
For while from life's fever my God sets me free,
Jehovah Tsidkenu my death-song shall be.

— *Robert Murray McCheyne*

ᐬ

THE UNKNOWN GOD

The Lord hath builded for Himself
　　He needs no earthly dome;
The universe His dwelling is,
　　Eternity His home.

Yon glorious sky His temple stands,
　　So lofty, bright and blue,
All lamped with stars, and curtained
　　round
　　With clouds of every hue.

Earth is His altar: Nature there
　　Her daily tribute pays;
The elements upon Him wait;
　　The seasons roll His praise.

Where shall I see Him? How describe
　　The Dread, Eternal One?
His foot-prints are in every place,
　　Himself is found in none.

He called the world, and it arose;
　　The heavens, and they appeared:

His hand poured forth the mighty
　　deep;
　　His arm the mountains reared.

He sets His foot upon the hills,
　　And earth beneath Him quakes;
He walks upon the hurricane,
　　And in the thunder speaks.

I search the rounds of space and time,
　　Nor find His semblance there:
Grandeur has nothing so sublime,
　　Nor Beauty half so fair.

— *Henry Francis Lyte*

ᐬ

RIGHT IS RIGHT

For right is right, since God is God,
　　And right the day must win;
To doubt would be disloyalty,
　　To falter would be sin.

— *Frederick William Faber*

OUT IN THE FIELDS WITH GOD

The little cares that fretted me
　I lost them yesterday,
Among the fields above the sea,
　Among the winds at play,
Among the lowing of the herds,
　The rustling of the trees,
Among the singing of the birds,
　The humming of the bees.

The foolish fears of what might
　　happen,
　I cast them all away
Among the clover-scented grass,
　Among the new-mown hay,
Among the husking of the corn,
　Where drowsy poppies nod
Where ill thoughts die and good are
　　born —
　Out in the fields with God.

　　　—*Elizabeth Barrett Browning*

O GOD, OUR HELP IN AGES PAST

O God, our help in ages past,
　Our hope in years to come,
Our shelter from the stormy blast,
　And our eternal home —

Under the shadow of thy throne
　Thy saints have dwelt secure;
Sufficient is thine arm alone,
　And our defense is sure.

Before the hills in order stood,
　Or earth received her frame,
From everlasting thou art God,
　To endless years the same.

A thousand ages in thy sight
　Are like an evening gone;
Short as the watch that ends the night
　Before the rising sun.

Time, like an ever-rolling stream
　Bears all its sons away;

They fly, forgotten, as a dream
　Dies at the opening day.

Our God, our help in ages past,
　Our hope in years to come,
Be thou our guard while troubles last,
　And our eternal home.

　　　— *Isaac Watts*

GREAT GOD!

Great God! beneath whose piercing eye
The earth's extended kingdoms lie;
Whose favoring smile upholds them
　all,
Whose anger smites them, and they
　fall.

We bow before Thy heavenly throne;
Thy power we see, Thy greatness own;
Yet, cherished by Thy milder voice,
Our bosoms tremble and rejoice.

Thy kindness to our fathers shown
Their children's children long shall
　own;
To Thee, with grateful hearts, shall
　raise
The tribute of exulting praise.

Great God, our Guardian, Guide and
　Friend!
O still Thy sheltering arm extend;
Preserved by Thee for ages past,
For ages let Thy kindness last!

　　　— *William Roscoe*

From THE BATTLE-FIELD

Truth, crushed to earth shall rise again;
　The eternal years of God are hers;
But Error, wounded, writhes with pain
　And dies among his worshipers.

　　　— *William Cullen Bryant*

THE MAJESTY AND MERCY OF GOD

Oh, worship the King all glorious above;
Oh, gratefully sing his power and his love;
Our shield and defender, the Ancient of Days
Pavilioned in splendor and girded with praise.

Oh, tell of his might, Oh, sing of his grace,
Whose robe is the light, whose canopy space;
His chariots of wrath the deep thunder clouds form,
And dark is his path on the wings of the storm.

The earth, with its store of wonders untold,
Almighty, thy power hath founded of old,
Hath stablished it fast by a changeless decree,
And round it hath cast, like a mantle, the sea.

Thy bountiful care what tongue can recite?
It breathes in the air, it shines in the light,
It streams from the hills, its descends to the plain,
And sweetly distills in the dew and the rain.

Frail children of dust and feeble as frail
In thee do we trust, nor find thee to fail.
Thy mercies how tender, how firm to the end,
Our Maker, Defender, Redeemer and Friend.

Oh, measureless Might, ineffable Love,
While angels delight to hymn thee above,
The humbler creation, though feeble their lays,
With true adoration shall lisp to thy praise.

—*Sir Robert Grant*

WEARY, LONELY, RESTLESS, HOMELESS

Weary hearts! weary hearts! by cares of life oppressed,
Ye are wandering in the shadows, ye are sighing for the rest;
There is darkness in the heavens, and the earth is bleak below,
And the joys we taste to-day may to-morrow turn to woe.
    Weary hearts! God is rest.

Lonely hearts! lonely hearts! 'tis but a land of grief;
Ye are pining for repose, ye are longing for relief;
What the world hath never given, kneel and ask of God above,
And your grief shall turn to gladness if you lean upon His love.
    Lonely hearts! God is love.

Restless hearts! restless hearts! ye are toiling night and day,
And the flowers of life, all withered, leave but thorns along your way;
Ye are waiting, ye are waiting till your toilings here shall cease,
And your ever-restless throbbing is a sad, sad prayer for peace.
    Restless hearts! God is peace.

Broken hearts! broken hearts! ye are desolate and lone,
And low voices from the past o'er your present ruins moan;
In the sweetest of your pleasures there was bitterest alloy,
And a starless night hath followed on the sunset of your joy.
    Broken hearts! God is joy.

Homeless hearts! homeless hearts! through the dreary, dreary years,
Ye are lonely, lonely wanderers, and your way is wet with tears;
In bright or blighted places, wheresoever ye may roam,
Ye look away from earthland, and ye murmur, "Where is Home?"
    Homeless hearts! God is home.

— Father Ryan

NEARER TO THEE

Nearer, my God, to Thee,
  Nearer to Thee!
E'en though it be a cross
  That raiseth me;
Still all my song shall be,
Nearer, my God, to Thee,
  Nearer to Thee!

Though like the wanderer,
  The sun gone down,
Darkness be over me
  My rest a stone;
Yet in my dreams I'd be
Nearer, my God, to Thee,
  Nearer to Thee!

There let the way appear
  Steps unto heaven;
All that Thou send'st to me
  In mercy given;
Angels to beckon me
Nearer, my God, to Thee,
  Nearer to Thee!

Then, with my waking thoughts
  Bright with Thy praise,
Out of my stony griefs
  Bethel I'll raise;
So by my woes to be
Nearer, my God, to Thee,
  Nearer to Thee!

Or if on joyful wing
  Cleaving the sky,
Sun, moon, and stars forgot,
  Upward I fly,
Still all my song shall be,
Nearer, my God, to Thee,
  Nearer to Thee!

— Sarah Flower Adams

AFTER ST. AUGUSTINE

Sunshine let it be or frost,
  Storm or calm, as Thou shalt choose;
Though Thine every gift were lost,
  Thee Thyself we could not lose.

— Mary Elizabeth Coleridge

GOD

There is an Eye that never sleeps
　Beneath the wing of night;
There is an Ear that never shuts
　When sinks the beams of light.

There is an Arm that never tires
　When human strength gives way;

There is a Love that never fails
　When earthly loves decay.

That Eye unseen o'erwatcheth all;
　That Arm upholds the sky;
That Ear doth hear the sparrows call;
　That Love is ever nigh.

　　　　　— James Cowden Wallace

GOD AND THE STRONG ONES

"We have made them fools and weak!" said the Strong Ones:
　"We have bound them, they are dumb and deaf and blind;
We have crushed them in our hands like a heap of crumbling sands,
　We have left them naught to seek or find:
They are quiet at our feet!" said the Strong Ones;
　"We have made them one with wood and stone and clod;
Serf and laborer and woman, they are less than wise or human!—"
　"I shall raise the weak!" saith God.

"They are stirring in the dark!" said the Strong Ones,
　"They are struggling, who were moveless like the dead.
We can hear them cry and strain hand and foot against the chain,
　We can hear their heavy upward tread. . . .
What if they are restless?" said the Strong Ones;
　"What if they have stirred beneath the rod?
Fools and weak and blinded men, we can tread them down again—"
　"Shall ye conquer Me?" saith God.

"They will trample us and bind!" said the Strong Ones;
　"We are crushed beneath the blackened feet and hands;
All the strong and fair and great they will crush from out the state;
　They will whelm it with the weight of pressing sands—
They are maddened and are blind!" said the Strong Ones;
　"Black decay has come where they have trod;
They will break the world in twain if their hands are on the rein—"
　"What is that to Me?" saith God.

"Ye have made them in their strength, who were Strong Ones,
　Ye have only taught the blackness ye have known:
These are evil men and blind?—Ay, but molded to your mind!
　How shall ye cry out against your own?
Ye have held the light and beauty I have given
　Far above the muddied ways where they must plod:
Ye have builded this your lord with the lash and with the sword—
　Reap what ye have sown!" saith God.

　　　　　— Margaret Widdemer

From THE ROCK

Men have left GOD not for other gods, they say, but for no god; and this
      has never happened before
That men both deny gods and worship gods, professing first Reason
And then Money, and Power, and what they call Life, or Race, or Dialectic.
The Church disowned, the tower overthrown, the bells upturned, what
      have we to do
But stand with empty hands and palms turned upwards
In an age which advances progessively backwards?

                              — T. S. Eliot

THE SUSTAINING POWER

Immense terrestrial ball
  Hanging in limitless space:
Oceans, mountains, forests, all
  Cling to its globular face.

Not one drop of water is spilled
  Over the rim of the world;
Not one mountain, not one tree
  To the bottomless deep is hurled.

No foundation but atmosphere
  Over, under, around.
Daily this globe on its axis turns
  By the laws of gravity bound.

O mighty God! Thy power sustains
  This earth. Each stream, tree, and
    hill
Obeys the laws of gravity —
  Subject to Thy will.

        — Anna-Modine Moran

A CLOSER WALK WITH GOD

O for a closer walk with God,
  A calm and heavenly frame;
A light to shine upon the road
  That leads me to the Lamb!
Where is the blessedness I knew
  When first I saw the Lord?
Where is the soul-refreshing view
  Of Jesus and His Word!
What peaceful hours I then enjoyed,
  How sweet their memory still!
But they have left an aching void
  The world can never fill.
Return, O Holy Dove, return,
  Sweet messenger of rest;
I hate the sins that made Thee mourn,
  And drove Thee from my breast!
The dearest idol I have known
  Whate'er that idol be;
Help me to tear it from Thy throne,
  And worship only Thee.

        — William Cowper

The City Beautiful

Sometimes when the day is ended
　And its round of duties done,
I watch at the western windows
　The gleam of the setting sun.
When my heart has been unquiet
　And its longings unbeguiled
By the day's vexatious trials
　And cannot be reconciled,
I look on the slope of the mountains
　And o'er the restless sea,
And I think of the beautiful city
　That lieth not far from me.

And my spirit is hushed in a moment
　As the twilight falls tender and
　　sweet;
And I cross in fancy the river,
　And kneel at the Master's feet.
And I rest in the shade that there fall-
　eth
　From the trees that with healing are
　　rife —
That shadow the banks of the river —
　The river of water of life.

And some time, when the day is ended,
　And the duties He gave me are done,
I shall watch at life's western windows
　The gleam of the setting sun.
I shall fall asleep in the twilight
　As I never have slept before,
To dream of the beautiful city,
　Till I waken to sleep no more.
There will fall on my restless spirit
　A hush, oh, so wondrously sweet,
And I shall cross over the river
　To rest at the Master's feet.

　　　　　　　— Boston Globe

Across the Great Divide

When I put out to sail the sea
　Across the Great Divide,
My heart shall have no fear or dread
　For I have faith — inside.

I know I shall not sail alone
　Nor shall I lose the way;
My Pilot shall be with me then
　Just as He is today.

When I put out to sail the sea,
　Let faith fill your heart, too,
For somewhere on that other shore —
　I'll watch and wait for you.

　　　　　　　— Phyllis C. Michael

　　　　　　　∞

Perhaps Today

Look up, God's child,
　This world of tragic sorrow
Might weigh thee down
　With its increasing woes!
Look up, and onward
　To that golden morrow,
To all the glory
　Which it will disclose.

Look up, and long for
　Our dear Lord's returning:
Look up and cry,
　"Lord Jesus, come, we pray!"
Look up — until for Him
　The heart is burning!
Look up! Look up!
　Perhaps He'll come today!

　　　　　　　— J. Danson Smith

"The Land of Beginning Again"

(Original Version)

I wish that there were some wonderful place
Called the "Land of Beginning Again,"
Where all our mistakes, and all our heartaches,
And all of our poor selfish griefs
Could be dropped like a shabby old coat at the door,
And never be put on again.

I wish we might come on it all unawares,
Like a hunter who finds a lost trail,
And I wish that the one whom our blunders had done
The greatest injustice of all —
Could be at the gates, like a friend who still waits
For the comrades he's gladdest to hail.

It wouldn't be possible not to be kind,
In the "Land of Beginning Again,"
And the ones we'd misjudged, and the ones we had grudged
Their moments of victory there,
Would find in the grasp of our loving handclasp,
More than penitent lips could explain.

(Christian Revision)

I have read in the Book of a wonderful place
Called the "Land of Beginning Again,"
Where the sins of the past are remembered no more,
And the years, locust-eaten, the Lord doth restore,
All our filthy rags change for a garment of grace,
And the soul is begotten again.

In that land (only found by those mariners true
Who will follow the Compass and Chart),
We do know that our Lord, against whom is all sin,
He who died on the Cross, our salvation to win,
We will find at the gates — our best Friend — He still waits
With a welcome for each seeking heart.

With the love shed abroad in our hearts by the Spirit
It is easy to love one another.
This love thinketh no evil, it envieth not;
Is so humble, unselfish, with kindness so fraught
That transformed by this love, as in Heaven above,
We shall eternally love each other.

— Carl F. Bruhn

I Shall See Them Again

I shall see them again in the light of the morning,
When the night has passed by with its tears and its mourning:
When the light of God's love is the sun ever shining
In the Land where the weary ones rest.

I shall know them again, though ten thousand surround them;
I shall hear their dear voice 'midst the blessed ones round them;
And the love that was theirs on the earth shall detect them
In the Land where the weary ones rest.

'Twas their lives in the past helped to fill me with gladness;
And the future in heaven, the home without sadness,
Where I see them today clad in bright robes of whiteness —
In the Land where the weary ones rest.

Would I wish for them back from their bright home in heaven!
No! in patience I'll wait till the veil shall be riven,
And the Saviour restores me the friends He has given —
In the Land where the weary ones rest.

— *E. Husband*

∾

The Judgment Is Near

The world is grown old, and her pleasures are past;
The world is grown old, and her form may not last;
The world is grown old, and trembles for fear;
For sorrows abound, and judgment is near;

The sun in the Heaven is languid and pale;
And feeble and few are the fruits of the vale:
And the hearts of the nations fail them for fear,
For the world is grown old, and judgment is near!

The king on his throne, the bride in her bower,
The children of pleasure all feel the sad hour;
The roses are faded, and tasteless the cheer,
For the world is grown old, and judgment is near!

The world is grown old! — but should we complain,
Who have tried her and know that her promise is vain?
Our heart is in Heaven, our home is not here,
And we look for our crown when judgment is near.

— *Reginald Heber*

SOMETIME, WE'LL UNDERSTAND

Not now, but in the coming years,
It may be in the Better Land,
We'll read the meaning of our tears,
And there, sometime, we'll understand.

We'll catch the broken thread again,
And finish what we here began;
Heaven will the mysteries explain,
And then, ah then, we'll understand.

We'll know why clouds instead of sun
Were over many a cherished plan;
Why song has ceased, when scarce begun;
'Tis there, sometime, we'll understand.

God knows the way, He holds the key,
He guides us with unerring Hand;
Sometime with tearless eyes we'll see;
Yes, there, up there, we'll understand.

Then trust in God thro' all thy days;
Fear not, for He doth hold thy hand;
Though dark the way, still sing and praise;—
Sometime, sometime, we'll understand.
— *Maxwell N. Cornelius*

ᐕ

LET ME GO

Let me go; my soul is weary
Of the chain which binds it here;
Let my spirit bend its pinions,
To a brighter, holier sphere.
Earth, 'tis true, hath friends who bless me
With their fond and faithful love;
But the hands of angels beckon
Me to brighter climes above.

Let me go; for earth hath sorrow,
Sin, and pain, and bitter tears;
All its paths are dark and dreary—
All its hopes are fraught with fears;
Short-liv'd are its brightest flowers;
Soon its cherished joys decay.
Let me go; I fain would leave it
For the realms of cloudless day.

Let me go; for earth's fond pleasures
Soon will vanish and decay,
But the soul has richer treasures;
Shining bright, as cloudless day.
Let me go; 'tis Jesus calling
Me from this vain world of care,
There to live forever with Him,
And the host already there.

Let me go; my heart hath tasted
Of my Saviour's wondrous grace;
Let me go; where I shall ever
See, and know Him, face to face;
Let me go; the trees of Heaven
Rise before me, waving bright,
And the distant crystal waters
Flash upon my failing sight.

Let me go; for songs seraphic
Now seem calling from the sky;
'Tis the welcome of the angels,
Which e'en now are hov'ring nigh;
Let me go; they wait to bear me
To the mansions of the blest,
Where the spirit, worn and weary,
Finds at last its long-sought rest.
— *W. H. Bucks*

ᐕ

MEANS AND ENDS

We till to sow, we sow to reap,
We reap and grind it by and by:
We grind to bake, we bake to eat,
We eat to live, we live to die.
We die with Christ to rest in joy
In heaven, made free from all annoy.
— *Humfrey Gifford*

ANTICIPATION

I wonder why God took such care
With all the things He made down
     here?
Why He took pains to beautify
The things which daily meet our eye?

A blooming cherry tree in spring,
The sheen upon a blackbird's wing;
A flowing streamlet, clear and cold,
A maple turned to red and gold.

How drab the whole earth would have
     been,
Had He not covered it with green!
How bare and dark the sky would be,
Were there no shining stars to see!

Perhaps God, in His wondrous love,
Would teach us thus of things above;
Some beauty to our eyes unfold,
Before He shows us streets of gold!

Had He not given the snowflakes
     white,
To softly fall on winter's night;
How could He tell us, help us know
His Blood can make us "white as
     snow"?

Had He not made the dazzling sun
To guide us 'til our day's work's done;
How could we understand that Light
Which makes the Heavenly City
     bright?

By trees which grow around so rife,
We understand the "Tree of Life";
By happy homes He gives us here,
We picture lovelier ones up there.

By man's poor, frail attempts at love,
We understand what God above
Means when He says, "Oh, child of
     Mine,
An *everlasting* love is thine!"

And by the torn, grief-stricken heart
Of mothers, when from sons they part,

We see how great a price God paid,
When all our sins on Christ He laid.

Because of sickness, toil and woe,
And loss of loved ones here below,
We long to see that blessed day
When all these trials shall pass away.

If earthly fellowships are sweet,
What will it be around His feet,
When finally we reach that shore
Where pain and heartaches are no
     more?

The brightness of His blessed face
Will illumine that glorious place;
And all earth's shadows take their flight
Before that blest, eternal Light.

— *Sarah Carter Lewis*

PEACE

My soul, there is a Countrie
     Far beyond the stars,
Where stands a winged centrie
     All skilfull in the wars.
There above noise and danger
     Sweet peace sits crowned with
          smiles,
And One born in a manger
     Commands the beauteous files.
He is thy gracious Friend,
     And (O my soul, awake!)
Did in pure love descend
     To die here for thy sake.
If thou canst get but thither,
     There growes the flowre of Peace,
The rose that cannot wither,
     Thy fortresse, and thy ease.
Leave then thy foolish ranges;
     For none can thee secure,
But One, who never changes,
     Thy God, thy life, thy cure!

— *Henry Vaughan*

A Little While

A little while to sow in tears and weakness
   The precious seed along the vernal plain,
'Til into life the tender blade expanding
   Fresh promise gives of summer's ripening grain.
A little while of patient, earnest labor,
   For His dear sake, our best and truest Friend;
A little while to wait for His Appearing,
   And then the joy that nevermore shall end.

A little while to bear the cross for Jesus
   And meet the foe that once He overcame;
To stand unmoved, the Sword of Truth uplifting,
   And through its power to conquer in His Name.
A little while around His throne to gather
   For one sweet hour within the house of prayer;
A little while when, heart with heart communing,
   We know by faith that He Himself is there.

A little while to weep for those we cherish
   As one by one they near the river's brink,
A little while to catch their sweet assurance
   That we in Heaven shall find each broken link.
A little while! and then the glorious dawning
   Of that fair morn beyond the swelling tide,
When we shall wake, and in our Saviour's likeness,
   Perfect and pure, we shall be satisfied.

                   —Fanny J. Crosby

We Shall Meet Them

We shall meet them in the morning,
   Meet the saved of other days;
Clasp again the hands of dear ones,
   Filled with wonder, love and praise.
Oh to see them in the Glory,
   Faces of the distant past!
Oh to meet them in the morning
   Safe at home in Heav'n at last!

We shall meet them in the morning,
   Friends who long have gone before,
They are waiting for our coming
   Where the trials of life are o'er;

Fathers, mothers, sisters, brothers,
   Children called in tender years;
Wives and husbands, friends and
      neighbours,
   Far beyond this vale of tears.

We shall meet them in the morning,
   In the Land of fadeless day,
Where there are no separations,
   Where all tears are wiped away.
We shall meet them, but the glory
   Of that meeting will be this:
That a Saviour waits to welcome
   Waits to share with us His bliss.

                   —Oswald J. Smith

A Wonderful Day

Glorious day when we stand in His presence,
  All of our heartaches and sorrows are past,
No more burdens too heavy to carry —
  We shall see Jesus at last!

Wonderful day when we shall be like Him,
  Features were marred by sin here below;
Now they are radiant, beautiful, glorious!
  Cleansed by His Blood, made whiter than snow.

Marvelous day, all suffering ended,
  Glorious bodies now, like to His own;
We will be kings and priests in God's Kingdom,
  With glory and honor around the great throne.

Radiant day — the day of His crowning —
  The thought of this day is immeasurably sweet;
Then we will stand transformed in His likeness,
  Casting our trophies and crowns at His feet.

Victorious day — the day of the Rapture,
  The Lamb who was slain is now become King!
The Bride of the Lamb, in garments all glorious,
  Is singing sweet songs the Bride only can sing.

Triumphant day — great day of His power!
  All the kingdoms of earth will crumble and fall;
The saints of all ages in garments of splendor
  Are crowning Him King to rule over all!
                                    — A. H. Dixon

The World of Light

They are all gone into the world of light,
  And I alone sit lingering here!
Their very memory is fair and bright,
  And my sad thoughts doth clear;

It glows and glitters in my cloudy breast,
  Like stars upon some gloomy grove —
Or those faint beams in which this hill is drest
  After the sun's remove.

I see them walking in an air of glory,
  Whose light doth trample on my days, —
My days which are at best but dull and hoary,
  Mere glimmering and decays.

O holy hope! and high humility,—
  High as the heavens above!
These are your walks, and you have showed them me
  To kindle my cold love.

Dear, beauteous death, the jewel of the just,
  Shining nowhere but in the dark!
What mysteries do lie beyond thy dust,
  Could man outlook that mark!

He that hath found some fledged bird's nest may know
  At first sight if the bird be flown;
But what fair grove or dell he sings in now,
  That is to him unknown.

And yet, as angels in some brighter dreams
  Call to the soul when man doth sleep,
So some strange thoughts transcend our wonted themes,
  And into glory peep.

If a star were confined into a tomb,
  Her captive flames must needs burn there;
But when the hand that locked her up gives room,
  She'll shine through all the sphere.

O Father of eternal life, and all
  Created glories under thee!
Resume thy spirit from this world of thrall
  Into true liberty.

Either disperse these mists, which blot and fill
  My perspective still as they pass;
Or else remove me hence unto that hill
  Where I shall need no glass.

                              —*Henry Vaughan*

ᴏⱳ

From ENDYMION

A thing of beauty is a joy for ever:
Its loveliness increases; it will never
Pass into nothingness, but still will keep
A bower quiet for us, and a sleep
Full of sweet dreams, and health, and quiet breathing. . . .
An endless fountain of immortal drink,
Pouring unto us from the heaven's brink.

                              —*John Keats*

THE VANISHERS

Sweetest of all childlike dreams
    In the simple Indian lore
Still to me the legend seems
    Of the shapes who flit before.

Flitting, passing, seen and gone,
    Never reached nor found at rest,
Baffling search, but beckoning on
    To the Sunset of the Blest. . . .

Doubt who may, O friend of mine!
    Thou and I have seen them too;
On before with beck and sign
    Still they glide, and we pursue. . . .

Glimpses of immortal youth,
    Gleams and glories seen and flown,
Far-heard voices sweet with truth,
    Airs from viewless Eden blown;

Beauty that eludes our grasp,
    Sweetness that transcends our taste,
Loving hands we may not clasp,
    Shining feet that mock our haste;

Gentle eyes we closed below,
    Tender voices heard once more,
Smile and call us, as they go
    On and onward, still before. . . .

Chase we still, with baffled feet,
    Smiling eye and waving hand,
Sought and seeker soon shall meet,
    Lost and found, in Sunset Land!
                — *John Greenleaf Whittier*

I WASN'T THERE

I wasn't there aboard that boat,
    That groaned as though in pain,
When Jesus spoke the quick command
    That hushed the hurricane.
But I was there another time
    And felt the dark tide roll
Upon my heart, and Jesus spoke,
    And peace came to my soul.

I didn't see the woman touch
    The Master's robe that day;
Nor see her face light up with joy
    As she went on her way.
But I put out my hand by faith,
    When life seemed bleak and vain;
I touched Him in the hopeless hour,
    And life seemed good again.

I wasn't there when Jesus sat
    Upon the mountainside
And gave to men the message that
    The ages could not hide.
But He has spoken to my heart,
    When life has seemed unkind;
And I have faced the future with
    Strange music in my mind.

I wasn't there upon that hill
    Where Jesus went to die;
I didn't see His agony,
    Or hear His lonely cry.
But nonetheless I've seen Him hang
    Upon that wretched tree,
And, somehow, in my inner mind
    I knew He died for me.

I wasn't there that Easter dawn,
    Beside the granite tomb,
When He whom they had crucified
    Walked from the ancient gloom.
But with a consciousness beyond
    The reasoning of men,
I know, somehow, He quit the grave,
    And that He lives again.

I've never seen that Other world,
    Beyond time's narrow shore,
Where He has pledged that we shall
        live
    With Him forevermore.
But tho' the map of that high world
    Be oddly-traced and dim,
Because He's there I'll be there, too,
    Sometime, somehow, with Him.
                — *Lon Woodrum*

HERE AND THERE

What no human eye hath seen,
    What no mortal ear hath heard,
What on thought hath never been
    In its noblest flights conferred —
This hath God prepared in store
For his people evermore!

When the shaded pilgrim-land
    Fades before my closing eye,
Then revealed on either hand
    Heaven's own scenery shall lie;
Then the veil of flesh shall fall,
Now concealing, darkening all.

Heavenly landscapes, calmly bright,
    Life's pure river murmuring low,
Forms of loveliness and light,
    Lost to earth long time ago;
Yes, mine own, lamented long,
Shine amid the angel throng!

Many a joyful sight was given,
    Many a lovely vision here —
Hill, and vale, and starry even,
    Friendship's smile, Affection's tear;
These were shadows, sent in love,
Of realities above!

When upon my wearied ear
    Earth's last echoes faintly die,
Then shall angel-harps draw near —
    All the chorus of the sky;
Long-hushed voices blend again,
Sweetly, in that welcome-strain.

Here were sweet and varied tones,
    Bird and breeze and fountain's fall,
Yet creation's travail-groans
    Ever sadly sighed through all.
There no discord jars the air —
Harmony is perfect there!

When this aching heart shall rest,
    All its busy pulses o'er,
Form her mortal robes undrest
    Shall my spirit upward soar.

Then shall unimagined joy
All my thoughts and powers employ.

Here devotion's healing balm
    Often came to soothe my breast —
Hours of deep and holy calm,
    Earnests of eternal rest.
But the bliss was here unknown,
Which shall there be all my own!

Jesus reigns, the Life, the Sun
    Of that wondrous world above;
All the clouds and storms are gone,
    All is light, and all is love.
All the shadows melt away
In the blaze of perfect day!

— Johann Peter Lange

ॐ

GLORIOUS MYSTERY

Oh glorious mystery of Love,
That I, a child of earth,
May dwell by faith with Christ above,
The Lamb of matchless worth!

My feet must tread earth's lowly way,
But on faith's wings I soar
To view that Land of Endless Day,
My home forevermore.

Though earth-bound for a little time,
My ransomed spirit sees
The glory which shall soon be mine
Within the Heavenlies.

So patiently I wait the day
When I shall be set free,
And leave this mortal house of clay
For all eternity.

To dwell within His Presence blest,
Who by His matchless grace
Hath brought me into Heavenly Rest,
There to behold His face.

— Avis B. Christiansen

ONE OF THESE DAYS

One of these days it will all be over,
  Sorrow and parting, and loss and gain,
Meetings and partings of friends and lover,
  Joy that was ever so edged with pain.
One of these days will our hands be folded,
  One of these days will the work be done,
Finished the pattern our lives have molded,
  Ended our labor beneath the sun.

One of these days will the heartaches leave us,
  One of these days will the burden drop;
Never again shall a hope deceive us,
  Never again will our progress stop.
Freed from the blight of vain endeavor,
  Winged with the health of immortal life,
One of these days we shall quit forever
  All that is vexing in earthly strife.

One of these days we shall know the reason,
  Haply, of much that perplexes now;
One of these days in the Lord's good season
  Light of His peace shall adorn the brow,
Blest, though out of tribulation,
  Lifted to dwell in His sun-bright smile,
Happy to share in the great salvation,
  Well may we tarry a little while.
                    — *Songs in the Night Watches*

WIND AND LYRE

Thou art the wind and I the lyre:
  Strike, O Wind, on the sleeping strings —
  Strike till the dead heart stirs and sings!
I am the altar and thou the fire:
  Burn, O Fire, to a snowy flame —
  Burn me clean of the mortal blame!

I am the night and thou the dream:
  Touch me softly and thrill me deep,
  When all is white on the hills of sleep.
Thou art the moon and I the stream:
  Shine to the trembling heart of me,
  Light my soul to the mother-sea.
                    — *Edwin Markham*

At Last

When on my day of life the night is falling,
And in the winds from unsunned spaces blown
I hear far voices out of darkness calling
My feet to paths unknown,—

Thou who hast made my home of life so pleasant,
Leave not its tenant when its walls decay;
O Love Divine, O Helper ever present,
Be Thou my strength and stay!

Be near me when all else is from me drifting:
Earth, sky, home's pictures, days of shade and shine,
And kindly faces to my own uplifting
The love which answers mine.

I have but Thee, O Father! Let Thy Spirit
Be with me then to comfort and uphold;
No gate of pearl, no branch of palm, I merit,
Nor street of shining gold.

Suffice it if, my good and ill unreckoned,
And both forgiven through Thine unbounding grace.
I find myself by hands familiar beckoned
Unto my fitting place:

Some humble door among Thy many mansions,
Some sheltering shade where sin and striving cease,
And flows forever through Heaven's green expansion
The river of Thy peace.

There from the music round about me stealing
I fain would learn the new and holy song,
And find at last, beneath Thy trees of healing,
The life for which I long.
— *John Greenleaf Whittier*

ოს

Whom Having Not Seen We Love

Not with our mortal eyes
    Have we beheld the Lord;
Yet we rejoice to hear His Name,
    And love Him in His Word.

On earth we want the sight
    Of our Redeemer's face;

Yet, Lord, our inmost thoughts delight
    To dwell upon Thy grace.

And when we taste Thy love,
    Our eyes Divinely grow,
Unspeakable, like those above,
    And Heav'n begins below.
— *Isaac Watts*

THE CITY GOD HATH MADE

Daily, daily sing the praises
  Of the city God hath made;
In the beauteous fields of Eden
  Its foundation-stones are laid.

All the walls of that dear city
  Are of bright and burnished gold;
It is matchless in its beauty,
  And its treasures are untold.

In the midst of that dear city
  Christ is reigning on his seat,
And the angels swing their censers
  In a ring about his feet.

From the throne a river issues,
  Clear as crystal, passing bright,
And it traverses the city
  Like a sudden beam of light.

Where it waters leafy Eden,
  Rolling over silver sands,
Sit the angels softly chiming
  On the harps between their hands.

There the meadows, green and dewy,
  Shine with lilies wondrous fair,
Thousand, thousand are the colors
  Of the waving flowers there.

There the forests ever blossom,
  Like our orchards here in May;
There the gardens never wither,
  But eternally are gay.

There are roses and carnations,
  There the honeysuckles twine;
There, along the river edges,
  Golden jonquils ever shine.

There the water-lilies open,
  Lying on the sea of glass,
There the yellow crocus glimmers
  Like a flame amidst the grass.

There the wind is sweetly fragrant,
  And is laden with the song
Of the seraphs and the elders
  And the great redeemed throng.

Oh, I would my ears were open
  Here to catch that happy strain;
Oh, I would my eyes some vision
  Of that Eden could attain.

Oh that I had wings of angels
  Here to spread and heavenward fly,
I would seek the gates of Zion
  Far beyond the starry sky.

— *Sabine Baring-Gould*

HAPPY ANY WAY

Lord, it belongs not to my care
  Whether I die or live;
To love and serve Thee is my share,
  And this Thy grace must give

If life be long, I will be glad
  That I may long obey;
If short, yet why should I be sad
  To soar to endless day?

Christ leads me thro' no darker rooms
  Than He went through before;
He that into God's kingdom comes
  Must enter by His door.

Come, Lord, when grace hath made
    me meet
  Thy blessed face to see;
For, if Thy work on earth be sweet,
  What will Thy glory be?

Then I shall end my sad complaints,
  And weary, sinful days,
And join with the triumphant saints
  Who sing Jehovah's praise.

My knowledge of that life is small;
  The eye of faith is dim;
But 'tis enough that Christ knows all,
  And I shall be with Him.

— *Richard Baxter*

THE GLAD HOME-COMING

I am waiting for the coming of the Bridegroom in the air,
I am longing for the gath'ring of the ransomed over there;
I am putting on the garments which the Heavenly Bride shall wear,
 For the glad home-coming draweth nigh.

I am letting go the pleasures and the treasures worldlings prize,
I am laying up my treasures and ambitions in the skies;
I am setting my affections where there are no broken ties,
 For the glad home-coming draweth nigh.

I am hasting on the coming of the Bridegroom in the air,
I am sending forth the Gospel of the Kingdom everywhere;
I am warning saints and sinners for the summons to prepare,
 For the glad home-coming draweth nigh.

I am watching for the rising of the morningstar's first ray,
In my heart its beams have risen as the harbinger of day;
Christ in me the hope of glory, every moment seems to say,
 "Lo! the glad home-coming draweth nigh."

Oh, the joy of meeting Jesus, and the loved ones gone before!
Oh, to be where sin and sorrow, pain and sickness come no more;
All my heart is turning ever to that everlasting shore,
 Where the glad home-coming draweth nigh.

— A. B. Simpson

HEAVEN

There is a blessed home
 Beyond this land of woe,
Where trials never come,
 Nor tears of sorrow flow;
Where faith is lost in sight,
 And patient hope is crowned,
And everlasting light
 Its glory throws around.

There is a land of peace,
 Good angels know it well,
Glad songs that never cease
 Within its portals swell;
Around its glorious throne
 Ten thousand saints adore
Christ, with the Father One
 And Spirit evermore.

O joy all joys beyond,
 To see the Lamb who died,
And count each sacred wound
 In hands and feet and side;
To give to him the praise
 Of every triumph won,
And sing through endless days
 The great things he hath done.

Look up, ye saints of God,
 Nor fear to tread below
The path your Saviour trod
 Of daily toil and woe;
Wait but a little while
 In uncomplaining love,
His own most gracious smile
 Shall welcome you above.

— Sir Henry William Baker

THE MORNING SHALL AWAKEN

The morning shall awaken,
Shadows flee away,
And each true-hearted servant
Shall shine as doth the day;

For God our King and Portion,
In fullness of His grace,
We then shall see forever
And worship face to face.

—*St. Bernard of Cluny*

TWO MOTHERS

Long, long ago, so I have been told,
Two saints once met on the streets paved with gold.
"By the stars in your crown," said the one to the other,
"I see that on earth, you too were a mother;
And by the blue-tinted halo you wear,
You too have known sorrow and deepest despair."
"Ah yes," came the answer, "I once had a son,
A sweet little lad, full of laughter and fun."

"But tell of your child—" "Oh, I knew I was blest
From the moment I first held him close to my breast;
And my heart almost burst with the joy of that day."
"Ah yes," sighed the other, "I felt the same way."
The former continued, "The first steps he took—
"So eager and breathless; the sweet, startled look
Which came over his face—he trusted me so—"
"Yes," sighed the other, "how well do I know!"

"But soon he had grown to a tall handsome boy,
So stalwart and kind, and it gave me such joy
To have him just walk down the street by my side."
"Ah yes," said the other, "I felt the same pride.
How often I shielded and spared him from pain;
And when he, for others, was cruelly slain,
When they crucified him and they spat in his face,
How gladly would I have hung there in His place!"

A moment of silence—"Oh, then you are *she,*
The mother of Christ?" and she fell on one knee.
But Mary raised her up, drawing her near,
And kissed from the cheek of the woman, a tear.
"Tell me the name of your son you loved so,
That I may share with you your grief and your woe."
She lifted her eyes, looking straight at the other,
"He was Judas Iscariot! I am his mother!"

—*Author Unknown*

THE SERAPHS' SONG

Crown him with many crowns,
  The Lamb upon his throne!
Hark, how the heavenly anthem
    drowns
  All music but its own!

Awake, my soul, and sing
  Of him who died for thee;
And hail him as the matchless King
  Through all eternity.

Crown him, the Virgin's Son!
  The God incarnate born,
Whose arms those crimson trophies
    won
  Which now his brow adorn.

Fruit of the mystic rose,
  As of that rose the stem;
The root whence mercy ever flows,
  The Babe of Bethlehem.

Crown him the Lord of love!
  Behold his hands and side,—
Rich wounds, yet visible above,
  In beauty glorified.

No angel in the sky
  Can fully bear that sight,
But downward bends his wondering
    eye
  At mysteries so bright.

Crown him the Lord of peace!
  Whose power a sceptre sways,
From pole to pole, that wars may cease,
  Absorbed in prayer and praise.

His reign shall know no end;
  And round his pierced feet
Fair flowers of paradise extend
  Their fragrance ever sweet.

Crown him the Lord of years,
  The Potentate of time,
Creator of the rolling spheres,
  Ineffably sublime!

Glassed in a sea of light
  Whose everlasting waves
Reflect his form—the Infinite!
  Who lives, and loves, and saves.

Crown him the Lord of heaven!
  One with the Father known,—
And the blest Spirit, thro' him given
  From yonder Triune throne!

All hail! Redeemer, hail!
  For thou hast died for me:
Thy praise shall never, never fail
  Throughout eternity.

— *Matthew Bridges*

ᥴᠣ

FOR ME

Love — uncaused, loving me
From all eternity
In sovereign mystery
Of thine election
Now in subjection,
Worship I Thee.

Blood — poured out full for me,
On dark Golgotha's tree,
Of Thy salvation.
In awful mystery
Faith's adoration
Bring I to Thee.

Grace — lavished still on me,
All worthless though I be,
In daily mystery
Of Thy heart's kindness!
Through all my blindness,
Praise be to Thee.

Heaven — opened wide for me
For all eternity!
Love's last, long mystery!
O consummation
Of God's redemption!
Wait I for Thee.

— *William R. Newell*

QUITE SUDDENLY

Quite suddenly — it may be at the turning of a lane,
Where I stand to watch a skylark from out the swelling grain,
That the trump of God shall thrill me, with its call so loud and clear,
And I'm called away to meet Him, whom of all I hold most dear.

Quite suddenly — it may be as I tread the busy street,
Strong to endure life's stress and strain, its every call to meet,
That through the roar of traffic, a trumpet, silvery clear,
Shall stir my startled senses and proclaim His Coming near.

Quite suddenly — it may be in His house I bend my knee,
When the kingly voice, long hoped for, comes at last to summon me;
And the fellowship of earth-life that has seemed so passing sweet,
Proves nothing but the shadow of our meeting round His feet.

Quite suddenly — it may be as I lie in dreamless sleep,
God's gift to many a sorrowing heart, with no more tears to weep,
That a call shall break my slumber and a Voice sound in my ear;
"Rise up, my love, and come away! Behold the Bridegroom's here!"

— Author Unknown

HOME

Come, says Jesus' sacred voice,
Come, and make My paths your
  choice;
I will guide you to your home,
Weary pilgrim, hither come!

Thou who, houseless, sole, forlorn,
Long hast borne the proud world's
  scorn,
Long hast roamed the barren waste,
Weary pilgrim, hither haste.

Ye who, tossed on beds of pain,
Seek for ease, but seek in vain;
Ye, by fiercer anguish torn,
In remorse for guilt who mourn —

Hither come! for here is found
Balm that flows for ev'ry wound,
Peace that ever shall endure,
Rest eternal, sacred, sure.

— Anna Letitia Barbauld

JAMES AND JOHN

Two brothers freely cast their lot
  With David's royal Son;
The cost of conquest counting not,
  They deem the battle won.

Brothers in heart, they hope to gain
  An undivided joy;
That man may one with man remain,
  As boy was one with boy.

Christ heard; and willed that James
  should fall,
  First prey of Satan's rage;
John linger out his fellows all,
  And die in bloodless age.

Now they join hands once more above,
  Before the Conqueror's throne;
Thus God grants prayer, but in his
  love
Makes times and ways his own.

— John Henry Newman

THE CHRISTIAN PILGRIM'S HYMN

Guide me, O thou great Jehovah,
  Pilgrim through this barren land:
I am weak but thou art mighty;
  Hold me with thy powerful hand:
    Bread of heaven! Bread of heaven!
    Feed me now and evermore!

Open now the crystal fountain
  Whence the healing streams do flow;
Let the fiery cloudy pillar
  Lead me all my journey through:
    Strong Deliverer! Strong Deliverer!
    Be thou still my strength and shield.

When I tread the verge of Jordan,
  Bid my anxious fears subside;
Death of deaths, and hell's destruction,
  Land me safe on Canaan's side:
    Songs of praises, songs of praises,
    I will ever give to thee.

Musing on my habitation,
  Musing on my heavenly home,
Fills my soul with holy longing;
  Come, my Jesus, quickly come!
    Vanity is all I see;
    Lord, I long to be with thee!

— *William Williams*

ᐯᔆ

ZION, CITY OF OUR GOD

Glorious things of thee are spoken,
  Zion, city of our God!
He, whose word cannot be broken,
  Formed thee for his own abode:
On the Rock of Ages founded,
  What can shake thy sure repose?
With salvation's wall surrounded,
  Thou may'st smile at all thy foes.

See, the streams of living waters,
  Springing from eternal love,
Well supply thy sons and daughters,
  And all fears of want remove:

Who can faint while such a river
  Ever flows their thirst t'assuage?
Grace, which like the Lord, the giver,
  Never fails from age to age.

Round each habitation hovering,
  See the cloud and fire appear,
For a glory and a covering,
  Showing that the Lord is near.
Thus deriving from their banner
  Light by night, and shade by day,
Safe they feed upon the manna
  Which he gives them when they
    pray.

Blest inhabitants of Zion,
  Washed in the Redeemer's blood!
Jesus, whom their souls rely on,
  Makes them kings and priests to
    God.
'Tis his love his people raises
  Over self to reign as kings,
And as priests, his solemn praises
  Each for a thank-offering brings.

Saviour, if of Zion's city
  I through grace a member am,
Let the world deride or pity,
  I will glory in thy name.
Fading is the worldling's pleasure,
  All his boasted pomp and show;
Solid joys and lasting treasure
  None but Zion's children know.

— *John Newton*

ᐯᔆ

JERUSALEM

Like the song of angel choirs,
Floating o'er the gleaming spires,
While as yet unseen to them
Comes the New Jerusalem.

Like the seer on Patmos gazing,
On the glory downward blazing,
Till upon earth's grateful sod
Rests the city of our God.

— *George Eliot*

AM I NEARER HEAVEN TO-NIGHT?

Sinks the sun and fades the light,
Evening darkens into night,
Deeper shadows gather fast,
And another day is past,
And another record made
Nevermore to change or fade
Till the Book shall be unsealed,
When the judgment is revealed.
Ere I give myself to rest
Let me make this solemn quest:
Have the hours that winged their flight
  Since the dawning of the day,
  Sped me on my homeward way,—
Am I nearer heaven to-night?

Have I since the opening morn
Faithfully my burden borne?
Has my strength on God been stayed?
Have I watched and have I prayed,
Seeking with a steadfast heart
Zealously the better part?
Have I run the Christian race
With a swift and tireless pace?
Have I conquered in the strife
Which besets my hourly life?
Have I kept my armor bright,—
Am I nearer heaven to-night?

Has my vision clearer grown
Of the things to faith made known,
And the heavenly and the true
Shone the world's illusions through?
Have I sought my thoughts to raise,
Redolent of grateful praise,
As I constantly have found
Every hour with mercies crowned,
And his kindness all-abounding
Evermore my path surrounding?
Have I loved with love unfeigned?
In my heart has Jesus reigned?
Spite of every adverse chance
Have I made a day's advance,
Gained some new celestial height,—
Am I nearer heaven tonight?

Have I learned to feel how near
Draws that day of hope and fear
When, the book of doom unsealed,
Every thought shall be revealed,
And the Judge upon his throne
Shall my destiny make known?

Tell me, oh, my anxious soul,
When that record shall unroll,
Shall I with the ransomed stand
Worshipping at God's right hand?
Shall I see the perfect light
In the land that knows no night?

— *Henry Dobbs Holt*

O BLESSED MOMENT

I am living for the moment
When my Saviour's face I see —
Oh, the thrill of that first meeting,
When His glory shines on me!
When His voice like sweetest music
Falls upon my waiting ear,
And my name, amid the millions,
From His precious lips I hear.

I am living for the moment
When His welcome smile I see
In that House of Many Mansions
He's preparing now for me.
Days of toil and nights of sorrow
From my memory will fade
As I enter that Fair City
Where the streets with gold are laid.

I am living for the moment
When before His feet I fall,
And with all the host of Heaven
Own Him Lord and King of all,
Evermore to sing the praises
Of the Lamb of Calvary,
And to worship and adore Him
Throughout all eternity.

— *Avis B. Christiansen*

HOPE IN DEATH

My life's a shade, my days
Apace to death decline;
My Lord is life, he'll raise
My dust again, e'en mine.
Sweet truth to me!
I shall arise,
And with these eyes
My Saviour see.

My peaceful grave shall keep
My bones till that sweet day,
I wake from my long sleep
And leave my bed of clay.
Sweet truth to me!
I shall arise,
And with these eyes
My Saviour see.

My Lord his angels shall
Their golden trumpets sound,
At whose most welcome call
My grave shall be unbound.
Sweet truth to me!
I shall arise,
And with these eyes
My Saviour see.

I said sometimes with tears,
"Ah me! I'm loath to die!"
Lord, silence thou these fears:
My life's with thee on high.
Sweet truth to me!
I shall arise,
And with these eyes
My Saviour see.

What means my trembling heart,
To be thus shy of death?
My life and I sha'n't part,
Though I resign my breath.
Sweet truth to me!
I shall arise,
And with these eyes
My Saviour see.

Then welcome, harmless grave:
By thee to heaven I'll go:
My Lord his death shall save
Me from the flames below.
Sweet truth to me!
I shall arise,
And with these eyes
My Saviour see.

— *Samuel Crossman*

∾

FOLLOWING FATHER HOME

Years ago, when I
    Was jest a little lad,
An' after school hours used to work
    Around the farm with Dad,
I used to be so wearied out
    When eventide was come,
That I got kinder anxious-like
    About the journey home;
But Dad, he used to lead the way,
An' once in awhile turn 'round an' say,
    So cheerin' like, so tender, "Come!
Come on, my son, you're nearly home!"
    That allers used to help me some;
An' so I followed Father home.

I'm old an' gray an' feeble now,
    An' trembly at the knee,
But life seems just the same today
    As then it seemed to me.
For while I am still so wearied out
    When eventide is come,
An' still git kinder anxious-like
    About the journey home,
But still my Father leads the way,
An' once in awhile I hear Him say,
    So cheerin' like, so tender, "Come!
Come on, My son, you're nearly
        home!"
    An' same as then, that helps me
        some,
And so I'm following Father home.

— *John Talman*

The Highlands

Oh, my heart is in the Highlan's
  O' the far and fair countree,
Where the King is waitin', waitin'
  For His ain, and e'en for me;
There He reigns in a' His glory,
  I shall see Him ane sweet day,
When He ca's me to the Highlan's
  Wi' Himself for aye to stay.

Ah, my heart was in the Lowlan's
  In the aulden, aulden time,
Midst the vapors and the shadows
  O' the lower, baser clime;
But the heavenly Man He sought me
  An' He deed for me straightwa';
Then He ga'ed back to the Highlan's
  An' He bore my heart awa'.

Oh, I love the bonnie Highlan's,
  Wi' its pure an' caller air,
Wi' its green fields an' its flowers
  An' its fragrance everywhere;
Ay, there's no place like the Highlan's
  For the soul frae sin set free;
'Tis a lan' o' wondrous beauty,
  'Tis the winsome lan' to me.

There's a palace in the Highlan's
  An' it glistens wi' the licht,
For the sun is ever shinin'
  An' there's never, never nicht,
An' there's music in the palace
  Sweeter far than a' the soun'
That e'er greets the list'nin' dwellers
  On the lower, Lowlan' groun'.

An' enthroned within the palace
  Is the King sae pure and fair,
Wi' His garments a' a-glist'nin'
  An' wi' shinin', snawy hair,
Wi' His face sae bricht, resplendent —
  'Bune the brichtness o' His croun —
That before Him a' the angels
  An' archangels fa' adoun.

Oh, my heart is in the Highlan's,
  Sae then dinna bid me stay,
For I canna but be hamesick
  For its gowden, blythesome day;
Ay, I'm wearyin' for its beauty,
  An' its licht that ne'er grows dim,
For the Ane wha's a' its glory
  An' a lastin' sicht o' Him!

— Henry W. Frost

Heaven

The waves unbuild the wasting shore;
  Where mountains towered, the billows sweep,
Yet still their borrowed spoils restore,
  And build new empires from the deep.
So while the floods of thought lay waste
  The proud domain of priestly creeds,
Its heaven-appointed tides will haste
  To plant new homes for human needs.
Be ours to mark with hearts unchilled
  The change an outworn church deplores;
The legend sinks, but Faith shall build
  A fairer throne on new found shores.

— Oliver Wendell Holmes

THE HOUSE OF MANY MANSIONS

There are glories up in Heaven
  That the world can never know;
There are joys beyond the telling
  Where the living waters flow.

There will be no sad repining,
  God shall wipe away all tears;
Neither sorrow, pain nor crying
  In the Land of endless years.

There no sin can ever enter,
  Grief at last shall be no more;
God Himself will dwell among them,
  And the reign of death be o'er.

There will be no pangs of hunger,
  Neither shall they thirst again,
For the Lamb of God will feed them,
  And they shall not drink in vain.

There the sun will shine no longer
  For the Lamb will be their light;
And the darkness will be vanquished
  For up there there'll be no night.

In the House of many mansions,
  In the palace of the blest,
There the wicked cease from troubling,
  And the weary are at rest.

—Oswald J. Smith

MORTALITY

We cannot kindle when we will
The fire that in the heart resides,
The spirit bloweth and is still,
In mystery our soul abides:
  But tasks in hours of insight will'd
  Can be thro' hours of gloom fulfill'd.

With aching hands and bleeding feet
We dig and heap, lay stone on stone;
We bear the burden and the heat
Of the long day, and wish 'twere done.
  Not till the hours of light return,
  All we have built do we discern.

Then, when the clouds are off the
    soul,
When thou dost bask in Nature's eye,
Ask, how *she* view'd thy self-control,
Thy struggling task'd mortality—
  Nature, whose free, light, cheerful
    air,
  Oft made thee, in thy gloom, despair.

And she, whose censure thou dost
    dread,
Whose eye thou wert afraid to seek,
See, on her face a glow is spread,
A strong emotion on her cheek.
  "Ah, child," she cries, "that strife
    divine—
  Whence was it, for it is not mine?

"There is no effort on *my* brow—
I do not strive, I do not weep.
I rush with the swift spheres, and glow
In joy, and, when I will, I sleep.—
  Yet that severe, that earnest air,
  I saw, I felt it once—but where?"

"I knew not yet the gauge of Time,
Nor wore the manacles of Space.
I felt it in some other clime—
I saw it in some other place.
  —'Twas when the heavenly house I
    trod,
  And lay upon the breast of God."

—Matthew Arnold

THE MYSTERY

He came and took me by the hand
  Up to a red rose tree,
He kept His meaning to Himself
  But gave a rose to me.

I did not pray Him to lay bare
  The mystery to me;
Enough the rose was Heaven to smell,
  And His own face to see.

—Ralph Hodgson

Nor Eye Has Seen

Nor eye has seen, nor ear has heard,
　　Nor sense nor reason known
What joys the Father has prepar'd
　　For those that love the Son.

But the good Spirit of the Lord
　　Reveals a heaven to come:
The beams of glory in His Word
　　Allure and guide us home.

Those holy gates forever bar
　　Pollution, sin and shame;
None shall obtain admittance there
　　But followers of the Lamb.

He keeps the Father's book of life,
　　There all their names are found;
The hypocrite in vain shall strive
　　To tread the heavenly ground.

— *Isaac Watts*

Heaven

There is a land of pure delight,
　　Where saints immortal reign;
Infinite day excludes the night,
　　And pleasures banish pain.

There everlasting spring abides,
　　And never-withering flowers;
Death like a narrow sea divides
　　This heavenly land from ours.

Sweet fields beyond the swelling flood
　　Stand dressed in living green;
So to the Jews old Canaan stood,
　　While Jordan rolled between.

But timorous mortals start and shrink
　　To cross this narrow sea,
And linger shivering on the brink,
　　And fear to launch away.

Oh! could we make our doubts remove,
　　These gloomy thoughts that rise,
And see that Canaan that we love
　　With unbeclouded eyes —

Could we but climb where Moses
　　　stood,
　　And view the landscape o'er,
Not Jordan's stream, nor death's cold
　　　flood,
　　Could fright us from the shore.

— *Isaac Watts*

Nearer Home

One sweetly solemn thought
　　Comes to me o'er and o'er:
I am nearer home to-day
　　Than I ever have been before;

Nearer my Father's house,
　　Where the many mansions be;
Nearer the great white throne,
　　Nearer the crystal sea;

Nearer the bound of life,
　　Where we lay our burdens down;
Nearer leaving the cross,
　　Nearer gaining the crown!

But lying darkly between,
　　Winding down through the night,
Is the silent, unknown stream,
　　That leads at last to the light.

Closer and closer my steps
　　Come to the dread abysm;
Closer Death to my lips
　　Presses the awful chrism.

Oh, if my mortal feet
　　Have almost gained the brink;
If it be I am nearer home
　　Even to-day than I think;

Father, perfect my trust;
　　Let my spirit feel in death,
That her feet are firmly set
　　On the rock of a living faith!

— *Phoebe Cary*

CHRISTIAN'S VICTORY — TRIUMPH

My latest sun is sinking fast,
  My race is nearly run,
My strongest trials now are past,
  My triumph is begun.

I'm nearing now the holy ranks
  Of friends and kindred dear,
For I brush the dews on Jordan's
    banks;
  The crossing must be near.

I've almost gained my heavenly home,
  My spirit loudly sings;
The holy ones, behold, they come!
  I hear the noise of wings.

Oh, bear my longing heart to Him
  Who bled and died for me;
Whose blood now cleanses from all sin,
  And gives me victory.

—*J. Haskell*

LEAD ME ON

Traveling to the better land,
O'er the desert's scorching sand,
Father! let me grasp Thy hand;
  Lead me on, lead me on!

When at Marah, parched with heat,
In the sparkling fountain greet,
Make the bitter water sweet;
  Lead me on!

When the wilderness is drear,
Show me Elim's palm grove near,
And her wells, as crystal clear;
  Lead me on!

Through the water, through the fire,
Never let me fall or tire,
Every step brings Canaan nigher;
  Lead me on!

Bid me stand on Nebo's height,
Gaze upon the land of light,
Then transported with the sight,
  Lead me on!

When I stand on Jordan's brink,
Never let me fear or shrink;
Hold me, Father, lest I sink;
  Lead me on!

When the victory is won,
And eternal life begun,
Up to Glory lead me on!
  Lead me on, lead me on!

—*Author Unknown*

A GLIMPSE OF GLORY

I have caught a glimpse of glory
  Never seen by mortal eyes,
Just beyond the blue horizon
  Of evening's transient skies;
But the ear of hope has heard it
  And the eye of faith can see
Sound and sign of heaven's nearness
  Just beyond mortality.

I have caught a glimpse of glory,
  Of that bright eternal day,
When the mists of Time have lifted
  And we lay aside his clay;
Then shall be the consummation
  Of our longing and desire,
For we'll sing the Song of Ages
  In the resurrection choir!

I have caught a glimpse of glory
  Just beyond the brink of Time,
And I travel toward the sunrise
  Of a better land and clime.
Soon I'll trade this earth for heaven
  And inside some golden door
I shall greet the ones I've cherished
  Safe with Jesus evermore.

—*Author Unknown*

THE PROMISED LAND

On Jordan's stormy banks I stand,
  And cast a wishful eye
To Canaan's fair and happy land,
  Where my possessions lie.

Oh the transporting, rapturous scene
  That rises to my sight!
Sweet fields arrayed in living green,
  And rivers of delight!

There generous fruits, that never fail,
  On trees immortal grow:
There rock and hill and brook and vale
  With milk and honey flow.

All o'er those wide-extended plains
  Shines one eternal day;
There God the Sun forever reigns,
  And scatters night away.

No chilling winds or poisonous breath
  Can reach that healthful shore:
Sickness and sorrow, pain and death,
  Are felt and feared no more.

When shall I reach that happy place,
  And be forever blest?
When shall I see my Father's face,
  And in his bosom rest?

Filled with delight, my raptured soul
  Can here no longer stay:
Tho' Jordan's waves around me roll,
  Fearless I'd launch away.
                    — Samuel Stennett

LORD JESUS, THINK ON ME

Lord Jesus, think on me,
And purge away my sin;
From earthborn passions set me free,
And make me pure within.

Lord Jesus, think on me,
Amid the battle's strife;
In all my pain and misery
Be Thou my health and life.

Lord Jesus, think on me,
Nor let me go astray;
Through darkness and perplexity
Point Thou the heavenly way.

Lord Jesus, think on me,
That, when this life is past,
I may th' eternal brightness see,
And share Thy joy at last.
                    — Bishop Synesius of Cyrene

THE WATCHER

She always leaned to watch for us,
  Anxious if we were late,
In winter by the window,
  In summer by the gate.

And though we mocked her tenderly
  Who had such foolish care,
The long way home would seem more
    safe
  Because she waited there.

Her thoughts were all so full of us.
  She never would forget;
And so I'm sure that where she is
  She must be watching yet!

Waiting till we come to her,
  Anxious if we are late —
Watching from heaven's window,
  Waiting at heaven's gate!
                    — Margaret Widdemer

STEPPING ASHORE

Oh! think to step ashore,
  And find it Heaven;
To clasp a hand outstretched,
  And find it God's hand!
To breathe new air,
  And that celestial air;
To feel refreshed,
  And find it immortality;
Ah, think to step from storm and stress
  To one unbroken calm:
To awake and find it Home.
                    — Robert E. Selle

HYMN TO THE HOLY SPIRIT

Come, O Creator Spirit blest!
And in our souls take up thy rest;
Come, with thy grace and heavenly
    aid,
To fill the hearts which thou hast
    made.

Great Paraclete! to thee we cry:
O highest gift of God most high!
O fount of life! O fire of love!
And solemn unction from above!

The sacred seven-fold grace is thine,
Dread finger of the hand divine!
The promise of the Father, thou!
Who dost the tongue with power
    endow.

Our senses touch with light and fire,
Our hearts with charity inspire:
And with endurance from on high
The weakness of our flesh supply.

Far back our enemy repel,
And let thy peace within us dwell,
So may we, having thee for guide,
Turn from each hurtful thing aside.

Oh, may thy grace on us bestow
The Father and the Son to know,
And evermore to hold confessed
Thyself of each the Spirit blest.

To God the Father praise be paid,
Praise to the Son, who from the dead
Arose, and perfect praise to thee,
O Holy Ghost, eternally.

    — Attributed to Charlemagne
    Translated by Edward Caswall

COME, HOLY SPIRIT, HEAVENLY DOVE

Come, Holy Spirit, heavenly Dove,
  With all Thy quick'ning powers;
Kindle a flame of sacred love
  In these cold hearts of ours.

Look, how we grovel here below,
  Fond of these trifling toys:
Our souls can neither fly nor go
  To reach eternal joys.

In vain we tune our formal songs,
  In vain we strive to rise:
Hosannas languish on our tongues,
  And our devotion dies.

Dear Lord, and shall we ever live
  At this poor, dying rate?
Our love so faint, so cold, to Thee,
  And Thine to us so great?

Come, Holy Spirit, heavenly Dove,
  With all Thy quick'ning powers;
Come, shed abroad a Saviour's love,
  And that shall kindle ours.

    — Isaac Watts

DROUGHT

My heart is parched by unbelief,
  My spirit sere from inward strife;
The heavens above are turned to brass,
  Arid and fruitless is my life.

Then falls Thy rain, O Holy One!
  Fresh is the earth, and young once
    more;
Then falls Thy Spirit on my heart;
  My life is green; the drought is o'er!

    — Betty Bruechert

THE HAPPY HOME

Happy the home when God is there,
  And love fills every breast,
Where one their wish, and one their
    prayer,
  And one their heavenly rest.
                    — *Author Unknown*
                    ∽

PRAYER TO THE HOLY SPIRIT

God the Holy Spirit,
  Reign within my heart;
Banish sin and sorrow;
  Bid all fear depart.
Rule o'er all my being,
  All that's wrong subdue;
Make me like my Saviour,
  Holy, strong and true.

God the Holy Spirit,
  Help me as I pray;
Make me mean most truly
  All the words I say.
Help me trust Thy promise
  Thou wilt hear my prayer;
Help me leave the answers
  In Thy holy care.

God the Holy Spirit,
  Teach Thy Word to me;
All its heavenly beauty
  Give me eyes to see.
Help me feed my spirit
  On Thy Truth each day;
And what Thou dost teach me
  Help me to obey.

God the Holy Spirit,
  Mould me to Thy will;
All my Saviour's pleasure
  In my life fulfill.
Heart and soul and body,
  All to Thee I bring:
Use me in the service
  Of my glorious King!
                — *E. Margaret Clarkson*

TRINITAS

At morn I prayed, "I fain would see
How Three are One, and One is
    Three;
Read the dark riddle unto me."

I wandered forth, the sun and air
I saw bestowed with equal care
On good and evil, foul and fair.

No partial favor dropped the rain;—
Alike the righteous and profane
Rejoiced above their headlong grain.

And my heart murmured, "Is it meet
That blindfold Nature thus should
    treat
With equal hand the tares and wheat?"

A presence melted thro' my mood,—
A warmth, a light, a sense of good,
Like sunshine through a winter wood.

I saw the presence, mailed complete
In her white innocence, pause to greet
A fallen sister of the street.

Upon her bosom snowy pure
The lost one clung, as if secure
From inward guilt or outward lure.

"Beware!" I said; "in this I see
No gain to her, but loss to thee:
Who touches pitch defiled must be."

I passed the haunts of shame and sin,
And a voice whispered, "Who therein
Shall these lost souls to Heaven's peace
    win?

"Who there shall hope and health dis-
    pense,
And lift the ladder up from thence
Whose rounds are prayers of peni-
    tence?"

I said, "No higher life they know;
These earth-worms love to have it so.
Who stoops to raise them sinks as low."

That night with painful care I read
What Hippo's saint and Calvin said,—
The living seeking to the dead!

In vain I turned, in weary quest,
Old pages, where (God give them rest!)
The poor creed-mongers dreamed and
    guessed.

And still I prayed, "Lord, let me see
How Three are One, and One is
    Three;
Read the dark riddle unto me!"

Then something whispered, "Dost
    thou pray
For what thou hast? This very day
The Holy Three have crossed thy way.

"Did not the gifts of sun and air
To good and ill alike declare
The all-compassionate Father's care?

"In the white soul that stooped to raise
The lost one from her evil ways,
Thou saw'st the Christ, whom angels
    praise!

"A bodiless Divinity,
The still small Voice that spake to thee
Was the Holy Spirit's mystery!

"O blind of sight, of faith how small!
Father, and Son, and Holy Call;—
This day thou hast denied them all!

"Revealed in love and sacrifice,
The Holiest passed before thine eyes,
One and the same, in threefold guise.

"The equal Father in rain and sun,
His Christ in the good to evil done,
His Voice in thy soul; — and the Three
    are One!"

I shut my grave Aquinas fast;
The monkish gloss of ages past,
The schoolman's creed aside I cast.

And my heart answered, "Lord, I see
How Three are One, and One is
    Three;
Thy riddle hath been read to me!"
    — *John Greenleaf Whittier*

ᐢᐪ

GRACIOUS SPIRIT

Gracious Spirit, dwell with me;
    I myself would gracious be;
And with words that help and heal
    Would Thy life in mine reveal;
And with actions bold and meek
Would for Christ my Saviour speak.

Truthful Spirit, dwell with me;
    I myself would truthful be;
And with wisdom kind and clear
Let Thy life in mine appear;
    And with actions brotherly
    Speak my Lord's sincerity.

Holy Spirit, dwell with me;
    I myself would holy be;
Separate from sin, I would
Choose and cherish all things good,
    And whatever I can be
Give to Him who gave me Thee!
    — *Thomas Toke Lynch*

ᐢᐪ

I AM IN CHRIST

I am in Christ
    Christ is in me,
My body his temple,
    Sin's captive set free;
My heart His altar,
    Divine love the flame,
Cleansing for service
    In His matchless Name;
My life and His life
    Co-mingled shall be,
With God's very Spirit
    Enthroned in me.
    — *Frances Rhoads La Chance*

ABANDONED

Utterly abandoned to the Holy Ghost!
Seeking all His fulness at whatever cost;
Cutting all the shore-lines, launching in the deep
Of His mighty power — strong to save and keep.

Utterly abandoned to the Holy Ghost!
Oh! the sinking, sinking, until self is lost!
Until the emptied vessel lies broken at His feet;
Waiting till His filling shall make the work complete.

Utterly abandoned to the will of God;
Seeking for no other path than my Master trod;
Leaving ease and pleasure, making Him my choice,
Waiting for His guidance, listening for His voice.

Utterly abandoned! no will of my own;
For time and for eternity, His, and His alone;
All my plans and purposes lost in His sweet will,
Having nothing, yet in Him all things possessing still.

Utterly abandoned! 'tis so sweet to be
Captive in His bonds of love, yet so wondrous free;
Free from sin's entanglements, free from doubt and fear,
Free from every worry, burden, grief or care.

Utterly abandoned! oh, the rest is sweet,
As I tarry, waiting, at His blessed feet;
Waiting for the coming of the Guest divine,
Who my inmost being shall perfectly refine.

Lo! He comes and fills me, Holy Spirit sweet!
I, in Him, am satisfied! I, in Him, complete!
And the light within my soul shall nevermore grow dim
While I keep my covenant — abandoned unto Him!

— *Author Unknown*

HOLY GHOST, DISPEL OUR SADNESS

Holy Ghost, dispel our sadness,
  Pierce the clouds of sinful night;
Come, thou source of sweetest glad-
    ness,
  Breathe thy life, and spread thy
    light!
Loving Spirit, God of peace!
Great distributer of grace!
  Rest upon this congregation,
  Hear, oh, hear our supplication!

From that height which knows no
    measure
  As a gracious shower descend,
Bringing down the richest treasure
  Men can wish or God can send!
O thou glory, shining down
From the Father and the Son,
  Grant us thy illumination!
  Rest upon this congregation!

Come, thou best of all donations
  God can give, or we implore;
Having thy sweet consolations,
  We need wish for nothing more.
Come with unction and with power;
On our souls thy graces shower;
  Author of the new creation,
  Make our hearts thy habitation.

Known to thee are all recesses
  Of the earth and spreading skies;
Every sand the shore possesses
  Thy omniscient mind descries.
Holy fountain, wash us clean
Both from error and from sin!
  Make us fly what thou refusest,
  And delight in what thou choosest!

Manifest thy love forever;
  Fence us in on every side;
In distress be our reliever,
  Guard and teach, support and guide!
Let thy kind effectual grace
Turn our feet from evil ways;
  Show thyself our new Creator,
  And conform us to thy nature!

Be our friend on each occasion,
  God, omnipotent to save!
When we die, be our salvation,
  When we're buried, be our grave!
And, when from the grave we rise,
Take us up above the skies,
  Seat us with thy saints in glory,
  There forever to adore thee!

— Paul Gerhardt

* HOME *

THE HOUSE IS NOT THE HOME

The house itself is not the home,
  Though beautiful it stands,
Designed by master architects
  And built by skillful hands;
For wealth may build a structure
    grand —
  A mansion, if you please —
But beauty doesn't make a home,
  Nor splendor, pomp and ease.

A home is made of loving hearts
  And faces bright with smiles,
Of gentle hands to help us on
  Along life's weary miles.
It has a lot of peace and cheer,
  And plenty of good-will;
A lot of joy to keep us well,
  Or sympathy when ill.

A house may be a lonely place,
  Or place of mere abode;
Instead of bringing joy and peace
  May add a greater load
Because of those who fret and frown,
  And hate instead of love;
Who bring a bitterness to life,
  Not bliss from God above.

A home is sweet, though rich or poor,
  If Jesus dwells within —
Abiding in our hearts and lives
  And overcoming sin;
Then bringing Heaven's sunshine
    down
  To cheer us on our way,
And lead us thro' this toilsome world
  To Heaven's golden day.

— *Walter Isenhour*

WEDDING PRAYER

Thou God, whose high, eternal Love
  Is the only blue sky of our life,
Clear all the Heaven that bends above
  The life-road of this man and wife.

May these two lives be but one note
  In the world's strange-sounding har-
    mony,
Whose sacred music e'er shall float
  Through every discord up to Thee.

As when from separate stars two beams
  Unite to form one tender ray:
As when two sweet but shadowy
    dreams
  Explain each other in the day:

So may these two dear hearts one light
  Emit, and each interpret each.
Let an angel come and dwell to-night
  In this dear double-heart, and teach!

— *Sidney Lanier*

∽

HOME

I turned an ancient poet's book
  And found upon the page,
"Stone walls do not a prison make
  Or iron bars a cage."
Yes, that is true, and something more
You will find where'er you roam
That marble floors and gilded walls
  Can never make a home.
But everywhere that love abides,
  And friendship is a guest
Is surely home, and home sweet home,
  For there the soul can rest.

— *Henry van Dyke*

362

O HAPPY HOUSE

O happy house! where thou art loved the best,
    Dear Friend and Saviour of our race,
Where never comes such welcome, honored Guest,
    Where none can ever fill thy place;
Where every heart goes forth to meet thee,
    Where every ear attends thy word,
Where every lip with blessing greets thee,
    Where all are waiting on their Lord.

O happy house! where man and wife in heart,
    In faith, and hope are one,
That neither life nor death can ever part
    The holy union here begun;
Where both are sharing one salvation,
    And live before thee, Lord, always,
In gladness or in tribulation,
    In happy or in evil days.

O happy house! whose little ones are given
    Early to thee, in faith and prayer,—
To thee, their Friend, who from the heights of heaven
    Guards them with more than mother's care.
O happy house! where little voices
    Their glad hosannas love to raise,
And childhood's lisping tongue rejoices
    To bring new songs of love and praise.

O happy house! and happy servitude!
    Where all alike one Master own;
Where daily duty, in thy strength pursued,
    Is never hard nor toilsome known;
Where each one serves thee, meek and lowly,
    Whatever thine appointment be,
Till common tasks seem great and holy,
    When they are done as unto thee.

O happy house! where thou art not forgot
    When joy is flowing full and free;
O happy house! where every wound is brought,
    Physician, Comforter, to thee.
Until at last, earth's day's work ended,
    All meet thee in that home above,
From whence thou camest, where thou hast ascended,
    Thy heaven of glory and of love!

        —*Karl Johann Philipp Spitta*

TO MAKE A HOME

It takes a heart to make a home,
   A heart that's warm and strong;
A heart with strength to live and love
   And ever keep its song;
A heart that flings the door back wide
   To all that's true and right,
But has the courage to withstand
   The wrong with all its might.

It takes a smile to make a home,
   A smile that's warm and real;
A smile that will not fade and die
   When fortune draws its steel;
A smile that, when the dark comes
    down
And stars no longer gleam,
Will lift a lamp against the night
   And kindle one more dream.

It takes a faith to make a home,
   A faith that's warm and sure,
That seeks the power of Him who
    makes
The human spirit pure;
A faith which enemies of life
   Can never overcome —
It takes a heart, a smile, a faith
   In God to make a home.

             — *Lon Woodrum*

HAPPY THE HOME

Happy the home where Jesus' name
   Is sweet to every ear;
Where children early lisp his fame,
   And parents hold him dear.

Lord, let us in this home agree,
   That thou alone shalt reign,
For those who love and worship thee,
   In joyous peace remain.

             — *Author Unknown*

HOLY MATRIMONY

A perfect, Heaven-made marriage,
   Is like a pair of shears;
So joined they cannot parted be,
   In all the coming years.
And tho' the points may oft diverge,
   They always come together
When there is good work to be done,
   In any kind of weather.

They fit together perfectly,
   And neither works alone;
Should someone try to come between,
   Their cutting edge is shown.
God surely meant they should be one,
   In life, thru weal or woe,
And He will bless their work for Him
   Together, here below.

             — *Maybell Whiting Leal*

WHAT MAKES A HOME

A man can build a mansion
   Anywhere this world about,
A man can build a palace
   Richly furnish it throughout.

A man can build a mansion
   Or a tiny cottage fair,
But it's not the hallowed place called
    "Home"
'Til Mother's dwelling there.

A man can build a mansion
   With a high and spacious dome,
But no man in this world can build
   That precious thing called "Home."

A man can build a mansion
   Carting treasures o'er the foam,
Yes, a man can build the building
   But a woman makes it "Home."

             — *Author Unknown*

PRAYER AT A WEDDING

Giver of good and perfect gifts,
Father and Shepherd of our souls,
Source of all life and joy;
Of Thee the family in heaven and earth is named;
From Thee come love and trust,
And all that knits together kindred minds
In unity of purpose and of thought.
Thou settest us in homes — in little groups —
In which we learn to share our joys and griefs —
"Two heads in counsel, two beside the hearth,
Two in the liberal offices of life."

Bless Thou the tie that now unites these hearts;
May their affection never change save as it grows
The deeper with the years.
Together they are young; so, too, may they grow old,
In step, each with the other, comrades all the way,
Through life's long march unto the journey's end.
If paths are rough and winds blow cold,
May they the closer draw, and hand in hand,
Appear before Thy face, serene and unashamed.
Grant Thou Thy help to keep inviolate their vows;
Endow them with the noble power to give and take —
The grace of "yieldingness" — the will to seek
Each in the other's self, self's perfect complement:
So may they come to know the meaning of the word
He spoke who said, "They two shall be as one."

— *Charles Carroll Albertson*

SEARCH

I sought Him in a great cathedral, dim
With age, where oft-repeated prayers arise,
But caught no glimpse of Him.

I sought Him then atop a lonely hill,
Like Moses once, but tho' I scanned the skies,
My search was fruitless still.

There was a little home where grief and care
Had bred but courage, love, and valiant will,
I sought — and found Him there.

— *Anne Marriott*

WE

May we be a happy family
Each moment throughout the day;
May we be friends to each other
In ev'ry sort of way.
Though it takes a lot of planning
And a lot of praying as well,
Though it takes a lot of forgiving
And more patience than tongue can
    tell,
May we be a happy family
With love enough and to spare —
We and ev'ry good neighbor
Who shares our humble fare.

— *Phyllis C. Michael*

A FATHER'S PRAYER

Father, today I bring to Thee
    This boy of mine whom Thou hast
        made;
In everything he looks to me;
    In turn I look to Thee for aid.

He knows not all that is before;
    He little dreams of hidden snares;
He holds my hand, and o'er and o'er
    I find myself beset with fears.

Father, as this boy looks up to me
    For guidance, and my help implores,
I bring him now in prayer to Thee;
    He trusts my strength and I trust
        Yours.

Hold Thou my hand as I hold his,
    And so guide that I may guide;
Teach me, Lord, that I may teach,
    And keep me free from foolish pride.

Help me to help this boy of mine,
    To be to him a father true;
Hold me, Lord, for every thing,
    As fast I hold my boy for You.

— *Mouzon W. Brabham*

LORD, BLESS OUR HOME

Lord, bless these sacred vows we take—
    Oh, keep us ever true;
Help us to look to Thee as one
    In all we say and do.

Lord, bless the bread we eat each day,
    Make this the bread of life;
Keep us forever in Thy care,
    Keep us from sin and strife.

Lord, bless our home with ties that
    bind
    Through joy or yet through woe;
Dwell Thou within our hearts, we
    pray,
    As moments come and go.

Lord, bless our home with perfect love,
    Bless Thou each thought and deed;
Fill both our hearts with Thy own
    grace.
    Unite us in our need.

Lord, bless our home, be ever near
    To guide us day by day;
Until we see Thee face to face,
    Oh, keep us in Thy way.

— *Phyllis C. Michael*

EVERY HOME AN ALTAR

If every home were an altar,
    Where hearts weighed down with
        care
Could find sustaining strength and
        grace
    In sweet uplift of prayer.

Then solved would be earth's prob-
        lems,
    Banished sin's curse and blight;
For God's own love would radiate
    From every altar light.

— *Author Unknown*

A House or a Home

The walls of a house may be builded of wood,
　　Its foundations of brick or of stone;
But a genuine home is an exquisite thing
　　For it's builded of hearthrobs alone.

The price of a house may be reckoned at once,
　　And paid with a handful of gold;
But the price of a home very few can compute,
　　And that price they have never yet told.

The rooms of a house may be stately and grand,
　　Their adornment a triumph of art;
But beauty of home is the final result
　　Of the toil of an unselfish heart.

A house may be burned, may be sold or exchanged,
　　Nor the loss of one's peace interfere;
But the loss of a home — how it crushes the heart!
　　For our homes we all love and revere.

Of houses a man may possess many scores,
　　Yet his poverty lead to despair;
But an honorable man, in a home of his own,
　　Must be counted a true millionaire.

— J. H. Sykes

ഛ

Prayer for a Bride's House

She is so young, dear Lord, so very young;
　　She is so wide-eyed and naively sweet;
She does not dream of great rooms, draped and hung
　　With master paintings, rugs where some queen's feet
Have lightly trod. She dreams of this instead:
　　A small, new house with freshly painted floors,
With hand-stitched curtains, and above her head
　　Bright dishes gleaming through wee cupboard doors.
She'll learn, some day, the value of old things,
　　When eagerness is still, and she is wise —
Knowing the disillusionment time brings —
　　But now, there's so much springtime in her eyes,
And this is her first house — Whate'er You do,
Let everything about it, Lord, be new!

— Christie Lund

THE HOUSEWIFE

Jesus, teach me how to be
Proud of my simplicity.

Sweep the floors, wash the clothes,
Gather for each vase a rose.

Iron and mend a tiny frock,
Keeping one eye on the clock.

Always having time kept free
For childish questions asked of me.

Grant me wisdom Mary had
When she taught her little Lad.

— *Catherine Cate Coblentz*

MY LITTLE ONE

God bless my little one! how fair
The mellow lamplight gilds his hair,
Loose on the cradle-pillow there,
    God bless my little one!

God love my little one! as clear,
Cool sunshine holds the first green
        spear
On April meadows, hold him dear.
    God love my little one!

When these fond lips are mute, and
        when
I slumber, not to wake again,
God bless, God guard, God love him
        then,
    My little one! Amen.

—*Edgar Fawcett*

PRAYER FOR A LITTLE HOME

God send us a little home
To come back to when we roam —
Low walls and fluted tiles;
Wide windows, a view for miles;

Red firelight and deep chairs;
Small white beds upstairs;
Great talk in little nooks;
Dim colors, rows of books;
One picture on each wall;
Not many things at all.

God send us a little ground —
Tall trees standing round,
Homely flowers in brown sod,
Overhead Thy stars, O God!
God bless, when winds blow,
Our home and all we know.

                    — *Florence Bone*

DEDICATION

O thou whose gracious presence blest
    The home at Bethany,
This shelter from the world's unrest,
This home made ready for its Guest,
    We dedicate to thee.

We build an altar here, and pray
    That thou wilt show thy face.
Dear Lord, if thou wilt come to stay,
This home we consecrate today
    Will be a holy place.

                    — *Louis F. Benson*

OUR HOME

May our home be a haven
Of peace
And contentment
Knowing laughter
And love
Without strife;
May our home be a harbor
Where we find
New courage
To sail
The sea
Of life.

                    — *Phyllis C. Michael*

A Prayer for the Household

Lord, behold our family here assembled.
We thank Thee for this place in which we dwell;
    for the love that unites us;
    for the peace accorded us this day;
    for the hope with which we expect the morrow;
    for the health, the work, the food and the bright skies
        that make our lives delightful;
    for our friends in all parts of the earth,
        and our friendly helpers in this foreign isle.
Let peace abound in our small company.
    Purge out of every heart the lurking grudge.
    Give us grace and strength to forbear and to persevere.
    Offenders,
        give us the grace to accept and to forgive offenders.
    Forgetful ourselves,
        help us to bear cheerfully the forgetfulness of others.
Give us courage and gaiety and the quiet mind.
    Spare to us our friends, soften to us our enemies.
    Bless us, if it may be, in all our innocent endeavors.
    If it may not,
        give us the strength to encounter that which is to come,
        that we be brave in peril,
        constant in tribulation,
        temperate in wrath and in all changes of fortune,
        and down to the gates of death loyal and loving one
        to another.
As the clay to the potter,
    as the windmill to the wind,
    as children of their sire,
    we beseech of Thee this help and mercy for Christ's sake.

— *Robert Louis Stevenson*

The Christian Home

How God must love a friendly home
Which has a warming smile
To welcome everyone who comes
To bide a little while!

How God must love a happy home
Where song and laughter show
Hearts full of joyous certainty
That life means ways to grow!

How God must love a loyal home
Serenely sound and sure!
When troubles come to those within,
They still can feel secure.

How God must love a Christian home
Where faith and love attest
That every moment, every hour,
He is the honored Guest!

— *Gail Brooks Burket*

GOD BLESS OUR HOME

Eternal Father, who hast given
To homes on earth foretaste of heaven,
Whose gentle Spirit from above
Doth breathe Thy peace in hearts that love;
    While here we bide, or far we roam,
      Hear this our prayer: God Bless Our Home!

O Saviour, who didst smile to see
The bridal feast in Galilee,
Whose grace we crave on all who bow,
For life and death to take their vow;
    While here we bide, or far we roam,
      Hear this our prayer: God Bless Our Home!

O Tender Shepherd, who dost hold
Each little lamb within Thy fold,
With rod and staff who followest still
The wandering sheep o'er vale and hill;
    While here we bide, or far we roam.
      Hear this our prayer: God Bless Our Home!

Eternal Father, ever near,
With arm outstretched and listening ear,
Whose mercy keeps whose power defends
Our sons, our daughters, and our friends,
    While here we bide, or far we roam,
      Hear this our prayer: God Bless Our Home.

— Robert Freeman

GOD BLESS THIS HOUSE

God bless this home and those who love it;
Fair be the skies which bend above it.
May never anger's thoughtless word
Within these sheltering walls be heard.
May all who rest beside this fire
And then depart, glad thoughts inspire;
And make them feel who close the door,
Friendship has graced their home once more.

God bless this house and those who keep it;
In the sweet oils of gladness steep it.
Endow these walls with lasting wealth,
The light of love, the glow of health,
The palm of peace, the charm of mirth,
Good friends to sit around the hearth;
And with each nightfall perfect rest —
Here let them live their happiest.

— Author Unknown

Only a Dad

Only a dad, with a tired face
Coming home from the daily race,
Bringing little gold or fame,
To show how well he has played the game,
But great in his heart that his own rejoice
To see him coming, and to hear his voice.

Only a dad, with a brood of four,
One of ten million men or more,
Plodding along in the daily strife,
Bearing the whips and the scorns of life,
With never a whimper of pain or hate
For the sake of those who at home await.

Only a dad, neither rich nor proud,
Merely one of the searching crowd,
Toiling, striving, from day to day,
Facing whatever may come his way.
Silent, whenever the harsh condemn,
And bearing it all for the love of them.

Only a dad, but he gives his all
To smooth the way for his children small
To do, with courage stern and grim,
The deeds that his father did for him,
This is the line that for him I pen,
Only a dad, but the best of men.

— Author Unknown

Bless This House

Bless this house, O Lord, we pray,
  Make it safe by night and day;
Bless these walls, so firm and stout,
  Keeping want and trouble out;
Bless the roof and chimneys tall,
  Let thy peace lie over all;
Bless this door, that it may prove
  Ever open to joy and love.

— Author Unknown

A House and a Home

A house is built of logs and stone,
  Of tiles and posts and piers;
A home is built of loving deeds
  That stand a thousand years.

— Victor Hugo

What Makes a Home

Men make a camp; a swarm of bees a
  comb;
Birds make a nest; a woman makes a
  home.

— Arthur Guiterman

Drop a Pebble in the Water

Drop a pebble in the water: just a splash and it is gone;
  But there's half-a-hundred ripples circling on and on and on,
Spreading, spreading from the center, flowing on out to the sea.
  And there is no way of telling where the end is going to be.
Drop an unkind word, or careless: in a minute you forget;
  But there's little waves a-flowing, and there's ripples circling yet,
And perhaps in some sad heart a mighty wave of tears you've stirred,
  And disturbed a life was happy where you dropped that unkind word.
Drop a word of cheer and kindness: in a minute you forget;
  But there's gladness still a-swelling, and there's joy a-circling yet,
And you've rolled a wave of comfort whose sweet music can be heard
  Over miles of water just by dropping one kind word.

— James W. Foley

Another If

If you can live as youth today is living, and keep your feet at such a dizzy pace;
If you can greet life's subtleties with candor, and turn toward all its cares a
     smiling face;
If you can feel the pulse of youthful vigor beat in your veins and yourself
     subdue;
If you can see untruth knee-deep about you, and still to God and home and
     self be true;
If you can cross the brimming flood of folly, and not dip from the stream to
     quench your thirst;
If you can note life's changing scales of values, and still in your own life keep
     first things first;
If you can feel the urge of disobedience, yet yield yourself to conscience's
     rigid rule;
If you can leave untouched the fruit forbidden, and daily learn in virtue's
     humble school;
If you can play the game of life with honor, and, losing, be inspired to strive
     the more;
If you can teach men how to live life the better, the world will beat a foot-
     path to your door.

— Author Unknown

"AIN'T IT FINE TODAY!"

Sure, this world is full of trouble —
　I ain't said it ain't.
Lord! I've had enough an' double
　Reason for complaint.
Rain an' storm have come to fret me
　Skies are often gray;
Thorns an' brambles have beset me
　On the road, but say,
　Ain't it fine today!

What's the use of always weepin',
　Makin' trouble last?
What's the use of always keepin'
　Thinkin' of the past?
Each must have his tribulation,
　Water with his wine.
Life ain't no celebration.
　Trouble? I've had mine —
　But today is fine.

It's today that I am livin',
　Not a month ago,
Havin', losin', takin', givin'
　As time will it so.
Yesterday a cloud of sorrow
　Fell across the way;
It may rain again tomorrow,
　It may rain — but, say,
　Ain't it fine today!

— *Douglas Malloch*

ᐁᔥ

THE LIFE THAT COUNTS

The life that counts must aim to rise
Above the earth to sunlit skies;
Must fix its gaze on Paradise —
That is the life that counts.
The life that counts must helpful be;
That cares and needs of others see;
Must seek the slave of sin to free —
That is the life that counts.

— *Author Unknown*

IF

If, as I live, I could become
　Immune to beauty's call
And never be affected
　By a lovely rose at all,
If I could watch a sunset
　And not become inspired
Nor by a burning bush
　That autumn flame has fired,
Or have a friend to play me false
　And never shed a tear,
And to another friend in pain
　I'd turn a deafened ear,
I'm sure, then, I'd suffer less
　If all of this were so;
But, if it were, I'd just as well
　Have died long years ago.

— *Daisy Moore Bynum*

ᐁᔥ

NEW THINGS

New mercies, new blessings,
　New light on the way;
New courage, new hope, and
　New strength for each day;
New notes of thanksgiving,
　New chords of delight;
New praise in the morning,
　New songs in the night;
New gifts from His treasures,
　New smiles from His face;
New streams from the fountain
　Of infinite grace;
New stars for thy crown,
　And new tokens of love;
New gleams of the glory
　That waits thee above;
New light of His countenance
　Full and unpriced —
All this be the joy of
　The new life in Christ!

— *Frances Ridley Havergal*

CHILDREN IN THE MARKET-PLACE

Like children in the market-place
    Who weary of their play,
We turn from folly's idle race
    And come to Thee today.
O Jesus, teller of the tale
    That never will grow old,
Thy words of living truth prevail
    Our listening hearts to hold.

Tell us of Father-love that speaks
    Peace to the wandering child
Of valiant Shepherd-love that seeks
    The lost sheep in the wild;
Of deep Redeemer-love that knows
    What sins we need forgiven,
And on the Magdalen bestows
    The purest joy of Heaven.

Tell us of faith that's like a sword,
    And hope that's like a star;
How great the patient soul's reward,
    How blest the loyal are.
Tell us of courage like a wall
    No storm can batter down;
Tell us of men who venture all
    For Thee, and win a crown.

Tell us that life is not a game,
    But real and brave and true;
A journey with a glorious aim,
    A quest to carry through.
Tell us that though our wills are weak
    And though we children be,
The everlasting good we seek
    We can attain through Thee.

                    — Henry van Dyke

                        ∽

MY WEALTH

God gave me eyes that I might thrill
To the rising sun beyond the hill;
A stately pine, a bird in flight,
Or the magic of a starlight night.

God gave me ears to know the thrush;
The startled partridge in the brush.
To hear the patter of tiny feet,
Tripping and dancing along the street.

God gave me hands to till the earth,
To weigh the gleanings; know their
    worth.
To feel the handclasp of a friend,
In truth and loyalty to blend.

God gave me tongue that I proclaim
His lavish blessings and his name,
To teach some stranger by the way
To see, and hear, and feel, and pray.
                    — Frank St. Way

                        ∽

CLOSER TO CHRIST

Draw thou my soul, O Christ,
    Closer to Thine!
Breathe into every wish
    Thy will Divine!
Raised my low self above,
Won by Thy deathless love,
    Ever, O Christ, through mine
    Let Thy life shine!

Not for myself alone
    May my prayer be;
Lift Thou Thy world, O Christ,
    Closer to Thee.
Cleanse it from guilt and wrong,
Teach it salvation's song,
    Make it alive in Thee,
    Perfect in Thee!

Nearer to Thee, O Christ,
    Nearer to Thee!
Till we in Thy dear face
    God's glory see.
Heavenward our hopes ascend,
Saviour and Lord and Friend;
    Oh! draw us all to Thee,
    Nearer to Thee.
                    — Lucy Larcom

STOCK-TAKING

I pause, amidst the clamor of the swiftly moving days
And write the ledger of my life, 'neath Thy all-seeing gaze,
I list in either column the profit and the loss,
The victories that were golden, the failures that were dross.

I look upon the credits with glowing heart and eye,
The faith and courage added as day by day went by;
The lessons Thou hast taught me as I journeyed on my way,
The patience Thou hast brought me through many a weary day,
The measure of Thy love which to others I have shown,
The wonder of Thy presence made manifest and known.

And then I scan the debits through swiftly falling tears,
The hours of fretful worry, beset by faithless fears.
The deeds, so often selfish, and just for men to see,
The motives, oft unworthy, that brought no joy to Thee.
The times when I have failed to show Thy love in word and deed,
To be a channel Thou couldst use to meet another's need;
The blotted entries, smudged and spoiled by sin and bitterness,
And marvel at Thy changeless love, and my unworthiness.

And for the stock on hand, two entries there I place,
My ever-present need — Thy never-failing grace.

Great Keeper of the Records, when Thou takest stock of me
What dost *Thou* see?

— Joan Suisted

CIRCUMSTANCES

Circumstances? How we pet them,
  How we give them right of way!
But the Master never planned that
  We should be beneath their sway.
We who know Him walk the highway
  Where the victors all have trod.
Circumstances cannot conquer
  In the presence of our God.

Paul made circumstances serve him,
  Made them glorify His Lord;
Turned each trial into blessing
  As he boldly preached the word.

"These things turned to my advantage"
  This old warrior used to say;
"For our good they work together,"
  Tho' the darkness shroud the day.

Why should Christians live beneath
  them,
  And not walk the heights with Him?
Circumstances? We're above them,
  Though they often seem so grim.
"More than victors"—this the promise,
  And Christ bids us cast out fear;
For we triumph o'er all testing
  With the Master ever near.

— Albert Simpson Reitz

So I Stay Near the Door: *An Apologia for My Life*

I stay near the door.
I neither go too far in, nor stay too far out,
The door is the most important door in the world —
It is the door through which men walk when they find God.
There's no use my going way inside, and staying there,
When so many are still outside and they, as much as I,
Crave to know where the door is.
And all that so many ever find
Is only the wall where the door ought to be.
They creep along the wall like blind men,
With outstretched, groping hands,
Feeling for a door, knowing there must be a door,
Yet they never find it . . .
So I stay near the door.

The most tremendous thing in the world
Is for men to find that door — the door to God.
The most important thing any man can do
Is to take hold of one of those blind, groping hands,
And put it on the latch — the latch that only clicks
And opens to the man's own touch.
Men die outside that door, as starving beggars die
On cold nights in cruel cities in the dead of winter —
Die for want of what is within their grasp.
They live, on the other side of it—live because they have found it.
Nothing else matters compared to helping them find it,
And open it, and walk in, and find Him . . .
So I stay near the door.

Go in, great saints, go all the way in —
Go way down into the cavernous cellars,
And way up into the spacious attics —
It is a vast, roomy house, this house where God is.
Go into the deepest of hidden casements,
Of withdrawal, of silence, of sainthood.
Some must inhabit those inner rooms,
And know the depths and heights of God,
And call outside to the rest of us how wonderful it is.
Sometimes I take a deeper look in,
Sometimes venture in a little farther;
But my place seems closer to the opening . . .
So I stay near the door.

There is another reason why I stay there.
Some people get part way in and become afraid
Lest God and the zeal of His house devour them;
For God is so very great, and asks all of us.
And these people feel a cosmic claustrophobia,
And want to get out. "Let me out!" they cry.
And the people way inside only terrify them more.
Somebody must be by the door to tell them that they are spoiled
For the old life, they have seen too much:
Once taste God, and nothing but God will do any more.
Somebody must be watching for the frightened
Who seek to sneak out just where they came in,
To tell them how much better it is inside.
The people too far in do not see how near these are
To leaving — preoccupied with the wonder of it all.
Somebody must watch for those who have entered the door,
But would like to run away. So for them, too,
I stay near the door.

I admire the people who go way in.
But I wish they would not forget how it was
Before they got in. Then they would be able to help
The people who have not yet even found the door,
Or the people who want to run away from God.
You can go in too deeply and stay in too long,
And forget the people outside the door.
As for me, I shall take my old accustomed place,
Near enough to God to hear Him, and know He is there,
But not so far from men as not to hear them,
And remember they are there, too.
Where? Outside the door —
Thousands of them, millions of them.
But — more important for me —
One of them, two of them, ten of them,
Whose hands I am intended to put on the latch.
So I shall stay by the door and wait
For those who see it.
"I had rather be a door-keeper . . ."
So I stay near the door.

— Samuel M. Shoemaker

∽

LIFE

Let me but live my life from year to year
With forward face and unreluctant soul,
Not hastening to, nor turning from, the goal;
Not mourning for the things that disappear
In the dim past, nor holding back in fear
From what the future veils; but with a whole
And happy heart that pays its toll
To Youth and Age, and travels on with cheer:
So let the way wind up the hill or down,
Through rough or smooth, the journey will be joy.
Still seeking what I sought when but a boy
New friendship, high adventure, and a crown,
I shall grow old, but never lose life's zest.
Because the road's last turn will be the best.

— *Henry van Dyke*

ALIVE

If I fail to catch the music in the gently falling rain,
If the splendors of the sunset spread their hues for me in vain,
If my heart sends back no echo to the bird in yonder tree —
Though my purse should hold a million, I would still a pauper be.

If the triumphs of my fellows wake no thrill within my breast,
If the task that waits the doing spurs me not to do my best,
If I do not find fresh courage with each day that passes by —
Then the beggar at the corner needs his crutches less than I.

— *Nellie Goode*

DRAW A LITTLE CLOSER

Draw a little closer to the Lord from day to day —
Draw a little closer, as you go along life's way,
Put your trust in Jesus, He will lead you all the way,
If you walk a little day by day.

He will keep you in all sorrow, and you'll never go astray,
Seek and you will find Him, if you only kneel and pray,
So walk a little closer, keep Him always by your side,
You will find your burdens lighter, if you will in Him abide.

— *Author Unknown*

A LITTLE FELLOW FOLLOWS ME

A careful man I ought to be,
A little fellow follows me,
I do not dare to go astray
For fear he'll go the selfsame way.

Not once can I escape his eyes;
Whate'er he sees me do he tries.
Like me says he's going to be
That little chap who follows me.

He thinks that I am good and fine;
Believes in every word of mine.
The base in me he must not see
That little chap who follows me.

I must remember as I go,
Thro' summer sun and winter snow,
I'm building for the years to be
That little chap who follows me.

— *Author Unknown*

WARN SOMEONE

If you have passed a dangerous place
    Somewhere along life's way,
And know that others, too, will face
    The same some future day,
You ought to place a red flag there,
    Or firmly set a stake,
Thus warning them with honest care
For God and Heaven's sake.

Then sound a strong, clear, warning
        note
    Revealing Satan's wiles,
Which may be done by word or vote,
    Or by some self-denials;
But if you save a soul from sin,
    A life from wreck and woe,
You'll help yourelf a crown to win
    Where Heaven's glories flow.

— *Author Unknown*

IN CHRIST WE HAVE:

A love that can never be fathomed;
A life that can never die;
A righteousness that can never be tar-
    nished;
A peace that can never be understood;
A rest than can never be disturbed;
A job that can never be diminished;
A hope that can never be disappointed;
A glory that can never be clouded;
A light that can never be darkened;
A purity that can never be defiled;
A beauty that can never be marred.

— *Author Unknown*

APPRECIATION

Despise no spot. There's not a place
From which joy hides its smiling face
Or whence a hero may not come,
Or greatness may not make its home.

Despise no hour. The drabbest time
May be the one to sound the chime
Of freedom from the toils, and tears,
And sorrows of a thousand years.

Despise no task, however small.
Life honors each and uses all.
What builds the story of the land?
The patient toil of unknown hands.

Despise no road that feet must go.
The roughest, hardest path you know
May be the one whose course is cast
Toward the fairest scene at last.

Despise no soul. God scorneth none.
His image is on every one.
In shadows where no trumpet swells
This moment many a great heart
        dwells.

— *Clarence Edwin Flynn*

Four Dogs

There were four dogs one summer day
　Went out for a morning walk,
And as they trotted along their way
　They began to laugh and talk!

Said Dog No. 1, "I really think
　My master is very wise;
For he builds houses tall and grand
　That reach clear up to the skies!"

Said Dog No. 2, in a scornful tone,
　"Ho! ho! That's wonderful — yes!
But listen to me — my master writes
　　books!
　He's sold a million, I guess!"

Then Dog No. 3 tossed his curly head
　And gave a sly little wink;
"That's nothing to tell! My master is
　　rich!
　He owns half the world, I think!"

The fourth little dog had been trotting
　　along,
　With a wise, reflective mind;
At last he said, with a happy smile,
　"My master — he is kind!"

Now, if your opinion should be asked,
　I wonder what you would say!
Which dog paid the sweetest compli-
　　ment
　To his master on that day?

— Author Unknown

Be With Me, Lord!

Through every minute of this day,
　Be with me, Lord!
Through every day of all this week,
　Be with me, Lord!
Through every week of all this year,
　Be with me, Lord!
Through all the years of all this life,
　Be with me, Lord!

So shall the days and week and years
Be threaded on a golden cord
And all draw on with sweet accord
　Unto Thy fullness, Lord;
That so, when time is past,
　By grace I may at last,
Be with Thee, Lord.

— John Oxenham

Begin With God

Begin the day with God!
　He is thy sun and day;
He is the radiance of thy dawn,
　To Him address thy lay.

Sing a new song at morn,
　Join the glad woods and hills;
Join the fresh winds, and seas, and
　　plains,
　Join the bright flowers and rills.

Sing thy first song to God,
　Not to thy fellow man:
Not to the creatures of His hand,
　But to the glorious One.

Cast every weight aside!
　Do battle with each sin;
Fight with the faithless world without,
　The faithless heart within.

Take thy first meal with God;
　He is thy Heavenly food;
Feed with and on Him; He with thee
　Will feast in brotherhood.

Take thy first walk with God!
　Let Him go forth with thee!
By stream, or sea of mountain path,
　Seek still His company.

Thy first transaction be
　With God Himself above;
So shall thy business prosper well,
　And all the day be love.

— Author Unknown

LOST

What? Lost your temper, did you say?
  Well, dear, I would not mind it.
It is not such a dreadful loss —
  Pray do not try to find it.

It chased the dimples all away,
  And wrinkled up your forehead.
And changed a pretty, smiling face
  To one — well, simply horrid.

It put to flight the cheery words,
  The laughter and the singing
And clouds upon the shining sky
  It would persist in bringing.

And now it's gone. Then, do, my dear,
  Make it your best endeavor
To quickly find a better one,
  And lose it never, never.

— Author Unknown

HOUSE CLEANING

I fling out fear and discontent
  And give my doubts the broom,
Then bring in cheer and merriment
  To fill each empty room.

The windows darkened by distress,
  I'll brighten up again
And wash with suds of cheerfulness
  To let the sunshine in.

I'll toss out selfishness and hate,
  Then buy a box of love
So big it barely clears the gate
  And ceiling high above.

Oh, yes, this year house-cleaning time
  Has me on reverent knees,
Scrubbing my heart of moral grime
  To win great victories.

— Nicholas Lloyd Ingraham

MYSELF

I live with myself each livelong day:
I know what I think; I hear what I say;
My mind is to me a secret book:
Its covers are closed; other eyes may not look;
Yet once in a while I pass on a thought
That comes from its pages so secretly wrought.

Today I was thinking of thoughts high and low,
When my ship, mental ship, was caught in the flow
Of eternity's stream flowing deep, sweeping wide,
And inwardly awed, I silently cried:
"How great are God's thoughts, how solemn, how high,
I cannot attain them, though hard I may try."

Then caught in the vortex of sin and despair,
I remembered His word and uttered this prayer:
"O God of dominion, eternal in power,
Remember Thy servant and free him this hour
From thoughts that are low to thoughts that are high,
And lift mine eyes to Thy limitless sky."

— Edwin C. Swanson

God Shows in Your Face

You don't have to tell how you live each day,
You don't have to say if you work or you play.
A tried, true barometer serves in the place:
However you live, it will show in your face.

The false, the deceit that you bear in your heart
Will not stay inside where it first got a start;
For sinew and blood are a thin veil of lace;
What you wear in your heart, you wear in your face.

If your life is unselfish, if for others you live,
For not what you get, but for how much you can give;
If you live close to God, in His infinite grace,
You don't have to tell it: it shows in your face.

—Author Unknown

Don't Find Fault

Pray don't find fault with the man who limps
    Or stumbles along the road,
Unless you have worn the shoes that he wears,
    Or struggled beneath his load.
There may be tacks in the shoes that hurt,
    Though hidden away from view;
Or burdens he bears placed on your back
    Might cause you to stumble, too.
Don't sneer at the man who's down today
    Unless you have felt the blow
That caused his fall, or felt the same
    That only the fallen know.
You may be strong but yet the blow
    That was his, if dealt to you
In the selfsame way, or at the selfsame time,
    Might cause you to stagger, too.
Don't be too harsh with the man who sins,
    Or pelt him with words or stones,
Unless you are sure — yea, doubly sure,
    That you have not sins of your own.
For you know, perhaps, if the tempter's voice
    Should whisper as soft to you
As it did to him when he went astray
    It would cause you to falter, too.

—Author Unknown

A SMILE

A smile costs nothing but gives much—
It takes but a moment, but the memory
Of it usually lasts forever.
None are so rich that can get along
Without it —
And none are so poor but that can
Be made rich by it.
It enriches those who receive
Without making poor those who give—
It creates sunshine in the home,
Fosters good will in business
And is a good antidote for trouble —
And yet it cannot be begged, borrowed
Or stolen, for it is of no value
Unless it is freely given away.
Some people are too busy to give
You a smile —
Give them one of yours —
For the good Lord knows that no one
Needs a smile so badly
As he or she who has no more
Smiles left to give.

— Author Unknown

HAND IN HAND WITH JESUS

I walked on the billows with Jesus
    And knew no fear of the sea;
Though waves of temptation surrounded,
    His grace was enough for me.
The spray touched my lips and my garments,
    'Twould never have caused me harm.
But the way seemed so rough and so endless
    My peace gave way to alarm.
When I should have counted my blessings,
    I counted my burdens each day.
And my eyes grew weary with weeping,
    My heart too discouraged to pray.
Almost I had sunk 'neath the waters,
    When I turned my eyes above
And saw that my Saviour was smiling,
    His eyes were tender with love.
I knew then He had not forsaken;
    "Save me, Lord Jesus!" I cried.
How quickly His arms were around me,
    I walked again at His side!
Though the waves are still all around me,
    The sea is still at my feet;
I walk hand in hand with my Saviour,
    And now the path has grown sweet.
No longer do doubts fill my being
    As I walk along with my Lord;
When I reach the ship with my Saviour,
    The winds shall cease at His word.

— Barbara Cornet Ryberg

DIAMONDS

Diamonds are only chunks of coal
  That stuck to their jobs, you see;
If they'd petered out, as most of us do,
  Where would the diamonds be?
It isn't the fact of making a start,
  It's the sticking that counts. I'll say,
It's the fellow that knows not the
    meaning of fall,
  But hammers and hammers away.
Whenever you think you've come to
    the end,
  And you're beaten as bad as can be,
Remember that diamonds are chunks
    of coal,
  That stuck to their jobs, you see.

— *Virginia Call*

DISAGREEING WITH GOD

We call Him "Lord" and believe His
    Word,
  We're careful all along our way.
And yet He says, "Why call Me 'Lord'
  And do not the things I say?"

He tells us to forgive our brother
  And we say we do, but, oh,
The lives we live speak out in truth,
  "Not so, my Lord, not so."

Believe in prayer? Of course we do.
  His great promises we know.
And yet, attendance at prayer meeting
  Speaks forth, "Not so, not so."

"And ye shall be witnesses unto Me,
  Wherever ye may go."
And yet, when that time comes, we say,
  "Not so, my Lord, not so."

We know He makes all grace abound,
  And gives us all we need.
And still we hold each penny dear,
  "Not so, my Lord," we plead.

We read the words, "Be anxious for
    naught."
  And yet we worry so.
We know the verse, believe its truth,
  And yet we say, "Not so."

My brother, what will He say to you,
  When the race of life is done?
"Depart from Me, I know you not"
  Or "Well done, My beloved one"?

— *Beverly Haglund*

IN MY PLACE

Thy Blood was shed for me.
  My life belongs to Thee.
With Thee I died, with Thee I rose.
  Thou livest now in me.

Thy body bruised for me.
  How can I thankless be,
Or hesitate to offer mine
  A sacrifice to Thee?

Blood from Thy thorn-pierced brow
  Washed my vile thoughts away.
Take captive ev'ry thought, O Christ,
  And teach them to obey.

Blood from Thy nail-pierced hands
  Cleansed all my evil deeds.
Now use my strength in youth, my
    Lord,
  To sow Thy precious seed.

Thy feet were pierced with nails
  Because mine went astray.
Lord, keep me walking in the light
  Of Thine eternal way.

Thy back was lashed that mine,
  Bent low beneath my sin,
Might lose its load at Calvary
  And I the race might win.

— *Esther Archibald*

PRAISE AT MIDNIGHT

The darkness still is deep'ning,
  O tried and weary heart,
No rift of morning brightness
  Bids midnight gloom depart;
The prison walls surround thee,
  No human help is nigh,
But blest is the assurance
  Thy Saviour reigns on high.

When shadowed in the darkness,
  And pressed by every foe,
Then let your gladdest carols
  And sweetest anthems flow;
The praise so sweet to Jesus,
  The "sacrifice of praise,"
Is when no earthly sunshine
  Pours forth its cheering rays.

'Tis then your song is wafted
  All human heights above,
And mingles with the angels,
  In realms of perfect love;
'Tis then the God of glory
  Makes Satan fear and flee,
And sends a mighty earthquake
  To set His ransomed free.

'Tis easy when the morning
  Appears at last to view
To praise thy strong Redeemer
  Who burst the bondage through,
But 'tis the praise at midnight
  That gives the foe alarm,
That glorifies thy Saviour,
  And bares His strong right arm.

A conqueror thou wouldst be?
  Yea, more than conqueror thou,
If thou wilt shout in triumph
  And claim the victory now;
The prison doors will open,
  The dungeon gleam with light,
And sin-chained souls around thee
  Shall see Jehovah's might.

— *Carrie Judd Montgomery*

YOU CAN BE ONE!

When you're looking for a Christian
  Who daily walks with God;
One who has a perfect conscience,
  Does not chafe beneath the rod;
One who keeps himself peculiar
  And unspotted from the world;
While his gaze is fixed on Heaven
  Tho' hell's darts at him be hurled —
    Well — you may not see one,
    But you can be one.

Tho' the church be far from perfect,
  As the members each you scan;
Some hypocrites you find and
  Others missing Heaven's plan;
Some are lazy, some too zealous,
  Some as stubborn as a mule —
Still you search for such a Christian
  As will measure to your rule —
    Well — you may not see one,
    But you can be one.

In God's people, oh, what patience,
  What tenderness you find;
What sincerity and meekness,
  What purity of mind;
But so many who are perfect
  In motive and in heart,
In performance may seem lacking,
  So remember from the start —
    Tho' you may not see one,
    Still you can be one.

God has never promised others
  Your demands would have to face;
But however high your standards,
  You can live them by His grace;
No ideals have yet depleted
  What God's grace can do for you;
But when checking for a Christian
  By the things *you* have to do —
    Tho' you may not see one,
    Still you can be one.

— *Edith C. Lilly*

INVENTORY

Busy? Yes, Lord, in the midst of the conflict,
  Working and striving Thy servant to be,
Pleading with sinners, helping the stumbling,
  Yet with my first love grown cold unto Thee.

Where is the thrill that once came with Thy presence?
  Where, Lord, the blessing once found in Thy Word?
Can it be I am so lost in Thy service
  That by Thyself I no longer am stirred?

Lord, let me no more grow dull to Thy presence,
  Fill my cold heart with the warmth of Thy love;
Never again need my poor soul go hungry,
  Satisfied daily with food from above.

— *Ellen McKay Trimmer*

IT MIGHT HAVE BEEN

An old man stood at eventide
  And looked across the bygone years;
For what he might have been he sighed;
  For what he was he shed great tears.
A misspent life — O that was it —
  His time was gone, his talent lost;
How sad to think and then admit
  It was too late to count the cost!

He might have been — O who can guess?
  No one indeed but God can know;
He might have been a saint — no less —
  To help, to lift, to shine and glow;
Or like a mighty ship at sea
  That's brought its cargo safe to land,
He might have brought to you and me
  Some blessings rich from God's great hand.

He studied of the golden days
  He lived in sin and wrongly spent;
Of how he walked in evil ways,
  And maybe others downward sent,
Whom he, perhaps, by word and deed,
  By prayer and good examples set,
Might in their lives have sown the seed
  That would have God's approval met.

Too late, alas! the time was spent,
  The opportunities were dead;
And though with tears he might repent,
  And God would save from fear and dread,
He can't recall the misspent past;
  It's gone to stay for evermore;
But who can tell the glories vast
  He's missed beyond this earthly shore?

— *Walter E. Isenhour*

SING!

There are hearts that are crushed by the cares of the road,
  And hurt by the strife of the day;
There are lonely souls who dwell apart,
  'Neath skies that are always grey.
Spirits that bear no friendly voice,
  Who are strangers to mirth and cheer;
Creatures who dwell in a barren world,
  Who weep through nights long and drear.

And perhaps, as we travel the highway of life —
  If our hearts are open to see,
We may meet these care-laden pilgrims
  And ministering spirits be.
For the joy of your heart was given to share —
  If imprisoned, it's destined to die;
And a weeping world will respond to your song,
  If you sing as the world goes by.

— *Author Unknown*

A MINUTE

Two or three minutes — two or three hours —
What do they mean in this life of ours?
Not very much if but counted as time,
But minutes of gold and hours sublime
If we will use them once in a while
To make someone happy, someone smile.
A minute may dry a little lad's tears;
An hour sweep aside the troubles of years.
Minutes of my time may bring to an end
Hopelessness, somewhere, and give me a friend!

— *Author Unknown*

IF I HAD BUT ONE YEAR TO LIVE

If I had but one year to live;
One year to help, one year to give;
One year to love, one year to bless;
One year of better things to stress;
One year to laugh, one year to smile;
To brighten earth a little while;
One year to sing my Maker's praise;
One year to fill with work my days;
I think that I should try to spend each
    day
In just the very selfsame way
That I do now.
For, from afar
The call may come across the bar
At anytime; and I must be
Prepared to spend eternity.
So, if I have a year to live
Or just one day in which to give
A pleasant smile, a helping hand;
A mind that tries to understand
A fellow traveler when in need,
'Tis one with me.
I'll take no heed,
But strive each day to fill
And serve my gracious Master's will.

— *Author Unknown*

GRACIOUS LIVING

If I should ask of him who holds
All good within his giving
Some special gifts, I think I'd ask
For grace in living.
That I might have a gentle heart,
O spirit brave and gay.
A comrade's sympathy for those
Who walk my way;
The proud humility that's best,
Receiving as in giving.
Lord, teach me daily, then, the art
Of gracious living.

— *Author Unknown*

RULES FOR DAILY LIFE

Begin the day with God,
Kneel down to Him in prayer;
Lift up thy heart to His abode,
And seek His love to share.

Open the Book of God,
And read a portion there;
That it may hallow all thy thoughts
And sweeten all thy care.

Go through the day with God,
Whate'er thy work may be;
Where'er thou art, at home, abroad,
He still is near to thee.

Converse in mind with God,
Thy spirit heavenward raise;
Acknowledge every good bestowed.
And offer grateful praise.

Conclude thy day with God,
Thy sins to Him confess;
Trust in the Lord's atoning blood,
And plead His righteousness.

Lie down at night with God,
Who gives His servants sleep,
And when thou tread'st the vale of
    death
He will thee guard and keep.

— *Author Unknown*

GOOD AND CLEVER

If all the good people were clever,
And all the clever people were good,
The world would be nicer than ever
We thought that it possibly could.
But alas it is seldom or never
The two hit it off as they should;
The good are so hard on the clever,
The clever so rude to the good.

— *Author Unknown*

BUILDING

I watched them tearing a building down —
A gang of men in a busy town —
With a yo-heave-ho and a lusty yell,
They swung a beam and the side wall fell.

I asked the foreman: "Are these men skilled —
The kind you would hire if you wanted to build?"
He laughed and said: "Why, no indeed,
Just common labour is all I need:
They can easily wreck in a day or two
What builders have taken years to do."

I asked myself, as I went my way,
Which of these roles have I tried today?
Am I a builder, who works with care,
Measuring life by the rule and square,
Shaping my deeds by the well-made plan,
Patiently doing the best I can?
Or am I a wrecker who walks the town,
Content with the labour of tearing down?

— *Gilbert Keith Chesterton*

DEEP LIVING

We love to spread our branches,
The root-life we neglect;
We love to shine in public,
And human praise expect;
While in our inner chamber,
Where creature voices cease,
We may meet God in silence,
And breathe in heaven's peace.

The secret of deep living
Lies in the secret place,
Where, time and sense forgotten,
We see God face to face,
Beyond mere forms and symbols,
Beyond mere words and signs,
Where, in that hidden temple,
The Light eternal shines.

— *Author Unknown*

MY HAND IN HIS

The day had gone: Alone and weak
I groped my way within a bleak
And sunless land
The path that led into the light,
I could not find . . . In that dark night
God took my hand
He led me that I might not stray
And brought me by a new safe way
I had not known.
By waters still through pastures green
I followed Him the path was clean
Of brier and stone.
The darkness lost its strength
My waiting eyes beheld at length
The streaking dawn.
On, safely on, through sunrise glow
I walked, my hand in His and lo,
The night had gone.

— *Author Unknown*

MUCH FOR LITTLE

How little it costs if we give it a thought,
  To make some heart happy each day!
Just one kind word or a tender smile
  As we go on our daily way.

Perhaps a look will suffice to clear
  The cloud from a neighbor's face;
And the press of a hand in sympathy
  A sorrowful tear efface.

It costs so little; I wonder why
  We give it so little thought.
A smile, kind words, a glance, a touch—
  What magic by them is wrought!

                          — *Author Unknown*

WORTHWHILE THINGS ARE FREE

The things of worth we pay for not at all:
  The shining dew at morning's dawn;
  The swaying leaves in the noonday breeze;
  The purple haze at evening's fall;
  The night with all its mystic pageantry
  Of fleecy clouds in moonlit sky.
For these our purse is far too small.
The things of worth we pay for not at all.

The joys of heaven need not be searched for afar:
  The waking in familiar room;
  The homely task and baby's laugh;
  The crackling flames of open fire;
  The waiting for the footsteps coming soon,
  The opening door, your grasp, your kiss.
Life's near at hand and ever new!
Is not heaven free and given here and now?

                          — *Charles R. Glazer*

HE CANNOT HEAL

He cannot heal who has not suffered much,
  For only sorrow, sorrow understands;
They will not come for healing at our touch
  Who have not seen the scars upon our hands.

                          —*Lillian R. Dickson*

The Secret of a Happy Day

Just to let thy Father do
  What He will;
Just to know that He is true,
  And be still.
Just to follow hour by hour
  As He leadeth;
Just to draw the moment's power
  As it needeth.
Just to trust Him, this is all!
  Then the day will surely be
Peaceful, whatsoe'er befall,
  Bright and blessed, calm and free.

Just to let Him speak to thee
  Through His Word,
Watching, that His voice may be
  Clearly heard.
Just to tell Him everything
  As it rises,
And at once to Him to bring
  All surprises.
Just to listen, and to stay
  Where you cannot miss His voice.
This is all! and thus today,
  Communing you shall rejoice.

Just to ask Him what to do
  All the day,
And to make you quick and true
  To obey.
Just to know the needed grace
  He bestoweth,
Every bar of time and place
  Overfloweth.
Just to take thy orders straight
  From the Master's own command.
Blessed day! when thus we wait
  Always at our Sovereign's hand.

Just to recollect His love,
  Always true;
Always shining from above,
  Always new.
Just to recognize its light,
  All-enfolding;

Just to claim its present might,
  All-upholding.
Just to know it as thine own,
  That no power can take away.
Is not this enough alone
  For the gladness of the day?

Just to trust, and yet to ask
  Guidance still;
Take the training or the task,
  As He will.
Just to take the loss or gain,
  As He sends it;
Just to take the joy or pain,
  As He lends it.
He who formed thee for His praise
  Will not miss the gracious aim;
So today and all thy days
  Shall be molded for the same.

Just to leave in His dear hand
  Little things,
All we cannot understand,
  All that stings.
Just to let Him take the care
  Sorely pressing,
Finding all we let Him bear
  Changed to blessing.
This is all! and yet the way
  Marked by Him who loves thee best:
Secret of a happy day,
  Secret of His promised rest.
          — *Frances Ridley Havergal*

Time

If I had time to find a place
And sit down, quietly and face
My better self, which cannot show
Because my days are crowded so;
And see my distant gleaming goal,
It might be I should find my soul.
And even thrill with thought sublime,
If I could only find the time.
          — *Author Unknown*

Things That Count

Not what we have, but what we use;
Not what we see, but what we choose.
These are the things that mar or bless
　The sum of human happiness.

The things near by, not things afar;
Not what we seem, but what we are.
These are the things that make or break
That give the heart its joy or ache.

Not what seems fair, but what is true;
Not what we dream, but the good we
　do,　　　　　　　　　　[gems,
These are the things that shine like
Like stars in fortune's diadems.

Not what we take, but what we give;
Not as we pray, but as we live,
These are the things that make for
　peace,
Both now and after time shall cease.
　　　　　　　　— *Author Unknown*

No Time for My Lord?

There's time for the mending and
　making;
There's time for the cooking and bak-
　ing;
　For the letter I write,
　Or the words I indite,
But what time do I give to my Lord?

There is time for trimming a hat;
There is time for a neighborly chat;
　There's time for some pleasure,
　But scarce any leisure
To give to my Master and Lord.

There's time for the book so compel-
　ling;
There's time for the buying and sell-
　ing;
　For the office or mart,
　For music or art,
But where is the time for my Lord?

There's time for the digging and hoe-
　ing;
There's time for the raking and mow-
　ing;
　For the sowing of seeds,
　And removing of weeds,
But what time do I give to my Lord?

There is time for the news on the air,
To which I must listen with care;
　For the claims of my health,
　Or the spending of wealth,
But what time do I give to my Lord?

Lord, Thou gavest Thy time here be-
　low,
Salvation and grace to bestow;
　Dost Thou wait for my voice?
　Can I make thee rejoice,
As I give of my time to Thee, Lord?

O Master, forgive me, I pray;
I'm sorry, repentant, today.
　From this hour make me wise,
　And teach me to prize
The time that I spend with my Lord.

　　　　　　— *Beth Coombe Harris*

I Take, He Undertakes

I clasp the hand of Love Divine,
I claim the gracious promise mine,
And this eternal countersign,
"I take, He undertakes."

I take salvation full and free,
Thro' Him who gave His life for me,
He undertakes my All to be,
"I take, He undertakes."

I simply take Him at His word,
I praise Him that my prayer is heard,
And claim my answer from the Lord,
"I take, He undertakes."

　　　　　　　　—*A. B. Simpson*

BLESSED SAVIOUR, THOU ART MINE

Blessed Saviour, Thou art mine,
All I have is wholly Thine;
Take, oh, take me now, I pray,
Wash my every sin away.
Let me of Thy fullness know,
Make me whiter than the snow;
Pure and holy let me be,
That my life may tell for Thee.

Every sin I now forsake,
As I of Thy fullness take;
Thou hast promised power Divine,
May it evermore be mine.
All in vain for peace I sigh,
Naught on earth can satisfy;
Thou alone canst be my rest,
Fold, O fold me to Thy breast.

Save me from the power of sin,
Give me victory within;
Grant me holiness of life,
Keep me spotless 'mid the strife.
May Thy Spirit fill my heart,
Power for service now impart;
Till I see Thee face to face,
Learn the secret of Thy grace.

— Oswald J. Smith

ॐ

THINGS WE CAN'T AFFORD

We can't afford to win the gain
　That means another's loss;
We can't afford to miss the crown
　By stumbling at the cross.

We can't afford the heedless jest
　That robs us of a friend;
We can't afford the laugh that finds
　In bitter tears an end.

We can't afford the feast today
　That brings tomorrow's fast.
We can't afford the farce that comes
　To tragedy at last.

We can't afford to play with fire
　Or tempt a serpent's bite.
We can't afford to think that sin
　Brings any true delight.

We can't afford with serious heed
　To treat the cynic's sneer;
We can't afford to wise men's words
　To turn a careless ear.

We can't afford for hate to give
　Like hatred in return;
We can't afford to feed such flame
　And make it fiercer burn.

We can't afford to lose the soul
　For this world's fleeting breath;
We can't afford to barter life
　In mad exchange for death.

But blind to good are we apart
　From Thee, all-seeing Lord;
O grant us light that we may know
　The things we can't afford.

— Author Unknown

ॐ

DESPISE NOT THOU THE CHASTENING OF THE ALMIGHTY

The sunshine to the flower may give
　The tints that charm the sight,
But scentless would that floweret live
　If skies were always bright;
Dark clouds and showers its scent bestow,
And purest joy is born of woe.

He who each bitter cup rejects,
　No loving spring shall quaff;
He whom thy rod in love corrects,
　Shall lean upon thy staff:
Happy, thrice happy, then, is he
Who knows his chastening is from thee.

— Bernard Barton

LIVE DAY BY DAY

Live day by day;
Why art thou bending toward the backward way?
One summit and another thou shalt mount.
Why stop at every round the space to count
The past mistakes if thou must still remember?
Watch not the ashes of the dying ember;
Kindle thy hope. Put all thy fears away —
Live day by day.

— Author Unknown

IN GRIEF

Strong Son of God, immortal Love,
    Whom we, that have not seen Thy face,
    By faith, and faith alone, embrace,
Believing where we cannot prove;

Thine are these orbs of light and shade;
    Thou madest life in man and brute;
    Thou madest Death; and lo, thy foot
Is on the skull which thou hast made!

Thou wilt not leave us in the dust:
    Thou madest man, he knows not why,
    He thinks he was not made to die:
And Thou hast made him: Thou art just.

Thou seemest human and divine,
    The highest, holiest manhood, Thou:
    Our wills are ours, we know not how;
Our wills are ours, to make them Thine.

Our little systems have their day;
    They have their day and cease to be:
    They are but broken lights of Thee,
And Thou, O Lord, art more than they.

We have but faith: we cannot know;
    For knowledge is of things we see;
    And yet we trust it comes from thee,
A beam in darkness: let it grow.

Let knowledge grow from more to more,
    But more of reverence in us dwell;
    That mind and soul, according well,
May make one music as before,

But vaster. We are fools and slight;
　　We mock thee when we do not fear:
　　But help thy foolish ones to bear;
Help thy vain worlds to bear thy light.

Forgive what seemed my sin in me;
　　What seemed my worth since I began:
　　For merit lives from man to man,
And not from man, O Lord, to thee.

Forgive my grief for one removed,
　　Thy creature, whom I found so fair.
　　I trust he lives in thee, and there
I find him worthier to be loved.

Forgive these wild and wandering cries,
　　Confusions of a wasted youth;
　　Forgive them where they fail in truth,
And in thy wisdom make me wise.

— Alfred, Lord Tennyson

'Twas a Sheep . . . Not a Lamb

It was a sheep—not a lamb, that strayed away
　　In the parable Jesus told:
A grown-up sheep that had gone astray
　　From the ninety and nine in the fold.

Out in the meadows, out in the cold,
　　'Twas a sheep the Good Shepherd sought:
Back to the flock and into the fold,
　　'Twas a sheep the Good Shepherd brought.

And why, for the sheep, should we earnestly long,
　　And so earnestly hope and pray?
Because there is danger, if they go wrong,
　　They will lead the young lambs astray.

For the lambs follow the sheep, you know,
　　Wherever the sheep may stray:
If the sheep go wrong, it will not be long
　　Till the lambs are as wrong as they.

So, with the sheep we earnestly plead,
　　For the sake of the lambs today:
If the lambs are lost, what a terrible cost
　　Some sheep may have to pay.

— Author Unknown

If I Knew

If I knew where the box of smiles was kept,
  No matter how large the key
Or strong the bolt, I would try so hard
  It would open, I know, for me.

Then over the land, the sea, broadcast
  I'd scatter the smiles to play,
That the children's faces might hold them fast
  For many and many a day.

If I knew a box was large enough
  To hold all the frowns I meet,
I would like to gather them every one
  From nursery, school, and street.

Then, folding and holding, I'd pack them in,
  And turning the monster key,
I'd hire a giant to drop the box
  In the depths of the deep, deep sea.

— *Phillips Brooks*

Rejoice, Be Glad

Rejoice, rejoice, O soul, be glad
And sing the Master's praise;
Let not your countenance be sad,
For pleasant are His ways.

Rejoice and let your witness show
Of Christ's redeeming love,
That all the world may come to know
His mercy from above.

Rejoice, be glad and have a part
With Zion's happy throng;
Express your love with all your heart,
And give to Him your song.

— *Carlton Buck*

Some Murmur When Their Sky Is Clear

Some murmur when their sky is clear
  And wholly bright to view,
If one small speck of dark appear
  In their great heaven of blue:
And some with thankful love are filled,
  If but one streak of light,
One ray of God's good mercy, gild
  The darkness of their night.

In palaces are hearts that ask,
  In discontent and pride,
Why life is such a dreary task,
  And all good things denied:
And hearts in poorest huts admire
  How Love has in their aid —
Love that not ever seems to tire —
  Such rich provision made.

— *Richard Chenevix Trench*

MUTUAL KINDNESS

Dear ties of mutual succor bind
   The children of our feeble race,
And, if our brethren were not kind,
   This earth were but a weary place.
We lean on others as we walk
   Life's twilight path with pitfalls
      strewn;
And 'twere an idle boast to talk
   Of treading that dim path alone.

Amid the snares misfortune lays
   Unseen, beneath the steps of all,
Blest is the Love that seeks to raise
   And stay and strengthen those who
      fall;
Till, taught by him who, for our sake,
   Bore every form of Life's distress,
With every passing year we make
   The sum of human sorrows less.

   —*William Cullen Bryant*

THE CROSS

'Tis my happiness below
   Not to live without the cross;
But the Saviour's power to know,
   Sanctifying every loss.

Trials must and will befall;
   But with humble faith to see
Love inscribed upon them all,—
   This is happiness to me.

Did I meet no trials here,
   No chastisement by the way,
Might I not with reason fear
   I should prove a castaway?

Trials make the promise sweet;
   Trials give new life to prayer;
Bring me to my Saviour's feet,
   Lay me low and keep me there.

   —*William Cowper*

OUT OF THIS LIFE

Out of this life I shall never take
Things of silver and gold I make.
All that I cherish and hoard away,
After I leave, on earth must stay.

Though I call it mine and I boast its worth,
I must give it up when I quit the earth.
All that I gather and all that I keep
I must leave behind when I fall asleep.

And I wonder often, just what I shall own,
In that other life when I pass alone,
What shall He find and what shall He see,
In the soul that answers the call for me?

Shall the great Judge learn when my task is through
That my soul had gathered some riches too?
Or shall at the last, it be mine to find,
That all I had worked for, I had left behind?

   —*Author Unknown*

LITTLE THINGS

What will it matter in a little while
That for a day we met and gave a word,
A touch, a smile upon the way?
What will it matter whether hearts
    were brave,
And lives were true, that you gave me
The sympathy I craved, as I gave you?
These trifles, can it be
They make or mar a human life?
Are souls as lightly waved as rushes
Are by storm or strife? Yea! Yea!
A look the failing heart may break,
Or make it whole
And just a word said for love's sweet
    sake
May save a soul.

                    — *Author Unknown*

THE WILL OF GOD

I worship thee, sweet will of God!
    And all thy ways adore,
And every day I live, I seem
    To love thee more and more.

Thou wert the end, the blessed rule
    Of our Saviour's toils and tears;
Thou wert the passion of his heart
    Those three and thirty years.

And he hath breathed into my soul
    A special love of thee,—
A love to lose my will in his,
    And by that loss be free.

I love to see thee bring to nought
    The plans of wily men;
When simple hearts outwit the wise,
    Oh, thou art loveliest then.

The headstrong world it presses hard
    Upon the church full oft,
And then how easily thou turnst
    The hard ways into soft.

I love to kiss each print where thou
    Hast set thine unseen feet;
I cannot fear thee, blessed will!
    Thine empire is so sweet.

When obstacles and trials seem
    Like prison walls to be,
I do the little I can do,
    And leave the rest to thee.

I know not what it is to doubt,
    My heart is ever gay;
I run no risk, for, come what will,
    Thou always hast thy way.

I have no cares, O blessed will!
    For all my cares are thine:
I live in triumph, Lord! for thou
    Hast made thy triumphs mine.

And when it seems no chance or
        change
    From grief can set me free,
Hope finds its strength in helplessness,
    And gayly waits on thee.

Man's weakness, waiting upon God,
    Its end can never miss,
For men on earth no work can do
    More angel-like than this.

Ride on, ride on triumphantly,
    Thou glorious will, ride on!
Faith's pilgrim sons behind thee take
    The road that thou hast gone.

He always wins who sides with God,
    To him no chance is lost;
God's will is sweetest to him, when
    It triumphs at his cost.

Ill that he blesses is our good,
    And unblest good is ill;
And all is right that seems most wrong,
    If it be his sweet will.

                    — *Frederick William Faber*

THE VILLAGE BLACKSMITH

Under a spreading chestnut tree
The village smithy stands;
The smith, a mighty man is he,
With large and sinewy hands;
And the muscles of his brawny arms
Are strong as iron bands.

His hair is crisp, and black, and long,
His face is like the tan;
His brow is wet with honest sweat,
He earns whate'er he can,
And looks the whole world in the face,
For he owes not any man.

Week in, week out, from morn till
night,
You can hear his bellows blow;
You can hear him swing his heavy
sledge,
With measured beat and slow,
Like a sexton ringing the village bell,
When the evening sun is low.

And children coming home from
school
Look in at the open door;
They love to see the flaming forge,
And hear the bellows roar,
And catch the burning sparks that fly
Like chaff from a threshing floor.

He goes on Sunday to the church,
And sits among his boys;
He hears the parson pray and preach,
He hears his daughter's voice,
Singing in the village choir,
And it makes his heart rejoice.

It sounds to him like her mother's
voice,
Singing in Paradise!
He needs must think of her once more,
How in the grave she lies;
And with his hard, rough hand he
wipes
A tear out of his eyes.

Toiling, — rejoicing, — sorrowing,
Onward through life he goes;
Each morning sees some task begun,
Each evening sees it close;
Something attempted, something done,
Has earned a night's repose.

Thanks, thanks to thee, my worthy
friend,
For the lesson thou hast taught!
Thus at the flaming forge of life
Our fortunes must be wrought;
Thus on its sounding anvil shaped
Each burning deed and thought!

— *Henry Wadsworth Longfellow*

BECAUSE YOU PASSED MY WAY —

My load's a little lighter now,
Because you passed my way —
The sun's a little brighter
And the clouds have passed away
I've found my Saviour nearer,
And each day He grows still dearer,
And I'm on my way to Glory,
Because you passed my way.

I was lost and no one seemed to care,
Until you passed my way,
You saw me, and led me to Christ
Oh, what a happy day,
Now I'm living all for Jesus,
And with Him I'll be some day,
For I found a new beginning,
Because you passed my way.

And when in realms of glory,
I see His precious face,
And hear the angel voices
Within that Heavenly place,
I'll remember that a sinner,
Who once had gone astray,
Might not be there in Glory,
Had you not passed my way.

— *Eleanor Taylor Rhodes*

The Beauty of Jesus in Me

My life touched yours for a very brief space,
    And what, oh, what did you see?
A hurried, a worried and anxious face,
    Or the beauty of Jesus in me?

Was I steeped so deep in the ways of the world
    That you couldn't detect one thing
That would set me apart and show that my heart
    Belonged to the Heavenly King?

Did I carry no banner for Jesus my Lord,
    Not one thing at all that could show
Whose side I am on in this glorious fight?
    I am His! But you wouldn't know.

Forgive me! And if we should e'er meet again
    Upon earth, oh, I pray you will see
No mark of this world, but His banner unfurled,
    And the beauty of Jesus in me!

                                    — *Alice Hansche Mortenson*

Help Me to Live!

If I have wounded any soul today,
If I have caused one foot to go astray,
If I have walked in my own willful way —
    Dear Lord, forgive!

If I have uttered idle words or vain,
If I have turned aside from want or pain
Lest I myself should suffer through the strain —
    Dear Lord, forgive!

If I have been perverse or hard or cold,
If I have longed for shelter in Thy fold,
When Thou hast given me some part to hold —
    Dear Lord, forgive!

Forgive the wrong I have confessed to Thee,
Forgive the wrong, the secret wrongs, I do not see;
That which I know not, Master, teach Thou me —
    Help me to live!

                                    — *Charles Gabriel*

THE LADDER OF SAINT AUGUSTINE

Saint Augustine! well hast thou said,
    That of our vices we can frame
A ladder, if we will but tread
    Beneath our feet each deed of shame!

All common things, each day's events,
    That with the hour begin and end,
Our pleasures and our discontents,
    Are rounds by which we may ascend.

The low desire, the base design,
    That makes another's virtues less;
The revel of the ruddy wine,
    And all occasions of excess;

The longing for ignoble things;
    The strife for triumph more than
        truth;
The hardening of the heart, that brings
    Irreverence for the dreams of youth;

All thoughts of ill; all evil deeds,
    That have their root in tho'ts of ill;
Whatever hinders or impedes
    The action of the nobler will:—

All these must first be trampled down
    Beneath our feet, if we would gain
In the bright fields of fair renown
    The right of eminent domain.

We have not wings, we cannot soar;
    But we have feet to scale and climb
By slow degrees, by more and more,
    The cloudy summits of our time.

The mighty pyramids of stone
    That wedge-like cleave the desert
        airs,
When nearer seen, and better known,
    Are but gigantic flights of stairs.

The distant mountains, that uprear
    Their solid bastions to the skies,
Are crossed by pathways, that appear
    As we to higher levels rise.

The heights by great men reached and
        kept
    Were not attained by sudden flight,
But they, while their companions
        slept,
    Were toiling upward in the night.

Standing on what too long we bore
    With shoulders bent and downcast
        eyes,
We may discern — unseen before —
    A path to higher destinies.

Nor deem the irrevocable Past
    As wholly wasted, wholly vain,
If, rising on its wrecks, at last
    To something nobler we attain.

        — *Henry Wadsworth Longfellow*

NO REGRETS

For doing good to all.
For speaking evil of none.
For hearing before judging.
For thinking before speaking.
For holding an angry tongue.
For being kind to the distressed.
For asking pardon for all errors.
For being patient toward everybody.
For disbelieving most of the ill reports.

        — *Author Unknown*

BE SUCH A MAN

Be such a man, and live such a life,
That if every man were such as you,
And every life a life like yours,
This earth would be God's Paradise.

        — *Phillips Brooks*

TEARS

Thank God, bless God, all ye who suffer not
More grief than ye can weep for. That is well —
That is light grieving! lighter, none befell,
Since Adam forfeited the primal lot.
Tears! what are tears? The babe weeps in its cot,
The mother singing; at her marriage bell
The bride weeps! and before the oracle
Of high-faned hills, the poet has forgot
Such moisture on his cheeks. Thank God for grace,
Ye who weep only! If, as some have done,
Ye grope tear-blinded in a desert place,
And touch but tombs, — look up! Those tears will run
Soon in long rivers down the lifted face,
And leave the vision clear for stars and sun.

— *Elizabeth Barrett Browning*

∽

OH, MAY I JOIN THE CHOIR INVISIBLE

Oh, may I join the choir invisible
Of those immortal dead who live again
In minds made better by their presence; live
In pulses stirred to generosity,
In deeds of daring rectitude, in scorn
Of miserable aims that end with self,
In thoughts sublime that pierce the night like stars,
And with their mild persistence urge men's minds
To vaster issues.
                    So to live is heaven:
To make undying music in the world,
Breathing a beauteous order, that controls
With growing sway the growing life of man.
So we inherit that sweet purity
For which we struggled, failed, and agonized
With widening retrospect that bred despair.
Rebellious flesh that would not be subdued,
A vicious parent shaming still its child,
Poor anxious penitence, is quick dissolved:
Its discords, quenched by meeting harmonies,
Die in the large and charitable air.
And all our rarer, better, truer self,
That sobbed religiously in yearning song,
That watched to ease the burden of the world,

Laboriously tracing what must be,
And what may yet be better, — saw within
A worthier image for the sanctuary,
And shaped it forth before the multitude,
Divinely human, raising worship so
To higher reverence more mixed with love, —
That better self shall live till human Time
Shall fold its eyelids, and the human sky
Be gathered like a scroll within the tomb,
Unread forever.
      This is life to come,
Which martyred men have made more glorious
For us, who strive to follow.
        May I reach
That purest heaven, — be to other souls
The cup of strength in some great agony,
Enkindle generous ardor, feed pure love,
Beget the smiles that have no cruelty,
Be the sweet presence of a good diffused,
And in diffusion ever more intense!
So shall I join the choir invisible,
Whose music is the gladness of the world.

            — *George Eliot*

       ◌

THE LAYMEN

Leave it to the ministers, and soon the church will die;
Leave it to the women folk, and some will pass it by;
For the church is all that lifts us from the coarse and selfish mob,
And the church that is to prosper needs the laymen on the job.
Now a layman has his business, and a layman has his joys;
But he also has the training of the little girls and boys;
And I wonder how he'd like it if there were no churches here
And he had to raise his children in a godless atmosphere.
It's the church's special function to uphold the finer things,
To teach the way of living from which all the noble springs;
But the minister can't do it single-handed and alone,
For the laymen of the country are the church's corner stone.
When you see a church that's empty, tho' its doors are opened wide,
It is not the church that's dying; it's the laymen who have died;
For it's not by song or sermon that the church's work is done;
It's the laymen of the country who for God must carry on.

            — *Edgar A. Guest*

HYMN — FOR MY BROTHER'S ORDINATION

Christ to the young man said: "Yet one thing more:
    If thou wouldst perfect be,
Sell all thou hast and give it to the poor,
    And come and follow me!"

Within this temple Christ again, unseen,
    Those sacred words hath said,
And his invisible hands to-day have been
    Laid on a young man's head.

And evermore beside him on his way
    The unseen Christ shall move,
That he may lean upon his arm and say,
    "Dost thou, dear Lord, approve?"

Beside him at the marriage feast shall be,
    To make the scene more fair;
Beside him in the dark Gethsemane
    Of pain and midnight prayer.

O holy trust! O endless sense of rest!
    Like the beloved John
To lay his head upon the Saviour's breast,
    And thus to journey on!

— Henry Wadsworth Longfellow

ᴏᴚᴏ

EXAGGERATION

We overstate the ills of life, and take
Imagination, given us to bring down
The choirs of singing angels overshone
By God's clear glory, — down our earth to rake
The dismal snows instead; flake following flake,
To cover all the corn. We walk upon
The shadow of hills across a level thrown,
And pant like climbers. Near the alder-brake
We sigh so loud, the nightingale within
Refuses to sing loud, as else she would.
O brothers! let us leave the shame and sin
Of taking vainly, in a plaintive mood,
The holy name of GRIEF! — holy herein,
That, by the grief of ONE, came all our good.

— Elizabeth Barrett Browning

UNAWARES

They said, "The Master is coming
  To honor the town today,
And none can tell at what house or
    home
The Master will choose to stay."
And I tho't while my heart beat wildly,
  What if He should come to mine,
How would I strive to entertain
  And honor the Guest Divine!

And straight I turned to toiling,
  To make my home more neat;
I swept, and polished and garnished,
  And decked it with blossoms sweet.
I was troubled for fear the Master
  Might come ere my work was done
And I hasted and worked the faster,
  And watched the hurrying sun.

But right in the midst of my duties
  A woman came to my door;
She had come to tell her sorrow
  And my comfort and aid to implore,
And I said, "I cannot listen,
  Nor help you any, today;
I have greater things to attend to."
  And the pleader turned away.

But soon there came another —
  A cripple, thin, pale and gray —
And said: "Oh, let me stop and rest
  A while in your house, I pray!
I have traveled far since morning,
  I am hungry and faint and weak;
My heart is full of misery,
  And comfort and help I seek."

And I cried, "I am grieved and sorry
  But I cannot help you today.
I look for a great and noble Guest,"
  And the cripple went away;
And the day wore onward swiftly —
  And my task was nearly done,
And a prayer was ever in my heart
  That the Master to me might come.

And I thought I would spring to meet
    Him,
  And serve Him with utmost care,
When a little child stood near me
  With a face so sweet and fair —
Sweet, but with marks of teardrops —
  And his clothes were tattered and
    old;
A finger was bruised and bleeding,
  And his little bare feet were cold.

And I said, "I'm sorry for you —
  You are sorely in need of care;
But I cannot stop to give it,
  You must hasten otherwhere."
And at the words, a shadow
  Swept o'er his blue-veined brow —
"Someone will feed and clothe you,
    dear,
  But I am too busy now."

At last the day was ended,
  And my toil was over and done;
My house was swept and garnished —
  And I watched in the dark — alone.
Watched — but no footfall sounded,
  No one paused at my gate;
No one entered my cottage door;
  I could only pray — and wait.

I waited till night had deepened,
  And the Master had not come.
"He has entered some other door," I
    said,
  "And gladdened some other home!"
My labor had been for nothing,
  And I bowed my head and I wept,
My heart was sore with longing —
  Yet — in spite of it all — I slept.

Then the Master stood before me,
  And His face was grave and fair;
"Three times today I came to your
    door,
  And I craved your pity and care;

Three times you sent me onward,
  Unhelped and uncomforted;
And the blessing you might have had
      was lost,
  And your chance to serve has fled."

"O Lord, dear Lord, forgive me!
  How could I know it was Thee?"
My very soul was shamed and bowed
  In the depths of humility,
And He said, "The sin is pardoned,
  But the blessing is lost to thee;
For, comforting not the least of Mine,
  You have failed to comfort Me."

  — *Emma A. Lent*

THE FINAL STRUGGLE

Tarry with me, O my Saviour!
  For the day is passing by;
See! the shades of evening gather,
  And the night is drawing nigh:
Deeper, deeper grow the shadows,
  Paler now the glowing west,
Swift the night of death advances;
  Shall it be the night of rest?

Lonely seems the vale of shadow;
  Sinks my heart with troubled fear;
Give me faith for clearer vision,
  Speak thou, Lord! in words of cheer;
Let me hear thy voice behind me,
  Calming all these wild alarms;
Let me, underneath my weakness,
  Feel the everlasting arms.

Feeble, trembling, fainting, dying,
  Lord! I cast myself on thee:
Tarry with me through the darkness;
  While I sleep, still watch by me.
Tarry with me, O my Saviour!
  Lay my head upon thy breast
Till the morning; then awake me;—
  Morning of eternal rest!

  — *Caroline Sprague Smith*

GOD'S BEST

Those things which might be counted
      gain
  Must oft be counted loss
That by God's grace I might attain
  The glory of the cross.

The seeming good life doth bestow,
  Appealing though it be,
I must reject if I would know
  My Saviour's best for me.

Lord, may I ne'er be satisfied
  With this world's second best,
When Thou hast blessings multiplied
  For those who stand the test.

Let me not deem it sacrifice
  To miss the joys of earth
To gain from Thee a higher prize
  Of everlasting worth.

  — *Avis B. Christiansen*

THE LORD'S CHARGE

A charge to keep I have,
  A God to glorify;
A never-dying soul to save,
  And fit it for the sky:

To serve the present age,
  My calling to fulfill;
Oh, may it all my powers engage
  To do my Master's will.

Arm me with jealous care,
  As in thy sight to live;
And oh, thy servant, Lord, prepare
  A strict account to give!

Help me to watch and pray,
  And on thyself rely!
Assured if I my trust betray,
  I shall forever die.

  — *Charles Wesley*

THE LOWEST PLACE

Give me the lowest place; not that I dare
  Ask for that lowest place, but thou hast died
That I might live and share
  Thy glory by thy side.

Give me the lowest place; or if for me
  That lowest place too high, make one more low
Where I may sit and see
  My God, and love thee so.

                               — *Christina G. Rossetti*

SLOW ME DOWN, LORD

Slow me down, Lord;
Ease the pounding of my heart
  by the quieting of my mind. . . .
Steady my hurried pace
  with a vision of eternal reach of time. . . .
Give me,
  amidst the confusion of my day,
    the calmness of the everlasting hills.

Slow me down, Lord;
Teach me the art of taking minute vacations . . .
  of lingering to study an azalea bush,
    or to chat with a new neighbor,
      or to pat an animal.

Slow me down, Lord;
That I may know
  the race is not always to
    the swift . . .
And that life consists of more
  than an increasing tempo.

Let me look into the branches of the towering elms
And learn that they grow tall
  because they rise slowly
    and ably.

Slow me down, Lord;
That I might send my roots
  deep into the soil of life's enduring values
And so reach toward the stars
  of an infinite destiny.

Let the still small voice
Of him who gave his Son for us all
   speak to me
      and through me
Of peace and victory that passes all understanding.

Then speed me on, Lord.
Arm me with a diligence
   and longing
To redeem each opportune moment for Thee,
To share with friend and stranger
The One who steadies my gait
As I walk this stony path
   toward the boundless reaches of his eternal love.

— Author Unknown

THE DAWNING

Ah! what time wilt thou come? when
   shall that cry
"The Bridegroom's coming!" fill the
   sky?
Shall it in the evening run
When our words and works are done?
Or will thy all-surprising light
Break at midnight,
When either sleep, or some dark
   pleasure
Possesseth mad man without measure?
Or shall these early, fragrant hours
Unlock thy bowers
And with their blush of light descry
Thy locks crowned with eternity?

Indeed, it is the only time
That with thy glory doth best chime;
All now are stirring, ev'ry field
Full hymns doth yield,
The whole Creation shakes off night,
And for thy shadow looks the light.
Stars now vanish without number,
Sleepy planets set and slumber,
The pursy clouds disband and scatter,
All expect some sudden matter;
Not one beam triumphs, but from far
That morning-star.

Oh at what time soever thou,
Unknown to us, the heavens wilt bow,
And with thy angels in the van
Descend to judge poor careless man,
Grant I may not like a puddle lie
In a corrupt security,
Where, if a traveller water crave,
He finds it dead, and in a grave.
But as this restless, vocal spring
All day and night doth run, and sing,
And tho' here born, yet is acquainted
Elsewhere, and flowing keeps un-
   tainted;
So let me all my busy age
In thy free services engage;
And tho' (while here) of force I must
Have commerce sometimes with poor
   dust,
And in my flesh, though vile and low,
As this doth in her channel flow,
Yet let my course, my aim, my love
And chief acquaintance be above;
So when that day and hour shall come,
In which thyself will be the sun,
Thou'lt find me dress'd and on my way,
Watching the break of thy great day.

— Henry Vaughan

SONG

Life with its weariness,
  Getting and spending,
Life with its fever,
  Its pomp and pretending,
Where would its meaning be,
Saviour, apart from Thee?
Saviour, apart from Thee
  Life were unending.

Life has brought much to me,
  Truly, of treasure,
Gladness of fellowship,
  Love in rich measure;
Yet is it naught to me,
Saviour, apart from Thee;
Saviour, apart from Thee
  Vain is earth's pleasure.

Life in Thy presence
  Is rest beyond telling,
Joy beyond human thought,
  Peace beyond quelling;
He who in Thee abides,
Saviour, has all besides:
Deep in Thy heart he hides —
  There is my dwelling!

— *E. Margaret Clarkson*

THE SHAPING OF A DISCIPLE

When God wants to drill a man,
And thrill a man, and skill a man,
When God wants to mold a man
To play for Him the noblest part,
When He yearns with all His heart
To build so great and bold a man
That all the world shall be amazed,
Then watch God's methods, watch
  His ways!
How He ruthlessly perfects
Whom He royally elects;
How He hammers him and hurts him,
And with mighty blows converts him,
Making shapes and forms which only
God Himself can understand,
Even while His man is crying,
Lifting a beseeching hand . . .
Yet God bends but never breaks
When man's good He undertakes;
When He uses whom He chooses,
And with every purpose fuses
Man to act, and act to man,
As it was when He began;
When God tries His splendor out,
Man will know what He's about!

— *Dale Martin Stone*

WITH THEE, O GOD!

Almighty Father, Son, and Holy Ghost,
Eternal ever-blessed gracious God,
To me, the least of saints, to me, allow
That I may keep a door in Paradise;
That I may keep even the smallest door,
The furthest door, the darkest, coldest door,
The door that is least used, the stiffest door,
If so it be but in Thine house, O God!
If so it be that I can see Thy glory
Even afar and hear Thy voice, O God!
And know that I am with Thee — Thee, O God.

— *Colomba of Iona*

TEMPER

When I have lost my temper
  I have lost my reason too.
I'm never proud of anything
  Which angrily I do.

When I have talked in anger,
  And my cheeks were flaming red,
I have always uttered something
  Which I wish I had not said.

In anger I have never
  Done a kindly deed or wise,
But many things for which I felt
  I should apologize.

In looking back across my life,
  And all I've lost or made,
I can't recall a single time
  When fury ever paid.

So I struggle to be patient,
  For I've reached a wiser age;
I do not want to do a thing
  Or speak a word in rage.

I have learned by sad experience
  That when my temper flies
I never do a worthy deed,
  A decent deed or wise.

—Author Unknown

SMILE

The thing that goes the farthest
  Towards making life worth while,
Which costs the least and counts the
    most,
  Is just a pleasant smile.
The smile that bubbles from a heart
  That loves its fellow men,
Will drive away the clouds of gloom
  And coax the sun again.
It is full of worth, and goodness too,
  With manly kindness blent;
It is worth a million dollars
  And it doesn't cost a cent.

There is no room for sadness
  When we see a cheery smile,
It always has the same good looks,
  It's never out of style.
It nerves us on to try again
  When failure makes us blue,
The dimples of encouragement
  Are good for me and you.
It pays a higher interest
  For it is merely lent;
It is worth a million dollars
  And a doesn't cost a cent.

A smile comes very easy,
  You can wrinkle up with cheer
A hundred times before you
  Can squeeze out a soggy tear.
It ripples out moreover
  To the heart-strings that will tug,
And always leaves an echo
  That is very like a hug;
So smile away, folks understand
  What by a smile is meant;
It is worth a million dollars
  And doesn't cost a cent.

—Author Unknown

ONLY A WORD

A word is such a potent thing;
  A careless word may break a heart;
A bitter word may burn and sting;
  A word can rip a home apart.
And yet a word can comfort bring.

A word can wound, a word can mend;
  Can lift the broken; lighten eyes,
A word can heal. A word can send
  The soul a touch of paradise.
A gentle word may win a friend.

So; Lord of Words, please grant to me
The speech that spreads tranquility.

—Lois Elizabeth Ridenour

For Those in Peril

Eternal Father, strong to save,
Whose arm doth bind the restless wave,
Who bidd'st the mighty ocean deep
Its own appointed limits keep;
Oh, hear us when we cry to thee
For those in peril on the sea.

O Saviour, whose almighty word
The winds and waves submissive heard,
Who walkedst in the foaming deep,
And calm amid its rage didst sleep;
Oh, hear us when we cry to thee
For those in peril on the sea.

O Sacred Spirit, who didst brood
Upon the chaos dark and rude,
Who bad'st its angry tumult cease,
And gavest light, and life, and peace;
Oh, hear us when we cry to thee
For those in peril on the sea.

O Trinity of love and power!
Our brethren shield in danger's hour;
From rock and tempest, fire and foe,
Protect them wheresoe'er they go.
And ever let there rise to thee
Glad hymns of praise from land and sea!

— *William Whiting*

Our Times Are in Thy Hand

Our times are in Thy hand;
Father, we wish them there!
Our life, our souls, our all we leave
Entirely to Thy care.

Our times are in Thy hand,
Whatever they may be;
Pleasing or painful, dark or bright,
As best may seem to Thee.

Our times are in Thy hand;
Why should we doubt or fear?
Our Father's hand will never cause
His child a needless tear.

Our times are in Thy hand,
Jesus the crucified!
The hand our many sins have pierced
Is now our guard and guide.

Our times are in Thy hand,
O Lord, our Advocate!
Nor is that hand outstretched in vain,
For us to supplicate.

Our times are in Thy hand;
We'll always trust in Thee,
Till we have left this weary land,
And all Thy glory see.

— *William F. Lloyd*

The Harvest and the Tempest

Deep in the shadow of slumber, one night I lay on my bed,
And dreamed I stood on a mountain, with valleys before me spread.
The valleys were wide, and yellow with beautiful waving grain.
And a cloud hung black in the distance, loaded with tempest and rain.

Looking, I saw in the valley, laborers — but, oh, so few!
I knew the gathering tempest would break before they were through.
Although they were all so busy, bending themselves to the work;
They saw the storm was approaching and knew that they dared not shirk.

Then near the foot of the mountain, I happened to turn my eyes.
And there stood a Man whose visage was brighter than sunset skies;

He spoke — in such tones of sorrow, it caused my heart to bleed;
"Behold, how white is the harvest — with reapers so few indeed."

"Why are the workers not many?" I thought to myself — and then
I glanced about me and noticed the mountains were full of men;
Men who were laughing and joking, playing some sort of a game;
Not seeing how ripe the harvest, or heeding the storm that came.

Soon I could stand it no longer, "Listen!" I shouted amain.
"The tempest shall soon be rushing over the beautiful grain;
Why waste your time in a frolic? Look at that gathering cloud!"
But one of them quickly answered, *"You're one of this idle crowd!"*

Then came the crash of the tempest, the rushing wind, and the rain,
Came howling over the valleys, ruining the yellow grain!
The heavens were rocked from thunder, the lightnings split the skies
Till we who stood on the mountain covered our poor, blinded eyes!

Above the crash of the tempest the voice of the Stranger broke;
"Behold, the ruin of the harvest — this is the heathen!" He spoke,
"The storm that so widely rages is God's great Judgment Day!"
And I woke, and wept in repentance as there on my bed I lay.

Calling on God in the heavens, with contrite spirit I prayed;
"O Lord, I will be a worker! Too long, too long have I played!
Because of the ripened harvest, I give You my heart and my arm;
I'll spend my strength in the valleys to save the grain from the storm!"

Lon Woodrum

ഔ

WHO PROFITS MOST?

Who profits most? It's not the man
Who, grasping every coin he can,
Unscrupulously crushes down
His weaker neighbor with a frown.
He is not worthy of his trust
And, friendless, knows his gold is dust.
He loses what he sought to gain
And finds instead of pleasure, pain.

Who profits most? It is not he
Of life's great opportunity.
He is not mourned. Why should he be
Who shirks responsibility,
Who hermit-like himself withdraws
To live apart from human flaws.
To scoff at human frailties,
He turns away, no vision sees.

Who profits most? It is the man
Who gives a boost where he can,
Who's on the square in all that's done
And trusts and helps the others on,
Who puts his task above mere self,
Who values friends and counts them
    wealth.

Who profits most? Is that your quest?
It is the man who serves the best.

— Author Unknown

UNTIL THE SHADOWS LENGTHEN

O Lord, support us all the day long
    of this troublous life,
Until the shadows lengthen,
And the evening comes,
And the busy world is hushed,
And the fever of life is over,
And our work is done.
Then of thy mercy
Grant us a safe lodging,
And a holy rest,
And peace at the last:
Thro' Jesus Christ our Lord. Amen.

— John Henry Newman

THE SINGERS

God sent his Singers upon earth
With songs of sadness and of mirth,
That they might touch the hearts of
    men,
And bring them back to heaven again.

The first, a youth, with soul of fire,
Held in his hand a golden lyre;
Through groves he wandered, and by
    streams,
Playing the music of our dreams.

The second, with a bearded face,
Stood singing in the market-place,
And stirred with accents deep and loud
The hearts of all the listening crowd.

A gray, old man, the third and last,
Sang in cathedrals dim and vast,
While the majestic organ rolled
Contrition from its mouths of gold.

And those who heard the Singers three
Disputed which the best might be;
For still their music seemed to start
Discordant echoes in each heart.

But the great Master said, "I see
No best in kind, but in degree;
I gave a various gift to each,
To charm, to strengthen, and to teach.

"These are the three great chords of
    might,
And he whose ear is tuned aright
Will hear no discord in the three,
But the most perfect harmony."

— Henry Wadsworth Longfellow

MY SAVIOUR

I am not skilled to understand
What God hath willed, what God
    hath planned;
I only know at His right hand
    Stands One who is my Saviour.

I take God at His word and deed:
"Christ died to save me" — this I read;
And in my heart I find a need
    Of Him to be my Saviour.

And was there then no other way
For God to take? — I cannot say;
I only bless Him, day by day,
    Who saved me through my Saviour.

That He should leave His place on
    high
And come for sinful man to die,
You count it strange? — so do not I,
    Since I have known my Saviour.

And O that He fulfilled may see
The travail of His soul in me,
And with His work contented be,
    As I with my dear Saviour!

Yea, living, dying, let me bring
My strength, my solace, from this
    spring,
That He who lives to be my King
    Once died to be my Saviour.

— Dora Greenwell

LITTLE THINGS

'Tis the little kindly acts you do
    That heartens one along,
And sends the friend away from you
    With glad and happy song.

'Tis the little word you're led to say
    Which touched that other life,
And gave it nerve and strength again
    To conquer in the strife.

'Tis just the secret little talk
    With Jesus by the way.
That keeps you loving, true to Him
    In all you do and say.

— *Maud Rose*

DON'T TROUBLE TROUBLE

Don't trouble trouble
    Till trouble troubles you.
Don't you look for trouble;
    Let trouble look for you.

Don't you borrow sorrow;
    You'll surely have your share.
He who dreams of sorrow
    Will find that sorrow's there.

Don't you hurry worry,
    By worrying lest it come.
To flurry is to worry,
    'Twill miss you if you're mum.

Who feareth hath forsaken
    The heavenly Father's side;
What He hath undertaken
    He surely will provide.

The very birds reprove thee
    With their happy song;
The very flowers teach thee
    That fretting is a wrong.

"Cheer up," the sparrow chirpeth,
    "Thy Father feedeth me;

Think how much He careth,
    O lonely child, for thee!"

"Fear not," the flowers whisper;
    "Since thus He hath arrayed
The buttercup and daisy,
    How canst thou be afraid?"

Then don't you trouble trouble,
    Till trouble troubles you;
You'll only double trouble,
    And trouble others, too.

— *Author Unknown*

THE SIN OF OMISSION

It isn't the thing you do;
    It's the thing you leave undone,
Which gives you a bit of heartache
    At the setting of the sun.

The tender word forgotten,
    The letter you did not write,
The flower you might have sent,
    Are your haunting ghosts at night.

The stone you might have lifted
    Out of a brother's way,
The bit of heartsome counsel
    You were hurried too much to say;

The loving touch of the hand,
    The gentle and winsome tone,
That you had no time or thought for
    With troubles enough of your own.

The little acts of kindness,
    So easily out of mind;
Those chances to be helpful
    Which everyone may find —

No, it's not the thing you do,
    It's the thing you leave undone,
Which gives you the bit of heartache
    At the setting of the sun.

— *Margaret E. Sangster*

A FAITHFUL PASTOR

He held the lamp each Sabbath day
So low that none could miss the way,
And yet so high to keep in sight
The picture fair of Christ the light;
The handle coming thus between,
The hand that held it was not seen.

He held the pitcher stooping low
To the lips of little ones below,
Then lifted to the weary saint,
And bade him drink when sick and
    faint;
The pitcher coming thus between,
The hand that held it was not seen.

He blew the trumpet loud and bold.
To storm the fort of Satan's hold,
Then with a tender note and clear
That trembling sinners need not fear;
The trumpet coming thus between,
The hand that held it was not seen.

But when the Master said, "Well done,
Thou good and faithful servant, come,
Lay down the trumpet, leave the
    camp,"
Thy hand is now most clearly seen,
Clasped in His pierced one, naught
    between.

— *Author Unknown*

ᔕᗯ

GOOD IN ILL

When gladness gilds our prosperous
    day,
    And hope is by fruition crowned,
"O Lord," with thankful hearts we say,
    "How doth thy love to us abound!"

But is that love less truly shown
    When earthly joys lie cold and dead,
And hopes have faded one by one,
    Leaving sad memories in their stead?

God knows the discipline we need,
    Nor sorrow sends for sorrow's sake;
And though our stricken hearts may
    bleed,
    His mercy will not let them break.

Oh, teach us to discern the good
    Thou sendest in the guise of ill;
Since all thou dost, if understood,
    Interpreteth thy loving will.

For pain is not the end of pain,
    Nor seldom trial comes to bless,
And work for us abundant gain,—
    The peaceful fruits of righteousness.

Then let us not, with anxious thought,
    Ask of to-morrow's joys or woes,
But, by his word and Spirit taught,
    Accept as best what God bestows.

— *William Henry Burleigh*

ᔕᗯ

PARADOX

When Thou hast mastered me,
    Then shall I be victor;
When Thou hast enslaved me,
    Then shall I be free.
When Thou hast humbled me,
    Then shall I be exalted;
When Thou hast prostrated me,
    Then shall I be lifted up.
When Thou hast impoverished me,
    Then shall I be wealthy;
When Thou hast emptied me,
    Then shall I be full.
When Thou hast taken all,
    Then shall I have all:

My Master, lo, I come to Thee —
Fulfill Thy paradox in me!

— *E. Margaret Clarkson*

Egypt Left Behind

Rise, my soul, thy God directs thee;
  Stranger hands no more impede;
Pass thou on, his strength protects thee,
  Strength that has the captive freed.

Is the wilderness before thee,
  Desert lands where drought abides?
Heavenly springs shall there restore
    thee,
  Fresh from God's exhaustless tides.

Light divine surrounds thy going,
  God himself shall mark thy way;
Secret blessings, richly flowing,
  Lead to everlasting day.

God, thine everlasting portion,
  Feeds thee with the mighty's meat;
Saved from Egypt's hard extortion,
  Egypt's food no more to eat.

Art thou weaned from Egypt's
    pleasures?
  God in secret shall thee keep;
There unfold his hidden treasures,—
  There his love's exhaustless deep.

In the desert God will teach thee
  What the God that thou hast
    found,—
Patient, gracious, powerful, holy;
  All his grace shall there abound.

On to Canaan's rest still wending,
  E'en thy wants and woes shall bring
Suited grace from high descending,—
  Thou shalt taste of mercy's spring.

Though thy way be long and dreary,
  Eagle strength he'll still renew;
Garments fresh, and feet unweary,
  Tell how God had bro't thee thro'.

When to Canaan's long-loved dwelling
  Love divine thy foot shall bring,
There, with shouts of triumph swell-
    ing,
  Zion's songs in rest to sing.

There no stranger-God shall meet
    thee;—
  Stranger thou in courts above!
He who to his rest shall greet thee,
  Greets thee with a well-known love.

          — *John Nelson Darby*

∽

Song of the Sojourner

A pilgrim and a stranger,
  I journey here below;
Far distant is my country,
  The home to which I go.
Here I must toil and travel,
  Oft weary and opprest,
But there my God shall lead me
  To everlasting rest.

I've met with storms and danger,
  Even from my early years,
With enemies and conflicts,
  With fightings and with fears.
There's nothing here that tempts me
  To wish a longer stay,
So I must hasten forwards,
  No halting or delay.

It is a well-worn pathway,—
  Many have gone before:
The holy saints and prophets,
  The patriarchs of yore.
They trod the toilsome journey
  In patience and in faith;
And them I fain would follow,
  Like them in life and death!

Who would share Abraham's blessing,
  Must Abraham's path pursue,
A stranger and a pilgrim,
  Like him, must journey through,
The foes must be encountered,
  The dangers must be passed;
Only a faithful soldier
  Receives the crown at last.

So I must hasten forwards,—
Thank God, the end will come!
This land of my sojourning
Is not my destined home.
That evermore abideth,
Jerusalem above,
The everlasting city,
The land of light and love.

There still my thoughts are dwelling,
'Tis there I long to be!
Come, Lord, and call thy servant
To blessedness with thee!
Come, bid my toils be ended,
Let all my wanderings cease;
Call from the wayside lodging,
To the sweet home of peace!

There I shall dwell forever,
No more a stranger guest,
With all thy blood-bought children
In everlasting rest.
The pilgrim toils forgotten,
The pilgrim conflicts o'er,
All earthly griefs behind us,
Eternal joys before!

— *Paul Gerhardt*

ↄ๏ට

To a Mute Musician

So music was "left out" of your make-
up.
You were just "not there"
When music was handed out.

It may be true
That you cannot sing, nor play an in-
strument.
Perhaps the mysteries of counterpoint
and harmony
Will always be a closed book
To you.

But I wonder
If that is all there is

To being a musician?
I think perhaps the violin
Is not conscious of the music
That lies hidden in its heart;
Yet countless multitudes
Rejoice
In the melodies that flow from it
When the Master takes his bow
And plays upon it.

I wonder
If you may not have lived
Closer to the Master of all Music
Than you know.
You have allowed Him to take
Life's dissonances,
And in you to resolve them
Into celestial concord.

You may not hear
The music that He makes;
Yet others hear the song
And bring Him praise.

One day
I think you will take your place
Among the truly great musicians
Of His court;
For you,
Who may not know earth's music,
Have learned the Song
Of Heaven.

— *E. Margaret Clarkson*

ↄ๏ට

Joy

Joy is a fruit that will not grow
In nature's barren soil;
All we can boast, till Christ we know,
Is vanity and toil.
But where the Lord hath planted grace,
And made His glories known,
These fruits of heavenly joy and peace
Are found, and there alone.

— *John Newton*

FORGIVENESS OF SINS

Weary of earth and laden with my sin,
I look at heaven and long to enter in,
But there no evil thing may find a home;
And yet I hear a voice that bids me "Come."

So vile I am, how dare I hope to stand
In the pure glory of that holy land?
Before the whiteness of that throne appear?
Yet there are hands stretched out to draw me near.

The while I fain would tread the heavenly way,
Evil is ever with me day by day;
Yet on mine ears the gracious tidings fall,
"Repent, confess, thou shalt be loosed from all."

It is the voice of Jesus that I hear,
His are the hands stretched out to draw me near,
And his the blood that can for all atone,
And set me faultless there before the throne.

'Twas he who found me on the deathly wild,
And made me heir of heaven, the Father's child,
And day by day, whereby my soul may live,
Gives me his grace of pardon, and will give.

O great Absolver, grant my soul may wear
The lowliest garb of penitence and prayer,
That in the Father's courts my glorious dress
May be the garment of thy righteousness.

Yea, thou wilt answer for me, righteous Lord:
Thine all the merits, mine the great reward;
Thine the sharps thorns, and mine the golden crown;
Mine the life won, and thine the life laid down.

Nought can I bring, dear Lord, for all I owe
Yet let my full heart what it can bestow;
Like Mary's gift let my devotion prove,
Forgiven greatly, how I greatly love.

—Samuel John Stone

PRAYER FOR HUMILITY

Humble, Lord, my haughty spirit,
　　Bid my swelling thoughts subside;
Strip me of my fancied merit:
　　What have I to do with pride?
Was my Saviour meek and lowly?
　　And shall such a worm as I,
Weak, and earthly, and unholy,
　　Dare to lift my head on high?

Teach me, Lord, my true condition;
　　Bring me childlike to thy knee;
Stripped of every low ambition,
　　Willing to be led by thee.
Guide me by thy Holy Spirit;
　　Feed me from thy blessed word:
All my wisdom, all my merit,
　　Borrowed from thyself, O Lord!

Like a little babe, confiding,
　　Simple, docile, let me be;
Trusting still to thy providing,
　　Willing to be led by thee.
Thus my all to thee submitting,
　　I am thine and not my own;
And when earthly hopes are flitting,
　　Rest secure on God alone.

　　　　　　— *Henry Francis Lyte*

၈

LIFE'S LESSONS

I learn, as the years roll onward
　　And leave the past behind,
That much I had counted sorrow
　　But proves that God is kind;
That many a flower I had longed for
　　Had hidden a thorn of pain,
And many a rugged bypath
　　Led to fields of ripened grain.

The clouds that cover the sunshine
　　They can not banish the sun;
And the earth shines out the brighter
　　When the weary rain is done.

We must stand in the deepest shadow
　　To see the clearest light;
And often thro' wrong's own darkness
　　Comes the very strength of light.

The sweetest rest is at even,
　　After a wearisome day,
When the heavy burden of labor
　　Has born from our hearts away;
And those who have never known sor-
　　row
　　Can not know the infinite peace
That falls on the troubled spirit
　　When it sees at last release.

We must live thro' the dreary winter
　　If we would value the spring;
And the woods must be cold and silent
　　Before the robins sing.
The flowers must be buried in dark-
　　ness
　　Before they can bud and bloom,
And the sweetest, warmest sunshine
　　Comes after the storm and gloom.

　　　　　　— *Author Unknown*

၈

THE DAY RETURNS

The day returns
And brings us the petty round
Of irritating concerns and duties.
Help us to play the man!
Help us to perform them
With laughter and kind faces.
Let cheerfulness abound with industry.
Give us to go blithely on our business
All this day.
Bring us to our resting beds
Weary, and content,
And undishonored,
And grant us in the end
The gift of sleep. Amen.

　　　　　　— *Robert Louis Stevenson*

THE CHURCH WITHIN

Who builds a church within his heart
And takes it with him everywhere,
Is holier far than he whose church
Is but a one-day house of prayer.

—*A. L. Alexander*

THE VOICE OF GOD

I sought to hear the voice of God
And climbed the topmost steeple.
But God declared: "Go down again,
I dwell among the people."

—*Louis I. Neeman*

BEGIN AGAIN

Every day is a fresh beginning,
  Every morn is the world made new;
You who are weary of sorrow and sinning,
  Here is a beautiful hope for you —
  A hope for me and a hope for you.

All the past things are past and over,
  The tasks are done and the tears are shed;
Yesterday's errors let yesterday cover;
  Yesterday's wounds, which smarted and bled,
  Are healed with the healing which night has shed.

Yesterday now is a part of forever,
  Bound up in a sheaf, which God holds tight;
With glad days and sad days and bad days which never
  Shall visit us more with their bloom and their blight,
  Their fullness of sunshine or sorrowful night.

Let them go, since we cannot relive them,
  Cannot undo, and cannot atone;
God in His mercy, receive, forgive them;
  Only the new days are our own,
  Today is ours, and today alone.

Here are the skies all burnished brightly,
  Here is the spent Earth all reborn,
Here are the tired limbs springing lightly
  To face the sun and to share with the morn,
  In the chrism of dew and the cool of dawn.

Every day is a fresh beginning;
  Listen, my soul, to the glad refrain,
And, spite of old sorrow and older sinning,
  And puzzles forecasted and possible pain,
  Take heart with the day, and begin again.

—*Susan Coolidge*

WAYFARER'S SONG

O wanderer, lost on the mountain bare,
Wearily treading ways rough and steep,
Borne on the breath of the midnight air,
This voice shall enter thy soul's despair —
  God gives His belovèd sleep.

O mariner, tossed on the raging sea,
When hope lies drowned in the waters deep
And naught avails but the bended knee,
The storm shall whisper these words to thee —
  God gives His belovèd sleep.

— *Henry W. Frost*

ᠬᠥ

PER PACEM AD LUCEM

I do not ask, O Lord, that life may be
    A pleasant road;
I do not ask that thou wouldst take from me
    Aught of its load;

I do not ask that flowers should always spring
    Beneath my feet;
I know too well the poison and the sting
    Of things too sweet.

For one thing only, Lord, dear Lord, I plead,
    Lead me aright —
Tho' strength should falter, and tho' heart should bleed —
    Through Peace to Light.

I do not ask, O Lord, that thou shouldst shed
    Full radiance here;
Give but a ray of peace, that I may tread
    Without a fear.

I do not ask my cross to understand,
    My way to see;
Better in darkness just to feel thy hand
    And follow thee.

Joy is like restless day; but peace divine
    Like quiet night:
Lead me, O Lord, till perfect day shall shine,
    Through Peace to Light.

— *Adelaide Anne Procter*

COMFORTED

As a fond mother, when the daylight fades
    And evening deepens into shadowy night,
Soothes her tired child, within the gath'ring shades,
    By lullaby and her sweet presence bright;

So God our Father, in His wondrous grace,
    When shadowing sorrows cover all our sky,
Draws near with tender word and shining face
    And calms our fears, while in His arms we lie.

Then, O my Father, I would ever choose
    Whatever grief or pain Thou sendest me;
Better o'erwhelming sorrows than to lose
    The joy of being comforted by Thee!

                — *Henry W. Frost*

THE SECRET

"And Enoch walked with God"
No other mortal ever trod
So bright a path, with such a Friend
To such a radiant, hallowed end,
We are not told the weary years,
The heartbreaks, maybe, and the tears,
But just — he walked with God.

And Enoch's path led home,
Not aimlessly to drift and roam,
To lose the way in mists of doubt,
Or pause to try earth's pleasures out,
But then, as now, one course to take
And every lesser goal forsake
And just walk home with God.

Together, day by day,
And step with step, they walked that
    way;
No feverish rushing to and fro,
Or with reluctant feet, and slow

To drag behind; — why should it be
So hard to travel patiently
And just keep step with God?

And Enoch's faith pleased God.
Thro' all the years the path they trod
Was made a fragrant, lovely place
By sweet communion, face to Face;
Why have we never time to spend
In fellowship with such a Friend
And just to talk with God?

But we — what fools we are,
We follow slowly from afar,
We stumble blindly thro' the night,
We miss the fellowship, the light,
So slow to learn, as learn we must
That all we need to do is trust,
And just to walk with God.

                — *Joan Suisted*

From *The Reaper* February 1968 issue published by the New Zealand Bible Training Institute, Auckland, New Zealand

KEEP SWEET

There's a little secret
  Worth its weight in gold,
Easy to remember,
  Easy to be told;
Changing into blessing
  Every curse we meet,
Turning hell to heaven,
  This is all — keep sweet.

Make us kind and gentle,
  Harmless as the dove;
Giving good for evil,
  Meeting hate with love;
What though trials press us,
  What though tempests beat,
Naught can move or harm us
  If we just keep sweet.

Storms may rage around us,
  Waves may sweep the deck,
But with hatches covered
  Naught our bark can wreck;
Sorrow cannot crush us,
  Satan must retreat
If within our spirit
  All is right and sweet.

Sweet when things are bitter,
  Sweet when hearts are sad;
Giving songs for sighing,
  Making others glad;
In the quiet household,
  On the bustling street,
Everywhere and always,
  Jesus, keep us sweet.

When our foes assail us,
  When our friends betray,
When our brightest prospects
  Wither and decay,
Christ can fill our sadness
  With a joy replete,
Turning grief to gladness,
  Making sorrow sweet.

Fountain in the desert,
  Song amid the night,
Beacon in the darkness,
  Star of hope and light;
Sunshine mid the tempest,
  Shadow from the heat —
Like the Blessed Master,
  Make us, keep us, sweet.

—*A. B. Simpson*

∽

THIS DO IN REMEMBRANCE OF ME

According to thy gracious word,
  In meek humility,
This will I do, my dying Lord,—
  I will remember thee.

Thy body, broken for my sake,
  My bread from heaven shall be;
Thy testamental cup I take,
  And thus remember thee.

Gethsemane can I forget?
  Or there thy conflict see,
Thine agony and bloody sweat,
  And not remember thee?

When to the cross I turn mine eyes,
  And rest on Calvary,
O Lamb of God, my sacrifice!
  I must remember thee:—

Remember thee, and all thy pains,
  And all thy love to me;
Yea, while a breath, a pulse remains,
  Will I remember thee.

And when these failing lips grow
      dumb,
  And mind and memory flee,
When thou shalt in thy kingdom come,
  Jesus, remember me!

— *James Montgomery*

COMPANIONSHIP

No distant Lord have I,
    Loving afar to be;
Made flesh for me, He cannot rest
    Unless He rests in me.

Brother in joy or pain,
    Bone of my bone was He;
Now — intimacy closer still —
    He dwells Himself in me.

I need not journey far,
    This dearest Friend to see;
Companionship is always mine,
    He makes His home with me.

I envy not the twelve,
    Nearer to me is He;
The life He once lived here on earth
    He lives again in me.

Ascended now to God,
    My witness there to be,
His witness here am I, because
    His Spirit dwells in me.

O glorious Son of God,
    Incarnate Deity,
I shall forever be with Thee
    Because Thou art with me.

                    — Maltbie D. Babcock

 o–o

REGRET

If I had known in the morning
How wearily all the day
The words unkind
Would trouble my mind
I said when you went away,
I had been more careful, darling,
Nor given you needless pain:
But we vex our own
With look and tone
We may never take back again.

For though in the quiet evening
You may give me the kiss of peace,
Yet it might be
That never for me
The pain of the heart should cease.
How many go forth in the morning
Who never come home at night,
And hearts are broken
For harsh words spoken
That sorrow can ne'er set right.

We have careful tho't for the stranger,
And smiles for the sometime guest,
But oft for our own
The bitter tone
Though we love our own the best.
Ah! lips with the curve impatient,
Ah! brow with that look of scorn,
'Twere a cruel fate
Were the night too late
To undo the work of morn!

                    — Margaret E. Sangster

o–o

EARLY MORN WITH JESUS

The early morn with Jesus,
    His happy, welcome guest!
The first glad thoughts for Jesus,
    The brightest and the best!

Alone, alone with Jesus,
    No other may intrude,
The secrets of Jehovah,
    Are told in solitude.

This is the time for worship,
    This is the time for prayer;
The sweetest time for laying
    The heart's petitions bare.

The time for holy wrestling,
    The time to intercede;
The time to win from Jesus
    The help and strength we need.

                    — Author Unknown

BY LIFE, OR BY DEATH

So this is life, this world with all its pleasures,
    Struggles and tears, a smile, a frown, a sigh,
Friendship so true, and love of kin and neighbor?
    Sometimes 'tis hard to live—always to die!

The world moves on, so rapidly the living
    The forms of those who disappear replace;
And each one dreams that he will be enduring—
    How soon that one becomes the missing face!

In life or death—and life is surely flying—
    The crib and coffin carved from the selfsame tree,
In life or death—and death so soon is coming—
    Escape I cannot, there's no place to flee.

But Thou, O God, hast life that is eternal;
    That life is mine, a gift through Thy dear Son;
Help me to feel its flush and pulse supernal,
    Assurance of the morn when life is done.

Help me to know the value of these hours;
    Help me the folly of all waste to see;
Help me to trust the Christ who bore my sorrows,
    And thus to yield for life or death to Thee.

In all my days be glorified, Lord Jesus;
    In all my ways guide me with Thine own eye;
Just when and as Thou wilt, use me, Lord Jesus,
    And then for me 'tis Christ, to live or die.

                                        —*Will H. Houghton*

∽

QUIETNESS

Passing one day beside Niagara's stream,
In the glad time of Nature's wakening,
When winter yields to spring and spring doth bring
Bright sunshine, fragrant flowers and singing birds,
I paused beside the river where its flow
Is most disturbed—the rapids in the gorge—
And watched the waters as they passed me by.
There I beheld, under the cloudless sky,
In sight of flowers, in sound of warbling birds,
The broad, deep torrent, rushing on and on,
Tossed to and fro, revolving round and round,

With whirlpools, and with waves which dashed themselves
Into white foam upon the blackened rocks,
Till all the river seemed alive and mad,
A very hell of waters, near and far,
Abysmal depths of discord and of pain.
And as I looked, I saw just opposite,
Right in the waters' midst, upon the wave,
A block of wood, resting all calm and still,
Not floating down the stream, nor moving round,
As still and calm as if on crystal sea.
Astonished at the sight I looked again.
And then again with steady, fixèd gaze,
Till all my doubts were gone, for there the wood
Remained quiescent as I saw it first.
Then studying the strange sight I found its cause;—
The block was held just at the central point
Of a great whirlpool's course, where, rushing round,
The waters met and formed a place of calm,
As if there were no whirlpool, nor mad rush
Of frenzied waters leaping to the sea.
And there I learned that day a lesson new,
Beneath bright heav'n, beside the troubled stream,
How deeply calm one's daily life may be,
In midst of all the torrent-rush of cares,
The pressing, maddening tides of daily tasks,
Which dash and whirl till sense is almost gone,
If only one can learn the lesson blest,
To hide within the all infolding will,
God's will for us, all perfect good and true;
For there, in midst of all, in spite of all,
We may find rest, abiding, deep, complete,
And thus find quietness, for ever more!

— *Henry W. Frost*

ᐁ

THE FINEST ENGLISH EPIGRAM

"Live while you live," the epicure would say,
And seize the pleasures of the present day.
"Live while you live," the sacred preacher cries,
And give to God each moment as it flies.
Lord, in my view, let both united be;
I live in pleasure while I live to thee.

— *Philip Doddridge*

ONE IN CHRIST

No form of human framing,
  No bond of outward might,
Can bind Thy Church together, Lord,
  And all her flocks unite;
But, Jesus, Thou hast told us
  How unity must be:
Thou art with God the Father one,
  And we are one in Thee.

The mind that is in Jesus
  Will guide us into truth,
The humble, open, joyful mind
  Of ever-learning youth;
The heart that is in Jesus
  Will lead us out of strife,
The giving and forgiving heart
  That follows love in life.

Wherever men adore Thee,
  Our souls with them would kneel;
Wherever men implore Thy help,
  Their trouble we would feel;
And where men do Thy service,
  Though knowing not Thy sign,
Our hand is with them in good work,
  For they are also Thine.

Forgive us, Lord, the folly
  That quarrels with Thy friends,
And draws us nearer to Thy heart
  Where every discord ends;
Thou art the crown of manhood,
  And Thou of God the Son;
O Master of our many lives,
  In Thee our life is one.

  — *Henry van Dyke*

COMMUNION HYMN

All praise to him of Nazareth,
  The Holy One who came,
For love of man, to die a death
  Of agony and shame.

Dark was the grave; but since he lay
  Within its dreary cell,
The beams of heaven's eternal day
  Upon its threshold dwell.

He grasped the iron veil, he drew
  Its gloomy folds aside,
And opened, to his follower's view,
  The glorious world they hide.

In tender memory of his grave
  The mystic bread we take,
And muse upon the life he gave
  So freely for our sake.

A boundless love he bore mankind;
  Oh, may at least a part
Of that strong love descend and find
  A place in every heart!

  — *William Cullen Bryant*

FEARS

Christ is on the throne;
Oh, may His blood atone;
May I not shrink and cry
When, 'neath His flashing eye,
I face Him all alone.

Christ is near at hand;
Oh, may His grace expand;
What else may be my plea
When He enquires of me
As I before Him stand?

Christ is at the door;
Oh, may I love Him more;
Mayhap, a moment's space
With sins which I deplore.

Christ will quickly come;
Oh, may His power o'ercome,
Lest in that awful day,
Because of sin's array,
I stand before Him dumb!

  — *Henry W. Frost*

COMMUNION OF SAINTS

Let party names no more
  The Christian world o'erspread;
Gentile and Jew, and bond and free,
  Are one in Christ, their Head.

Among the saints on earth
  Let mutual love be found;
Heirs of the same inheritance,
  With mutual blessings crowned.

Let envy, child of hell!
  Be banished far away:
Those should in strictest friendship
    dwell,
  Who the same Lord obey.

Thus will the church below
  Resemble that above;
Where streams of endless pleasure flow,
  And every heart is love.

                — *Benjamin Beddome*

CALM

O Sabbath rest by Galilee!
  O calm of hills above,
Where Jesus knelt to share with thee
The silence of eternity,
  Interpreted by love!

Drop thy still dews of quietness
  Till all our strivings cease;
Take from our souls the strain and
    stress,
And let our ordered lives confess
  The beauty of thy peace.

Breathe through the heats of our desire
  Thy coolness and thy balm;
Let sense be dumb, let flesh retire:
Speak through the earthquake, wind
    and fire,
  O still small voice of calm.

                — *John Greenleaf Whittier*

ALL THINGS ARE THINE

All things are Thine; no gift have we,
Lord of all gifts, to offer Thee;
And hence with grateful hearts today,
Thine own before Thy feet we lay.

Thy will was in the builders' thought;
Thy hand unseen amidst us wrought;
Through mortal motive, scheme and plan,
Thy wise eternal purpose ran.

In weakness and in want we call
On Thee for whom the heavens are small;
Thy glory is Thy children's good,
Thy joy Thy tender Fatherhood.

O Father, deign these walls to bless;
Fill with Thy love their emptiness;
And let their door a gateway be
To lead us from ourselves to Thee.

                — *John Greenleaf Whittier*

How Much I Owe

When this passing world is done,
When has sunk yon glowing sun,
When we stand with Christ in Glory,
Looking o'er life's finished story,
Then, Lord, shall I fully know —
Not till then — how much I owe.

When I stand before the throne,
Dressed in beauty not my own,
When I see Thee as Thou art,
Love Thee with unsinning heart,
Then, Lord, shall I fully know —
Not till then — how much I owe.

When the praise of Heaven I hear,
Loud as thunder to the ear,
Loud as many waters' noise,
Sweet as harp's melodious voice,
Then, Lord, shall I fully know —
Not till then — how much I owe.

Even on earth, as through a glass
Darkly, let Thy glory pass;
Make forgiveness feel so sweet;
Make Thy Spirit's help so meet;
Even on earth, Lord, make me know
Something of how much I owe.

— *Robert Murray McCheyne*

The Busy Man

If you want to get a favor done
   By some obliging friend,
And want a promise safe and sure
   On which you may depend,
Don't go to him who always has
   Much leisure time to plan,
But if you want your favor done,
   Just ask the busy man.

The man of leisure never has
   A moment he can spare;
He's busy "putting off" until
   His friends are in despair;

But he whose every waking hour
   Is crowded full of work,
Forgets the art of wasting time —
   He cannot stop to shirk.

So when you want a favor done,
   And want it right away,
Go to the man who constantly
   Works twenty hours a day.
He'll find a moment, sure, somewhere
   That has not other use,
And fix you while the idle man
   Is framing an excuse.

— *Author Unknown*

Passing Through

"When thou passest thro' the waters,"
   Deep the waves may be, and cold,
But Jehovah is our refuge
   And His promise is our hold;
For the Lord Himself hath said it,
   He the faithful God and true:
"When thou comest to the waters,
   Thou shalt *not go down*, but *thro'.*"

Seas of sorrow, seas of trial,
   Bitterest anguish, fiercest pain,
Rolling surges of temptation,
   Sweeping over heart and brain,
They shall never overflow us,
   For we know His word is true;
All His waves and all His billows
   He will *lead us safely through.*

Threatening breakers of destruction,
   Doubt's insidious undertow,
Shall not sink us, shall not drag us
   Out to ocean depths of woe;
For His promise shall sustain us,
   Praise the Lord, whose word is true!
We shall not go down nor under,
   He hath said, "Thou passest *thro'.*"

— *Annie Johnson Flint*

WEEPING

Weep, sorrowing one, for God would have thee weep,
  He did not make thee stone, but very man,
Yea, He did form thy soul a fountain deep,
    Seek not to close it up, weep whilst thou can;
      Yea, weep and weep, weep tears on tears until
      Thy weeping heart has ta'en its bitter fill.

Ne'er think thy weeping sin, since Christ did weep,
  Who held His life in such long, strong restraint;
Mark there, at Lazarus' tomb, how tears upleap,
    Hear yonder Garden's mournful, bitter plaint;
      Grieve not, then, if deep grief thine eyes bedim;
      As Master, so disciple; — weep with Him.

And yet this learn, weep not amidst the crowd;
  Weeping is sacred; shut thy closet door;
There, only there, put on thy mourner's shroud
    Where thou canst speak with Christ, and help implore;
      Then, on the breast of Him who weeps with thee,
      Pour out thy sorrow's bitterest agony.

And grieve not Christ; weep not as without hope;
  Despair is trustlessness, and, therefore, sin;
However deep thy darkness, never grope,
    Lift up thine head and see the Light within;
      Weep on, belovèd, weep till sorrow's end,
      But ne'er forget that Christ is thy good Friend.

Weep, sorrowing one; but e'er remember this:
  Weeping will not endure beyond the night;
There is in store for thee a rapturous bliss,
    God's joy will greet thee with the morning light;
      For God's own hand will wipe each weeping eye!

                                        — *Henry W. Frost*

                      ᘯ

A CONFESSION

Did I not know there is in heaven above
A God of wisdom and of changeless love,
In spite of all one earth which makes life glad,
    I should be ever sad.

Life masters me, I cannot master it,
Before its problems I e'er helpless sit
Like witless dullard in a crowded school,
    Confessed by all a fool.

Within my heart are longings infinite,
And yet, like fearful child in darksome night,
I start, I shrink, I grope but cannot find,
    A child, indeed, and blind.

The more I seek, the more is mystery;
The dark e'er deepens in intensity;
I yearn for wisdom, light, for these I cry,
    They stand far off, not nigh.

I grasp at substance, and I find it air;
I place my foot on rock, and naught is there;
I think high thoughts, they turn to foolishness
    And add to my distress.

E'en love is e'er imperfect here below;
The fondest hopes are often turned to woe;
At heart of sweetest joy lies secret pain,
    And life is loss, not gain.

Yea, I have seen life's ideals pass away,
As passes into night some brightsome day,
Till what is left is disappointment keen
    For things which might have been.

I will not cease my quest, but this I see
There is no solving here of mystery;
I will pursue life's ideals, but I know
    The best is not below.

Life, at its best, is brightness shadowed o'er;
Life, 'spite of life, lies ever on before;
Not here, but there in heaven, may hearts abide
    For ever satisfied.

This, then, I've surely found; with God above
Is everlasting life and light and love;
And this — in spite of all that makes life sad —
    This keeps me ever glad!

              — *Henry W. Frost*

RELIGION

Religion's all or nothing; it's no mere smile
Of contentment, sigh of aspiration, sir —
No quality o' the finelier-tempered clay
Like its whiteness or its lightness; rather, stuff
O' very stuff, life of life, and self of self.

              — *Robert Browning*

WHAT GOD HATH PROMISED

God hath not promised
  Skies always blue,
Flower-strewn pathways
All our lives through;
God hath not promised
Sun without rain,
Joy without sorrow,
  Peace without pain.

But God hath promised
  Strength for the day,
Rest for the labor,
  Light for the way,
Grace for the trials,
  Help from above,
Unfailing sympathy,
  Undying love.
                — *Annie Johnson Flint*

ɷ

HEART-BREAK

I have lost my Love to-day,
  Lost Him in the crowded way,
While I turned aside to see
  Life in its festivity;
Oh, to look into His face
And to find His pard'ning grace!

Ah, my heart, how fair this world
  When its beauties are unfurled,
How they glitter, dazzle, blind,
  How they 'snare the heart and mind!
Tell me, and oh, tell me true,
Has my Love been seen by you?

I did take my wanton way
  With the throngs all thro' the day,
Seeking pleasures, sweet and rare,
  Joyful, without thought or care;
Now 'tis night; oh, can you tell
Where my grievèd Love doth dwell?

Days are long and full of light,
  Pleasures sweet and joyance bright;
But the night, how dark and drear,
And how full of dread and fear!
Oh, that I could find my Love,
Then I would no longer rove!

If you see my Love, do you
  Tell Him that my love is true,
That grief's tears my eyes bedim
  As I seek and call for Him;
Will you, in sweet charity,
Help to find my Love for me?

Ah, I wander all alone;
  Would I could for sin atone,
I would give my very heart,
  With my very life would part,
If in giving, dying, I
Might but find my Love was nigh!

Hear me, Love; I cry, I moan,
  Thee I long for, Thee alone;
If Thou wilt return to me
  I will never part from Thee;
Hear me all, below, above,
Tell my Love, I die from love!

                — *Henry W. Frost*

ɷ

EARTH IS ENOUGH

We men of Earth have here the stuff
Of Paradise — we have enough!
We need no other stones to build
The Temple of the Unfulfilled —
No other ivory for the doors —
No other marble for the floors —
No other cedar for the beam
And dome of man's immortal dream.

Here on the paths of every-day —
Here on the common human way
Is all the stuff the gods would take
To build a Heaven, to mold and make
New Edens. Ours the stuff sublime
To build Eternity in time!

                — *Edwin Markham*

DRIFTING

Why do I drift on a storm-tossed sea,
With neither compass, nor star, nor chart,
When, as I drift, God's own plan for me
Waits at the door of my slow-trusting heart?

Down from the heavens it drops like a scroll,
Each day a bit will the Master unroll,
Each day a mite of the veil will He lift.
Why do I falter? Why wander and drift?

Drifting, while God's at the helm to steer;
Groping, when God lays the course so clear;
Swerving, though straight into port I might sail;
Wrecking, when heaven lies just within hail.

Help me, O God, in the plan to believe;
Help me my fragment each day to receive.
Oh, that my will may with Thine have no strife!
God-yielded wills find the God-planned life.

— *James McConkey*

❦

PEACEFULNESS

A forest dim and grand, with mile on mile
    Of tangled undergrowth and arching trees,
    Where sunlight rests upon the matted leaves
But never reaches earth to flowers beguile;
        There footsteps never fell
        To break the silent spell,
        There always, all around
        Is stillness deep, profound;—
            And there is peace.

An ocean's wide expanse, with leagues untold
    Of untracked waters, 'neath a tropic sun,
    Where every passing day, till day is done,
The sea lies glittering bright, like burnished gold;
        There storm-winds never blow,
        There storm-waves never flow,
        There crystal waters lie
        Beneath a cloudless sky;—
            And there is peace.

A lake half-hidden, near a mountain's crest,
  Surrounded by great trees with foliage bright,
  O'er which the wild-duck wings his circling flight,
Near which the eagle builds his lofty nest;
      There, 'neath the sun's bright beam,
      Wavelets like jewels gleam;
      There, lilies white and rare
      Perfume the still soft air;—
        And there is peace.

A heart all-sensitive, 'midst city din,
  Pressed hard upon by selfish, jostling crowds,
  Touched by dark lives which wickedness enshrouds,
Forced always, everywhere, to look on sin;
      Yet kept by God's great power,
      Rejoicing hour by hour,
      Uplifting prayer and psalm,
      Dwelling in heav'nly calm;—
        Ah, *there* is peace!
                    — *Henry W. Frost*

ᕔᓆ

PEACE

I longed for peace and quiet,
  But Jesus chose for me
A path through storm and tempest,
  A wild and boisterous sea.
But while the raging billows
  In fury round me tore
And threatened with destruction
  My frail bark o'er and o'er,
I glimpsed amid the darkness
  A trail of heavenly light,
And one came walking toward me,
  Whose voice dispelled my night.
In accents soft and tender,
  He bade my fears to cease,
As to the roaring tempest
  He whispered words of peace.
Oh hallowed are life's conflicts,
  And blest its every storm,
If they but draw me closer
  To His encircling arm!
                — *Avis B. Christiansen*

ALL'S WELL

The clouds, which rise with thunder,
    slake
  Our thirsty souls with rain;
The blow most dreaded falls to break
  From off our limbs a chain;
And wrongs of man to man but make
  The love of God more plain,
As through the shadowy lens of even,
The eye looks farthest into heaven,
On gleams of star and depths of blue
The glaring sunshine ever knew!
            — *John Greenleaf Whittier*

ᕔᓆ

ABUNDANT LIFE

To do God's will from day to day,
To follow Christ and not to stray,
To have the Spirit's power alway,
    This is abundant life!
                — *Henry W. Frost*

WANDERER'S SONG

Jesus, I am far astray
From the straight and narrow way;
Bring me back, I humbly pray;
    Jesus, hear and save me!

Draw me with Thy cords of love,
Fix my heart on Thee above,
That I may no longer rove;
    Jesus, hear and save me!

Save me from life's snare and sin,
Make me Thine, without, within,
Grant me strength the race to win;
    Jesus, hear and save me!

Keep me ever at Thy side,
Held by Thee, whate'er betide,
Loved and blessed, and satisfied;
    Jesus, hear and save me!

Take me when I come to die
To Thyself, in heaven on high,
There to dwell, e'er safe and nigh;
    Jesus, hear and save me!

        — *Henry W. Frost*

GETHSEMANE

In golden youth when seems the earth
A summer-land of surging mirth,
When souls are glad and hearts are
    light,
And not a shadow lurks in sight,
We do not know it, but there lies
Somewhere veiled 'neath evening skies
A garden which we all must see —
The garden of Gethsemane.

With joyous steps we go our ways,
Love lends a halo to our days;
Light sorrows sail like clouds afar,
We laugh, and say how strong we are,
We hurry on: and hurrying, go
Close to the borderland of woe
That waits for you, and waits for me —
Forever waits Gethsemane.

Down shadowy lanes, across strange
    streams
Bridged over by our broken dreams;
Behind the misty caps of years,
Beyond the great salt fount of tears,
The garden lies. Strive, as you may,
You cannot miss it in your way;
All paths that have been, or shall be
Pass somewhere through Gethsemane.

All those who journey, soon or late,
Must pass within the garden's gate;
Must kneel alone in darkness there,
And battle with some fierce despair,
God pity those who cannot say,
"Not mine, but Thine," who only pray,
"Let this cup pass," and cannot see
The purpose of Gethsemane.

        — *Ella Wheeler Wilcox*

IN HOC SIGNO

The Kingdoms of the Earth go by
    In purple and in gold;
They rise, they triumph, and they die,
    And all their tale is told.

One Kingdom only is divine,
    One banner triumphs still;
Its King a servant, and its sign
    A gibbet on a hill.

        — *Godfrey Fox Bradby*

PEACE

There is a life deep hid in God
Where all is calm and still,
Where, listening to His holy Word,
One learns to trust, until
All anxious care is put away
And there is peace, profound, alway;
    Grant us Thy peace, O God!

        — *Henry W. Frost*

Day by Day

Day by day manna fell:
O to learn this lesson well.
Still by constant mercy fed,
Give me, Lord, my daily bread.

"Day by day," the promise reads,
Daily strength for daily needs:
Cast foreboding fears away;
Take the manna of today.

Lord! my times are in Thy hand:
All my sanguine hopes have planned,
To Thy wisdom I resign,
And would make Thy purpose mine.

Thou my daily task shalt give:
Day by day to Thee I live;
So shall added years fulfill,
Not my own, my Father's will.

— *Josiah Conder*

ↄ⃝

Words

Words are things of little cost,
Quickly spoken, quickly lost;
We forget them, but they stand
Witnesses at God's right hand.

Grant us, Lord, from day to day,
Strength to watch and grace to pray;
May our lips, from sin set free,
Love to speak and sing of thee.

— *Author Unknown*

ↄ⃝

Not Growing Old

They say that I am growing old,
I've heard them tell it times untold
In language plain and bold —
But I'm not growing old.
This frail old shell in which I dwell
Is growing old, I know full well,
But I'm not growing old!

What if my hair *is* turning gray?
Gray hair is honorable, they say.
What *if* my eyesight's growing dim?
I still can see to follow Him
Who sacrificed His life for me
There on the Cross at Calvary!
What should I care if Time's old plow
Has dug its furrows in my brow?
Another house, not made with hand,
Awaits me in the Glory Land.

My hearing may not be as keen
As in the past it might have been,
Still I can hear my Saviour say,
"Come, faltering child, this is the way!"
The outward man, do what I can
To lengthen out this life's short span,
Shall perish and return to dust,
As everything in nature must.

But the inward man, the Scriptures
    say,
Is growing stronger every day!
Then how can I be growing old?
I'm safe within my Saviour's fold.
E'er long my soul shall fly away
And leave this tenement of clay!
This robe of flesh I'll drop and rise
To seize the everlasting prize!
I'll meet you on the streets of gold
And prove that I'm *not* growing old!

— *Author Unknown*

ↄ⃝

The Christian Life

To me, O Lord, be thou "The Way,"
    To me be thou "The Truth";
To me, my Saviour, be "The Life,"
    Thou Guardian of my youth!

So shall that Way be my delight,
    That Truth shall make me free;
That Life shall raise me from the dead,
    And then I'll live to thee.

— *Author Unknown*

THE CHARACTER OF A HAPPY LIFE

How happy is he born and taught
   That serveth not another's will;
Whose armour is his honest thought,
   And simple truth his utmost skill!

Whose passions not his masters are;
   Whose soul is still prepared for death,
Untied unto the world by care
   Of public fame or private breath;

Who envies none that chance doth raise;
   Nor vice hath ever understood
(How deepest wounds are given by praise!)
   Nor rules of State, but rules of good;

Who hath his life from rumours freed;
   Whose conscience is his strong retreat,
Whose state can neither flatterers feed,
   Nor ruin make oppressors great;

Who God doth late and early pray,
   More of his grace, than gifts, to lend,
And entertains the harmless day
   With a religious book or friend!

This man is freed from servile bands
   Of hope to rise or fear to fall!
Lord of himself, though not of lands;
   And having nothing, yet hath all!
                              — *Sir Henry Wotton*

THE VALLEY OF SILENCE

I walk down the Valley of Silence
   Down the dim, voiceless valley alone;
And I hear not the fall of a footstep
   Around me — Save God's and my own,
And the hush of my heart is as holy
   As hovers where angels have flown.

Long ago was I weary of voices,
   Whose music my heart could not win;
Long ago was I weary of noises,
   That fretted my soul with their din;
Long ago was I weary of places,
   Where I met but the human and sin.

And still I pined for the perfect,
    And still found the false with the true,
I sought mid the human for heaven,
    But caught a mere glimpse of the blue;
I wept as the clouds of the world veiled
    Even that glimpse from my view.

I toiled on heart-tired of the human,
    I moaned mid the mazes of men,
Till I knelt, long ago, at an Altar,
    And heard a Voice call me; since then
I walk down the Valley of Silence,
    That lies far beyond mortal ken.

Do you ask what I found in the Valley?
    'Tis my trysting place with the Divine.
When I fell at the feet of the Holy,
    And about me the Voice said, "Be Mine,"
There arose from the depths of my spirit,
    An echo, "My heart shall be Thine."

Do you ask how I live in the Valley?
    I weep, and I dream, and I pray:
But my tears are as sweet as the dew drops,
    That fall on the roses of May;
And my prayer like a perfume from censer
    Ascendeth to God night and day.

In the hush of the Valley of Silence,
    I dream all the songs that I sing;
And the music floats down the dim valley,
    Till each finds a word for a wing,
That to men, like the doves of the deluge,
    The message of Peace they may bring.

But far out on the deep there are billows,
    That never shall break on the beach;
And I have heard songs in the Silence,
    That never shall float into speech;
And I have had dreams in the Valley,
    Too lofty for language to reach.

And I have seen forms in the Valley,
    Ah, me! how my spirit was stirred;
And they wear holy veils on their faces,
    Their footsteps can scarcely be heard
They pass through the Valley like virgins,
    Too pure for the touch of a word.

Do you ask me the place of the Valley,
   Ye hearts that are harrowed by care?
It lieth afar between Mountains,
   And God and His angels are there;
And one is the dark Mount of Sorrow,
   The other the bright Mount of Prayer.

                  — *Father Ryan*

THE LITTLE STAR

A little star shone singly in the night,
And thought "How very feeble is my light!
There's not a traveler who will see his way,
Who will be guided by my tiny ray.
But I will not go out — the more will I
Attempt to shine in this vast, darkened sky."

Down in the world there was a weary soul
Striving alone to see the clouded goal.
Full of despair, she wrestled all the night,
But saw no shining of a guiding light.
She said, "There is no moon, I am so sad,"
And lost the very little hope she had.

But through her narrow window did she see
A point of brightness gleaming fervently.
It was the single star. She cried aloud,
And hoped anew for passing of the cloud.
When morning came, with all its golden light,
She said, "I found the Saviour in the night.

"I found Him through a star — it must have been
The Star of Bethlehem that I have seen,
For to the Lord it led — and so I came
And saw the hills of Heaven all aflame,
All shining with the glory of that star,
Whose small but steady light had called afar."

O little star! be not afraid thy light
Will be too feeble to be seen at night.
However small, if steady, it will be
Lighting the roadway to Eternity.
They know in Heaven, where the angels are,
A soul was lighted by a little star.

                — *Vivien Jameson*

PILGRIMAGE

A few more miles and a few more tears
    And I'll be at home with the blest;
A few more struggles and doubts and fears
    And I'll be for ever at rest;
Then steady, my soul, till the day is done;
Go bravely on till the setting sun
    Has sunk 'neath the hills in the west.

My way is the way that the Master went,
    With His feet full weary and sore,
Where, for love of me, He was sorely spent
    As He bowed 'neath the cross which He bore;
Yet He journeyed on, though His sun sank red,
Till He reached the portal which straightly led
    To the rest of the other shore.

Then follow on, though the way be rough;
    Ne'er pause till the journey is done;
For the weary miles there'll be strength enough
    Till the heavenly welcome is won;
    And if I keep steady, whatever betide,
My soul will be fully satisfied
    At the going down of the sun!
                                        — *Henry W. Frost*

ov

THE EMMAUS ROAD

The road was dreary and rough and long
And their hearts were sad and lone;
Gone was their once triumphant song
And the joy that they once had known.
Their footsteps lagged as they journeyed on,
And their eyes with tears were dim,
But One came and walked beside them there,
And they found new hope in Him.
His words were as balm to their troubled souls,
And His smile dispelled their fears,
And their hearts were warmed as His voice of love
Fell like music on their ears.
Their world was changed as they talked with Him,
And their way so dark and lone,
As they journey on with their risen King,
In the light of His presence shone.

And thus it is on our homeward way,
So rugged, and oft so drear,
One walks by our side each passing day,
And we thrill at His voice so dear.
Though our tear-dimmed eyes are holden at times,
And His smile we fail to see,
He is ever near, and in love divine
Watches o'er us tenderly.
Sweet words of comfort and hope and cheer
He whispers along the way,
And our very hearts within us burn
'Neath their blessed healing ray.

Yea, life is like the Emmaus road,
And we tread it not alone,
For beside us walks the Son of God,
To uphold and keep His own.
And our hearts within us thrill with joy
At His words of love and grace,
And the blessed hope that when day is done
We shall see His blessed face.

— Avis B. Christiansen

༄

There Is a Stillness

There is a stillness in the Christian's life:
An inner stillness only known to him
Who has so gladly laid at Jesus' feet
His all, and now He reigns alone within,
Master of every motion, wish, and plan.
In stillness crowned, He rules supreme as King,
And in that inner chamber of the heart
Has made a little sanctuary within.

There is a stillness in the Christian's life:
The corn of wheat must fall into the ground
And die, then if it die, out of that death
Life, fullest life, will blessedly abound.
It is a mystery no words can tell,
But known to those who in this stillness rest;
Something divinely incomprehensible:
That for my nothingness, I get God's best!

— Author Unknown

SPIRITUAL CONFLICT

Down, deeper down, thou sinful, sensual Self
  Back to low earth from which thou would'st arise;
Thou robber-fiend, keep thine ill-gotten pelf
  Of my misdeeds, it is thy lawful prize;
But henceforth know thou shalt not rule o'er me,
For a sweet Voice calls me to victory.

Up, higher up, thou better, nobler one,
  Rise up in strength, with face turned toward the skies;
Faint not, nor fear, the conflict will be won,
  Behold, before thee is the victor's prize;
Thy God who calleth thee will strength maintain
And turn all earthly loss to heavenly gain.

— *Henry W. Frost*

CHANCE AND CHANGE

  What if a day, or a month, or a year,
Crown thy delights, with a thousand sweet contentings!
  Cannot a chance of a night, or an hour,
Cross thy desires, with as many sad tormentings?
Fortune, honour, beauty, youth,
  Are but blossoms dying!
Wanton pleasure, doting love,
  Are but shadows flying!
All our joys are but toys;
  Idle thoughts deceiving!
None have power, of an hour,
  In their life's bereaving.

  Earth's but a point to the world; and a man
Is but a point to the world's comparèd centre!
  Shall then, a point of a point be so vain
As to triumph in a silly point's adventure!
All is hazard that we have!
  There is nothing biding!
Days of pleasure are like streams,
  Through fair meadows gliding!
Weal and woe, Time doth go!
  Time is never turning!
Secret fates guide our states;
  Both in mirth and mourning!

— *Thomas Campion*

BROTHERLY LOVE

Blest be the tie that binds
  Our hearts in Christian love:
The fellowship of kindred minds
  Is like to that above.

Before our Father's throne
  We pour our ardent prayers;
Our fears, our hopes, our aims are one,
  Our comforts and our cares.

We share our mutual woes;
  Our mutual burdens bear;
And often for each other flows
  The sympathizing tear.

When we asunder part,
  It gives us inward pain;
But we shall still be joined in heart,
  And hope to meet again.

This glorious hope revives
  Our courage by the way;
While each in expectation lives,
  And longs to see the day.

From sorrow, toil, and pain,
  And sin we shall be free;
And perfect love and friendship reign
  Through all eternity.
                    — *John Fawcett*

SHUT IN

I

Shut in; a prisoner;
  Within four walls confined;
Counting the weary hours
  Of days and nights combined.

Shut in; enclosed around;
  Sick, helpless, and alone;
In pain and suffering,
  Each sigh almost a moan.

Shut in; in idleness;
  No duties to fulfil;
Served, but not serving now;
  My service to lie still.

II

And is there nought beside?
  Ah, yes, thrice-blessèd word;
Shut into Jesus Christ,
  "A prisoner in the Lord."

Shut in where there's no fear
  With walls of radiant light;
Where days all golden are
  And there is never night.

Shut in where music is
  And there is deepest peace;
Where love fore'er abounds
  And joys fore'er increase.

Shut in where there's no fear
  And nought of earth's alarms;
Where there's unbroken rest
  In everlasting arms.

Shut in? Yes, all shut in,
  Whatever ill betide;
Shut into Christ, my Lord;
  And oh, so satisfied!
                    — *Henry W. Frost*

THE BUSINESS OF THE DAY

It's just the way we carry through
The business of the day
That makes and molds the character —
The things we do and say;
The way we act when we are vexed;
The attitude we take;
The sort of pleasures we enjoy;
The kind of friends we make.
It's not the big events alone
That make us what we are;
And not the dizzy moments when
We're swinging on a star.
It's just the things that happen as
Along the road we plod.
The little things determine what
We're really worth to God.
                    — *Patience Strong*

TEARS

Ashamed of tears? This world of ours
Might be as well ashamed of flowers
Skies of their stars when night appears
As mortals be ashamed of tears.
For then, if ever, when we weep,
We waken who have been asleep
And let the flood of feeling roll
Across the desert of the soul.

We live so much the dull drab days,
We walk so much life's treadmill ways,
With heart so dumb, with mind so
    mute
We're little better than the brute.
And then some day there comes a grief
That only tears can give relief.
And then the beauty floods our eyes
That God has put in rain-washed skies!

Ashamed of tears, when even He
Knelt weeping in Gethsemane?
We never see God quite so clear
As through the prism of a tear!
If purity we ever know
It is our tears that made us so;
And only they need blush with shame
To whom emotion never came!

        — *Author Unknown*

THINGS THAT NEVER DIE

The pure, the bright, the beautiful,
    That stirred our hearts in youth,
The impulses to wordless prayer,
    The dreams of love and truth;
The longings after something lost,
    The spirit's yearning cry,
The strivings after better hopes —
    These things can never die.

The timid hand stretched forth to aid
    A brother in his need,
A kindly word in grief's dark hour
    That proves a friend indeed;

The plea for mercy softly breathed,
    When justice threatens nigh,
The sorrow of a contrite heart —
    These things shall never die.

Let nothing pass, for every hand
    Must find some work to do;
Lose not a chance to waken love —
    Be firm, and just and true:
So shall a light that cannot fade
    Beam on thee from on high,
And angel voices say to thee —
    These things shall never die.

        — *Author Unknown*

BE THE BEST

If you can't be a pine
    on the top of the hill,
Be a scrub in the valley — but be
The best little scrub
    by the side of the rill:
Be a bush if you can't be a tree.

If you can't be a bush,
    be a bit of the grass,
Doing something for somebody's sake;
If you can't be a muskie,
    then just be a bass —
But the liveliest bass in the lake!

We can't all be captains,
    some have to be crew,
There's something for all of us here,
There's big work and little
    for people to do,
And the task we must do is the near.

If you can't be the highway,
    then just be a trail,
If you can't be the sun, be a star;
It isn't by size that you
    win or you fail —
Be the best of whatever you are!

        — *Douglas Malloch*

FOURSCORE YEARS

My hands are gnarled and my hair is gray
And I'm just eighty years old today.
My friends are coming my hand to shake,
My children are bringing a birthday cake.
A candle for every year? — Ah no,
A cake can hold but thirty or so.

Yet I shall enjoy the thoughts they bring,
The ties and socks, and the songs they sing.
Eighty years have passed me since my birth,
A right long time to be here on earth.
I'm tired and I've had almost enough.
Life hasn't been easy — the road was rough.

Yet I know as I 'wait Time's knock on my door,
I'd like to remain a year or two more,
To see what becomes of my Billy and Bess,
But the chances are slim that I may, I guess.
With the back of my hand I brush a tear
As I open a well-worn book that's near.

There I see on a page once turned down by my wife —
"I come that you may have eternal life."
And then turning over a page or two —
"I go to prepare a place for you."
Once more I turn and the lines now say —
"For a thousand years are but a day."

Old Book, you've never been known to be wrong,
And according to you, I've not lived very long.
So I get out my pencil and soon it is clear
Though I've spent eighty years on this earthly sphere,
Though they've worn my body and stiffened my knee —
Yet I'm but two hours old in eternity!

So at last I know, though my frame is old,
Though my eyes are dim and my hands are cold,
Why it is that inside I'm still young and gay —
It's because I'm just starting on my way:
A babe in the eyes of time to be,
Just two hours old in Eternity!

— Author Unknown

FOLLOW ME!

"Child, follow me," the Master said,
    As he knocked full loud at my chamber door;
        But the morn was fair, and my heart was gay,
        "I'll dally a while on the primrose way,
    And I'll come" said I, "when the morning's o'er."

"Child, follow me," the Master said,
    As he lingered patiently at the gate;
        Gray shadows were falling, the night was near;
        "Life's joys are so sweet, and my friends so dear,
    "I will come," said I, "when the night is late."

"Child follow me," the Master cried,
    As he walked away through the darkness deep;
        And the night had fallen, and the birds were still;
        "Linger," said I, "at the foot of the hill,
    And I'll come when the world is hushed in sleep."

"Master, I come," I cried at length,
    "Heart weary to serve at thine own dear side,
        Thou hast called me long, but I come at last."
        (But his eyes were dim and his strength was past,
    And not long could he follow the Crucified).

                                        — *Author Unknown*

TEACH ME

Morning by morning waken me, my Father,
    Let Thy voice be the first my soul to greet,
Bidding my spirit rise from earthly slumber,
    And sit a learner at Thy sacred feet.

There, in the stillness, open Thy good treasure,
    The precious things of Christ unfolding still,
And, as Thy Spirit brings them to remembrance,
    Let gratitude and love my spirit fill.

Teach me to do Thy will, Thy pattern show me;
    Reveal Thy purpose for my life each day.
Then for Thy service with fresh oil anoint me,
    And with Thy presence hallow all my way.

                                        — *Freda Hanbury Allen*

FORBEARANCE

Lord, grant me the gift of forbearance,
A merciful spirit I pray.
That suffers the wrongs of another
And seeks not the ill to repay.

Lord, help me be kind and forgiving—
I who Thy forgiveness have known
So oft for my many transgressions.
Grant me, Lord, a love like Thine own.

Thou who didst once suffer for sinners
Such bitter reproach and disdain,
Fill me with that same gentle spirit,
That reviled, still reviles not again.

Lord, grant me the gift of forbearance,
Thy tender, compassionate grace,
That others beholding my visage
The light of Thy likeness may trace.

— *Avis B. Christiansen*

LIFE AND DEATH FOR THE CHRISTIAN

What is this thing called life —
This short swift span of years
So veiled with mystery,
So filled with toil and tears?
What is this thing called life,
Dear friend, you ask of me?
'Tis but the threshold to
A blest eternity.

A time to love and serve
The Saviour we adore,
A time to trust and pray,
And prove Him o'er and o'er;
A time to glorify
His great and holy name —
The wonders of His grace
To sinners to proclaim.

A time to walk by faith
And trust His pow'r to keep;
A time to watch and wait
While others fain would sleep;

A time to yield to Him
The sacrifice of love,
E'er He shall ope' the gate
To Glory up above.

And what is death you ask?
'Tis but the open door
To yon fair Land of Light,
Our Home forevermore,
Where we shall gaze on Him
With Whom we've walked below,
And sing His endless praise,
While ages come and go.

— *Avis B. Christiansen*

SOME MINUTES IN THE MORNING

Some minutes in the morning,
Ere the cares of life begin,
Ere the heart's wide door is open
For the world to enter in.
Oh, then alone with Jesus,
In the silence of the morn,
In heavenly, sweet communion
Let your every day be born,
In the quietude that blesses,
With a prelude of repose,
Let your soul be soothed and softened
As the dew revives the rose.

Some minutes in the morning
Take your Bible in your hand,
And catch a glimpse of glory
From the peaceful promised land.
It will linger still before you
When you seek the busy mart,
And like flowers of hope will blossom
Into beauty in your heart.
The precious words like jewels
Will glisten all the day
With a rare refulgent glory
That will brighten all the way!

— *Author Unknown*

KEEP LOOKING UP

When life's cares around you gather,
And you can't see through,
Find the Way by looking up;
When disturbed by adverse weather
And you don't know what to do,
Keep looking up.

There's an antidote for worry,
Discontent and strife,
Find the Way by looking up;
It will help when things are blurry,
It's a principle of life,
Keep looking up.

It's the upward look that frees us
From the snares of earth,
Find the Way by looking up;
When we look to God, He sees us,
And in Christ He gives New Birth,
Keep looking up.

Keep looking up —
For the uplook is the soul's way out of
    sorrow;
Keep looking up —
And God will bring a glory-filled to-
    morrow;
Look thou to God,
And brightness will break through
    your clouded sky;

Keep looking up,
And your faith will find its answer
    by and by.
                            — Carlton Buck

                    ～

IF THOU DOST NEED

If Thou dost need a hand today
To clasp another hand on life's rough
    way;
Take mine, dear Lord, take mine.
If Thou art needing feet to tread
In paths where sin to woe is wed;
Use mine, dear Lord, use mine.
If thou art needing lips today

For words that help and heal, to say;
Fill mine, dear Lord, fill mine.
If Thou art needing eyes to see
When souls begin to stray from Thee;
Fit mine, dear Lord, fit mine.
But cleanse, dear Lord, and purify,
And then each talent sanctify;
Of mine, dear Lord, of mine.
                        — Mary E. Kendrew

                    ～

THEY HAVE BEEN WITH JESUS

Yes, they are changed —
How kindly do they speak;
The crippled beggar stands erect
Since they have passed,
And surely, yonder blind man
Is gazing toward the mountain seeing!

So spoke the ones who scoffed
When those who had left all
To follow Him passed by.
These men had been with Jesus,
Had seen His mighty works
And heard His words.

So, too, may we be changed by Him
When earnestly we strive.
'Twas not for them alone
He broke the bread of Life,
Still storm-tossed wave,
And banished pain and sorrow.

O may it be
That some who scorn, today
Are speaking thus of you — and me:
Some wonder has been wrought —
Where once she was so cold,
She now is kind!

And thankfully we say —
Though none but God may hear:
"Rejoice! Rejoice!
For He is guiding me —
I, too,
Have been with Jesus."
                        — Author Unknown

THE THREADS YOU USE

Of what are you weaving your life today,
Of fast-fading pleasures or joys that stay?
Do you want it completed in lovely hues?
It will all depend on the threads you use!

Take only the best from the maze you find,
The threads that will strengthen your heart and mind;
Just threads you are sure of, beyond a doubt,
Durable threads that will not wear out.

You will want some colorful, gay and bright,
Beautiful, too, but they must be right;
No snags, no knots, no colors that run,
To make you ashamed in the days to come.

Some of the threads should be sturdy and plain
The better, we know, to withstand the strain
Of the noonday sun and the scalding tears
That are sure to come with the passing years.

To all of your threads you must add some gold,
The wealth of God's Love — it will make them hold;
For, in weaving a life of beautiful hues,
It always depends on the threads you use!

— *Alice Hansche Mortenson*

I NEED WIDE SPACES

I need wide spaces in my heart
Where faith and I can go apart
And grow serene.

Life gets so choked by busy living,
Kindness so lost in fussy giving,
That love slips by unseen.

I want to make a quiet place
Where those I love can see God's face,
Can stretch their hearts across the
earth,
Can understand what spring is worth,
Can count the stars,
Watch violets grow,
And learn what birds and children
know.

— *Author Unknown*

FAITH, HOPE, LOVE

In the lone places of my soul
The far dim depths, where none can
see,
I hear a little singing bird,
For faith has come to live with me.

And o'er the dimness of my way,
The vast, gray reaches of my sea,
There lies a trembling shaft of light,
For hope has drifted in to me.

And in this wintry house of mine,
Where grief and gloom at home
would be,
A tender hand has lit a fire,
For love has come to stay with me.

— *Margaret Matthews*

MARKED FOR HIS OWN

How lovely are the faces of
  The men who talk with God —
Lit with an inner sureness of
  The path their feet have trod;
How gentle is the manner of
  A man who walks with Him!
No strength can overcome him, and
  No cloud his courage dim,
Keen are the hands and feet—ah, yes—
  Of those who wait His will,
And clear as crystal mirrors are
  The hearts His love can fill.

Some lives are drear from doubt and
      fear
  While others merely plod;
But lovely faces mark the men
  Who walk and talk with God.

          — *Pauline Prosser-Thompson*

FOUND IN THEE

O Christ, in Thee my soul hath found,
And found in Thee alone,
The peace, the joy I sought so long;
The bliss till now unknown.

I sighed for rest and happiness,
I yearned for them, not Thee;
But while I passed my Saviour by,
His love laid hold on me.

I tried the broken cisterns, Lord,
But ah! the waters failed.
E'en as I stooped to drink they'd fled,
And mocked me as I wailed.

Now none but Christ can satisfy,
None other name for me;
There's love, and life, and lasting joy,
Lord Jesus, found in Thee!

          — *Author Unknown*

THE KINGDOM OF GOD ON EARTH

Eternal Ruler of the ceaseless round
Of circling planets singing on their way;
Guide of the nations from the night profound
Into the glory of the perfect day:
Rule in our hearts, that we may ever be
Guided and strengthened and upheld by Thee.

We are of Thee, the children of Thy love,
The brothers of Thy well beloved Son;
Descend, O Holy Spirit, like a dove
Into our hearts, that we may be as one;
As one with Thee, to whom we ever tend;
As one with Him our Brother and our Friend.

We would be one in hatred of all wrong
One in our love of all things sweet and fair,
One with the joy that breaketh into song,
One with the grief that trembles into prayer,
One in the power that makes Thy children free
To follow truth, and thus to follow Thee.

          — *John W. Chadwick*

Tomorrow

He was going to be all that a mortal could be —
    Tomorrow;
No one should be kinder nor braver than he —
    Tomorrow;
  A friend who was troubled and weary he knew
  Who'd be glad of a lift and who needed it, too;
On him he would call and see what he could do —
    Tomorrow.

Each morning he stacked up the letters he'd write —
    Tomorrow;
And he thought of the folks he would fill with delight —
    Tomorrow;
  It was too bad, indeed, he was busy today,
  And hadn't a minute to stop on his way;
"More time I'll have to give others," he'd say —
    "Tomorrow."

The greatest of workers this man would have been —
    Tomorrow;
The world would have known him had he ever seen —
    Tomorrow;
  But the fact is he died, and he faded from view,
  And all that he left here when living was through
Was a mountain of things he intended to do —
    Tomorrow.

              — Author Unknown

Move to the Fore

Move to the fore;
Say not another is fitter than thou.
Shame to thy shrinking! Up! Face thy task now.
Own thyself equal to all a soul may,
Cease thy evading — God needs thee today.
Move to the fore!

God Himself waits, and must wait till thou come;
Men are God's prophets though ages lie dumb.
Halts the Christ Kingdom with conquest so near?
Thou art the cause, thou soul in the rear.
Move to the fore!

              — Author Unknown

I Broke My Tryst With God

At such an hour on such a day
I had a tryst with God;
I was to put all things away
And keep that tryst with God.
But a friend of mine just happened in —
To go with him was sure no sin —
So I ran along, a friend to win,
But I broke my tryst with God.

My friends all know my word is good,
Yet I broke my tryst with God.
They know I'd keep my word if I could,
Yet I broke my tryst with God.
But somehow I felt when that day was done,
And my spirit sank with the setting sun
That I'd lost much more than I had won
By breaking my tryst with God.

O let us keep that meeting place —
The secret tryst with God.
At such a time He shows His face,
O holy tryst with God.
Never mind though friends and others call,
His love impels our best, our all;
Let us come alone, before Him fall
And keep our tryst with God.

— *Author Unknown*

Joy Is Built of Little Things

Joy is built of little things like this —
A woman's smile, and a baby's kiss;
A single rose, a slender vase,
The slant of sunlight on a happy face;
A child's sigh, a father's fond caress,
Just simple things, but they bring happiness.

A lilt of song that lingers through the years,
A bit of sunshine and a bit of tears;
A silhouette of pines against the sky,
A silver star, a nightbird's cry;
A good night prayer and faith within your breast,
Just simple things, but they make — happiness!

— *Alice Hansche Mortenson*

My Chum

He stood at the crossroads all alone,
　With the sunrise in his face;
He had no fear for the path unknown;
　He was set for a manly race.
But the road stretched east, and the road stretched west;
There was no one to tell him which way was the best;
So my chum turned wrong and went down, down, down,
Till he lost the race and the victor's crown
And fell at last in an ugly snare,
Because no one stood at the crossroads there.

Another chum on another day
　At the selfsame crossroads stood;
He paused a moment to choose the way
　That would stretch to the greater good.
And the road stretched east, and the road stretched west;
But I was there to show him the best;
So my chum turned right and went on and on,
Till he won the race and the victor's crown;
He came at last to the mansions fair,
Because I stood at the crossroads there.

Since then I have raised a daily prayer
That I be kept faithful standing there.
To warn the runners as they come,
And save my own or another's chum.

　　　　　　　　　　　　　— Author Unknown

A Cowboy's Prayer

Oh, Lord, I've never lived where churches grow,
　I love creation better as it stood
That day You finished it so long ago,
　And looked upon Your work and called it good.

I know that others find You in the light
　That filters down through tinted window panes,
And yet I seem to feel You near tonight
　In this dim, quiet starlight on the plains.

I thank You, Lord, that I am placed so well;
　That You have made my freedom so complete,
That I'm no slave of whistle, clock or bell,
　Or weak-eyed prisoner of wall or street.

Just let me live my life as I've begun,
  And give me work that's open to the sky;
Make me a partner of the wind and sun,
  And I won't ask a life that's soft or high.

Let me be easy on the man that's down;
  And make me square and generous with all;
I'm careless sometimes, Lord, when I'm in town,
  But never let them say I'm mean or small.

Make me as big and open as the plains,
  As honest as the horse between my knees,
Clean as the wind that blows behind the rains,
  Free as the hawk that circles down the breeze.

Forgive me, Lord, when I sometimes forget,
  You understand the reasons that are hid,
You know the little things that gall and fret,
  You know me better than my mother did.

Just keep an eye on all that's done and said,
  Just right me sometimes when I turn aside,
And guide me on the long, dim trail ahead
  That stretches upward toward the Great Divide.

— Author Unknown

oɬꙅ

BE CAREFUL

Be careful of the little deeds you do,
For oftentime they echo back to you
    Across the years.
The tiny note you sent one sorry day,
The coin that helped a beggar on his way,
Oh! Always take the time to stop and say
    The word that cheers!
Perhaps some little deed will bring you fame,
Perhaps the world will learn to love your name,
    Because of tears
You dried for others; and when life is through
Perhaps the little deeds you, thoughtless, do
Will be a glowing monument to you
    For countless years.

— Author Unknown

FINISH THY WORK

Finish thy work, the time is short;
　The sun is in the west,
The night is coming down; till then
　Think not of rest.

Rest? Finish thy work, then rest;
　Till then, rest never.
The rest prepared for thee by God
　Is rest forever.

Finish thy work, then sit thee down
　On some celestial hill,
And of heaven's everlasting bliss
　Take thou thy fill.

Finish thy work, then go in peace,
　Life's battle fought and won;
Hear from the throne the Master's
　　voice,
　"Well done! Well done!"

Finish thy work, then take the harp,
　Give praise to God above;
Sing a new song of mighty joy
　And endless love!

　　　　　　　— Author Unknown

WE TWO

I cannot do it alone;
　The waves run fast and high,
And the fogs close chill around,
　And the light goes out in the sky;
But I know that We Two shall win —
　　in the end:
　　　　　— Jesus and I.

I cannot row it myself —
　The boat on the raging sea —
But beside me sits Another,
　Who pulls or steers — with me;
And I know that We Two shall come
　safe into port,
　　　　　— His child and He.

Coward and wayward and weak,
　I change with the changing sky;
Today, so eager and brave,
　Tomorrow, not caring to try:
But He never gives in; so We Two
　　shall win!
　　　　　— Jesus and I.

Strong and tender and true,
　Crucified once for me;
Ne'er will He change, I know,
　Whatever I may be.
But all He says I must do —
　Ever from sin to keep free;
We shall finish our course, and reach
　　Home at last!
　　　　　— His child and He.

　　　　　　　— Author Unknown

JESUS, THE MASTER OF MY FATE

I am not the master of my fate;
　That lies in wiser, abler hands;
And I am captain of my soul
　Only if He beside me stands.

He alone knows the quiet lanes
　Thro' which my little bark must steer;
The rocks and shoals to me unknown
　To that keen eye are plain and clear.

Black though the night be, as the pit,
　Unlighted by a single star,
Steadfast He guides me on; to Him
　Alike the light and darkness are.

Wild blasts upon my vessel sweep,
　From my weak grasp the wheel
　　would tear,
I feel beside my hands His hands,
　Master of sky and sea and air.

I cannot plot my onward way;
　He holds all things in His control,
Jesus, Master of my fate,
　Pilot and Captain of my soul.

　　　　　　　— Author Unknown

Good Timber

The tree that never had to fight
For sun and sky and air and light,
That stood out in the open plain
And always got its share of rain,
Never became a forest king,
But lived and died a scrubby thing.

The man who never had to toil
To heaven from the common soil,
Who never had to win his share
Of sun and sky and light and air,
Never became a manly man,
But lived and died as he began.

Good timber does not grow in ease;
The stronger wind, the tougher trees;
The farther sky, the greater length;
The more the storm, the more the
    strength;
By sun and cold, by rain and snows,
In tree or man, good timber grows.

Where thickest stands the forest
    growth
We find the patriarchs of both;
And they hold converse with the stars
Whose broken branches show the scars
Of many winds and of much strife —
This is the common law of life.

— *Douglas Malloch*

ᴄ∾ᴏ

The Rose Leaf

Oh, beautiful rose, please tell me,
    For I would like to know,
Why I must crush your petals
    That sweet perfume may flow.

Oh, life that is clothed in beauty,
    Perhaps like that beautiful rose,
You will need to be crushed by suffer-
    ing
    Ere you give out your best; who
        knows?

A life that is crushed by sorrow
    Can feel for another's grief,
And send out that sweet perfume of
        love
    That will bring some heart relief.

Oh, do not repine at your testing,
    When called to pass under the rod,
It is that life might the sweeter be,
    And comes from the Hand of God.

He knows how much we are needing,
    Of sorrow, or suffering, or test,
And only gives to His children
    The things that He knoweth are
        best.

Then let us rejoice when He sendeth
    Some sorrow or hardship that tries,
And be glad to be crushed as the rose
        leaf,
    That a sweeter perfume may arise.

— *Flora L. Osgood*

ᴄ∾ᴏ

I Dare Not Be Defeated

I dare not be defeated
    Since Christ, my conquering King,
Has called me to the battle
    Which He did surely win.
Come, Lord, and give me courage,
    Thy conquering Spirit give,
Make me an overcomer,
    In power within me live.

I dare not be defeated,
    Just at the set of sun,
When Jesus waits to whisper,
    "Well done, beloved, well done!"
Come, Lord, bend from the Glory,
    On me Thy Spirit cast,
Make me an overcomer,
    A victor to the last.

— *The Verses of a Pilgrim*

BE TRUE TO YOURSELF

Be true to yourself at the start, young man,
    Be true to yourself and God;
Ere you build your house, mark well the spot,
Test all the ground, and build you not
    On the sand or the shaking sod.

Dig, dig the foundation deep, young man,
    Plant firmly the outer wall;
Let the props be strong and the roof be high,
Like an open turret toward the sky,
    Through which heaven's dews may fall.

Let this be the room of the soul, young man —
    When shadows shall herald care,
A chamber with never a roof or thatch
To hinder the light — or door or latch
    To shut in the spirit's prayer!

Build slow and sure; 'tis for life, young man,
    A life that outlives the breath;
For who shall gainsay the Holy Word?
"Their works do follow them," said the Lord,
    Therein there is no death.

Build deep, and high, and broad, young man,
    As the needful case demands;
Let your title-deeds be clear and bright,
Till you enter your claim to the Lord of Light,
    For the "house not made with hands."

— Author Unknown

ɔⱷ

UNIQUE

Toil-worn I stood and said,
"O Lord, my feet have bled,
My hands are sore,
I weep, my efforts vainly poor.
With fainting heart I pray of Thee,
Give some brave other, work designed for me."

But my Lord answer made,
"O child of Mine,
I have looked through space and searched through time,
There is none can do the work called thine."

Soul-sick I knelt and cried,
"Let me forever hide
My little soul
From sight of Him who made me whole,
My one small spirit in the vast,
Vast throngs of like mean myriads, present, past!"

But my Lord answer made,
"O child of Mine,
I have looked through space and searched through time,
But I find no soul is like to thine!"

— Frances Bent Dillingham

WHERE THE LEPROSY BEGINS

When Nations are to perish in their sins,
'Tis in the Church the leprosy begins:
The priest, whose office is, with zeal sincere
To watch the foundation and preserve it clear,
Carelessly nods and sleeps upon the brink,
While others poison what "the flock" must drink;
Or waking at the call of lust alone,
Infuses lies and errors of his own:
His unsuspecting sheep believe it pure,
And, tainted by the very means of cure,
Catch from each other a contagious spot,
The foul forerunner of a general rot.
Then Truth is hush'd that heresy may preach,
And all is trash that reason cannot reach;
Then God's own image on the soul impress'd
Becomes a mockery and a standing jest;
And Faith, the root whence only can arise
The graces of a life that wins the skies,
Loses at once all value and esteem,
Pronounced by greybeards a pernicious dream;
Then Ceremony leads her bigots forth,
Prepared to fight for shadows of no worth;
While Truths, on which Eternal Things depend,
Finds not, or hardly finds a single friend:
As soldiers watch the signal of command,
They learn to bow, to kneel, to sit, to stand;
Happy to fill Religion's vacant place
With hollow form, and gesture, and grimace.

— William Cowper

HE CAME

He came to you, for in His gentle voice
  He'd much that He would say.
Your ears were turned to earth's discordant sounds,
  And so — He went away.

He came; and in His hand He had a task
  That He would have you do,
But you were occupied with other things,
  And so you missed that too.

He would have touched you; and His touch could thrill,
  And give you quickening power;
But earthly things enveloped, and you could
  Not feel Him in that hour.
                            — *Author Unknown*

ตพ

TAKE A MAN (*Mark 8:23-25*)

Take a man!
Take any man,
And touch his life
With the redeeming love of Christ,
And something happens.
Something good happens.
He sees more clearly.
He hears more distinctly.
He loves more deeply.
He comes to a self-realization
In proper perspective to others.
His sensitivity to need is sharpened.

Vague human shapes
Become people;
Real people who feel, suffer,
Rejoice, love.
Suddenly there is kinship
With all of life.
Statistics of suffering
Begin to breathe.
Vision enlarges, interest expands.
The world has meaning,
And he is no longer orphaned
In a cold universe.

Take a man!
Take any man;
It is true.   — *Carlton Buck*

ตพ

SOMEONE'S BIBLE

Thy life is someone's Bible, where
  Each day adds one new page;
Where chapters rise from little deeds
  That fill thy youth and age.

The friend who meets thee now and
    then
  Will read a line therein,
And find some cheer to strive anew,
  Or pretext for his sin.

Someday these speeding years —
  Their work of record done —
May show how often reading thee,
  His soul was lost or won.

A godless act may fix his doom;
  Thy thoughtlessness he heeds;
Be careful friend, for where thou art,
  Someone his Bible reads.
                            — *E. C. Kurtz*

In Heavenly Love Abiding

In heav'nly love abiding,
No change my heart shall fear;
And safe is such confiding,
For nothing changes here.
The storm may roar without me,
My heart may low be laid,
But God is round about me,
And can I be dismayed?

Wherever He may giude me,
No want shall turn me back;
My Shepherd is beside me,
And nothing can I lack.

His wisdom ever waketh,
His sight is never dim,
He knows the way He taketh,
And I will walk with Him.

Green pastures are before me,
Which yet I have not seen;
Bright skies will soon be o'er me,
Where darkest clouds have been.
My hope I cannot measure,
My path to life is free,
My Savior has my treasure,
And He will walk with me.

— *Anna L. Waring*

Lord, I Would Follow

Lord, I would follow, but —
First I would see what means that wondrous call
That peals so sweetly through life's rainbow hall,
That thrills my heart with quivering golden chords,
And fills my soul with joys seraphical.

Lord, I would follow, but —
First I would leave things straight before I go —
Collect my dues, and pay the debts I owe;
Lest when I'm gone, and none is here to tend,
Time's ruthless hand my garnering o'erthrow.

Lord, I would follow, but —
First I would see the end of this high road
That stretches straight before me fair and broad;
So clear the way I cannot go astray,
It surely leads me equally to God.

Who answers Christ's insistent call
Must give himself, his life, his all,
Without one backward look.
Who sets his hand upon the plow,
And glances back with anxious brow,
His calling hath mistook;
Christ claims him wholly for His own;
He must be Christ's and Christ's alone.

— *Author Unknown*

Wilt Thou Follow Me?

"Wilt thou follow Me?"
The Saviour asked.
The road looked bright and fair,
And filled with youthful hope and zeal
I answered, "Anywhere."

"Wilt thou follow Me?"
Again He asked.
The road looked dim ahead;
But I gave one glance at His glowing
      face
"To the end, dear Lord," I said.

"Wilt thou follow Me?"
I almost blanched,
For the road was rough and new,
But I felt the grip of His steady Hand,
And it thrilled me thro' and thro'.

"Still followest thou?"
'Twas a tender tone,
And it thrilled my inmost heart.
I answered not, but He drew me close,
And I knew we would never part.
                    — *Author Unknown*

This Is Today

Yesterday ended when the shadows
Caught up each faint trace of its light
And God tenderly covered His
      children
With the warm cloud soft blanket of
      night.
Tomorrow is yet in the making;
It may be all gloomy or all bright.

But this is today — the true treasure
God made just for you and for me;
Then out of its bright dewey fresh-
      ness —
Let be whatever must be.
God planned it and on past its
      boundaries
I'm certain we *need* not see.

No man should ever cross over
The threshold of God's tomorrow
Nor yet retrace his own footsteps
Through yesterday's portals to borrow
A quart or even a cupful
Of human joy or sorrow.

This is today, the true treasure
God made just for you and for me;
Out of its bright dewey freshness —
Let be whatever must be.
God planned it and on past its
      boundaries
I'm certain we *need* not see.
                    — *Phyllis C. Michael*

Life's Cross

I heard a voice so softly calling:
   "Take up thy cross and follow me."
A tempest o'er my heart was falling,
   A living cross this was to me.

His cross I took, which, cross no longer,
   A hundred-fold brings life to me;
My heart is filled with joy o'erflowing,
   His love and life are light to me.

                    — *Author Unknown*

My Life

O God, not like a stagnant pool
   With tepid depths, let my life be;
But like a stream, undaunted, cool,
   That plunges, surges toward the sea.

O God, not like a sodden log,
   Now, dead, tho' once a stately tree;
But pushing high above the bog
   Still upward yearning, let life be!
                    — *J. Gordon Howard*

Come

Come ye yourselves apart and rest awhile,
  Weary, I know it, of the press and throng,
Wipe from your brow the sweat and dust of toil,
  And in My quiet strength again be strong.

Come ye aside from all the world holds dear,
  For converse which the world has never known,
Alone with Me, and with My Father here,
  With Me and with My Father not alone.

Come, tell Me all that ye have said and done,
  Your victories and failures, hopes and fears.
I know how hardly souls are wooed and won:
  My choicest wreaths are always wet with tears.

Come ye and rest; the journey is too great,
  And ye will faint beside the way and sink;
The bread of life is here for you to eat,
  And here for you the wine of love to drink.

Then fresh from converse with your Lord return,
  And work till daylight softens into even:
The brief hours are not lost in which ye learn
  More of your Master and His rest in Heaven.

                                        — *Author Unknown*

Old Age

Ah nothing is too late till the tired heart shall cease to palpitate.
Cato learned Greek at eighty; Sophocles wrote his grand
        Oedipus, and Simonides
Bore off the prize of verse from his compeers
When each had numbered more than fourscore years.

Chaucer, at Woodstock with the nightingales,
At sixty wrote the *Canterbury Tales;*
Goethe at Weimar, toiling to the last
Completed *Faust* when eighty years were past.

For age is opportunity no less
Than youth itself, though in another dress,
And as the evening twilight fades away
The sky is filled with stars, invisible by day.

                                — *Henry Wadsworth Longfellow*

THE BLUEBIRD

I heard a bluebird in the field today,
  Shouting aloud its springtime joy;
My heart leaped backward thro' the
      years
  And knelt before a laughing boy.

"Oh boy," I pray, "give back to me
  My laughter of that other day;
Give me the spirit, glad and free,
  That once I knew along the way."

He saw me not! Yet in his eye
  I read the answer to my plea;
"Joy lives not in the yesterdays,
  But in the living now," said he.

"Seize thou the joy of every day,
  For gladness thrills the common sod,
And every brook and every bird
  May sing to you the joy of God."

— *Author Unknown*

HAVE I?

I have never seen God's Face —
Or have I? I don't know —
I have seen a rose's grace
And watched it bud and bloom and
      grow,
I have seen a violet burst
And capture from the sky,
The glorious beauty of the color
Of heaven on high,
I have seen a baby's smile,
I have seen a sea gull's grace,
Just simple things, but all the while,
Have I not glimpsed, through them,
    God's Face?

I have never heard God's Voice —
Or have I? I don't know —
I have heard a singing bird,
And listened to the north wind blow,
I have heard the patter of

Spring rain upon awakening grass,
I have heard the silver voice
Of friendship, when a friend I pass,
I have heard a baby's cry,
And the word, "Mother," from my
    boys;
Just simple things, but all the while,
Have I not heard, through them,
    God's Voice?

I have never touched God's Hand —
Or have I? I don't know —
I have felt the wondering softness
Of the pure, white winter snow,
I have touched a tiny seed
Where-in great mysteries dwell,
I have touched a baby's cheek,
Softer than mere words can tell.
I have touched my sons' sweet faces,
I have felt the rich, brown land;
Just simple things, but all the while,
Have I not touched, through them,
    God's Hand?

— *Jessie Cannon Eldridge*

LIGHT FOR THE NORTH ROOM

While lying in a north room
  Where no sun came at all
Quite suddenly I saw a light
  Reflected on the wall;
Delightedly I turned to see
  Whence such a thing had come,
When through the open door I spied
  A mirror in the sun.

Oh, what a precious lesson
  For Christians — you and me;
Our lives perhaps are all the light
  Of Christ that some may see.
Let's keep our mirrors facing Him,
  All clear and shining bright;
For someone in the north room
  Is sure to need our light!

— *Alice Hansche Mortenson*

The Zigzag Path

We climbed the height by the zigzag path
    And wondered why — until
We understood it was made zigzag
    To break the force of the hill.

A road straight up would prove too steep
    For the traveler's feet to tread;
The thought was kind in its wise design
Of a zigzag path instead.

It is often so in our daily life;
    We fail to understand
That the twisting way our feet must tread
    By love alone was planned.

Then murmur not at the winding way,
    It is our Father's will
To lead us Home by the zigzag path,
    To break the force of the hill.

         — *Author Unknown*

Make Me Thy Mountaineer

Make me Thy mountaineer; I would not linger
    On the lower slope.
Fill me afresh with hope, O God of hope,
    That undefeated
I may climb the hill
As seeing Him who is invisible.

Make me to be Thy happy mountaineer,
    O God most high;
My climbing soul would welcome the austere;
    Lord, crucify
On rock or scree, ice-cliff or field of snow,
The softness that would sink to things below.

Thou art my Guide; where Thy sure feet have trod
    Shall mine be set;
Thy lightest word my law of life, O God;
    Lest I forget,
And slip and fall, teach me to do Thy will,
Thy mountaineer upon Thy holy hill.

         — *Amy Carmichael*

It's a Beautiful Day!

It's a beautiful day! These are the words
   I heard at the edge of dawn.
And waking, I tried to fathom out why
   This inner glow and this song
Enfolding me, lifting me, leaving my cares
   Like a mantle discarded and torn?
Then I remembered! What cause to rejoice!
   Why I am a sinner reborn!

It's a beautiful day! Though clouds may arise,
   No Christian is ever alone.
Though "penniless, poor and rejected of men,"
   We're heirs and joint-heirs to a throne!
It's a beautiful day! Christ dwelling within,
   Let me walk with a conqueror's tread,
Just doing His will! It's a beautiful day!
   And — Heaven is just ahead!

                   — *Alice Hansche Mortenson*

Of Preachers

I venerate the man whose heart is warm,
Whose hands are pure, whose doctrine and whose life,
Coincident, exhibit lucid proof
That he is honest in the sacred cause,
To such I render more than mere respect,
Whose actions say that they respect themselves,
But, loose in morals, and in manners vain,
In conversation frivolous, in dress
Extreme, at once rapacious and profuse;
Frequent in park with lady at his side,
Ambling and prattling scandal as he goes;
But rare at home, and never at his books,
Or with his pen, save when he scrawls a card;
Constant at routs, familiar with a round
Of ladyships — a stranger to the poor;
Ambitious of preferment for its gold,
And well-prepar'd, by ignorance and sloth,
By infidelity and love of world,
To make God's work a sinecure; a slave
To his own pleasures and his patron's pride:
From such apostles, oh, ye mitred heads,
Preserve the church! And lay not careless hands
On sculls that cannot teach, and will not learn.

Would I describe a preacher, such as Paul,
Were he on earth, would hear, approve, and own —
Paul should himself direct me. I would trace
His master-strokes, and draw from his design.
I would express him simple, grave, sincere;
In doctrine uncorrupt; in language plain,
And plain in manner; decent, solemn, chaste,
And natural in gesture; much impress'd
Himself, as conscious of his awful charge,
And anxious mainly that the flock he feeds
May feel it too; affectionate in look,
And tender in address, as well becomes
A messenger of grace to guilty men.
Behold the picture! — Is it like? — Like whom?
The things that mount the rostrum with a skip,
And then skip down again; pronounce a text;
Cry — hem: and, reading what they never wrote,
Just fifteen minutes, huddle up their work,
And with a well-bred whisper close the scene!

— *William Cowper*

As I Go Down the Sunset Hill

As I go down the sunset hill,
   I pray, O Lord, that I
Will sweeter and more loving grow
   Until the day I die.
May trouble serve to mellow me,
   And weakness make me kind
To slowness in another's step;
   And let me not be blind
To beauty in the simple things
   That all around me lie —
In people and their loving deeds,
   As well as field and sky.

Oh, make me slow to criticize,
   And quicker to forgive,
And brush away each fancied slight
   As long as I shall live.
Let me take time to savor well
   The good things as I go
Along this (sometimes rugged) path
   Ablaze with sunset glow.

And may the brightness of Thy love
   Within my heart erase
All earthiness — preparing me
   To look upon Thy face!

— *Alice Hansche Mortenson*

Age Is a Quality of Mind

Age is a quality of mind —
If you have left your dreams behind,
If hope is lost,
If you no longer look ahead,
If your ambitions' fires are dead —
   Then you are old.

But if from life you take the best
And if in life you keep the jest,
If love you hold —
No matter how the years go by,
No matter how the birthdays fly,
   You are not old!

— *Author Unknown*

THE INWARD LIFE

Oh, sacred union with the Perfect Mind,
Transcendent bliss, which Thou alone canst give;
How blest are they this Pearl of Price who find,
And, dead to earth, have learnt in Thee to live.

Thus in Thine arms of love, O God, I lie,
Lost, and for ever lost to all but Thee.
My happy soul, since it hath learnt to die,
Hath found new life in Thine Infinity.

Go then, and learn this lesson of the Cross,
And tread the way the saints and prophets trod:
Who, counting life and self and all things loss,
Have found in inward death the life of God.

— *Author Unkown*

THE CROSS A CROWN

God laid upon my back a grievous load,
A heavy cross to bear along the road.

I staggered on, and lo! one weary day,
An angry lion sprang across my way.

I prayed to God, and swift at His command
The cross became a weapon in my hand.

It slew my raging enemy, and then
Became a cross upon my back again.

I reached a desert. O'er the burning track
I persevered, the cross upon my back.

No shade was there, and in the cruel sun
I sank at last, and thought my days were done.

But lo! the Lord works many a blest surprise —
The cross became a tree before my eyes!

I slept; I woke, to feel the strength of ten.
I found the cross upon my back again.

And thus through all my days from then to this,
The cross, my burden, has become my bliss.

Nor ever shall I lay the burden down,
For God some day will make the cross a crown!

— *Amos R. Wells*

AUTUMN DAYS

Today I saw a slender locust tree
With misty white all sprinkled, as in May;
And giving forth to all who passed that way
Its delicate, rare fragrance lavishly.
The maples newly tipped with red might be;
The golden-rod in glowing waves might sway;
But the locust heeded not October's day—
It dressed itself for spring, and smiled at me.

Oh grant that when the autumn days of life
Shall come to me, my spirit then may bloom
And deck itself in white; recall its spring;
Remember battles won, forget the strife;
Forget old enemies, remember whom
It loved, be joyful in these thoughts—and sing!

— Margaret Knowled Speidel

CROWN OF AGE

Why speak of those whom age is crowning,
   As going slowly down hill,
When on the heights above them shining
   Stands One who beckons upwards still?

No sad descent to death and darkness
   Is life when lived with love as guide;
But ever climbing toward the hilltop,
   Each summit gained brings visions wide.

'Tis always up the Pilgrims travel;
   While love rejoices at their side,
To feel the press of faith more strongly,
   To know He's near, whate'er betide.

As love the pilgrims forward leadeth,
   Footsteps may falter, eyes grow dim,
But ev'ry sigh He quickly heareth,
   And not a pain is hid from Him.

The steepest crags lie all behind them;
   By gentle slopes He guides the way;
Then one last step—still up—He bears them,
   To find the joy of perfect day.

—M. H.

When I Grow Old

Lord, keep me sweet when I grow old,
  And things in life seem hard to bear;
When I feel sad and all alone,
  And people do not seem to care.

O keep me sweet when time has caused
  This body, which was once so strong,
To droop beneath its load of years,
  And suffering and pain have come.

And keep me sweet when I have grown
  To worry so, at din and noise;
And help me smile, the while I watch
  The noisy play of girls and boys.

Help me remember how that I,
  When I was younger than today,
And full of life and health and joy,
  Would romp and shout in happy
    play.

Help me to train my heart each day,
  That it will only sweetness hold;
And as the days and years roll on
  May I keep sweet, as I grow old.

O keep me sweet, and let me look
  Beyond the frets that life must hold,
To see the glad eternal joys.
  Yes, keep me sweet in growing old.

          — Author Unknown

                ☙

Humility

Lord, let me do the little things,
  Which may fall to my lot,
Those little inconspicuous ones,
  By others, oft forgot,

A staff, for others to lean upon,
  Strong hands to help the weak,
A loving heart with open door,
  To all, who solace seek,

To hold my tongue, when hot words
    arise,
  Speak kindly ones instead,
Nor harshly judge my fellowmen,
  In what they've done, or said,

To share another's heavy load,
  By word, or courage given,
To help a fallen brother rise,
  And bring him nearer Heaven.

If, like the Master, I can give,
  Myself, for those I love,
Rich joy, and peace, shall come to me,
  Sweet rest, in Heaven above.

I know not, when today shall close,
  But when life's curfew rings,
I want my Lord to find me then,
  Still doing little things.

          — Author Unknown

                ☙

The Passing Years

Day by day the years are fleeting,
  Grain by grain the sands still fall.
One by one the hours are passing,
  Shadows lengthen on the wall.

From their places round our hearthside,
  Forms and faces fade away.
Like the briefness of a candle
  Each lives out his little day.

O'er the green mounds on the hillside
  Sounds again the tolling knell,
Life is brief, and time is fleeing,
  Live it Godly, live it well!

Riches, pleasure, idle pastimes,
  All these vanish with the grave.
Give your heart complete to Jesus,
  He alone your soul can save.

Just one life — 'tis all He offers
  Just one life — 'twill soon be past.
Only in His boundless mercy
  Can we find true peace at last.

One by one we make our exit,
  One by one we pass away.
Do not risk your soul's destruction
  Say "Yes" to Jesus Christ today!

— *James McGinlay*

∽

LORD, I LOVE THY MORNING

Lord, I love Thy morning
  When the sun breaks through:
When the birds are glad with singing,
  And the grass is wet with dew:
When all the world is full of living,
  And all nature seems to pray,
"Thou hast kept us thro' the darkness,
  Father, guide us through the day!"
For it always will remind me
  It was morning in my soul,
On the day I met my Saviour,
  When He touched and made me
    whole.

— *Barbara E. Cornet*

∽

VICTORIA

Thy victory is in the heart,
  Thy kingdom is within;
When outward pride and pomp depart,
  Thy glory doth begin.

Thine army, ever in the field,
  Is led by love and light;
Thy followers fall but never yield,
  Triumphant in the right.

O King most meek and wonderful,
  Grant us among Thy host,
To follow Thee, to fight for Thee,
  Knights of the Holy Ghost.

— *Henry van Dyke*

LEAN ON ME

"Is there no other way, O God,
  Except thro' sorrow, pain and loss,
To stamp Christ's image on my soul?
  No other way except the Cross?"

And then a voice stills all my soul,
  As stilled the waves on Galilee:
"Canst thou not bear the furnace heat,
  If 'mid the flames I walk with thee?

"I bore the Cross, I know its weight,
  I drank the cup I hold for thee;
Canst thou not follow where I lead?
  I'll give the strength — lean thou on
    me."

— *Author Unknown*

∽

THAT WAS ALL!

Why were the saints, saints?
It is quite simple.
Because they were cheerful
When it was difficult to be cheerful.
Patient, when it was difficult to be
  patient.
Because they pushed on
When they wanted to stand still.
And kept silent
When they wanted to talk.
And were agreeable when they wanted
  to be disagreeable.
    That was all!

— *Author Unknown*

∽

LIVING

To live with saints in heaven
  Will be eternal glory;
But to live with them on earth
  Is quite a different story!

— *Author Unknown*

THE OLD VIOLIN

I never knew the old, brown violin,
    That was so long in some dark corner thrust,
Its strings broken or loose, its pegs run down,
    Could ever be of use again. The dust
Of years lay on its shabby case, until
    One day a Master took the instrument,
And with caressing fingers touched the wood,
    Adjusted pegs and strings; his mind intent
On making music as he drew his bow.
    Then from the violin, long silent, sprang
Once more arpeggios, runs, trills. The wood
    Quivered, leapt into life, and joyous sang.

I now believe that any broken life,
    Jangling with discords, unadjusted, tossed
In some far corner, wasted, thrown aside,
    Can yet be of some use; need not be lost
From Heaven's orchestra. A Master's Hand
    Scarred with old wounds, can mend the broken thing
If yielded to Him wholly; and can make
    The dumb life speak again, and joyous sing
In praise of One who gave His life that none
    Need perish. And this message, glad, most blest,
I now believe; for placing in His Hand
    My life, I find my world is now at rest.

                                        — *Dorothy M. Barter-Snow*

ॐ

THE TOILS OF THE ROAD

My life is a wearisome journey,
    I'm sick with the dust and the heat.
The rays of the sun beat upon me,
    The briers are wounding my feet;
But the city to which I am going,
    Will more than my trials repay;
For the toils of the road will seem nothing
    When I get to the end of the way.

There are so many hills to climb upward,
    That I often am longing for rest;
But He who has marked out my pathway
    Knows just what is needful and best.
I know in His word He's promised

My strength will be as my day
And the toils of the road will seem nothing
    When I get to the end of the way.

When the last feeble step has been taken,
    And the gates of the city appear,
And the beautiful songs of the angels
    Float out on my listening ear;
Then all that seemed so mysterious
    Will be clear and plain as the day
And the toils of the road will seem nothing
    When we get to the end of the way.

Cooling fountains are there for the weary;
    There are cordials for those who are faint;
There are robes that are whiter
    Than any that fancy can paint.
Then I'll cheerfully press hopefully onward
    Knowing now through each wearisome day
That the toils of the road will seem nothing
    When we get to the end of the way.

                              — *Author Unknown*

                        ∾

IT TAKES SO LITTLE

It takes so little to make us sad:
Just a slighting word or a doubting sneer,
Just a scornful smile on some lips held dear;
And our footsteps lag, tho' the goal seemed near,
And we lose the courage and hope we had —
So little it takes to make us sad.

It takes so little to make us glad:
Just a cheering clasp of a friendly hand,
Just a word from one who can understand;
And we finish the task we long had planned
And we lose the doubt and the fear we had —
So little it takes to make us glad.

                              — *Author Unknown*

WHEN I THINK OF HIS LOVE

When I think of the cross where my Saviour died,
  'Neath the frown of the darkened skies,
When I hear the groan of the Crucified,
  And I look on those death-closed eyes,
When I know that for me He the anguish bore,
  From sin He might set me free,
Oh, I know that I'll love Him forevermore,
  When I think of His love for me.

When I think of the grave where they laid my Lord,
  And they sealed Him within the gloom,
When I think how according to His Word,
  He arose from that vanquished tomb,
Oh, I know that for me He endured it all,
  My eyes with tears grow dim,
While low at His feet in love I fall,
  Whenever I think of Him.

— Louis Paul Lehman, Jr.

ॐ

THE SPIRIT

Here must I be forever intimate,
Nor ever be a stranger to your mind;
So bar me not from secret door or gate,
Nor close to me the corridors that wind
Into the chambers of your treasured themes.
For I must look through closets, and must peer
In crypts that keep the tracings of old dreams.
So, with abandonment, make all things clear.
Surrender all the keys into My hand,
Nor seek to stay me in this urgent quest.
Here in this house I cannot be both Friend
And Foe, both Resident and transient Guest.
I cannot with each mood remain or move.
Here must I be at home; for I am LOVE.

— Lon Woodrum

THE CALL OF THE CHRISTIAN

Not always as the whirlwind's rush
   On Horeb's mount of fear,
Not always as the burning bush
   To Midian's shepherd seer,
Nor as the awful voice which came
   To Israel's prophet bards,
Nor as the tongues of cloven flame,
   Nor gift of fearful words,—

Not always thus, with outward sign
   Of fire or voice from Heaven,
The message of a truth divine,
   The call of God is given!
Awaking in the human heart
   Love for the true and right,—
Zeal for the Christian's better part,
   Strength for the Christian's fight.

Nor unto manhood's heart alone
   The holy influence steals:
Warm with a rapture not its own,
   The heart of woman feels!
As she who by Samaria's wall
   The Saviour's errand sought,—
As those who with the fervent Paul
   And meek Aquila wrought:

Or those meek ones whose martyrdom
   Rome's gathered grandeur saw:
Or those who in their Alpine home
   Braved the Crusader's war,
When the green Vaudois, trembling,
     heard,
   Through all its vales of death,
The martyr's song of triumph poured
   From woman's failing breath.

And gently, by a thousand things
   Which o'er our spirits pass,
Like breezes o'er the harp's fine strings,
   Or vapors o'er a glass,
Leaving their token strange and new
   Of music or of shade,
The summons to the right and true
   And merciful is made.

Oh, then, if gleams of truth and light
   Flash o'er thy waiting mind,
Unfolding to thy mental sight
   The wants of human-kind;
If, brooding over human grief,
   The earnest wish is known
To soothe and gladden with relief
   An anguish not thine own;

Though heralded with nought of fear,
   Or outward sign or show;
Though only to the inward ear
   It whispers soft and low;
Though dropping, as the manna fell,
   Unseen, yet from above,
Noiseless as dew-fall, heed it well,—
   Thy Father's call of love!

         — *John Greenleaf Whittier*

ᏇᎥ

THE PRODIGAL

He came back from the gray dust
of alien streets and the smell
of the swinecote, back to love.
Two things he would never under-
    stand:
why he had fled love for the dark
   streets
and the black wine, or why,
when he quit the swinecote, love
ran to meet him on the road.

But he did not need to understand.
It was enough that music from the
   house
washed over him, and that he was
   kissed,
and that the words fell on his spirit:
*This, my son, was dead, and is alive
   again:*
he was lost, and is found.

         — *Lon Woodrum*

Hymn

My God, I love thee, not because
I hope for heaven thereby;
Nor because they who love thee not
Must burn eternally.

Thou, O my Jesus, thou didst me
Upon the cross embrace;
For me didst bear the nails and spear,
And manifold disgrace;

And griefs and torments numberless;
And sweat of agony;
E'en death itself, — and all for me
Who was thine enemy.

Then why, O blessed Jesu Christ!
Should I not love thee well;
Not for the sake of winning heaven,
Or of escaping hell:

Not with the hope of gaining aught;
Not seeking a reward;
But as thyself hast loved me,
Oh, ever-loving Lord!

E'en so I love thee, and will love
And in thy praise will sing;
Solely because thou art my God,
And my eternal King.

— St. Francis Xavier

cxo

I Love All Beauteous Things

I love all beauteous things,
I seek and adore them;
God hath no better praise,
And man in his hasty days
Is honoured for them.

I too will something make
And joy in the making;
Altho' to-morrow it seem
Like the empty words of a dream
Remembered on waking.

— Robert Bridges

The Choice of Love

"Love seeketh not her own," and so
He did not stay as God above,
But chose a manger and a cross
To show that He was Love.

— Marion Wilmshurst

cxo

Divine Love

Love divine, all love excelling,
Joy of heaven, to earth come down;
Fix in us thy humble dwelling;
All thy faithful mercies crown.
Jesus, thou art all compassion,
Pure, unbounded love thou art;
Visit us with thy salvation,
Enter every trembling heart.

Breathe, O breathe thy loving spirit
Into every troubled breast;
Let us all in thee inherit,
Let us find the promised rest;
Take away the love of sinning,
Alpha and Omega be,
End of faith, as its beginning,
Set our hearts at liberty.

Come, Almighty to deliver,
Let us all thy life receive;
Suddenly return, and never,
Nevermore thy temples leave.
Thee we would be always blessing;
Serve thee as thy hosts above;
Pray, and praise thee without ceasing;
Glory in thy perfect love.

Finish, then, thy new creation,
Pure and spotless may we be;
Let us see thy great salvation
Perfectly restored in thee;
Changed from glory into glory,
Till in heaven we take our place:
Till we cast our crowns before thee,
Lost in wonder, love and praise!

— Charles Wesley

A Christian Mother's Love

A Christian mother's love contains
　Such priceless, added grace —
Her healing touch that verifies
　His presence in her face,
The firm yet quiet loveliness
　She always undergirds
With constant prayer that we may
　know
　The Force that forms her words.
And though she had a gentle part
　And cradled us with psalms,
Gladly she gave us back to Him
　Who placed us in her arms.
A Christian mother's love contains
　A Gospel all its own,
Because the King of love has found
　Her heart an ample throne.

— *Raymond H. Crawford*

☙

God's Provident Love

When we meet God every morning,
　As the dark flees from the light,
And the stars that were adorning
　Heaven's skies bid us goodnight,
High above, the sun-lit ceiling,
　Far beyond the unseen air,
Creates in our hearts the feeling
　That His love is everywhere.

God's love, as the day is dying,
　Lights the candles of the skies,
From His unseen source, supplying,
　Till the morning sun shall rise,
Light to those in darkness groping,
　That they may, with true delight,
See His presence, and keep hoping,
　As He guides them thro' the night.

As the Sun shines on, forever,
　In his splendor, from the skies,
God's love for His children never
　Changes, and it never dies,

Thrilling us with joy and pleasure,
　And inspiring us anew,
With hopes, which we love to treasure,
　For His promises are true.

— *Horace C. Carlisle*

☙

Love

I love you,
Not only for what you are,
But for what I am
When I am with you.

I love you,
Not only for what
You have made of yourself,
But for what
You are making of me.

I love you
For the part of me
That you bring out;
I love you
For putting your hand
Into my heaped-up heart
And passing over
All the foolish, weak things
That you can't help
Dimly seeing there,
And for drawing out
Into the light
All the beautiful belongings
That no one else had looked
Quite far enough to find.

I love you because you
Are helping me to make
Of the lumber of my life
Not a tavern
But a temple;
Out of the works
Of my every day
Not a reproach
But a song. . . .

— *Author Unknown*

O BROTHER MAN

O brother man, fold to thy heart thy brother
Where pity dwells, the peace of God is there;
To worship rightly is to love each other,
Each smile a hymn, each kindly deed a prayer.

Follow with reverent steps the great example
Of Him whose holy work was doing good:
So shall the wide earth seem our Father's temple,
Each loving life a psalm of gratitude.

Then shall all shackles fall; the stormy clangor
Of wild war-music o'er the earth shall cease;
Love shall tread out the baleful fire of anger,
And in its ashes plant the tree of peace.

— John Greenleaf Whittier

O BOTTOMLESS DEPTHS OF GOD'S INFINITE LOVE

O bottomless depths of God's infinite love,
   In Jesus our Saviour revealed!
Its motions how burning, how glowing they prove,
   Though from all man's wisdom concealed.
Whom dost thou love? It is sinners. Vile race!
Whom dost thou bless? Children scorning thy grace.
O Being most gracious, whom angels adore,
Thou takest delight in things worthless and poor.

Our thirsting can never, O merciful God,
   Be great as thy love, rich and sure.
On us thou more blessings and love has bestowed
   Than the stripes we so rightly endure.
On the rock of thy truth teach us firmly to stand.
Keep us ever near Christ by thy merciful hand.
In all things the spirit's kind teachings we'll prove,
And serve thee and honor thy infinite love.

Oh, show us, thou Being most gracious and mild,—
   By the light of the heavenly flame,—
In the face of Immanuel, thine image and child,
   How great is thy glorious name!
Oh, show us how blessed a task 'tis to bear
Thy yoke, and to trust in thy Fatherly care,
That, till the short period of trial shall end,
Our faith and our love may their Author commend.

— Nikolaus L. von Zinzendorf

ABOVE THE HILLS OF TIME

Above the hills of time the Cross is gleaming,
 Fair as the sun when night has turned to day;
And from it love's pure light is richly streaming,
 To cleanse the heart and banish sin away.
To this dear Cross the eyes of men are turning
 To-day as in the ages lost to sight;
And for the love of Christ men's hearts are yearning
 As shipwrecked seamen yearn for morning light.

The Cross, O Christ, Thy wondrous love revealing,
 Awakes our hearts as with the light of morn,
And pardon o'er our sinful spirits stealing
 Tells us that we, in Thee, have been re-born.
Like echoes to sweet temple bells replying,
 Our hearts, O Lord, make answer to Thy love;
And we will love Thee with a love undying,
 Till we are gathered to Thy home above.

         — *Thomas Tiplady*

COMPASSION

Compassion is love, plus desire to share
The trouble and tears that come from despair;
Compassion is love, plus sympathy, too,
With a will to help, to heal and renew.

Compassion is love, plus pity enough
To walk with the weary when the going is rough;
Compassion is love, plus the spirit to do
For others, our Lord had compassion, do you?

         — *James A. Sanaker*

WHAT IS LOVE?

Love is an attitude — Love is a prayer,
For a soul in sorrow, a heart in despair.
Love is good wishes for the gain of another,
Love suffers long with the fault of a brother.
Love giveth water to a cup that's run dry.
Love reaches low, as it can reach high.
Seeks not her own at expense of another.
Love reaches God when it reaches our brother.

         — *Author Unknown*

Leave God to Order

Leave God to order all thy ways,
  And hope in Him whate'er betide;
Thou'lt find Him, in the evil days,
  Thine all-sufficient Strength and
    Guide.
Who trusts in God's unchanging love
Builds on the Rock that naught can
    move!

Only thy restless heart keep still,
  And wait in cheerful hope, content
To take whate'er His gracious will,
  His all-discerning love hath sent,
Nor doubt our inmost wants are
    known
To Him who chose us for His own.

He knows when joyful hours are best,
  He sends them as He sees it meet,
When thou hast borne the fiery test,
  And now art freed from all deceit,
He comes to thee all unaware,
And makes thee own His loving care.

Sing, pray and swerve not from His
    ways;
  But do thine own part faithfully.
Trust His rich promises of grace,
  So shall they be fulfilled in thee.
God never yet forsook at need
The soul that trusted Him indeed.

— George Neumark
(Translated by Catherine Winkworth)

༨

Love Ship

If all the ships I have at sea
Should come a-sailing home to me,
Weighed down with gems and silks
    and gold —
Ah, well! the harbor could not hold
So many sails as there would be
If all my ships came in from sea.

If half my ships came home from sea,
And brought their precious freight to
    me,
Ah, well! I would have wealth as great
As any king who sits in state,
So rich the treasures that would be
In half my ships now out at sea.

If just one ship I have at sea
Should come a-sailing home to me,
Ah, well! the storm-clouds then might
    frown,
For, if the others all went down,
Still, rich and proud and glad I'd be
If that one ship came home to me.

If that one ship went down at sea,
And all the rest came home to me,
Weighed down with gems and wealth
    untold,
With glory, honor, riches, gold,
The poorest soul on earth I'd be
If that one ship came not to me.

O skies, be calm! O winds, blow free,
Blow all my ships safe home to me!
But if thou sendest some a-wreck,
To never more come sailing back,
Send any, all, that skim the sea,
But bring my love ship home to me!

— Ella Wheeler Wilcox

༨

Love for All

God loved the world of sinners lost,
  And ruined by the fall.
Salvation full, at highest cost,
  He offers free to all.

Love brings the glorious fulness in,
  And to His saints makes known
The blessed rest from inbred sin,
  Through faith in Christ alone.

— Mrs. M. Stockton

O Love Divine

O Love divine and golden,
Mysterious depth and height,
To Thee the world beholden
Looks up for life and light;
O Love divine and gentle,
The Blesser and the Blest,
Beneath Thy care parental
The world lies down in rest.

O Love divine and tender,
That through our homes does move,
Veiled in the softened splendor
Of holy household love,
A throne without Thy blessing
Were labor without rest,
And cottages possessing
Thy blessedness are blest.

God bless these hands united;
God bless these hearts made one!
Unsevered and unblighted
May they through life go on,
Here in earth's home preparing
For the bright home above,
And there forever sharing
Its joy where God is Love.

— *John S. B. Monsell*

O Love That Wilt Not Let Me Go

O Love that wilt not let me go,
  I rest my weary soul in Thee;
I give Thee back the life I owe,
That in Thine ocean depths its flow
  May richer, fuller be.

O Light that followest all my way,
  I yield my flickering torch to Thee;
My heart restores its borrowed ray,
That in Thy sunshine's blaze its day
  May brighter, fairer be.

O Joy that seekest me through pain,
  I cannot close my heart to Thee;
I trace the rainbow through the rain,
And feel the promise is not vain
  That morn shall tearless be.

O Cross that liftest up my head,
  I dare not ask to fly from Thee;
I lay in dust life's glory dead,
And from the ground there blossoms
  red
  Life that shall endless be.

O Hope that lightens all my way,
  I cannot choose but cleave to Thee;
And wrestle till the break of day,
Disclose the wisdom of the way
  In blessings yet to be.

— *George Matheson*

Love of God

Love through me, Love of God,
There is no love in me,
Oh Fire of love, light thou the love,
That burns perpetually.

Flow through me, Peace of God,
Calm river, flow until
No wind can blow, no current stir
A ripple of self-will.

Shine through me, Joy of God,
Make me like Thy clear air
Which Thou dost pour Thy colours
  thro'
As though it were not there.

Oh blessed Love of God,
That all may taste and see
How good Thou art, once more I pray:
Love through me, even me.

— *Amy Carmichael*

Midnight

God help the homeless ones who lack this night
    A roof for shelter and a couch for sleep;
God help the sailormen who long for light
    As restlessly they toss upon the deep.

God keep the orphaned children who are left
    Unmothered in this world of chill and dole;
God keep the widowed hearts, of joy bereft;
    God make all weary broken spirits whole.

Dark broods the midnight over sea and land,
    No star illumes the blackness of the sky.
But safe as nested birds within Thy hand,
    God of our Fathers, we Thy children lie.

— Margaret E. Sangster

∽

I Was Found of Thee

I sought the Lord, and afterward I knew
He moved my soul to seek Him, seeking me;
It was not I that found, O Saviour true;
No, I was found of Thee.

Thou didst reach forth Thy hand and mine enfold;
I walked and sank not on the storm-vexed sea,
'Twas not so much that I on Thee took hold,
As Thou, dear Lord, on me.

I find, I walk, I love, but, O the whole
Of love is but my answer, Lord, to Thee!
For Thou wert long beforehand with my soul;
Always Thou lovedst me.

— Author Unknown

∽

How Do I Love Thee?

How do I love thee? Let me count the ways.
I love thee to the depth and breadth and height
My soul can reach, when feeling out of sight
For the ends of Being and ideal Grace.
I love thee to the level of everyday's
Most quiet need, by sun and candle-light.

I love thee freely, as men strive for Right;
I love thee purely, as they turn from Praise.
I love thee with the passion put to use
In my old griefs, and with my childhood's faith.
I love thee with a love I seemed to lose
With my lost saints, — I love thee with the breath,
Smiles, tears, of all my life! — and, if God choose,
I shall but love thee better after death.

— Elizabeth Barrett Browning

ᢙᩔ

THE MASTER-PLAYER

An old, worn harp that had been played
Till all its strings were loose and frayed,
Joy, Hate, and Fear, each one essayed,
To play. But each in turn had found
No sweet responsiveness of sound.

Then Love the Master-Player came
With heaving breast and eyes aflame;
The Harp he took all undismayed,
Smote on its strings, still strange to song,
And brought forth music sweet and strong.

— Paul Laurence Dunbar

ᢙᩔ

HIS LOVE

The love of Christ doth me constrain
To seek the wandering souls of men;
With cries, entreaties, tears, to save,
To snatch them from the gaping grave.

For this let men revile my name;
No cross I shun, I fear no shame:
All hail, reproach! and welcome, pain!
Only thy terrors, Lord, restrain.

My life, my blood, I here present,
If for thy truth they may be spent:
Thy faithful witness will I be:
'Tis fix'd! I can do all through thee.

— Author Unknown

MY SAVIOUR'S LOVE FOR ME

The height of the highest mountain
The depth of the deepest sea
Is far too small a measure
Of the Saviour's love for me.

The glorious beauty of sunsets
That no artist can hope to paint
Is nothing compared to the glory
Awaiting the ransomed saint.

The mountains and seas shall vanish
And the sunsets fade from view,
But the believer shall live forever
In the land that's always new.

— William C. Fisher

MOTHER'S LOVE

Her love is like an island
  In life's ocean, vast and wide.
A peaceful, quiet shelter
  From the wind, the rain, the tide.

'Tis bound on the north by Hope,
  By Patience on the West,
By tender Counsel on the South
  And on the East by Rest.

Above it like a beacon light
  Shine Faith, and Truth, and Prayer;
And thro' the changing scenes of life
  I find a haven there.

— *Author Unknown*

O LOVE OF GOD

O love of God, how strong and true,
Eternal, and yet ever new;
Uncomprehended and unbought,
Beyond all knowledge and all thought.

O heavenly love, how precious still,
In days of weariness and ill,
In nights of pain and helplessness,
To hear, to comfort, and to bless!

O wide-embracing, wondrous love,
We read thee in the sky above;
We read thee in the earth below,
In seas that swell, and streams that
  flow.

We read thee best in Him who came
To bear for us the cross of shame,
Sent by the Father from on high,
Our life to live, our death to die.

O love of God, our shield and stay
Through all the perils of our way;
Eternal love, in Thee we rest,
Forever safe, forever blest.

— *Horatius Bonar*

SAVIOUR, TEACH ME DAY BY DAY

Saviour, teach me day by day,
Love's sweet lesson to obey;
Sweeter lesson cannot be —
Loving Him who first loved me.

With a childlike heart of love,
At Thy bidding may I move;
Prompt to serve and follow Thee —
Loving Him who first loved me.

Teach me all Thy steps to trace,
Strong to follow in Thy grace;
Learning how to love from Thee —
Loving Him who first loved me.

Love in loving finds employ,
In obedience all her joy;
Ever new that joy will be —
Loving Him who first loved me.

— *Jane E. Leesom*

MEDITATION

Holding a beggar's child
Against my heart,
Through blinding tears I see
That as I love the tiny, piteous thing,
So God loves me!

— *Toyohiko Kagawa*

LOVE

  My God is Love;
  My God is Love,
  Tender and deep;
I feel His close, sweet presence
  Looking down to see
  The beggar-baby
  Lying in my arms asleep.

— *Toyohiko Kagawa*

LOVE'S AIM

Love ever gives,
Forgives, outlives,
And ever stands with open hands,
And while it lives it gives.
For this is Love's prerogative
To give — and give — and give.

— Author Unknown

THE BEST CHOICE

He knows, He loves, He cares,
  Nothing this truth can dim,
He gives the very best to those
  Who leave the choice with Him.

— Author Unknown

ഗ

THE LOVE OF GOD

My God, how endless is thy love:
  Thy gifts are every evening new;
And morning mercies from above
  Gently distil like early dew.

Thou spread'st the curtains of the
    night,
  Great Guardian of my sleeping
    hours;
The sovereign word restores the light,
  And quickens all my drowsy powers.

I yield my powers to thy command;
  To thee I consecrate my days;
Perpetual blessings from thy hand
  Demand perpetual songs of praise.

— Isaac Watts

LOVE IS OF GOD

Beloved, let us love: love is of God;
In God alone hath love its true abode.

Beloved, let us love: for they who love,
They only, are His sons, born from
    above.

Beloved, let us love: for love is rest,
And he who loveth not abides unblest.

Beloved, let us love: for love is light,
And he who loveth not dwelleth in
    night.

Beloved, let us love: for only thus
Shall we behold that God who loveth
    us.

— Horatius Bonar

ഗ

HE CARES

I know that I can trust the Lord
  To keep the stars in place,
To grant the lark, the rose, the oak
  His wisdom and His grace.

I know that I can trust the Lord
  To send the morning light,
To turn each winter into spring,
  To rule each depth, each height.

I know that ev'rywhere I look
  I see His guiding hand,
More beauty, mercy, love, and faith
  Than I can understand.

Then why should I refuse to trust
  Those things I cannot see
To Him who knows tomorrow's needs?
  He cares for you and me.

— Phyllis C. Michael

ON WITH THE MESSAGE! ON, ON, AND ON!

On with the message! On with the light!
On to the regions still shrouded in night.
On to the nations which never have heard;
On with the life-giving, soul-saving Word.

On with the message! message of pow'r
Message to meet ev'ry need of the hour
On with the message o'er land and o'er sea;
On with the truth that can set sinners free.

On with the message! Carry it on.
Millions in darkness still pray for the dawn.
Millions for whom Christ's own Blood did atone
Die in their darkness, unreached, and alone.

On with the message! Haste thee away;
Soon cometh night, haste thee while 'tis day.
On with the message, by love's passion stirred;
On till each creature of Jesus has heard.

On with the message; strive more and more;
Soon will the days for proclaiming be o'er.
On to all lengths, to where none have yet gone;
On with the message! On, *on, and on!*

— *Wesley Duewel*

MISSIONARIES

Away in foreign lands they wondered how
    Their single word had power!
At home, the Christians, two or three, had met
    To pray an hour.

The weary ones had rest, the sad had joy
    That day; I wondered how!
A ploughman, singing at his work had prayed;
    Lord help them now.

— *Author Unknown*

485

THE MISSIONARY

An unknown dreamer dreamed concerning men,
  And what he saw in vision came to pass,
  For he, by faith, had stood on sea of glass
And heard the Voice, and then had said, Amen!
Thereat, he quickly turned from heaven to earth,
  The light of glory burning in his eyes,
  To speak what he had heard within the skies,
To preach redemption through the heavenly birth:

And so he saw what God saw from His throne,
  And thus he wrought according to God's plan,
And thence through years, though oft rejected, lone,
  He voiced God's message to his fellow-man:—
The dreamer died; they laid him 'neath the sod;
But now a countless host adores his God!

                                    —*Henry W. Frost*

STIR INTO FLAME

Stir me, oh, stir me, Lord — I care not how,
  But stir my heart in passion for the world;
Stir me to give, to go, but most to pray;
  Stir till the blood-red banner be unfurled
O'er lands that still in heathen darkness lie,
O'er deserts where no cross is lifted high.

Stir me, oh, stir me, Lord, till all my heart
  Is filled with strong compassion for these souls,
Till Thy compelling "must" drives me to pray,
  Till Thy constraining love reach to the poles.
Far North and South, is burning deep desire,
Till East and West are caught in love's great fire.

Stir me, oh, stir me, Lord, till prayer is pain;
  Till prayer is joy; till prayer turns into praise;
Stir me till heart and will and mind, yea, all
  Is wholly Thine to use through all the days;
Stir till I learn to pray exceedingly;
Stir till I learn to pray expectantly.

Stir me, oh, stir me, Lord; Thy heart was stirred
  By love's intensest fire, till Thou didst give
Thine only Son, Thy best beloved One,

E'en to the dreadful Cross, that I might live.
Stir me to give myself so back to Thee,
That Thou canst give Thyself again through me.

Stir me, oh, stir me, Lord, for I can see
    Thy glorious triumph day begin to break;
The dawn already gilds the eastern sky;
    O Church of Christ, awake! awake!
Oh, stir us, Lord, as heralds of that day,
For night is past — our King is on His way.

— Author Unknown

SICK

The world is sick —
Hot, with burning brow; now fevered, and now cold!
Seeking for things that only rust and mold;
Giving all it has for joys that soon grow old —
    The world is sick.

The world is sick —
Seeking for things that only hurt the soul,
Striving to obtain but reaching not its goal;
Like some storm-toss'd wave that breaks on yonder shoal —
    The world is sick.

The world is sick —
Having great desire for joys that last a day,
Madly seeking wealth that soon must know decay;
Blind to all the worth of things that last for aye —
    The world is sick.

The world is sick —
Hearing not the voice of God amid its din —
Seeking not the hand once nail-pierced for its sin —
Knowing not the peace of those who let Him in —
    The world is sick.

The world is sick —
Lo, a healing hand now waits to touch its brow,
Tenderly He speaks, "Oh, come to Me just now."
When at His feet the world shall humbly bow
    It shall be well.

— Haldor Lillenas

NOT GRIEVED FOR ISRAEL

"Not grieved for Israel!" canst thou
  stand
  Rejoicing in the light;
And nothing care for those who stray
  In darkest shades of night?

"Not grieved for Israel!" having lost
  Thy load of sin and shame,
Should'st thou not their salvation seek
  Through whom thy Saviour came?

"Not grieved for Israel!" thou wast
  healed,
  When broken, sick and sore,
How deep their wounds! Hast thou no
  balm
  On their sad hearts to pour?

"Not grieved for Israel!" When thy
  cup
  With mercy overflows,
Wilt thou not give from thy full store
  Some comfort for their woes?

Lo, Jesus grieves His flock to see
  All ruined, lost, undone,
And bids thee in the desert go
  To seek them one by one.

Oh, holy task, His Name to bear
  In all its healing power,
To "these His brethren," thus to haste
  Their glad redemption hour.

                    — Jesse F. Webb

THE CRIES!

Hark! the awful cries I hear,
Cries of sorrow, pain and fear,
Sounding far across the sea,
Crying, crying unto me.
In lone watches of the night,
In the dawn of morning's light,
In my work, in my prayer,
I can hear them everywhere.

Cries of little ones I hear,
Wails of mothers pierce my ear,
Groans from souls that long to know
Freedom from their awful woe.
Conscience sounds the awful knell
That their souls are doomed to hell;
Day and night they never cease
Seeking to obtain release.

To gods of wood and stone they pray,
Burning incense night and day;
Vows and vigils do they keep,
Vainly at the graves they weep;
But in these they cannot find
Power to break the chains that bind.
On in darkness still they grope,
Without God and without hope.

As I hear these wails of woe,
Jesus calls for me to go
Preach the Year of Jubilee;
Set the sin-bound captives free.
Tell them that the price is paid,
Every sacrifice is made;
If they only will believe
Peace and pardon they'll receive.

Dare I vain excuses make
While my Saviour's heart doth ache?
Aches to tell them of His love,
How He left His throne above,
And upon the cursed Tree
Shed the Blood that makes them free.
No! my talents now I bring
To the service of my King.

Gold and silver, with their shine,
Cannot quench this love of mine!
Friends and loved ones with their pleas
Tempt me not to live in ease!
For the wails of sin and woe,
And the Voice that calls to go
Fill my heart and spirit so
That I never will say no!

                    — Author Unknown

ONWARD!

Onward, Christian soldiers,
    Marching as to war,
With the cross of Jesus
    Going on before.
Christ, the royal Master,
    Leads against the foe;
Forward into battle,
    See, his banners go.

At the sign of triumph
    Satan's host doth flee;
On, then, Christian soldiers,
    On to victory!
Hell's foundations quiver
    At the shout of praise;
Brothers, lift your voices,
    Loud your anthems raise.

Like a mighty army
    Moves the Church of God;
Brothers, we are treading
    Where the saints have trod;
We are not divided,
    All one body we,
One in hope and doctrine,
    One in charity.

Crowns and thrones may perish,
    Kingdoms rise and wane,
But the Church of Jesus
    Constant will remain;
Gates of hell can never
    'Gainst that Church prevail;
We have Christ's own promise,
    And that cannot fail.

Onward, then, ye people,
    Join our happy throng,
Blend with ours your voices,
    In the triumph-song;
Glory, laud, and honor,
    Unto Christ the King;
This through countless ages
    Men and angels sing.

— *Sabine Baring-Gould*

THE CHRISTIAN HERALD

Ye Christian heralds, go, proclaim
Salvation through Immanuel's name;
To distant climes the tidings bear,
And plant the Rose of Sharon there.

He'll shield you with a wall of fire,
With flaming zeal your breast inspire,
Bid raging winds their fury cease,
And hush the tempest into peace.

And when our labors all are o'er,
Then we shall meet to part no more;
Meet, with the blood-bought throng to
    fall,
And crown our Jesus Lord of all.
                                — *Voke*

IN SPITE OF SORROW

In spite of sorrow, loss, and pain,
    Our course be onward still;
We sow on Burmah's barren plain,
    We reap on Zion's hill.
                    — *Adoniram Judson*

COMMISSIONED

Out from the realm of the glory-light
Into the far-away land of night;
Out of the bliss of worshipful song
Into the pain of hatred and wrong;
Out from the holy rapture above
Into the grief of rejected love;
Out from the life at the Father's side
Into the death of the crucified;
Out of high honor and into shame
The Master, willingly, gladly came:—
    And now, since He may not suffer
        anew,
    As the Father sent Him, so sendeth
        He you!
                        — *Henry W. Frost*

DISCIPLESHIP

I thought it hard that Christ should ask of me
To walk through life along a blood-marked way,
And thus it was, I shrank back, tremblingly,
Then paused, and bowed my head, and said Him, Nay!
But looking down I saw, with tear-dimmed eyes,
That all the blood-marks came from piercèd feet,
At which I learned, with sad yet glad surprise,
That they were proofs of love, enduring, sweet;
'Twas thus again I looked on Christ's dear face,
And once again began to follow on;—
Since then I've only thought of His great grace,
And fear of blood-marked ways is wholly gone.

— Henry W. Frost

ல

TRANSFORMED

A single touch of a gentle hand,
  A single word of a winsome voice,
And fishermen turned from sea to land
  To follow a Stranger, by willing choice;
They left their nets by the sunlit sea
To walk in the deserts of Galilee.

The Master led them by dusty ways
  And over the lonely mountain heights;
The sun beat hot through the lifeless days
  And crowds pressed close thro' the long-drawn nights;
They were bond-slaves now, where once they were free,
But they ne'er turned back to their nets by the sea.

They followed on to the city fair,
  On Judah's heights with its walls and towers,
With its glittering temple in whitened square
  Where priests said prayers thro' the countless hours;
They went with their Master to Calvary,
And they clave to Him there in His agony.

They were left alone; but they still pressed on —
  E'en as He had said — to the distant lands,
Yea, on and on, till their strength was gone
  And they sank to die on the desert sands;—
Ah, they never forgot blest Galilee
And the voice and the hand by the sunlit sea!

— Henry W. Frost

AFRICA

I slept. I dreamed. I seemed to climb a hard, ascended track
And just behind me labored one whose face was black.
I pitied him, but hour by hour he gained upon my path.
He stood beside me, stood upright, and then I turned in wrath:
"Go back," I cried, "what right have you to stand beside me here?"
I paused, struck dumb with fear, for lo! the black man was not there—
But Christ stood in his place!
And oh! the pain, the pain, the pain that looked from that dear face!

— *Author Unknown*

COMPASSION FOR THE LOST

Sudden, before my inward, open vision,
  Millions of faces crowded up to view —
Sad eyes that said, "For us is no provision,
  Give us your Saviour, too."

Sorrowful women's faces, hungry, yearning,
  Wild with despair, or dark with sin and dread,
Worn with long weeping for the unreturning,
  Hopeless, uncomforted.

"Give us," they cry, "your cup of consolation,
  Never to our outstretched hands is passed;
We long for the Desire of every nation,
  And, oh, we die so fast."

"Does He not love us, too, this gracious Master?
  'Tis from your hand alone we can receive
The bounty of His grace; oh, send it faster
  That we may take and live."

"Master," I said, as from a dream awaking,
  "Is this the service Thou dost show to me?
Dost Thou to me entrust Thy Bread for breaking
  To those who cry for Thee?

"Dear heart of love, canst Thou forgive the blindness
  That let Thy child sit selfish and at ease
By the full table of Thy lovingkindness,
  And take no thought for these?

"As Thou hast loved me let me love, returning
  To those dark souls the grace Thou givest me;
And, oh, to me impart Thy deathless yearning,
  To draw the lost to Thee."

— *Author Unknown*

ALONE?

"If I have eaten my morsel alone,"
 The patriarch spoke with scorn;
What would he think of the Church
  were he shown
Heathendom — huge, forlorn,
Godless, Christless, with soul unfed,
While the Church's ailment is fullness
  of bread,
 Eating her morsel alone?

"Freely ye have received, so give,"
 He bade, who hath given us all.
How shall the soul in us longer live
 Deaf to their starving call,
For whom the blood of the Lord was
  shed,
And His body broken to give them
  bread,
 If we eat our morsel alone!

— *Archbishop Alexander*

A MISSIONARY CRY

A hundred thousand souls a day,
Are passing one by one away,
 In Christless guilt and gloom.
Without one ray of hope or light,
With future dark as endless night,
 They're passing to their doom.

O Holy Ghost, Thy people move,
Baptize their hearts with faith and love,
 And consecrate their gold.
At Jesus' feet their millions pour,
And all their ranks unite once more,
 As in the days of old.

Armies of pray'r your promise claim,
Prove the full pow'r of Jesus' name,
 And take the victory.
Your conq'ring Captain leads you on,
The glorious fight may still be won,
 This very century.

The Master's coming draweth near,
The Son of man will soon appear,
 His kingdom is at hand.
But ere that glorious day can be,
This Gospel of the kingdom, we
 Must preach in ev'ry land.

Oh, let us then His coming haste,
Oh, let us end this awful waste
 Of souls that never die.
A thousand millions still are lost,
A Saviour's blood has paid the cost,
 Oh, hear their dying cry.

They're passing, passing fast away,
A hundred thousand souls a day,
 In Christless guilt and gloom,
O Church of Christ, what wilt thou
  say
When in the awful judgment day,
 They charge thee with their doom?

— *A. B. Simpson*

EVANGELIZE!

Give us a watchword for the hour,
A thrilling word, a word of power,
A battlecry, a flaming breath
That calls to conquest or to death.

A word to rouse the Church from rest,
To heed the Master's high behest,
The call is given: Ye hosts arise,
Our watchword is, *Evangelize!*

The glad Evangel now proclaim,
Through all the earth, in Jesus' Name.
This word is ringing through the skies:
Evangelize! Evangelize!

To dying men, a fallen race,
Make known the gift of Gospel grace.
The world that now in darkness lies,
Evangelize! Evangelize!

— *Author Unknown*

WHAT WOULD HE SAY?

If He should come today,
And find my hands so full
Of future plans, however fair,
In which my Savior has no share,
What would He say?

If He should come today,
And find my love so cold,
My faith so very weak and dim,
I had not even looked for Him,
What would He say?

If He should come today,
And find I had not told
One soul about my Heavenly Friend
Whose blessings all my way attend,
What would He say?

If He should come today,
Would I be glad — quite glad?
Remembering He had died for all,
And none, thro' me, had heard His call,
What would He say?

— *Grace E. Troy*

ors

SOLDIERS OF THE CROSS, ARISE

Soldiers of the cross, arise,
  Gird you with your armor bright;
Mighty are your enemies,
  Hard the battle ye must fight.
O'er a faithless fallen world
  Raise your banner in the sky,
Let it float there wide unfurled,
  Bear it onward, lift it high!

'Mid the homes of want and woe,
  Strangers to the living Word,
Let the Saviour's herald go,
  Let the voice of hope be heard.
Where the shadows deepest lie,
  Carry truth's unsullied ray;
Where are crimes of blackest dye,
  There the saving sign display.

To the weary and the worn
  Tell of realms where sorrows cease;
To the outcast and forlorn
  Speak of mercy and of peace.
Guard the helpless, seek the strayed,
  Comfort trouble, banish grief;
With the Spirit's sword arrayed,
  Scatter sin and unbelief.

Be the banner still unfurled,
  Bear it bravely still abroad,
Till the kingdoms of the Lord.
Praise with songs of holy glee,
  Saints of earth and heavenly host,
Godhead one in persons three,
  Father, Son, and Holy Ghost.

— *William Walsham How*

ors

THY NEIGHBOR

Who is thy neighbor? He whom thou
  Hast power to aid or bless,
Whose aching heart or burning brow
  Thy soothing hand may press.

Thy neighbor? 'Tis the fainting poor
  Whose eye with want is dim.
Oh, enter thou his humble door
  With aid and peace for him.

Thy neighbor? He who drinks the cup
  When sorrow drowns the brim;
With words of high sustaining hope
  Go thou and comfort him.

Thy neighbor? 'Tis the weary slave,
  Fettered in mind and limb;
He hath no hope this side the grave.
  Go thou and ransom him.

Thy neighbor? Pass no mourner by.
  Perhaps thou canst redeem
A breaking heart from misery.
  Go share thy lot with him.

— *Author Unknown*

OBEDIENCE

If ever Jesus has need of me,
  Somewhere in the field of sin,
I'll go where the darkest places be,
  And let the sunshine in,
I'll be content with the lowliest place
  To earth's remotest rim;
I know I'll see His smiling face,
  If it's done with a thought of Him.

I'll fill each day with little things
  As the passing moments fly,
The tendril which to the great oak
    clings
  Grows strong as it climbs on high.
I'll trust my Lord, tho' I cannot see,
  Nor e'er let my faith grow dim;
He'll smile, and that's enough for me,
  If it's done with a thought of Him.

— *Author Unknown*

HARK! THE VOICE OF JESUS CALLING

Hark! the voice of Jesus calling —
  "Who will go and work today?
Fields are white, the harvest waiting—
  Who will bear the sheaves away?"
Loud and long the Master calleth,
  Rich reward He offers free:
Who will answer, gladly saying,
  "Here am I, O Lord: send me"?
Who will answer, gladly saying,
  "Here am I, O Lord; send me"?

If you cannot cross the ocean,
  And the other lands explore,
You can find the needy nearer,
  You can help them at your door;
If you cannot speak like angels,
  If you cannot preach like Paul,
You can tell the love of Jesus,
  You can say He died for all.
You can tell the love of Jesus,
  You can say He died for all.

While the souls of men are dying,
  And the Master calls for you,
Let none hear you idly saying,
  "There is nothing I can do."
Gladly take the task He gives you,
  Let His work your pleasure be;
Answer quickly when He calleth,
  "Here am I, O Lord: send me."
Answer quickly when He calleth,
  "Here am I, O Lord: send me."

— *Daniel March*

THE MASTER'S CALL

Have you heard the Master's Call?
  Will you go forsaking all?
Millions still in sin and shame
  Ne'er have heard the Saviour's
    Name
Some may give and some may pray,
  But for you He calls today;
Will you answer: "Here am I,"
  Or must Jesus pass you by?

Have you heard their bitter cry?
  Can you bear to see them die,
Thousands who in darkest night,
  Never yet have seen the Light?
Soon 'twill be too late to go
  And your love for Jesus show;
Oh, then, quickly speed away,
  Tarry not another day.

What if you refuse to go?
  Someone then will never know
Of the Saviour kind and true,
  And the blame will rest on you.
Will you then, forsaking all,
  Gladly heed the Master's Call;
Answer quickly, "Lord, send me
  To the lands beyond the sea"?

— *Oswald J. Smith*

A SOUL

A living soul, how priceless!
    Its value is untold.
Invisible, immortal,
    Worth more than purest gold.
And oh, the souls are countless
    Upon life's busy way
Who know not Christ, our Savior,
    Who never stop to pray.
They rush toward sin's gay glitter,
    Its glaring, garish light
These souls of men are marching
    To everlasting night.

O go ye into all the world,
    Is his divine command.
I hear his voice so tender,
    I see his loving hand
Outstretched in power and blessing
    The fallen ones to raise.
Then may we do his bidding
    Through all our early days;
And when the sheaves are gathered
    Before his throne that day,
May there be souls most precious
    Whom we have shown the way.

— *Bertha Prince Vander Ark*

SUCCESS OF THE GOSPEL

The morning light is breaking;
    The darkness disappears;
The sons of earth are waking
    To penitential tears.
Each breeze that sweeps the ocean
    Brings tidings from afar,
Of nations in commotion,
    Prepared for Zion's war.

Rich dews of grace come o'er us
    In many a gentle shower,
And brighter scenes before us
    Are opening every hour:

Each cry, to Heaven going,
    Abundant answer brings,
And heavenly gales are blowing,
    With peace upon their wings.

See heathen nations bending
    Before the God we love,
And thousand hearts ascending
    In gratitude above;
While sinners, now confessing,
    The gospel call obey,
And seek the Saviour's blessing,
    A nation in a day.

Blest river of salvation,
    Pursue thy onward way;
Flow thou to every nation,
    Nor in thy richness stay:
Stay not till all the lowly
    Triumphant reach their home;
Stay not till all the holy
    Proclaim, "The Lord is come!"

— *S. F. Smith*

I KNOW A NAME

I know a soul that is steeped in sin,
    That no man's art can cure;
But I know a Name, a Name, a Name
    That can make that soul all pure.

I know a life that is lost to God,
    Bound down by the things of earth;
But I know a Name, a Name, a Name
    That can bring that soul new birth.

I know of lands that are sunk in
        shame,
    Of hearts that faint and tire;
But I know a Name, a Name, a Name
    That can set those lands on fire.

Its sound is a brand, its letters flame,
    Like glowing tongues of fire.
But I know a Name, a Name, a Name
    Of which the world ne'er tires.

— *Author Unknown*

FROM GREENLAND'S ICY MOUNTAINS

From Greenland's icy mountains,
    From India's coral strand,
Where Afric's sunny fountains
    Roll down their golden sand;
From many an ancient river,
    From many a palmy plain,
They call us to deliver
    Their land from error's chain.

What though the spicy breezes
    Blow soft o'er Ceylon's isle,
Though every prospect pleases,
    And only man is vile;
In vain with lavish kindness
    The gifts of God are strown;
The heathen, in his blindness,
    Bows down to wood and stone.

Shall we, whose souls are lighted
    With wisdom from on high,
Shall we to men benighted
    The lamp of life deny?
Salvation! O Salvation!
    The joyful sound proclaim,
Till earth's remotest nation
    Has learned Messiah's name.

Waft, waft, ye winds, his story,
    And you, ye waters, roll,
Till, like a sea of glory,
    It spreads from pole to pole;
Till o'er our ransomed nature,
    The Lamb for sinners slain,
Redeemer, King, Creator,
    In bliss returns to reign.

— *Reginald Heber*

MISSIONS

Heralds of Christ, who bear the King's commands,
Immortal tidings in your mortal hands,
Pass on and carry swift the news ye bring:
Make straight, make straight the highway of the King.

Through desert ways, dark fen, and deep morass,
Through jungles, sluggish seas, and mountain pass,
Build ye the road, and falter not, nor stay;
Prepare across the earth the King's highway.

Where once the crooked trail in darkness wound
Let marching feet and joyous song resound,
Where burn the funeral pyres, and censers swing,
Make straight, make straight the highway of the King.

Lord, give us faith, and strength the road to build,
To see the promise of the day fulfilled,
When war shall be no more and strife shall cease
Upon the highway of the Prince of Peace.

— *Laura S. Copenhaver*

THE CALL OF THE EAST

Do you hear the East a-calling,
  Day by day?
Do you hear its plaint a-falling,
  Far away?
Crying out, since sore distrest,
Pleading, pleading to be blest,
Needy East to tardy West;—
  "Do not stay!"

See, the peach-trees high a-growing,
  Fresh and fair;
See, the cherry blossoms blowing
  Through the air;
Lo, the spices breathe forth balm,
Sweet the shade of fronded palm,
In the bright, warm tropic calm,
  Over there.

Hark, the sound of merry laughter,
  Bright and clear,
Happy tale, and then the after
  Happier cheer;
Boys and girls with sparkling eyes,
Women showing glad surprise,
Men more grave, since gravely wise,
  Far and near.

But beneath the beauteous brightness,
  Dark and death,
And behind the heart's glad lightness,
  Bated breath;—
Ah, they bow to gods of stone
Which for sin can ne'er atone;
Hear ye not the cry and moan,
  As God saith?

Yea, the East is calling, calling
  'Cross the seas,
For the shadows are a-falling
  As life flees;
Dark the day, in spite of light,
Darker still the long-drawn night,
Shadows sinful souls affright,
  Such as these.

Coming, coming, I am coming,
  I'll not stay,
Love shall conquer fear benumbing,
  I'll away;—
Yea, the East shall meet the West,
Hear, O East, thou shalt be blest,
Jesus, yet will give thee rest;
  Glorious day!

  — Henry W. Frost

Ⱄⲟ

INTERCESSION

Oh, for a passionate passion for souls!
  Oh, for a pity that yearns!
Oh, for a love that loves unto death!
  Oh, for a fire that burns!
Oh, for the pure prayer power that
    prevails,
  That pours itself out for the lost;
Victorious prayer in the Conqueror's
    Name,
  Oh, for a Pentecost!

Infinite Saviour, in mighty compassion
  Take Thy poor child tonight!
That which she hath not in tenderness
    give her,
  Teach her to pray and to fight.
Cost what it may of self crucifixion
  So that Thy will be done;
Cost what it may of loneliness after
  So only souls be won!

Jesus, my Saviour, beyond telling rare
  The jewel I ask of Thee.
So much it meaneth, this talisman,
    prayer —
  Wilt Thou give it to me?

Thou art speaking now. Dost Thou
    give to me
  A choice, as in olden time?
Dear Lord, wilt Thou put the end of
  the rope

That pulleth God's prayer-bell chime
Into my hand, with Thine enfolding,
   That nothing may be of me?
When it soundeth above, our Father
      will know
   It is rung, O Beloved, by Thee.

— Author Unknown

ᕦᕤ

HE SENT THEM OUT

He sent them, disinherited,
despised, unknown, dispossessed;
he sent them out as strangers
in the world, east and west.

He sent them forth to change the
      world,
these unimpressive peasants matched
against the mind of Greece; he hurled
them at the iron breast of Rome.

And having set them in array against
such odds, he saw them wrest
the world from the grip of darkness;
he watched them set the cross like fire
upon a thousand hills.
                  He saw them span
the years, their names like stars
burned in the history of man.

Ask not only whether
we believe in Christ; but ask again
if we will share His faith in men!

—Lon Woodrum

ᕦᕤ

THERE IS A MAN ON THE CROSS

Whenever there is silence around me
By day or by night —
I am startled by a cry.
It came down from the cross —
The first time I heard it.
I went out and searched —
And found a Man in the throes of
      crucifixion,

And I said, "I will take You down,"
And I tried to take the nails out of His
      feet.
But He said, "Let them be
For I cannot be taken down
Until every man, every woman, and
      every child
Come together to take Me down."
And I said, "But I cannot hear You
      cry.
What can I do?"
And He said, "Go about the world —
Tell everyone that you meet —
There is a Man on the cross
Waiting for them to take Him down."

— Elizabeth Cheney

ᕦᕤ

SPREAD THE WORD

Lord of all pow'r and might,
Father of love and light,
Speed on Thy Word:
O let the Gospel sound
All the wide world around,
Wherever man is found;
God speed His Word.

Lo, what embattled foes,
Stern in their hate, oppose
God's holy Word:
One for His truth we stand,
Strong in His own right hand,
Firm as a martyr band;
God shield His Word.

Onward shall be our course,
Despite of fraud or force;
God is before;
His Word ere long shall run
Free as the noonday sun;
His purpose must be done;
God bless His Word.

— Hugh Stowell

NATURE

As a fond mother, when the day is o'er
  Leads by the hand her little child to bed,
  Half willing, half reluctant to be led,
  And leave his broken playthings on the floor,
Still gazing at them through the open door,
  Nor wholly reassured and comforted
  By promises of others in their stead,
  Which, though more splendid, may not please him more;
So Nature deals with us, and takes away
  Our playthings one by one, and by the hand
  Leads us to rest so gently, that we go
Scarce knowing if we wish to go or stay,
  Being too full of sleep to understand
  How far the unknown transcends the what we know.

                — Henry Wadsworth Longfellow

TAKE MY HEART

Take my heart
and pull it all apart
and you will find these things:
the sudden whir of wings,
flame-red and lemon-yellow flowers,
dusk and dawn and arrowy showers . . . .
you will find a few symphonies,
and the wind leaning against tall trees . . . .
mountains asleep in moon-fire,
white stars flickering over an old church-spire,
the wild gander's bugle-cry . . . .
sails quivering on a lilac sky . . . .
winding-roads and river-bends . . .
the smell of new-turned sod . . . .
but mostly you will find
the faces of my friends
and the dream of God.

                —Lon Woodrum

HIGH FLIGHT

Oh! I have slipped the surly bonds of earth
   And danced the skies on laughter-silvered wings;
Sunward I've climbed, and joined the tumbling mirth
   Of sun-split clouds — and done a hundred things
You have not dreamed of — wheeled and soared and swung
   High in the sunlit silence. Hov'ring there,
I've chased the shouting wind along, and flung
   My eager craft through footless halls of air.

Up, up the long, delirious, burning blue
   I've topped the wind-swept heights with easy grace
Where never lark, or even eagle flew —
   And, while with silent lifting mind I've trod
The high untrespassed sanctity of space,
   Put out my hand and touched the face of God.

         — *Pilot Officer John Gillespie Magee, Jr., R.C.A.F.*

                ∽

GOD'S AFTERMATH

The mower's scythe had passed o'er summer fields,
   The grass lay bleeding 'neath the summer sun;
Strong hands swift stored the harvest's wealthy yields,
   And left the fields deserted, one by one,

Their glory gone, their beauty swept away,
   Still smarting from the swift, keen cut of death,
Their woe the sharp, short work of one brief day
   That dawned with sunshine in its balmy breath.

Methought they pleaded to the gentle sky
   That smiled above them, bending o'er their grief,
A voiceless pleading in a tearless cry,
   A soundless sob soft sighing for relief.

And heaven heard the fervour of their call,
   And sent them healing balm at eventide,
Sweet raindrops breathing blessing in their fall,
   And weeping gently o'er their wounded pride.

Thus shall He come as rain on new-mown grass,
   And withered hopes spring up to grace His path,
New life be born where'er His footsteps pass,
   And tender grass spring forth — "God's Aftermath."

         — *Frances Brook*

Who Runs May Read

There is a book, who runs may read,
  Which heavenly truth imparts,
And all the lore its scholars need,
  Pure eyes and Christian hearts.

The works of God above, below,
  Within us and around,
Are pages in that book, to show
  How God himself is found.

The glorious sky, embracing all,
  Is like the Maker's love,
Wherewith encompassed, great and
    small
In peace and order move.

The moon above, the Church below,
  A wondrous race they run,
But all their radiance, all their glow,
  Each borrows of its sun.

The Saviour lends the light and heat
  That crowns his holy hill;
The saints, like stars, around his seat,
  Perform their courses still.

The saints above are stars in heaven—
  What are the saints on earth?
Like trees they stand whom God has
    given,
Our Eden's happy birth.

Faith is their fixed unswerving root,
  Hope their unfading flower,
Fair deeds of charity their fruit,
  The glory of their bower.

The dew of heaven is like thy grace,
  It steals in silence down;
But where it lights, the favored place
  By richest fruits is known.

One Name above all glorious names
  With its ten thousand tongues,
The everlasting sea proclaims,
  Echoing angelic songs.

The raging fire, the roaring wind,
  Thy boundless power display:
But in the gentler breeze we find
  Thy spirit's viewless way.

Two worlds are ours: 'tis only sin
  Forbids us to descry
The mystic heaven and earth within,
  Plain as the sea and sky.

Thou, who hast given me eyes to see
  And love this sight so fair,
Give me a heart to find out thee,
  And read thee everywhere.

        — John Keble

Spring Forever

Spring has returned again this year,
  In spite of long delay,
For near the garden's edge I saw
  A robin yesterday.

Although the scene to which he came
  Is rather rough and bleak,
He hopes, as I, that it will be
  Much brighter by next week.

I heard him sing at dawn today,
  As if his heart would burst
With joy, because he sees ahead
  The best, and not the worst.

And as above the melting snow
  Those tones of triumph float,
I find within my heart today,
  A warm responsive note,

A note of joy no sorrow's night
  Or wintry wind can sever;
I sing — for in my Father's house
  It will be spring forever!

      — Alice Hansche Mortenson

O Love of God Most Full

O Love of God most full,
O Love of God most free,
Come warm my heart, come fill my
    soul,
Come lead me unto Thee!

Warm as the glowing sun
So shines Thy love on me,
It wraps me 'round with kindly care,
It draws me unto Thee.

The wildest sea is calm,
The tempest brings no fear,
The darkest night is full of light,
Because Thy love is near.

I triumph over sin,
I put temptation down;
The love of God doth give me strength
To win the victor's crown.
— *Oscar Clute*

ༀ

The Olive-Tree

Said an ancient hermit, bending
    Half in prayer upon his knee,
"Oil I need for midnight watching,
    I desire an olive-tree."

Then he took a tender sapling,
    Planted it before his cave,
Spread his trembling hands above it,
    As his benison he gave.

But he thought, the rain it needeth,
    That the root may drink and swell:
"God! I pray thee send thy showers!"
    So a gentle shower fell.

"Lord! I ask for beams of summer,
    Cherishing this little child."
Then the dripping clouds divided,
    And the sun looked down and
        smiled.

"Send it frost to brace its tissues,
    O my God!" the hermit cried.

Then the plant was bright and hoary,
    But at evensong it died.

Went the hermit to a brother
    Sitting in his rocky cell:
"Thou an olive-tree possessest;
    How is this, my brother, tell?

"I have planted one, and prayed,
    Now for sunshine, now for rain;
God hath granted each petition,
    Yet my olive-tree hath slain!

Said the other, "I intrusted
    To its God my little tree;
He who made knew what it needed
    Better than a man like me.

"Laid I on him no condition,
    Fixed not ways and means; so I
Wonder not my olive thriveth,
    Whilst thy olive-tree did die."
        — *Sabine Baring-Gould*

ༀ

To This Lilac-Scented Room

I cannot roam the woods this year,
    I cannot climb the hills,
But still there's something in the spring
    That all my being thrills.

I cannot lie upon the grass
    And look up through the trees,
But through the open window
    I can feel the fragrant breeze.

And all the places that I love
    And somehow long to see,
Through memory's wide open door
    Have come to visit me.

And, looking out, the swaying trees,
    Like comrades wave and call
A friendly greeting, while the birds
    Spread music over all.

And though I'm very quiet now,
    My heart is on the wing,
For to this lilac-scented room
    Dear God has brought the spring!
        — *Alice Hansche Mortenson*

LOVE TO GOD

Praise to God, immortal praise,
For the love that crowns our days!
Bounteous source of every joy,
Let thy praise our tongues employ.

For the blessings of the field,
For the stores the gardens yield;
For the vine's exalted juice,
For the generous olive's use;

Flocks that whiten all the plain;
Yellow sheaves of ripened grain;
Clouds that drop their fattening dews;
Suns that temperate warmth diffuse:

All the Spring with bounteous hand
Scatters o'er the smiling land;
All that liberal Autumn pours
From her rich o'erflowing stores:

These to thee, my God, we owe,
Source whence all our blessings flow;
And for these my soul shall raise
Grateful vows and solemn praise.

Yet, should rising whirlwinds tear
From its stem the ripening ear;
Should the fig-tree's blasted shoot
Drop her green, untimely fruit;

Should the vine put forth no more,
Nor the olive yield her store;
Tho' the sickening flocks should fall,
And the herds desert the stall;

Should thine altered hand restrain
The early and the latter rain;
Blast each opening bud of joy,
And the rising year destroy;—

Yet to thee my soul should raise
Grateful vows and solemn praise;
And, when every blessing's flown,
Love thee for thyself alone.

— *Anna Letitia Barbauld*

NATURE NO SELF-ACTING INSTRUMENT

So soberly and softly
The seasons tread their round,
So surely seeds of autumn
In spring-time clothe the ground,
Amid their measured music
What watchful ear can hear
God's voice amidst the garden?
Yet, hush! for he is here!

No mere machine is nature,
Wound up and left to play,
No wind-harp swept at random
By airs that idly stray;
A spirit sways the music,
A hand is on the chords,
Oh, bow thy head and listen,—
That hand, it is the Lord's!

— *Elizabeth (Rundle) Charles*

❧

IN THE EARLY HOURS

Did He smell the scents of the morn-
ing,
The dew-wet grass and the hay,
As down He came in the dawning,
From the hill where He went to pray?
Did He hear the birds in the branches,
And the soft little sounds of sheep,
As He passed the quiet houses,
Where the people lay asleep?

Sometimes in the early morning hours,
As I watch the stars grow dim,
I smell the scent of the unseen flowers,
And I often think of Him.
When He prayed for those who should
believe,
All down the years to be,
I like to think as He turned to leave,
That He spared a thought for me.

— *Dawn Finlay*

UNDER THE SNOW

It is pleasant to think, just under the snow,
  That stretches so bleak and blank and cold,
Are beauty and warmth that we cannot know,—
  Green fields and leaves and blossoms of gold.

Yes, under this frozen and dumb expanse,
  Ungladdened by bee or bird or flower,
A world where the leaping fountains glance,
  And the buds expand, is waiting its hour.

It is hidden now; not a glimmer breaks
  Thro' the hard blue ice and the sparkling drift,
The world shrinks back from the downy flakes
  Which out of the folds of the night-cloud sift.

But as fair and real a world it is
  As any that rolls in the upper blue;
If you wait, you will hear its melodies,
  And see the sparkle of fount and dew.

And often now when the skies are wild,
  And hoarse and sullen the night winds blow.
And lanes and hollows with drifts are piled,
  I think of the violets under the snow.

I look in the wild-flower's tremulous eye,
  I hear the chirp of the ground bird brown;
A breath from the budding grove steals by,
  And the swallows are dipping above the town.

So there, from the outer sense concealed,
  It lies, shut in by a veil of snow;
But there, to the inward eye revealed,
  Are boughs that blossom, and flowers that glow.

The lily shines on its bending stem,
  The crocus opens its April gold,
And the rose up-tosses its diadem
  Against the floor of the winter's cold.

And that other world, to my soul I say,
  That veiled and mystic world of the dead,
Is no farther away on any day
  Than the lilies just under the snow we tread.

                                        —T. Hempstead

THE CAMP HYMN

God, who touchest earth with beauty,
  Make me lovely too;
With Thy Spirit re-create me,
  Make my heart anew.

Like Thy springs and running waters,
  Make me crystal pure;
Like Thy rocks of towering grandeur,
  Make me strong and sure.

Like Thy dancing waves in sunlight,
  Make me glad and free;
Like the straightness of the pine trees
  Let me upright be.

Like the arching of the heavens,
  Lift my thoughts above;
Turn my dreams to noble action —
  Ministries of love.

God, who touchest earth with beauty,
  Make me lovely too;
Keep me ever, by Thy Spirit,
  Pure and strong and true.

— *Mary S. Edgar*

DAY IS DYING IN THE WEST

Day is dying in the west;
Heaven is touching earth with rest;
Wait and worship while the night
Sets her evening lamps alight
  Through all the sky.
Holy, holy, holy, Lord God of Hosts!
Heaven and earth are full of thee!

Lord of life, beneath the dome
Of the universe, thy home,
Gather us who seek thy face
To the fold of thy embrace,
  For thou art nigh.
Holy, holy, holy, Lord God of Hosts!
Heaven and earth are full of thee!

When forever from our sight
Pass the stars, the day, the night,
Lord of angels, on our eyes
Let eternal morning rise,
  And shadows end.
Holy, holy, holy, Lord God of Hosts!
Heaven and earth are full of thee!

— *Mary A. Lathbury*

OMNIPRESENCE

A thousand sounds, and each a joyful sound;
The dragon flies are humming as they please,
The humming birds are humming all around,
The clithra all alive with buzzing bees,
Each playful leaf its separate whisper found,
As laughing winds went rustling thro' the grove;
And I saw thousands of such sights as these,
And heard a thousand sounds of joy and love.

And yet so dull I was, I did not know
That He was there who all this love displayed,
I did not think how He who loved us so
Shared all my joy, was glad that I was glad;
And all because I did not hear the word
In English accents says, "It is the Lord."

— *Edward Everett Hale*

THE LEAVES

The leaves are fading and falling,
  The winds are rough and wild,
The birds have ceased their calling,
  But let me tell you, my child.

Though day by day as it closes,
  Doth darker and colder grow,
The roots of the bright red roses,
  Will keep alive in the snow.

And when the winter is over,
  The boughs will get back new leaves,
The quail come back to the clover,
  And the swallows back to the eaves;

The robin will wear on his bosom,
  A vest that is bright and new,
And the loveliest wayside blossom
  Will shine with the sun and dew.

The leaves, today, are swishing,
  The brooks are all dry and dumb;
But let me tell you, darling,
  The spring will surely come.

There must be rough cold weather,
  And winds and rains so wild;
Not all good things together,
  Come to us here, my child.

So, when some dear joy loses
  Its beauteous summer glow,
Think how the roots of the roses
  Are kept alive in the snow.

— *Alice Cary*

ᐦᐧ

ANEMONE
(Written on "Gordon's Calvary")

I gathered a red anemone,
On the very slopes of Calvary,
Red as the blood He shed for me,
When I was yet His enemy!

— *Dawn Finlay*

MY GARDEN

A garden is a lovesome thing, God wot!
Rose plot,
Fringed pool,
Ferned grot —
The veriest school
Of peace; and yet the fool
Contends that God is not —
Not God! in gardens! when the eve is
  cool?
Nay, but I have a sign;
'Tis very sure God walks in mine.

— *Thomas Edward Brown*

ᐦᐧ

TREES

In every path of timber you
Will always find a tree or two
That would have fallen long ago,
Borne down by wind or age or snow,
Had not another neighbor tree
Held out its arms in sympathy
And caught the tree that the storm had
  hurled
To earth. So, neighbors, is the world.
In every patch of timber stand
Samaritans of forest land,
The birch, the maple, oak and pine,
The fir, the cedar, all in line!
In every wood unseen, unknown,
They bear their burdens of their own
And bear as well another form,
Some neighbor stricken in the storm.
Shall trees be nobler to their kind
Than men, who boast the noble mind;
Shall there exist within the wood
This great eternal brotherhood
Of oak and pine, of hill and fen,
And not within the hearts of men?
God grant that men are like to these,
And brothers, brotherly as trees.

— *Author Unknown*

EVERY YEAR

Oh, every year hath its winter,
  And every year hath its rain —
But a day is always coming
  When the birds go north again.

When new leaves swell in the forest,
  And grass springs green on the plain,
And alders' veins turn crimson —
And the birds go north again.

Oh, every heart hath its sorrow,
  And every heart hath its pain —
But a day is always coming
  When the birds go north again.

'Tis the sweetest thing to remember,
  If courage be on the wane,
When the cold, dark days are over —
  Why, the birds go north again.

— *Author Unknown*

A PRAYER

Teach me, Father, how to go
Softly as the grasses grow;
Hush my soul to meet the shock
Of the wild world as a rock;
But my spirit, propt with power,
Make as simple as a flower.
Let the dry heart fill its cup,
Like a poppy looking up;
Let life lightly wear her crown,
Like a poppy looking down,
When its heart is filled with dew,
And its life begins anew.

Teach me, Father, how to be
Kind and patient as a tree.
Joyfully the crickets croon
Under shady oak at noon;

Beetle, on his mission bent,
Tarries in that cooling tent.
Let me, also, cheer a spot,
Hidden field or garden grot —
Place where passing souls can rest
On the way and be their best.

— *Edwin Markham*

FOR THE BEAUTY OF THE EARTH

For the beauty of the earth,
For the glory of the skies,
For the love which from our birth
Over and around us lies:

For the wonder of each hour
Of the day and of the night,
Hill and vale, and tree and flower,
Sun and moon, and stars of light:

For the joy of human love,
Brother, sister, parent, child,
Friends on earth, and friends above;
For all gentle thoughts and mild:

For Thy church, that evermore
Lifteth holy hands above,
Off'ring up on every shore
Her pure sacrifice of love:

For Thyself, best Gift Divine!
To our race so freely given;
For that great, great love of Thine,
Peace on earth, and joy in heaven:

Lord of all, to Thee we raise
This our hymn of grateful praise.
  Amen.

— *Folliott S. Pierpont*

Even in These Dying Leaves

The many-colored fires of fall
upon a thousand hills confess
a burning creed: that beauty, too,
is God's, along with all
things true and holy; even in
these dying leaves is loveliness.

Is not this autumn-death prophetic
that the resurrection, Spring,
will give us leaves again, and bring
us back the other things that live
and leap and fly and sing?

Did not high beauty burn in Him
who turned the cross on which He
        bled
into a shining glory? Even His great
        dying
was the certain prophesying
of His triumph over death, thus giving
men assurance God is God, not of the
        dead,
but of the living.   — Lon Woodrum

The Heavens (Psalm 19)

The spacious firmament on high,
With all the blue ethereal sky,
And spangled heavens, a shining frame,
Their great Original proclaim.
The unwearied sun, from day to day,
Does his Creator's power display,
And publishes to every land
The work of an Almighty hand.

Soon as the evening shades prevail,
The moon takes up the wondrous tale,
And nightly to the listening earth
Repeats the story of her birth;
Whilst all the stars that round her
        burn,
And all the planets in their turn,
Confirm the tidings as they roll,
And spread the truth from pole to pole.

What though in solemn silence all
Move round the dark terrestrial ball;
What though no real voice or sound
Amidst their radiant orbs be found;
In reason's ear they all rejoice,
And utter forth a glorious voice,
Forever singing as they shine,
"The hand that made us is divine."

                    — Joseph Addison

Pippa's Song

The year's at the spring,
And day's at the morn;
Morning's at seven;
The hill-side's dew-pearl'd;
The lark's on the wing;
The snail's on the thorn;
God's in His heaven —
All's right with the world!

                    — Robert Browning

Twenty-third Psalm

Beside still waters,
To lie, in pastures green . . .
But no, we go more often
Where grass is seldom seen.
On super-ways, or sky-ways
On super-sonic planes;
We hunt in concrete jungles,
For small material gains;
Promotion and preferment,
Political intrigue,
Resultant restless boredom,
Frustration, and fatigue . . .
He leads beside still waters,
Where pastures in the hollow
Are green with living waters . . .
He leads, but do we follow?

                    — Dawn Finlay

CONSIDER

Consider
The lilies of the field, whose bloom is
  brief—
We are as they;
Like them we fade away,
  As doth a leaf.

Consider
The sparrows of the air, of small ac-
  count:
Our God doth view
Whether they fall or mount—
  He guards us too.

Consider
The lilies, that do neither spin nor toil,
Yet are most fair—
What profits all this care,
  And all this coil?

Consider
The birds, that have no barn nor har-
  vest-weeks:
God gives them food—
Much more our Father seeks
  To do us good.

— *Christina Rossetti*

SHADE

The kindliest thing God ever made
His hand of very healing laid
Upon a fevered world, is shade.

His glorious company of trees
Throw out their mantles, and on these
The dust-stained wanderer finds ease.

Green temples, closed against the beat
Of noontime's blinding glare and heat
Open to any pilgrim's feet.

The white road blisters in the sun;
Now, half the weary journey done,
Enter and rest, oh, weary one!

And feel the dew of dawn still wet
Beneath thy feet and so forget
The burning highway's ache and fret.

This is God's hospitality,
And whoso rests beneath a tree
Hath cause to thank Him gratefully.

— *T. Harrison*

GOD OF THE GALLANT TREES

God of the gallant trees
  Give to us fortitude:
Give as Thou givest to these,
  Valorous hardihood.
We are the trees of Thy planting, O
  God,
  We are the trees of Thy wood.

Now let the life-sap run
  Clean through our every vein,
Perfect what Thou hast begun,
  God of the sun and rain.
Thou who dost measure the weight of
  wind,
  Fit us for stress and strain!

— *A. W. C.*

MY HEART LEAPS UP

My heart leaps up when I behold
  A rainbow in the sky;
So was it when my life began;
So is it now I am a man;
So be it when I shall grow old.
  Or let me die!
The Child is father of the Man;
And I could wish my days to be
Bound each to each by natural piety.

— *William Wordsworth*

I Love a Tree

I love a tree,
A brave, upstanding tree!
When I am wearied in the strife,
Beaten by storms and bruised by life,
I look up at a tree and it refreshes me.
If it can keep its head held high,
And look the storms straight in the eye,
Ready to stand, ready to die,
Then by the grace of God, can I —
At least with Heaven's help, I'll try;
I love a tree, for it refreshes me.

I love a tree.
When it seems dead,
Its leaves all shorn and bared its head,
When winter flings its cold and snow,
It stands there undismayed by woe;
It stands there waiting for the spring —
A tree is such a believing thing.
I love a tree.
For it refreshes me.

— *Ralph Spaulding Cushman*

A Yellow Daffodil

Oh the glowing beauty
    Of a yellow daffodil,
Bringing springtime freshness
    To a winter window sill.

Like a living promise
    Of garden, song and sun,
Joyous little prelude
    Of lovely days to come.

Like a note of laughter
    Upon a dreary day,
Breaking through the winter's gloom
    With melodies of May.

Strange how notes of beauty
    Can change our world about,
Bits of loveliness in life
    We cannot do without.

Oh, the loving kindness
    Of God whose sovereign will
Could pause to make, for you and me,
    A yellow daffodil!

— *Alice Hansche Mortenson*

All Nature Sings

All nature sings her song of praise,
She shows her thanks in many ways;
Can I, for all God's gifts do less
Than sing my hymn of gratefulness?

The brook which gaily babbles on
Sings day and night her cheerful song;
She sings her praise to God on high
For grandeur which she passes by.

The joyous song of tall pine trees
Through soft caress of evening breeze
Sends forth true thanks for constant
        love
For constant blessing from above.

The tulip stretches forth its cup,
The lowly shrubs turn branches up;
They, too, would faithful homage pay
By speaking in their faultless way.

The peaceful drone of lowing herds,
The clear, sweet tones of singing birds
Each thank the God who never sleeps
For ev'ry loving watch He keeps.

The valleys fair, the purple hills,
The mountain rocks, the spring that
        fills,
All silently show forth His care
Whose love and power is everywhere.

The springtime buds, the autumn
        glow,
The summer rain, the winter snow,
All speak of His protecting hand,
All say, " 'Twas wisely, safely
        planned."

— *Phyllis C. Michael*

Battle-Hymn of the Republic

Mine eyes have seen the glory of the coming of the Lord;
He is trampling out the vintage where grapes of wrath are stored!
He hath loosed the fateful lightning of his terrible swift sword;
    His truth is marching on.

I have seen him in the watch-fires of a hundred circling camps;
The have builded him an altar in the evening dews and damps:
I have read his righteous sentence by the dim and flaring lamps:
    His day is marching on.

I have read a fiery gospel writ in burnished rows of steel:
"As ye deal with my contemners, so with you my grace shall deal:
Let the Hero, born of woman, crush the serpent with his heel,
    Since God is marching on."

He has sounded forth the trumpet that shall never call retreat;
He is sifting out the hearts of men before his judgment-seat;
Oh, be swift, my soul, to answer him! be jubilant, my feet!
    Our God is marching on.

In the beauty of the lilies Christ was born across the sea,
With a glory in his bosom that transfigures you and me:
As he died to make men holy, let us die to make men free,
    While God is marching on.

                     — Julia Ward Howe

Lest We Lack True Men

God give us women, women of such mould,
Preferring ever honor unto gold;
Women unspoiled by luxury and ease,
Of nobler type than ancient Rome or Greece.
Women who wear their beauty as a flower,
Whose homely virtues are their richest dower.
Say you "The age needs men?" I say again
"God give us women, lest we lack true men."

                     — Author Unknown

ARMY HYMN

O Lord of Hosts! Almighty King!
Behold the sacrifice we bring!
To every arm thy strength impart,
Thy spirit shed through every heart.

Wake in our breasts the living fires,
The holy faith that warmed our sires;
Thy hand hath made our Nation free:
To die for her is serving thee.

Be thou a pillared flame to show
The midnight snare, the silent foe;
And when the battle thunders loud,
Still guide us in its moving cloud.

God of all Nations! Sovereign Lord!
In thy dread name we draw the sword;
We lift the starry flag on high
That fills with light our stormy sky.

From treason's rent, from murder's
        stain,
Guard thou its folds till Peace shall
        reign,—
Till fort and field, till shore and sea,
Join our loud anthem, Praise to Thee!

                    — *Oliver Wendell Holmes*

ᕗ

PEACE HYMN OF THE REPUBLIC

O Lord, our God, Thy mighty hand
    Hath made our country free;
From all her broad and happy land
    May praise arise to Thee.
Fulfill the promise of her youth,
    Her liberty defend;
By law and order, love and truth,
    America befriend!

The strengh of every state increase
    In Union's golden chain;
Her thousand cities fill with peace,
    Her million fields with grain.

The virtues of her mingled blood
    In one new people bend;
By unity and brotherhood
    America befriend!

O suffer not her feet to stray;
    But guide her untaught might,
That she may walk in peaceful day,
    And lead the world in light.
Bring down the proud, lift up the poor,
    Unequal ways amend;
By justice, nation-wide and sure,
    America befriend!

Through all the waiting land proclaim
    Thy gospel of good-will;
And may the music of Thy name
    In every bosom thrill.
O'er hill and vale, from sea to sea,
    Thy holy reign extend;
By faith and hope and charity,
    America befriend!

                    — *Henry van Dyke*

ᕗ

PATRIOTISM

Breathes there a man with soul so dead
Who never to himself hath said,
"This is my own, my native land!"
Whose heart hath ne'er within him
        burned
As home his footsteps he hath turned
From wandering on a foreign strand?
If such there breathe, go, mark him
        well!
For him no minstrel raptures swell;
High tho' his titles, power, and pelf,
The wretch, concentred all in self,
Living, shall forfeit fair renown,
And, doubly dying, shall go down
To the vile dust from whence he
        sprung,
Unwept, unhonored, and unsung.

                    — *Sir Walter Scott*

TRUTH AND FALSEHOOD

Once to every man and nation comes the moment to decide,
In the strife of Truth with Falsehood, for the good or evil side;
Some great cause, God's new Messiah, offering each the bloom or blight,
Parts the goats upon the left hand, and the sheep upon the right,
And the choice goes by forever 'twixt that darkness and that light.

Careless seems the great Avenger; history's pages but record
One death-grapple in the darkness 'twixt old systems and the Word;
Truth forever on the scaffold, Wrong forever on the throne —
Yet that scaffold sways the future, and, behind the dim unknown,
Standeth God within the shadow, keeping watch above his own.

Then to side with Truth is noble when we share her wretched crust,
Ere her cause bring fame and profit, and 'tis prosperous to be just;
Then it is the brave man chooses, while the coward stands aside,
Doubting in his abject spirit, till his Lord is crucified,
And the multitude make virtue of the faith they had denied.

Count me o'er earth's chosen heroes — they were souls that stood alone
While the men they agonized for hurled the contumelious stone;
Stood serene, and down the future saw the golden beam incline
To the side of perfect justice, mastered by their faith divine,
By one man's plain truth to manhood and to God's supreme design.

By the light of burning heretics Christ's bleeding feet I track,
Toiling up new Calvaries ever with the cross that turns not back,
And these mounts of anguish number how each generation learned
One new word of that grand *Credo* which in prophet-hearts hath burned
Since the first man stood God-conquered with his face to heaven upturned.

For Humanity sweeps onward: where to-day the martyr stands,
On the morrow crouches Judas with the silver in his hands;
Far in front the cross stands ready and the crackling fagots burn,
While the hooting mob of yesterday in silent awe return
To glean up the scattered ashes into History's golden urn.

'Tis as easy to be heroes as to sit the idle slaves
Of a legendary virtue carved upon our fathers' graves;
Worshipers of light ancestral make the present light a crime;—
Was the Mayflower launched by cowards, steered by men behind their time?
Turn those tracks toward Past or Future that make Plymouth Rock sublime?

They have rights who dare maintain them; we are traitors to our sires,
Smothering in their holy ashes Freedom's new-lit altar-fires;
Shall we make their creed our jailer? shall we in our haste to slay,
From the tombs of the old prophets steal the funeral lamps away
To light up the martyr-fagots round the prophets of to-day?

New occasions teach new duties; Time makes ancient good uncouth;
They must upward still, and onward, who would keep abreast of Truth;
Lo, before us gleam her camp-fires! we ourselves must Pilgrims be,
Launch our Mayflower, and steer boldly through the desperate winter sea,
Nor attempt the Future's portal with the Past's blood-rusted key.

— *James Russell Lowell*

REDEMPTION

Loving man, I have wearied of the ways of men:
They have shut themselves up within strong walls of self,
The rich from the poor, the poor from the rich.
They have given themselves over to the pursuit of gold,
The rich and the poor.
They have lost their desire for high things;
Knowledge and wisdom and human sympathy
Have lost their ministrants. Greed and lust and pride
Have set up altars in the market-places and the homes,
And gossiping crowds throng them.

Blow, O fresh winds of God, blow through our prairie lands,
Dotted with towns and villages;
Sweep, mighty tempests, through our wide city deserts;
Let the blasts from the river-cleansed Rockies
Sweep eastward to our white halls of state,
Where giant Greed has builded her shrine,
Where laws are made for a few.
Flaming fires of war, smoldering fires of peace,
Burn, burn from the heart of our life
The decay of death. Let there come forth
From the furnace of flames
A nation, God-loving, God-inspired, God-led,
Purified, transformed — a redeemed people.

— *Thomas Curtis Clark*

THREE THINGS

I know three things must always be
To keep a nation strong and free.
One is a hearthstone bright and dear,
With busy, happy loved ones near.
One is a ready heart and hand
To love, and serve, and keep the land.
One is a worn and beaten way
To where the people go to pray.
So long as these are kept alive,
Nation and people will survive.
God keep them always, everywhere —
The home, the heart, the place of
    prayer.

— *Author Unknown*

HAWAIIAN NATIONAL HYMN

Eternal Father, mighty God,
Behold us from thy blest abode;
To thee we turn, for thou wilt care
To listen to our humble prayer.

May gentle peace forever reign
O'er these fair islands of the main,
Hawaii's peaks to Niihau's strand,
The peace of God o'er all the land!
Forever be our country free,
Our laws and heaven's in harmony
All hearts respond, all voices sing,
God save, God save our gracious
king!

And may our chieftains ever be
Guided, O Lord, by love to thee,
And all the people join to raise
One universal song of praise.

God save the people of our land,
Uphold by thine Almighty hand;
Thy watchful care defends from harm,
Faithful and sure thy sovereign arm.
Forever be our country free,
Our laws and heaven's in harmony.
All hearts respond, all voices sing,
God save, God save our gracious
king!
— *Lilia K. Dominis*
(*Translated by H. L. Sheldon*)

လ

LANDING OF THE PILGRIM FATHERS

The breaking waves dashed high
On a stern and rock-bound coast,
And the woods against a stormy sky
Their giant branches tossed.

And the heavy night hung dark
The hills and waters o'er,
When a band of exiles moored their
bark
On the wild New England shore.

Not as the conqueror comes,
They, the true-hearted, came;
Not with the roll of the stirring drums,
And the trumpet that sings of fame.

Not as the flying come,
In silence and in fear;—
They shook the depths of the desert
gloom
With their hymns of lofty cheer.

Amidst the storm they sang,
And the stars heard, and the sea:
And the sounding aisles of the dim
woods rang
To the anthem of the free!

The ocean eagle soared
From his nest by the white wave's
foam:
And the rocking pines of the forest
roared,—
This was their welcome home!

There were men with hoary hair
Amidst that pilgrim band:—
Why had *they* come to wither there,
Away from their childhood's land?

There was woman's fearless eye,
Lit by her deep love's truth;
There was manhood's brow serenely
high,
And the fiery heart of youth.

What sought they thus afar?
Bright jewels of the mine?
The wealth of seas, the spoils of war?—
They sought a faith's pure shrine!

Ay, call it holy ground,
The soil where first they trod:
They have left unstained what there
they found,—
Freedom to worship God.

— *Felicia Hemans*

ON THE BUILDING OF SPRINGFIELD

Let not our town be large, remembering
That little Athens was the Muses' home,
That Oxford rules the heart of London still,
That Florence gave the Renaissance to Rome.

Record it for the grandson of your son —
A city is not builded in a day:
Our little town cannot complete her soul
Till countless generations pass away.

Now let each child be joined as to a church
To her perpetual hopes, each man ordained:
Let every street be made a reverent aisle
Where Music grows and Beauty is unchained.

Let Science and Machinery and Trade
Be slaves of her, and make her all in all,
Building against our blatant, restless time
An unseen, skilful, medieval wall.

Let every citizen be rich toward God.
Let Christ, the beggar, teach divinity.
Let no man rule who holds his money dear.
Let this, our city, be our luxury.

We should build parks that students from afar
Would choose to starve in, rather than go home,
Fair little squares, with Phidian ornament,
Food for the spirit, milk and honeycomb.

Songs shall be sung by us in that good day,
Songs we have written, blood within the rhyme
Beating, as when Old England still was glad —
The purple, rich, Elizabethan time.

Say, is my prophecy too fair and far?
I only know, unless her faith be high,
The soul of this, our Nineveh, is doomed,
Our little Babylon will surely die.

Some city on the breast of Illinois
No wiser and no better at the start
By faith shall rise redeemed, by faith shall rise
Bearing the western glory in her heart.

The genius of the Maple, Elm and Oak,
The secret hidden in each grain of corn,
The glory that the prairie angels sing
At night when sons of Life and Love are born,

Born but to struggle, squalid and alone,
Broken and wandering in their early years;
When will they make our dusty streets their goal,
Within our attics hide their sacred tears?

When will they start our vulgar blood athrill
With living language, words that set us free?
When will they make a path of beauty clear
Between our riches and our liberty?

We must have many Lincoln-hearted men —
A city is not builded in a day —
And they must do their work, and come and go
While countless generations pass away.

— Vachel Lindsay

ABRAHAM LINCOLN

The weary form, that rested not,
    Save in a martyr's grave;
The careworn face that none forgot,
    Turned to the kneeling slave.

We rest in peace, where his sad eyes
    Saw perils, strife, and pain;
His was the awful sacrifice,
    And ours the priceless gain.

— John Greenleaf Whittier

IN GOD WE TRUST

In God we trust, O nation highly favoured,
    We trust in God to save us from our foes;
Our Victor He, almighty to deliver,
    What need we more? our ev'ry need He knows.

In God we trust, let others trust their rulers,
    We trust in God to save us from alarm;
Like broken reeds, the works of man will fail us,
    Our God alone can keep us from all harm.

In God we trust, O people of His choosing,
    We trust in God to save us from our greed,
That we unselfishly may live for others,
    And to His Word may hearken and take heed.

In God we trust, O land of Heaven's blessing,
    We trust in God to save us from our sin;
Our fleshly walk, our laws and standards, broken,
    Proclaim our need of righteousness within.

— Oswald J. Smith

THE PEOPLE'S PRAYER

God bless our dear United States,
Preserve the land from evil fates,
Lift high her banner fair and free,
And guard her bounds from sea to sea.

From foe without and foe within,
From open shame and hidden sin,
From boastful pride and greedy store,
God keep our nation evermore.

Forever may her friendly hands
Receive the poor of other lands
In kindliness of sisterhood,
And fill their arms with ample good.

Assailed by battle hosts of wrong,
God help our country to be strong.
Assailed by falsehood's crafty crew,
God help our country to be true.

God hold the nation's aim sincere,
God save her heart from coward fear.
God prosper her in true succes.
And crown her head with worthiness.

God bless our dear United States,
Preserve the land from evil fates,
Lift high her banner fair and free,
And ever guard her liberty.

— *Amos R. Wells*

A PRAYER FOR PEACE

Dear Father, whom we cannot see,
  We know that Thou art near;
With longing hearts we turn to Thee,
And ask that Thou wilt set us free
  From war and hate and fear.

Dear Father, King of love and peace,
  We know that Thou art strong;
Make conflicts everywhere to cease,
Let mercy everywhere increase,
  And kindness conquer wrong.

Dear Father, Lord of sea and land,
  We know that Thou art wise;
Oh, make the nations understand
That only by Thy guiding hand
  Can splendid peace arise.

— *John Oxenham*

THE WAY TO PEACE

If there is righteousness
  in the heart,
There will be beauty
  in the character.
If there is beauty
  in the character,
There will be harmony
  in the home.
If there is harmony
  in the home,
There will be order
  in the nation.
If there is order
  in the nation,
There will be peace
  in the world.

— *Chinese Proverb*

OUR COUNTRY

God bless our native land!
Firm may she ever stand
  Through storm and night;
When the wild tempests rave,
Ruler of winds and wave,
Do thou our country save
  By thy great might.

For her our prayer shall rise
To God, above the skies;
  On him we wait:
Thou who art ever nigh,
Guarding with watchful eye,
To thee aloud we cry,
  God save the State!

— *John Sullivan Dwight*

A NATION'S STRENGTH

What makes a nation's pillars high
  And its foundations strong?
What makes it mighty to defy
  The foes that round it throng?

It is not gold. Its kingdoms grand
  Go down in battle shock;
Its shafts are laid on sinking sand,
  Not on abiding rock.

Is it the sword? Ask the red dust
  Of empires passed away;
The blood has turned their stones to
    rust,
  Their glory to decay.

And is it pride? Ah, that bright crown
  Has seemed to nations sweet;
But God has struck its luster down
  In ashes at his feet.

Not gold but only men can make
  A people great and strong;
Men who for truth and honor's sake
  Stand fast and suffer long.

Brave men who work while others
    sleep,
  Who dare while others fly —
They build a nation's pillars deep
  And lift them to the sky.
              — *Ralph Waldo Emerson*

∽

FOUR THINGS

Four things in any land must dwell,
If it endures and prospers well:
One is manhood true and good;
One is noble womanhood;
One is child life, clean and bright;
And one an altar kept alight.

              — *Author Unknown*

NATIONAL HYMN

My country, 'tis of thee,
Sweet land of liberty,
  Of thee I sing;
Land where my fathers died,
Land of the pilgrim's pride,
From every mountain-side
  Let freedom ring.

My native country, thee,
Land of the noble, free,
  Thy name I love;
I love thy rocks and rills,
Thy woods and templed hills;
My heart with rapture thrills
  Like that above.

Let music swell the breeze,
And ring from all the trees
  Sweet freedom's song:
Let mortal tongues awake,
Let all that breathe partake,
Let rocks their silence break,
  The sound prolong.

Our father's God, to thee,
Author of liberty,
  To thee we sing:
Long may our land be bright
With freedom's holy light;
Protect us by thy might,
  Great God, our King.

              — *Samuel Francis Smith*

∽

THE GLORY OF PATRIOTISM

Far dearer, the grave or the prison,
  Illumed by one patriot name,
Than the trophies of all who have risen
  On Liberty's ruins to fame.

              — *Thomas Moore*

PRAYER AND PROMISES

I will not therefore minimize my prayer,
But make it large as are the promises.
Since God is willing thus to bless,
No less an answer would I share.
Alas, for my small faith,
Compared with what He saith.

Therefore, henceforth, shall prayer be heard
From me according to God's word.
I will request, as long as I shall live,
All God has shown His willingness to give.
As are the love and power His truth declares,
So shall faith make the measure of my prayers.

— *William Olney*

PRAYER FOR STRENGTH

Father, in Thy mysterious presence kneeling,
  Fain would our souls feel all Thy kindling love,
For we are weak, and need some deep revealing
  Of trust and strength and calmness from above.

Lord, we have wandered forth through doubt and sorrow,
  And Thou hast made each step an onward one;
And we will ever trust each unknown morrow,—
  Thou wilt sustain us till its work is done.

In the heart's depths a peace serene and holy
  Abides; and when pain seems to have its will,
Or we despair, O may that peace rise slowly,
  Stronger than agony, and we be still!

Now, Father, now, in Thy dear presence kneeling,
  Our spirits yearn to feel Thy kindling love:
Now make us strong, we need Thy deep revealing
  Of trust and strength and calmness from above.

— *Samuel Johnson*

A Blind Man Prays

I pray for courage to receive the light
When, with amaze and awful fear, I find
In truth's resplendent blaze
Old thoughts, old ways, old creeds
Must be abandoned with all haste; for they
Accepted once with mild credulity
As hiding places for my furtive soul —
Though pretty castles, were not built by God.

One man is robbed of sight by grim disease,
Another shuts his eyes and turns from light.
Both are bereft of beauty; both are blind!
I have not known disease, but I have lived
By choice in shadowy shelters, undisturbed.
Now, drenched in loneliness, I face the dawn
And pray for courage to receive the light.

— Catherine Baird

For This Child I Prayed

For this child I prayed — now God be praised
   That He has hearkened to my prayer;
In tender grace and bounteous love,
   Has sent this little son so fair.

For this child I prayed — and I have vowed
   To grant him always to the Lord;
Cost what it may in pain and tears
   I gladly keep my solemn word.

For this child I prayed — O God Most High,
   E'er guide his eager steps aright;
Surround him with Thy love, and speak
   To him in visions of the night.

For this child I prayed — his growing years
   Make pure and true and brave and strong;
Endue him with Thy Spirit's power
   To choose the right and conquer wrong.

For this child I prayed — my fairest hopes
   And dreams have more than been fulfilled;
I thank Thee for this noble son,
   And all the good that Thou hast willed.

— J. Harold Gwynne

The Fault Is Mine

Sometimes God seems so far away,
  The mists between so dense,
My heart is filled with sudden dread,
  Foreboding, and suspense.
The very prayers I utter
  Come straightway back thro' space—
Too weak to make their faltering way
  Up to the throne of grace.

And then again, God seems so near,
  I cannot but believe;
His faintest whisper rings as clear
  As vesper chimes at eve.
"I never leave thee nor forsake,"
  His gentle whisper saith;
And what had caused my sudden
    dread
    Was just my lack of faith!

                            —*Edith M. Lee*

A Father's Prayer

Dear God, my little boy of three
Has said his nightly prayer to Thee;
Before his eyes were closed to sleep,
He asked that Thou his soul would
    keep.
And I, still kneeling at his bed,
My hand upon his tousled head,
Do ask with deep humility,
That Thou, dear Lord, remember me.
Make me, kind Lord, a worthy Dad,
That I may lead this little lad
In pathways ever fair and bright,
That I may keep his steps aright.
O God, his trust must never be
Destroyed or even marred by me.
So, for the simple things he prayed
With childish voice so unafraid,
I, trembling, ask the same from Thee.
Dear Lord, kind Lord, remember me.

                            —*Author Unknown*

Secret Prayer

There is an hour of calm relief
  From every throbbing care;
'Tis when before a throne of grace,
  I kneel in secret prayer.

When one by one, like threads of gold,
  The hues of twilight fall,
Oh, sweet communion with my God,
  My Saviour and my all!

I hear seraphic tones that float
  Amid celestial air,
And bathe my soul in streams of joy,
  Alone in secret prayer.

Oh, when the hour of death shall
    come,
  How sweet from thence to rise,
With prayer on earth my latest breath,
  My watchword to the skies.

                            —*Fanny J. Crosby*

A Prayer

'Mid all the traffic of the ways,
  Turmoils without, within,
Make in my heart a quiet place,
  And come and dwell therein;

A little shrine of quietness,
  All sacred to Thyself,
Where Thou shalt all my soul possess,
  And I may find myself;

A little shelter from life's stress,
  Where I may lay me prone,
And bare my soul in loneliness,
  And know as I am known.

A little place of mystic grace,
  Of self and sin swept bare,
Where I may look upon Thy face,
  And talk with Thee in prayer.

                            —*John Oxenham*

The Secret Place

There is a place where thou canst touch the eyes
  Of blinded men to instant, perfect sight;
There is a place where thou canst say, "Arise!"
  To dying captives, bound in chains of night;
There is a place where thou canst reach the store
  Of hoarded gold and free it for the Lord;
There is a place — upon some distant shore —
  Where thou canst send the worker or the Word;
There is a place where Heaven's resistless power
  Responsive moves to thine insistent plea;
There is a place — a silent, trusting hour —
  Where God Himself descends and fights for thee.
Where is that blessed place — dost thou ask, "Where?"
  O soul, it is the secret place of prayer.

— *Author Unknown*

ᐤᑌᓀ

The Larger Prayer

At first I prayed for Light:
  Could I but see the way,
How gladly, swiftly, would I walk
  To everlasting day!

And next I prayed for strength,
  That I might tread the road
With firm, unfaltering feet, and win
  The heavens' serene abode.

And then I asked for faith:
  Could I but trust my God,
I'd live enfolded in His peace,
  Though foes were all abroad.

But now I pray for love:
  Deep love to God and man;
A living love that will not fail,
  However dark His plan.

And light and strength and faith
  Are opening everywhere!
God only waited for me till
  I prayed the larger prayer.

— *Edith Dean Cheney*

Forgiveness

Remorsefully,
Upon my bed,
With tears, not words,
My prayers I said.

God's listening ear,
Heard my distress;
Knew the regret
I would express.

Then lovingly,
He washed away
The debt of sin
I could not pay.

He raised me up,
My hope restored,
And armed me with
His Spirit's sword.

With courage then,
I tried once more,
To make, with Him,
A better score.

— *Lois Duffield*

LIKE ORPHANS

We kneel down to pray
And right earnestly say,
"Dear Father in Heaven above,"
Then rising, we go
So mournful, so slow,
Like orphans without any love.

— *Opal Leonore Gibbs*

ᘏᗯ

CYRUS BROWN'S PRAYER

"The proper way for man to pray,"
Said Deacon Lemuel Keyes,
"And the only proper attitude,
Is down upon his knees."

"No, I should say the way to pray,"
Said Rev. Dr. Wise,
"Is standing straight with outstretched
    arms,
And rapt and upturned eyes."

"Oh, no, no, no!" said Elder Slow,
"Such posture is too proud;
A man should pray with eyes fast
    closed,
And head contritely bowed."

"It seems to me his hands should be
Austerely clasped in front.
With both thumbs pointing toward
    the ground,"
Said Rev. Dr. Blunt.

"Las' year I fell in Hodgkin's well
Head first," said Cyrus Brown,
"With both my heels a-stickin' up,
My head a-pintin' down;

"An' I made a prayer right then an'
    there —
Best prayer I ever said,
The prayin'est prayer I ever prayed,
A-standin' on my head."

— *Sam Walter Foss*

WHERE A DOGWOOD STOOD

Today while walking in the wood,
I stopped short where a dogwood stood,
Arrayed in its fragile white lace,
In a lovely, springtime-painted place.
So stirred was I by the beauty there
That I joined the dogwood in prayer,
Realizing that no one else but God
Could lift snowy blooms from the sod.
And, as we prayed, an Unseen Power
Pervaded the enchanted green bower;
No longer were there just the tree and I
But the Holy Spirit, too, with Heaven
    nigh.
Never shall I forget meeting God in
    the wood
When I stopped and prayed where a
    dogwood stood!

— *Earle J. Grant*

ᘏᗯ

REMEMBRANCE

I prayed, "Lord, take away the pain."
"Remember, child," He said, "the stain
Upon the Cross, the stain of red."
With quickening tears I hung my
    head.

"Oh, take away the sorrow, Lord,"
I prayed. "Remember, child, the sword
That pierced my heart," the Saviour
    said,
"When those I loved and trusted fled."
In deepest shame I hung my head.

At last I prayed, "Lord, sanctify
The suffering and grief." Then I
Knew the peace and joy, that I might
    share
Gethsemane; and lingering there,
I glimpsed beyond the darkened sod
The shining citadel of God.

— *Grace V. Watkins*

PENMAN'S PRAYER

The pen of a ready writer, Lord,
  O grant it may be mine,
To show the deep things of Thy
    Word,
  Or drop a friendly line.

I'll yield its dedicated nib
  To magnify Thy grace;
Or, with an understanding touch,
  Some loneliness erase.

O steel its point with strength Divine
  To face the field of wrong;
Then soften it that saddened souls
  May catch the lilt of song.

When righteousness requires a sword,
  May it be swift to start;
Yet oft be dipped in sympathy
  To heal a wounded heart.

I do not ask for eloquence
  To sway the minds of men;
Grant me that fiery, friendly flame —
  A ready writer's pen.

— *Charles E. Bayley*

ஒ

A PRAYER

Dear Lord, for all in pain,
  We pray to thee:
O come and smite again
  Thine enemy.
Give to thy servants skill
  To sooth and bless,
And, to the tired and ill.
  Give quietness.
And Lord, to those who fear
  Come near that even though
Pain may not cease,
  They, too, find peace.

— *Amy Carmichael*

REGRET

I bow my head in sorrow,
  My eyes they fill with tears,
When I look back across my life,
  And see the wasted years.

Down through the years I wandered,
  Without a goal in mind,
Until at last He found me,
  My Saviour good and kind.

He left His realm of Glory,
  Of Heaven far above,
And came to die on Calvary,
  To prove His gracious love.

God knows that I am sorry,
  And He's forgiven me;
But how I wish the wasted years
  Were given back to me.

That I might live each one again
  In service for my King;
And for the wealth He's given me,
  Some small gift I could bring.

— *Mrs. Mabel Murray*

ஒ

SANCTUARY

Hast thou within a care so deep,
It chases from thine eyelids sleep?
To thy Redeemer take that care
And change anxiety to prayer.

Hast thou a hope, with which thy
    heart
Would almost feel it death to part?
Entreat thy God that hope to crown,
Or give thee strength to lay it down.

Whate'er the care that breaks thy rest,
Whate'er the wish that swells thy
    breast,
Spread before God that wish, that care,
And change anxiety to prayer.

— *Author Unknown*

A THANKSGIVING

For all Thy blessings given there are many to thank Thee, Lord,
But for the gifts withholden I fain would add my word.
For the good things I desired that barred me from the best,
The peace at the price of honor, the sloth of a shameful rest;
The poisonous sweets I longed for to my hungering heart denied,
The staff that broke and failed me when I walked in the way of pride;
The tinsel joys withheld that so content might still be mine,
The help refused that might have made me loose my hand from Thine;
The light withdrawn that I might not see the dangers of my way;
For what Thou hast not given, I thank Thee, Lord, today.

— *Annie Johnson Flint*

ო·ი

"IF I HAD PRAYED"

Perhaps the day would not have seemed so long,
    The skies would have not seemed so gray,
If on my knees in humble prayer
    I had begun the day.

Perhaps the fight would not have seemed so hard —
    Prepared, I might have faced the fray,
If I had been alone with Him
    Upon my knees, to pray.

Perhaps I might have cheered a broken heart
    Or helped a wand'rer on the way.
If I had asked to be a light
    To some dark soul today.

I would remember just the pleasant things,
    The harsh words that I meant to say
I would forget, if I had prayed
    When I began the day.

I think I would have met life's harder trials
    With hopeful heart and cheerful smile,
If I had spoken with my Lord
    Just for a little while.

And, if I pray, I find that all is well;
    All cares at His dear feet are laid.
My heart is glad, the load is light,
    Because I first have prayed.

— *M. Joyce Roder*

MY PRAYER

Teach me to love — for what is wealth or fame
But foam upon the restless sea of life,
A fading flower, a soon-forgotten name,
A sense of sore defeat ending the strife?

Help me to live — for living I shall grow;
Denying self — perhaps my deepest grief
Is nought when balanced with another's woe
Wherein is neither respite nor relief.

Teach me humility — casting the beam
From mine own eye of prejudice and pride;
So may I see, through love's revealing gleam
In other lives the beauty long denied.

Lord, make me pure in thought, in word and deed,
My deepest motives under Thy control;
Upon the sea of life in joy or need
Be Thou the gracious Pilot of my soul!

— Flora Emily Smith

A PRAYER FOR THE DAY

Lord, may I enter this day without hurry;
May I bear its burdens without complaint.
May I face its tasks without fear,
May I meet its temptations without dishonor,
May I rest at its close without shame.
And this prayer I make to Thee, let Thy Kingdom
come today in me.

— Author Unknown

STORMY NIGHT

Bronze daggers pierced the darkened night;
Thunder beat on conscience' quaking door.
"Lord, take away all harm and fright . . .
Then, tomorrow I shall sin no more!"

Morning came out washed bright and blue,
Filled with new peace and tranquil too.
Perhaps it takes Life's storm-washed night
To cleanse God's earth and make hearts right.

— Barbara Drake Johnston

PRESCRIPTION

When your heart is heavy laden
And your spirit's tide ebbs low
When you are perplexed with prob-
    lems
To your secret prayer room go
Humbly fall upon your knees
And lose yourself in fervent prayer
You will find relief and comfort
And the Christ will meet you there!
When your heart is sore discouraged
With some task you have begun
And your dreams are wishful longings
Of the laurels you might have won
When the day is full of conflict
And the night is dark and long
Ask for deeper faith and courage
Sing a song . . . sing a song!
                          — A. L. Guerard

A PRAYER OF THANKSGIVING

Not for the joys that I have known,
    Not for the past that has been sweet,
    Today I kneel, God, at your feet,
I kneel, though tired and alone,
    To thank you for the mystery
    Of hours to come; and that the fire
    Of youth still burns . . . For the
        desire
To meet the years that are to be!

The path — it may be hard to go,
    I may know poverty and pain;
    I may be bowed by springtime rain,
Beneath the weight of winter snow.
I may find loss and sore distress,
    Vague disappointment may be mine;
    But still the far horizon's line
Will hold frail dreams for me to guess!

And — with a drifting, keen delight,
    My eager searching eyes may see
    The flame that lights an autumn
        tree . . .
I may be sure that stars, at night,
Will shine for me when all the way
    Is hard to go. That there is mirth,
    To veil the sorrows of the earth.
So, Father, not for yesterday,

Do I give thanks . . . although it made
    My heart and soul know rapture's
        thrill,
For, God, tomorrow waits me still.
Ah, may I meet it unafraid!
The past is done — its tapestry
    Is background for new scenes that
        shift;
    Today I thank you for the gift
Of all the years that are to be!
                        — Margaret E. Sangster

AN ANCIENT PRAYER

Give me a good digestion, Lord,
And also something to digest;
Give me a healthy body, Lord,
And sense to keep it at its best.
Give me a healthy mind, good Lord,
To keep the good and pure in sight,
Which, seeing sin, is not appalled,
But finds a way to set it right.

Give me a mind that is not bound,
That does not whimper, whine or sigh.
Don't let me worry overmuch
About the fussy thing called I.
Give me a sense of humor, Lord;
Give me the grace to see a joke,
To get some happiness from life
And pass it on to other folk.
                        — Thomas H. B. Webb

The Way I Pray

I knelt to pray when day was done,
And prayed, "O God, bless everyone,
Lift from each burdened heart the
     pain,
And let the sick be well again."
And then I woke another day,
And carelessly went on my way,
And all day long I did not try
To wipe the tear from any eye.
I did not try to bear the load
Of any brother on the road.
I did not even go to see
The sick man just next door to me.

And then again when day was done
I prayed, "O God, bless everyone."
And as I prayed, into my ear
There came a voice which whispered
     clear,
"Whom have you tried to bless to-
     day?
Pause, hypocrite, before you pray;
God's richest blessings always go
By hands that serve Him, here be-
     low."
And then I hid my face and cried,
"Forgive me, Lord, for I have lied;
Let me but see another day,
And I will live the way I pray."

— *Whitney Montgomery*

A Prayer

Lord, I come, and simply resting
In Thy faithful, changeless Word,
I believe the Blood hath cleansed me,
And that Christ is crownèd Lord.
Grant henceforth a secret outflow
Of Thy life and love through me,
Reaching those who dwell in darkness,
Reaching priceless souls for Thee!

— *Author Unknown*

Heart Prayer

For an understanding heart, I pray,
For quiet strength to help each day,
Any in need who come my way.

For a happy heart, I ask in prayer,
For cheerfulness that I may share
With any who may be bowed with
     care.

For a grateful heart, for a heart that is
     true,
I humbly ask that I may do
Your work, dear Lord, on earth for
     You.

— *Enola Chamberlin*

A Breath of Prayer

A breath of prayer in the morning
Means a day of blessing sure;
A breath of prayer in the evening
Means a night of rest secure;
A breath of prayer in our weakness
Means a clasp of a Mighty Hand;
A breath of prayer when we're lonely
Means Someone to understand.
A breath of prayer in our doubtings
Assures us the Lord knows best.
A breath of prayer in our sorrows
Means comfort and peace and rest;
A breath of prayer in rejoicing
Gives joy an added delight.
For they that remember God's good-
     ness
Go singing far into the night.
There's never a year nor a season
That prayer may not bless every
     hour,
And never a soul need be helpless
When linked with God's infinite
     power.

— *Frances McKinnon Morton*

FROM THE RECESSES

From recesses of a lowly spirit
My humble prayer ascends: O Father! hear it.
Upsoaring on the wings of fear and meekness,
        Forgive its weakness.

I know, I feel, how mean and how unworthy
The trembling sacrifice I pour before thee;
What can I offer in thy presence holy,
        But sin and folly?

For in thy sight, who every bosom viewest,
Cold are our warmest vows, and vain our truest;
Thoughts of a hurrying hour, our lips repeat them,
        Our hearts forget them.

We see thy hand,— it leads us, it supports us;
We hear thy voice,— it counsels and it courts us;
And then we turn away,— and still thy kindness
        Forgives our blindness.

And still thy rain descends, thy sun is glowing,
Fruits ripen round, flowers are beneath us blowing,
And, as if man were some deserving creature,
        Joy covers nature.

Oh, how long-suffering, Lord! but thou delightest
To win with love the wandering; thou invitest,
By smiles of mercy, not by frowns or terrors,
        Man from his errors.

Who can resist thy gentle call, appealing
To every generous thought and grateful feeling,—
That voice paternal, whispering, watching ever,—
        My bosom? — never.

Father and Saviour! plant within this bosom
The seeds of holiness; and bid them blossom
In fragrance and in beauty bright and vernal,
        And spring eternal!

Then place them in those everlasting gardens,
Where angels walk, and seraphs are the wardens;
Where every flower that climbs through death's dark portal
        Becomes immortal.
                    — Sir John Bowring

HOURS OF PRAYER

Yesterday my cross seemed heavy,
  I was sunken in despair,
The way stretched out before me
  And there were no hours of prayer.

It seemed I could not carry on,
  'Neath all my earthly strife,
Till Jesus whispered sweetly,
  "I am the Way, the Truth, and . . .
    Life."

"Ask in My Name, ye shall receive,"
  There is comfort from all care,
If believing you will seek
  In hours of earnest prayer.

'Twas then I dropped my burden
  Unloaded all my care,
As I knelt before the throne of God,
  For hours of earnest prayer.

I felt His presence near me,
  My cross He carried away,
He soothed that weary feeling,
  When I began to pray.

And now the way seems brighter,
  With Him my joys I share,
And sweet communion have we two,
  Because of earnest prayer.
          — *Julia Biebesheimer*

MY FATHER CARES

My Father leads my day by day,
Thro' darkness, cloud, or misty way;
I cannot always understand,
But I am sure He holds my hand.

My Father trains me tenderly,
Both in the storm and silently;
In daily tests, reproach, alarm,
He teaches, cheers, and brings His
  calm.

My Father strengthens with His power
In every conflict, every hour.

No man can pluck me from His hand,
For He enables me to "stand."

My Father wipes away each tear,
By faith, His gentle voice I hear;
Some glad bright day, I'll see His face,
And praise His wondrous love and
  grace.
          — *Margaret Spencer Johnson*

THE HOUR OF PRAYER

My God! is any hour so sweet,
  From blush of morn to evening star,
As that which calls me to thy feet,—
  The hour of prayer?

Blest is the tranquil hour of morn,
  And blest that solemn hour of eve,
When, on the wings of prayer upborne,
  The world I leave.

For then a dayspring shines on me,
  Brighter than morn's ethereal glow;
And richer dews descend from thee
  Than earth can know.

Then is my strength by thee renewed;
  Then are my sins by thee forgiven;
Then dost thou cheer my solitude
  With hopes of heaven.

No words can tell what sweet relief
  Here for my every want I find;
What strength for warfare, balm for
  grief,
  What peace of mind!

Hushed is each doubt, gone every fear;
  My spirit seems in heaven to stay;
And e'en the penitential tear
  Is wiped away.

Lord! till I reach yon blissful shore,
  No privilege so dear shall be
As thus my inmost soul to pour
  In prayer to thee.
          — *Charlotte Elliott*

PRAYER

If, when I kneel to pray,
With eager lips I say:
"Lord, give me all the things that I desire;
Health, wealth, fame, friends, brave heart, religious fire,
The power to sway my fellow-men at will,
And strength for mighty works to banish ill";
In such a prayer as this
The blessing I must miss.

Or if I only dare
To raise this fainting prayer:
"Thou seest, Lord, that I am poor and weak,
And cannot tell what things I ought to seek;
I therefore do not ask at all, but still
I trust thy bounty all my wants to fill";
My lips shall thus grow dumb,
The blessing shall not come.

But if I lowly fall,
And thus in faith I call:
"Through Christ, O Lord, I pray thee give to me
Not what I would, but what seems best to thee,
Of life, of health, of service, and of strength,
Until to thy full joy I come at length";
My prayer shall then avail,
The blessing shall not fail.

— Charles Francis Richardson

A PRAYER IN THE NIGHT

O Thou who seest all my grief,
  The anguish of my heart,
The disappointments, trials and cares
  That make the teardrops start;
O Thou whose love has never failed
  Though dark the night and long,
To Thee I turn my weary eyes
  And hope springs forth in song.

O Thou who knowest all my thoughts,
  The hunger of my soul,
The blighted hopes of bygone years,
  The dreams of life's lost goal;

The aching void, the loneliness,
  And all the thornclad way,
To Thee I turn with faith undimmed
  And 'mid the darkness pray.

O Thou who givest grace and strength
  For ev'ry trying hour,
Who understandest when I fall
  Before the tempter's pow'r;
O Thou who dwellest in my heart,
  Whose will is my delight,
To Thee I turn, Thy face I see
  And all again is bright.

— Oswald J. Smith

LET US COME BOLDLY

Let us come boldly
　　Now to the Throne,
Here where the Saviour
　　Meets with His own;
Here let us worship,
　　Here seek His face;
Here bring our needy hearts,
　　Here find His grace.

Let us come boldly
　　Blessings to claim,
Bringing our weakness,
　　Pleading His Name;
Here for His children
　　Praying He stands,
Love in His burning heart,
　　Grace in His hands.

Let us come boldly,
　　Filled with His praise;
Sure are His judgments,
　　Perfect His ways;
All our heart's treasure
　　Here to outpour,
Low at His wounded feet
　　Let us adore!

His arms are open
　　Gifts to bestow,
Strength for our weakness,
　　Joy for our woe;
Grace for our trials,
　　Peace for our fear —
Bold to the Mercy Seat
　　Let us draw near!

— *E. Margaret Clarkson*

BECAUSE YOU PRAYED

Because you prayed for me
I found the strength I needed for my task,
The courage I lacked before, the faith to see
Beyond my narrow world; new joy for pain
I found, and zeal
To press on forward strong of heart again —
Because you prayed.

Because you prayed today
I found it was not hard to face the dawn,
Take up again the work I laid away
But yesterday, and shoulder it, and dare
To smile a bit
And find a blessing I'd not dreamed was there —
Because you prayed.

Because you prayed for me
Tonight, I seemed to reach and find your hand
Close by as I had known it would be,
And somehow toil and turmoil needs must cease: —
It was as though
God to our hearts had softly whispered, "Peace" —
Because you prayed.

— *Ruth Margaret Gibbs*

THE ECLIPSE

Whither, O whither didst thou fly
When I did grieve thine holy eye,
When thou didst mourn to see me lost,
And all thy care and counsels crost.
O do not grieve, where'er thou art!
Thy grief is an undoing smart,
Which doth not only pain, but break
My heart, and makes me blush to
    speak.
Thy anger I could kiss, and will:
But O thy grief, thy grief doth kill!

— *Henry Vaughan*

HE TAKES MY HAND

She's just a little kiddie
    Who walks by her mother's side,
And she'd rather go out walking
    Than to take a little ride.

She likes to skip and hop along,
    To run ahead and wait
For mother to catch up to her
    Down by the garden gate.

But sometimes when they go walking
    It gets hard for her to stand,
And when the road gets rocky,
    She says, "Mother, take my hand."

It's all right when paths are easy
    For her to skip along,
But when it's getting hard to walk
    She wants a hand so strong,

To reach down and take hold of hers
    To help her find the way,
"Mother, mother, hold my hand";
    Is what you'll hear her say.

I guess that we're all children,
    Sometimes the way is bright,
Then we like to run along;
    But when the day grows night,

When the shadows lengthen,
    When the sky is overcast —
Or when we walk the valley
    When the day is done at last:

I think that we shall reach right up,
    I know He'll understand,
And we'll cry like weary children,
    "Lord Jesus, take my hand."

I know that He will reach right down
    To help us in our need,
For when we cannot help ourselves
    He'll always intercede.

Then when the journey's over
    And we stand on yonder strand,
Methinks that we shall ask again,
    "Lord Jesus, take my hand."

— *Louis Paul Lehman, Jr.*

KEEPING VICTORY

Meet your Saviour in the morning
    In the secret place of prayer,
And obtain the strength and courage
    You shall need for ev'ry care.
Meet your loved ones and your neigh-
    bors,
    Meet your friends and meet your
    foes;
Meet the sinners and the Christians
    With sweet peace that overflows.

Meet your trials and your problems,
    Meet your heartaches and your
    sighs;
Meet your many disappointments,
    And whatever sorely tries,
With a heart of love and kindness
    And with faith that reaches God,
Knowing that His hand will lead you
    Up the way that saints have trod.

— *Walter E. Isenhour*

ANGUISH

My God and King! to thee
I bow my knee;
I bow my troubled soul, and greet
With my foul heart thy holy feet.
Cast it, or tread it! it shall do
Even what thou wilt, and praise thee
    too.

My God, could I weep blood,
Gladly I would,
Or if thou wilt give me that art,
Which through the eyes pours out the
    heart,
I will exhaust it all, and make
Myself all tears, a weeping lake.

O! 'tis an easy thing
To write and sing;
But to write true, unfeignèd verse
Is very hard! O God, disperse
These weights, and give my spirit leave
To act as well as to conceive!

O my God, hear my cry;
Or let me die! . . .
                            — *Henry Vaughan*

∽

SECOND CRUCIFIXION

They crushed the thorns into His brow
    And struck harsh blows that day.
Oh, Lord, I would not treat Thee so —
    I only walked away.

They drove the nails into His hands,
    And raised the cross on high.
Oh, Lord, that men could be so vile —
    I only passed Thee by.

But blinded eyes and heart of stone
    Will spurn a love like Thine.
Oh, Lord, I struck the cruelest blows,
    The sharpest thorns were mine.

                  — *Victoria Beaudin Johnson*

THE MERCY-SEAT

From every stormy wind that blows,
From every swelling tide of woes,
There is a calm, a sure retreat;
'Tis found beneath the mercy-seat.

There is a place where Jesus sheds
The oil of gladness on our heads.
A place than all beside more sweet;
It is the blood-stained mercy-seat.

There is a spot where spirits blend,
Where friend holds fellowship with
    friend;
Tho' sundered far, by faith they meet
Around the common mercy-seat.

Ah, whither could we flee for aid,
When tempted, desolate, dismayed,
Or how the hosts of hell defeat,
Had suffering saints no mercy-seat?

There, there on eagle wings we soar,
And time and sense seem all no more;
And heaven comes down, our souls to
    greet,
And glory crowns the mercy-seat.

Oh, may my hand forget her skill,
My tongue be silent, cold, and still,
This bounding heart forget to beat,
If I forget the mercy-seat!

                            — *Hugh Stowell*

∽

PRAYER

Lord, the newness of this day
Calls me to an untried way:
Let me gladly take the road,
Give me strength to bear my load,
Thou my guide and helper be —
I will travel through with Thee.

                        — *Henry van Dyke*

From MORTE D'ARTHUR

The old order changeth, yielding place to new,
And God fulfils himself in many ways,
Lest one good custom should corrupt the world.
Comfort thyself: what comfort is in me?
I have lived my life, and that which I have done
May He within himself make pure! but thou,
If thou shouldst never see my face again,
Pray for my soul. More things are wrought by prayer
Than this world dreams of. Wherefore, let thy voice
Rise like a fountain for me night and day.
For what are men better than sheep or goats
That nourish a blind life within the brain,
If, knowing God, they lift not hands of prayer
Both for themselves and those who call them friend?
For so the whole round earth is every way
Bound by gold chains about the feet of God. . . .

— *Alfred, Lord Tennyson*

EARLY RISING AND PRAYER

When first thine eyes unveil, give thy soul leave
    To do the like; our bodies but forerun
The spirit's duty; true hearts spread and heave
    Unto their God, as flowers do to the sun.
Give him thy first thoughts, then, so shalt thou keep
Him company all day, and in him sleep.

Yet never sleep the sun up; prayer should
    Dawn with the day; there are set awful hours
'Twixt Heaven and us; the manna was not good
    After sun-rising; far day sullies flowers.
Rise to prevent the sun: sleep doth sins glut,
And heaven's gate opens when this world's is shut.

Walk with thy fellow-creatures: note the hush
    And whisperings amongst them. Not a spring
Or leaf but hath his morning hymn; each bush
    And oak doth know I AM. Canst thou not sing?
Oh, leave thy cares and follies! go this way,
And thou art sure to prosper all the day.

Serve God before the world; let him not go
    Until thou hast a blessing; then resign
The whole unto him, and remember who

Prevailed by wrestling ere the sun did shine;
Pour oil upon the stones, weep for thy sin,
Then journey on, and have an eye to heaven.

Mornings are mysteries: the world's first youth,
 Man's resurrection, and the future's bud,
Shroud in their births; the crown of life, light, truth,
 Is styled their star, the store and hidden food:
Three blessings wait upon them; one of which
Should move: they make us holy, happy, rich.

When the world's up, and every swarm abroad,
 Keep well thy temper, mix not with each clay;
Despatch necessities; life hath a load
 Which must be carried on, and safely may.
Yet keep those cares without thee; let the heart
Be God's alone, and choose the better part.

       — Henry Vaughan

Save Me

Save me, O God, Thou God of my redemption;
My life is forfeit, 'tis in Thee I live;
Thy grace has brought me penalty's exemption;
Oh, do Thou also, daily sins forgive.

Save me, O God, Thou God of my defending;
My soul is base, it clings to things below;
Hold me to Thee, where Thy great power befriending,
I may be Thine, and all Thy fulness know.

Save me, O God, Thou God of my sustaining;
My heart is vagrant, 'tis afar from Thee;
Lift me and keep me, till Thy love obtaining,
From self's desires I am for ever free.

Save me, O God, Thou God of my sure guiding;
My eyes are veiled, I dare not walk alone;
Show me Thy path, the way of Thy providing;
Lead me straight onward till I reach Thy throne.

Save me, O God, Thou God of my dread judging;
Forgive my sins, I fear to see Thy face;
For Thy dear Son, Thy mercy not begrudging,
Save me, and give me in Thy heaven a place.

       — Henry W. Frost

O Do Not Go

O do not go, thou know'st I'll die;
My spring and fall are in thy book;
Or, if thou goest, do not deny
To lend me, though from far, one look.

My sins long since have made thee strange,
A very stranger unto me;
No morning meetings since this change,
Nor evening walks have I with thee.

Why is my God thus slow and cold,
When I am most, most sick and sad?
Well fare those blessed days of old,
When thou didst hear the weeping lad.

O do not thou do as I did,
Do not despise a love-sick heart;
What though some clouds defiance bid,
Thy sun must shine in every part.

Though I have spoiled, O spoil not thou,
Hate not thine own dear gift and token,
Poor birds sing best, and prettiest show,
When their nest is fallen and broken.

Dear Lord, restore thy ancient peace,
Thy quickening friendship, man's bright wealth;
And if thou wilt not give me ease
From sickness, give my spirit health.

— *Henry Vaughan*

VESPERS

(Written in memory of a Vesper Service attended in Wales)

Beyond the square of the old church tower,
Where the bell is tolling the evening hour.
The sun sinks low in its glory red
To a long night's rest in its ocean-bed:
The sunlight falls on the ancient fane,
On arch and lintel and window-pane,
On lofty roof and on high-peaked choir,
On tower and turret and slender spire,
Till the old, stone church, with its ivy green,
Seems aglow in a flame of celestial sheen.
Through the stained-glass windows the sunset bright
Throws its measureless rays of radiant light,

Touching with lustre carved saints of old
And wingèd angels with harps of gold,
Making resplendent the chilly gloom
Of darkened recess and shadowy tomb,
And, flashing glory, the nave across,
Through the chancel's length to the brazen cross,
It falls upon it, a crimson flood,
Till the cross seems bathed in a tide of blood.

The tones of the bell are now dying away,
And, at last, they pass, as passes the day,
When out from the church sounds the vesper-hymn,
As the worshipping saints sing praise to Him
Who is Lord of all, of the day and the night,
Who watches His own from the heavenly height.
Then follow the words of the evening prayer,
Which fall on the hearts of the worshippers there
All peaceful and still, with the blessing of God,
As the dew falls soft on the waiting sod;
And to all, the worshipping women and men,
With heads bowed low, say a glad Amen!

Beyond the square of the old church tower,
The bell is tolling the curfew hour;
And the sun goes down in its glory red,
To its long night's rest in its ocean-bed.

— Henry W. Frost

ॐ

ADEQUACY

Now by the verdure on thy thousand hills,
Beloved England,— doth the earth appear
Quite good enough for men to overbear
The will of God in, with rebellious wills!
We cannot say the morning sun fulfils
Ingloriously its course; nor that the clear
Strong stars without significance insphere
Our habitation. We, meantime, our ills
Heap up against this good; and lift a cry
Against this work-day world, this ill-spread feast,
As if ourselves were better certainly
Than what we come to. Maker and High Priest,
I ask thee not my joys to multiply,—
Only make me worthier of the least.

— Elizabeth Barrett Browning

THE PURPOSE OF PRAYER

The camel, at the close of day,
  Kneels down upon the sandy plain
To have his burden lifted off
  And rest to gain.

My soul, thou, too, shouldst to thy
      knees
  When daylight draweth to a close,
And let the Master lift the load
  And grant repose.

The camel kneels at break of day
  To have his guide replace his load,
Then rises up anew to take
  The desert road.

So thou shouldst kneel at morning's
      dawn
  That God may give thee daily care,
Assured that He no load too great
  Will make thee bear.

                — *Author Unknown*

ᕗ

WHAT IS PRAYER?

Prayer is the soul's sincere desire,
  Uttered or unexpressed;
The motion of a hidden fire
  That trembles in the breast.

Prayer is the burden of a sigh,
  The falling of a tear,
The upward glancing of the eye,
  When none but God is near.

Prayer is the simplest form of speech
  That infant's lips can try;
Prayer the sublimest strains that reach
  The Majesty on high.

Prayer is the contrite sinner's voice,
  Returning from his ways;
While angels in their songs rejoice,
  And cry, "Behold, he prays!"

Prayer is the Christian's vital breath,
  The Christian's native air,
His watchword at the gates of death:
  He enters heaven with prayer.

The saints in prayer appear as one
  In word and deed and mind,
While with the Father and the Son
  Sweet fellowship they find.

Nor prayer is made by man alone,—
  The Holy Spirit pleads,
And Jesus on the eternal throne
  For sinners intercedes.

O thou by whom we come to God,
  The Life, the Truth, the Way!
The path of prayer thyself hast trod:
  Lord, teach us how to pray!

                — *James Montgomery*

ᕗ

THE HELPER

The little sharp vexations,
  And the briars, that catch and fret,
Why not take all to The Helper
  Who has never failed us yet?
Tell Him about the heartache,
  And tell Him the longings too;
Tell Him the baffled purpose
  When we scarce know what to do;
Then leaving all our weakness
  With the One divinely strong;
Forget that we bore the burden,
  And carry away the song.

                — *Phillips Brooks*

ᕗ

AS WE PRAY

Only, O Lord, in Thy dear love
Fit us for perfect rest above;
And help us this and every day,
To live more nearly as we pray.

                — *John Keble*

A PRAYER FOR HELP

When temptations fierce assail me
  And my heart is filled with fear,
Blessed Saviour, do not fail me,
  Let me know that Thou art near;
Do, oh do as Thou hast promised,
  Turn to me Thy list'ning ear.

Lead me through this world of sorrow
  To the Land of fadeless day;
Give me strength for each tomorrow
  As I journey on my way;
Be my helper, Lord, I pray Thee,
  Ever be my Strength and Stay.

Thou wilt never leave me, never,
  Till the trials of life are o'er;
I am Thine and Thine forever,
  Oh, to serve and love Thee more!
With the prophets and the martyrs
  I would all Thy works adore.

Clouds of darkness all around me,
  Songs and praises in my soul;
God of Heaven, still surround me
  With Thy grace, and make me
    whole;
Let me rise to realms of glory
  While Thy blessings o'er me roll.

— *Author Unknown*

EXHORTATION TO PRAYER

What various hindrances we meet
In coming to a mercy-seat!
Yet who, that knows the worth of
    prayer,
But wishes to be often there?

Prayer makes the darkened cloud with-
    draw;
Prayer climbs the ladder Jacob saw,
Gives exercise to faith and love,
Brings every blessing from above.

Restraining prayer, we cease to fight;
Prayer makes the Christian's armor
    bright;
And Satan trembles when he sees
The weakest saint upon his knees.

While Moses stood with arms spread
    wide,
Success was found on Israel's side;
But when thro' weariness they failed,
That moment Amalek prevailed.

Have you no words? Ah! think again,
Words flow apace when you complain,
And fill your fellow-creature's ear,
With the sad tale of all your care.

Were half the breath, thus vainly
    spent,
To Heaven in supplication sent,
Your cheerful song would oftener be,
"Hear what the Lord has done for me!"

— *William Cowper*

DO I REALLY PRAY?

I often say my prayers,
  But do I really pray?
And do the wishes of my heart
  Go with the words I say?

I may as well kneel down
  And worship gods of stone,
As offer to the living God
  A prayer of words alone.

For words without the heart
  The Lord will never hear;
Nor will He to those lips attend
  Whose prayer is not sincere!

Lord, show me what I need
  And teach me how to pray,
And help me when I seek Thy grace
  To mean the words I say.

— *John Burton*

PRAYER FOR GUIDANCE

Father, lead me on, I pray,
Through the long and narrow way,
Till the sunlight fades away
    And the day is done.

May my heart from sin be free,
Keep it in all purity,
So that I may walk with Thee,
    Thee the holy One.

Give me vision true and keen,
May none else but Thee be seen,
Thee and me, with naught between,
    Till my rest is won.

Bring me to Thy home at last,
Toils and dangers overpast,
Grant me there Thy glories vast,
    Through Thy blessed Son.

Then may I be filled with praise
For Thy care through devious ways,
For the end of journeying days
    And for heav'n begun.

                    — Henry W. Frost

✓✓ PRAYER

How prone we are
    To ask for answers
To our prayer,
    To take our care,
And lay it all at Jesus' feet,
    To then expect — complete
Response,
    Without a time of trust,
A time to know the peace,
    And sweet release,
Of prayer, whose answer may
    Be on the way,
But not as yet in sight;
    To know the pure delight,
Of trusting Him,
    From day to day,

Thro' storms, and trial along the way;
    How prone we are
To know despair,
    When really God doth know and
        care,
But wants to see
    If we can bear
The test.
    Our Lord knows best!
And we must bow — and humbly ask,
    With trust,
That He shall do the task,
    As in a childlike faith
We bask,
    Untouched with care;
The knowledge deep within,
    He answers prayer!

                    — Connie Calenberg

A MORNING PRAYER

I ask thee not to withhold grief
Thou hast in store for me;
I only ask for courage, Lord,
    To bear it patiently.

To always tread the flowery path?
Not this my earnest plea;
I only ask my hand in thine,
    Then I'll wait patiently.

I pray thee not to smooth one wave
From off my troubled sea;
Only give my frail bark strength
    To sail through patiently.

I ask thee not to always place
Sweet fruit upon life's tree,
But of the bitter fruit — dear Lord,
    To partake patiently.

Some day the azure sky will break
And Thy dear face I'll see;
I pray that Thou wilt find me, Lord,
    Waiting patiently.

                    — Betty Perpetuo

PRAYER IN THE SPIRIT

Spirit of God, descend upon my heart;
Wean it from earth; through all its pulses move;
Stoop to my weakness, mighty as Thou art,
And make me love Thee as I ought to love.

I ask no dream, no prophet ecstasies,
No sudden rending of the veil of clay,
No angel visitant, no opening skies;
But take the dimness of my soul away.

Hast Thou not bid us love Thee, God and King
All, all Thine own, soul, heart, and strength, and mind;
I see Thy cross — there teach my heart to cling:
O let me seek Thee, and O let me find!

Teach me to feel that Thou art always nigh;
Teach me the struggles of the soul to bear,
To check the rising doubt, the rebel sigh;
Teach me the patience of unanswered prayer.

— *George Croly*

A PRAYER FOR MISSIONARIES

O God of grace, Thou God of free salvation,
Who sent Thy Son to die for those who sin,
Be with Thy servants, gone to every nation,
Give them Thy power rebellious souls to win.

O God of life, Thou God of life abounding,
Grant to Thy chosen length of days and years,
Protect their lives from every ill surrounding,
Deliver them from all depressing fears.

O God of light, Thou God of light effulgent,
Lighten their darkness as they follow Thee,
Lead them and guide them, in Thy care indulgent,
Give them in all Thy blessed will to see.

O God of love, Thou God of love constraining,
Draw them to Thee and hold them very near,
That filled with Thee, their lives Thy love containing,
May unto others make Thee very dear.

O God of power, Thou God of power victorious,
Make Thy dear servants bold to speak for Thee.
So that lost men, beholding Thee all-glorious,
May worship Thee alone, eternally!

— *Henry W. Frost*

PRAYER AT EVENTIDE

For hasty word and secret sin
  For needful task undone,
We pray Thy full forgiveness, Lord,
  At setting sun.

The day to us has beauty brought,
  Thy smile has blessed our way,
Now as the evening hours come,
  For rest we pray.

Keep us beneath Thy wings tonight
  Where peace alone is found,
For in Thy love we rest secure
  Thy arms around.

And when tomorrow's duties call,
  With joy or sorrow sown,
May we in full surrender seek
  Thy will alone. Amen.

— *Author Unknown*

ᏻᎧ

AN EVENING PRAYER

Curfew bells are softly pealing,
Shades across the earth are stealing,
Dark'ning night is drawing near;
O my God, my heart upraising,
I would give Thee prayer and praising,
Thou art infinitely dear.

Let no night-shades hide Thee from
  me,
Let no night-fears overcome me,
Keep me safe from every harm;

May I sleep with Thee defending,
May I rest with Thee befriending,
Sheltered by Thy mighty arm.

Like the bird, I would be nesting
'Neath Thy wings, as I am resting,
Still and calm and close to Thee;
E'en in sleep, Thy power confining,
I would know Thy sweet enshrining,
Held in love's captivity.

Strengthen me while I am sleeping,
Strengthen me for joy or weeping,
Make me ready for Thy will;
So that in the morn awaking,
Thy full life afresh partaking,
I may Thy behests fulfil.

Now the sun is past its setting;
In the dark, all ills forgetting,
I would praise Thy faithfulness;
In Thy power and love abiding;
To Thy care my soul confiding,
Grant me sleep's unconsciousness!

— *Henry W. Frost*

ᏻᎧ

A PRAYER

God, give me sympathy and sense,
  And help me keep my courage high;
God, give me calm and confidence,
  And—please—a twinkle in my eye.
    Amen.

— *Margaret Bailey*

ᏻᎧ

√ A MOTHER'S PRAYER

Father in Heaven, make me wise, so that my gaze may never meet
A question in my children's eyes. God, keep me always sweet
And patient too, before their need; let each vexation know its place;
Let gentleness be all my creed, let laughter live upon my face.
A mother's day is very long, there are so many things to do;
But never let me lose my song before the hardest day is through.

— *Author Unknown*

Go From Me

Go from me. Yet I feel that I shall stand
Henceforward in thy shadow. Nevermore
Alone upon the threshold of my door
Of individual life, I shall command
The uses of my soul, nor lift my hand
Serenely in the sunshine as before,
Without the sense of that which I forbore —
Thy touch upon the palm. The widest land
Doom takes to part us, leaves thy heart in mine
With pulses that beat double. What I do
And what I dream include thee, as the wine
Must taste of its own grapes. And when I sue
God for myself, He hears that name of thine,
And sees within my eyes the tears of two.

— *Elizabeth Barrett Browning*

Thy Peace, O God

We bless Thee for Thy peace, O God,
  Deep as th' unfathomed sea,
Which falls like sunshine on the road
  Of those who trust in Thee.

We ask not, Father, for repose
  Which comes from outward rest,
If we may have through all life's woes,
  Thy peace within our breast.

That peace which suffers and is strong,
  Trusts where it cannot see,
Deems not the trial way too long,
  But leaves the end with Thee.

That peace which flows serene and
    deep,
  A river in the soul,
Whose banks a living verdure keep,
  God's sunshine o'er the whole.

O Father, give our hearts this peace,
  Whate'er may outward be,
Till all life's discipline shall cease,
  And we go home to Thee.

— *Author Unknown*

Thou Art Coming to a King

Thou art coming to a King,
Large petitions with thee bring
For His grace and power are such
None can ever ask too much.

— *John Newton*

The Search

I sought his love in sun and stars,
  And where the wild seas roll,
And found it not. As mute I stood,
  Fear overwhelmed my soul;
But when I gave to one in need,
I found the Lord of Love indeed.

I sought his love in lore of books,
  In charts of science' skill;
They left me orphaned as before —
  His love eluded still;
Then in despair I breathed a prayer;
The Lord of Love was standing there!

— *Thomas Curtis Clark*

PRAYER OF A PATRIOT

Lord of the land,
The sea, the air,
Extend Thy hand
In watchful care!

Lord of the sea,
The air, the land,
Guard liberty,
For which we stand!

Lord of the air,
The land, the sea,
Our humble prayer —
Forever free!

— Henry J. von Schlichten

ॐ

WHEN FATHER PRAYS

When father prays he doesn't use
  The words the preacher does;
There's different things for different
    days,
  But mostly it's for us.

When father prays the house is still,
  His voice is slow and deep.
We shut our eyes, the clock ticks loud,
  So quiet we must keep.

He prays that we may be good boys,
  And later on good men;
And then we squirm, and think we
    won't
  Have any quarrels again.

You'd never think, to look at Dad,
  He once had tempers, too.
I guess if father needs to pray,
  We youngsters surely do.

Sometimes the prayer gets very long
  And hard to understand,
And then I wiggle up quite close,
  And let him hold my hand.

I can't remember all of it,
  I'm little yet, you see;
But one thing I cannot forget,
  My father prays for me!

— Author Unknown

ॐ

THE WORTH OF PRAYER

Prayer is the breath of God in man,
  Returning whence it came;
Love is the sacred fire within,
  And prayer the rising flame.

It gives the burdened spirit ease,
  And soothes the troubled breast;
Yields comfort to the mourners here,
  And to the weary rest.

When God inclines the heart to pray,
  He hath an ear to hear;
To him there's music in a groan,
  And beauty in a tear.

The humble suppliant cannot fail
  To have his wants supplied,
Since he for sinners intercedes,
  Who once for sinners died.

— Benjamin Beddome

ॐ

THE TEACHER'S PRAYER

O Lord of Life and God of Love,
  Make us to know, we ask,
The beauty of the trust we bear,
  The glory of our task!

Strengthen our hands and cleanse our
    hearts,
  Lighten our eyes, and make
Us worthy of our calling, for
  The children's Master's sake!

— Nancy Byrd Turner

Evening Hymn

Sun of my soul, Thou Saviour dear,
It is not night if Thou be near;
Oh! may no earth-born cloud arise
To hide Thee from Thy servant's eyes.

When the soft dews of kindly sleep
My wearied eyelids gently steep,
Be my last thought how sweet to rest
Forever on my Saviour's breast.

Abide with me from morn till eve,
For without Thee I cannot live;
Abide with me when night is nigh,
For without Thee I dare not die.

If some poor wandering child of Thine
Have spurned today the voice divine,
Now, Lord, the gracious work begin;
Let him no more lie down in sin.

Watch by the sick, enrich the poor
With blessings from Thy boundless
      store;
Be every mourner's sleep tonight,
Like infant's slumbers, pure and light.

Come near and bless us when we wake,
Ere thro' the world our way we take:
Till, in the ocean of Thy love,
We lose ourselves in heaven above.

— *John Keble*

The Blessings of God

Mercy abundantly given
Help for the difficult place
Courage when it's sorely needed,
Strength for the problems we face!
Comfort when grief assails us,
Love when we need someone to care
These are the blessings of God
That He gives in answer to prayer!

— *Mary D. Hughes*

A Prayer

Not more of light I ask, O God,
   But eyes to see what is;
Not sweeter songs, but power to hear
   The present melodies.

Not greater strength, but how to use
   The power that I possess;
Not more of love, but skill to turn
   A frown to a caress.

Not more of joy, but power to feel
   Its kindling presence near,
To give to others all I have
   Of courage and of cheer.

Give me all fears to dominate,
   All holy joys to know;
To be the friend I wish to be,
   To speak the truth I know.

— *Florence Holbrook*

Be Still

Be still, my soul and listen,
For God would speak to thee,
And while the tempest's raging
Thy refuge He would be.

Be still, and cease to struggle,
Seek not to understand;
The flames will not destroy thee,
Thou'rt in the Father's hand.

And when the burden's heavy
He seeks to make thee pure,
To give thee faith and patience
And courage to endure.

The way is not too hard for thee,
Endure the chastening rod;
Thy gold shall only be refined,
Be still, submit to God.

— *G. W. S.*

Begin the Day With God

Every morning lean thine arms awhile
Upon the window sill of heaven
And gaze upon thy Lord.
Then, with the vision in thy heart,
Turn strong to meet thy day.

— *Author Unknown*

Two Prayers

Last night my little boy confessed to
me
Some childish wrong;
And kneeling at my knee,
He prayed with tears —
"Dear God, make me a man
Like Daddy — wise and strong;
I know you can."

Then while he slept
I knelt beside his bed,
Confessed my sins,
And prayed with low-bowed head.
"O God, make me a child
Like my child here —
Pure, guileless,
Trusting Thee with faith sincere."

— *Andrew Gillies*

The Solitary Place (Mark 1:35)

Before the work and toil of day,
Before our tasks we face,
We need to take the time to pray
In the solitary place.

The Master went at early morn
Before the break of day;
Before the hours were spent or worn
He sought a place to pray.

We need the solitary place
For study, thought and prayer:
We need the strength and added grace
He gives while kneeling there.

With courage then we start the day,
With smiles our tasks we face,
For we have taken time to pray
In the solitary place.

— *Carlton Buck*

The Teacher

Lord, who am I to teach the way
    To little children day by day,
    So prone myself to go astray?

I teach them knowledge, but I know
    How faint the flicker and how low
    The candles of my knowledge glow.

I teach them love for all mankind
    And all God's creatures, but I find
    My love comes lagging far behind.

Lord, if their guide I still must be,
    Oh, let the little children see
    The teacher leaning hard on Thee.

— *Leslie Pinckney Hill*

Evening

Softly now the light of day
Fades upon my sight away;
Free from care, from labor free,
Lord, I would commune with Thee:

Thou, whose all-pervading eye,
    Naught escapes, without, within,
Pardon each infirmity,
    Open fault and secret sin.

Soon, for me, the light of day
Shall for ever pass away;
Then, from sin and sorrow free,
Take me, Lord, to dwell with Thee:

Thou, who, sinless, yet hast known
    All of man's infirmity;
Then, from Thine eternal throne,
    Jesus, look with pitying eye.

— *George Washington Doane*

THE MORNING LIGHT

The twilight deepens o'er the sleeping hills,
　　The hush of ev'ning calms my troubled breast;
I hear a voice, it is the voice of God,
　　And all my being enters into rest.

The clouds hang motionless against the sky,
　　Eternal music echoes through my soul;
I hear a song; it is the angel choir,
　　And o'er my spirit Heaven's anthems roll.

I draw yet nearer as the night grows dark,
　　And hear Him whisper, "Be thou not afraid";
The morn awakens and I see His face,
　　He gently murmurs, "I will be thine aid."

The darkness settles over hill and vale,
　　I feel the presence of my Saviour near;
He bids me trust, and though I cannot see,
　　I know that He my cry will surely hear.

The way is lonely but He ne'er forsakes,
　　My heart is burdened, yet He still is near;
I feel His presence when I cannot see,
　　His voice, it ever soundeth in my ear.

Some day I'll see my Saviour face to face,
　　Till then I'll walk by faith and not by sight;
And when at last the long, dark night is gone,
　　My weary eyes will greet the morning light.

　　　　　　　　　　　　　— Author Unknown

WATCH AND PRAY

The God that stopped the sun on high
And sent the manna from the sky,
Laid flat the walls of Jericho,
And put to flight old Israel's foe;
Why can't he answer prayer today,
And drive each stormy cloud away?

Who turned the water into wine,
And healed a helpless cripple's spine,
Commanded tempest, "Peace, be still,"
And hungry multitudes did fill;
His power is just the same today,
So why not labor, watch and pray?

He conquered in the lions' den,
Brought Lazarus back to life again,
He heard Elijah's cry for rain,
And freed the sufferers from pain.
If He could do those wonders then,
Let's prove our mighty God again.

Why can't the God who raised the
　　dead,
Gave little David Goliath's head,
Cast out the demons with a word,
Yet sees the fall of one wee bird,
Do signs and miracles today,
In that same, good, old-fashioned way?
He can! He's just the same today!

　　　　　　　　　　　　　— Martin Luther

PRAYER IN SORROW

Father, to Thee we look in all our sorrow,
　　Thou art the fountain whence our healing flows;
Dark though the night, joy cometh with the morrow;
　　Safely they rest who in Thy love repose.

When fond hopes fail and skies are dark before us,
　　When the vain cares that vex our life increase —
Comes with its calm the thought that Thou art o'er us,
　　And we grow quiet, folded in Thy peace.

Naught shall affright us on thy goodness leaning,
　　Low in the heart Faith singeth still her song;
Chastened by pain, we learn life's deepest meaning,
　　And in our weakness Thou dost make us strong.

Patient, O heart, though heavy be thy sorrows!
　　Be not cast down, disquieted in vain;
Yet shalt thou praise Him when these darkened furrows,
　　Where now He plougheth, wave with golden grain.

　　　　　　　　　　　　　— *Frederick L. Hosmer*

THE SHUT DOOR

I need not leave the jostling world,
　　Or wait till daily tasks are o'er,
To fold my palms in secret prayer
　　Within the close-shut, closet door.
There is a viewless, cloistered room,
　　As high as heaven, as fair as day,
Where though my feet may join the
　　　　throng,
　　My soul can enter in and pray.

　　　　　　　　　　　Author Unknown

PRAYER

To worship Him who is my Father-God,
  In the all-worthy name of Christ, the Son,
  Through the blest Spirit, ever Holy One,
Bowing the knee, with heart all hushed and awed;
To come to Him, confessing all my sin,
  And seek forgiveness through the precious blood;
  To ask that He, in love's o'erflowing flood,
Will bless my needy life, without, within:
To intercede for all my kinsmen, friends,
  For the elect who love our Saviour-Lord,
  For the great world, e'en to its farthest ends,
That Christ may be by men obeyed, adored;
  And then to praise, always and everywhere;—
  Be this my fervent and effectual prayer!

— Henry W. Frost

NIGHT-WATCH PRAYER

Lord, Thy peaceful gift restore,
Give my body sleep once more:
While I wait my soul will rest
Like a child upon Thy breast.

— Henry van Dyke

AT PRAYER MEETING

There were only two or three of us
  Who came to the place of prayer;
Came in the teeth of a driving storm;
  But for that we did not care,
Since after our hymns of praise had
    risen,
  And our earnest prayers were said,
The Master Himself was present there
  And gave us the living bread.

We knew His look in our leader's face,
  So rapt and glad and free;
We felt His touch when our heads we
    bowed,
  We heard His "Come to Me!"

Nobody saw Him lift the latch,
  And none unbarred the door;
But peace was His token to every heart,
  And how could we ask for more?

It was only a handful gathered in
  To the little place of prayer,
Outside was struggle and pain and sin,
  But the Lord Himself was there;
He came to redeem the pledge He gave
  Wherever His loved ones be,
To stand Himself in the midst of them,
  Tho' they count but two or three.

And forth we fared in the bitter rain.
  And our hearts had grown so warm,
It seemed like the pelting of summer
    flowers
  And not the crash of a storm;
" 'Twas a time of the dearest privilege
  At the Lord's right hand," we said,
And we thought how Jesus Himself
    had come
  To feed us the Living Bread.

— Margaret E. Sangster

A PRAYER

Oh, not for more or longer days, dear Lord,
 My prayer shall be —
But rather teach me how to use the day
 Now given to me.

I ask not more of pleasure or of joy
 For this brief while —
But rather let me for the joys I have
 Be glad and smile.

I ask not ownership of vast estates
 Nor piles of gold —
But make me generous with the little store
 My hands now hold.

Nor shall I ask that life should give to me
 Another friend —
Just keep me true to those I have, dear Lord,
 Until the end.

         — *B. Y. Williams*

EVENING PRAYER

God of Mercy:
The day with all its choices, good or ill,
Is now beyond recall;
And I am alone with Thee,
To make answer for deed and word and thought,
I cannot play the hypocrite with Thee,
I cannot excuse or justify the blots that stained the day;
I cannot lightly laugh at my transgressions now;
For Thou dost know me altogether:
But Thou dost know the good in me, and not the evil only;
Dost see my struggles, mark my resolutions,
Hear my silent prayers in heaven, Thy dwelling place.
Thy heart is kind.
There is forgiveness with Thee.
It was for men like me that Jesus died.
For His sake, let me know Thy peace tonight,
And with the morrow make me to be
A new and worthier man.

         — *Robert Freeman*

Too Busy

Forgive me, Lord, that I allow
My days and hours to be
So filled with trifling tasks, that oft
I find no time for Thee.

My thoughts so oft are occupied
With countless earthly things,
When Thou wouldst have them
        mount on High
By faith with eagle wings.

So many duties round me press,
That rob me of the time
I fain would spend with Thee, my
        Lord,
In fellowship divine.

Too busy — O forbid, dear Lord,
That I should ever be
Too much engrossed in worldly tasks
To spend an hour with Thee!

That I should let the din of life
Drown out Thy voice of love,
And, grovelling in the "sands of time,"
Lose out on things Above.

O help me, Lord, to take the time —
To set all else aside,
That in the Secret Place of prayer
I may with Thee abide;

To hear what Thou wouldst say to me,
And hold communion sweet;
To praise Thy precious worthy Name
And worship at Thy feet:

To hearken to Thy holy will,
To feel Thy cleansing pow'r —
O may I ne'er let aught deprive
My soul of this blest hour!
            — *Avis B. Christiansen*

The Place of Prayer

The place of prayer is not confined
To a chapel by the way.
The place of prayer is anywhere
The soul will pause to pray.

The cathedral with its altar,
A shop or a prison cell,
Or a house of lath by a garden path
Will serve the purpose well.

At kitchen sink or mountain stream
Or distant desert place,
God is there and the earnest prayer
Will tap the source of grace.

So pray, O heart, remembering
That God is everywhere;
In town or field just quietly yield
And let love lift your prayer.
            — *Carlton Buck*

Hast Thou Spoken, Blessed Master?

Hast Thou spoken, blessed Master,
Hast Thou whispered in my ear,
And have I because of dullness
Failed Thy precious voice to hear?

Hast Thou sought to bring some
        message
From Thy heart of love to mine,
Which I've missed because earth's
        clatter
Has drowned out Thy voice divine?

Have my hands been over-active
With a thousand lesser deeds,
While my heart has been oblivious
To my spirit's greater needs?

Have I been so bent on asking
For Thy help each passing day,
That I've had not time to listen
To what Thou, O Lord, wouldst say?

O forgive me, precious Saviour!
Still the tumult in my heart,
That my soul might hear the message
Thou art waiting to impart!
            — *Avis B. Christiansen*

FATHER, WE THANK THEE

For flowers that bloom about our feet,
Father, we thank Thee,
For tender grass so fresh and sweet,
Father, we thank Thee,
For song of bird and hum of bee,
For all things fair we hear or see,
Father in heaven, we thank Thee.

For blue of stream and blue of sky,
Father, we thank Thee,
For pleasant shade of branches high,
Father, we thank Thee,
For fragrant air and cooling breeze,
For beauty of the blooming trees,
Father in heaven, we thank Thee.

For this new morning with its light,
Father, we thank Thee,
For rest and shelter of the night,
Father, we thank Thee,
For health and food, for love and
friends,
For everything Thy goodness sends,
Father in heaven, we thank Thee.

— *Author Unknown*

ᏩᏯ

THANKFULNESS

My God, I thank Thee who hast made
The earth so bright;
So full of splendor and of joy,
Beauty and light;
So many glorious things are here,
Noble and right!

I thank Thee, too, that Thou hast
made
Joy to abound;
So many gentle thoughts and deeds
Circling us round,
That in the darkest spot of Earth
Some love is found.

I thank Thee more that all our joy
Is touched with pain;
That shadows fall on brightest hours;
That thorns remain;
So that Earth's bliss may be our guide,
And not our chain.

I thank Thee, Lord, that Thou hast
kept
The best in store;
We have enough, yet not too much
To long for more:
A yearning for a deeper peace,
Not known before.

I thank Thee, Lord, that here our souls,
Though amply blest,
Can never find, although they seek,
A perfect rest,—
Nor ever shall, until they lean
On Jesus' breast!

— *Adelaide Anne Procter*

ᏩᏯ

LIGHT AT EVENING TIME

Holy Father, cheer our way
With thy love's perpetual ray;
Grant us every closing day
Light at evening time.

Holy Saviour, calm our fears
When earth's brightness disappears;
Grant us in our later years
Light at evening time.

Holy Spirit, be thou nigh
When in mortal pains we lie;
Grant us, as we come to die.
Light at evening time.

Holy, blessèd Trinity,
Darkness is not dark to thee;
Those thou keepest always see
Light at evening time.

— *R. H. Robinson*

A PRAYER

Lord, in mercy pardon me
  All that I this day have done:
Sins of every kind 'gainst Thee,
  Oh, forgive them, thro' Thy Son.

Make me, Jesus, like to Thee,
  Gentle, holy, meek, and mild,
My transgressions pardon me,
  Oh, forgive a sinful child.

— *Frances Ridley Havergal*

ༀ

HEARD

What if I cry in midnight gloom,
  Shall I be heard?
Will there be found in God's heart
      room
  For my poor word?
My soul is breaking, I must cry;
Hear me, O Father, or I die!

I cried aloud in midnight gloom,
  With pleading word;
I spoke of sorrow's threat'ning doom,
  Of hope deferred;
And lo, God heard my anguished cry—
And e'en my lowest, faintest sigh!

— *Henry W. Frost*

ༀ

MY PRAYER

  I kneel to pray,
But know not what to say:
  I cannot tell
What may be ill or well:
  But as I look
Into Thy Face or Book
  I see a love
From which I cannot move:
  And learn to rest
In this — Thy will is best:

Therefore I pray
Only have Thine own way
  In everything
My all wise God and King.
  Grant me the grace
In all to give Thee place:
  This liberty
Alone I ask of Thee:
  This only gift,
Have Thy way perfectly.

— *Mark Guy Pearse*

ༀ

A MISSIONARY PRAYER

Thy mercy, Lord, to us dispense,
  Thy blessing on us pour;
Lift up Thy gracious countenance
  Upon us evermore:
Oh, may we fully know Thy mind,
  Thy saving word proclaim,
That many heathen-tribes may find
  Salvation in Thy Name.

Let tongues and kindreds praise the
      Lord,
  Let every nation praise,
Let all the earth with one accord
  A glad thanksgiving raise,
That sin no more its sway maintains,
  For Christ the Lord is King,
His word defends, His law sustains;
  Shout all ye lands and sing!

Then shall the earth her increase bring,
  Her fruits be multiplied;
Then shall Thy scepter rule, O King,
  Thy word be glorified:
And God, our God, with blessings
      crown,
  His faithful Church again,
And earth's remotest bounds shall own
Him, Lord and God! Amen!

— *Martin Luther*

PRAYER

Prayer is the mightiest force that men can wield;
A power to which Omnipotence doth yield;
A privilege unparalleled, a way
Whereby the Almighty Father can display
His interest in His children's need and care.

Jehovah's storehouse is unlocked by prayer,
And faith doth turn the key. Oh! would that men
Made full proof of this wondrous means, for then
Would mightier blessings on the Church be showered,
Her witness owned, her ministers empowered,
And souls ingathered. Then the Gospel's sound
Would soon be heard to earth's remotest bound.
All things are possible if men but pray,
And if God did but limit to a day,
The time in which He'd note the upward glance,
Or fix the place, or name the circumstance,
When, where, or why petition could be brought,
Methinks His presence would by all be sought.

—*Author Unknown*

THE TOYS

My little son, who look'd from thoughtful eyes
And moved and spoke in quiet grown-up wise,
Having my law the seventh time disobey'd,
I struck him, and dismiss'd
With hard words and unkiss'd,—
His Mother, who was patient, being dead.
Then, fearing lest his grief should hinder sleep,
I visited his bed,
But found him slumbering deep,
With darken'd eyelids, and their lashes yet
From his late sobbing wet.
And I, with moan,
Kissing away his tears, left others of my own;
For, on a table drawn beside his head,
He had put, within his reach,
A box of counters and a red-vein'd stone,
A piece of glass abraded by the beach,
And six or seven shells,
A bottle with bluebells,

And two French copper coins, ranged there with careful art,
To comfort his sad heart.
So when that night I pray'd
To God, I wept, and said:
Ah, when at last we lie with trancèd breath,
Not vexing Thee in death,
And Thou rememberest of what toys
We made our joys,
How weakly understood
Thy great commanded good,
Then, fatherly not less
Than I whom Thou hast moulded from the clay,
Thou'lt leave Thy wrath, and say,
"I will be sorry for their childishness."

                                        — *Coventry Patmore*

ᕤ

A PRAYER

We know the paths wherein our feet should press,
Across our hearts are written Thy decrees,
Yet now, O Lord, be merciful to bless
        With more than these.

Grant us the will to fashion as we feel,
Grant us the strength to labor as we know,
Grant us the purpose, ribbed and edged with steel,
        To strike the blow.

Knowledge we ask not — knowledge Thou hast lent,
But, Lord, the will — there lies our bitter need,
Give us to build above the deep intent
        The deed, the deed.

                                        — *John Drinkwater*

ᕤ

MAN'S PLEA

Man's plea to man is, that he nevermore
Will beg, and that he never begged before:
Man's plea to God is, that he did obtain
A former suit, and therefore sues again.
How good a God we serve, that, when we sue,
Makes His old gifts the examples of His new.

                                        — *Francis Quarles*

PRAYER TIME

The while she darns her children's socks,
  She prays for little stumbling feet;
Each folded pair within its box
  Fits faith's bright sandals, sure and fleet.

While washing out, with mother pains,
  Small dusty suits and frocks and slips,
She prays that God may cleanse the stains
  From little hearts and hands and lips.

And when she breaks the fragrant bread,
  Or pours each portion in its cup,
For grace to keep their spirits fed,
  Her mother-heart is lifted up.

O busy ones, whose souls grow faint,
  Whose tasks seem longer than the day,
It doesn't take a cloistered saint
  To find a little time to pray!

— *Ruby Weyburn Tobias*

TOO BUSY?

"I'm busy!
  No, I cannot stay,
A thousand things
  Call me away;
To-morrow
  I will stop to pray."
And so I lost me
  One great day!

"I'm busy!
  Yes, so I must wait,
A thousand things
  Without my gate
Warn that to-morrow
  Is too late
To pray."
  Is too late to pray."
And so I saved me
  One great day!

— *Ralph S. Cushman*

GRACE FOR THE NOONDAY MEAL

Dear Lord, we bow our heads to pray
At noontime of this happy day.
Thus far Thy love has kept us true
Half of this wondrous daytime through.

We thank Thee for the food we eat
And for our happy homes so sweet;
For all of those who love us so,
For all adventuring ways we go.

For cloud and sun and wind and showers,
For grass and trees and birds and flowers;
For clothes to wear and tasks to do
This whole glad happy daytime through.

Be with us all this afternoon,
And may we ever keep in tune
  With all Thy love and all Thy ways,
Through all these happy, happy days.
  Amen.

— *William L. Stidger*

TONIGHT

For all who watch tonight — by land or sea or air —
O Father, may they know that Thou art with them there.

For all who weep tonight, the hearts that cannot rest,
Reveal Thy love, that wondrous love which gave for us Thy best.

For all who wake tonight, love's tender watch to keep,
Watcher Divine, Thyself draw nigh, Thou who dost never sleep.

For all who fear tonight, whate'er the dread may be,
We ask for them the perfect peace of hearts that rest in Thee.

Our own belov'd tonight, O Father, keep, and where
Our love and succor cannot reach, now bless them through our prayer.

And all who pray tonight, Thy wrestling hosts, O Lord,
Make weakness strong, let them prevail according to Thy word.

— Author Unknown

PRAY WITH FAITH

Prayer is appointed to convey
  The blessings God designs to give:
Long as they live should Christians pray;
  They learn to pray when first they live.

'Tis prayer supports the soul that's weak;
  Though thought be broken, language lame,
Pray, if thou canst or canst not speak;
  But pray with faith in Jesus' name.

Depend on him; thou canst not fail;
  Make all thy wants and wishes known;
Fear not; his merits must prevail:
  Ask but in faith, it shall be done.

— Joseph Hart

A GRACE

Reveal Thy Presence now, O Lord,
  As in the Upper Room of old;
Break Thou our bread, grace Thou our board,
  And keep our hearts from growing cold.

— Thomas Tiplady

THE STAIRWAY TO THE STARS

There's a stairway leading upward —
  Which the weariest may climb
Far above the highest mountain
  To an altitude sublime,
Where a Comforter awaits us,
  For the Father's home is there;
And the way to mount that stairway
  Is the simple way of prayer!

There's a stairway leading upward —
  Though the distance may be far,
Though the lowest step's a valley,
  And the highest step a star;
'Tis the measure of an instant,
  Lowly vale to starry height —
Just a little prayer will lift us
  From the darkness to the light.

— *William Ludlum*

THE UNSEEN BRIDGE

There is a bridge, whereof the span
Is rooted in the heart of man,
And reaches, without pile or rod,
Unto the Great White Throne of God.

Its traffic is in human sighs
Fervently wafted to the skies;
'Tis the one pathway from Despair;
And it is called the Bridge of Prayer.

— *Gilbert Thomas*

I LOVE TO STEAL AWHILE AWAY

I love to steal awhile away
  From every cumbering care,
And spend the hours of setting day
  In humble, grateful prayer.

I love in solitude to shed
  The penitential tear,
And all his promises to plead,
  Where none but God can hear.

I love to think on mercies past,
  And future good implore,
And all my cares and sorrows cast
  On him whom I adore.

— *Phoebe H. Brown*

PRAYER

Prayer — the fragrance of a flower
After the refreshing shower;
'Tis the dew that soars again,
Mist ascending after rain;
'Tis the life-blood of the tree;
Oft it bleeds in agony.
Oh, the agony of prayer!
How it wrings the soul with care;
One of God's true witnesses,
This true sign: "Behold, he prays."

— *Robert Maguire*

PRAYER FOR PURITY

Thou didst teach the thronging people
  By blue Galilee;
Speak to us, Thy erring children;
  Teach us purity.

Thou whose touch could heal the leper,
  Make the blind to see;
Touch our hearts and turn from sin-
    ning,
  Into purity.

Thou whose word could still the tem-
    pest,
  Calm the raging sea,
Hush the storm of human passion,
  Give us purity.

Thou didst sinless meet the tempter.
  Grant, O Christ, that we
May o'ercome the bent to evil,
  By thy purity.

— *Jemima Luke*

THE THREE PRAYERS

I

"Lord, help me," so we pray,
  "Help me my work to do;
I am so ignorant and weak,
  Make me more wise and true."

II

"Lord, help me to do Thy work,"
  We pray when wiser grown,
When on the upward way
  Our feet have farther gone.

III

"Lord, do Thy work through me";
  So when all self we lose;
His doing and His work, and we
  The tools His hand can use.

— Annie Johnson Flint

ᏨᏩ

A WOMAN'S PRAYER

O Lord, who knowest every need of
    mine,
Help me to bear each cross and not
    repine;
Grant me fresh courage every day,
Help me to do my work alway
    Without complaint!

O Lord, Thou knowest well how dark
    the way,
Guide Thou my footsteps, lest they
    stray;
Give me fresh faith for every hour,
Lest I should ever doubt Thy power
    And make complaint!

Give me a heart, O Lord, strong to
    endure,
Help me to keep it simple, pure,
Make me unselfish, helpful, true,
In every act, whate'er I do,
    And keep content!

Help me to do my woman's share,
Make me courageous, strong to bear
Sunshine or shadow in my life!
Sustain me in the daily strife
    To keep content!

— Author Unknown

ᏨᏩ

THE UNDISCOVERED COUNTRY

Lord, for the erring thought
Not unto evil wrought:
Lord, for the wicked will
Betrayed and baffled still:
For the heart from itself kept,
Our thanksgiving accept.
For ignorant hopes that were
Broken to our blind prayer:
For pain, death, sorrow sent
Unto our chastisement:
For all loss of seeming good,
Quicken our gratitude.

— William Dean Howells

ᏨᏩ

A PRAYER

Give me the faith that asks not "Why?"
I shall know God's plan by and by.

Give me the faith that looks at pain
And says all will be right again.

Give me the faith to bow my head
Trustfully waiting to be led.

Give me the faith to face my life
With all its pain and wrong and strife,

And then with the day's setting sun
I'll close my eyes when life is done.

My soul will go without a care
Knowing that God is waiting there.

— Author Unknown

BLESSED

He prayed for strength that he might achieve;
He was made weak that he might obey.
He prayed for wealth that he might do greater things;
He was given infirmity that he might do better things,
He prayed for riches that he might be happy;
He was given poverty that he might be wise.
He prayed for power that he might have the praise of men;
He was given infirmity that he might feel the need of God.
He prayed for all things that he might enjoy life;
He was given life that he might enjoy all things.
He had received nothing that he asked for — all that he hoped for;
His prayer was answered — he was most blessed.

— *Author Unknown*

ojo

SHALL I PRAY ON?

For years I've prayed, and yet I see no change.
The mountain stands exactly where it stood;
  The shadows that it casts are just as deep;
  The pathway to its summit e'en more steep.
    Shall I pray on?

Shall I pray on with ne'er a hopeful sign?
Not only does the mountain still remain
  But, while I watch to see it disappear,
  Becomes the more appalling year by year.
    Shall I pray on?

I will pray on. Though distant it may seem,
The answer may be almost at my door,
  Or just around the corner on its way.
  But whether near or far, yea, I shall pray —
    I will pray on.

— *Edith L. Mapes*

ojo

PRAYER

I asked for bread; God gave a stone instead.
Yet, while I pillowed there my weary head,
The angels made a ladder of my dreams,
Which upward to celestial mountains led.

And when I woke beneath the morning's beams,
Around my resting-place fresh manna lay;
And, praising God, I went upon my way,
    For I was fed.

God answers prayer; sometimes, when hearts are weak,
He gives the very gifts believers seek.
But often faith must learn a deeper rest,
And trust God's silence when He does not speak;
For He whose name is Love will send the best.
Stars may burn out, nor mountain walls endure,
But God is true, His promises are sure.
    For those who seek.

               — *Author Unknown*

MY NAME IN MOTHER'S PRAYER

'Twas in the years of long ago
When life was fair and bright
And ne'er a tear and scarce a fear
O'ercast my day or night,
That often in the eventide
I found her kneeling there
And just one word, my name, I heard:
    My name in mother's prayer!

I thought but little of it then,
Though reverence touched my heart
For her whose love sought from above
For me, the better part.
But when the sterner battles came
With many a subtle snare,
'Twas then one word, my name, I
    heard:
    My name in mother's prayer.

I wandered on and heeded not
God's oft-repeated call
To turn from sin, to live for Him,
And give to Him my all;
Until at last of sin convinced
I sank in deep despair:
My hope awoke when mem'ry spoke
    My name in mother's prayer!

That pleading heart; that soul, so tired,
Has reached the shining shore,
But now the spirit of her life
Doth guide me more and more;
And when I enter heaven's rest
And greet her over there
I'll praise the Lord, because He heard
    My name in mother's prayer!

               — *Author Unknown*

THIS I KNOW

I know not by what methods rare,
But this I know, God answers prayer.
I know that He has given His Word,
Which tells me prayer is always heard,
And will be answered, soon or late.
And so I pray and calmly wait.

I know not if the blessing sought
Will come in just the way I thought;
But leave my prayers with Him alone,
Whose will is wiser than my own,
Assured that He will grant my quest,
Or send some answer far more blest.
           — *Eliza M. Hickok*

FATHER, WHATE'ER OF EARTHLY BLISS

Father, whate'er of earthly bliss
  Thy sovereign will denies,
Accepted at thy throne of grace,
  Let this petition rise:

Give me a calm and thankful heart,
  From every murmur free,
The blessings of thy love impart,
  And help me live to thee.

Let the sweet hope that thou art mine
  My life and death attend;
Thy presence thro' my journey shine,
  And crown my journey's end.

— *Anne Steele*

༝

LITTLE JESUS

Little Jesus, wast Thou shy
Once, and just so small as I?
And what did it feel like to be
Out of Heaven, and just like me?
Didst Thou sometimes think of there,
And ask where all the angels were?
I should think that I would cry
For my house all made of sky;
I would look about the air,
And wonder where my angels were;
And at waking 'twould distress me —
Not an angel there to dress me!
Hadst Thou ever any toys,
Like us little girls and boys?
And didst Thou play in Heaven with
  all
The angels that were not too tall,
With stars for marbles? Did the things
Play *Can you see me?* through their
  wings?
And did Thy Mother let Thee spoil
Thy robes, with playing on *our* soil?
How nice to have them always new
In Heaven, because 'twas quite clean
  blue!

Didst Thou kneel at night to pray,
And didst Thou join Thy hands, this
  way?
And did they tire sometimes, being
  young,
And make the prayer seem very long?
And dost Thou like it best, that we
Should join our hands to pray to
  Thee?
I used to think, before I knew,
The prayer not said unless we do.
And did Thy Mother at the night
Kiss Thee, and fold the clothes in
  right?
And didst Thou feel quite good in bed,
Kissed, and sweet, and Thy prayers
  said?

Thou canst not have forgotten all
That it feels like to be small:
And Thou know'st I cannot pray
To Thee in my father's way —
When Thou wast so little, say,
Couldst Thou talk Thy Father's way?
So, a litle Child, come down
And hear a child's tongue like Thy
  own;
Take me by the hand and walk,
And listen to my baby-talk.
To Thy Father's show my prayer
(He will look, Thou art so fair),
And say: "O Father, I, Thy Son,
Bring the prayer of a little one."

And He will smile, that children's
  tongue
Has not changed since Thou wast
  young!

— *Francis Thompson*

PRAYER

Dear Refuge of my weary soul,
  On Thee, when sorrows rise,
On Thee, when waves of trouble roll,
  My fainting hope relies.

To Thee I tell each rising grief,
  For Thou alone canst heal;
Thy word can bring a sweet relief,
  For every pain I feel.

— *Anne Steele*

∼

MY PRAYER

I do not ask that I may steer
  My bark by peaceful shores alone,
Nor that I linger, harbor-bound,
  And sail no stormy seas unknown;
I only ask this boon of Thee:
Be ever in the ship with me.

I do not ask that I may dwell
  From din of battle far removed,
Nor ever feel temptation's force,
  Nor ever know mine armor proved;
I only ask, through Life's long fight,
Grant me the power of Thy might.

I do not ask that I may walk
  Only on smoothly trodden grass,
Nor ever climb the mountain's height
  And trembling, through its dangers
    pass;
I only ask, on rocks or sand,
The sure upholding of Thy hand.

I dare not pray for any gift
  Upon my pligrim path to Heaven;
I only ask one thing of Thee:
  Give Thou Thyself and all is given.
I am not strong nor brave nor wise;
  Be Thou with me — it shall suffice.

— *Annie Johnson Flint*

MY PRAYER

If the way be rough with thorns and
    stones,
  May faith provide a balm
To soothe my weary, bleeding feet
  And fill my soul with calm.

— *Lucy Carruth*

∼

LORD, GIVE ME FAITH

Lord, give me faith,
Enlightening faith,
  That I may see
    The things unseen
  With vision clear
    And crystalline.

Lord, give me faith,
Far-seeing faith,
  That I may tell
    My soul at night
  That in the sky
    The stars are bright.

Lord, give me faith,
Assuring faith,
  That when I pass
    Deep glades of fear
  I'll realize
    That Thou art near.

Lord, give me faith,
Outreaching faith,
  That I, when tried,
    May flee to Thee,
  And find Thy strength
    My victory.

Lord, give me faith,
Revealing faith,
  That when I go
    Through cloud and storm
  I'll hear Thy voice
    And see Thy form.

— *Dwight Edwards Marvin*

A Prayer

Lord, when on my bed I lie,
Sleepless unto Thee I cry;
When my brain works overmuch,
Stay the wheels with Thy soft touch.
Just a quiet thought of Thee,
And of Thy sweet charity,
Just a little prayer, and then
I will turn to sleep again.

— *John Oxenham*

Evening

O Lord, the sun is low;
    With me abide;
Dark shadows 'neath their wings
    Bring eventide.

Thy presence, Lord, was mine
    The livelong day;
I welcome night, for Thou
    Hast heard me pray.

— *Robert J. Craig*

I Have a Rendezvous With God

I have a rendezvous with God!
Upon His blessèd day of rest,
To His loved house I go, and meet
With others on the Holy Quest;
Whose presence fill His holy place,
Our spiritual eyes behold
The radiance of our Father's face;
Then at the midweek hour of prayer
What strength flows down our need to
    meet,
As unto Him in prayer we turn,
United at the mercy seat!
How can I to my faith be true
If I keep not this rendezvous?

— *Author Unknown*

Our Prayer

Thou that hast given so much to me,
Give one thing more—a grateful heart;
Not thankful when it pleaseth me,
As if Thy blessings had spare days;
But such a heart, whose pulse may be
    Thy praise.

— *George Herbert*

A Prayer to Make Your Own

Look from thy sphere of endless day,
    O God of mercy and of might;
In pity look on those who stray,
    Benighted, in this land of light.

In peopled vale, in lonely glen,
    In crowded mart, by stream or sea,
How many of the sons of men
    Hear not the message sent from
        Thee!

Send forth thy heralds, Lord, to call
    The thoughtless young, the hard-
        ened old,
A scattered, homeless flock, till all
    Be gathered to thy peaceful fold.

Send them thy mighty word to speak,
    Till faith shall dawn, and doubt de-
        part,
To awe the bold, to stay the weak,
    And bind and heal the broken heart.

— *William Cullen Bryant*

Morning Prayer for Day's Work

May Jesus' grace and blessing
Attend me without ceasing;
Thus I stretch out my hand,
And do that work with pleasure,
Which is my call and measure,
My God for me to do ordained.

— *John Matthesius*

He Prayeth Well

He prayeth well who loveth well
Both man and bird and beast.
He prayeth best who lovest best
    All things both great and small;
For the dear God, who loveth us,
    He made and loveth all.

        — S. T. Coleridge

Pharisee and Publican

Two went to pray? O, rather say
One went to brag, the other to pray;
One stands up close and treads on high,
Where the other dares not lend his eye;
One nearer to God's altar trod,
The other to the altar's God.

        — Richard Crashaw

Our Share in Calvary

I see the crowd in Pilate's hall,
    I mark their wrathful mien;
Their shouts of "Crucify!" appall,
    With blasphemy between.
And of that shouting multitude
    I feel that I am one;
And in that din of voices rude
    I recognize my own.
'Twas I that shed the sacred blood;
    I nailed him to the tree;
I crucified the Christ of God;
    I joined the mockery.
Around the cross the throng I see
    Mocking the Sufferer's groan;
Yet still my voice, it seems to be
    As if I mocked alone.
But not the less that blood avails
    To cleanse away my sin;
And not the less that cross prevails
    To give me peace within.

        — Horatius Bonar

My Prayer

Lord Jesus, make Thyself to me
A living, bright reality;
More present to faith's vision keen
Than any outward object seen;
More dear, more intimately nigh
Than e'en the sweetest earthly tie.

        — Author Unknown

Vesper Bells

The days are filled with duties;
    Each moment has its care:
But evening bids us worship
    And kneel in humble prayer

The vesper bells now softly
    Caress the fading day;
Their silver tones are pleading
    With men to kneel and pray.

        — Dwight Edwards Marvin

Prayer Is a Power

Prayer is a power omnipotent —
    Prayer has wrought great things!
No man can bar the flight of prayer
    When once it takes its wings.

Prayer is a power omnipotent
    That rules on earth and sea;
No prayer is ever prayed in vain
    By either you or me.

We cannot change the will of God
    Nor shorten any road;
But just one earnest, heartfelt prayer
    Can lighten *any* load.

Prayer is a power omnipotent!
    It draws all mankind near
To God and all His mighty love —
    It makes His purpose clear.

        — Phyllis C. Michael

Buried Thy Sins

In the deep silent depths far away from the shore,
Where they never shall rise to trouble thee more,
Where no far-reaching tide with its powerful sweep
May stir the dark waves of forgetfulness deep,
      I have buried them there —
      Where no mortal can see!
      I have cast all thy sins
      In the depths of the sea!

In the depths, in the depths, where the storm cannot come,
Where its faint echo falls like a musical drum,
Where no mortal can enter, thy faults to deride —
For above them forever flows love's mighty tide!
      In the sepulchral vaults
      Of which God holds the key!
      He has buried thy sins
      In the depths of the sea!
                     — Author Unknown

The Touch of the Master's Hand

'Twas battered and scarred, and the auctioneer
Thought it scarcely worth his while
To waste much time on the old violin,
But he held it up with a smile.
"What am I bidden, good folks," he cried,
"Who'll start the bidding for me?"
"A dollar, a dollar"; then, "Two! Only two?
Two dollars, and who'll make it three?
Three dollars, once; three dollars, twice;
Going for three——" But no,
From the room, far back, a gray-haired man
Came forward and picked up the bow;
Then, wiping the dust from the old violin,
And tightening the loose strings,
He played a melody pure and sweet
As a caroling angel sings.

The music ceased, and the auctioneer,
With a voice that was quiet and low,
Said: "What am I bid for the old violin?"
And he held it up with the bow.
"A thousand dollars, and who'll make it two?
Two thousand! And who'll make it three?
Three thousand, once; three thousand, twice,
And going, and gone," said he.
The people cheered, but some of them cried,
"We do not quite understand
What changed its worth." Swift came the reply:
"The touch of a master's hand."

And many a man with life out of tune,
And battered and scarred with sin,
Is auctioned cheap to the thoughtless crowd,
Much like the old violin.
A "mess of pottage," a glass of wine;
A game — and he travels on.
He is "going" once, and "going" twice,
He's "going" and almost "gone."
But the Master comes, and the foolish crowd
Never can quite understand
The worth of a soul and the change that's wrought
By the touch of the Master's hand.

— *Myra Brooks Welch*

ᴄᴍᴏ

Success

I tried, myself, to bring to pass
    That which I thought should be,
I felt the Lord would profit by
    A little help from me.
And so I worried and despaired
    And vainly labored on
Until my fairest plans had crashed,
    My choicest visions gone;
And then I knelt before my Lord,
    Chastened, humbled, still,
Ready to let Him work through me,
    Ready to do His will.
And there it was I found success,
For then alone my Lord could bless.

I tried to win a soul for Christ;
    How earnestly I pleaded
That he had sinned and gone astray
    And Christ was all he needed.
I begged him to forsake the world,
    Repent and be forgiven —
I tried to coax him to the Lord,
    To woo him into Heaven.
And then I realized that Christ
    Longed for him more than I,
That He alone could make one care,
    Who cared enough to die.
Upon my knees I fought the fight —
My friend was born again that night.

— *Barbara E. Cornet*

WHICH DO YOU CHOOSE?

You don't have to go to heaven,
  You don't have to live for God;
You don't have to be forgiven
  Nor be cleansed in Jesus' blood.
When beyond the shining portals
  All the ransomed meet at last,
You don't have to be among them
  When the fight on earth is past.

Tho' the Saviour died on Calv'ry,
  Yet His pardon none need know.
Tho' the Spirit now is striving,
  To the Lord you need not go.
Tho' a mother up in glory
  For your soul may plead and pray,
You don't have to go to heaven,
  Need not tread the narrow way.

You can choose eternal anguish,
  Live the life that suits you best;
Turn your back on heav'nly treasures;
  Vainly seek for peace and rest.
God will never make you serve Him,
  Never force you to be saved.
You can go to judgment Christless,
  Tho' your path with prayers be
        paved!
                — Harry A. Ironside
        (Written at the age of 17)

∽

CHOSEN

"Ye have not chosen me," He said,
  "But I have chosen you,"
When from the hurrying multitudes
  He called the list'ning few.
And day by day Himself He poured
  Into each seeking mind,
Till through their eyes His loving gaze
  Embraced a lost mankind.
'Twas from their lips His voice rang
        out
  A challenge naught could stay;

It pierced the fortresses of years —
  It quickens us today.
They did not choose Him — nor did I;
  But He has chosen me,
That thro' my yielded worthlessness
  The world His worth may see.

                — Catherine Baird

∽

HOW OLD OUGHT I TO BE?

"Dear Mother," said a little maid,
  "Please whisper it to me,
Before I am a Christian,
  How old ought I to be?"

"How old ought you to be, dear child,
  Before you can love me?"
"I always love you, Mother mine,
  Since I was tiny wee."

"I love you now, and always will,"
  The little daughter said.
And on her mother's shoulder laid
  Her golden, curly head.

"How old, my girlie, must you be,
  Before you trust my care?"
"Oh, Mother dear, I do, I do —
  I trust you everywhere."

"How old ought you to be, my child,
  To do the things I say?"
The little girl looked up and said,
  "I can do that today."

"Then you can be a Christian, too,
  Don't wait till you are grown.
Tell Jesus now you come to Him,
  To be His very own."

Then as the little maid knelt down,
  And said, "Lord, if I may,
I'd like to be a Christian now,"
  He answered, "Yes, today."

                — Author Unknown

I Heard the Voice of Jesus Say

I heard the voice of Jesus say,
  "Come unto me and rest;
Lay down, thou weary one, lay down
  Thy head upon My breast."
I came to Jesus as I was,
  Weary, and worn, and sad;
I found in Him a resting place,
  And He has made me glad.

I heard the voice of Jesus say,
  "Behold! I freely give
The living water; thirsty one,
  Stoop down and drink and live."
I came to Jesus, and I drank
  Of that life-giving stream;
My thirst was quenched, my soul re-
      vived,
  And now I live in Him.

I heard the voice of Jesus say,
  "I am this dark world's light;
Look unto Me, thy morn shall rise,
  And all thy day be bright."
I looked to Jesus, and I found
  In Him my star, my sun;
And in that light of life I'll walk
  Till traveling days are done.

  — *Horatius Bonar*

"Accepted"

'Tis not for works which I have wro't,
'Tis not for gifts which I have bro't,
Nor yet for blessings that I sought,
  That I have been "Accepted."

'Tis not for tears that I have shed,
'Tis not for prayers that I have said,
Nor yet for slavish fear or dread,
  That I have been "Accepted."

'Tis not for these, however right,
  That God has formed intense de-
      light,

Nor is it these that have made white
  The robes of those "Accepted."

From these I turn my eyes to Him,
  Who bore the judgment due to sin,
And by His blood I enter in,
  And share in His "Acceptance."

His precious blood was shed for me,
  And in that precious blood I see
The righteous ground, the perfect plea,
  For my complete "Acceptance."

And as I gaze, my joys abound,
  For now on resurrection ground
I see the Lamb with glory crowned
  Who died for my "Acceptance."

And when within that circle sweet,
  Where God's eternal smile I meet,
I'll praise Him for the work complete,
  Through which I am "'Accepted."
      — *Author Unknown*

I Have Found It!

I have found the perfect treasure,
  Richer than my fondest dream;
It is mine and mine forever,
  Safe from every selfish scheme.

Wealth as vast as all of heaven!
  Beauty fairer than the day!
Joy with no corrupting leaven
  Shall go with me all the way!

Long I sought this wondrous blessing,
  Sought by labor under law,
Till God's grace reached down, caress-
      ing,
  Touched my faith—and then I saw!

Will you share with me this treasure—
  Gift of God's amazing grace?
'Twill be more than all earth's measure
  Just to look upon His face!
      — *L. M. Hearn*

Profit or Loss

What will it profit when life here is o'er,
　　Though great worldly wisdom I gain,
If, seeking knowledge, I utterly fail
　　The wisdom of God to obtain?

What will it profit, when life here is o'er,
　　Though gathering riches and fame,
If, gaining the world, I lose my own soul,
　　And in Heav'n unknown is my name?

What will it profit, when life here is o'er,
　　Though earth's farthest corners I see,
If, going my way and doing my will,
　　I miss what His love planned for me?

What will it profit, when life here is o'er,
　　Though earth's fleeting love has been mine,
If, seeking its gifts, I fail to secure
　　The riches of God's love divine?

What will it profit? My soul, stop and think!
　　What balance that day will declare:
Life's record laid bare, will gain turn to loss,
　　And leave me at last to despair?

— Grace E. Troy

No Time for God

You've time to build houses, and in them to dwell,
And time to do business, to buy and to sell;
But none for repentance, or deep, earnest prayer;
To seek your salvation you've no time to spare.

You've time for earth's pleasures, for frolic and fun,
For her glittering treasures how quickly you run;
But care not to seek the fair mansions above,
The favor of God or the gift of His love.

You've time to take voyages over the sea,
And time to take in the world's jubilee;
But soon your bright hopes will be lost in the gloom
Of the cold, dark river of death, and the tomb.

You've time to resort to the mountain and glen,
And time to gain knowledge from books and of men.
Yet no time to search for the wisdom of God;
But what of your soul when you're under the sod?

For time will not linger when helpless you lie:
Staring death in the face you will take time to die!
Then, what of the judgment? Pause, think, I implore!
For time will be lost on eternity's shore.

— *Author Unknown*

THE DERELICT

I

Storm tossed and driv'n,
Hither and yon;
Sails black and riv'n,
The rudder gone;
Smashed at the side,
Swept by the wave,
Borne by the tide,
With none to save;
No crew at hand,
No pilot near,
Far from the land
On waters drear;
Fixed to the mast
Flag of distress;
All beauty past,
All usefulness;
Past voyages,
Gone the conflict,
The sport of seas,
A derelict!

II

Out from the night
Into the morn,
Gleaming with light,
Like gull up-borne,
A man-of-war,
Strong, brave and free,
Come from afar,
Over the sea;
A hawser strong
Made taut and fast;
A cheer and song,
A whistle-blast;
Off and away,

Steamer and ship,
Through night and day
On homeward trip;
A harbor vast,
A hull remade,
A reset mast
And sails relaid;
Out on the seas,
Beauteous in form,
Borne by the breeze,
Fearless of storm;
Made all anew,
Fit for conflict;
No one e'er knew
The derelict!

— *Henry W. Frost*

UNPAYABLE DEBT

Some from their income tithe the gross,
    While others pay one-tenth the net.
Some deduct for flowers they bought
    At the demise of their "Aunt Bet."
What Uncle Sam withholds, they claim,
    Is not the Lord's for them to share.
And they deduct the cash they pay
    For taxi to the house of prayer.

Christ counted not the price He paid:
His lifeblood on dark Calvary.
How could one ever over-pay
In love or gold sin's ransom fee.

— *Barbara Drake Johnston*

OUR ROCK

If life's pleasures cheer thee,
    Give them not thy heart,
Lest the gifts ensnare thee
    From thy God to part;
His praises speak, His favor seek,
    Fix there thy hope's foundation,
Love Him, and He shall ever be
    The Rock of thy salvation.

If sorrow e'er befall thee,
    Painful though it be,
Let not fear appall thee:
    To thy Saviour flee;
He, ever near, thy prayer will hear,
    And calm thy perturbation;
The waves of woe shall ne'er o'erflow
    The Rock of thy salvation.

Death shall never harm thee,
    Shrink not from his blow,
For thy God shall arm thee
    And victory bestow;
For death shall bring to thee no sting,
    The grave no desolation;
'Tis gain to die with Jesus nigh —
    The Rock of thy salvation.

— *Francis Scott Key*

ᴄᴧᴐ

THE MASTER BUILDER

The children builded in the sand
A tiny city, nicely planned.
For that their work might be complete
They laid it out with block and street,
And made the buildings fine and tall
With smoothly finished roof and wall.
And when 'twas done, quite satisfied
They sought their homes. But how
        they cried
When with the early morning dew
The master builder and his crew
Despoiled their city — all for naught

The things their patient efforts
        wrought.
Yet when they saw the structure fair
Upbuilded by the master there
In afterdays, they quite forgot
They once had claimed the building
        spot.

Like little children, so are we;
Building, building thoughtlessly,
Mere gain our goal, with small concern
That things of dust to dust return.
So nations rise, but after all,
With God left out rise but to fall.
Then from the ruined heaps of sand
He builds a structure fine and grand,
A kingdom that's conceived in love
As far beyond and far above
Man's plans, to rule the universe
And override sin's awful curse,
As buildings reared by workmen
        skilled
O'ershadow those that children build.
And when our pigmy minds unfold
And clouds and mist have backward
        rolled,
We'll understand beyond a doubt
That they who plan and leave God
        out,
Will fail, like children who have tho't
To claim the owner's building spot.

— *Myra Brooks Welch*

ᴄᴧᴐ

FLYING TO CHRIST

Jesus, the sinner's Friend, to Thee,
Lost and undone, for aid I flee;
Weary of earth, myself, and sin,
Open Thine arms and take me in.

What can I say Thy grace to move?
Lord, I am sin, — but Thou art love;
I give up every plea beside,
Lord, I am lost, — but Thou hast died!

— *Author Unknown*

WHAT LACK I YET?

While with the living I remain,
　And I have some success,
I have enough of earthly gain
　And health for happiness.
　　What lack I yet?

Of many friendships I'm assured
　To cheer my every day;
I go to church and hear the Word,
　And oftentimes I pray.
　　What lack I yet?

If earthly gain I count but loss,
　If giving is my goal;
If all my sins are at the Cross,
　God's Spirit in my soul —
　　Then nothing lack I yet!

　　　　— Pearl Burnside McKinney

ᕫᕫ

THE FOUR CALLS

The Spirit came in *childhood,*
　And pleaded, "Let me in."
But Oh! the door was bolted,
　By thoughtlessness and sin;
"I am too young," the child replied,
　"I will not yield today,
There's time enough tomorrow";
　The Spirit went away.

Again He came and pleaded,
　In *youth's* bright happy hour,
He came, but heard no answer,
　For lured by Satan's power,
The youth lay dreaming then,
　And saying, "Not today,
Nor till I've tried earth's pleasures";
　The Spirit went away.

Again He called in mercy,
　In *manhood's* vigorous prime,
But still he found no welcome,
　The merchant had no time;

No time for true repentance,
　No time to think or pray,
And so, repulsed and saddened,
　The Spirit went away.

Once more He called and waited
　The man was *old* and ill,
He scarcely heard the whisper,
　His heart was cold and still;
"Go leave me, when I need thee,
　I'll call for thee," he cried;
Then sinking on his pillow,
　Without a hope, he died.

　　　　— Author Unknown

ᕫᕫ

WHY WILL YE DIE?

Sinners, turn; why will ye die?
God, your maker, asks you why;
God, who did your being give,
Made you with Himself to live;
He the fatal cause demands,
Asks the work of His own hands:
Why, ye thankless creatures, why
Will ye cross His love, and die?

Sinners, turn; why will ye die?
God, your Saviour, asks you why;
God, who did your souls retrieve,
Died Himself, that ye might live.
Will ye let Him die in vain?
Crucify your Lord again?
Why, ye ransomed sinners, why
Will ye slight His grace, and die?

Sinners, turn; why will ye die?
God, the Spirit, asks you why;
He, who all your lives hath strove,
Wooed you to embrace His love;
Will ye not His grace receive?
Will ye still refuse to live?
Why, ye long-sought sinners, why
Will ye grieve your God, and die?

　　　　— Charles Wesley

PENITENCE

Were not the sinful Mary's tears
An offering worthy Heaven,
When o'er the faults of former years
She wept — and was forgiven?

When bringing every balmy sweet
Her day of luxury stored,
She o'er her Saviour's hallow'd feet,
The precious perfume pour'd!

Were not those sweets, so humbly
　　shed,—
That hair,— those weeping eyes,—
And the sunk heart, that inly bled,—
Heaven's noblest sacrifice?

Thou, that hast slept in error's sleep,
Oh! would'st thou wake in heaven,
Like Mary kneel, like Mary weep,
"Love much," — and be forgiven!

— *Thomas Moore*

∽

THE SOUL WHEREIN GOD DWELLS

The soul wherein God dwells,
What church could holier be?
Becomes a walking-tent
Of heavenly majesty.
How far from here to heaven?
Not very far, my friend.
A single hearty step
Will all the journey end.
Though Christ a thousand times
In Bethlehem be born,
If He's not born in thee,
Thy soul is still forlorn.
The cross of Golgotha
Will never save thy soul:
The cross in thine own heart
Alone can make thee whole.
Hold thou — where runnest thou?
Know heaven is in thee —
Seek'st thou for God elsewhere,

His face thou'lt never see.
Oh, would thy heart but be
A manger for His birth;
God would once more become
A child upon the earth.
Go out, God will go in;
Die thou — and let Him live;
Be not — and He will be;
Wait, and He'll all things give.
O shame, a silk-worm works
And spins till it can fly;
And thou, my soul, wilt still
On thine old earth-clod lie!

— *Angelus Silesius*

∽

I LAY MY SINS ON JESUS

I lay my sins on Jesus,
　　The spotless Lamb of God;
He bears them all and frees us
　　From the accursed load:
I bring my guilt to Jesus,
　　To wash my crimson stains
White in His blood most precious,
　　Till not a stain remains.

I lay my wants on Jesus;
　　All fullness dwells in Him;
He healeth my diseases,
　　He doth my soul redeem:
I lay my griefs on Jesus,
　　My burdens and my cares;
He from them all releases,
　　He all my sorrows shares.

I long to be like Jesus,
　　Meek, loving, lowly, mild;
I long to be like Jesus,
　　The Father's holy Child:
I long to be with Jesus
　　Amid the heavenly throng,
To sing with saints His praises,
　　And learn the angels' song.

— *Horatius Bonar*

BLIND BARTIMAEUS

Blind Bartimaeus at the gates
Of Jericho in darkness waits;
He hears the crowd—he hears a breath
Say, "It is Christ of Nazareth!"
And calls in tones of agony,
"Jesus, have mercy now on me!"

The thronging multitudes increase;
Blind Bartimaeus, hold thy peace!
But still, above the noisy crowd,
The beggar's cry is shrill and loud:
Until they say, "He calleth thee!"
"Fear not; arise, He calleth thee!"

Then saith the Christ, as silent stands
The crowd, "What wilt thou at my
hands?"
And he replies, "O give me light!
Rabbi, restore the blind man's sight."
And Jesus answers, "Go in peace
Thy faith from blindness gives release!"

Ye that have eyes yet cannot see,
In darkness and in misery,
Recall those mighty Voices Three,
"Jesus, have mercy now on me!"
"Fear not, arise, and go in peace!
Thy faith from blindness gives release!"

— *Henry Wadsworth Longfellow*

LINES WRITTEN IN HER BREVIARY

Let nothing disturb thee,
Nothing affright thee;
All things are passing;
God never changeth;
Patient endurance
Attaineth to all things;
Who God possesseth
In nothing is wanting;
Alone God sufficeth.

— *St. Teresa of Avila*

FAITH

Father, I stretch my hands to Thee;
 No other help I know:
If Thou withdraw Thyself from me,
 Ah! whither shall I go?

What did Thine only Son endure,
 Before I drew my breath!
What pain, what labor, to secure
 My soul from endless death!

Surely Thou canst not let me die;
 O speak, and I shall live;
And here I will unwearied lie,
 Till Thou Thy Spirit give.

Author of faith! to Thee I lift
 My weary, longing eyes:
O let me now receive that gift!
 My soul without it dies.

— *Charles Wesley*

HIS SALVATION

Of Him who did salvation bring,
I could forever think and sing;
Arise, ye needy, He'll relieve;
Arise, ye guilty, He'll forgive.

Ask but His grace, and lo, 'tis given!
Ask, and He turns your hell to heaven:
Tho' sin and sorrow wound my soul,
Jesus, Thy balm will make it whole.

To shame our sins He blushed in blood;
He closed His eyes to show us God:
Let all the world fall down and know
That none but God such love can
show.

Insatiate to this spring I fly;
I drink, and yet am ever dry;
Ah! who against Thy charms is proof?
Ah! who that loves, can love enough?

— *Bernard of Clairvaux*
Translated by Anthony W. Boehm

CHRIST AT THE DOOR

Behold, a stranger's at the door!
He gently knocks, has knocked before;
Has waited long, is waiting still;
You treat no other friend so ill.

But will He prove a friend indeed?
He will; the very friend you need;
The Man of Nazareth, 'tis He,
With garments dyed at Calvary.
If thou art poor, and poor thou art,
Lo, He has riches to impart;
Not wealth in which mean avarice
    rolls;
Oh, better far the wealth of souls!

Thou'rt blind, He'll take the scales
    away,
And let in everlasting day:
Naked thou art, but He shall dress
Thy blushing soul in righteousness.

Art thou a weeper? Grief shall fly,
For who can weep with Jesus by?
No terror shall thy hopes annoy,
No tear, except the tear of joy.

Admit Him, for the human breast
Ne'er entertained so kind a guest:
Admit Him, for you can't expel;
Where'er He comes, He comes to
    dwell.
Admit Him, ere His anger burn;
His feet depart ne'er to return;
Admit Him; or the hour's at hand,
When, at His door, denied you'll
    stand.

— *Joseph Grigg*

NO, NOT DESPAIRINGLY

No, not despairingly
    Come I to Thee;
No, not distrustingly
    Bend I the knee:
Sin hath gone over me,
Yet is this still my plea,
    Jesus hath died.

Ah! mine iniquity
    Crimson has been,
Infinite, infinite
    Sin upon sin;
Sin of not loving Thee,
Sin of not trusting Thee,
    Infinite sin.

Faithful and just art Thou,
    Forgiving all;
Loving and kind art Thou
    When poor ones call:
Lord, let the cleansing blood,
Blood of the Lamb of God,
    Pass o'er my soul.

Then all is peace and light
    This soul within:
Thus shall I walk with Thee,
    The loved Unseen;
Leaning on Thee, my God,
Guided along the road,
    Nothing between.

— *Horatius Bonar*

He Was Alone

They came for Him with sword and
stave,
   They cut His heart with hate.
No one stood by to help or save,
   Or even share His fate.

They left Him all alone to face
   The cursing, spitting crowd,
And rulers, some of whom were base
   But more of whom were proud.

His Cross alone He had to bear —
   How much alone was He!
Perhaps that's why He's always near
   To help and comfort me!

           — *Lois Duffield*

His Way

God bade me go when I would stay
   ('Twas cool within the wood);
I did not know the reason why.
   I heard a boulder crashing by
Across the pathway where I stood.

He bade me stay when I would go;
   "Thy will be done," I said.
They found one day at early dawn,
Across the way I would have gone,
   A serpent with a mangled head.

No more I ask the reason why,
   Although I may not see
The path ahead, His way I go;
For tho' I know not, He doth know,
   And He will choose safe paths for
     me.

           — *Author Unknown*

Hymn

When storms arise
And dark'ning skies
   About me threat'ning lower,
To Thee, O Lord, I raise mine eyes,
To Thee my tortured spirit flies
   For solace in that hour.

Thy mighty arm
Will let no harm
   Come near me nor befall me;
Thy voice shall quiet my alarm,
When life's great battle waxeth warm:
   No foeman shall appall me.

Upon Thy breast
Secure I rest
   From sorrow and vexation;
No more by sinful cares oppressed,
But in Thy presence ever blest,
   O God of my salvation.

           — *Paul Laurence Dunbar*

I'm Not Alone

I'm not alone, though others go
   A different way from what I choose;
I'm not alone, though I say "No!"
   I know that I will never lose.
I'm not alone, though others tease
   And urge that I should go their way;
I'm not alone, though I displease
   My friends by what I'll never say.
I'm not alone, for I now choose —
   Though other folk may call me odd,
Tho' now it seems that I might lose —
   To go the way that Jesus trod.

           — *L. E. Dunkin*

Comfort

Speak low to me, my Saviour, low and sweet
From out the hallelujahs, sweet and low,
Lest I should fear and fall, and miss Thee so,
Who art not missed by any that entreat.
Speak to me as to Mary at Thy feet!
And if no precious gems my hands bestow,
Let my tears drop like amber, while I go
In reach of Thy divinest voice complete
In humanest affection — thus, in sooth,
To lose the sense of losing. As a child,
Whose song-bird seeks the wood for evermore,
Is sung to in its stead by mother's mouth,
Till, sinking on her breast, love-reconciled,
He sleeps the faster that he wept before.

— *Elizabeth Barrett Browning*

He Keeps the Key

Is there some problem in your life to solve,
    Some passage seeming full of mystery?
God knows, Who brings the hidden things to light.
        He keeps the key.

Is there some door closed by the Father's hand
    Which widely opened you had hoped to see?
Trust God and wait — for when He shuts the door,
        He keeps the key.

Is there some earnest prayer unanswered yet,
    Or answered *not* as you had thought 'twould be!
God will make clear His purpose by-and-by.
        He keeps the key.

Have patience with your God, your patient God,
    All wise, all knowing, no longer tarrier He,
And of the door of all thy future life
        He keeps the key.

Unfailing comfort, sweet and blessed rest,
    To know of *every* door He keeps the key.
That He at last when just *He* sees 'tis best,
        Will give it *thee.*

— *Author Unknown*

SEND FORTH, O GOD, THY LIGHT AND TRUTH

Send forth, O God, Thy light and truth,
And let them lead me still,
Undaunted, in the paths of right,
Up to Thy holy hill:
Then to Thy altar will I spring,
And in my God rejoice;
And praise shall tune the trembling string,
And gratitude my voice.

O why, my soul, art thou cast down?
Within me why distressed?
Thy hopes the God of grace shall crown;
He yet shall make thee blessed:
To Him, my never failing Friend, I bow,
And kiss the rod;
To Him shall thanks and praise ascend,
My Savior and my God.

— John Quincy Adams

A QUIET MIND

What room is there for troubled fear?
  I know my Lord, and He is near;
And He will light my candle, so
  That I may see the way I go.

There need be no bewilderment
  To one who goes where he is sent;
The trackless plain, by night and day
  Is set with signs lest he should stray.

My path may cross a waste of sea,
  But that need never frighten me —
Or rivers full to very brim,
  But they are open ways to Him.

My path may lead thro' wood at night,
  Where neither moon nor any light
Of guiding star or beacon shines;
  He will not let me miss my signs.

Lord, grant to me a quiet mind,
  That, trusting Thee — for Thou art
    kind —
I may go on without a fear,
  For Thou, my Lord, art always near.

— Amy Carmichael

"IN A MOMENT"

A moment more and I may be
Caught up in glory, Lord, with Thee:
And, raptured sight, Thy beauty see
  For evermore!

A moment more — what joy to wear
Thy likeness, Saviour, and to share
With Thee the place prepared there,
  Where Thou art gone!

A moment more — upon Thy throne,
Thy place by right, then made our
  own;
Thou wilt not fill that seat alone,
  But with Thy saints!

— Author Unknown

SOWING AND REAPING

In spite of sorrow, loss, and pain,
  Our course be onward still;
We sow on Burma's barren plain,
  We reap on Zion's hill.

— Adoniram Judson

PLACE OF REPAIR

Place of repair: O blessed place of refuge!
How gladly will I come to meet Him there,
To cease awhile from all the joy of service
To find a deeper joy with Him to share.

Place of repair: for tired brain and body!
How much I need that place just out of sight
Where only He can talk, and be beside me,
Until again made strong by His great might.

Place of repair: when trials press upon me
And God permits the unexpected test,
'Tis there I learn some lesson sweet and precious
As simply on His faithfulness I rest.

Place of repair: the place to take my sorrow,
The thing that hurts and would be hard to bear,
But somehow in the secret place I'm finding
That all the hurt is healed since He is there.

Place of repair: to wait for fresh enduement
I silently with Him alone would stay
Until He speaks again, and says, "Go forward
To help some other sheep to find the way."

Place of repair: O trysting-place most hallowed,
The Lord Himself is just that place to me,
His grace, His strength, His glory and His triumph,
Himself alone my all-sufficiency.

— *Author Unknown*

I GO ALONE

I go alone
Upon the narrow way that leads
Through shadowed valleys, over rocky heights,
To glorious plains beyond;
And sometimes when the way is very lone
I cry out for companionship, and long
For fellow-travelers on the toilsome path,
Until a Voice of sweetest music whispers,
"My grace sufficient is, no other guide thou needst
But Me." And then the path grows brighter as
I go alone.

My Saviour knows
The way I take. Himself has trod
The selfsame road. He knows each stone,
Temptations, pitfalls hid by blossoms fair,
The hour of darkness that my life must share,
The wilderness of sorrow, doubt, and fear,
Renunciation's agony, and every pang
Of loneliness and labor's wear; enough for me
That He has known it all, that now He stays
To strengthen, guide and help me. I am glad
My Saviour knows.

Thy will be done
Whether on pleasant paths I walk along,
Or crouch amid the lightnings of the storm,
Whether for me the larks of springtime sing,
Or winter's icy blasts my being sting;
Whatever Thou dost send is best for me,
With joyful heart I take it all from Thee,
Rejoicing in Thy sovereignty, and pray
That Thou wilt lead me on my upward way;
The road grows smoother as I travel on.
Thy will be done.
— *Amy L. Person*

ༀ

Rest Where You Are

When, spurred by tasks unceasing or undone,
  You would seek rest afar,
And cannot, though repose be rightly won —
  Rest where you are.

Neglect the needless; sanctify the rest;
  Move without stress or jar;
With quiet of a spirit self-possessed
  Rest where you are.

Not in event, restriction, or release,
  Not in scenes near or far,
But in ourselves are restlessness or peace:
  Rest where you are.

Where lives the soul lives God; His day, His world,
  No phantom mists need mar;
His starry nights are tents of peace unfurled:
  Rest where you are.
— *Author Unknown*

TRUSTING GOD

Jeroboam failed to do
The things the Lord had asked him to.
He did not walk within God's light;
He did not rule his kingdom right.
He did not follow in God's way,
So things went wrong for him each day.
Until at last his son was dead,
The crown was taken from his head.
Let us not be as this sad king —
Let us trust God in everything.

— Enola Chamberlin

BE STILL

"*Stand still,*" my soul, for so thy Lord commands:
E'en when thy way seems blocked, leave it in His wise hands;
His arm is mighty to divide the wave.
"Stand still," my soul, "stand still" and thou shalt see
How God can work the "impossible" for thee,
For with a great deliverance He doth save.

Be not impatient, but in stillness stand,
Even when compassed 'round on every hand,
In ways thy spirit does not comprehend.
God cannot clear thy way till thou art still,
That He may work in thee His blessed will,
And all thy heart and will to Him do bend.

"*Be still,*" my soul, for just as thou art still,
Can God reveal Himself to thee; until
Through thee His love and light and life can freely flow;
In stillness God can work through thee and reach
The souls around thee. He then through thee can teach
His lessons, and His power in weakness show.

"*Be still*" — a deeper step in faith and rest.
"Be still and know" thy Father knoweth best
The way to lead His child to that fair land,
A "summer" land, where quiet waters flow;
Where longing souls are satisfied, and "know
Their God," and praise for all that He has planned.

— Author Unknown

MY TRUST

Whate'er my God ordains is right;
    His will is ever just;
Howe'er He orders now my cause,
    I will be still and trust.
        He is my God;
        Though dark my road,
He holds me that I shall not fall,
Wherefore to Him I leave it all.

Whate'er my God ordains is right;
    My light, my life is He,
Who cannot will me aught but good;
    I trust Him utterly;
        For well I know,
        In joy or woe,
We soon shall see, as sunlight clear,
How faithful was our guardian here.

Whate'er my God ordains is right;
    Here will I take my stand,
Tho' sorrow, need, or death make earth
    For me a desert land.
        My Father's care
        Is round me there,
He holds me that I shall not fall;
And so to Him I leave it all.

    — *Samuel Rodigast*

ono

MORE THAN

Thou art more than a clod;
    More than a rough-spun dress;
More than a sheltering pod
    For a soul's homelessness;

More than a fettered slave
    Bound to a master;
Destined to fill a grave;
    Born to disaster.

Thou art a thought of God;
    A long-planned implement,

Designed to fill His hand
    And made for His content.

Angels with watchful eyes
    Have charge of thee,
Lest uncouth hand should chip
    Thy frail mortality.

Lest uncouth hand should chip
    The vase of clay;
Or underling let slip
    The pitcher by the way.

When thou art broken — when
    Thy lamp is lifted high,
Will He who made thee, leave thee
        then,
    Or, heedless, put thee by?

        — *Fay Inchfawn*

ono

IT'S NEVER EASY

It's never easy when one must go
    And one must stay — behind;
It's never easy, I know, I know —
    It sears both heart and mind.

It's never easy, but go one must
    When comes the day, the hour;
It's never easy, but if we trust,
    God will give strength and power.

It's never easy! God knows this, too;
    That's why He stays quite near
To help us as we stumble through
    The vale of grief and fear.

It's never easy, but take God's hand
    And pray till night has passed;
Just trust nor ask to understand —
    And peace will come — at last.

        — *Phyllis C. Michael*

I'M STANDING, LORD"

"I'm standing, Lord.
There is a mist that blinds my sight.
Steep jagged rocks, front, left, and
     right,
Lower, dim, gigantic, in the night.
     Where is the way?

"I'm standing, Lord.
The black rock hems me in behind.
Above my head a moaning wind
Chills and oppresses heart and mind.
     I am afraid!

"I'm standing, Lord.
The rock is hard beneath my feet.
I nearly slipped, Lord, on the sleet.
So weary, Lord, and where a seat?
     Still must I stand?"

He answered me, and on His face
A look ineffable of grace,
Of perfect, understanding love,
Which all my murmuring did remove.

"I'm standing, Lord.
Since Thou hast spoken, Lord, I see
Thou hast beset; these rocks are Thee;
And since Thy love encloses me,
     I stand and sing!"

                         — *Betty Stam*

THE RAINFALL FOLLOWS THE PLOUGH

I heard an old farmer talk one day,
     Telling his listeners how
In the wide, new country far away
     The rainfall follows the plough.
"As fast as they break it up, you see,
     And turn the heart to the sun,
As they open the furrow deep and free
     And the tillage is begun,
The earth grows mellow, and more
     and more
     It holds and sends to the sky
A moisture it never had before,

When its face was hard and dry.
And so wherever the ploughshares run
     The clouds run overhead,
And the soil that works and lets in
     the sun
     With water is always fed."
I wonder if that old farmer knew
     The half of his simple word,
Or guessed the message that, heavenly
     true,
     Within it was hidden and heard.
It fell on my ear by chance that day,
     But the gladness lingers now,
To think it is always God's dear way
     That the rainfall follows the plough.

                         — *Author Unknown*

COMFORT

Say not, my soul, "From whence
     Can God relieve my care?"
Remember that Omnipotence
     Hath servants everywhere.

His help is always sure,
     His methods seldom guessed;
Delay will make our pleasure pure:
     Surprise will give it zest.

His wisdom is sublime,
     His heart profoundly kind;
God never is before His time,
     And never is behind.

Hast thou assumed a load
     Which none will bear with thee?
And art thou bearing it for God,
     And shall He fail to see?

Be comforted at heart,
     Thou art not left alone;
Now thou the Lord's companion art —
     Soon thou shalt share His throne.

                         — *J. J. Lynch*

SLEEP

I'm too tired to trust and too tired to pray,
Said one, as the over-taxed strength gave way.
The one conscious thought by my mind possessed,
Is, oh, could I just drop it all and rest.

Will God forgive me, do you suppose,
If I go right to sleep as a baby goes,
Without an asking if I may,
Without ever trying to trust and pray?

Will God forgive you? why think, dear heart,
When language to you was an unknown art,
Did a mother deny you needed rest,
Or refuse to pillow your head on her breast?

Did she let you want when you could not ask?
Did she set her child an unequal task?
Or did she cradle you in her arms,
And then guard your slumber against alarms?

Ah, how quick was her mother love to see,
The unconscious yearnings of infancy.
When you've grown too tired to trust and pray,
When over-wrought nature has quite given way:

Then just drop it all, and give up to rest,
As you used to do on a mother's breast,
He knows all about it — the dear Lord knows,
So just go to sleep as a baby goes;

Without even asking if you may,
God knows when His child is too tired to pray.
He judges not solely by uttered prayer,
He knows when the yearnings of love are there.

He knows you do pray, He knows you do trust,
And He knows, too, the limits of poor weak dust.
Oh, the wonderful sympathy of Christ,
For His chosen ones in that midnight tryst,

When He bade them sleep and take their rest,
While on Him the guilt of the whole world pressed —
You've given your life up to Him to keep,
Then don't be afraid to go right to sleep.

— *Ella Conrad Cowherd*

My Will

My wild will was captured, yet under the yoke
  There was pain and not peace at the press of the load;
Till the glorious burden the last fibre broke,
  And I melted like wax in the furnace of God.

And now I have flung myself recklessly out,
  Like a chip on the stream of His infinite will;
I pass the rough rocks with a smile and a shout,
  And just let my God His dear purpose fulfil.

— *Author Unknown*

Wings

The little bird sat on a slender limb,
    Upward swinging,
And though wind and rain were rough with him,
    Still kept singing.
"O little bird, quick, seek out your nest!"
I could not keep from calling;
"The bleak winds tear your tender breast,
Your tiny feet are falling."
    "More need for song
    When things go wrong,
I was not meant for crying;
    No fear for me,"
    He piped with glee,
"My wings were made for flying!"

My heart had been dark as the stormy sky
    In my sorrow,
With the weight of troubles long passed by,
    And the morrow.
"O little bird, sing!" I cried once more,
    "The sun will soon be shining.
See, there's a rainbow arching o'er
    The storm cloud's silver lining."
    I, too, will sing
    Through everything;
It will teach blessing double;
    Nor yet forget.
    When rude winds fret,
To fly above my trouble.

— *Author Unknown*

LAID ON THINE ALTAR

Laid on Thine altar, O my Lord, divine,
Accept this day my gift for Jesus' sake.
I have no jewels to adorn Thy shrine,
Nor any world-famed sacrifice to make;
But here I bring within my trembling hand
This will of mine: a thing that seemeth small;
And only Thou dear Lord, canst understand
That when I yield Thee this, I yield Thee all.
It hath been wet with tears and dimmed with sighs,
Clenched in my clasp, till beauty it hath none.

Now from Thy footstool, where it vanquished lies,
The prayer ascendeth: "Let Thy will be done."
Take it, O Father, ere my courage fail,
And blend it so with Thine own will, that e'en
If in some desperate hour my cry prevail,
And Thou giv'st back my gift, it may have been
So changed, so purified, so fair have grown,
So one with Thee, so filled with peace divine,
I may not know nor feel it as my own,
But gaining back my will may find it Thine.

— *Author Unknown*

ოა

A LITTLE CHILD

A little child at mother's knee
    Plies woolen strands and needles bright.
Small, eager hands strive earnestly
    To fasten every stitch aright.

But soon perplexing knots appear
    Which vex and hinder progress' flow;
Impatient fingers pull and tear,
    While ever worse the tangles grow.

How surely then in wiser hands
    The roughest places are made plain!
How easy now the task's demands,
    How wonderful the lesson's gain!

Thus, God, we bring our snarls to Thee;
    Though human sense and stubborn will
Oft clamor loud for mastery,
    We hear alone Thy "Peace, be still."

— *Edith Shaw Brown*

LORD, MAKE ME STRONG

Lord, make me strong! Let my soul rooted be
　　Afar from vales of rest,
　　Flung close to heaven upon a great Rock's breast,
Unsheltered and alone, but strong in Thee.

What though the lashing tempests leave their scars?
　　Has not the Rock been bruised?
　　Mine, with the strength of ages deep infused,
To face the storms, and triumph with the stars!

Lord, plant my spirit high upon the crest
　　Of Thine eternal strength!
　　Then, though life's breaking struggles come at length,
Their storm shall only bend me to Thy breast.

　　　　　　　　　　　　　— Dorothy Clark Wilson

DELIVERANCE

Thou servant of the living God,
　　Whilst lions round thee roar,
Look up and trust and praise His
　　　　Name,
　　And all His ways adore;
For even now, in peril dire,
　　He works to set thee free,
And in a way known but to Him,
　　Shall thy deliverance be.

Dost wait while lions round thee stand?
　　Dost wait in gloom, alone,
And looking up above thy head
　　See but a sealed stone?
Praise in the dark! Yea, praise His
　　　　Name,
　　Who trusted thee to see
His mighty power displayed again
　　For thee, His saint, for thee.

Thou servant of the living God,
　　Thine but to wait and praise;
The living God, Himself, will work,
　　To Him thine anthem raise;
Though undelivered thou dost wait,
The God Who works for thee,
When His hour strikes, will with a
　　　　word
　　Set thee for ever free.

　　　　　　　　　　　　　— M. E. B.

REST

Not so in haste, my heart!
Have faith in God and wait:
Although He linger long
He never comes too late.

Until He cometh, rest,
Nor grudge the hours that roll,
The feet that wait for God
Are soonest at the goal.

Are soonest at the goal
That is not gained by speed.
Then hold thee still, my heart,
For I shall wait His lead.

　　　　　　　　　　　　　— Bayard Taylor

An Exchange of Wills

I want my heart so cleared of self
That my dear Lord can come
And set up His own furnishings,
And make my heart — His home.

And since I know what this requires,
Each morning while it's still,
I slip into that secret room,
And leave with Him — My *will*,

He always takes it graciously,
Presenting me with His;
I'm ready then to meet the day
And any task there is.

And this is how my Lord controls
My interest, my ills,
Because we meet at break of day,
For an *exchange of wills*.

— *Anna Jane Granniss*

When Thou Hast Shut Thy Door

When thou hast shut thy door,
Shut out from thee its anxious care
With all its sharp temptations sore,
   For He is there.

When thou hast shut thy door,
Shut out from thee its pain and grief,
Bereavements — pressures to the core;
   He gives relief.

When thou hast shut thy door,
And left all there behind that wall
Of God's own care, forevermore —
   He takes it all.

When thou hast shut thy door,
Shut out thyself — He only in,
Nothing for thee but to adore —
   He works within.

— *L. S. P.*

Still With Thee

Still, still with Thee, when purple morning breaketh,
   When the bird waketh, and the shadows flee;
Fairer than morning, lovelier than daylight,
   Dawns the sweet consciousness, I am with Thee.

Alone with Thee, amid the mystic shadows,
   The hush of nature newly born;
Alone with Thee in breathless adoration,
   In the calm dew and freshness of the morn.

As in the dawning o'er the waveless ocean,
   The image of the morning-star doth rest,
So in this stillness, Thou beholdest only
   Thine image in the waters of my breast.

When sinks the soul, subdued by toil, to slumber,
   Its closing eyes look up to Thee in prayer;
Sweet the repose, beneath Thy wings o'er shadowing,
   But sweeter still to wake and find Thee there.

— *Harriet Beecher Stowe*

LEAN HARD

Child of My love, lean hard,
And let Me feel the pressure of thy care;
I know thy burden, child. I shaped it;
Poised it in Mine Own hand; made no proportion
In its weight to thine unaided strength,
For even as I laid it on, I said,
"I shall be near, and while she leans on Me,
This burden shall be Mine, not hers;
So shall I keep My child within the circling arms
Of My Own love." Here lay it down, nor fear
To impose it on a shoulder which upholds
The government of worlds. Yet closer come:
Thou art not near enough. I would embrace thy care;
So I might feel My child reposing on My breast.
Thou lovest Me? I knew it. Doubt not then;
But loving Me, lean hard.

— Author Unknown

GOD OF ALL COMFORT

I have been through the valley of weeping,
    The valley of sorrow and pain;
But the "God of all comfort" was with me,
    At hand to uphold and sustain.

As the earth needs the clouds and sunshine,
    Our souls need both sorrow and joy;
So He places us oft in the furnace,
    The dross from the gold to destroy.

When he leads through some valley of trouble,
    His omnipotent hand we trace;
For the trials and sorrows He sends us,
    Are part of His lessons in grace.

Oft we shrink from the purging and pruning,
    Forgetting the Husbandman knows
That the deeper the cutting and paring,
    The richer the cluster that grows.

Well He knows that affliction is needed;
    He has a wise purpose in view,
And in the dark valley He whispers,
    "Hereafter thou'lt know what I do."

As we travel through life's shadow'd valley,
  Fresh springs of His love ever rise;
And we learn that our sorrows and losses,
  Are blessings just sent in disguise.

So we'll follow wherever He leadeth,
  Let the path be dreary or bright;
For we've proved that our God can give comfort;
  Our God can give songs in the night.

— *Author Unknown*

WHERE YOU'VE PUT ME

I'll stay where You've put me; I will, dear Lord,
  Though I wanted so badly to go;
I was eager to march with the 'rank and file,'
  Yes, I wanted to lead them, You know.
I planned to keep step to the music loud,
  To cheer when the banner unfurled,
To stand in the midst of the first straight and proud,
  But I'll stay where You've put me.

I'll stay where You've put me; I'll work, dear Lord,
  Though the field be narrow and small,
And the ground be fallow, and the stones lie thick,
  And there seems to be no life at all.
The field is Thine own, only give me the seed,
  I'll sow it with never a fear;
I'll till the dry soil while I wait for the rain,
  And rejoice when the green blades appear;
    I'll work where You've put me.

I'll stay where You've put me; I will, dear Lord,
  I'll bear the day's burden and heat,
Always trusting Thee fully; when even has come
  I'll lay heavy sheaves at Thy feet.
And then, when my earth work is ended and done,
  In the light of eternity's glow,
Life's record all closed, I surely shall find
  I was better to stay than to go;
    I'll stay where You've put me.

— *Author Unknown*

THE WILL OF GOD

Thou sweet, beloved will of God,
    My anchor ground, my fortress hill,
My spirit's silent, fair abode,
    In Thee I hide me and am still.

Thy beautiful sweet will, my God,
    Holds fast in its sublime embrace
My captive will, a gladsome bird,
    Prison'd in such a realm of grace.

Upon God's will I lay me down,
    As child upon its mother's breast,
No silken couch, nor softest bed,
    Could ever give me such deep rest.

    — *Gerhardt Tersteegen*

∿

AGAINST A THORN

Once I heard a song of sweetness,
    As it cleft the morning air,
Sounding in its blest completeness,
    Like a tender, pleading prayer;
And I sought to find the singer,
    Whence the wondrous song was
        borne;
And I found a bird, sore wounded,
    Pinioned by a cruel thorn.

I have seen a soul in sadness,
    While its wings with pain were
        furl'd,
Giving hope, and cheer and gladness
    That should bless a weeping world;
And I knew that life of sweetness,
    Was of pain and sorrow borne,
And a stricken soul was singing,
    With its heart against a thorn.

Ye are told of One who loved you,
    Of a Saviour crucified,
Ye are told of nails that pinioned,
    And a spear that pierced His side;

Ye are told of cruel scourging,
    Of a Saviour bearing scorn,
And He died for your salvation,
    With His brow against a thorn.

Ye "are not above the Master."
    Will you breathe a sweet refrain?
And His grace will be sufficient,
    When your heart is pierced with
        pain.
Will you live to bless His loved ones,
    Tho' your life be bruised and torn,
Like the bird that sang so sweetly,
    With its heart again a thorn?

    — *Author Unknown*

∿

THAT ODD LITTLE SPARROW

Just think of that odd little sparrow,
    Uncared for by any but God,
It surely must bring thee some comfort
    To know that He loved it—tho' odd.

That one little odd little sparrow,
    The object of God's tender care?
Then surely thou art of more value,
    Thou need'st not give way to de-
        spair.

It may be thou art an "odd sparrow,"
    But God's eye of love rests on thee,
And He understands what to others,
    Will always a mystery be.

Thou thinkest thy case so peculiar
    That nobody can understand.
Take life's tangled skein to Thy
        Saviour
    And leave it in His skilful Hand.

Believe in His love and His pity
    Confide in His wisdom and care,
Remember the little odd sparrow,
    And never give way to despair.

    — *Author Unknown*

He Holds My Hand

It isn't that I cling to Him
    Or struggle to be blest;
He simply takes my hand in His
    And there I let it rest.

So I dread not any pathway,
    Dare to sail on any sea,
Since the handclasp of Another
    Makes the journey safe for me.

— *Author Unknown*

ൟ

The Potter

    The potter worked at his task
With patience, love and skill.
    A vessel, marred and broken,
He altered again to his will.
    It was blackened, bent and old
But with traces of beauty left,
    So he worked, this mender of pottery,
To restore the charm bereft,
    Till at last it stood transformed
And he viewed it with tender eyes,
    The work of his hands and love,
This potter, patient and wise.

    I know a Mender of broken hearts,
And of lives that are all undone;
    He takes them all, as they come to
        Him
And He loves them, every one.
    With patience, love and skill
That surpasses the knowledge of men,
    This Master Potter gathers the lost
And restores to His image again.
    O Lover of folk with broken lives,
O wonderful Potter Divine,
    I bring my soul for Thy healing
        touch;
In me, let Thy beauty shine.

— *Author Unknown*

He Will Silently Plan for Thee

He will silently plan for thee,
    Object thou of omniscient care;
God Himself undertakes to be
    Thy Pilot thro' each subtle snare.

He *will* silently plan for thee,
    So certainly, He cannot fail!
Rest on the faithfulness of God,
    In Him thou surely shalt prevail.

He will *silently* plan for thee
    Some wonderful surprise of love.
Eye hath not seen, nor ear hath heard,
    But it is kept for thee above.

He will silently *plan* for thee,
    His purposes shall all unfold;
The tangled skein shall shine at last,
    A masterpiece of skill untold.

He will silently plan *for thee,*
    Happy child of a Father's care,
As though no other claimed His love,
    But thou alone to Him wert dear.

— *E. Mary Grimes*

ൟ

Shut In

Shut in? Ah, yes, that's so,
As far as getting out may go,
Shut in away from earthly cares,
But not shut out from Him who cares.

Shut in from many a futile quest,
But Christ can be your daily Guest.
He's not shut out by your four walls,
But hears and answers all your calls.

Shut in with God. Oh that should be
Such a wonderful opportunity.
Then after you have done your best,
In God's hands safely leave the rest.

— *Author Unknown*

COME UNTO ME, YE WEARY

"Come unto me, ye weary,
And I will give you rest."
O blessed voice of Jesus,
Which comes to hearts oppressed!
It tells of benediction,
Of pardon, grace, and peace,
Of joy that hath no ending,
Of love which cannot cease.

"Come unto me, ye wanderers,
And I will give you light."
O loving voice of Jesus,
Which comes to cheer the night!
Our hearts were filled with sadness,
And we had lost our way;
But morning brings us gladness,
And songs, the break of day.

"Come unto me, ye fainting,
And I will give you life."
O cheering voice of Jesus,
Which comes to aid our strife!
The foe is stern and eager,
The fight is fierce and long;
But Thou hast made us mighty,
And stronger than the strong.

"And whosoever cometh,
I will not cast him out."
O welcome voice of Jesus,
Which drives away our doubt!
Which calls us, very sinners,
Unworthy though we be
Of love so free and boundless,
To come, dear Lord, to Thee!

—*William C. Dix*

MY BOAT

I owned a little boat a while ago
  And sailed a Morning Sea without a fear,
And whither any breeze might fairly blow
  I'd steer the little craft afar or near.

      Mine was the boat, and mine the air,
      And mine the sea; not mine, a care.

My boat became my place of nightly toil.
  I sailed at sunset to the fishing ground.
At morn the boat was freighted with the spoil
  That my all-conquering work and skill had found.

      Mine was the boat, and mine the net,
      And mine the skill, and power to get.

One day there passed along the silent shore,
  While I my net was casting in the sea,
A man, who spoke as never man before;
  I followed Him—new life begun in me.

      Mine was the boat, but His the voice,
      And His the call; yet mine, the choice.

Ah, 'twas a fearful night out on the lake,
   And all my skill availed not at the helm,
Till Him asleep I waken, crying "Take,
   Take Thou command, lest waters overwhelm!"

     His was the boat, and His the Sea,
     And His the Peace o'er all and me.

Once from His boat He taught the curious throng,
   Then bade me let down nets out in the Sea;
I murmured, but obeyed, nor was it long
   Before the catch amazed and humbled me.

     His was the boat, and His the skill,
     And His the catch — and His, my will.
                       — Joseph Addison Richards

INTO THE DARK

    Into the dark, Lord Jesus,
    Into the dark with Thee,
There hath come to my heart a calling apart,
    And a whispered, "Follow Me."

    Take Thou my hand, Lord Jesus,
    In Thy mighty clasp divine;
    Hold it close, Lord Jesus,
    That it tremble not in Thine;
For my heart shrinks back from the unknown track,
    And my feet tread falteringly;
    And into the dark I follow —
    Into the dark with Thee.

    Into the dark, Lord Jesus,
    Is it the dark with Thee?
Nay, Thou makest the night about me light,
    And mine eyes — mine eyes shall see —
    Shall "see the King in His beauty,"
    In the land that is far away;
    Shall see in the heavenly sunshine,
    The path that is hid today.

Then why should I fear what the untried year
    May bring to mine or me?
    Into the dark I follow —
    Nay, into the Light, with Thee!
                      — Edith Gilling Cherry

GOD WILL ANSWER

God will answer when to thee,
Not a possibility
Of deliverance seems near;
It is when He will appear.

God will answer when you pray;
Yea, though mountains block thy way,
At His word, a way will be
E'en thro' mountains, made for thee.

God who still divides the sea,
Willingly will work for thee;
God, before whom mountains fall,
Promises to hear thy call.

— M. E. B.

ONE LOWLY PATH

One place have I in heaven above —
    The glory of His throne;
On this dark earth, whence He is gone,
    I have one place alone;

And if His rest in heaven I know,
    I joy to find His path below.

One lowly path across the waste,
    The lowly path of shame;
I would adore Thy wondrous grace
That I should tread the same.
The Stranger and the Alien, Thou —
And I the stranger, alien, now.

— G. T. S.

"WIT'S END CORNER"

Are you standing at "Wit's End Corner,"
    Christian, with troubled brow?
Are you thinking of what is before you,
    And all you are bearing now?
Does all the world seem against you,
    And you in the battle alone?
Remember — at "Wit's End Corner"
    Is just where God's power is shown.

Are you standing at "Wit's End Corner,"
    Blinded with wearying pain,
Feeling you cannot endure it,
    You cannot bear the strain,
Bruised through the constant suffering,
    Dizzy, and dazed, and numb?
Remember — at "Wit's End Corner"
    Is where Jesus loves to come.

Are you standing at "Wit's End Corner"?
    Your work before you spread,
All lying begun, unfinished,
    And pressing on heart and head,
Longing for strength to do it,
    Stretching out trembling hands?
Remember — at "Wit's End Corner"
    The Burden-bearer stands.

Are you standing at "Wit's End Corner"?
  Then you're just in the very spot
To learn the wondrous resources
  Of Him who faileth not;
No doubt to a brighter pathway
  Your footsteps will soon be moved,
But only at "Wit's End Corner"
  Is the "God who is able" proved.

— Antoinette Wilson

ᝍᝋ

Be Still My Heart

Be still my heart! We murmur, you and I,
We fret and fret, while precious hours fly,
Be still — the silent are truly blest;
There is no rapture for a heart distressed.

Be still my heart! the deep, dark night is still,
The trees in prayer, the star above the hill.
Be still — and to this promise softly cling,
The silent hear the great archangels sing.

— Rosco Gilmore Scott

ᝍᝋ

He Goes Before

Dark is the sky! and veiled the unknown morrow!
  Dark is life's way, for night is not yet o'er;
The longed-for glimpse I may not meanwhile borrow;
  But, this I know, *He goeth on before.*

Dangers are nigh! and fears my mind are shaking;
  Heart seems to dread what life may hold in store;
But I am His — He knows the way I'm taking,
  More blessed still — *He goeth on before.*

Doubts cast their weird, unwelcome shadows o'er me,
  Doubts that life's best — life's choicest things are o'er;
What but His Word can strengthen, can restore me,
  And this blest fact; that still *He goes before.*

He goes before! Be this my consolation!
  He goes before! On this my heart would dwell!
He goes before! This guarantees salvation!
  He goes before! And therefore all is well.

— J. Danson Smith

MY LOAD

One day when walking down the
  street,
On business bent, while thinking hard
About the "hundred cares" which
  seemed
Like thunder clouds about to break
In torrents, Self-pity said to me:
"You, poor, poor thing, you have too
  much
To do. Your life is far too hard.
This heavy load will crush you soon."
A swift response of sympathy
Welled up within. The burning sun
Seemed more intense. The dust and
  noise
Of puffing motors flying past
With rasping blast of blowing horn
Incensed still more the whining nerves,
The fabled last back-breaking straw
To weary, troubled, fretting mind.

"Ah, yes, 'twill break and crush my life;
I cannot bear this constant strain
Of endless, aggravating cares;
They are too great for such as I."
So thus my heart condoled itself,
"Enjoying misery," when lo!
A "still small voice" distinctly said,
" 'Twas sent to lift you—not to crush."
I saw at once my great mistake.
My place was not beneath the load
But on the top! God meant it not
That I should carry it. He sent
It here to carry me. Full well
He knew my incapacity
Before the plan was made. He saw
A child of His in need of grace
And power to serve; a puny twig
Requiring sun and rain to grow;
An undeveloped chrysalis;
A weak soul lacking faith in God.
He could not help but see all this

And more. And then, with tender
  thought
He placed it where it had to grow—
Or die. To lie and cringe beneath
One's load means death, but life and
  power
Await all those who dare to rise above.
Our burdens are our wings; on them
We soar to higher realms of grace;
Without them we must roam for aye
On planes of undeveloped faith,
(For faith grows but by exercise
In circumstance impossible).

Oh, paradox of Heaven. The load
We think will crush was sent to lift us
Up to God! Then, soul of mine,
Climb up! for naught can e'er be
  crushed
Save what is underneath the weight.
How may we climb! By what ascent
Shall we surmount the carping cares
Of life! Within His word is found
The key which opes His secret stairs;
Alone with Christ, secluded there,
We mount our loads, and rest in Him.

— *Mary Butterfield*

∽

THE GUIDE

My path lies in obscurity,
Through winding ways, and on,
And yet I feel security . . .
This way my guide has gone.
By lonely seas of sorrow, lie
The imprints of His feet;
I sometimes trace them in the dust,
Of my own city street.
And if I climb the mountain,
I see the impress, where
Among the mountain flowers,
The Master knelt in prayer.

— *Dawn Finlay*

THE NIGHT HAD GONE

The day had gone; alone and weak
I groped my way within a bleak
    And sunless land.
The path that led into the light
I could not find! In that dark night
    God took my hand.

He led me that I might not stray,
And brought me by a new, safe way
    I had not known.
By waters still, through pastures green
I followed Him — the path was clean
    Of briar and stone.

The heavy darkness lost its strength,
My waiting eyes beheld at length
    The streaking dawn.
On, safely on, through sunrise glow
I walked, my hand in His, and lo,
    The night had gone.

— Annie Porter Johnson

ↄↄ

O THOU OF LITTLE FAITH

O thou of little faith,
    God hath not failed thee yet!
When all looks darks and gloomy,
    Thou dost so soon forget —

Forget that He has led thee,
    And gently cleared thy way;
On clouds has poured His sunshine,
    And turned thy night to day.

And if He's helped thee hitherto,
    He will not fail thee now;
How it must wound His loving heart
    To see thy anxious brow!

Oh! doubt not any longer,
    To Him commit thy way,
Whom in the past thou trusted,
    And is "just the same today."

— Author Unknown

OVERANXIOUS

I said: "The desert is so wide!"
I said: "The desert is so bare!
What springs to quench my thirst are
    there?
Whence shall I from the tempest hide?"

I said: "The desert is so lone!
Nor gentle voice, nor loving face
Will brighten any smallest space."
I paused or ere my moan was done!

I heard a flow of hidden springs;
Before me palms rose green and fair;
The birds were singing; all the air
Did shine and stir with angels' wings!

And One said mildly: "Why, indeed,
Take over-anxious thought for that
The morrow bringeth! See you not
The Father knoweth what you need?"

— Author Unknown

ↄↄ

SUSTAINMENT

If wind or wave swept all away
    Those things I now hold dear;
If health should flee
    And sickness come,

Or loved ones leave me here;
    Should fortune change
And hardship come,
    If dreams should fade away:

If tests and trials
    Should plague me sore,
And troubles haunt my day;
    When all had gone,

This still I know
    Christ's love will never leave us,
For when all things have passed away
    We still can count on Jesus.

— Author Unknown

THE EYE OF THE STORM

Fear not that the whirlwind shall carry thee hence,
Nor wait for its onslaught in breathless suspense,
Nor shrink from the whips of the terrible hail,
But pass through the edge to the heart of the gale,
For there is a shelter, sunlighted and warm,
And Faith sees her God through the eye of the storm.

The passionate tempest with rush and wild roar
And threatenings of evil may beat on the shore,
The waves may be mountains, the fields battle plains,
And the earth be immersed in a deluge of rains,
Yet, the soul, stayed on God, may sing bravely its psalm,
For the heart of the storm is the center of calm.

Let hope be not quenched in the blackness of night,
Though the cyclone awhile may have blotted the light,
Far behind the great darkness the stars ever shine,
And the light of God's heavens, His love shall make thine,
Let no gloom dim thine eyes, but uplift them on high
To the face of thy God and the blue of the sky.

The storm is thy shelter from danger and sin,
And God Himself takes thee for safety within;
The tempest with Him passeth into deep calm,
And the roar of the winds is the sound of a psalm.
Be glad and serene when the tempest clouds form;
God smiles on His child in the eye of the storm.

                                        — *Author Unknown*

ↄ๏

HEART-HUSHINGS

Oh, ask in faith! Against the ill thou dreadest,
    Comes white-robed Peace, sweet angel of God's will;
Folding her wings beside thee as thou pleadest,
    Whispering as God's own word to thee, "Be still!"

"Be still!" how fearfully soever blended
    Thy day with dark, like twilight's flickering bars;
For God will make thy deepest midnight splendid,
    With all His countless wealth of glittering stars.

                                        — *Swan*

BE HOPEFUL

Fain would I hold my lamp of life aloft
Like yonder tower built high above the reef;
Steadfast, though tempests rave or winds blow soft;
Clear, though the sky dissolve in tears of grief.

For darkness passes; storms shall not abide:
A little patience and the storm is past.
After the sorrow of the ebbing tide
The singing flood returns in joy at last.

The night is long and pain weighs heavily;
But God will hold His world above despair.
Look to the east, where up the lucid sky
The morning climbs! The day shall yet be fair.

— Celia Thaxter

A LITTLE WAY

A little way — I know it is not far
To that dear home where my beloved are;
And yet my faith grows weaker, as I stand
A poor, lone pilgrim in a dreary land,
Where present pain the future bliss obscures;
And still my heart sits like a bird upon
The empty nest, and mourns its treasures gone;
  Plumed for their flight,
  And vanished quite,
Ah me! where is the comfort? — though I say
They have but journeyed on a little way!

A little way! — this sentence I repeat,
Hoping and longing to extract some sweet
To mingle with the bitter. From Thy hand
I take the cup I cannot understand,
And in my weakness give myself to Thee!
Although it seems so very, very far
To that dear home where my beloved are,
  I know, I know,
  It is not so;
Oh! give me faith to feel it when I say
That they are gone — gone but a little way.

— Author Unknown

He Will Not Fail

The withered flowers hold the seeds of promise,
  The winter days are harbingers of spring;
The trials that may often seem most bitter
  May bring to you the joys that make you sing.

The sorrows that have come to you unbidden
  Have often brought a peace before unknown;
The Maker of your destiny is striving
  To fit your heart to be His royal throne.

Your roses may have thorns, but don't forget —
  Your thorns may have some roses, too;
The Lord of great compassion loves you yet,
  And He will never fail to see you through.

— Author Unknown

Alone With God

When storms of life are round me beating,
  When rough the path that I have trod,
Within my closet doors retreating,
  I love to be alone with God.

What though the clouds have gathered o'er me
  What though I've passed beneath the rod?
God's perfect will there lies before me,
  When I am thus alone with God.

'Tis there I find new strength for duty,
  As o'er the sands of time I plod,
I see the King in all His beauty,
  While resting there alone with God.

Alone with God the world forbidden,
  Alone with Him, O blest retreat!
Alone with God and in Him hidden,
  To hold with Him communion sweet.

— Johnson Oatman, Jr.

I Thank Thee

I thank Thee, Lord, for cloudy weather,
  We soon would tire of blue;
I thank Thee, Lord, for Pain, our brother,
  Whose rude care holds us true.

I thank Thee for the weary morrow,
  That makes the past more sweet;
I thank Thee for our sister, Sorrow.
  Who leads us to Thy feet.

—F. L. Knowles

CALLED ASIDE

Called aside —
From the glad working of thy busy life,
From the world's ceaseless stir of care and strife,
Into the shade and stillness by thy Heavenly Guide
For a brief space thou hast been called aside.

Called aside —
Perhaps into a desert garden dim;
And yet not alone, when thou hast been with Him,
And heard His voice in sweetest accents say:
"Child, wilt thou not with Me this still hour stay?"

Called aside —
In hidden paths with Christ thy Lord to tread,
Deeper to drink at the sweet Fountainhead,
Closer in fellowship with Him to roam,
Nearer, perchance, to feel thy Heavenly Home.

Called aside —
Oh, knowledge deeper grows with Him alone;
In secret oft His deeper love is shown,
And learnt in many an hour of dark distress
Some rare, sweet lesson of His tenderness.

Called aside —
We thank Thee for the stillness and the shade;
We thank Thee for the hidden paths Thy love hath made,
And, so that we have wept and watched with Thee,
We thank Thee for our dark Gethsemane.

Called aside —
Oh, restful thought — He doeth all things well;
Oh, blessed sense, with Christ alone to dwell;
So in the shadow of Thy cross to hide,
We thank Thee, Lord, to have been called aside.

— *Author Unknown*

THE UPWARD PLACE

He stood aside from his playmates,
    His sightless eyes to the sky,
And the cord in his hands was tightly drawn
    By the kite that flew so high.
In his big eyes, wondering, beautiful,

On his pale little slender face,
There shone such a rapture, such keen delight,
    That someway it seemed out of place.
And I could not forbear to pause and ask,
    "My laddie, what pleases you so,
As you hold your kite in the far-off sky,
    Since its motion you cannot know?"

He turned and smiled as he softly said,
    And his voice with joy was full,
"I can't just explain, but it makes me glad,
    When I feel that upward pull."

That Upward Pull; it comes to us
    In the weariness of strife.
When we stand bewildered, blinded and hurt,
    Mid the fall of our cherished dream.
It is good to know that we cannot fail,
    If we follow the heavenly gleam.
And never an hour may be so sad,
    Nor ever a sky so dull
But we may, if we will, reach out and find
    That God-given, Upward Pull.
                              — *Helen M. Wilson*

ᘒ

LONELY? — TIRED? — AFRAID?

Lonely? Yes, sometimes when the night is dark
    And silence wraps the spirit in its gloom;
But then his angels, watching ever nigh,
    Supply the place of friendship's room.

Tired? Yes, often when the day is done,
    And sun rays sink behind the distant west;
But then my Saviour walks beside; and He
    Can give the wearied heart its rest.

Afraid? Oh yes, when mountain paths are steep,
    Too steep for feet unused to rugged ways;
But then His promise cheers me, and the fear
    Is turned to joyful hymns of praise.

So on I press, the loneliness and fear
    But bind me closer to the love divine;
Within the deepest darkness faith can see;
    And so I pray: "Thy will, not mine."
                              — *R. Hare*

I TELL THE KING

Once in an Eastern palace wide
  A little child sat weaving;
So patiently her task she plied,
The men and women at her side
  Flocked around her almost grieving.

"How is it, little one," they said,
  "You always work so cheerily?
You never seem to break your thread,
Or snarl or tangle it, instead
  Of working smooth and clearly."

"I only go and tell the King,"
  She said, abashed and meekly;
"You know He said, 'In everything.'"
"Why so do we!" they cried. "We
    bring
  Him all our troubles weekly."

She turned her little head aside;
  A moment let them wrangle;
"Ah, but," she softly then replied,
"I go and get the knot untied
  At the first little tangle!"

— *Author Unknown*

GOD PLOUGHED

God ploughed one day with an earth-
    quake,
  And drove His furrows deep!
The huddling plains upstarted,
  The hills were all aleap!

But that is the mountains' secret,
  Age-hidden in their breast;
"God's peace is everlasting,"
  Are the dream-words of their rest.

He made them the haunts of beauty,
  The home elect of His grace;
He spreadeth His mornings upon
    them,
  His sunsets light their face.

His winds bring messages to them —
  Wild storm-news from the main;
They sing it down the valleys
  In the love-song of the rain.

They are nurseries for young rivers,
  Nests for His flying cloud,
Homesteads for new-born races,
  Masterful, free, and proud.

The people of tired cities
  Come up to their shrines and pray;
God freshens again within them,
  As He passes by all day.

And lo, I have caught their secret!
  The beauty deeper than all!
This faith — that life's hard moments,
  When the jarring sorrows befall,

Are but God ploughing His moun-
    tains;
  And those mountains yet shall be
The source of His grace and freshness,
  And His peace everlasting to me.

— *William C. Gannett*

WHY WORRY?

Why do we worry about the nest?
  We only stay for a day;
Or a month, or a year, at the Lord's
    behest,
  In this habitat of clay.

Why do we worry about the road,
  With its hills or deep ravine?
In a dismal path, or heavy load,
  We are helped by hands unseen.

Why do we worry about the years
  That our feet have not yet trod?
Who labors with courage and trusts,
    not fears,
  Has fellowship with God.

— *Author Unknown*

LONGING

I longed to walk along an easy road,
   And leave behind the dull routine of home,
Thinking in other fields to serve my God;
   But Jesus said, "My time has not yet come."

I longed to sow the seed in other soil,
   To be unfettered in the work, and free,
To join with other laborers in their toil;
   But Jesus said, " 'Tis not My choice for thee."

I longed to leave the desert, and be led
   To work where souls were sunk in sin and shame,
That I might win them; but the Master said,
   "I have not called thee, publish here My name."

I longed to fight the battles of my King,
   Lift high His standards in the thickest strife;
But my great Captain bade me wait and sing
   Songs of His conquests in my quiet life.

I longed to leave the uncongenial sphere,
   Where all alone I seemed to stand and wait,
To feel I had some human helper near,
   But Jesus bade me guard one lonely gate.

I longed to leave the round of daily toil,
   Where no one seemed to understand or care;
But Jesus said, "I choose for thee this soil,
   That thou might'st raise for Me some blossoms rare."

And now I have no longing but to do
   At home, or else afar, His blessed will,
To work amid the many or the few;
   Thus, "choosing not to choose," my heart is still.

                      — *Author Unknown*

HAST THOU A CLOUD?

   Hast thou a cloud?
Something that is dark and full of dread;
A messenger of tempest overhead?
A something that is darkening the sky;
A something growing darker bye and bye;
A something that thou fear'st will burst at last;
A cloud that doth a deep, long shadow cast,
   God cometh in that cloud.

Hast thou a cloud?
It is Jehovah's triumph car: in this
He rideth to thee, o'er the wide abyss.
It is the robe in which He wraps His form;
For He doth gird Him with the flashing storm.
It is the veil in which He hides the light
Of His fair face, too dazzling for thy sight.
God cometh in that cloud.

Hast thou a cloud?
A trial that is terrible to thee?
A black temptation threatening to see?
A loss of some dear one long thine own?
A mist, a veiling, bringing the unknown?
A mystery that unsubstantial seems:
A cloud between thee and the sun's bright beams?
God cometh in that cloud.

Hast thou a cloud?
A sickness — weak old age — distress and death?
These clouds will scatter at thy last faint breath.
Fear not the clouds that hover o'er thy barque,
Making the harbour's entrance dire and dark;
The cloud of death, though misty, chill and cold,
Will yet grow radiant with a fringe of gold.
God cometh in that cloud.

— *Author Unknown*

∽

I PROMISE THEE

I promise thee
That I, to whom the pillars of the earth belong,
Will bear thee up and keep thy spirit strong.

I promise thee
That none shall add a furlong to the mile
That thou must walk, through this long little while.

I promise thee
Thy private shadow shall not shadow ever
The path of thy beloved fellow-lover.

I promise thee
That though it tarry, yet the day will come
When I shall call thee Home.

— *Amy Carmichael*

Hush!

Then hush! oh, hush! for the Father knows what thou knowest not,
The need and the thorn and the shadow linked with the fairest lot;
Knows the wisest exemption from many an unseen snare,
Knows what will keep thee nearest, knows what thou could'st not bear.

Hush! oh, hush! for the Father portioneth as He will,
To all His beloved children, and shall they not be still?
Is not His will the wisest, is not His choice the best?
And in perfect acquiescence is there not perfect rest?

Hush! oh, hush! for the Father, whose ways are true and just,
Knoweth and careth and loveth, and waits for thy perfect trust;
The cup He is slowly filling shall soon be full to the brim,
And infinite compensations for ever be found in Him.

— *F. R. Havergal*

The Storm Thrush

There's a sweet little bird in a far-off isle —
    The isle where the shamrocks grow;
And of all the birds in that dear old land,
    He's the dearest that I know;
He is dressed in a suit of sober brown,
    And a speckled breast has he;
But his eyes is bright and his voice is tuned
    To heaven's own minstrelsy.
He sits and sings when the sun shines fair
    To his mate in her downy nest,
But the topmost twig of the tallest tree
    Is the place where he sings best!
When the rain pours down and the floods are out,
    And the wild winds rage and roar,
Then, clear and high, o'er the shrieking gale,
    The storm thrush sings the more.

That frail little bird on the swaying twig,
    As his clear voice pierced the gales,
Dropped a message sweet at my faltering feet,
    Of a Love that never fails:
Though many a storm has crossed my life,
    And many a grief and fear;
Yet with heart and voice did my soul rejoice,
    For my Lord was always near.
So when dark clouds are about *your* path,

Like the storm thrush, learn to sing;
For from topmost height of a lofty faith
　　You can always see the King!
And with eyes that gaze on His blessed face,
　　You never need fear or fail.
The gales may *prove*, but they *cannot move*,
　　The anchor "within the vail."

— *Mrs. C. L. de Cheney*

He Leads

He leads us on by paths we did not know;
Upward He leads us, though our steps be slow,
Though oft we faint and falter on the way,
Though storms and darkness oft obscure the day;
　　Yet when the clouds are gone,
　　We know He leads us on.

He leads us on through all the unquiet years;
Past all our dreamland hopes, and doubts and fears,
He guides our steps, through all the tangled maze
Of losses, sorrows, and o'erclouded days;
　　We know His will is done;
　　And still He leads us on.

— *N. L. Zinzendorf*

Thy Look

I sit alone and watch the dark'ning years,
　　And all my heart grows dim with doubts and fear,
Till out of deepest gloom a Face appears,—
　　The only one of all that shineth clear.

Make white thy wedding-garments, O my soul!
　　And sigh no longer for thy scanty dower;
For if He loves thee, He will crown thee whole
　　With nobler beauty and immortal power.

O mighty Angel of the secret name!
　　Come, for my heart doth answer Thy All-hail:
Come with the new name and the mystic stone,
　　And speak so low that none shall hear the call.—
O beautiful, beloved, and still unknown,
　　I ask Thee naught:— Thy look hath promised all!

— *Spencer*

LORD, KEEP ME STILL

Lord, keep me still,
Though stormy winds may blow,
And waves my little bark may overflow,
Or even if in darkness I must go,
Yet keep me still, yet keep me still.

Lord, keep me still,
The waves are in Thy hand,
The roughest winds subside at Thy
  command.
Steer Thou my bark in safety to the
  land,
And keep me still, and keep me still.

Lord, keep me still,
And may I ever hear Thy still small
  voice
To comfort and to cheer;
So shall I know and feel Thee ever
  near.
And keep me still, and keep me still.

— *Author Unknown*

I SHALL SEE HIM

In the bitter waves of woe
  Beaten and tosssed about
By the sullen winds that blow
  From the desolate shores of doubt,
Where the anchors that faith has cast
  Are dragging in the gale,
I am quietly holding fast
  To the things that cannot fail.

And fierce tho' the fiends may fight,
  And long though the angels hide,
I know that truth and right
  Have the universe on their side;
And that somewhere beyond the stars
  Is a love that is better than fate.
When the night unlocks her bars
  I shall see Him — I will wait.

— *Washington Gladden*

TRUST

O there are heavenly heights to reach
  In many a fearful place,
While the poor, timid heir of God
  Lies blindly on his face.
Lies languishing for light Divine
  That he shall never see
Till he goes forward at Thy sign
  And trusts himself to Thee.

— *C. A. Fox*

IT NEVER COMES

Many a stormcloud gathering o'er us
  Never comes to bring us rain;
Many a grief we see before us
  Never comes to give us pain.

Ofttimes in the feared tomorrow
  Sunshine comes, the cloud is gone;
Look not then in foolish sorrow
  For the trouble yet to come.

— *Author Unknown*

I KNOW THAT MY REDEEMER LIVES

I know that my Redeemer lives,
And ever prays for me;
A token of his love he gives,
A pledge of liberty.
He lives, triumphant o'er the grave,
At God's right hand on high.
My ransomed soul to keep and save,
To bless and glorify.
He lives, that I may also live,
And now his grace proclaim;
He lives that I may honor give
To his most holy Name.
Let strains of heavenly music rise,
While all their anthem sing
To Christ, my precious sacrifice,
And everliving King.

— *Charles Wesley*

WHILE PASSING THROUGH THIS VALLEY (*Psalm 84:6*)

While passing through this valley
   Let me make it
A deep refreshing well
   That there may be
Reflected in its depths
   With tender mercy,
One star of faith to shine
   Eternally!

And may it be so clear and bright
   That others,
Bewildered by the darkness
   Of their night,
May, thirsty, drawing near, drink deep
   And find Him
Who is the Author of
   Eternal light!
                — *Alice Hansche Mortenson*

ᕽᕽ

THIS PEACE HE GIVES

I know not why my pathway leads
   Through valleys rough and steep,
But this I know, while walking there
   I've found communion sweet
With those I love, and, best of all,
   With Him who climbed for me,
Beneath a heavy cross, the hill
   That led to Calvary.

I know not why so many props
   Have gently been removed,
But I do know through every loss
   His arms unfailing proved.
I have no reason, none at all,
   To doubt His Precious Word;
Though all I loved be swept away,
   His Voice would still be heard
Above the storm, and as I lift
   My tear-filled eyes to Him,
The Great Creator, Lord of all,
   He whispers "Peace," within.

So as I look beyond today,
   I pray that I may share
This peace He gives with those who have
   A greater cross to bear.
I know not now how long 'twill be
   Before He calls me home,
But this I know — beneath His wings
   I'll never be alone!

                — *Alice Hansche Mortenson*

ᕽᕽ

TRUST IS BEST

I think if thou couldst know,
   O soul that will complain,
What lies concealed below
   Our burden and our pain;
How just our anguish brings
Nearer those longed-for things,
We seek for now in vain —
I think thou wouldst rejoice and not
   complain.

I think if thou couldst see,
   With thy dim mortal sight,
How meanings dark to thee
   Are shadows hiding light;
Truth's efforts crossed and vex'd,
Life-purpose all perplex'd —
If thou could see them right,
I think that they would seem all clear,
   and wise and bright.

And yet thou canst not know,
   And yet thou canst not see;
Wisdom and sight are slow
   In poor humanity,
If thou couldst *trust*, poor soul,
In Him who rules the whole,
Thou wouldst find peace and rest;
Wisdom and right as well, but trust
   is best.

                — *Author Unknown*

I Look Up

I look not back — God knows the fruitless effort,
The wasted hours, the sinning and regrets;
I leave them all with Him that blots the record
And graciously forgives and then forgets.

I look not forward, God sees all the future,
The road that short or long, will lead me home;
And He will face with me its every trial,
And bear for me the burden that may come.

I look not 'round me — then would fears assail me,
So wild the tumult of life's restless sea;
So dark the world, so filled with war and evil,
So vain the hope of comfort and of ease.

I look not inward, that would make me wretched,
For I have naught on which to stay my trust;
Nothing I see but failures and shortcomings,
And weak endeavors crumbling into dust.

But I look up — into the face of Jesus!
For there my heart can rest, my fears are stilled;
And there is joy, and love and light for darkness,
And perfect peace, and every hope fulfilled.

— J. H. Hunt

That's All

Whom the Lord loveth He chasteneth often.
What a comforting thought, all hardness to soften!
Quiet it brings to a questioning heart.
"Why was it this cruel thing did befall?"
Quickly God answers, "I love you," that's all.

"All things must work for the good of God's lovers."
Like a tree's leafy shade, this Bible word covers
Hearts hot with grieving and ready to break.
"Why is it grief made this unwelcome call?"
Softly God answers, "I love you," that's all.

"Whom the Lord loveth His scourging correcteth."
As rain coming down on scorched grass, so affecteth
This saying the soul that God's furnace has seared.
"Why came on me all these woes that appall?"
Kindly God answers, "I love you." That's all.

— Author Unknown

THE PATH IN THE SKY

The woods were dark and the night was black
And only an owl could see the track;
But the cheery driver made his way
Through the great pine woods as if it were day.

I asked him, "How do you manage to see?
The road and the forest are one to me."
"To me as well," he replied, "And I
Can only drive by the path in the sky."

I looked above, where the tree tops tall
Rose from the road, like an ebon wall;
And lo! a beautiful starry lane
Wound as the road wound and made it plain.

And since when the path of my life is drear,
And all is blackness and doubt and fear,
When the horrors of midnight are here below
And I see not a step of the way to go,
Then, oh! then, I can look on high
And walk on earth by the light in the sky.

— Amos R. Wells

THE CROSSROADS

I seem to have come to the cross-roads,
    And know not which way to turn,
So look into my Father's face,
    My direction from Him to learn.

I seem to have come to the cross-roads,
    And overhead clouds dark as night,
Then quickly I call to my Father
    To ask Him to send the light.

I seem to have come to the cross-roads,
    But the voice that I hear comforts me;
"Fear not! Be not afraid! I am with Thee
    As thy day, so shall thy strength be!"

I seem to have come to the cross-roads,
    But with words such as these, need I more,
For grace and courage to follow
    My Guide, Whose knowledge is sure!

— E. Randall

WALK CLOSE BESIDE ME

Lord, walk close beside me
As I walk the narrow way.
Lord, walk close beside me
And direct my path each day.
Lord, walk close beside me
For I know the tempter's power.
Lord, walk close beside me
Every day and every hour.

Lord, walk close beside me
As I walk life's lonely way.
Lord, walk close beside me
Lest my steps should go astray.
Lord, walk close beside me
Till my journey here is done.
Lord, walk close beside me
Till my race in life is won.

— *Roy J. Wilkins*

COME, MY SHEEP

Come, my sheep,
Shadows deep
Fall o'er land and sea.
Fast the day
Fades away,
Come and rest with me.
Come, and in my fold abide,
Dangers lurk on every side
Till at last
Night has passed
In my fold abide.

Come, my sheep,
I will keep
Watch, the long night through,
Safe from harm
And alarm
I will shelter you.
Thro' the night, my lambs shall rest
Safe upon their Shepherd's breast.
Folded there,
Free from care,
Through the night, shall rest.

Come, my sheep,
Calmly sleep
Sheltered in the fold.
Weary one,
Homeward come,
Winds are blowing cold.
Rest until the dawn shall break,
Then with joy my flocks shall wake.
Pastures new
Wait for you
When the dawn shall break.

— *Dorothy B. Polsue*

THE BLESSED SECRET
Philippians 4:11

I have learned the blessed secret
  Of the soul that's satisfied,
Since the Savior dwells within me,
  And in Him I now abide.
I have learned the joy of trusting
  In the sureness of His Word,
Knowing that each promise spoken,
  Will be honored by my Lord.

In the silence I have heard Him:
  (O, the music of His voice!)
"Peace I give thee, be not troubled,
  Let thy heart and soul rejoice."
Yes, I've found my Lord sufficient,
  For He meets my ev'ry need;
Satisfies my soul's deep longings,
  Guards and guides each thought and
     deed.

Peace that passeth understanding
  Is His gift of grace so free.
And the power of His presence
  Is His promise unto me.
Blessed peace, divine contentment
  From the heart of God above!
All the shadows turn to sunshine,
  Walking with the Lord of love.

—*Albert Simpson Reitz*

"Believe Ye That I Am Able to Do This?"
Matthew 9:28

Why should I doubt,
When loaves and fish
Are multiplied, if so He wish;
When storms are stilled,
If so He willed?
His were the hands that raised the
    dead,
His was the voice *Creation*, said;
Why should I doubt that He can do
This thing that now I ask Him to?

— *Dawn Finlay*

ᔐ

God's Ways

God's ways are ways of pleasantness,
    And all His paths are peace
        (Proverbs 3:17).
How often this seems quite untrue
    When life's glad songs must cease,
And in their place come anguished sobs
    Of grief and bitter tears;
And disappointing pain and loss
    That lasts, and lasts, for years.

God's ways are ways of pleasantness,
    And all His paths are peace.
How often this seems quite untrue
    When He grants no release
From circumstances, hard, unjust,
    When we had tried to win
His approbation for our lives,
    And keep unstained from sin.

God's ways are ways of pleasantness,
    And all His paths are peace.
How often this seems quite untrue
    As galling wrongs increase
When we supposed all trials past,
    And thought we saw ahead
A quiet home of peace and rest
    Toward which our pathway led.

God's ways *are* ways of pleasantness,
    And all His paths *are* peace!
They may lead thro' distracting cares,
    And trials that increase;
But they lead through all earthly woes,
    Yes, through earth's saddest night,
And up, in gladness, joy and peace,
    To regions of delight.

God's ways *are* ways of pleasantness,
    And all His paths *are* peace!
They all lead to that longed-for-land
    Where glad songs never cease;
Where anguished sobs are never heard;
    Where tears are wiped away;
Where life holds all that Heaven
        means;
    And lasts, and lasts, for aye (Psalm
        16:11).

— *Albert C. Stewart*

ᔐ

Quietness

"Be still and know that I am God,"
That I who made and gave thee life
Will lead thy faltering steps aright;
That I who see each sparrow's fall
Will hear and heed thy earnest call.
    I am God.

"Be still and know that I am God,"
When aching burdens crush thy heart,
Then know I form thee for thy part
And purpose in the plan I hold.
Thou art the clay that I would mold.
    Trust in God.

"Be still and know that I am God,"
Who made the atom's tiny span
And set it moving to my plan,
That I who guide the stars above
Will guide and keep thee in my love.
    Be thou still.

— *Author Unknown*

MY SAVIOUR'S FACE

Tho' the road may be rough where He leads me,
    Still His footprints I plainly can trace,
And the trials I meet will seem nothing,
    When I look in my dear Saviour's face.

So I keep my eyes fixed upon Jesus,
    While I'm running life's wearisome race;
I'll forget the hard pathway I traveled,
    When I look in my dear Saviour's face.

Tho' the shadows around me may gather,
    Safe I rest in my Lord's secret place,
For I know there'll be glorious sunshine,
    When I look in my dear Saviour's face.

When I look in His face, His wonderful face,
    In Heaven, that beautiful place!
All the hardships of earth will seem nothing —
    When I look in my dear Saviour's face.

— Author Unknown

DON'T QUIT

When things go wrong as they sometimes will,
When the road you're trudging seems all up hill,
When the funds are low and the debts are high
And you want to smile, but you have to sigh,
When care is pressing you down a bit,
Rest, if you must — but don't you quit.

Life is queer with its twists and turns,
As everyone of us sometimes learns,
And many a failure turns about
When he might have won had he stuck it out;
Don't give up though the pace seems slow —
You may succeed with another blow.

Success is failure turned inside out —
The silver tint of the clouds of doubt
And you never can tell how close you are,
It may be near when it seems afar;
So stick to the fight when you're hardest hit —
It's when things seem worst that you must not quit.

— Author Unknown

I Bow My Forehead to the Dust

I bow my forehead to the dust,
I veil mine eyes for shame,
And urge, in trembling self distrust,
A prayer without a claim.
No off'ring of mine own I have,
Nor works my faith to prove;
I can but give the gifts He gave,
And plead His love for love!

I know not what the future hath
Of marvel or surprise,
Assured alone that life and death
His mercy underlies.

And so beside the silent sea
I wait the muffled oar;
No harm from Him can come to me
On ocean or on shore.

I know not where His islands lift
Their fronded palms in air;
I only know I cannot drift
Beyond His love and care.
And Thou, O Lord, by whom are seen
Thy creatures as they be,
Forgive me if too close I lean
My human heart on Thee.

— *John Greenleaf Whittier*

Be Still and Sleep

Be still and sleep, my soul!
  Now gentle-footed night,
In softly shadowed stole,
  Holds all the day from sight.

Why shouldst thou lie and stare
  Against the dark, and toss,
And live again thy care,
  Thine agony and loss?

'Twas given thee to live,
  And thou hast lived it all;
Let that suffice, nor give
  One thought what may befall.

Thou hast no need to wake,
  Thou art no sentinel;
Love all the care will take,
  And Wisdom watcheth well.

Weep not, think not, but rest!
  The stars in silence roll;
On the world's mother-breast,
  Be still and sleep, my soul!

— *Edward Rowland Sill*

Calm Me, My God

Calm me, my God, and keep me calm,
  While these hot breezes blow;
Be like the night-dew's cooling balm
  Upon earth's fevered brow!

Calm me, my God, and keep me calm,
  Soft resting on Thy breast;
Soothe me with holy hymn and psalm,
  And bid my spirit rest.

Calm me, my God, and keep me calm.
  Let Thine outstretched wing
Be like the shade of Elim's palm
  Beside her desert spring.

Yes, keep me calm, tho' loud and rude
  The sounds my ear that greet,—
Calm in the closet's solitude,
  Calm in the bustling street;

Calm as the ray of sun or star
  Which storms assail in vain,—
Moving unruffled through earth's war,
  The eternal calm to gain.

— *Horatius Bonar*

WAIT, MY SOUL

Wait, my soul, upon the Lord,
  To His gracious promise flee,
Laying hold upon His Word,
  "As thy days thy strength shall be."

If the sorrows of thy case
  Seem peculiar still to thee,
God has promised needful grace,
  "As thy days thy strength shall be."

Days of trial, days of grief,
  In succession thou mayst see;
This is still thy sweet relief,
  "As thy days thy strength shall be."

Rock of Ages, I'm secure,
  With Thy promise full and free;
Faithful, positive, and sure —
  "As thy days thy strength shall be."

— Author Unknown

HOPE'S SONG

I hear it singing, singing sweetly,
  Softly in an undertone,—
Singing as if God had taught it,
  "It is better farther on!"

Night and day it sings the same song,
  Sings it while I sit alone,
Sings so that the heart may hear it,
  "It is better farther on!"

Sits upon the grave and sings it,
  Sings it when the heart would groan,
Sings it when the shadows darken,
  "It is better farther on!"

Farther on? Oh, how much farther?
  Count the milestones one by one —
No, not counting, only trusting,
  "It is better farther on!"

— Author Unknown

BE STILL MY HEART

I will commit my way, O Lord, to Thee,
Nor doubt Thy love, though dark the way may be,
Nor murmur, for the sorrow is from God,
And there is comfort also in Thy rod.

I will not seek to know the future years,
Nor cloud today with dark tomorrow's fears;
I will but ask a light from heaven, to show
How, step by step, my pilgrimage should go.

And if the distant perils seem to make
The path impossible that I must take,
Yet as the river winds through mountains lone,
The way will open up — as I go on.

Be still, my heart; for faithful is thy Lord,
And pure and true and tried His Holy Word;
Through stormy flood that rageth as the sea,
His promises thy stepping-stones shall be.

— Author Unknown

PEACE

"There is a peace that cometh after sorrow,"
  Of hope surrendered, not of hope fulfilled;
A peace that looketh not upon tomorrow,
  But calmly on a tempest that is stilled.

A peace which lives not now in joy's excesses,
  Nor in the happy life of love secure;
But in the strength the heart possesses
  Of conflicts won while learning to endure.

A peace there is, in sacrifice secluded;
  A life subdued, from will and passion free;
'Tis not the peace which over Eden brooded,
  But that which triumphed in Gethsemane.

— *Jessie Rose Gates*

ᨀ

CHILD OF MY LOVE

Child of My love, fear not the unknown morrow,
  Dread not the new demand life makes of thee;
Thy ignorance doth hold no cause for sorrow
  Since what thou knowest not is known to Me.

Thou canst not see today the hidden meaning
  Of My command, but thou the light shalt gain;
Walk on in faith, upon My promise leaning,
  And as thou goest all shall be made plain.

One step thou seest — then go forward boldly,
  One step is far enough for faith to see;
Take that, and thy next duty shall be told thee,
  For step by step thy Lord is leading thee.

Stand not in fear, thy adversaries counting,
  Dare every peril, save to disobey;
Thou shalt march on, all obstacles surmounting,
  For I, the Strong, will open up the way.

Wherefore go gladly to the task assigned thee,
  Having My promise, needing nothing more
Than just to know, where'er the future find thee,
  In all thy journeying I go before.

— *Frank J. Exeley*

TRUST

Though the rain may fall and the wind is blowing,
   And cold and chill is the wintry blast,
Though the cloudy sky is still cloudier growing,
   And the dead leaves tell that summer has passed.
My face I hold to the stormy heaven,
   My heart is as calm as the summer sea,
Glad to receive what God has given,
      Whate'er it be.

When I feel the cold I can say, "He sends it,"
   And His wind blows blessing I surely know,
For I've never a want but that He attends it,
   And my heart beats warm though the winds may blow.
The soft sweet summer was warm and glowing;
   Bright were the blossoms on every bough;
I trusted Him when the roses were blowing;—
      I trust Him now.

Small were my faith should it weakly falter,
   Now that the roses have ceased to grow;
Frail were the trust that now should alter,
   Doubting His love when storm clouds blow.
If I trust Him once, I must trust Him ever,
   And His way is best, though I stand or fall,
Through wind and storm, He will leave me never,—
      He sends it all.

Why should my heart be faint and fearing?
   Mighty He rules above the storm;
Even the wintry blast is cheering,
   Showing his power to keep me warm.
Never a care on my heart is pressing,
   Never a fear can disturb my breast,
Everything that He sends is blessing,
      For He knows best.
          — *Song of a Bird in a Winter Storm*

WHEN THE STARS ARE GONE

The stars shine over the mountains, the stars shine over the sea,
The stars look up to the mighty God, the stars look down on me;
The stars shall last for a million years, a million years and a day,
But God and I will live and love when the stars have passed away.

          — *Robert Louis Stevenson*

I Will Guide Thee

Benighted on a lone and dreary wild,
Perplexed, exhausted, helpless, in despair,
I cast me down, and thought to perish there.
When through the gloom a Face appeared and smiled;
And a sweet Voice said, "Courage! rise, My child!
And I will guide thee safely by the way."

As to night-watchers comes the morning ray,
So came that voice to me; and on that Face
I seemed a loving tenderness to trace,
That soothed and cheered me as, forlorn, I lay;
I felt as feels the child whose throbbing grief
A mother's love assuages in its source;
And asking strength of Him who gave relief,
I straightway rose, and onward held my course.

—*W. L. Alexander*

∾

The Everlasting Arms — *Deuteronomy* 33:27

There is a place of safe retreat
    When the shadows of life hang low;
Where rest and peace and comfort meet —
    'Tis ours to learn, 'tis ours to know
        The Everlasting Arms!

There is a calm when billows roll,
    And angry waves would crush the weak;
There is a solace for the soul —
    He bids us come, He bids us seek
        The Everlasting Arms!

There is a balm in Gilead still;
    Rest for the heart, peace for the mind.
It's good to know His way and will —
    It's good to have, it's good to find
        The Everlasting Arms!

There is a shelter in the storm;
    Grace has bestowed in gracious measure.
When foes assail and fears alarm —
    We find our help: this greatest treasure,
        The Everlasting Arms!

There is a Mount above the plains
  Of earthly care and worldly strife.
No more the wounds, no more the pains —
  Eternal joy, eternal life
    In His Everlasting Arms!
                — *William M. Scholfield*

Trust

The little birds trust God, for they go singing
  From Northern woods where autumn winds have blown.
With joyous faith their trackless pathway winging
  To summer lands of song, afar, unknown.

And if He cares for them through wintry weather,
  And will not disappoint one little bird,
Will He not be as true a heavenly Father
  To every soul who trusts His holy word?

Let us go singing then, and not go sighing
  Since we are sure our times are in His hand.
Why should we weep, and fear, and call it dying? —
  'Tis only flitting to a Summer land!
                — *Annie Johnson Flint*

What of That?

  Dark! Well what of that?
Didst fondly dream the sun would never set?
Dost fear to lose thy way? take courage yet!
Learn thou to walk by faith and not by sight
Thy steps will guided be, and guided right.

  Lonely! And what of that?
Some must be lonely. 'Tis not given to all
To feel a heart responsive rise and fall,
To blend another life into his own;
Work may be done in loneliness; work on!

  No help! Nay, it's not so!
Though human help be far, thy God is nigh;
Who feeds the ravens, hears His children's cry;
He's near thee, wheresoe'er the footsteps roam,
And He will guide thee, light thee, help thee home.

                — *Author Unknown*

I Will Take Thy Hand

The way is dark, My child! but leads to light:
I would not always have thee walk by sight.
My dealings now thou canst not understand,
I meant it so; but I will take thy hand.

The day goes fast, My child! But is the night
Darker to Me than day? In Me is light!
Keep close to Me, and every spectral band
Of fears shall vanish. I will take thy hand.

The way is long, My Child! But it shall be
Not one step longer than is best for thee;
And thou shalt know, at last, when thou shalt stand
Safe at the goal, how I did take thy hand.

— *Author Unknown*

Songs in the Night

My songs have been the songs of the daylight,
    Of the sunshine of His face,
Of the hours of blest communion,
    And the wonders of His grace.

In my song has been unremembered
    The touch of His hand in my plight.
Oh! how easy to sing in the sunshine —
    He alone can give songs in the night.

The weight of an awful darkness,
    Hung over my soul like a pall;
And everything round me seemed blackness —
    No help but to struggle and fall.

But treasures are found in the darkness,
    And riches are hidden in store;
And sorrow oft gives us a song to sing,
    Unknown to us heretofore.

Our God gives us songs in the midnight,
    When our feet are held fast in the stocks;
And sends with the praises He giveth,
    The unloosing of bars and locks.

— *J. Lyall*

Know That I Am God

Of all the words that have been borne
  From ancient sea or distant sod;
These are the eight that shine as stars:
  Be still, and know that I am God.

Be still —. There is a storm of noise
  That beats from every plain and hill;
But I have found the blessedness
  Of peace that comes from being still!

Be still and know—. The earth is full
  Of theories; but I seek to find
The never-failing wisdom from
  The fountain of Eternal Mind.

In meditation gleams the way
  Of truth and peace and love and
    good!
There are eight words to save the
    world:
  Be still, and know that I am God!

         — *Lon Woodrum*

God Knoweth Best

Sometimes God, who knoweth best,
Gives us joy and peace and rest,
Sometimes days glide swiftly by
Filled with sunshine from on high.

Sometimes God, who knoweth best,
Sends us sorrow as a test,
Sometimes He doth wound a heart
Greater sweetness to impart.

Oft a heart bowed down in grief
Looks to Jesus for relief,
Seeks the Saviour's loving care,
Learns to have more faith in pray'r.

Well we know whate'er betide,
If we let the Spirit guide,
Will but prove God knoweth best,
Then fear not, though hard the test.

So we leave in His dear hand
All we cannot understand,
While our God with heart of love
Leads His own to heights above.

         — *Emily Donaghy*

Rise, My Soul

Rise, my soul, and stretch thy wings,
  Thy better portion trace;
  Rise from transitory things
Toward heaven thy destined place.
  Sun and moon and stars decay,
Time shall soon this earth remove;
  Rise, my soul, and haste away
  To seats prepared above.

Rivers to the ocean run,
  Nor stay in all their course;
Fire ascending seeks the sun;
  Both speed them to their source
So my soul, derived from God,
  Longs to view His glorious face,
Forward tends to His abode,
  To rest in His embrace.

Cease, my soul, then, cease to mourn,
  Press onward to the prize;
Soon the Saviour will return
  Triumphant in the skies:
Yet a season, and we know
  Happy entrance will be given,
All our sorrows let below,
  And earth exchanged for heaven.

         — *Robert Seagrave*

"He Careth" — *I Peter* 5:7

What can it mean? Is it aught to Him
That the nights are long, and the days are dim?
Can He be touched by the griefs I bear,
Which sadden the heart, and whiten the hair?
Around His throne are eternal calms,
And glad, strong music of happy psalms,
And bliss unruffled by any strife,
How can He care for my little life?

And yet I want Him to care for me
While I live in this world where the sorrows be;
When the lights are down from the path I take;
When strength is feeble, and friends forsake;
When love and music that once did bless
Have left me to silence and loneliness;
And my life-song changes to sobbing prayers,
When my heart cries out for a God who cares.

When shadows hang o'er me the whole day long,
And my spirit is bowed 'neath shame and wrong;
When I am not good, and the deepening shade
Of conscious sin makes my heart afraid;
And the busy world has too much to do
To stay in its course to help me through;
And I long for a Saviour — Can it be
That the God of the universe cares for me.

Oh, the wonderful story of deathless love!
Each child is dear to that heart above;
He fights for me when I cannot fight,
He comforts me in the gloom of night,
He lifts the burden for He is strong,
He stills the sigh, and awakens the song;
The burdens that bow me down He bears,
And loves and pities because He cares.

Oh, all that are sad, take heart again!
You are not alone in your hour of pain;
The Father stoops from His throne above
To soothe and comfort us with His love.
He leaves us not when the storm beats high,
And we have safety, for He is nigh.
Can it be trouble when He doth share?
Oh, rest in peace, for your Lord does care!

— Author Unknown

RIVER OF LIFE

"Please, may I hold your hand, dear Lord?
There's a river of life that I must ford.
The way is hard and the road is steep.
I'll need some help through the waters deep."

I took God's hand and on we went,
But I slipped and fell 'ere the day was spent.
We tried again but it didn't work.
I lost my grasp and was often hurt.

Once more I called on the Lord for help.
I had failed in my tries to save myself.
"Dear Lord," I cried, "You understand.
This time *You* better hold *my* hand."

— *Elayne Tedder*

CHRIST'S INVITATION

Oh, sweetest invitation this sin-worn earth hath known,
In yearning supplication the Lord calls back His own;
From toil and grief and failure, from strivings all unblest,
"Come, weary, heavy laden, and I will give you rest!"

Was ever such appealing from such a suppliant heard?
Love infinite, revealing, in one majestic word:
The mighty heart of Jesus in tenderness expressed —
"Come unto Me, ye weary, and I will give you rest!"

Not only as a guerdon for lifelong labor done,
But in the heat and burden, this blessedness is won —
I offer rest at noontide, and ease when foes molest:
"Come, take My yoke upon you, and I will give you rest."

From hopes that fail and falter amidst the crowding years,
From friends that change and falter when pleasure disappears;
From plans and projects broken, and birthrights unpossessed —
"Come, weary, heavy laden, and I will you give you rest."

When life's last voices calling are hushed at close of day,
When dews of death are falling and strength has passed away,
Oh, heirs of many mansions, made free among the blest —
"Come unto Me forever, and I will give you rest."

— *Author Unknown*

GOD'S PLOW OF SORROW

God's plow of sorrow! Sterile is
The field that is not turned thereby;
And but a scanty harvest his
Whom the great Plowman passeth
by.
God's plow of sorrow! All in vain
His richest seed bestrews the sod;
And spent for naught the sun and rain
On globes that are not plowed of
God.
He ploweth well, He ploweth deep,
And where He ploweth, angels reap.

God's plow of sorrow! Gentle child,
I do not ask that He may spare
Thy tender soul, though undefiled,
Nor turn it with His iron share;
Be thine His after-rain of love,

And where His heavy plow hath
passed
May mellow furrows bear above
A holier harvest at the last!
He ploweth well, He ploweth deep,
And where He ploweth, angels reap.

God's plow of sorrow! Do not think
Oh, careless soul, that thou shalt
lack.
God is afield, He will not shrink —
God is afield, He turns not back.
Deep driven, shall the iron be sent
Through all thy fallow fields, until
The stubborn elements relent
And lo, the Plowman hath His will!
He ploweth well, He ploweth deep,
And where He ploweth, angels reap.

— *Robert Clarkson Tongue*

ↄﻭ

AFTER

After the winter, so cold and so drear,
Cometh the springtime with gladness and cheer;
After the shadows have all passed away,
Sunshine will follow in God's perfect day.

After the sorrow, the grief and the loss,
After the anguish and shame of the cross;
After the darkness, the conflict and strife
Cometh the joy of victorious life.

After the heart has been robbed of its love,
God in great goodness His mercy will prove;
After the loneliness, after the night
Teardrops will vanish and faith turn to sight.

After the flowers have all withered and died
Hope will yet linger whatever betide,
Life cannot perish, God's Word is still true,
What He has promised He surely will do.

— *Oswald J. Smith*

How Could I Face the Future?

How could I face the future
  Were Christ not real to me,
With stormy clouds appearing
  On land, in air and sea?
Though I know not the meaning
  Of all mine eyes can see,
I know God's ways eternal
  Are always best for me.

The darkness may grow darker,
  But I shall know no fear,
For Christ my Lord is with me,
  His presence is so near.
My heart shall not be troubled
  With all the stress and strife,
For God has oft assured me,
  In Him is all my life.

The foe would have me frightened
  With what may soon take place;
But I shall hide in Jesus,
  And trust His saving grace.
And so through all the journey,
  My hope in Him is stayed;
My heart will not be troubled,
  Nor will it be afraid.

           — *Alma Hoellein*

God Uses Broken Things

It takes the broken soil to grow
And ripen fields of grain;
And overspreading broken clouds
To give refreshing rain.
'Tis broken grain that gives us bread;
And broken bread that gives
Us strength for every moment, hour;
By broken things man lives.
A broken spirit, contrite heart,
Our God will ne'er despise;
For pleasing are these things to him,
Therein repentance lies.
It was the alabaster box

As broken, emptied, poured
A fragrant, rich, and rare perfume
Anointing Christ, our Lord.
It was the heart of him who died
Upon Mount Calvary;
As broken, bleeding thereupon,
That ransomed even me.

           — *Eva Gray*

Grace Sufficient

Friend, never give up;
  The day may be long;
The hill may be steep;
  The enemy strong.

But you have been promised,
  Abundant and free,
God's wonderful grace,
  Sufficient for thee.

Then take it, my friend;
  Drink deep of the cup,
His grace is sufficient,
  So never give up.

           — *Charles E. Bayley*

My Heart Is Fixed

My heart is fixed, my mind is made,
I shall not ever be afraid,
Love conquers fear, our God will do
What He has promised me — and you.

My heart is fixed, the things on earth
May lose their luster or their worth,
No anxious moments need be mine,
I rest in strength and power Divine.

My heart is fixed, I trust His Name,
Forever and a day the same,
His Holy Spirit from above
Will fill my soul with perfect love.

           — *James A. Sanaker*

WHY THEN SO FEARFUL?

Fear is faith in Satan
  Faith is fearing God.
Ever see it that way?
Does look rather odd.

Fear says, "God may fail me."
  Faith knows He keeps His Word;
"Hitherto the Lord hath helped us";
  Doubting now would be absurd.

"He careth for the sparrows."
  And are ye not more than these?
Why are ye then so fearful?
  Stay longer on your knees.

Dismiss your doubts and feelings,
  "Stand still" and see it through:
And the God who fed Elijah
  Will do the same for you.

— *Author Unknown*

ⴳⴰⴰ

MY PRESENCE SHALL GO WITH THEE

My presence shall go with thee —
  So calm thy troubled fears;
My promise is unchanging
  Throughout the changeful years.
'Mid scenes of gloom or gladness,
  When weary or distressed,
My presence shall go with thee,
  And I will give thee rest.
My presence shall go with thee —
  Most blest assurance here,
While in this lower valley
  Beset by doubt and fear.
No evil shall befall thee,
  Close sheltered to My breast;
My presence shall go with thee,
  And I will give thee rest.
My presence shall go with thee —
  Though in a foreign land;
Afar from home and kindred
  This covenant shall stand.

Nor time, nor space can sever,
  Love knows not East or West;
My presence shall go with thee,
  And I will give thee rest.

— *H. Isabel Graham*

ⴳⴰⴰ

HAST THOU CONSIDERED JOB'S WIFE?

"Curse God, and die," Job's wife ad-
    vised,
Her heart o'erwhelmed with strife
When trouble came.
Whom did she blame?
"Curse God and end your life."

In bitterness of soul she spoke,
With grief her breast was filled.
Mother bereft —
No children left.
All ten the storm had killed.

Her home and luxuries were gone.
She placed the blame on God.
She did not know
While here below
We need His chast'ning rod.

Impatient with her patient Job,
Resentful of this trust.
Though robbed of health
And all his wealth
Yet love his God he must.

"Trust God and live through good and
    ill,"
Job taught this fretful wife.
He passed the test.
She, too, was blessed
Through his victorious life.

God gave to them ten children more,
Job's health and wealth restored.
His patient life
Convinced his wife
'Twas best to trust the Lord.

— *Esther Archibald*

ONE DAY AT A TIME

One day at a time, with its failures and fears,
With its hurts and mistakes, with its weakness and tears,
With its portion of pain and its burden of care;
One day at a time we must meet and must bear.

One day at a time to be patient and strong,
To be calm under trial and sweet under wrong;
Then its toiling shall pass and its sorrow shall cease;
It shall darken and die, and the night shall bring peace.

One day at a time — but the day is so long,
And the heart is not brave and the soul is not strong.
O Thou pitiful Christ, be Thou near all the way;
Give courage and patience and strength for the day.

Swift cometh His answer, so clear and so sweet;
"Yea, I will be with thee, thy troubles to meet;
I will not forget thee, nor fail thee, nor grieve;
I will not forsake; I never will leave."

Not yesterday's load we are called on to bear,
Nor the morrow's uncertain and shadowy care;
Why should we look forward or back with dismay?
Our needs, as our mercies, are but for the day.

One day at a time, and the day is His day;
He hath numbered its hours, though they haste or delay.
His grace is sufficient, we walk not alone;
As the day, so the strength that He giveth His own.

— Annie Johnson Flint

MY FATHER CARES

My Father cares. He cares for me,
Should I then ever careful be?
What if the way to me looks dark,
Has it not all by Him been marked?
And will He not give grace to me,
To walk in it, whate'er it be?
He knows my weakness, knows my need,
Knows every thought and word and deed,
Knows all my longings and desires,
Oh, yes, He knows, but more He cares.
He cares, God cares. How grand the thought

In all my life that there is not
One detail not observed by Him!
Surely my cup o'erflows the brim,
Goodness and mercy, all my days,
Shall follow me. To Him be praise!
He makes all things work for my good.
Oh, may I trust Him as I should!
My Father *knows,* He *loves,* He *cares.*
My Father hears and answers prayers.
Though iron gates my way doth block,
At His command, it will unlock.
No matter what my sight may dim,
I always have recourse to Him.
And, with Him, all my care will cease,
And He will fill me with His peace,
And conscious knowledge of His love,
Which day to day, to me He'll prove.
My wants I will make known in prayer,
Then trust a loving Father's care.
His power, so great, His love, so strong,
Will fill my soul with endless song.

— *Mabel E. Brown*

ↂ

OPPORTUNITY

Yesterday, I dreamed of tomorrow:
In it I saw completion of little tasks;
Little duties, needing but an idle minute's gift of time.

I listened, in this dream of mine,
And I heard the sweet piping of tree-top carolers
Piping music grand enough
To make these routine cares, a joy.

And also, in this dream of mine,
I felt the peace of work well done,
Accomplished in those fleeting moments
When hand and heart were stirred by garden harmony.

My dream of yesterday faded:
'Twas then I realized, and knew,
That yesterday's tomorrow was today,
And I, this hour, could make my dream come true.

—*W. Audrey P. Good*

The Future

I know not what the future holds,
  No, not one single hour.
But I know One who knoweth well,
  And has it in His power.
The universe is all His own
  For all eternity
He fashioned all its laws in love,
  By grace He shares with me.

Now He who all the future holds
  Knows what will be today,
So I can place my hand in His
  And walk with Him, His way.
The things confronting all the world
  Are dark as blackest night;
Yet in the Christ who is the way
  There is a shining light.

I thank my God that by His grace
  There is no need to fear,
For, howsoever dark the way,
  My Lord is always near.
Because I trusted in the Blood
  Poured out on Calvary,
In Him my future is secure
  For all eternity.

— *Edward Cane*

Fret Not Thyself — *Psalm 37:1*

Far in the future
Lieth a fear,
Like a long, low mist of grey,
Gathering to fall in dreary rain,
Thus doth thy heart within thee
    complain;
And even now thou art afraid, for
    round thy dwelling
The flying winds are ever telling
Of the fear that lieth grey,
Like a gloom of brooding mist upon
    the way.

But the Lord is always kind,
Be not blind,
To the shining of His face,
To the comforts of His grace.
Hath He ever failed thee yet?
Never, never: wherefore fret
O fret not thyself, nor let
Thy heart be troubled,
Neither let it be afraid.

— *Amy Carmichael*

The Shadow of His Wings

The evening comes, the sun is sunk and gone,
  And all things lie in stillness and in rest;
And thou, my soul, for thee one rest alone
  Remaineth ever, on the Father's breast.

The wanderer rests at last each weary limb;
  Birds to their nests return from health and hill;
The sheep are gathered from the pastures dim —
  In Thee, my God, my restless heart is still.

Lord, gather from the regions dim and far
  Desires and thoughts that wandered far from Thee;
To home and rest lead on, O guiding Star,
  No other home or nest but God for me.

The daily toil of this worn body done,
  The spirit for untiring work is strong;
Still hours of worship and of love begun,
  Of blessed vision and eternal song.

In darkness and in silence still and sweet
  With blessed awe my spirit feels Thee near;
Within the Holiest, worships at .Thy feet:
  Speak Thou, and silence all my soul to hear.

To Thee my heart as incense shall arise;
  Consumed upon Thine altar all my will;
Love, Praise, and Peace, an evening sacrifice,
  And in the Lord I rest, and I am still.

  — *Gerhardt Tersteegen*

ॐ

He Maketh No Mistake

My Father's way may twist and turn,
  My heart may throb and ache,
But in my soul I'm glad I know,
  He maketh no mistake.

My cherished plans may go astray
  My hopes may fade away,
But still I'll trust my Lord to lead
  For He doth know the way.

Though night be dark and it may seem
  That day will never break;
I'll pin my faith, my all in Him,
  He maketh no mistake.

There's so much now I cannot see,
  My eyesight's far too dim;
But come what may, I'll surely trust
  And leave it all to Him.

For by and by the mist will lift
  And plain it all He'll make
Through all the way, tho' dark to me,
  He made not one mistake.

  — *Author Unknown*

O Lonely Heart

O lonely heart and sad,
  Look up, look up, be glad;
The night will soon be past,
  The morn will come at last.
The sorrows of thy soul
  On Christ the Saviour roll;
His love can never fail
  No matter what assail.

O hungry heart, be still,
  God's will can ne'er be ill;
Trust Him and thou shalt see
  His plan was best for thee.
Thou shalt be satisfied
  No matter what betide;
No good will He withhold,
  His love can ne'er be told.

O aching heart, rejoice,
  It is thy Saviour's voice;
He fills the vacancy
  And comes to sup with thee.
He cares, thy Father cares,
  And every heartache shares;
Take courage then and prove
  The greatness of His love.
  — *Oswald J. Smith*

WHY SHOULD I FEAR?

I will trust Him, yea, I will trust,
  For He never hath failed me yet,
And never a day nor an hour,
  But mine uttermost need is met.
Though I dwell in the midst of foes,
  Yet there is my table spread,
And His presence wraps me round
  And His wings are o'er my head.
Father and infinite God,
  My refuge and Fortress Rock,
Where I hide from the tempest's
    wrath,
  And feel not the earthquake shock;
So I abide with a soul serene,
  And a heart that is undismayed,
He is my strength and my shield;
  Of whom shall I be afraid?

I will not be afraid, for I know
  That He keepeth me safe from
    harm,
And He shall defend His own
  With a strong and a stretched-out
    arm;
Though I grope in perilous paths
  In darkness and danger and doubt,
I know as He brought me in,
  So He surely will bring me out.

For the God I serve today,
  Is one with the God of old;
Still does He guide my steps,
  And still doth His hand uphold.
He giveth me rest from fear,
  For on Him my mind is stayed,
He is the strength of my life;
  Of what shall I be afraid?

I will trust and not be afraid.
  I have seen, I have heard, I have
    known,
This mighty and terrible God,
  Hath called me and made me His
    own.
"Dread not! Faint not!" He hath said,
  For the battle belongs to Me,
Go forth with a song of praise,
  And My victory thou shalt see."
And where I go, He will go,
  And He knoweth the way I take;
He is with me unto the end,
  And He will not fail nor forsake;
They that trust in the Lord
  Shall never be moved nor swayed.
"Fear not!" He hath said unto me,
  And why should I be afraid?

— Annie Johnson Flint

STILL WILL I TRUST — *Isaiah 41:10*

Still will I trust, though all my hopes lie shattered
  In broken fragments at my feet;
Though all my plans, like driven leaves, are scattered
  By winds of darkness and defeat.
For in my need I hear my Savior saying,
  In answer to my pleading and my praying,
    "I am thy God, be not afraid,
    I will be near; be not dismayed."

Yea, in the deepest shadows of death's valley,
  Where sorrows circle me around;
When all the powers of darkness seem to rally,
  And scarce a ray of light is found;

Then will I trust in Christ with great rejoicing,
In Him who once again His love is voicing —
  "I am thy God, be not afraid,
  I will be near; be not dismayed."

So will I walk with Christ, in faith believing,
  With child-like trust, whate'er betide;
And from His hand His strength and love receiving,
  As in His presence I abide.
Thus shall I journey on to His glad morrow,
Where I shall hear Him say, "Lay down thy sorrow,
  Come dwell with Me in realms above,
  Where all is light, and life, and love."

— Albert Simpson Reitz

ͻͽ

THE BETTER WAY

God never would send you the darkness
  If He thought you could bear the light;
But you would not cling to His guiding hand,
  If the way were always bright;
And you would not care to walk by faith
  Could you always walk by sight.

'Tis true He has many an anguish
  For your sorrowing heart to bear,
And many a cruel thorn crown
  For your tired head to wear;
He knows how few would reach Heaven at all
  If pain did not guide them there.

So He sends you the blinding darkness,
  And the furnace of sevenfold heat;
'Tis the only way, believe me,
  To keep you close to His feet,
For 'tis always so easy to wander
  When our lives are glad and sweet.

Then nestle your hand in your Father's,
  And sing if you can, as you go,
Your song may cheer someone behind you
  Whose courage is sinking low;
And, well, well if your lips do quiver
  God will love you better so.

— Author Unknown

GOD'S WAYS AND MINE

Two bonny pilgrims of the air — a songbird and his wife,
(A pair untouched by time they seemed — unlearned in ways of life)
Came to my home — the welcome guests — one sunny day of spring,
Hunting a place where they might build and rear their young and sing.

The chosen spot soon proved to be within my spouted eave!
How subtle is the serpent's power the guileless to deceive!
Persistently they labored there from dawn till set of sun,
When lovingly my hand destroyed the home they had begun.

And then it was with fallen crests, and spirits truly broke,
They sought a safe, a high retreat within a sturdy oak;
Yet, I believe, they saw no love, no wisdom in my hand —
That why they had been dealt with thus, they failed to understand.

God's ways and mine! His thoughts and mine! Our plans, how far apart!
The wisdom of His hand corrects the errors of my heart!
My sight and His! Throughout a day, an hour I cannot see,
For me He views, with loving care, a vast eternity!

And this I know, that crosses raise, that sorrow lifts me high
Above the storm-swept caves of earth to "mansions in the sky."
With others I, at last, have learned to trust Him for His grace,
Behind a "frowning Providence" to find "His smiling face."

And when His ways I cannot trace, I've learned to trust Him still —
And to submit this will of mine to His unerring will!
Then, when "that which is perfect" comes — the faulty "done away"
I shall no longer "know in part" — I'll understand — some day!

— Grace Canfield Halladay

ოഄ

FEAR NOT!

The landscape, brown and sere beneath the sun,
Needs but the cloud to lift it into life;
The dews may damp the leaves of tree and flower,
But it requires the cloud-distilled shower
To bring rich verdure to the lifeless life.

Ah, how like this, the landscape of a life:
Dews of trial fall like incense, rich and sweet;
But bearing little in the crystal tray —
Like nymphs of night, dews lift at break of day
And transient impress leave, like lips that meet.

But clouds of trials, bearing burdens rare,
Leave in the soul, a moisture settled deep:
Life kindles by the magic law of God;
And where before the thirsty camel trod,
There richest beauties to life's landscape leap.

Then read thou in each cloud that comes to thee
The words of Paul, in letters large and clear:
So shall those clouds thy soul with blessing feed,
And with a constant trust as thou dost read,
All things together work for good. Fret not, nor fear!

— *Author Unknown*

ↄ⎯ↄ

DAY AND NIGHT ARE THINE

The day is Thine —
The long bright summer day
From the first dawning till evening closes,
And all its merry birds and blooming roses,
And all its golden beauty bids us say
    The day, O Lord, is Thine!

And life's brief day
Is also Thine, when we
Must work, while light doth last, for our dear Master.
Oh, that our sluggish feet could travel faster,
And we with readier service give to Thee
    Our life's fast-fleeting day!

The night is Thine —
The long, dark winter's night,
Hushing our birds to sleep, our flowers concealing;
But, by its host of glowing stars, revealing
Through the deep sky, Thy glory and Thy might;
    The night, O Lord, is Thine!

That darker night
Is also Thine, O Lord,
When Thou sweet sleep to Thy beloved givest,
For while they needs must sleep, Thou ever livest,
And o'er Thy dear ones keepest watch and ward,
    Till darkness ends in light.

— *Author Unknown*

By Candlelight

"O Lord," I cried, "the shadows are deep,
  And my journey is only begun.
I cannot walk all the way in the dark;
  Give me the light of the sun.
Thou canst give me light, for all light is Thine."
Then I waited in hope, but the sun did not shine.

"O Lord," I said, "I do not ask
  For the golden brightness of noon.
But scatter the shadows and lighten my way
  With the silver light of the moon.
Thou canst, for the moon like the sun is Thine."
Then I waited in hope, but the moon did not shine.

"O Lord," I said, "Thou art God of Light.
  Thy glory no shadow mars.
But I am alone in the darkness here;
  Give me the light of the stars.
For the stars, like the sun and the moon, are Thine."
Then I waited in hope, but the stars did not shine.

"O Lord," I said, "if it be Thy will
  I will walk all the way in the night."
Then He answered, "Impetuous child, be still;
  Thy walk is by faith, not by sight.
Yet I give thee a candle called patience.
  Light it, and walk by its light."

                        — *Lorie C. Gooding*

Content With Thee

Thou hast not *that,* My child, but thou hast Me,
And am not I alone enough for thee?
I know it all, know how thy heart was set
Upon this joy which is not given yet.

And well I know how through the wistful days
Thou walkest all the dear familiar ways,
As unregarded as a breath of air,
But there in love and longing, always there.

I know it all; but from thy briar shall blow
A rose for others. If it were not so
I would have told thee come, then, say to Me,
My Lord, my Love, I am content with Thee.

                        — *Amy Carmichael*

REST

The year just past
  Hast been so blest,
For I have learned
  To know His rest.

He teaches me
  To look above;
And day by day
  I prove His love.

The troubled waves
  Are dropped to calm;
And in the night
  He gives a psalm.

Long years I spent
  Unsatisfied
But now I keep
  Close by His side.

My seeking soul
  Has found her rest,
And I can sing
  Upon His breast.

No earth-love now
  My stay can be —
This is my song:
  He loveth me!

  — *Annie Clarke*

ᐯ

TRUST

The clouds hang heavy around my
    way,
But through the darkness I believe
  God leadeth me.
'Tis sweet to keep my hand in His
  While all is dim,
To close my weary, aching eyes
  And follow Him.

Through many a thorny path He leads
  My tired feet,
Through many a path of tears I go,
  But it is sweet

To know that He is close to me
  My Guard, my Guide;
He leadeth me; and so I walk
  Quite satisfied.
    — *Author Unknown*

ᐯ

WHY FEAR?

God is *before* me, He will be my guide;
God is *behind* me, no ill can betide;
God is *beside* me to comfort and cheer;
God is *around* me, so why should I fear?
    — *Author Unknown*

ᐯ

SAVIOR, WHILE MY HEART IS TENDER

Savior, while my heart is tender,
I would yield that heart to Thee;
All my pow'rs to Thee surrender,
Thine and only Thine to be.
Take me now, Lord Jesus, take me,
Let my youthful heart be Thine,
Thy devoted servant make me,
Fill my soul with love divine.

Send me, Lord, where Thou wilt send
    me,
Only do Thou guide my way,
May Thy grace thro' life attend me,
Gladly then shall I obey.
Let me do Thy will, or bear it,
I would know no will but Thine,
Shouldst Thou take my life, or spare it,
I that life to Thee resign.

May this solemn consecration
Never once forgotten be;
Let it know no revocation,
Registered, confirmed by Thee.
Thine I am, O Lord, forever
To Thy service set apart;
Suffer me to leave Thee never,
Seal Thine image on my heart.

    — *John Burton, Jr.*

Afraid?

Afraid?
Why should I be afraid?
The path I choose is but to follow Thee.
If I am blind —
The things that are not seen, dear Lord, I see.
If I am deaf —
Lord, Thou dost put within my heart a song.
If I am lame —
Thy hand is there to lead me safe along.

Afraid?
Why should I be afraid?
Today new sorrows come, I know not why,
But Thou dost lead me oft o'er mountains high,
And valleys deep, I cannot understand.
I only walk the way that Thou hast planned.

Afraid?
Why should I be afraid?
The world shakes, and the powers of darkness rise
To paint a threat of doom across the skies.
I do not know, dear Lord, just when that hour shall be.
I only know that I am safe because I walk with Thee.

— Esther P. Moore

I Needed the Quiet

I needed the quiet, so He took me aside,
    Into the shadows where we could confide;
Away from the bustle, where all the day long
    I hurried and worried, when active and strong.
I needed the quiet, though at first I rebelled,
    But gently, so gently, my cross He upheld,
And whispered so sweetly of spiritual things,
    Though weakened in body, my spirit took wings.

To heights never dreamed of when active and gay,
    He loved me so greatly, He drew me away.
I needed the quiet, no prison my bed —
    But a beautiful valley of blessing instead,
A place to grow richer, in Jesus to hide,
    I needed the quiet, so He drew me aside.

— Alice Hansche Mortenson

BE STILL!

Be still! Just now be still!
Something thy soul hath never heard,
Something unknown to any song of bird,
Something unknown to any wind, or wave, or star,
A message from the Fatherland afar,
That with sweet joy the homesick soul shall thrill,
Cometh to thee if thou canst but be still.

Be still! Just now be still!
There comes a presence very mild and sweet,
White are the sandals of His noiseless feet.
It is the Comforter whom Jesus sent
To teach thee what the words He uttered meant.
The willing, waiting spirit He doth fill.
If thou wouldst hear His message,
Dear soul, be still!

—*Author Unknown*

MY BOY AND HIS SAVIOUR

They walked along together side by side,
My boy and his Saviour, Shepherd, and Guide.
One day they kept walking straight ahead
Into God's country. They said he was dead.

They were mistaken. God couldn't lie.
The soul that believeth shall never die.
My boy has gone home to be with his God;
His soul was not buried under the sod.

The bliss that is his will be ours someday,
If we walk with the Saviour the selfsame way.
And one day they will say that we too are dead,
When into God's country we've walked straight ahead.

—*William C. Fisher*

TRUST

Sure, it takes a lot of courage
  To put things in God's hands,
To give ourselves completely,
  Our lives, our hopes, our plans;
To follow where He leads us
  And make His will our own,
But all it takes is foolishness
  To go the way alone.

—*Betsey Kline*

SECOND BENEFIT!

O Hallelujah! — now I see
This gracious gift was meant for me.
A witness clear, and plainly given,
Cleansed for service, filled for Heaven.
A heart that's clean, my joy complete
While tarrying at the mercy seat.

Yes — fully yielded, doubly blest,
For such as I, remains a rest!
This life shall sound with holy tone,
And will be lived for God alone!
Ah, Spirit tide, Thy work complete,
While tarrying at the mercy seat!
                                    — *Mary Ferguson*

ᔕ

PEACE, BE STILL

"Carest Thou not" — how many times the cry
Has winged its way up to the throne on high!
As from the boat upon the rolling deep,
Where Jesus, wearied, found sweet rest in sleep.
"Why are ye fearful" of the raging sea?
It is the Master who is calling thee.

Fear not the fury of the breaking gale,
The pilot is with thee — He cannot fail;
He who rebuked the waves can calm the soul,
Dispel our fears and guide us to the goal.

No harm can come with Jesus at the helm,
Nothing can conquer, nothing overwhelm.
Then rest within His blessed will,
And hear Him saying, "Peace, be still."
                                    — *Maude Steenburg*

ᔕ

LEARNED TO TRUST

I have no answer for myself or thee,
Save that I learned beside my mother's knee:
"All is of God that is, and is to be;
And God is good." Let this suffice us still,
Resting in childlike trust upon His will
Who moves to His great ends unthwarted by the ill.
                                    — *William Cowper*

GOD HOLDS THE KEY

God holds the key of all unknown,
  And I am glad;
If other hands should hold the key,
Or if He trusted it to me,
  I might be sad.

What if tomorrow's cares were here
  Without its rest?
I'd rather He unlocked the day,
And, as the hours swing open, say,
  "My will is best."

The very dimness of my sight
  Makes me secure;
For, groping in my misty way,
I feel His hand, I hear Him say,
  "My help is sure."

I cannot read His future plans;
  But this I know:
I have the smiling of His face,
And all the refuge of His grace
  While here below.

Enough! This covers all my wants;
  And so I rest!
For what I cannot, He can see,
And in His care I saved shall be,
  For ever blest.

             — *J. Parker*

IN QUIETNESS — *Isaiah 30:15*

In quietness let me abide
  When light is growing dim,
From earth's distractions would I hide,
  Shut in alone with Him.

In perfect peace then let me turn
  My thoughts to heights above,
And there anew life's lessons learn
  From Him who speaks in love.

There, while I in His presence wait,
  He makes the storm a calm,
And on my heart so desolate
  He pours His healing balm.

He gives me grace to preserve
  New courage to go on;
His love dispels the clouds of fear
  And fills my heart with song.

             — *Grace E. Troy*

"WHAT IF"

What if your way is stormy
  As you travel on life's road;
What if your path is thorny,
  And your back is bent with its load?
What if the day is dreary,
  And your way is dark as night;
What if your soul is weary,
  And there seems to be no light?

There's One who knows your sorrows,
  Who's acquainted with all your
    grief;
He knows your path for tomorrow,
  And will surely bring relief.
Your back for you He'll lighten,
  He knows your every care;
Your way He'll bless and brighten,
  If you go to Him in prayer.

What if He sometimes chastens,
  It proves His love for you;
He may not always hasten,
  But He'll surely see you through.
For we know there is no other,
  Who'll be with us to the end;
So trust your all, my brother
  To this never failing Friend.

             — *Author Unknown*

Then God Bends Low

When, in the sky, my Star of Hope
    In dazzling splendor gleams,
When verdant fields in beauty lie
    As exquisite as dreams,
When joy o'erflows its brimming cup
    And Love my way attends,
I know that God is hovering near,
    As tender care He lends.

When skies are dark with mounting
        storm
    And sullen clouds hang low,
When all my ways are desert ways
    And hours drag leaden-slow,
When pain-filled nights are dark and
        long
    And dawn no respite brings,
*Then God bends low to touch my
        hand —*
    And, oh, my glad heart sings!

— *Dorothy Conant Stroud*

ᔿ

Suffering

If flowers reasoned, would they under-
        stand
Why suddenly the gardener's hand
        Uproots,
        Selects,
        Transplants
To give their roots more room, their
        leaves more air —
Would flowers misconstrue this care
        As wrath,
        Contempt,
        Disdain?
Or be content to let their beauty show
His wisdom . . . or demand to know
        His plan,
        Intent,
        Design?

— *Jane W. Lauber*

God's Will

It is God's will that I should cast
    All care on Him each day;
He also bids me not to cast
    My confidence away.
My soul, what folly then is thine,
    When taken unawares,
To cast away thy confidence,
    And carry all thy cares!

— *Author Unknown*

ᔿ

Tomorrow's Way

I know not if tomorrow's way
    Be steep or rough;
But when His hand is guiding me,
    That is enough.
And so, although the veil has hid
    Tomorrow's way,
I walk with perfect faith and trust,
    Through each today.

The love of God has hung a veil
    Around tomorrow.
That we may not its beauty see
    Nor trouble borrow.
But, oh, 'tis sweeter far, to trust
    His unseen hand,
And know that all the paths of life,
    His wisdom planned.

— *Author Unknown*

ᔿ

My All

Not mine, not mine the choice
    In things or great or small;
Be Thou my guide, my strength,
    My wisdom and my all.

— *Horatius Bonar*

God Understands

It is so sweet to know,
When we are tired and when the hand of pain
Lies on our hearts, and we look in vain
For human comfort, that the heart Divine
Still understands these cares, both yours and mine:

Not only understands, but day by day,
Lives with us while we tread the earthly way;
Bears with us all our weariness, and feels
The shadows of the faintest cloud steal
Across our sunshine; ever learns again
The depths and bitterness of human pain.

There is no sorrow that He will not share,
No cross, no burden, for our hearts to bear
Without His help, no care of ours too small
To cast on Jesus: let us tell Him all —
Lay at His feet the story of our woes,
And in His sympathy find sweet repose.

— Author Unknown

Enough for Me

I am so weak, dear Lord, I cannot stand
  One moment without Thee;
But, oh, the tenderness of Thine enfolding!
And, oh, the faithfulness of Thine upholding!
And, oh, the strength of Thy right hand!
  That strength is enough for me.

I am so needy, Lord, and yet I know
  All fullness dwells in Thee;
And hour by hour, that never-failing treasure
Supplies and fills in overflowing measure,
My least and greatest need, and so
  Thy grace is enough for me.

It is so sweet to trust Thy Word alone.
  I do not ask to see
The unveiling of Thy purposes, or the shining
Of future light on mysteries untwining.
Thy promise-roll is all my own —
  Thy Word is enough for me.

— Frances Ridley Havergal

DAY BY DAY

Charge not thyself with the weight of a year,
Child of the Master, faithful and dear:
Choose not the cross for the coming week,
For that is more than He bids thee seek.

Bend not thine arms for tomorrow's load;
Thou mayest leave that to thy gracious God.
"Daily," only He saith to thee,
"Take up thy cross and follow Me."

—Author Unknown

ംഏ

DWELL DEEP, MY SOUL

Dwell deep, my soul, dwell deep!
The little things that chafe and fret
    O waste not golden hours to give them heed!
The slight, the thoughtless wrong do thou forget;
    Be self-forgot in serving other's need
Thou faith in God through love for man shalt keep—
    Dwell deep, my soul, dwell deep!

— Author Unknown

ംഏ

PERFECT PEACE

Like a river glorious is God's perfect peace;
Over all victorious in its bright increase;
Perfect, yet it floweth fuller every day,
Perfect, yet it groweth deeper all the way.

Hidden in the hollow of His blessed hand,
Never foe can follow, never traitor stand;
Not a surge of worry, not a shade of care,
Not a blast of hurry touch the spirit there.

Every joy or trial falleth from above,
Traced upon our dial by the Sun of Love,
We may trust Him fully, all for us to do;
They who trust Him wholly find Him wholly true.

— Frances Ridley Havergal

DUSK FOR ME

Dusk for me, but when the shadows lengthen
  Know this, that in the shadows deep
God comes my faltering heart to strengthen
  And gently cradles me in sleep.

But such a dusk as falls o'er life's brief day
  Must in the morning vanish with the sun,
God will waken me to endless life I pray,
  When night at last is done.

Dusk for me, and the taps are sounding,
  And over hill and plain
From the silent dusk rebounding,
  Comes the death-call's sad refrain.

But God, who uses shades of night
  To veil the day's reborning,
Can change the taps that now affright
  Into the reveille of morning.

Dusk for me, and may there be no tears
  When someday I have my leave-taking,
For God doth quiet all my fears,
  And the dawn — the dawn is breaking!

— Louis Paul Lehman, Jr.

REPOSE

The shadows of the evening hours
  Fall from the darkening sky;
Upon the fragrance of the flowers
  The dews of evening lie:
Before Thy throne, O Lord of heaven,
  We kneel at close of day;
Look on Thy children from on high,
  And hear us while we pray.

The sorrows of Thy servants, Lord,
  O do not Thou despise,
But let the incense of our prayers
  Before Thy mercy rise.

The brightness of the coming night
  Upon the darkness rolls;
With hopes of future glory chase
  The shadows from our souls.

Let peace, O Lord, Thy peace, O God,
  Upon our souls descend;
From midnight fears and perils, Thou
  Our trembling hearts defend:
Give us a respite from our toil,
  Calm and subdue our woes;
Through the long day we labor, Lord,
  O give us now repose.

— Adelaide Anne Procter

He Giveth Peace!

He giveth peace!
Tho' storms may rage—the billows roll
And beat upon thy weary soul;
Though skies be dark and overcast,
The storm will not forever last,
He giveth peace!

Dear restless heart, be still and know
That He who walked life's path below
Will surely understand and care,
And all thy heavy burden share.

Thy loving Father knows thy heart;
He sees the tears that often start;
With arms outstretched He yearns for
     thee
To come to Him that you might see—
He giveth peace!

Whatever He may send—'tis best!
It may be that it's meant to test
Thy willingness to follow Him.
Press onward then—tho' faith be dim!
He giveth peace!

—*Georgia B. Adams*

ᏝᎾ

He Will Never Fail

Can the sun forget its rising?
   Can the stars forget to shine?
Can the moon forget its duty?
   Then can God His will resign.

Can the sea forget to roar?
   Can the waves cease and be still?
Can the waters stop giving?
   Then God can forget His will.

Can the skies above be measured?
   Can the foes of God prevail?
Can a man earth's structure fathom?
   Then God's promises can fail.

—*H. H. Savage*

O Thou Whose Compassionate Care

O Thou, whose compassionate care
   Forbids my sad heart to complain,
Now graciously teach me to bear
   The weight of affliction and pain.
Tho' cheerless my days seem to flow,
   Tho' weary and wakeful my nights,
What comfort it gives me to know
   'Tis the hand of a Father that smites.

A tender physician Thou art,
   Who woundest in order to heal,
And comfort Divine dost impart
   To soften the anguish we feel.
Oh, let this correction be blest,
   And answer Thy gracious design;
Then grant that my soul may find rest
   In comforts so healing as Thine.

—*W. H. Bathurst*

ᏝᎾ

Peace

Peace is not an elusive thing
Darting about on hurried wing . . .
Just out of reach, or off afar;
It's everywhere, where people are.

No need for an extended search,
For peace abides within each church
Where friendly folks in every pew
Show love and faith in God and you.

Then there are homes richly blessed
With peace and joy and happiness;
Where sound of strife is never heard
And folks are fed upon His Word.

Yet, peace needs no confining wall,
For it's within the grasp of all;
Not to be gained by war, you'll see
For peace is Love . . . unleashed . . . set
     free.

—*Barbara Drake Johnson*

ALL THE WAY MY SAVIOUR LEADS ME

All the way my Saviour leads me;
What have I to ask beside?
Can I doubt His tender mercy,
Who through life has been my Guide?
Heavenly peace, divinest comfort,
Here by faith in Him to dwell!
For I know, whate'er befall me,
Jesus doeth all things well.

All the way my Saviour leads me,
Cheers each winding path I tread,
Gives me grace for every trial,
Feeds me with the living bread.
Though my weary steps may falter,
And my soul athirst may be,
Gushing from the Rock before me,
Lo! a spring of joy I see.

All the way my Saviour leads me;
Oh, the fullness of His love!
Perfect rest to me is promised
In my Father's house above.
When my spirit, clothed immortal,
Wings its flight to realms of day;
This my song through endless ages:
Jesus led me all the way.

— *Fanny J. Crosby*

❧

LINES WRITTEN THE NIGHT BEFORE HIS EXECUTION

E'en such is time; which takes on trust
  Our youth, our joys, our all we have,
And pays us but with earth and dust;
  Which in the dark and silent grave,
When we have wandered all our ways,
Shuts up the story of our days:
But from this earth, this grave, this
    dust,
My God shall raise me up, I trust.

— *Sir Walter Raleigh*

PROGRESS

Until I learned to trust
  I never learned to pray,
Nor did I learn to fully trust
  Till sorrows came my way.
Until I felt my weakness,
  His strength I never knew,
Nor dreamed till I was stricken
  That He could see me through.

Who deepest drinks of sorrow,
  Drinks deepest too of grace;
He sends the storm so He Himself
  Can be our hiding place.
His heart, that seeks our highest good,
  Knows well when things annoy;
We would not long for heaven
  If earth held only joy!

— *Barbara C. Ryberg*

❧

JESUS, SAVIOUR, PILOT ME

Jesus, Saviour, pilot me
Over life's tempestuous sea:
Unknown waves before me roll,
Hiding rocks and treacherous shoal;
Chart and compass come from Thee,
Jesus, Saviour, pilot me.

As a mother stills her child,
Thou canst hush the ocean wild;
Boisterous waves obey Thy will
When Thou say'st to them, "Be still!"
Wondrous Sovereign of the sea,
Jesus, Saviour, pilot me.

When at last I near the shore,
And the fearful breakers roar
'Twixt me and the peaceful rest,
Then, while leaning on Thy breast,
May I hear Thee say to me,
"Fear not, I will pilot thee."

— *Edward Hopper*

I CAN TRUST

I cannot see, with my small human sight,
Why God should lead this way or that for me;
I only know He saith, "Child, follow me."
    But I can trust.

I know not why my path should be at times
So straitly hedged, so strongly barred before;
I only know God could keep wide the door;
    But I can trust.

I find no answer, often, when beset
With questions fierce and subtle on my way,
And often have but strength to faintly pray;
    But I can trust.

I often wonder, as with trembling hand
I cast the seed along the furrowed ground,
If ripened fruit will in my life be found;
    But I can trust.

I cannot know why suddenly the storm
Should rage so fiercely round me in its wrath;
But this I know — God watches all my path,
    And I can trust.

I may not draw aside the mystic veil
That hides the unknown future from my sight;
Nor know if for me waits the dark or light;
    But I can trust.

I have no power to look across the tide,
To see, while here, the land beyond the river;
But this I know, I shall be God's forever;
    So, I can trust.

— Author Unknown

KEPT EVERY MOMENT

If Christ is mine, then all is mine,
  And more than angels know;
Both present things, and things to
    come,
  And grace and glory too.

If He is mine, let friends forsake,
  And earthly comforts flee;

He the Dispenser of all good,
  Is more than all to me.

Let Christ assure me He is mine;
  I nothing want beside.
My soul shall at the fountain live
  When all the streams are dried.

— John Roberts

SECURITY

More secure is no one ever
Than the loved ones of the Saviour;
Not yon star, on high abiding,
Nor the bird in home-nest hiding.

God His own doth tend and nourish,
In His holy courts they flourish;
Like a father kind He spares them,
In His loving arms He bears them.

Neither life nor death can ever
From the Lord His children sever;
For His love and deep compassion
Comfort them in tribulation.

Little flock, to joy then yield thee!
Jacob's God will ever shield thee;
Rest secure with this Defender,
At His will all foes surrender.

What He takes or what He gives us
Shows the Father's love so precious;
We may trust His purpose wholly —
'Tis His children's welfare solely.

— *Lina Sandell*

ᐁ

THORNS

Strange gift indeed! a thorn to prick,
To pierce into the very quick,
To cause perpetual sense of pain,
Strange gift — and yet, 'twas given for
gain.
Unwelcome, yet it came to stay,
Nor could it e'en be prayed away.
It came to fill its God-planned place,
A life-enriching means of grace.

God's grace-thorns — oh, what forms
they take;
What piercing, smarting pain they
make!
And yet, each one in love is sent,
And always just for blessing meant.

And so, whate'er thy thorn may be
From God, accept it willingly.
But reckon Christ — His life — His
power
To keep in thy most trying hour.

And sure — thy life will richer grow,
He grace sufficient will bestow,
And in Heav'n's morn thy joy 'twill be
That, by His thorn, He strengthened
thee.

— *J. Danson Smith*

ᐁ

WONDERFUL IS MY SAVIOUR

Wonderful is my Saviour,
Wondrous the peace in my soul,
Since I at the fountain of cleansing
Was redeemed and fully made whole.
Wondrous the joy He bestoweth,
Since I from my guilt am free;
But the wonder of wonders forever,
Is the love of my Saviour for me.

Wonderful is His power,
Who holdeth the earth in His hands.
Angels in Heaven adore Him,
And bow at His holy commands.
Wonderful is His glory,
Great is His majesty,
But the wonder of wonders forever
Is the love of my Saviour for me.

Wonderful are the heavens,
The work which my Father hath
wrought.
Sun, moon, stars He hath fashioned,
Whose daily course changeth not.
Wonderful is all nature,
Mountains and plains and sea,
But the wonder of wonders forever
Is the love of my Saviour for me.

— *Avis B. Christiansen*

This I Know

I do not know the depths of love
  It took to die on Calvary;
I do not know the shame and grief
  He suffered there to set me free.
Nor can I tell how bitter was
  His cup in dark Gethsemane,
The pain He bore—heartbroken, poor;
  But this I know: He died for me!

I know not why that for my sins
  His precious blood so freely flows,
Nor fathom why the Lord of All
  Did not such cruel death oppose.
I cannot understand the power
  Which triumphed over death and
    foes.
They sealed His tomb 'midst dark'ning
    gloom;
  But this I know: for me He rose!

I do not know why oftentimes
  The skies are dark and overcast;
Nor why, in grave temptations, all
  My problems seem so hard, so vast.
I cannot tell what things may come—
  Sore heartaches, all my hopes to
    blast
The shades of night obscure the light;
  But this I know: He'll hold me fast.

        — *Grace M. Watkins*

The King of Love

The King of love my Shepherd is,
Whose goodness faileth never;
I nothing lack if I am His,
And He is mine forever.

Where streams of living water flow,
My ransomed soul He leadeth,
And where the verdant pastures grow,
With food celestial feedeth.

Perverse and foolish oft I strayed
But yet in love He sought me,
And on His shoulder gently laid,
And home, rejoicing, brought me.

In death's dark vale I feel no ill
With Thee, dear Lord, beside me;
Thy rod and staff they comfort still,
Thy cross before to guide me.

And so through all the length of days,
Thy goodness faileth never;
Good Shepherd, may I sing Thy praise
Within Thy house forever.

        — *Henry W. Baker*

My Friend

I've found a Friend whose equal
  This world has never known,
And for His loss no treasure
  Of earth could e'er atone.
He bids me bring my burdens,
  However, great or small,
To Him in full assurance
  That He will bear them all.

I've found a Friend whose equal
  This world has never known,
Whose Blood for my transgressions
  So freely doth atone.
He bids me come for cleansing
  To His dear pierced side,
Where e'en for me there floweth
  The precious crimson tide.

I've found a Friend whose equal
  This world has never known;
He understands my trials,
  And counts them as His own.
He comforts me in sorrow,
  He cheers me when oppressed,
He takes my griefs and burdens,
  And gives me peace and rest.

        — *Author Unknown*

GOD'S WILL

"Remove this thorn, dear Lord," in vain I cried;
"Sufficient is My grace," my Lord replied.

"Not this, dear Lord," I prayed, "another way";
"Remember," spake my Lord, "I am thy Stay."

"My plans, dear Lord," I sighed, "they vanish, all";
"My plans are best," He said, "whate'er befall."

Then to His will I bowed, and found it best;
Henceforth I walked with Him, my heart at rest.

— Oswald J. Smith

RETIREMENT

Far from the world, O Lord, I flee,
　From strife and tumult far;
From scenes where Satan wages still
　His most successful war.

The calm retreat, the silent shade,
　With prayer and praise agree;
And seem by thy sweet bounty made
　For those who follow thee.

There, if thy Spirit touch the soul,
　And grace her mean abode,
Oh, with what peace and joy and love
　She communes with her God!

There like the nightingale she pours
　Her solitary lays;
Nor asks a witness of her song,
　Nor thirsts for human praise.

Author and Guardian of my life,
　Sweet source of light divine,
And (all harmonious names in one)
　My Saviour, thou art mine.

What thanks I owe thee, and what
　　love,
　A boundless, endless store,
Shall echo through the realms above
　When time shall be no more.

— William Cowper

I AM TRUSTING THEE

I am trusting Thee, Lord Jesus,
　Trusting only Thee!
Trusting Thee for full salvation,
　Great and free.

I am trusting Thee for pardon
　At Thy feet I bow;
For Thy grace and tender mercy,
　Trusting now.

I am trusting Thee for cleansing,
　In the crimson flood;
Trusting Thee to make me holy,
　By Thy blood.

I am trusting Thee to guide me,
　Thou alone shalt lead,
Every day and hour supplying
　All my need.

I am trusting Thee for power,
　Thine can never fail;
Words which Thou Thyself shalt give
　　me,
　Must prevail.

I am trusting Thee, Lord Jesus,
　Never let me fall!
I am trusting Thee for ever,
　And for all.

— Frances Ridley Havergal

GOD IS IN EVERY TOMORROW

God is in every tomorrow,
    Therefore I live for today,
Certain of finding at sunrise,
    Guidance and strength for the way;
Power for each moment of weakness;
    Hope for each moment of pain,
Comfort for every sorrow,
    Sunshine and joy after rain.

God is in every tomorrow,
    Planning for you and for me;
E'en in the dark will I follow,
    Trust where my eyes cannot see.
Stilled by His promise of blessing,
    Soothed by the touch of His hand,
Confident in His protection,
    Knowing my life path is planned.

God is in every tomorrow,
    Life with its changes may come,
He is behind and before me,
    While in the distance shines Home!
Home—where no thought of tomorrow
    Ever can shadow my brow,
Home — in the presence of Jesus,
    Through all eternity — now!

                    — *Author Unknown*

တသ

SUFFICIENCY

His grace is sufficient,
    Then why need I fear,
Though the testing be hard,
    And the trial severe?
He tempers each wind
    That upon me doth blow,
And tenderly whispers,
    "Thy Father doth know."

His pow'r is sufficient,
    Then why should I quail,
Though the storm clouds hang low,
    And though wild is the gale?

His strength will not falter,
    Whatever betide,
And safe on His bosom
    He bids me to hide.

His love is sufficient,
    Yea, boundless and free;
As high as the mountains,
    As deep as the sea.
Ah, there I will rest
    Till the darkness is o'er
And wake in His likeness,
    To dwell evermore.

                    — *Avis B. Christiansen*

တသ

HIS PRESENCE

His presence is wealth,
    His grace is a treasure,
His promise is health
    And joy out of measure.
His Word is my rest,
    His Spirit my guide;
In him I am blest
    Whatever betide,

Since Jesus is mine,
    Adieu to all sorrow;
I ne'er shall repine,
    Nor think of to-morrow;
The lily so fair,
    And raven so black,
He nurses with care;
    Then how shall I lack?

Each promise is sure
    That shines in his Word,
And tells me, though poor,
    I'm rich in my Lord.
Hence, sorrow and fear!
    Since Jesus is nigh.
I'll dry up each tear
    And stifle each sigh.

                    — *Patrick Brontë*

My God Is Near

My God is near when morning dawn is breaking,
When day is new and all is turned to light;
He speaks to me in love; new hope awaking
And sends me forth to face the world aright.

When I am weak beneath the daytime burden,
He, through His power, brings added strength to me;
I trust in Him and share His matchless word in
Renewing faith that sets the laden free.

When dims the sun as daylight hours are ebbing,
I sense anew my Father's loving care:
Then golden thoughts and memories awebbing
Bring thanks to Him in heartfelt evening prayer.

My God is near when morning sunbeams strengthen,
My God is near in brightest noontime hour:
My God is near when evening shadows lengthen,
And in the night time I can sense His power.

— Carlton Buck

 caro

How Firm a Foundation

How firm a foundation, ye saints of the Lord,
Is laid for your faith in His excellent Word!
What more can He say than to you He hath said,
To you, who for refuge to Jesus have fled?

"Fear not, I am with thee, O be not dismayed,
For I am thy God, I will still give thee aid;
I'll strengthen thee, help thee, and cause thee to stand,
Upheld by My gracious, omnipotent hand.

"When through the deep waters I call thee to go,
The rivers of sorrow shall not overflow;
For I will be with thee Thy trials to bless,
And sanctify to thee thy deepest distress.

"When through fiery trials thy pathway shall lie,
My grace, all sufficient, shall be thy supply;
The flames shall not hurt thee, I only design
Thy dross to consume, and thy gold to refine."

— George Keith

TO-MORROW

'Tis late at night, and in the realm of sleep
  My little lambs are folded like the flocks;
  From room to room I hear the wakeful clocks
  Challenge the passing hour, like guards that keep
Their solitary watch on tower and steep;
  Far off I hear the crowing of the cocks,
  And through the opening door that time unlocks
Feel the fresh breathing of To-morrow creep.
To-morrow! the mysterious, unknown guest,
  Who cries to me: "Remember Barmecide,
  And tremble to be happy with the rest."
And I make answer: "I am satisfied;
  I dare not ask; I know not what is best;
  God hath already said what shall betide."

— Henry Wadsworth Longfellow

SOLITUDE

There is in stillness oft a magic power
To calm the breast, when struggling passions lower;
Touched by its influence, in the soul arise
Diviner feelings, kindred with the skies.
By this the Arab's kindling thoughts expand,
When circling skies enclose the desert sand;
For this the hermit seeks the thickest grove,
To catch the inspiring glow of heavenly love.
It is not solely in the freedom given
To purify and fix the heart on heaven;
There is a spirit singing aye in air
That lifts us high above all mortal care.
No mortal measure swells that mystic sound.
No mortal minstrel breathes such tones around,—
The angels' hymn,— the sovereign harmony
That guides the rolling orbs along the sky,—
And hence perchance the tales of saints who viewed
And heard angelic choirs in solitude.
By most unheard,— because the earthly din
Of toil or mirth has charms their ears to win,
Alas for man! he knows not of the bliss,
The heaven that brightens such a life as this.

— John Henry Newman

On Leaving My Native Land

Unto the winds and waves I now commit
My body, subject to the will of Heaven;
Its resting-place may be the watery pit—
'Tis his alone to take, who life has given.
But, O ye elements! the deathless soul,
Impalpable, outsoaring time and space,
Submits not to your mightiest control,
Nor meanly dwells in any earthly place.
Ocean may bleach, earth crumble, worms devour,
Beyond identity, its wondrous frame;
Decay blights not the spiritual flower,
Nor age suppresses the ethereal flame:
Thus thy dread sting, O death! I dare to brave;
Thus do I take from thee the victory, O grave!

—*William Lloyd Garrison*

A Waterfall

Beside a lofty waterfall I've stood,
  Formed by a torrent from a mountain height,
And gazed far up to where the foaming flood
  Burst from the sky-line on my awe-struck sight.

So vast its volume, and so fierce its shock,
  No power at first its headlong course might stay;
It seemed as if the everlasting rock
  Before its furious onset would give way.

But as it fell it lingered in mid-air,
  And melted into lace-like wreaths of mist,
Decked by the sun with rainbow colors fair,
  And swayed by passing breezes as they'd list.

And when at last it reached the dimpled pool,
  Hid in its granite basin far below,
Its spray fell softly as the showers that cool
  The sultry languor of the summer glow.

The aspen leaf scarce quivered to its sound,
  The bluebell smiled beneath its benison;
And all the verdure of the forest round
  A fresher green from its baptism won.

So have I watched for coming sorrow's dread,
  With heavy heart for many a weary day,
Foreboding that the torrent overhead
  Would bear me with o'erflowing flood away.

But when the threatened evil came, I found
  That God was better than my foolish fears;
The furious flood fell gently to the ground,
  And blessed my soul with dew of grateful tears.

God mingles mercy with each judgment stern,
  Brings goodness out of evil things we see;
Then let us from our past experience learn
  That as our day our promised strength shall be.

                     — *Hugh McMillan*

MILTON'S PRAYER FOR PATIENCE

    I am old and blind!
Men point at me as smitten by God's frown:
Afflicted and deserted of my kind,
    Yet am I not cast down.

    I am weak, yet strong;
I murmur not that I no longer see;
Poor, old, and helpless, I the more belong,
    Father supreme, to Thee!

    All-merciful One!
When men are furthest, then art Thou most near;
When friends pass by, my weaknesses to shun,
    Thy chariot I hear.

    Thy glorious face
Is leaning toward me; and its holy light
Shines in upon my lonely dwelling place,—
    And there is no more night.

    On my bended knee
I recognized Thy purpose clearly shown:
My vision Thou hast dimmed, that I may see
    Thyself, Thyself alone.

    I have naught to fear;
This darkness is the shadow of Thy wing;
Beneath it I am almost sacred; here
    Can come no evil thing.

Oh, I seem to stand
Trembling, where foot of mortal ne'er hath been,
Wrapt in that radiance from the sinless land,
Which eye hath never seen!

Visions come and go:
Shapes of resplendent beauty around me throng;
From angel lips I seem to hear the flow
Of soft and holy song.

It is nothing now,
When heaven is opening on my sightless eyes,
When airs from Paradise refresh my brow,
That earth in darkness lies.

In a purer clime
My being fills with rapture, — waves of thought
Roll in upon my spirit, — strains sublime
Break over me unsought.

Give me now my lyre!
I feel the stirrings of a gift divine:
Within my bosom glows unearthly fire,
Lit by no skill of mine.

— *Elizabeth Lloyd Howell*

ᕲᕳ

ALL THINGS IN JESUS

I've found a joy in sorrow,
    A secret balm for pain;
A beautiful tomorrow
    Of sunshine after rain;
I've found a branch of healing
    Near every bitter spring;
A whispered promise stealing
    O'er every broken string.

I've found a glad hosannah
    For every woe and wail;
A handful of sweet manna
    When grapes of Eschol fail;
I've found a Rock of Ages
    When desert wells were dry;
And after weary stages,
    I've found an Elim nigh.

An Elim with its coolness,
    Its fountain and its shade;
A blessing in its fulness,
    When buds of promise fade;
O'er tears of soft contrition
    I've seen a rainbow light;
A glory and fruition
    So near, yet out of sight.

My Saviour, Thee possessing,
    I have the joy, the balm,
The healing, and the blessing,
    The sunshine and the psalm;
The promise for the fearful,
    The Elim for the faint,
The rainbow for the tearful,
    The glory for the saint.

— *J. Danson Smith*

A Christian's Testimony

Not half the storms that threaten me
    E'er broke upon my head.
Not half the pains I've waited for
    E'er reached me or my bed.
Not half the clouds that drifted by
    Have overshadowed me —
Not half the dangers ever came
    I fancied I could see.

Dear Heavenly Father, hold my hand
    Each moment lest I fall.
Thine is the power to keep — my part
    To let Thee, that is all.
I dare not take one step alone,
    And, oh, how sweet it is to know
Thy loving, mighty, tender clasp
    Will never let me go.

— *Author Unknown*

Treasures of Darkness

He giveth me treasures of darkness;
Before the day dawns He's so nigh;
It is then we have wordless com-
            munion —
    He hovers above me;
    His love, it enfolds me;
    His joy is within me.
    And I know that He holds me.
I see my past spread out before me,
And know what I could not know
            then:
How the bright and the dark worked
            together
For good; and I praise Him, and praise
            Him,
    And praise Him again.
He knoweth what lies in the darkness,
While the light dwelleth ever with
            Him.
And the Father in whom is no dark-
            ness

Will make clear what now is so dim.
For the treasures that lie in the dark-
            ness,
And the riches that now are concealed
By the One who doth hold all the
            secrets
Will some day by Him be revealed.

— *Sarah Faris*

A Sure Trust

Do not fear to claim His promise
    He will not your trust betray;
While on earth He healed them gladly,
    And He's just the same today.

— *Author Unknown*

"With Whom Is No Shadow of Turning" — *James 1:17*

Above earth's bloody battlefields
The sun still shines at noon,
At eventide the starlight gleams;
Night after night the moon

Still climbs the peaceful, silent sky.
The white tides rise and fall,
Their pulse unchanged. Above the
            dead
The waving grass grows tall

And still the skylark sings of God,
And still comes on the spring,
Pregnant with life, and busy with
Her lovely burgeoning.

As sure as time and tide, shall come
The day when wars shall cease.
God's clock ticks on, God's plans
            change not.
Come, blessed Prince of Peace!

— *Martha Snell Nicholson*

PEACE AFTER A STORM

When darkness long has veiled my
    mind,
  And smiling day once more appears,
Then, my Redeemer, then I find
  The folly of my doubts and fears.

Straight I upbraid my wandering heart,
  And blush that I should ever be
Thus prone to act so base a part,
  Or harbor one hard thought of thee!

Oh, let me then at length be taught
  What I am still so slow to learn:
That God is love, and changes not,
  Nor knows the shadow of a turn.

Sweet truth, and easy to repeat!
  But when my faith is sharply tried
I find myself a learner yet,
  Unskilful, weak, and apt to slide.

But, O my Lord, one look from thee
  Subdues my disobedient will;
Drives doubt and discontent away,
  And thy rebellious worm is still.

Thou art as ready to forgive
  As I am ready to repine:
Thou, therefore, all the praise receive;
  Be shame and self-abhorrence mine.

        — William Cowper

MY TRUST

He that hath made his refuge God
Shall find a most secure abode,
Shall walk all day beneath his shade,
And there at night shall rest his head.

Then will I say, "My God, thy power
Shall be my fortress and my tower:
I, that am form'd of feeble dust,
Make thine almighty arm my trust."

        — Author Unknown

WAIT PATIENTLY FOR HIM

God doth not bid thee wait
  To disappoint at last;
A golden promise, fair and great,
  In precept-mould is cast;
Soon shall the morning gild
  The dark horizon rim,
Thy heart's desire shall be fulfilled —
  "Wait patiently for Him."

He doth bid thee wait,
  Like driftwood on the wave,
For fickle chance or fixed fate
  To ruin or to save.
Thine eyes shall surely see,
  No distant hope or dim,
The Lord thy God arise for thee,
  "Wait patiently for Him."

      — Frances Ridley Havergal

A REFUGE AND PRESENT HELP

God is the refuge of His saints,
  When storms of sharp distress in-
    vade;
Ere we can offer our complaints,
  Behold Him present with His aid.

        — Isaac Watts

WHEN WE SEE . . .

When we see the lilies
  Spinning in distress,
Taking thought to
  Manufacture loveliness;
When we see the birds all
  Building barns for store,
'Twill be time for us to worry —
  Not before!

        — Author Unknown

GOD COMFORTS

God counts the sorrows of his saints,
  Their groans affect his ears;
Thou hast a book for my complaints,
  A bottle for my tears.

When to thy throne I raise my cry,
  The wicked fear and flee:
So swift is prayer to reach the sky;
  So near is God to me.

In thee, most holy, just and true,
  I have reposed my trust;
Nor will I fear what man can do,
  The offspring of the dust.

— *Author Unknown*

HE KNOWS

He knows it all — the winding path,
  The sky o'ercast and grey,
The steepness of the mountainside,
  The roughness of the way.

He knows it all — the haunting fear,
  The doubtings that distress,
The wond'rings and perplexities,
  And all the strain and stress.

He knows it all — each troubled tho't,
  Each anxious wave of care,
And every burden, every grief,
  Or cross that thou dost bear.

He knows it all — thy weight of woe,
  Thine often tear-dimmed eye,
The stabbing pain, the slow, dull ache,
  And sorrow's broken cry.

He knows it all — by His to choose,
  And thine to take His choice!
He knows it all! He planned it so!
  Then trust Him, and rejoice!

— *E. Margaret Clarkson*

THE WEAVER

My life is but a weaving
  Between my Lord and me;
I cannot choose the colors
  He worketh steadily.

Ofttimes He weaveth sorrow
  And I in foolish pride,
Forget that He seeth the upper,
  And I the under side.

Not till the loom is silent
  And the shuttles cease to fly,
Shall God unroll the canvas
  And explain the reason why.

The dark threads are as needful
  In the Weaver's skillful hand,
As the threads of gold and silver
  In the pattern He has planned.

— *Author Unknown*

WINGS OF THE MORNING

Tho' I take the wings of the morning
  And dwell by the farthest sea,
Even there, Lord, Thou art with me,
  And Thy right hand guideth me.

If I mount up with wings, as an eagle,
  And stand on the mountain peak,
Thy presence fills and thrills me,
  Lord, as Thy face I seek.

If I abide in the lowest depths,
  Burdened with grief and pain,
Even there, Lord, Thou art with me,
  To lift me up again.

In height or depth, my Father,
  In darkness or in light,
Thy matchless love surrounds me,
  O God of grace and might.

— *Mabel Custis*

IN A GARDEN

God walks in my garden
In the early dawn,
But when I rise to greet Him
He is always gone,

Though I can trace His footprints
In beds of violet,
And in a lily's perfume
His presence lingers yet.

Hush, my soul, be patient
For yet a little space —
Some day you will see Him,
Will meet Him face to face;

Some day, earth forgotten,
You will fare abroad,
And in heaven's gardens
You will walk with God.

— *Martha Snell Nicholson*

ᢒᡃᢀ

COMMIT THY WAY

Commit thy way to God,
  The weight which makes thee faint;
Worlds are to him no load,
  To him breathe thy complaint.
He who for winds and clouds
  Maketh a pathway free,
Through wastes or hostile crowds,
  Can make a way for thee.

Thou must in him be blest
  Ere bliss can be secure;
On his works must thou rest
  If thy work shall endure.
To anxious, prying thought,
  And weary, fretting care,
The highest yieldeth naught:
  He giveth all to prayer.

Father, thy faithful love,
  Thy mercy, wise and mild,
Sees what will blessing prove,
  Or what will hurt thy child;

And what thy wise foreseeing
  Doth for thy children choose
Thou bringest into being,
  Nor sufferest them to lose.

Hope, then, though woes be doubled;
  Hope and be undismayed;
Let not thy heart be troubled,
  Nor let it be afraid.
This prison where thou art —
  Thy God will break it soon,
And flood with light thy heart
  In his own blessed noon.

Up! up! the day is breaking;
  Say to thy cares, Good night!
Thy troubles from thee shaking
  Like dreams in day's fresh light.
Thou wearest not the crown,
  Nor the best course can tell;
God sitteth on the throne
  And guideth all things well.

— *Paul Gerhardt*
(Translated by Elizabeth Rundle Charles)

ᢒᡃᢀ

MANNA

'Twas in the night the manna fell
That fed the hosts of Israel.

Enough for each day's fullest store
And largest need; enough, no more.

For willful waste, for prideful show,
God sent not angels' food below.

Still in our nights of deep distress
The manna falls our heart to bless.

And, famished, as we cry for bread,
With heavenly food our lives are fed,

And each day's need finds each day's
  store
Enough. Dear Lord, what want we
  more!

— *Margaret E. Sangster*

PEACE, PERFECT PEACE

Peace, perfect peace, in this dark world of sin?
The blood of Jesus whispers peace within.

Peace, perfect peace, by thronging duties pressed?
To do the will of Jesus, this is rest.

Peace, perfect peace, with sorrows surging round?
On Jesus' bosom naught but calm is found.

Peace, perfect peace, with loved ones far away?
In Jesus' keeping we are safe, and they.

Peace, perfect peace, the future all unknown?
Jesus we know, and He is on the throne.

Peace, perfect peace, death shadowing us and ours?
Jesus has vanquished death and all its powers.

It is enough; earth's struggles soon shall cease,
And Jesus call us to Heaven's perfect peace.

— Edward Henry Bickersteth

UPWARD

Upward where the stars are burning,
Silent, silent in their turning
Round the never changing pole;
Upward where the sky is brightest,
Upward where the blue is lightest,
Lift I now my longing soul.

Where the Lamb on high is seated,
By ten thousand voices greeted,
Lord of lords, and King of kings.
Son of Man, they crown Him,
Son of God, they own Him;
With His Name the palace rings.

Blessing, honor, without measure,
Heavenly riches, earthly treasure,
Lay we at His blessed feet:
Poor the praise that now we render,
Loud shall be our voices yonder,
When before His throne we meet.

— Horatius Bonar

IF ASKED WHEREON I REST MY CLAIM

If asked whereon I rest my claim
   To full salvation's joy,
If nothing more I need to name,
   Or other words employ,
Besides our Savior's blood and wounds,
To me all satisfying grounds;
I answer then, "My claim is good!
'Tis based on Jesus' blood."

This is my hope's foundation firm,
   Which ever shall endure;
Yea, at the end of life's brief term,
   I'll rest thereon secure,
And dreaded death shall lose its sting,
As of my Savior's wounds I sing;
His precious blood shall be the key
That opens heav'n for me.

— A. Samuel Wallgren

THE CHRISTIAN LIFE

I look to Thee in ev'ry need,
  And never look in vain;
I feel Thy strong and tender love,
  And all is well again;
The thought of Thee is mightier far
Than sin and pain and sorrow are.

Discouraged in the work of life,
  Disheartened by its load,
Shamed by its failures or its fears,
  I sink beside the road;
But let me only think of Thee,
And then new heart springs up in me.

Thy calmness bends serene above,
  My restlessness to still,
Around me flows Thy quickening life
  To nerve my faltering will;
Thy presence fills my solitude,
Thy providence turns all to good.

Embosomed deep in Thy great love,
  Held in Thy law, I stand;
Thy hand in all things I behold,
  And all things in Thy hand;
Thou leadest me by unsought ways,
And turn'st my mourning into praise.

— Samuel Longfellow

HOW WE NEED THE SECRET PLACE

In this world of toil and turmoil,
How we need the Secret Place!
How we need the calm reflection
Of our blessed Saviour's face!
How we need to gaze upon Him

Till our troubled souls grow still,
And find rest in sweet surrender
To our Heavenly Father's will.

In this world of grief and sadness,
How we need a safe retreat,
Where our wounded hearts may enter
And find comfort blest and sweet!
How we need to hear the whisper
Of the Saviour, "Have no fear!"
And to rest in the assurance
That His loving arms are near.

In this world of sin and evil,
How we need a mighty Tow'r,
Where for help and for deliv'rance
We may flee in danger's hour!
How we need the strength and power
He is waiting to bestow!
How we need His glorious Presence
At the battle's front to know!

— Avis B. Christiansen

IF YOU BELIEVE

The thorns we see just up ahead
God knows will be a rose instead;

He sees our needs from up above
And we can safely trust His love!

What seems just now a cross to bear
May be, in truth, a crown to wear;

So walk by faith and not by sight,
Trust God to lead thro' day or night,

His perfect peace you shall receive
If you believe — if you believe.

— Phyllis C. Michael

RESTING

Once my hands were always trying,
  Trying hard to do my best;
Now my heart is sweetly trusting,
  And my soul is all at rest.

Once my brain was always planning,
  And my heart, with cares oppressed;
Now I trust the Lord to lead me,
  And my life is all at rest.

Once my life was full of effort,
  Now 'tis full of joy and zest;
Since I took His yoke upon me,
  Jesus gives to me His rest.

— *A. B. Simpson*

LOOKING BACKWARD

The young cannot look back and say,
  "He led me thus and so;
Here is the blueprint of my life."
  But as we older grow

It is a sweet and precious thing
  In retrospect to see
How thro' the myriad maze of roads
  We might have taken, He

Kept our oft wayward feet upon
  The road He chose for us.
Now just around the bend there lies
  The City Glorious,

And He who kept us safe thus far
  And would not let us roam,
Will lead us gently by the hand,
  And take us safely home.

The young can only trust to Him,
  And walk by faith, but we,
Those who have traveled longer roads,
  And older grown, — can *see!*

— *Martha Snell Nicholson*

THE LORD'S MY SHEPHERD

The Lord's my shepherd, I'll not want;
  He makes me down to lie
In pastures green; he leadeth me
  The quiet waters by.

My soul he doth restore again;
  And me to walk doth make
Within the paths of righteousness,
  E'en for his own name's sake.

Yea, tho' I walk in death's dark vale,
  Yet will I fear no ill,
For thou art with me, and thy rod
  And staff me comfort still.

My table thou hast furnished
  In presence of my foes
My head thou dost with oil anoint,
  And my cup overflows.

Goodness and mercy all my life
  Shall surely follow me;
And in God's house for evermore
  My dwelling place shall be.

— *Scottish Psalter*

THE PRECEPT OF SILENCE

I know you: solitary griefs,
Desolate passions, aching hours!
I know you: tremulous beliefs,
Agonized hopes, and ashen flowers!

The winds are sometimes sad to me;
The starry spaces, full of fear;
Mine is the sorrow on the sea,
And mine the sigh of places drear.

Some players upon plaintive strings
Publish their wistfulness abroad:
I have not spoken of these things,
Save to one man, and unto God.

— *Lionel Johnson*

BE STILL, MY SOUL

Be still, my soul: the Lord is on thy side;
  Bear patiently the cross of grief or pain;
Leave to thy God to order and provide;
  In every change the faithful will remain.
Be still, my soul: thy best, thy heavenly Friend
Through thorny ways leads to a joyful end.

Be still, my soul: thy God doth undertake
  To guide the future as he has the past.
Thy hope, thy confidence let nothing shake;
  All now mysterious shall be bright at last.
Be still, my soul: the waves and winds still know
His voice who ruled them while he dwelt below.

— Katharina von Schlegel
(Translated by Jane L. Borthwick)

∽

TO A WATERFOWL

Whither, midst falling dew,
While glow the heavens with the last steps of day,
Far, through their rosy depths, dost thou pursue
  Thy solitary way?

Vainly the fowler's eye
Might mark thy distant flight to do thee wrong,
As, darkly seen against the crimson sky,
  Thy figure floats along.

Seek'st thou the plashy brink
Of weedy lake, or marge of river wide,
Or where the rocking billows rise and sink
  On the chafed ocean-side?

There is a Power whose care
Teaches thy way along that pathless coast —
The desert and illimitable air —
  Lone wandering, but not lost.

All day thy wings have fanned,
At that far height, the cold, thin atmosphere,
Yet stoop not, weary, to the welcome land,
  Though the dark night is near.

And soon that toil shall end;
Soon shalt thou find a summer home, and rest,
And scream among thy fellows; reeds shall bend,
    Soon, o'er thy sheltered nest.

Thou'rt gone, the abyss of heaven
Hath swallowed up thy form; yet, on my heart
Deeply has sunk the lesson thou hast given,
    And shall not soon depart.

He who from zone to zone,
Guides through the boundless sky thy certain flight,
In the long way that I must tread alone,
    Will lead my steps aright.

— *William Cullen Bryant*

CHANGE OF RAIMENT

Lord Jesus, all my sin and guilt
    Love laid of old on Thee,
Thy love the cross and sorrow willed,
    Love undeserved by me.
The victory over death and hell
    Thou, Lord, for me didst win;
And Thou hast nailed upon Thy Cross
    All, all my sin.

The way into the Holiest Place
    Stands open now to me;
Where I can see Thy glorious Face,
    Nor trembled thus to see.
For as I am to Thee I come,
    I clasp Thy blessed Feet,
And learn the mystery of love
    So deep, so sweet.

Enfolded, O my Lord, in Thee,
    And hid in Thee I rest,
Enwrapped in Christ's own purity
    Secure upon Thy breast.
Had I an Angel's raiment — fair
    With heavenly gems unpriced,
That glorious garb I would not wear,
    My robe is Christ.

— *Gerhardt Tersteegen*

THIS I KNOW

I do not know what next may come
    Across my pilgrim way;
I do not know tomorrow's road,
    Nor see beyond today.
But this I know — my Saviour knows
    The path I cannot see;
And I can trust His wounded hand
    To guide and care for me.

I do not know what may befall,
    Of sunshine or of rain;
I do not know what may be mine,
    Of pleasure and of pain;
But this I know — my Saviour knows,
    And whatsoe'er it be,
Still I can trust His love to give
    What will be best for me.

I do not know what may await,
    Or what the morrow brings;
But with the glad salute of faith,
    I hail its opening wings;
For this I know — that in my Lord
    Shall all my needs be met;
And I can trust the heart of Him
    Who has not failed me yet.

— *E. Margaret Clarkson*

CHOSEN LESSONS

In the way that He shall choose
  He will teach us;
Not a lesson we shall lose,
  All shall reach us.

Strange and difficult indeed
  We may find it,
But the blessing that we need
  Is behind it.

All the lessons He shall send
  Are the sweetest,
And His training, in the end,
  Is completest.

     — *Frances Ridley Havergal*

ᏩᏙ

THE QUIET MIND

I have a treasure which I prize;
  The like I cannot find;
There's nothing like it in the earth:
  It is a quiet mind.

But 'tis not that I'm stupefied,
  Or senseless, dull, or blind:
'Tis God's own peace within my soul
  Which forms my quiet mind.

I found this treasure at the Cross.
  'Tis there to every kind
Of heavy-laden, weary souls
  Christ gives a quiet mind.

My Saviour's death and risen life
  To give this were designed;
And that's the root and that's the
    branch,
  Of this my quiet mind.

The love of God within my heart
  My heart to his doth bind;
This is the mind of heaven on earth;
  This is my quiet mind.

I've many a cross to take up now,
  And many left behind;
But present trials move me not,
  Nor shake my quiet mind.

And what may be to-morrow's cross
  I never seek to find;
My Saviour says, Leave that to Me,
  And keep a quiet mind.

And well I know the Lord hath said,
  To make my heart resigned,
That mercy still shall follow such
  As have this quiet mind.

I meet with pride of wit and wealth,
  And scorn and looks unkind,
It matters naught: I envy not,
  For I've a quiet mind.

I'm waiting now to see the Lord,
  Who's been to me so kind:
I want to thank him face to face
  For this my quiet mind.

     — *Author Unknown*

ᏩᏙ

THE REVIVAL

Unfold, unfold! take in his light,
Who makes thy cares more short than
    night.
The joys which with his day-star rise
He deals to all but drowsy eyes;
And (what the men of this world miss)
Some drops and dews of future bliss.

Hark, how the winds have chang'd
    their note,
And with warm whispers call thee out.
The frosts are past, the storms are gone,
And backward life at last comes on.
The lofty groves in express joys
Reply unto the turtle's voice;
And here in dust and dirt, O here
The lilies of his love appear!

     — *Henry Vaughan*

The Place of Peace

At the heart of the cyclone tearing the
    sky
And flinging the clouds and the towers
    by,
Is a place of central calm;
So here in the roar of mortal things,
I have a place where my spirit sings,
In the hollow of God's palm.

— *Edwin Markham*

God's Way Is Perfect

As for God, His way is perfect!
Oh to grasp this truth divine!
Oh to rest upon His promise,
And accept His will as mine!

As for God, His way is perfect,—
Love divine my path has planned.
I can safely leave the future
In my Saviour's mighty hand.

As for God, His way is perfect!
May I never doubt it, Lord.
May I lean in sweet assurance
On Thy precious Holy Word.

As for God, His way is perfect!
Some day I shall clearly see
All His purposes unfolded,
And rejoice eternally.

— *Avis B. Christiansen*

Reflections

Stars lie broken on a lake
Whenever passing breezes make
    The wavelets leap;
But when the lake is still, the sky
Gives moon and stars that they may lie
    On that calm deep.

If, like the lake that has the boon
Of cradling the little moon
    Above the hill,
I want the Infinite to be
Reflected undisturbed in me,
    I must be still.

— *Edna Becker*

Sheer Joy

Oh the sheer joy of it!
    Living with Thee,
God of the universe,
    Lord of a tree,
Maker of mountains,
    Lover of me!

Oh the sheer joy of it!
    Breathing Thy air;
Morning is dawning,
    Gone every care,
All the world's singing,
    "God's everywhere."

Oh the sheer joy of it!
    Walking with Thee,
Out on the hilltop,
    Down by the sea,
Life is so wonderful,
    Life is so free.

Oh the sheer joy of it!
    Working with God,
Running His errands,
    Waiting His nod,
Building His heaven,
    On common sod.

Oh the sheer joy of it!
    Ever to be
Living in glory,
    Living with Thee,
Lord of tomorrow,
    Lover of me!

— *Ralph Spaulding Cushman*

SILENCE MY HEART

Silence my heart, Lord Jesus;
Bid the tumult within be still.
Quiet the raging billows,
And a holy hush instill.

I would hear Thy voice, O Jesus;
But the tempest's ceaseless roar
Doth oft drown out the message
That my soul so longeth for.

Silence my heart, Lord Jesus,
That I may hear Thy voice,
Yea, even Thy faintest whisper,
And in Thy great love rejoice.

May Thy all pervading presence
My waiting soul infill,
Till my every thought is captive
Unto Thy blest holy will.

Grant me Thy peace, O Jesus,
That nothing can molest;
So shall my heart be silenced,
So shall my spirit rest.

— *Avis B. Christiansen*

ↄ

CONTRASTS

Clouds, then the glory of sunset;
Darkness, then burst of the morn;
Dearth, then the gentle shower;
Sacrifice — Truth is born!

The earth-throe, then comes the harvest;
Silence, and then the word;
Mist, before the full starlight;
Discord, ere music is heard!

Erring, and then the forgiveness;
Heart's-ease, after the strife;
Passion, and then the refining —
Death, then the wonder of life!

— *Henry Meade Bland*

JESUS, PRICELESS TREASURE

Jesus, priceless treasure,
Source of purest pleasure,
Truest Friend to me;
Long my heart hath panted
Till it well-nigh fainted,
Thirsting after Thee.
Thine I am, O spotless Lamb,
I will suffer nought to hide Thee,
Ask for nought beside Thee.

In Thine arm I rest me;
Foes who would molest me
Cannot reach me here.
Though the earth be shaking,
Every heart be quaking,
God dispels our fear;
Sin and hell in conflict fell
With their heaviest storms assail us:
Jesus will not fail us.

Hence, all thoughts of sadness!
For the Lord of gladness,
Jesus, enters in:
Those who love the Father,
Though the storms may gather,
Still have peace within;
Yea, whate'er we here must bear,
Still in Thee lieth purest pleasure,
Jesus, priceless treasure!

— *Johann Franck*

ↄ

TODAY

Build a little fence of trust
Around today;
Fill the space with loving deeds,
And therein stay.
Look not through the sheltering bars
Upon tomorrow;
God will help thee bear what comes
Of joy or sorrow.

— *Mary Frances Butts*

God's Garden

God works in His garden, I'm told, ev'ry day
With the roses He needs for His heavenly bouquet.

There are times when He picks all the withered, the old
And gathers them lovingly into His fold.

There are times when He prunes where some other must grow
That He on the weak ones more strength may bestow.

But some days He chooses the fairest in sight;
He needs certain buds to make heaven look bright.

How sweet, oh how beautiful is His bouquet!
God works in His garden and best is His way.

— *Phyllis C. Michael*

The Red Sea Place in Your Life

Have you come to the Red Sea place in your life,
    Where, in spite of all you can do,
There is no way out, there is no way back,
    There is no other way but — through?
Then wait on the Lord with a trust serene,
    Till the night of your fear is gone,
He will send the wind, He will heap the floods,
    He says to your soul, "Go on!"

And His hand will lead you through — clear through —
    Ere the watery walls roll down,
No foe can reach you, no wave can touch,
    No mightiest sea can drown;
The tossing billows may rear their crests,
    Their foam at your feet may break,
But over their bed you may walk dry shod,
    In a path that your Lord will make.

In the morning watch, 'neath the lifted cloud,
    You shall see but the Lord alone,
Where He leads you on from the place by the sea,
    To the land that you have not known;
And your fears shall pass as your foes have passed,
    You shall be no more afraid;
You shall sing His praise in a better place,
    A place that His hand has made.

— *Annie Johnson Flint*

THE PILLAR OF THE CLOUD

Lead, Kindly Light, amid the encircling gloom,
    Lead Thou me on!
The night is dark, and I am far from home —
    Lead Thou me on!
Keep Thou my feet; I do not ask to see
The distant scene, — one step enough for me.

I was not ever thus, nor pray'd that Thou
    Shouldst lead me on.
I lov'd to choose and see my path; but now
    Lead Thou me on!
I lov'd the garish day, and, spite of fears,
Pride rul'd my will: remember not past years.

So long Thy power hath bless'd me, sure it still
    Will lead me on,
O'er moor and fen, o'er crag and torrent, till
    The night is gone;
And with the morn those angel faces smile
Which I have lov'd long since, and lost awhile.

— John Henry Newman

TRUST AND WAIT

Just wait upon the Lord and you will know
The reason for the way you suffered so;
He only seeks your faith in Him to prove
And teach you more about His wondrous love.

Then trust in God no matter what befall,
And ev'ry day upon the Saviour call;
Believe His Word and you will surely see
That He is all He promised He would be.

Your darkest night will someday pass away
If you but put your trust in Him and pray;
He promised He would see you safely through,
And ev'ry promise in His Word is true.

So wait upon the Lord, be not afraid,
For He Himself will be your Strength and Aid;
Just rest in Him, your never-failing Friend,
And peace and joy will all your way attend.

— Oswald J. Smith

Our Burden Bearer

The little sharp vexations
  And the briars that cut the feet,
Why not take all to the Helper
  Who has never failed us yet?
Tell Him about the heartache,
  And tell Him the longings too,
Tell Him the baffled purpose
  When we scarce know what to do.
Then, leaving all our weakness
  With the One divinely strong,
Forget that we bore the burden
  And carry away the song.

— *Phillips Brooks*

ᴄᴡ

Art Thou Weary?

Art thou weary, heavy laden,
  Art thou sore distrest?
"Come to Me," saith One, "and com-
  ing,
  Be at rest."

Hath He marks to lead me to Him,
  If He be my Guide?
"In His feet and hands are wound
  prints,
  And His side."

Is there diadem, as Monarch,
  That His brow adorns?
"Yea, a crown, in very surety,
  But of thorns."

If I find Him, if I follow,
  What His guerdon here?
"Many a sorrow, many a labor,
  Many a tear."

If I still hold closely to Him
  What hath He at last?
"Sorrow vanquished, labor ended,
  Jordan passed."

If I ask Him to receive me,
  Will He say me nay?
"Not till earth and not till heaven
  Pass away."

Finding, following, keeping, strug-
  gling,
  Is He sure to bless?
"Saints, apostles, prophets, martyrs,
  Answer yes."

— *John M. Neale*

ᴄᴡ

Guidance

How wonderful to lay my hand
In Thine, dear Lord, today,
And with complete assurance walk
With Thee life's unknown way!
Content though but one step I see,
To follow without fear,
Since 'tis Thy love that leadeth me,
And Thy sweet voice I hear.

How wonderful to take each hour
Thou dost intrust to me,
And seek to make it by Thy pow'r
Count for eternity!
Rejoicing, Lord, whate'er the cost,
To follow day by day
Until the final vale is crossed,
And glory crowns my way.

How wonderful, dear Lord, to lay
The tangled threads of life,—
The trials of my pilgrim way,—
The turmoil and the strife,
Each bitter ill, each stern demand,
Each burden great and small
Within Thy precious nail-scarred
  hand,
And trust Thy grace for all!

How wonderful to walk with Thee!
How wonderful to know
The hand once pierced on Calvary
Doth guide me as I go!

— *Avis B. Christiansen*

BEYOND TODAY

If we could see beyond today
  As God can see;
If all the clouds should roll away,
  The shadows flee,
O'er present griefs we would not fret,
Each sorrow we would soon forget,
For many joys are waiting yet
  For you and me.

If we could know beyond today
  As God doth know,
Why dearest treasures pass away
  And tears must flow;
And why the darkness leads to light,
Why dreary paths will soon grow
      bright;
Some day life's wrongs will be made
      right
  Faith tells us so.

"If we could see, if we could know,"
  We often say,
But God in love a veil doth throw
  Across our way;
We cannot see what lies before
And so we cling to Him the more,
He leads us till this life is o'er;
  Trust and obey.

— *Author Unknown*

REST

There is a rest that deeper grows,
  In midst of pain and strife;
A mighty, conscious, willed repose,
  The breath of deepest life.

To have and hold the precious prize,
  No need of jealous bars,
But windows open to the skies,
  And power to see the stars.

— *George Macdonald*

GOOD-NIGHT

The sun has sunk within the west;
The shades have fallen, still and blest;
'Tis time for weary souls to rest;
  Good-night, good-night.

God never sleeps, His eye doth see;
God ever cares, He keepeth thee;
In His safe guarding, peaceful be;
  Good-night, good-night.

Sleep deep and long, let care be past;
On God thy every burden cast;
His arms will hold thee close and fast;
  Good-night, good-night.

Good-night, belovèd, God is near;
Good-night, belovèd, thou art dear;
Let God and love, then, banish fear;
  Good-night, good-night.

— *Henry W. Frost*

FOUR THINGS

Four things a man must learn to do
If he would make his record true:
To think without confusion clearly;
To love his fellowmen sincerely;
To act from honest motives purely;
To trust in God and Heaven securely.

— *Henry van Dyke*

SYMPATHY

I am no trumpet, but a reed,—
A broken reed the wind indeed
  Left flat upon a dismal shore:
Yet if a little maid or child
Should sigh within it earnest-mild,
  This reed will answer evermore.

— *Elizabeth Browning*

"Lean Hard On Me"

In the midst of roaring cannon
As the bombs begin to fall,
I can hear His sweet voice whisper
"I will be your All in All."

In the midst of pealing thunder,
When the lightning will not cease,
As the storm still rages round me
I can hear Him whisper, "Peace."

In the midst of darkest midnight
When the moon and stars are dim,
For my light and consolation
I draw the closer unto Him.

In the midst of deepest sorrow
He still listens to my plea,
Speaking words of hope and comfort,
"Fear thou not; lean hard on me."

In the midst of world confusion
When I cannot understand,
By faith I gaze with rapture
To my blessed Promised Land.

— *Clifford Lewis*

Joy and Peace in Believing

Sometimes a light surprises
    The Christian while he sings;
It is the Lord who rises
    With healing in his wings:
When comforts are declining,
    He grants the soul again
A season of clear shining
    To cheer it after rain.

In holy contemplation,
    We sweetly then pursue
The theme of God's salvation,
    And find it ever new:
Set free from present sorrow,
    We cheerfully can say,
E'en let th' unknown tomorrow
    Bring with it what it may.

It can bring with it nothing
    But he will bear us through;
Who gives the lilies clothing
    Will clothe his people too:
Beneath the spreading heavens,
    No creature but is fed;
And he who feeds the ravens
    Will give his children bread.

Though vine, nor fig tree neither,
    Their wonted fruit should bear,
Though all the fields should wither,
    Nor flocks, nor herds, be there:
Yet God the same abiding,
    His praise shall tune my voice;
For while in him confiding,
    I cannot but rejoice.

— *William Cowper*

For the Blind

A special tenderness and love
Within my heart I find
For you whose light is blotted out,
For you whom men call blind,

Because you grope thro' darkened days.
Yet often I have seen
Your sightless faces glow with light
As though you long had been

Alone with God, as though you dwelt
In some bright place apart,
Where glowing candles lighted all
The chambers of your heart.

Give me your vision! These my eyes
Too often look on sin
And human woe, and must until
My heavenly life begin.

O patient eyelids, closed and still,
How blessed it must be
To know His face will be the next
Your opened eyes will see!

— *Martha Snell Nicholson*

Hymn of Trust

O Love Divine, that stooped to share
  Our sharpest pang, our bitterest tear,
On Thee we cast each earth-born care,
  We smile at pain while Thou art near!

Though long the weary way we tread,
  And sorrow crown each lingering year,
No path we shun, no darkness dread,
  Our hearts still whispering, Thou art near!

When drooping pleasure turns to grief,
  And trembling faith is changed to fear,
The murmuring wind, the quivering leaf,
  Shall softly tell us, Thou art near!

On Thee we fling our burdening woe,
  O Love Divine, forever dear,
Content to suffer while we know,
  Living and dying, Thou art near!

— Oliver Wendell Holmes

The Lord Is My Shepherd

The Lord is my Shepherd, no want shall I know,
  I feed in green pastures, safe folded I rest;
He leadeth my soul where the still waters flow,
  Restores me when wandering, redeems when oppressed.

Through the valley and shadow of death though I stray,
  Since Thou art my Guardian, no evil I fear;
Thy rod shall defend me, Thy staff be my stay;
  No harm can befall, with my Comforter near.

In the midst of affliction my table is spread;
  With blessings unmeasured my cup runneth o'er;
With perfume and oil Thou anointest my head;
  Oh, what shall I ask of Thy providence more?

Let goodness and mercy, my bountiful God,
  Still follow my steps till I meet Thee above;
I seek by the path which my forefathers trod,
  Through the land of their sojourn, Thy kingdom of love.

— James Montgomery

THE LORD WILL PROVIDE

Though troubles assail, and dangers affright,
Though friends should all fail, and foes all unite,
Yet one thing secures us, whatever betide,
The promise assures us, "The Lord will provide."

The birds, without barn or storehouse, are fed;
From them let us learn to trust for our bread:
His saints what is fitting shall ne'er be denied,
So long as 'tis written, "The Lord will provide."

No strength of our own, nor goodness we claim;
Our trust is all thrown on Jesus' name:
In this our strong tower for safety we hide;
The Lord is our power, "The Lord will provide."

When life sinks apace, and death is in view,
The word of His grace shall comfort us through:
Not fearing or doubting, with Christ on our side,
We hope to die shouting, "The Lord will provide."

— *John Newton*

❧

CAREFUL FOR NOTHING

Careful for nothing — dear Lord, can it be
That this is the life Thou desirest for me?
A life free from worry, though troubles abound,
A spirit at rest, 'mid the tumult around?

Careful for nothing, ah yes, blessed Lord,
Like a beacon of light it shines forth in Thy Word:
"Cast on Me thy burdens, the weight of thy care,
Yea, bring every need to Thy Father in prayer."

Be careful for nothing. Let Him undertake
The problems that press thee for His dear Name's sake;
And as thou dost watch His blest purpose unfold,
New glory His love and His mercy will hold.

Be careful for nothing. Yea, rest and be still,
As you wait the fulfillment of His perfect will:
Secure in His love He would have thee abide,
With no anxious thought His blest visage to hide.

— *Avis B. Christiansen*

L'ENVOI

When earth's last picture is painted, and the tubes are twisted and dried,
When the oldest colors have faded, and the youngest critic has died,
We shall rest, and — faith, we shall need it, — lie down for an aeon or two,
Till the Master of all Good Workmen shall set us to work anew!

And those that were good shall be happy: they shall sit in a golden chair;
They shall splash at a ten-league canvas with brushes of comets' hair;
They shall find real saints to draw from — Magdalen, Peter, and Paul;
They shall work for an age at a sitting, and never be tired at all!

And only the Master shall praise us, and only the Master shall blame;
And no one shall work for money, and no one shall work for fame;
But each for the joy of the working, and each in his separate star
Shall draw the Thing as he sees It for the God of the Things as They are!

— Rudyard Kipling

STRENGTH — HUMAN

For though the giant ages heave the hill
   And break the shore, and evermore
Make and break, and work their will;
   Though world on world in myriad myriads roll
     Round us, each with different powers,
     And other forms of life than ours,
What know we greater than the Soul?
On God and godlike men we build our trust.

— Alfred, Lord Tennyson

THE REFINER'S FIRE

He sat by a furnace of sevenfold heat,
   As He watched by the precious ore;
And closer He bent, with a searching gaze,
   As He heated it more and more.

He knew He had ore that could stand the test;
   And He wanted the finest of gold —
To mould as a crown for the king to wear,
   Set with gems of a price untold.

So He laid our gold in the burning fire,
   Though we fain would have said Him nay;
And He watched the dross that we had not seen,
   As it melted and passed away.

And the gold grew brighter, and yet more bright;
  But our eyes were so dim with tears,
We saw but the fire — not the Master's hand,
  And questioned with anxious fears.

Yet our gold shone out with a richer glow,
  As it mirrored a form above
That bent o'er the fire — though unseen by us —
  With looks of ineffable love.

Can we think that it pleases His loving heart
  To cause us a moment's pain?
Ah! no, but He saw through the present loss
  The bliss of eternal gain.

So He waited there with a watchful eye,
  With a love that is strong and sure;
And His gold did not suffer a whit more heat
  Than was needed to make it pure.

                    — *Author Unknown*

The Centuries Are His

The centuries are His. I will not be
  Dismayed when evil men and days prevail,
Though God may seem to be on Calvary,
  And peace may walk alone a midnight trail.

God does not balance books along the way,
  Yet always there will be a judgment day.
The centuries are His and He is just;
  His Kingdom shall yet rule though stars be dust.

                    — *Georgia Moore Eberling*

Unafraid

My presence shall go with thee,
  Beloved child of Mine!
Then why should'st thou be fearful,
  Or why should'st thou repine?
No danger can o'ertake thee
  When I am at thy side —
My presence shall go with thee,
  And I will be thy guide!

My presence shall go with thee!
  Though heavy be thy load,
Though dark may be the midnight,
  Though rough may be the road,
In sunshine and in shadow
  Commit thine all to Me —
My presence shall go with thee,
  And I will care for thee!

                    —*E. Margaret Clarkson*

"My Grace Is Sufficient for Thee"

When, sin-stricken, burdened, and
    weary,
  From bondage I longed to be free,
There came to my heart the sweet mes-
    sage:
  "My grace is sufficient for thee."

Tho' tempted and sadly discouraged,
  My soul to this refuge will flee,
And rest in the blessed assurance:
  "My grace is sufficient for thee."

My bark may be tossed by the tempest
  That sweeps o'er the turbulent sea—
A rainbow illumines the darkness:
  "My grace is sufficient for thee."

O Lord, I would press on with courage,
  Tho' rugged the pathway may be,
Sustained and upheld by the promise:
  "My grace is sufficient for thee."

Soon, soon will the warfare be over,
  My Lord face to face I shall see,
And prove, as I dwell in His presence:
  "His grace was sufficient for me."

                 — *Author Unknown*

Satisfaction

I have tasted heaven's manna,
And I want no other bread.
In green pastures I am dwelling,
And my hung'ring soul is fed.
At the living Fount of waters,
I have quenched my thirst for aye.
I am living in God's glory,
And my sins are washed away.

I have seen the face of Jesus,
I have felt His touch divine;
I have heard His voice so tender,
As He whispered, "Thou art Mine."

Oh the sweetness of His presence,
Oh the glory of His love;
Oh the wonder of salvation —
Matchless gift from God above!

                 — *Avis B. Christiansen*

Crossing the Bar

Sunset and evening star,
  And one clear call for me!
And may there be no moaning of the
    bar,
  When I put out to sea,

But such a tide as moving seems asleep,
  Too full for sound and foam,
When that which drew from out the
    boundless deep
  Turns again home.

Twilight and evening bell,
  And after that the dark!
And may there be no sadness of fare-
    well,
  When I embark;

For tho' from out our bourne of Time
    and Place
  The flood may bear me far,
I hope to see my Pilot face to face
  When I have crossed the bar.

                 — *Alfred, Lord Tennyson*

Trust

Always place in God thy trust,
Will and do what's right and true;
Let thy soul be brave and just;
Show thy Lord a humble mind;
Thou shalt thus his favor find;
Love but few and simple things;
Simple life much comfort brings.

                 — *Thomas à Kempis*

LORD, GIVE US LIFE

Have you knelt in the garden
where the feet of Jesus trod
and lifted your heart in quiet prayer
to an ever-loving God?

'Twas here our Savior agonized
and strength to Him was given
to bear our sins on Calv'ry's cross
and open wide the gates of heaven.

He agonized! Oh, He agonized
but strength to Him was given!
He overcame our guilt and shame
and sits with God in heaven.

Now it's glory! Oh, what glory!
Christ our Lord is risen.
God the Father and the Son
new life to us has given!

—*Helen Eberhard*

ON ANOTHER'S SORROW

Can I see another's woe,
And not be in sorrow too?
Can I see another's grief,
And not seek for kind relief?

Can I see a falling tear,
And not feel my sorrow's share?
Can a father see his child
Weep, nor be with sorrow filled?

Can a mother sit and hear
An infant groan, an infant fear?
No, no! never can it be!
Never, never can it be!

And can He who smiles on all
Hear the wren with sorrows small,
Hear the small bird's grief and care,
Hear the woes that infants bear—

And not sit beside the nest,
Pouring pity in their breast,
And not sit the cradle near,
Weeping tear on infant's tear?

And not sit both night and day,
Wiping all our tears away?
O no! never can it be!
Never, never can it be!

He doth give His joy to all:
He becomes an infant small,
He becomes a man of woe,
He doth feel the sorrow too.

Think not thou canst sigh a sigh,
And thy Maker is not by:
Think not thou canst weep a tear,
And thy Maker is not near.

Oh, He gives to us His joy,
That our grief He may destroy:
Till our grief is fled and gone
He doth sit by us, and moan.

—*William Blake*

PEACE, BE STILL!

Jesus, Fountain of my days,
Well-spring of my heart's delight,
Brightness of my morning rays,
Solace of my hours of night!
When I see Thee I arise
To the hope of cloudless skies.

Lord, Thy presence on the deep
Calms the pulses of the sea,
And the waters sink to sleep
In the rest of seeing Thee,
And my oft rebellious will
Hears the mandate, "Peace, be still!"

Now Thy will and mine are one,
Heart in heart and hand in hand;
All the clouds have touched the sun,
All the ships have reached the land;
For thy love has said to me,
"No more night!" and "No more sea!"

—*George Matheson*

Trust — *Habakkuk 3:17-18*

Though the fig tree shall not ripen,
  And no fruit be on the vine,
Tho' the shades of night be gath'ring,
  And the sun hath ceased to shine,
Still in Christ, my blessed Saviour,
  Joy may still my portion be,
For His love abideth ever
  Unto all eternity.

Though the fields be parched and
      withered,
  And the flocks no longer graze,
Tho' the singing birds have vanished
  With their bright and tuneful lays,
Still in Christ my soul is resting,
  And my cup o'erflow its brim.
He my every need supplieth —
  I am satisfied in Him.

Though afflictions press me sorely,
  And abound on every hand,
On His everlasting promise,
  He hath bid me firmly stand,
Casting all my care upon Him,
  Who hath died to set me free,
And in Christ, my risen Saviour,
  To rejoice exceedingly.

— Avis B. Christiansen

ᧁ

What a Friend We Have in Jesus

What a Friend we have in Jesus,
All our sins and griefs to bear!
What a privilege to carry
Everything to God in prayer!
O what peace we often forfeit,
O what needless pain we bear,
All because we do not carry
Everything to God in prayer!

Have we trials and temptations?
Is there trouble anywhere?
We should never be discouraged,
Take it to the Lord in prayer.
Can we find a friend so faithful
Who will all our sorrows share?
Jesus knows our every weakness,
Take it to the Lord in prayer.

Are we weak and heavy laden,
Cumbered with a load of care? —
Precious Saviour, still our refuge,—
Take it to the Lord in prayer.
Do thy friends despise, forsake thee?
Take it to the Lord in prayer;
In His arms He'll take and shield thee,
Thou wilt find a solace there.

— Joseph Scriven

ᧁ

Confidence

Fear not, my soul, in peace abide,
Though threat'ning clouds hang low,
And rumblings grim on every side
Each hour intenser grow.

The dread of coming doom pervades
The very atmosphere,
But they whose hearts on Christ are
    stayed
Need have no anxious fear.

He holds the planets in His hands,
And all the universe.
What pow'r can alter His commands,
Or change His holy course?

He watches from Mt. Zion's Hill
Men's schemes to conquer all,
But without His permissive will
Not one dread blow can fall.

And they who trust in Him may rest
In calm and sweet repose
Upon His promise sure and blest.
He loves, He cares, He knows.

— Avis B. Christiansen

GIVE TO THE WINDS THY FEARS

Give to the winds thy fears;
  Hope and be undismayed;
God hears thy sighs and counts thy
    tears,
  God shall lift up thy head.

Through waves and clouds and storms
  He gently clears thy way;
Wait thou His time; so shall this night
  Soon end in joyous day.

Leave to His sovereign sway
  To choose and to command;
So shalt thou, wondering, own His
    way,
  How wise, how strong His hand!

Far, far above thy thought
  His counsel shall appear,
When fully He the work hath
    wrought
  That caused thy needless fear.
                    — *Paul Gerhardt*

TAKE THOU MY HAND

Oft times it seem my load of care
Is so much more than I can bear;
Then I look up and Thou art there —
O precious Saviour, walk with me.

Take Thou my hand and be my Guide,
Then I'll not fear what may betide;
For Thou, O Lord, art by my side —
Take Thou my hand, be Thou my
    Guide.

Lord, help me walk more patiently,
Until the day when I shall see
That out of pain comes victory —
O precious Saviour, walk with me.

Life's road ahead is veiled and grey,
I cannot seem to find my way;
Lord, heed my helpless cry, I pray —
O precious Saviour, walk with me.

Time holds from me the things I
    planned
And barriers rise on ev'ry hand;
But I'll not ask to understand,
I'll simply trust in Thy command.

Take Thou my hand and be my Guide,
Then I'll not fear what may betide;
For Thou, O Lord, art by my side —
Take Thou my hand, be Thou my
    Guide.

Let each day dawn with strength anew
That I Thy perfect will may do;
I *can* go on and bravely, too —
O precious Saviour, walk with me.

Take Thou my hand and be my Guide,
Then I'll not fear what may betide;
For Thou, O Lord, art by my side —
Take Thou my hand, be Thou my
    Guide.
                    — *Phyllis C. Michael*

GOD IS

Some things are hard to understand
  And harder still to bear;
But oh, how sweet to know God *is*
  About us ev'rywhere.

How sweet to know His way is best —
  To make His will our own
And calmly trust His tender care
  The future all unknown.

Some things are hard to understand
  And to accept as right;
But rest assured no joy or grief
  Escapes God's precious sight.

He sees beyond the secret veil,
  He knows tomorrow's needs;
So put your hand in His just now
  And follow where He leads.
                    — *Phyllis C. Michael*

IN THE HOUR OF TRIAL

In the hour of trial,
Jesus, plead for me;
Lest by base denial,
I depart from Thee.
When Thou seest me waver,
With a look recall,
Nor for fear or favor
Suffer me to fall.

With forbidden pleasures
Would this vain world charm,
Or its sordid treasures
Spread to work me harm,
Bring to my remembrance
Sad Gethsemane,
Or, in darker semblance,
Cross-crowned Calvary

Should Thy mercy send me
Sorrow, toil and woe;
Or should pain attend me
On my path below,
Grant that I may never
Fail Thy hand to see,
Grant that I may ever
Cast my care on Thee.

— *James Montgomery*

RULE ON

O God of ev'ry kind of earth,
Rule on in majesty;
Thy hand hath made each star, each
world
That is or e'er shall be.

O God of wisdom and of love,
Rule on in pow'r this day;
Fulfill in us Thy perfect will,
Rule on in truth, we pray.

O God of all we cannot see,
Rule on o'er night and day;
Let all creation sound Thy praise,
Rule on in Thine own way.

O God of all our future days,
Rule on just as before;
Whatever things each dawn may bring,
Rule on for evermore.

— *Phyllis C. Michael*

DEAR LORD AND FATHER OF MANKIND

Dear Lord and Father of mankind!
Forgive our foolish ways!
Reclothe us in our rightful mind,
In purer lives Thy service find,
In deeper reverence, praise.

In simple trust like theirs who heard,
Beside the Syrian sea,
The gracious calling of the Lord,
Let us, like them, without a word,
Rise up and follow Thee.

O Sabbath rest by Galilee!
O calm of hills above,
Where Jesus knelt to share with Thee
The silence of eternity
Interpreted by love!

With that deep hush subduing all
Our words and works that drown
The tender whisper of Thy call,
As noiseless let Thy blessing fall
As fell Thy manna down.

Drop Thy still dews of quietness,
Till all our strivings cease;
Take from our souls the strain and
stress,
And let our ordered lives confess
The beauty of Thy peace.

Breathe thro' the heats of our desire
Thy coolness and Thy balm;
Let sense be dumb, let flesh retire;
Speak thro' the earthquake, wind and
fire,
O still small voice of calm!

— *John Greenleaf Whittier*

My Friend

Since Jesus is my Friend,
  And I to Him belong,
It matters not what foes intend,
  However fierce and strong.

He whispers in my breast
  Sweet words of holy cheer:
How they who seek in God their rest
  Shall ever find Him near.

How God hath built above,
  A city fair and new,
Where eye and heart shall see and
    prove
  What faith has counted true.

My heart for gladness springs,
  It cannot more be sad;
For very joy it laughs and sings
  Sees nought but sunshine glad.

The Sun that lights mine eyes
  Is Christ, the Lord I love;
I sing for joy for that which lies
  Stored up for me above.

                — *Paul Gerhardt*

∽

Thy Way, Not Mine

Thy way, not mine, O Lord,
  However dark it be!
Lead me by Thine own hand,
  Choose out the path for me.

Smooth let it be or rough,
  It will be still the best;
Winding or straight, it leads
  Right onward to Thy rest.

I dare not choose my lot;
  I would not, if I might;
Choose Thou for me, my God;
  So shall I walk aright.

The kingdom that I seek
  Is Thine; so let the way
That leads to it be Thine;
  Else I must surely stray.

Take Thou my cup, and it
  With joy or sorrow fill,
As best to Thee may seem;
  Choose Thou my good and ill;

Choose Thou for me my friends,
  My sickness or my health;
Choose Thou my cares for me,
  My poverty or wealth.

Not mine, not mine the choice,
  In things or great or small;
Be Thou my guide, my strength,
  My wisdom, and my all!

                — *Horatius Bonar*

∽

How Can I Doubt?

How can I ever doubt God is
  When all around I see
The wonders of the universe
  God made for you and me?

How can I ever doubt God's love
  When time and time again
His mercy has been shown to me —
  Ah, yes, and to all men!

How can I ever grieve my Lord?
  How can I fail to praise
When day by day He shows His love
  In oh, so many ways?

How can I fear? How can I doubt?
  What else have I beside?
God holds the key, the only key
  That rules both Time and Tide.

                — *Phyllis C. Michael*

✳ WORK ✳

ONE HERE AND THERE

Of all we meet on life's great stream
  There's but one here and there,
Who treasures most the better things
Each man to self most tightly clings,
For self he toils, of self he sings,
  Except one here and there.

The earth would be a darker place
  But for one here and there,
Whose heart with self has not been
    filled,
Whose love for God has not been
    killed,
Whose thankful praise has not been
    stilled;
  There's one such here and there.

And this has been the Lord's wise will
  To find one here and there,
Who counting earthly gain but dross,
Would daily take the Christian cross
E'en at the risk of any loss;
  God finds one here and there.

'Tis not the many that He seeks,
  But just one here and there,
He seeks not all, but jewels fair;
For those who will His sufferings
    share,
And for His sake reproaches bear;
  They're few — one here and there.

But oh! the grandeur of the work
  For this one here and there!
To cheer those weary in the race,
To sinners speak of pardoning grace,
To shed Heav'n's light in every place,
  Let's be one here and there!

— *Author Unknown*

THE HARDER TASK

It's not so hard to ask You, Lord,
To bless all humankind —
The greater task for me may be
To grow more color blind.

It's not so hard to share, dear Lord,
With those in other lands —
It may be lonely folks next door
Who need my helping hands.

It's easy, Lord, to smile at friends
Who wear our kind of clothes —
But smiles I share with humbler souls
May lighten unseen woes.

O stir me, Lord, so that I rise
From prayer and plainly see
The harder tasks right here at home,
The tasks You give to me!

— *Katherine L. Ramsdell*

ϡ

UP, THEN DOWN

Go up unto the mountain of blessing,
Alone with the Master in prayer;
In fellowship sweet
To sit at His feet,
And tarry awhile with Him there.

Then down to the work
In the valley below;
Your face with the love light of Jesus
    aglow.
Then down to the work
In the valley below,
Fearless and freely go.

— *Author Unknown*

689

BE KIND NOW

If you have a kind word, say it,
  Throbbing hearts soon sink to rest;
If you owe a kindness, pay it,
  Life's sun hurries to the west.

Can you do a kind deed? Do it,
  From despair a soul to save;
Bless each day as you pass through it,
  Marching onward to the grave.

If of something for tomorrow
  You are dreaming, do it now;
From the future do not borrow;
  Frost soon gathers on the brow.

Days for deeds are few, my brother,
  Then today fulfill thy vow;
If you mean to help another,
  Do not dream it, do it now.

— *Author Unknown*

THE PATIENT POTTER

The potter stood at his daily work,
  One patient foot on the ground;
The other with never slackening speed,
  Turning his swift wheel round.
Silent we stood beside him there,
  Watching the restless knee,
Till my friend said low, in pitying
    voice,
  "How tired his foot must be."

The potter never paused in his work,
  Shaping the wondrous thing;
'Twas only a common flower pot,
  But perfect in fashioning.
Slowly he raised his patient eyes
  With homely truth inspired:
"No, ma'am; it isn't the foot that kicks,
  The one that stands gets tired."

— *Author Unknown*

THE SECOND MILE

Stern Duty said, "Go walk a mile
  And help thy brother bear his load."
I walked reluctant, but, meanwhile,
  My heart grew soft with help be-
    stowed.
Then Love said, "Go another mile."
  I went, and Duty spake no more,
But Love arose and with a smile
  Took all the burden that I bore.
'Tis ever thus when Duty calls;
  If we spring quickly to obey,
Love comes, and whatso'er befalls,
  We're glad to help another day.
The second mile we walk with joy;
  Heaven's peace goes with us on the
    road,
So let us all our powers employ
  To help our brother bear life's load.

— *Stephen Moore*

O TO BE UP AND DOING

O to be up and doing, O
Unfearing and unshamed to go
In all the uproar and the press
About my human business! . . .
For still the Lord is Lord of might:
In deeds, in deeds he takes delight;
The plough, the spear, the laden barks,
The field, the founded city, marks;
He marks the smiler of the streets,
The singers upon garden seats; . . .
Those he approves that ply the trade,
That rock the child, that wed the
    maid,
That with weak virtues, weaker hands,
Sow gladness on the peopled lands,
And still with laughter, song and
    shout,
Spin the great wheel of earth about.

— *Robert Louis Stevenson*

WHEN THINGS GO WRONG

Do not spend your time in fretting;
Spend it, rather, in forgetting
    Little things that wound you so.
    Do not let the whole world know
That you'd rather sit a-grieving
When you might be out relieving
    Pain and care. Rise up, be true!
    Just find something good to do.

When your days are full of sighing,
Don't give up, but keep on trying
    Some good cause to help along,
    You will soon forget the wrong
That the dismal days are bringing,
If you time your work to singing.
    When your skies are dark in hue,
    Just find something good to do.

When your life seems full of trouble,
Pain and care will always double,
    If you talk about your woes;
    Also will your skies disclose
Brighter tints upon the morrow,
When the lessons taught by sorrow
    Help instead of hinder you.
    Just find something good to do.

Spend no time in dull repining;
Everywhere the sun is shining.
    And the future ways are bright,
    If we truly see aright.
Life is what we make it, truly,
And 'twill seldom go unruly
    If the right course we pursue —
    Just find something good to do.

— *Author Unknown*

∽

MY PRAYER

Oh, Lord, I cannot teach another
    Of his need for Thee.
I cannot tell him nor convince him,
    Not I; but Thou in me.

I cannot do my daily tasks
    And still from fear be free.
I can't stop worrying at maybes.
    Not I; but Thou in me.

I cannot let tomorrow beckon
    And yet from care be free.
I cannot let past be forgotten.
    Not I; but Thou in me.

I cannot live the way of Jesus
    Loving tenderly
All in the world, good or sinful.
    Not I; but Thou in me.

I cannot serve Thee as I ought.
    I make this giant plea:
My Lord, please lead me, guide me,
        use me;
    The rest I leave to Thee.

— *Loraine Burdick*

∽

YOUR CORNER

Are you busy in the corner
    God entrusted to your care?
One small portion of God's vineyard
    Is appointed as your share.

Each man has his work assigned him,
    Each one has his special task.
"What have you accomplished,
        brother?"
    Christ will soon return to ask.

Have you sowed the seed, or watered
    What another man has sown?
Have you brought some soul to Jesus?
    Has God's love to him been shown?

Oh, God wants your little corner
    To reflect His loving care;
And He wants its fruit to ripen
    For the harvest "over there."

— *Mary Harrington*

SERVICE

I asked the Lord to let me do
  Some mighty work for Him;
To fight amidst His battle hosts,
  Then sing the victor's hymn;
I longed my ardent love to show,
But Jesus would not have it so.

He placed me in a quiet home,
  Whose life was calm and still,
And gave me little things to do
  My daily round to fill;
I could not think it good to be
Just put aside so silently.

Small duties gathered 'round my way;
  They seemed of earth alone.
I, who had longed for conquest bright
  To lay before His throne,
Had common things to do and bear,
To watch and strive with daily care.

So as I thought my prayer unheard,
  And asked the Lord once more
That He would give me work for Him,
  And open wide the door —
Forgetting that my Master knew
Just what was best for me to do.

Then quietly the answer came —
  "My child, I hear thy cry;
Think not that mighty deeds alone
  Will bring the victory;
The battle has been planned by Me,
Let daily life thy conquests see."

— *Author Unknown*

I DO NOT FEAR TOMORROW

I do not fear tomorrow
  For I have lived today
And though my course was stormy,
  My Pilot knew the way.

I do not fear tomorrow —
  I shall not sail alone.
The same true Pilot shall be with me
  For He never forsakes His own.

I do not fear tomorrow!
  If the sails set east or west,
On sea or safe in harbor,
  In Him, secure, I rest.

— *Phyllis C. Michael*

YOUR FIELD OF LABOR

If you cannot on the ocean
  Sail among the swiftest fleet,
Rocking on the highest billows,
  Laughing at the storms you meet,
You can stand among the sailors
  Anchored yet within the bay;
You can lend a hand to help them,
  As they launch their boats away.

If you are too weak to journey
  Up the mountain steep and high,
You can stand within the valley
  While the multitudes go by;
You can chant in happy measure
  As they slowly pass along,
Though they may forget the singer,
  They will not forget the song.

Do not, then, stand idly waiting
  For some greater work to do;
Fortune is a lazy goddess,
  She will never come to you;
Go, and toil in any vineyard,
  Do not fear to do or dare;
If you want a field of labor,
  You can find it anywhere.

— *Ellen H. Cotes*

SPEAK OUT

We are not here to play, to dream, to drift,
We have hard work to do, and loads to lift.
Shun not the struggle; face it. 'Tis God's gift.
Say not the days are evil — who's to blame?
And fold the hands and acquiesce — O shame!
Stand up, speak out, and bravely, in God's name.
It matters not how deep entrenched the wrong,
How hard the battle goes, the day how long,
Faint not, fight on! Tomorrow comes the song.

— Maltbie D. Babcock

👁

LINGER NOT!

The time is short!
If thou would'st work for God it must be now;
If thou would'st win the garland for thy brow,
Redeem the time!

Shake off earth's sloth!
Go forth with staff in hand while yet 'tis day,
Set out with girded loins upon the way;
Up! linger not!

Fold not thy hands!
What has the pilgrim of the cross and crown
To do with luxury or couch of down?
On! pilgrim on!

With His reward
He comes; He tarries not; His day is near;
When men least look for Him will He be here.
Prepare for Him!

Let not the flood
Sweep thy firm feet from the eternal rock;
Face calmly, solemnly, the billow's shock,
Nor fear the storm.

Withstand the foe!
Die daily, that thou mayest forever live,
Be faithful unto death; thy Lord will give
The crown of life.

— Horatius Bonar

THE WHOLE ARMOR

Soldiers of Christ, arise,
  And put your armor on,
Strong in the strength which God sup-
      plies
  Through his eternal Son;
Strong in the Lord of Hosts,
  And in his mighty power;
Who in the strength of Jesus trusts,
  Is more than conqueror.

Stand, then, in his great might,
  With all his strength endued;
But take, to arm you for the fight,
  The panoply of God:
That, having all things done,
  And all your conflicts past,
Ye may o'ercome, thro' Christ alone,
  And stand entire at last.

Stand, then, against your foes,
  In close and firm array:
Legions of wily fiends oppose
  Throughout the evil day:
But meet the sons of night,
  But mock their vain design,
Armed in the arms of heavenly light,
  Of righteousness divine.

Leave no unguarded place,
  No weakness of the soul;
Take every virtue, every grace,
  And fortify the whole:
Indissolubly joined,
  To battle all proceed;
But arm yourselves with all the mind
  That was in Christ your Head.

But above all lay hold
  On faith's victorious shield;
Armed with that adamant and gold,
  Be sure to win the field:
If faith surround your heart,
  Satan shall be subdued;
Repelled his every fiery dart,
  And quenched with Jesus' blood.

Jesus hath died for you;
  What can his love withstand?
Believe, hold fast your shield, and who
  Shall pluck you from his hand?
Believe that Jesus reigns;
  All power to him is given:
Believe, till freed from sin's remains;
  Believe yourselves to heaven.

To keep your armor bright,
  Attend with constant care,
Still walking in your Captain's sight,
  And watching unto prayer.
Ready for all alarms,
  Steadfastly set your face,
And always exercise your arms,
  And use your every grace.

Pray, without ceasing pray,
  Your Captain gives the word;
His summons cheerfully obey,
  And call upon the Lord:
To God your every want
  In instant prayer display;
Pray always; pray, and never faint;
  Pray, without ceasing pray.

In fellowship alone,
  To God with faith draw near;
Approach his courts, besiege his throne
  With all the power of prayer:
His mercy now implore,
  And now show forth his praise;
In shouts, or silent awe, adore
  His miracles of grace.

To God your spirits dart;
  Your souls in words declare;
Or groan, to him who reads the heart,
  The unutterable prayer:
His mercy now implore,
  And now show forth his praise;
In shouts, or silent awe, adore
  His miracles of grace.

Pour out your souls to God,
And bow them with your knees;
And spread your heart and hands
abroad,
And pray for Zion's peace:
Your guides and brethren bear
Forever on your mind;
Extend the arms of mighty prayer,
In grasping all mankind.

From strength to strength go on;
Wrestle and fight and pray;
Tread all the powers of darkness down,
And win the well-fought day:
Still let the Spirit cry,
In all his soldiers, — Come,
Till Christ the Lord descend from
high,
And take the conquerors home.

— *Charles Wesley*

ZEAL IN LABOR

Go, labor on; spend and be spent,
Thy joy to do the Father's will;
It is the way the Master went;
Should not the servant tread it still?

Go, labor on; 'tis not for naught;
Thine earthly loss is heavenly gain;
Men heed thee, love thee, praise thee
not;
The Master praises — what are men?

Go, labor on; your hands are weak;
Your knees are faint, your soul cast
down;
Yet falter not; the prize you seek
Is near -- a kingdom and a crown!

Toil on, faint not; keep watch and
pray!
Be wise the erring soul to win;
Go forth into the world's highway;
Compel the wanderer to come in.

Toil on, and in thy toil rejoice;
For toil comes rest, for exile home;
Soon shalt thou hear the Bridegroom's
voice
The midnight peal, "Behold, I
come!"

— *Horatius Bonar*

THE FAITHFUL FEW

In every church, in every clime,
When there's some work to do,
It very likely will be done
By just the Faithful Few.

While many folks will help to sing,
And some of them will talk,
When it comes down to doing things,
A lot of them will balk.

"We can't do this, we can't do that,
Excuse us, please, this time.
We'd be so glad to help you out,
But it's not in our line."

So when a leader casts about
To find someone "who'll do,"
Although he's done it oft before,
He asks the Faithful Few.

Of course they're very busy, too,
And always hard at work,
But well he knows they'll not refuse,
Nor any duty shirk.

They never stop to make excuse,
But promptly try to do
The very, very best they can
To smooth the way for you.

God bless, I pray, the Faithful Few,
And may their tribe increase;
They must be very precious to
The blessed Prince of Peace!

— *Author Unknown*

THEY WHO TREAD THE PATH OF LABOR

They who tread the path of labor follow where My feet have trod;
They who work without complaining do the holy will of God;

Where the many toil together, there am I among My own;
Where the tired workman sleepeth, there am I with him alone.

I, the peace that passeth knowledge, dwell amid the daily strife;
I, the bread of heaven, am broken in the sacrament of life.

Every task, however simple, sets the soul that does it free;
Every deed of love and mercy, done to man, is done to Me.

* ·* * * *

Nevermore thou needest seek Me; I am with thee everywhere;
Raise the stone, and thou shalt find Me; cleave the wood, and I am there.

— Henry van Dyke

MY BEST

Though others far exceed me,
In the things that they can do,
I shall not blush when I bring in my sheaves,
If it is the best that I can do.

It is only when we fail to try,
And never when we try and fail,
That we should dread our King's return,
Or in His presence pale.

So look up brother, sister, friend.
Take courage in your trial,
The Savior was with you at your start,
He'll be there in that last long mile.

And when life's sun for you has set,
And the final curtain drawn,
May God be able to say these words,
"My child, your work's well done."

And should I leave ere Jesus comes
And my body be laid to rest,
I would ask no greater words than these:
"On earth she did her best."

— Annabelle Jones

HOLY FORTITUDE

Am I a soldier of the cross,
    A follower of the Lamb?
And shall I fear to own his cause,—
    Or blush to speak his name?

Must I be carried to the skies
    On flowery beds of ease,
While others fought to win the prize,
    And sailed through bloody seas?

Are there no foes for me to face?
    Must I not stem the flood?
Is this vile world a friend to grace,
    To help me on to God?

Sure I must fight if I would reign;
    Increase my courage, Lord!
I'll bear the toil, endure the pain,
    Supported by thy word.

Thy saints, in all this glorious war,
    Shall conquer though they die:
They see the triumph from afar,
    And seize it with their eye.

When that illustrious day shall rise,
    And all thy armies shine
In robes of victory through the skies,
    The glory shall be thine.

— *Isaac Watts*

YOUR PLACE

Is your place a small place?
    Tend it with care!—
        He set you there.

Is your place a large place?
    Guard it with care!—
        He set you there.

Whate'er your place, it is
    Not yours alone, but His
        Who set you there.

— *John Oxenham*

ONLY A LITTLE TIME

I only have a little time
    To love and serve the Lord;
I only have a little time
    To read and learn His Word.

I only have a little time
    To talk to men for Him;
They only have a little time
    To turn their hearts from sin.

So since the time is short for all
    And shorter still each day,
We seek to learn His blessed will
    We strive to know His way.

For when to fairer realms we go
    And there behold His face,
We'll praise our God for time we gave
    To live and serve by grace.

— *Author Unknown*

NOT TO BE MINISTERED TO

O Lord, I pray
That for this day
I may not swerve
    By foot or hand
    From Thy command
Not to be served, but to serve.

This, too, I pray,
That from this day
No love of ease
    Nor pride prevent
    My good intent
Not to be pleased, but to please.

And if I may,
I'd have this day
Strength from above
    To set my heart
    In heavenly art
Not to be loved, but to love.

— *Maltbie D. Babcock*

The Servant's Path

Servant of Christ, stand fast amid the scorn
   Of men who little know or love the Lord;
Turn not aside from toil; cease not to warn,
   Comfort and teach. Trust Him for thy reward.
A few more moments' suffering, and then
Cometh sweet rest from all thy heart's deep pain.

Have friends forsaken thee and cast thy name
   Out as a worthless thing? Take courage then;
Go tell thy Master; for they did the same
   To Him, who once in patience toiled for them,
Yet He was perfect in all service here;
Thou oft hast failed; this maketh Him more dear.

Self-vindication shun; if in the right,
   What gainest thou by taking from God's hand
Thy cause? If wrong, what dost thou but invite
   Satan himself thy friend in need to stand?
Leave all with God. If right, He'll prove thee so;
If not, He'll pardon; therefore to Him go.

"The time is short"; seek little here below;
   Earth's goods would cumber thee and drag thee down.
Let daily food suffice; care not to know
   Thought for tomorrow — it may never come.
Thou canst not perish, thy Lord is nigh,
And His own care will all thy need supply.

— Author Unknown

The Minister's Wife

You may sing of your heroes of war and of peace,
Your soldiers of fortune or strife;
When the tumult shall die, and the shouting shall cease,
Let me sing of the minister's wife.

You may laud to the skies all the learned and wise,
The servants with dignities rife;
My heart says amen, but I take up my pen
In praise of the minister's wife.

Oh, the minister's wife is a cook and a clerk;
A dressmaker, mother, and nurse;
A wonderful teacher, a maid-of-all-work,
And a player and singer, of course!

She must listen, with nerves that are raw to the quick
To heartaches and troubles galore;
She must welcome the stranger, and visit the sick,
Wearing dresses her sister once wore.

She must work with the Aid, and the junior Hi-Y;
She must help with the Sunday school stunts;
Be a leader in missions, or tell us all why;
And not miss a prayer meeting once!

She must comfort her husband when Monday's are blue
And smooth out his trials — and coats;
Be ready to move every twelvemonth or two
When he shepherds new sheep, (and new goats).

And whether the weather be cloudy or bright;
In season or out — all the while,
If her heart it be heavy, or if it be light —
She must smile, smile, smile!

Oh, sing of the noble, the great, and the good,
Whom you meet in the course of your life;
I take up the strain, be it here understood,
In praise of the minister's wife!

— *Author Unknown*

ॐ

WORK

Let me but do my work from day to day
   In field or forest, at desk or loom,
   In roaring market-place or tranquil room;
Let me but find it in my heart to say,
When vagrant wishes beckon me astray,
   "This is my work; my blessing, not my doom;
   Of all who live, I am the one by whom
This work can best be done in the right way."

Then shall I see it not too great, nor small,
   To suit my spirit and to prove my powers;
   Then shall I cheerful greet the labouring hours,
And cheerful turn, when the long shadows fall
At eventide, to play and love and rest,
Because I know for me my work is best.

— *Henry van Dyke*

WORKING IN THE VINEYARD

In the vineyard of our Father
　Daily work we find to do;
Scattered gleanings we may gather,
　　Though we are but young and few;
　　Little clusters
　Help to fill the garners too.

Toiling early in the morning,
　Catching moments through the day,
Nothing small or lowly scorning,
　　While we work, and watch, and
　　　　　pray;
　　Gathering gladly
　Free-will offerings by the way.

Not for selfish praise or glory,
　Not for objects nothing worth,
But to send the blessed story
　　Of the gospel o'er the earth,
　　Telling mortals
　Of our Lord and Saviour's birth.

Up and ever at our calling,
　Till in death our lips are dumb,
Or till, sin's dominion falling,
　　Christ shall in his kingdom come,
　　And his children
　Reach their everlasting home.

Steadfast, then, in our endeavor,
　Heavenly Father, may we be;
And forever, and forever,
　　We will give the praise to thee;
　　Hallelujah
　Singing, all eternity!

　　　　　— *Thomas MacKellar*

ᢍ

REST

Rest is not quitting
　This busy career;
Rest is the fitting
　Of self to one's sphere.

'Tis the brook's motion,
　Clear without strife,
Fleeing to the ocean
　After its life.

'Tis loving and serving
　The highest and best;
'Tis onward, unswerving:
　And this is true rest.

　　　　　— *Johann Wolfgang von Goethe*

ᢍ

A SURE PROMISE

In the common round of duty
　Lift thy heart in praise;
For the Lord hath surely promised
　Strength for all thy days.

　　　　　— *Herbert G. Tovey*

ᢍ

LESSON OF LOVE

O how can they look up to heaven,
　And ask for mercy there,
Who never soothed the poor man's
　　　　　pang,
　Nor dried the orphan's tear?

The dread omnipotence of heaven
　We every hour provoke;
Yet still the mercy of our God
　Withholds the avenging stroke.

And Christ was still the healing friend
　Of poverty and pain;
And never did imploring soul
　His garment touch in vain.

May we with humble effort take
　Example from above;
And thence the active lesson learn
　Of charity and love!

　　　　　— *Simon Browne*

DAILY WORK

In the name of God advancing,
Sow thy seed at morning light;
Cheerily the furrows turning,
  Labor on with all thy might.
Look not to the far-off future,
  Do the work which nearest lies;
Sow thou must before thou reapest,
  Rest at last is labor's prize.

Standing still is dangerous ever,
  Toil is meant for Christians now;
Let there be, when evening cometh,
  Honest sweat upon thy brow;
And the Master shall come smiling,
  At the setting of the sun,
Saying, as he pays thy wages,
  "Good and faithful one, well done!"

          — Author Unknown

WORK — *A Song of Triumph*

Work!
Thank God for the might of it,
The ardor, the urge, the delight of it—
Work that springs from the heart's desire,
Setting the brain and the soul on fire—
Oh, what is so good as the heat of it,
And what is so glad as the beat of it,
And what is so kind as the stern command,
Challenging brain and heart and hand?

Work!
Thank God for the pride of it,
For the beautiful, conquering tide of it,
Sweeping the life in its furious flood,
Thrilling the arteries, cleansing the blood,
Mastering stupor and dull despair,
Moving the dreamer to do and dare.
Oh, what is so good as the urge of it,
And what is so glad as the surge of it,
And what is so strong as the summons deep,
Rousing the torpid soul from sleep?

Work!
Thank God for the pace of it,
For the terrible, keen, swift race of it;
Fiery steeds in full control,
Nostrils a-quiver to greet the goal.
Work. the Power that drives behind,
Guiding the purpose, taming the mind,
Holding the runaway wishes back,
Reining the will to one steady track,
Speeding the energies faster, faster,
Triumphing over disaster.
Oh, what is so good as the pain of it,
And what is so great as the gain of it?
And what is so kind as the cruel goad,
Forcing us on thro' the rugged road?

Work!
Thank God for the swing of it,
For the clamoring, hammering ring of it,
Passion of labor daily hurled
On the mighty anvils of the world.
Oh, what is so fierce as the flame of it?
And what is so huge as the aim of it?
Thundering on through dearth and doubt,
Calling the plan of the Maker out.
Work, the Titan; Work, the friend,
Shaping the earth to a glorious end,
Draining the swamps and blasting the hills,
Doing whatever the Spirit wills —
Rending a continent apart,
To answer the dream of the Master heart.
Thank God for a world where none may shirk —
Thank God for the splendor of work!

          — Angela Morgan

O MASTER OF THE LOVING HEART

O Master of the loving heart,
  The Friend of all in need,
We pray that we may be like Thee
  In thought and word and deed.

Thy days were full of kindly acts;
  Thy speech was true and plain;
And no one ever sought Thee, Lord,
  Or came to Thee in vain.

Thy hand was warm with sympathy;
  Thy hand God's strength revealed;
Who saw Thy face or felt Thy touch
  Were comforted and healed.

O grant us hearts like Thine, dear
    Lord;
  So joyous, true, and free
That all Thy children everywhere
  Be drawn by us to Thee.

          — Calvin W. Laufer

WATCH, MY SOUL, AND PRAY

Watch, my soul, and pray,
Arm for life's affray.
When the danger least thou fearest,
Watch, the tempter's snares are
    nearest,

Such is e'er his way:
Watch, my soul, and pray.

Watch and pray, my soul,
Flesh and blood control;
When the world, in tempting story,
Tells of pleasure, wealth, and glory,
Be not led astray:
Watch, my soul, and pray.

See the goodly land
On the heav'nly strand;
See God's people, thither tending,
Through the sea and desert wending,
Led by Joshua's hand:
Seek the godly land.

Through thy pilgrimage
Guard thy heritage:
Pray and fight, on Christ relying,
Live to Him, thyself denying;
Onward to the goal,
Win the crown, my soul!

Watch, and fight, and pray
Through this mortal day;
Soon thy Canaan thou attainest,
Soon the crown and palm thou gainest,
Peace is won for aye;
Watch, my soul, and pray.

          — Johan Olof Wallin

ON HIS BLINDNESS

When I consider how my light is spent
Ere half my days in this dark world and wide,
And that one talent, which is death to hide,
Lodged with me useless, though my soul more bent
To serve therewith my Maker, and present
My true account, lest He returning chide;
"Doth God exact day-labor, light denied?"
I fondly ask. But Patience, to prevent
That murmur, soon replies, "God doth not need

Either man's work or his own gifts; who best
Bear his mild yoke, they serve him best; his state
Is kingly; thousands at his bidding speed,
And post o'er land and ocean without rest;
They also serve who only stand and wait."

— *John Milton*

Work, for the Night Is Coming

Work, for the night is coming, Work thro' the morning hours;
Work while the dew is sparkling, Work 'mid springing flowers
Work when the day grows brighter, Work in the glowing sun;
Work, for the night is coming, When man's work is done.

Work, for the night is coming, Work thro' the sunny noon;
Fill brightest hours with labor, Rest comes sure and soon.
Give every flying minute Something to keep in store:
Work, for the night is coming, When man works no more.

Work, for the night is coming, Under the sunset skies;
While their bright tints are glowing, Work, for daylight flies.
Work till the last beam fadeth, Fadeth to shine no more;
Work while the night is darkening, When man's work is o'er.

— *Annie L. Coghill*

Lord of All Pots and Pans and Things

Lord of all pots and pans and things, since I've not time to be
A saint by doing lovely things or watching late with Thee,
Or dreaming in the dawn light or storming Heaven's gates,
Make me a saint by getting meals and washing up the plates.

Although I must have Martha's hands, I have a Mary mind
And when I black the boots and shoes, Thy sandals, Lord, I find.
I think of how they trod the earth, what time I scrub the floor;
Accept this meditation, Lord, I haven't time for more.

Warm all the kitchen with Thy love, and light it with Thy peace.
Forgive me all my worrying and make my grumbling cease.
Thou who didst love to give men food, in room or by the sea,
Accept this service that I do, I do it unto Thee.

*This poem has been attributed to various authors but appears to be
reworked from "The Divine Office of the Kitchen" by Cecily Hallack.*

The Master's Touch

"He touched her hand, and the fever left her."
  He touched her hand as He only can,
With the wondrous skill of the great Physician,
  With the tender touch of the Son of Man,
And the fever pain in the throbbing temples
  Died out with the flush on brow and cheek;
And the lips that had been so parched and burning
  Trembled with thanks that she could not speak;
And the eyes, where the fever light had faded,
  Looked up — by her grateful tears made dim;
And she rose and ministered to her household —
  She rose and ministered unto Him.

"He touched her hand, and the fever left her."
  Oh blessed touch of the Man Divine!
So beautiful then to rise and serve Him
  When the fever is gone from your life and mine;
It may be the fever of restless serving,
  With heart all thirsty for love and praise,
And eyes all aching and strained with yearning
  Toward self-set goals in the future days;
Or it may be a fever of spirit anguish,
  Some tempest of sorrrow that dies not down
Till the cross at last is in meekness lifted
  And the head stoops low for the thorny crown;
Or it may be a fever of pain and anger,
  When the wounded spirit is hard to bear,
And only the Lord can draw forth the arrows
  Left carelessly, cruelly ranking there.

Whatever the fever, His touch can heal it;
  Whatever the tempest, his voice can still;
There is only joy as we seek His pleasure;
  There is only a rest as we seek His will —
And some day after life's fitful fever,
  I think we shall say in the home on high:
"If the hands that He touched but did His bidding
  How little it matters what else went by!"

Ah, Lord! Thou knowest us altogether,
  Each heart's sore sickness, whatever it be,
Touch Thou our hands! Let the fever leave us —
  And so shall we minister unto Thee!

              — *Author Unknown*

GOD'S VIEW OF SERVICE

All service ranks the same with God:
If now, as formerly he trod
Paradise, his presence fills
Our earth, each day only as God wills
Can work — God's puppets, best and
   worst,
Are we; there is no last nor first.

Say not "a small event"! Why "small"?
Costs it more pain than this, ye call
A "great event," should come to pass,
Than that? Untwine me from the
   mass
Of deeds which make up life, one deed
Power shall fall short in or exceed!

— Robert Browning

NOT MINE

It is not mine to run
  With eager feet
Along life's crowded ways,
  My Lord to meet.

It is not mine to pour
  The oil and wine,
Or bring the purple robe
  And linen fine.

It is not mine to break
  At his dear feet
The alabaster-box
  Of ointment sweet.

It is not mine to bear
  His heavy cross,
Or suffer, for his sake,
  All pain and loss.

If I, in harvest-fields
  Where strong ones reap,
May bind one golden sheaf
  For Love to keep;

May speak one quiet word
  When all is still,
Helping some fainting heart
  To bear thy will;

Or sing one high, clear song,
  On which may soar
Some glad soul heavenward,
  I ask no more!

— Julia C. R. Dorr

GRACE TO SHARE

Lord, give me grace to share from day to day
In office, home or in the market place
Some love, good will, a loaf, a smiling face
With those I chance to meet along the way;
Let me by Christian faith and works portray
Thy love by what I do, and help erase
Some wrong and lift some load without a trace
Of bigotry; this is the prayer I pray.

Forbid that I should close my heart or hands
Before Thy altar or my brother's need;
Renew the vision that my soul may heed
The call to share in this and other lands;
Give me faith to pray, "Thy kingdom come,"
And sharing grace for world-wide Christendom.

— Carlton Buck

THE WATERED LILIES

The Master stood in His garden,
  Among the lilies so fair,
Which His own right hand had
      planted
  And trained with tend'rest care;

He looked at their snowy blossoms,
  And marked with observant eye
That His flow'rs were sadly drooping,
  For their leaves were parched and
      dry.

"My lilies have need to be watered,"
  The Heavenly Master said;
"Wherein shall I draw it for them,
  And raise each drooping head?"

Close, close to His feet, in the path-
      way,
  All empty and frail and small,
Was an earthen vessel lying,
  Which seemed of no use at all.

But the Master saw and raised it
  From the dust in which it lay,
And smiled as He gently whispered,
  "My work it shall do today."

"It is but an earthen vessel,
  But close it is lying to me;
It is small, but clean, and empty —
  That is all it needs to be."

So forth to the fountain He bore it,
  And filled it full to the brim;
How glad was the earthen vessel
  To be of some use to Him!

He poured forth the living water
  All over His lilies so fair,
Till empty was the vessel,
  And again He filled it there.

The drooping lilies were watered
  Until all revived again;
And the Master saw with pleasure
  That His labor had not been in vain.

His own hand drew the water
  Which refreshed the thirsty flow'rs;
But He used the earthen vessel
  To convey the living show'rs.

And so to itself it whispered,
  As He laid it aside once more,
"Still will I lie in His pathway,
  Just where I did before.

"Close would I keep to the Master,
  And empty would I remain;
Perhaps some day He may use me
  To water His flow'rs again."

                    — *Author Unknown*

JESUS THE CARPENTER

If I could hold within my hand
  The hammer Jesus swung,
Not all the gold in all the land,
Nor jewels countless as the sand,
  All in the balance flung,
Could weigh the value of that thing
Round which His fingers once did
      cling.

If I could have the table Christ
  Once made in Nazareth,
Not all the pearls in all the sea,
Nor crowns of kings or kings to be
  As long as men have breath,
Could buy that thing of wood He
      made —
The Lord of Lords who learned a trade.

Yea, but His hammer still is shown
  By honest hands that toil,
And round His table men sit down;
And all are equals, with a crown
  Nor gold nor pearls can soil;
The shop of Nazareth was bare —
But brotherhood was builded there.

                    — *Charles M. Sheldon*

TOMORROW

He was going to be all that a mortal could be —
    Tomorrow.
No one should be kinder or braver than he —
    Tomorrow.
A friend who was weary and troubled he knew
Who'd be glad of a laugh and who needed it, too,
On him he would call and see what he could do
    Tomorrow.

Each morning he stacked up the letters he'd write —
    Tomorrow.
And thought of the folks he would fill with delight —
    Tomorrow.
It was too bad, indeed, he was busy today,
And hadn't a minute to stop on his way;
More time I will have to give others, he'd say,
    Tomorrow.

The greatest of workers this man would have been —
    Tomorrow.
The world would have known him had he ever seen
    Tomorrow.
But the fact is, he died and he faded from view,
And all that he left here when living was through
Was a mountain of things he intended to do
    Tomorrow.

— Author Unknown

ᕲᕳ

LIFTERS AND LEANERS

There are two kinds of people on earth to-day,
Just two kinds of people, no more, I say.
Not the rich and the poor, for to count a man's wealth
You must first know the state of his conscience and health.
Not the humble and proud, for, in life's little span,
Who puts on airs is not counted a man.
Not the happy and sad, for the swift flying years
Bring each man his laughter and each man his tears.
No, the two kinds of people on earth I mean
Are the people who lift and the people who lean.
Wherever you go you will find the world's masses
Are always divided in just these two classes;

And oddly enough you will find, too, I ween,
There's only one lifter to twenty who lean.
In which class are you? Are you easing the load
Of overtaxed lifters who toil down the road?
Or are you a learner who lets others bear
Your portion of labor and worry and care?

— Ella Wheeler Wilcox

ↄ

Send Me

Use me, God, in Thy great harvest field,
Which stretcheth far and wide like a wide sea;
The gatherers are so few; I fear the precious yield
Will suffer loss. Oh, find a place for me!
A place where best the strength I have will tell:
It may be one the older toilers shun;
Be it a wide or narrow place, 'tis well
So that the work it holds be only done.

— Christina Rossetti

ↄ

God's Saints

Stars are of mighty use: the night
  Is dark and long
The road foal — and where one goes
  right,
  Six may go wrong.
  One twinkling ray
  Shot o'er some cloud,
  May clear much way
  And guide a crowd.

God's saints are shining lights: who
  stays
  Here long, must pass
O'er hills, swift streams, and steep
  ways
  As smooth as glass;
  But these, all night,
  Like candles, shed
  Their beams, and light
  Us into bed.

— Henry Vaughan

ↄ

Teach Us to Serve Thee, Lord

Teach us, good Lord, to serve Thee as Thou deservest:
To give and not to count the cost;
To fight and not to heed the wounds;
To toil and not to seek for rest;
To labor and not ask for any reward
    save that of knowing that we do Thy will. Amen.

— St. Ignatius of Loyola

MY OFFERING

Master, no offering
Costly and sweet,
May we, like Magdalene,
Lay at Thy feet;
Yet may love's incense rise,
Sweeter than sacrifice,
Dear Lord, to Thee.

Daily our lives would show
Weakness made strong,
Toilsome and gloomy ways
Brightened with song;
Some deeds of kindness done,
Some souls by patience won,
Dear Lord, to Thee.

Some word of hope for hearts
Burdened with fears,
Some balm of peace for eyes
Blinded with tears,
Some dews of mercy shed,
Some wayward footsteps led,
Dear Lord, to Thee.

Thus, in Thy service, Lord,
Till eventide
Closes the day of life,
May we abide;
And when earth's labors cease,
Bid us depart in peace,
Dear Lord, to Thee.

— *Edwin P. Parker*

CHRISTIAN SOUL

Christian soul, the times are calling,
Altars falling,
Men's hearts failing them for fear;
Unto thee their eyes are turning,
Spirits yearning,
For the word of faith and cheer.

Christian soul, great deeds await thee,
Consecrate thee
To the task that nearest lies;

Question not that God will use thee,
Nor refuse thee
Blessing on thy sacrifice.

Walk thou not as one benighted,
Nor affrighted,
Where the foolish see no God;
Thine to glimpse the fiery column,
Thine the solemn
Comfort of His staff and rod!

— *Louise Betts Edwards*

HERE AM I

I ask no heaven till earth be Thine;
No glory crown while work of mine
   Remaineth here.

When earth shall shine among the
   stars,
Her sins wiped out, her captives free,
Her voice a music unto Thee,
For crown, more work give Thou to me,
   Lord, here am I.

— *Author Unknown*

WORK

Time worketh; let me work too.
Time undoeth; let me do.
Busy as time, my work I ply
Till I rest in the rest of eternity.

Sin worketh; let me work too.
Sin undoeth; let me do.
Busy as sin, my work I ply
Till I rest in the rest of eternity.

Death worketh; let me work too.
Death undoeth; let me do.
Busy as death, my work I ply
Till I rest in the rest of eternity.

— *Horatius Bonar*

GOD'S GARDENER

Oft times I kneel among the hilltop pine trees,
    In chapel fair, out underneath God's sky;
'Tis here I bring my ev'ry joy and sorrow
    To share with Him who lives and reigns on high;
'Tis here I see the wonders of God's garden,
    Through graceful boughs, like windows arched above;
'Tis here I sing with all God's lowly creatures,
    "I thank Thee, God, for all these things I love."

And as my hands caress the velvet carpet,
    The eager shoots of precious lacy moss
Bespeak the care of One with matchless mercy —
    The One who died for me upon the cross.
The huge carved rocks that form my chapel doorway,
    The crystal spring that is my sacred fount,
The beaten path that leads to fields below me,
    These are among the blessings I can count.

Oh I'm so glad the loving Master chose me
    To work out there among His growing corn!
What joy to feel the soft brown earth at seed-time,
    And know it's mine to till this very morn!
What bless to watch the grain in God's own garden
    All sprouting forth in gladness of rebirth;
Each blade proclaims the resurrection story
    Fulfilled once more in all God's pulsing earth!

This be my pray'r — "Till ev'ning shadows veil me,
    Lord, may I ne'er betray Thy trust in me!
Oh let me be a faithful, humble gard'ner
    Who seeks to bring a harvest home to Thee.
Then with the dawn, O Lord, may I tend gardens
    In other fields, somewhere beyond the sun;
And may I sing Thy praise in other chapels
    Atop a hill, when all my work is done.
                                    — *Phyllis C. Michael*

WANTED — A MESSENGER

The Lord Christ wanted a tongue one day,
    To speak a message of cheer
To a heart that was weary and worn and sad,
    Weighed down with a mighty fear.
He asked for mine, but, 'twas busy quite,
With my own affairs from morn till night.

The Lord Christ wanted a hand one day
  To do a loving deed;
He wanted two feet on an errand for Him,
  To run with gladsome speed,
But I had need of my own that day;
To His gentle beseeching I answered, "Nay."

So all that day I used my tongue,
  My hands, and my feet as I chose;
I said some hasty, bitter words
  That hurt one heart, God knows.
I busied my hands with worthless play,
And my willful feet went a crooked way.

While the dear Lord grieved, with His work undone,
  For the lack of a willing heart!
Only through men does He speak to men,
  Dumb must He be apart.
I do not know, but I wish today,
I had let the Lord Christ have His way.

— Author Unknown

∾

SERVICE

The bread that bringeth strength I want to give;
The water pure that bids the thirsty live;
I want to help the fainting day by day;
I'm sure I shall not pass again this way.

I want to give the oil of joy for tears,
The faith to conquer crowding doubts and fears;
Beauty for ashes may I give alway;
I'm sure I shall not pass again this way.

I want to give good measure running o'er,
And into angry hearts I want to pour
The answer soft that turneth wrath away;
I'm sure I shall not pass again this way.

I want to give to others hope and faith;
I want to do all that the Master saith;
To meet the needs of others every day;
I'm sure I shall not pass again this way.

—D. S. Ford

Our Work

O hearts are bruised and dead,
  And homes are bare and cold,
And lambs for whom the Shepherd
    bled
  Are straying from the fold!

To comfort and to bless,
  To find a balm for woe,
To tend the lone and fatherless,
  Is angels' work below.

The captive to release,
  To God the lost to bring,
To teach the way of life and peace —
  It is a Christlike thing.

And we believe Thy Word,
  Though dim our faith may be;
Whate'er for Thine we do, O Lord,
  We do it unto Thee.

          —*William W. How*

In the Carpenter Shop

I wish I had been His apprentice,
  To see Him each morning at seven,
As He tossed His gray tunic about Him,
  The Master of earth and of Heaven.
When He lifted the lid of His work-
    chest,
  And opened His carpenter's kit,
And looked at His chisels and augers,
  And took the bright tools out of it;
When He gazed at the rising sun tinting
  The dew on the opening flowers,
And He smiled at the thought of His
    Father
  Whose love floods this fair world of
    ours;
Then fastened the apron about Him,
  And put on His workingman's cap,
And grasped the smooth haft of His ham-
    mer
  To give the bent woodwork a tap,

Saying, "Lad, let us finish this ox yoke,
  The farmer must finish his crop."
Oh, I wish I had been His apprentice
  And worked in the Nazareth shop.

But, still as of old we may serve Him,
  For did not the Carpenter say,—
"Inasmuch . . ." as ye aid my littlest one,
  Ye do it, my friend, for me.
His poor we have always with us
  The lonely, the sick, and the driven
To these we may give of our succor,
  For of such is His Kingdom of Heaven.
The drive of our world is terrific,
  There are many who fall by the way,
We may find them in the street and the
    alley,
  Of our cluttered-up cities today.
They feed on the crumbs from the table
  As did dogs in the Master's day;
Yet we live in plenty and comfort,
  Nor drop them a crumb by the way.
If the Carpenter's yearning for others
  Lived in our hearts, we'd hear Him
    say —
"Give! Give! do not hoard, my brother,
  For this is the abundant way."

          —*Author Unknown*

My Daily Prayer

If I can do some good today,
If I can serve along life's way,
If I can something helpful say,
  Lord, show me how.

If I can right a human wrong,
If I can help to make one strong,
If I can cheer with smile or song,
  Lord, show me how.

If I can aid one in distress,
If I can make a burden less,
If I can spread more happiness,
  Lord, show me how.

          —*Grenville Kleiser*

THE CORN AND THE LILIES

Said the corn to the lilies:
  "Press not near my feet.
You are only idlers,
  Neither corn nor wheat.
Does one earn a living
  Just by being sweet?"

Naught answered the lilies,
  Neither yea nor nay,
Only they grew sweeter
  All the livelong day.
And at last the Teacher
  Chanced to come that way.

While his tired disciples
  Rested at his feet,
And the proud corn rustled,
  Bidding them to eat,
"Children," said the Teacher,
  "The life is more than meat.

"Consider the liles,
  How beautiful they grow!
Never king had such glory,
  Yet no toil they know."
Oh, happy were the lilies
  That he loved them so!

       — *Emily A. Braddock*

GOD'S SYMPHONY

God ever keeps a watchful eye
  Upon the world below;
There is no grief beyond His sight,
  No care He does not know.

There is no prayer He fails to hear
  Or fails to answer soon;
But sometimes He must say, "Not yet!
  All earth must be in tune!"

This world's a kind of symphony
  And we the violins;
The Great Conductor knows the score,
  The note where each begins.

He knows some folks must rest awhile,
  Must listen night and day
Until their hearts find peace within—
  Until they learn His way.

He knows if some play melody
  In tones flute like and clear,
Then some must play the harmony
  To make it sweet to hear.

God ever keeps a watchful eye!
  Have faith! Just wait your cue
Then play with all your heart and soul
  The part God gives to you.

       — *Phyllis C. Michael*

BUILDERS

A builder builded a temple;
  He wrought with care and skill.
Pillars and groins and arches
  Were fashioned to meet his will;
And men said when they saw its
    beauty:
  "It shall never know decay.
Great is thy skill, O builder,
  Thy fame shall endure for aye."

A teacher builded a temple;
  She wrought with skill and care,
Forming each pillar with patience,
  Laying each stone with prayer.
None saw the unceasing effort;
  None knew of the marvelous plan;
For the temple the teacher builded
  Was unseen by the eyes of man.

Gone is the builder's temple;
  Crumbled into the dust,
Pillar and groin and arches
  Food for consuming rust;
But the temple the teacher builded
  Shall endure while the ages roll;
For that beautiful, unseen temple
  Was a child's immortal soul.

       — *Author Unknown*

In the Presence of the King!

I thought that I stood in His presence —
  My bosom storm-shaken with sighs;
I loved Him; ah, yes, how I loved Him,
  And trembled with joy 'neath His eyes!
I walked, with His Spirit around me
  Like sunshine, for years and for years;
His strength and His love had upheld me,
  And banished my sorrows and tears.

And now, as I stood in His presence,
  Unmindful of glories around,
So He, my Beloved, was near me,
  And I sank to my knees, for I found
His hand, with the marks of the nail-points,
  Received for my sins, and for me,
Was stretched o'er my head, as I whispered,
  "Dear Lord, keep me ever by Thee."

I yearned with a rapture of longing
  To feel that blest Hand on my head,
And waited — when, lo, through the silence
  His gentle voice tenderly said:
"What fruit dost thou bring, of thy service?
  What sheaves at My feet canst thou lay?
The fields have long whitened to harvest —
  Hast thou toiled thro' the heat of the day?"

I trembled, and started; the service
  I thought I had rendered to Him,
Seemed naught, with that question before me —
  His love filled my heart to the brim.
I saw at a glance all the millions
  Who knew not of Him — and I wept;
For, oh, there was blood on my garments,
  And grief thro' my whole being swept!

"Dear Master," I whispered, "I love Thee!
  Have pity and mercy, I pray;
I'll carry Thy Name to the millions,
  If Thou wilt but show me the way.

I'll tell of Thy love and compassion —
  The joy when a sinner is saved;
Thy Blood that was shed for their cleansing,
  Thy Name on their foreheads engraved.

"Oh, grant me still time for Thy service,
  And seal me with strength from above;
Touch my lips with a coal from Thine altar,
  And fill me, O Fountain of Love!"
And then came this blessed assurance,
  To thrill me and calm my distress:
"Thy strength is made perfect in weakness,
  And, lo! I am with thee to bless."

                              — *Author Unknown*

 large

Thanksgiving for National Peace

Great Ruler of the earth and skies,
  A word of thine almighty breath
Can sink the world, or bid it rise:
  Thy smile is life, thy frown is death.

When angry nations rush to arms,
  And rage, and noise, and tumult reign,
And war resounds its dire alarms.
  And slaughter dyes the hostile plain.

Thy sovereign eye looks calmly down,
  And marks their course, and bounds their power;
Thy law the angry nations own,
  And noise and war are heard no more.

Then peace returns from balmy wing;
  Sweet peace, with her what blessings fled!
Glad plenty laughs, the valleys sing,
  Reviving commerce lifts her head.

To thee we pay our grateful songs;
  Thy kind protection still implore;
O may our hearts, and lives, and tongues,
  Confess thy goodness, and adore.

                              — *Anne Steele*

THE RISEN LORD

He rose as Mediator strong,
　Redeemer of the race,
And all the great angelic throng
　Fall down before His face.

He rose to heal the broken heart,
　To dry the mourner's tears,
To take the helpless widow's part,
　And drive away her fears.

Disease and death shall both expire,
　And burst shall be the prison,
And men shall be baptized with fire,
　For Jesus Christ is risen.

The earth's a garden of our Lord,
　Instead of thorn the flower.
And men shall preach the living Word
　With pentecostal power.

And all the thunderbolts of wrath
　Are with Him fully stored.
Across the guilty rebel's path
　He is the Risen Lord.

— *H. J. McKinnell*

THANKSGIVING AND PRAISE

Lord, we thank Thee for the beauty
　Of the land in which we live;
Thank Thee for the friends and loved
　　ones
　Thou so graciously doth give.

Lord, we thank Thee for the blessings
　That Thy presence doth impart,
Peace that passeth understanding,
　Joy that satisfies the heart.

Lord, we praise Thee for the Giver
　Who has claimed us as His own,
Who, though Lord of highest heaven,
　Make our humble hearts His home.

— *Neva Brien*

SING TO THE LORD OF HARVEST

Sing to the Lord of harvest,
　Sing songs of love and praise;
With joyful hearts and voices
　Your alleluias raise:
By Him the rolling seasons
　In fruitful order move;
Sing to the Lord of harvest
　A song of happy love.

By Him the clouds drop fatness,
　Deserts bloom and spring,
The hills leap up in gladness,
　The valleys laugh and sing:
He filleth with His fullness
　All things with large increase,
He crowns the year with goodness,
　With plenty, and with peace.

— *John Samuel Bewley Monsell*

SUNDAY

When the worn spirit wants repose,
　And sighs her God to seek,
How sweet to hail the evening's close,
　That ends the weary week!

How sweet to hail the early dawn,
　That opens on the sight,
When first that soul-reviving morn
　Sheds forth new rays of light!

Sweet day! thine hours too soon will
　　cease;
　Yet, while they gently roll,
Breathe, Heavenly Spirit, source of
　　peace,
　A Sabbath o'er my soul!

When will my pilgrimage be done,
　The world's long week be o'er,
That Sabbath dawn which needs no
　　sun,
　That day which fades no more?

— *James Edmeston*

IN THE QUIET

In the quiet of the moments
  We devote to worship God
Comes the peace that passes knowledge
  Where old restless doubtings trod.
We relax the tangled tensions
  Of the hours of fret and fear,
And we know the warming presence
  Of the God who's always near.
As we bow in deep devotion
  In the quiet ways of prayer
For the far and hungry-hearted,
  He is here — and he is there.
So we come before him often
  When our hearts are anxious, sad;
And we never leave that hour
  But our hearts are strangely glad.

  — *T. Moore Atkinson*

FULL REDEMPTION

Thou wilt to us Thy Name impart,
  Thou bear'st it not in vain;
What Thou art called Thou surely art,
  Saviour of sinful man;
Into Thy Name, Thy nature, we
  Assuredly believe,
Jesus, from sin, Thee, only Thee,
  Our Jesus we receive.

Our Jesus, Thou from future woe,
  From present wrath Divine,
Shalt save us from our sins below,
  And make our souls like Thine;
Jesus, from all the power of sin,
  From all the being, too,
Thy grace shall make us thro'ly clean,
  And perfectly renew.

Jesus, from pride, from wrath, from
    lust,
  Our inward Jesus be,
From every idle thought, we trust
  To be redeemed by Thee;

When Thou dost in the flesh appear,
  We shall the promise prove,
Saved into all perfection here,
  Renewed in sinless love.

Come, O Thou Prophet, Priest and
    King,
  Thou Son of God and man!
Into our souls Thy fullness bring,
  Instruct, atone, and reign;
Holy and pure, as just and wise,
  We would be in Thy sight:
Less than Thine all cannot suffice,
  We grasp the Infinite.

Our Jesus, Thee, entire and whole,
  With willing heart we take;
Fill ours and every faithful soul
  For Thine own mercies' sake.
We wait to know Thy utmost Name
  The nature's Heavenly powers;
One undivided Christ we claim,
  And all Thou art is ours.

  — *John Wesley*

HOW WONDROUS ARE THY WORKS

How wondrous and great Thy works,
  God of praise!
How just, King of saints,
  And true are Thy ways!
O who shall not fear Thee,
  And honor Thy Name?
Thou only art holy,
  Thou only supreme.

To nations long dark
  Thy light shall be shown;
Their worship and vows
  Shall come to Thy throne;
Thy truth and Thy judgments
  Shall spread all abroad,
Till earth's every people
  Confess Thee their God.

  — *Henry Ustic Onderdonk*

I Stood Alone

I stood alone at sunset
  And watched the clouds drift by;
Each was tinted, shaped and shaded
  By the Painter of the sky.
The heavens were a glory
  With their ever-changing scene,
And the symphony of the color
  Made the landscape calm, serene.

I stood alone at twilight
  Beside a shadowed lake
And listened to the music
  That the woodland creatures make,
The singing of the crickets,
  The whippoorwill's sweet call,
And I reveled in God's presence,
  He who "marks the sparrow's fall."

I stood alone at nightfall
  As the last blush of the day
Had surrendered to the darkness
  On the hilltops far away —
And there on the horizon,
  Brilliant as a fabled gem,
Was the evening star, God's handwork,
  Shining forth its praise to him.

— G. Kearnie Keegan

ᐂ

The Potter's Face

The Potter's face above the clay
  I had not seen before.
My gaze had been upon the pots
  Around the Potter's door.
For some of them were beautiful,
  Their colors won my heart;
And some were simple, useful things
  Designed to play their part.
I saw the wheel that turned and
    turned,
  The hands that deftly pressed:
I saw the growing forms take shape,

And said, "He knoweth best."
But then I saw the Potter's face.
  I looked into his eyes —
The wisdom and the love therein,
  They thrilled me with surprise!
"Indeed, He does know best," I cried,
  "Whose mind designs each vase!"
There is no fear at all for those
  Who watch the Potter's face.

— Hazel H. Simon

ᐂ

Hymn of Praise

Come, thou Fount of every blessing,
  Tune mine heart to sing thy grace;
Streams of mercy, never ceasing,
  Call for songs of loudest praise.

Teach me some melodious sonnet,
  Sung by flaming tongues above;
Praise the mount; I'm fixed upon it!
  Mount of God's unchanging love.

Here I raise my Ebenezer;
  Hither, by thine help, I'm come;
And I hope, by thy good pleasure,
  Safely to arrive at home.

Jesus sought me when a stranger,
  Wandering from the fold of God;
He, to rescue me from danger,
  Interposed with precious blood.

Oh, to grace how great a debtor
  Daily I'm constrained to be!
Let that grace now, like a fetter,
  Bind my wandering heart to thee.

Prone to wander, Lord, I feel it;
  Prone to leave the God I love;
Here's mine heart—oh, take and seal it!
  Seal it from thy courts above.

— Robert Robinson

THE GAIN OF LOSSES

My anxious soul tonight is stirred,
Like some content yet cagéd bird.
I live surrounded by the wealth of pleasure —
Friends, home, delights, enjoyment without measure.
God's voice unto my soul His peace hath spoken;
Our bond of union hath remained unbroken.
Yet, when some heart-loved treasure He denies,
In agony my longing spirit cries:
"Lord, when can I attain to this —
To thank Thee for the things I miss?"

My yielded heart would not rebel;
He doeth all His dealings well.
His watchful eye is o'er His children ever;
His promised care and strength have failed me never.
I know the way Omnipotence hath planned
Must far exceed that formed by man's own hand.
Yet to be really glad He wills it so
Seems more than I can ever feel or know.
I surely cannot utter this —
A prayer of thanks for what I miss.

I wish through grace that He applies
To cease to crave what He denies;
Still, were the gaping wound so truly hidden
That not again would tears gush forth unbidden,
His love henceforth would have no void to fill;
His peace would have no clamoring voice to still;
And I should never feel His love and power
Flooding my soul in every lonely hour.
So, if through loss I find His bliss,
I'll thank Him for the things I miss.

— *Sadie Louise Miller*

FIRST-DAY THOUGHTS

In calm and cool and silence, once again
    I find my old accustomed place among
    My brethren, where, perchance, no human tongue
    Shall utter words; where never hymn is sung,
    Nor deep-toned organ blown, nor censer swung,
Nor dim light falling through the pictured pane!
There, syllabled by silence, let me hear

The still small voice which reached the prophet's ear;
Read in my heart a still diviner law,
Than Israel's leader on this tables saw!
There let me strive with each besetting sin,
     Recall my wandering fancies, and restrain
     The sore disquiet of a restless brain;
     And, as the path of duty is made plain,
May grace be given that I may walk therein,
     Not like the hireling, for his selfish gain,
With backward glances and reluctant tread,
Making a merit of his coward dread,—
     But, cheerful, in the light around me thrown,
     Walking as one to pleasant service led;
     Doing God's will as if it were my own,
Yet trusting not in mine, but in his strength alone!

— *John Greenleaf Whittier*

THE PRINCE OF PEACE

Hark! the glad sound! the Saviour
          comes,
    The Saviour promised long:
Let every heart prepare a throne,
    And every voice a song.

He comes, the prisoners to release
    In Satan's bondage held;
The gates of brass before Him burst,
    The iron fetters yield.

He comes, from the thick films of vice
    To clear the mental ray,
And on the eyeballs of the blind
    To pour celestial day.

He comes, the broken heart to bind,
    The bleeding soul to cure,
And, with the treasures of His grace,
    To enrich the humble poor.

Our glad hosannas, Prince of Peace,
    Thy welcome shall proclaim,
And Heaven's eternal arches ring
    With Thy beloved name.

— *Philip Doddridge*

A SUN-DAY HYMN

Lord of all being! throned afar,
Thy glory flames from sun and star:
Centre and soul of every sphere,
Yet to each loving heart how near!

Sun of our life, thy quickening ray
Sheds on our path the glow of day;
Star of our hope, thy softened light
Cheers the long watches of the night.

Our midnight is thy smile withdrawn;
Our noontide is thy gracious dawn;
Our rainbow arch thy mercy's sign;
All, save the clouds of sin, are thine.

Lord of all life, below, above,
Whose light is truth, whose warmth is
          love,
Before thy ever-blazing throne
We ask no lustre of our own.

Grant us thy truth to make us free,
And kindling hearts that burn for thee,
Till all thy living altars claim
One holy light, one heavenly flame.

— *Oliver Wendell Holmes*

THANKFUL HEARTS

For all that God in mercy sends —
For health and children, home and
    friends,
For comforts in the time of need,
For every kindly word and deed,
For happy thoughts and holy talk,
For guidance in our daily walk —
    In everything give thanks!

For beauty in this world of ours,
For verdant grass and loyal flowers,
For song of birds, for hum of bees,
For the refreshing summer breeze,
For hill and plain, for stream and
    wood,
For the great ocean's mighty flood —
    In everything give thanks!

For the sweet sleep which comes with
    night,
For the returning morning light,
For the bright sun that shines on high,
For the stars glittering in the sky —
For these and everything we see,
O Lord, our hearts we lift to Thee,
    In everything give thanks!

— Author Unknown

HE SHALL BEAR THE GLORY

Sing to God, my spirit, sing
Joyful praise and worship bring
He whom sinners mocked as King —
    He shall bear the glory.

He in lowly guise who came,
Bore the spitting and the shame;
His the highest place and name —
    He shall bear the glory.

He who sorrows pathway trod,
He that every good bestowed,
Son of Man and Son of God,
    He shall bear the glory.

Monarch of the smitten cheek,
Scorn of both the Jew and Greek,
Priest and King, divinely meek —
    He shall bear the glory.

Where the thorn-wreath pressed His
    brow,
Sits the priestly mitre now;
With the many crowns, O how
    He shall bear the glory.

His the grand "eternal weight,"
His the priestly-regal state;
He the Father maketh great —
    He shall bear the glory.

He who died to set me free;
He who lives and loveth me;
He who comes — whom I shall see,
Jesus only, only He —
    He shall bear the glory.

— William Blane

THANKSGIVING

I thank Thee, dear Lord, for my eyes
That see the color of the skies —
The spell that Autumn softly weaves,
The beauty of the changing leaves.

I thank Thee I have ears to hear
The sounds of Nature, sweet and clear;
A robin singing up above,
The voice of someone that I love.

I thank Thee for these lips of mine
That from Thy chalice sip the wine
Of heaven, and their power to sing
My gratitude to Thee, my King.

Oh may these lips and ears and eyes
Be kept from vanity and lies,
That what is beautiful to Thee
I only speak and hear and see.

— Author Unknown

A Thanksgiving Psalm

As the trees shake off their leaves and lift their branches to heaven;
  So my soul sheds its cares and its thoughts of the world and reaches up
    to Thee in adoration;
As the geese, flying southward before the winter wind,
  Seek the warmth of the sun,
So my soul flies to the warmth of Thy love.
  As the black bulbs lie in the warm earth awaiting the spring,
So do I rest in Thy love and Thy law, awaiting Thy bidding to service;
  As the harvest is gathered into the barns against the winter,
So into my soul is gathered Thy bounty and Thy provision.
  Therefore will I praise Thee and will offer thanks in Thy sanctuary;
Every day will I bless Thy holy name and sing a hymn of praise;
  I will thank Thee for Jesus, Thy Son, my Saviour. Amen.

— Author Unknown

Thank Thee, Lord

Lord, we thank Thee for affliction
  How it draws our hearts to Thee!
Though the road be hard and thorny
  Yet Thy face we still can see.

Thank Thee, Lord, for every trial
  Though we do not understand,
Lead us gently step by step
  And hold us by Thy hand.

Alone, we are most needy and
  No worthiness possess;
In Christ we find our All in All,
  Our strength, our righteousness.

We hear Thy kind, constraining voice
  That bids us trust in Thee,
And only in Thy strength we find
  Our all-sufficiency.

Though all of life seems hopeless, still
  God's faithfulness remains;
Thy Holy Word has bathed our hearts
  Thy precious peace sustains.

— Georgia B. Adams

Because of Thy Great Bounty

Because I have been given much,
  I, too, shall give;
Because of Thy great bounty, Lord,
  Each day I live
I shall divide my gifts from Thee
With every brother that I see
Who has the need of help from me.

Because I have been sheltered, fed,
  By Thy good care,
I cannot see another's lack
  And I not share
My glowing fire, my loaf of bread,
My roof's shelter overhead,
That he, too, may be comforted,

Because love has been lavished so
  Upon me, Lord,
A wealth I know that was not meant
  For me to hoard,
I shall give love to those in need,
The cold and hungry clothe and feed,
Thus shall I show my thanks indeed.

— Grace Noll Crowell

WE THANK THEE

We thank Thee, Lord,
That of Thy tender grace,
In our distress
Thou hast not left us wholly comfort-
less.

We thank Thee, Lord,
That of Thy wondrous might,
Into our night
Thou hast sent down the glory of the
Light.

We thank Thee, Lord,
That all Thy wondrous ways,
Through all our days
Are wisdom, right, and ceaseless ten-
derness.

— *John Oxenham*

A LORD'S DAY

O day of rest and gladness,
  O day of joy and light,
O balm of care and sadness,
  Most beautiful, most bright;
On thee, the high and lowly,
  Through ages joined in tune,
Sing, Holy, Holy, Holy,
  To the great God Triune.

On thee, at the creation,
  The light first had its birth;
On thee, for our salvation,
  Christ rose from depths of earth;
On thee, our Lord victorious
  The Spirit sent from heaven,
And thus, on thee most glorious,
  A triple light was given.

Thou art a port protected
  From storms that round us rise,
A garden intersected
  With streams of paradise;

Thou art a cooling fountain,
  In life's dry, dreary sand;
From thee, like Pisgah's mountain,
  We view our promised land.

Thou art a holy ladder,
  Where angels go and come;
Each Sunday finds us gladder,
  Nearer to heaven, our home.
A day of sweet refection
  Thou art, a day of love,
A day of resurrection
  From earth to things above.

To-day on weary nations
  The heavenly manna falls;
To holy convocations
  The silver trumpet calls,—
Where gospel light is glowing
  With pure and radiant beams,
And living water flowing
  With soul-refreshing streams.

New graces ever gaining,
  From this our day of rest,
We reach the rest remaining
  To spirits of the blest;
To Holy Ghost be praises,
  To Father and to Son;
The Church her voice upraises
  To thee, blest Three in One.

— *Christopher Wordsworth*

THANKS

Thank God for Dirty Dishes,
  They have a tale to tell;
While others may go hungry
  We're eating very well,
With Home, Health and Happiness
  I shouldn't want to fuss;
By the stack of Evidence,
  God's been very good to us.

— *Author Unknown*

"THOU ART WORTHY"

Lamb of God! Behold Him ready
  To be offered, waiting there,
Dwelling in a human body,
  Son of God, to Heaven heir!

Master, speak and I will follow,
  Thy disciple gladly be,
Calling others till they enter
  Into fellowship with Thee.

Come and see the wonder-worker.
  He, the Christ of Galilee,
Is the Lord of light and glory,
  King of Israel soon to be!

All for Thee! Heavenly Bridegroom,
  Let Thy pleasure now be mine;
Let me serve Thee here and ever
  For the joy of being Thine.

Thy commands shall be enablings,
  All Thy words becoming deeds,
By the power of love indwelling,
  Whereso'er Thy Spirit leads.

— *Author Unknown*

TESTIMONY

When I lift up my eyes on high
  And see eternal wonders shine,
Can I a glorious God deny,
  Or doubt His sovereignty Divine?

Can I believe these hosts of night
  Just came by chance in time and
    space?
That it so happened that each light
  Just fortunately found its place?

Unnumbered splendors from on high
  The great Creator's hand proclaim
And spread abroad from sky to sky
  The glories of His sovereign Name.

— *Mark Bullock*

AN HOSANNA FOR THE LORD'S DAY

This is the day the Lord hath made,
  He calls the hours his own;
Let heaven rejoice, let earth be glad,
  And praise surround the throne.

To-day he rose and left the dead,
  And Satan's empire fell;
To-day the saints his triumphs spread,
  And all his wonders tell.

Hosanna to the anointed King,
  To David's holy Son;
Help us, O Lord, descend and bring
  Salvation from the throne.

Blest be the Lord, who comes to men
  With messages of grace;
Who comes in God his Father's name,
  To save our sinful race.

Hosanna, in the highest strains
  The Church on earth can raise;
The highest heavens, in which he
    reigns,
  Shall give him nobler praise.

— *Isaac Watts*

BEFORE HIS THRONE

Come, ye that love the Saviour's name,
  And joy to make it known;
The Sovereign of your heart proclaim,
  And bow before His throne.

Lo, He on David's ancient throne,
  His power and grace displays,
While Salem with its echoing hills,
  Sends forth the voice of praise.

Sing, ye redeem'd! Before the throne,
  Ye white-robed myriads fall;
Sing, for the Lord of glory reigns,
  The Christ, the heir of all.

— *Author Unknown*

DEVOTION

If I had met in Galilee
The Man of sweet humility,
And He had turned and looked on me
And called me to His side;
What would have been my answ'ring word?
Should I have said, "My Saviour, Lord,
Thou art beyond all else adored,
Be Thou my Friend and Guide?"

If He had led me, day by day,
In burning heat, 'neath shadows gray,
By dusty path, through tortuous way,
And asked me to be true;
What would have been my choosing then?
Should I have followed on, e'en when,
He took me from loved home and men,
To scenes I never knew?

If He had gone before me till
My day was done, and night's cold chill
Had fallen, with its startling thrill,
Upon my weary soul;
If He had asked me then to lie
In some drear place, 'neath starless sky,
And there, alone, to suffer, die,
Would He have had control?

Yea, if e'en this had been my lot,
Knowing my name would be forgot
And my dead body left to rot,
I should have followed on;
If only, in sweet charity,
My Friend and Guide had stayed with me
And granted me His face to see
Till life's hard toil had gone.

For love does what the Lover saith,
For love transcends the fear of death,
For love loves on till latest breath,
And I do love my Friend;—
Then lead me on, my Master-Guide,
Lead where Thou wilt, Thou Crucified,
Since Thou art mine, what e'er betide,
I'll follow to the end!

—*Henry W. Frost*

HOLY, HOLY, HOLY!

Holy, Holy, Holy! Lord God Almighty!
  Early in the morning our song shall rise to thee;
Holy, Holy, Holy! merciful and mighty!
  God in Three Persons, Blessed Trinity!

Holy, Holy, Holy! all the saints adore thee,
  Casting down their golden crowns around the glassy sea;
Cherubim and seraphim falling down before thee,
  Which wert, and art, and evermore shalt be!

Holy, Holy, Holy! though the darkness hide thee,
  Though the eye of sinful man thy glory may not see,
Only thou art Holy, there is none beside thee,
  Perfect in power, in love, in purity!

Holy, Holy, Holy! Lord God Almighty!
  All thy works shall praise thy name, in earth and sky and sea:
Holy, Holy, Holy! merciful and mighty!
  God in Three Persons, Blessed Trinity!

— Reginald Heber

BLESSING, AND HONOR

Blessing, and honor, and glory, and power,
  Wisdom, and riches, and strength evermore,
Give ye to Him who our battle hath won,
  Whose are the Kingdom, the crown, and the throne.

Dwelleth the light of the glory with Him,
  Light of a glory that cannot grow dim,
Light in its silence and beauty and calm,
  Light in its gladness and brightness and balm.

Ever ascendeth the song and the joy,
  Ever descendeth the love from on high,
Blessing, and honor, and glory, and praise,
  This is the theme of the hymns that we raise.

Life of all life, and true Light of all light,
  Star of the dawning, unchangingly bright,
Sing we the song of the Lamb that was slain,
  Dying in weakness, but rising to reign.

— Horatius Bonar

THE HUNDREDTH PSALM

All people that on earth do dwell,
Sing to the Lord with cheerful voice;
Him serve with fear, his praise forth
tell,
Come ye before him and rejoice.

The Lord, ye know, is God indeed;
Without our aid he did us make:
We are his flock, he doth us feed,
And for his sheep he doth us take.

Oh, enter, then, his gates with praise,
Approach with joy his courts unto;
Praise, laud, and bless his name always,
For it is seemly so to do.

For why? the Lord our God is good,
His mercy is forever sure;
His truth at all times firmly stood,
And shall from age to age endure.

—William Kethe

☙

GOD PRAISED FOR HIS GOODNESS AND TRUTH

I'll praise my Maker with my breath;
And when my voice is lost in death,
Praise shall employ my nobler
powers;
My days of praise shall ne'er be past,
While life and thought and being last,
Or immortality endures.

Why should I make a man my trust?
Princes must die and turn to dust:
Vain is the help of flesh and blood:
Their breath departs, their pomp and
power,
And thoughts all vanish in an hour;
Nor can they make their promise
good.

Happy the man whose hopes rely
On Israel's God: he made the sky,
And earth, and seas, with all their
train;
His truth forever stands secure;
He saves the opprest, he feeds the poor,
And none shall find his promise
vain.

The Lord hath eyes to give the blind;
The Lord supports the sinking mind;
He sends the laboring conscience
peace
He helps the stranger in distress,
The widow and the fatherless,
And grants the prisoner sweet re-
lease.

He loves his saints, he knows them
well;
But turns the wicked down to hell:
Thy God, O Zion, ever reigns:
Let every tongue, let every age,
In this exalted work engage:
Praise him in everlasting strains.

I'll praise him while he lends me
breath;
And when my voice is lost in death,
Praise shall employ my nobler
powers:
My days of praise shall ne'er be past,
While life and thought and being last,
Or immortality endures.

— Isaac Watts

☙

A HEART TO PRAISE THEE

Thou hast given so much to me,
Give one thing more—a grateful heart:
Not thankful when it pleaseth me,
As if thy blessings had spare days,
But such a heart whose Pulse may be
Thy Praise.

— George Herbert

I Sing the Mighty Power of God

I sing the mighty power of God,
That made the mountains rise,
That spread the flowing seas abroad,
And built the lofty skies.
I sing the wisdom that ordained
The sun to rule the day;
The moon shines full at his command,
And all the stars obey.

I sing the goodness of the Lord,
That filled the earth with food;
He formed the creatures with his word,
And then pronounced them good.
Lord, how thy wonders are displayed,
Where'er I turn my eye:
If I survey the ground I tread,
Or gaze upon the sky!

There's not a plant or flower below,
But makes thy glories known;
And clouds arise, and tempests blow,
By order from thy throne,
While all that borrows life from thee
Is ever in thy care,
And everywhere that man can be,
Thou, God, art present there.

— *Isaac Watts*

Sunday Evening

The Sabbath day has reached its close;
Yet, Saviour, ere I seek repose,
Grant me the peace thy love bestows:
    Smile on my evening hour!

O heavenly Comforter, sweet guest!
Hallow and calm my troubled breast;
Weary, I come to thee for rest:
    Smile on my evening hour!

If ever I have found it sweet
To worship at my Saviour's feet,
Now to my soul that bliss repeat:
    Smile on my evening hour!

Let not the gospel seed remain
Unfruitful, or be lost again!
Let heavenly dews descend like rain:
    Smile on my evening hour!

Oh, ever present, ever nigh,
Jesus, on thee I fix mine eye;
Thou hearest the contrite spirit's sigh:
    Smile on my evening hour!

My only Intercessor thou,
Mingle thy fragrant incense now
With every prayer and every vow:
    Smile on my evening hour!

And oh, when life's short course shall
    end,
And death's dark shades around im-
    pend,
My God, my everlasting Friend,
    Smile on my evening hour!

— *Charlotte Elliott*

Summer Days Are Come Again

The summer days are come again;
    Once more the glad earth yields
Her golden wealth of ripening grain,
    And breath of clover fields,
And deepening shade of summer
    woods,
    And glow of summer air,
And winging tho'ts, and happy moods
    Of love and joy and prayer.

The summer days are come again;
    The birds are on the wing;
God's praises, in their loving strain,
    Unconsciously they sing.
We know who giveth all the good
    That doth our cup o'erbrim;
For summer joy in field and wood
    We lift our song to Him.

— *Samuel Longfellow*

LET US WITH A GLADSOME MIND

Let us with a gladsome mind
Praise the Lord, for he is kind;
For his mercies aye endure,
Ever faithful, ever sure.

He, with all commanding might,
Filled the new-made world with light;
For his mercies aye endure,
Ever faithful, ever sure.

He the golden tressèd sun
Caused all day his course to run;
For his mercies aye endure,
Ever faithful, ever sure.

The hornèd moon to shine by night,
'Mid her spangled sisters bright;
For his mercies aye endure,
Ever faithful, ever sure.

All things living he doth feed;
His full hand supplies their need;
For his mercies aye endure,
Ever faithful, ever sure.

Let us with a gladsome mind
Praise the Lord, for he is kind;
For his mercies aye endure,
Ever faithful, ever sure.

— *John Milton*

THIS IS MY FATHER'S WORLD

This is my Father's world,
And to my list'ning ears,
All nature sings, and round me rings
The music of the spheres.
This is my Father's world,
I rest me in the thought
Of rocks and trees, of skies and seas —
His hand the wonders wrought.

This is my Father's world,
The birds their carols raise,
The morning light, the lily white,
Declare their Maker's praise.
This is my Father's world,
He shines in all that's fair;
In the rustling grass I hear Him pass,
He speaks to me ev'rywhere.

This is my Father's world,
O let me ne'er forget
That though the wrong seems oft so strong,
God is the Ruler yet.
This is my Father's world,
The battle is not done,
Jesus who died shall be satisfied,
And earth and heav'n be one.

— *Maltbie D. Babcock*

"I WILL SEND THEM PROPHETS AND APOSTLES"

All that in this wide world we see,
Almighty Father! speaks of thee;
And in the darkness or the day
Thy monitors surround our way.

The fearful storms that sweep the sky,
The maladies by which we die,
The pangs that make the guilty groan,
Are angels from thy awful throne.

Each mercy sent when sorrows lower,
Each blessing of the winged hour,
All we enjoy, and all we love,
Bring with them lessons from above.

Nor thus content, thy gracious hand,
From midst the children of the land,
Hath raised, to stand before our race,
Thy living messengers of grace.

We thank thee that so clear a ray
Shines on thy straight, thy chosen way,
And pray that passion, sloth, or pride
May never lure our steps aside.

— *William Cullen Bryant*

THANKSGIVING

For all true words that have been spoken,
 For all brave deeds that have been done,
For every loaf in kindness broken,
 For every race in valor run,
For martyr lips which have not failed
 To give God praise and smile to rest,
For knightly souls which have not quailed
 At stubborn strife or lonesome quest;
Lord unto whom we stand in thrall
 We give Thee thanks for all, for all.

For each fair field where golden stubble
 Hath followed wealth of waving grain;
For every passing wind of trouble
 Which bends Thy grass that lifts again;
For gold in mine that men must seek,
 For work which bows the sullen knee;
For strength, swift sent to aid the weak,
 For love by which we climb to Thee;
Thy freemen, Lord, yet each Thy thrall,
 We give Thee praise for all, for all.

         — *Margaret E. Sangster*

THE POET

Why hast thou breathed, O God, upon my thoughts
And tuned my pulse to thy high melodies,
Lighting my soul with love, my heart with flame,
Thrilling my ear with songs I cannot keep —
Only to set me in the market place
Amid the clamor of the bartering throng,
Whose ears are deaf to my impassioned plea,
Whose hearts are heedless of the word I bring?

And yet — dear God, forgive! I will sing on.
I will sing until that shining day
When one, perchance, one only may it be —
Shall turn aside from out the sordid way,
List'ning with eager ears that understand
Until that day — thy day — help me to bear
The hurt of cold indifference and the pain
Of seeing all the multitude rush by,
Drowning thy music with their cry for gold!

         — *Angela Morgan*

Have We Not Seen Thy Shining Garment's Hem?

Have we not seen Thy shining garment's hem
Floating at dawn across the golden skies,
Through thin blue veils at noon, bright majesties,
Seen starry hosts delight to gem
The splendour that shall be Thy diadem?

O Immanence, that knows nor far nor near,
But as the air we breathe is with us here,
Our Breath of Life, O Lord, we worship Thee.

Worship and laud and praise Thee evermore,
Look up in wonder, and behold a door
Opened in heaven, and One set on a throne;
Stretch out a hand, and touch Thine own,
O Christ, our King, our Lord whom we adore.

— *Amy Carmichael*

The Name

There is a name, a wondrous name,
Of infinite and endless fame,
By God beloved, by saints revered,
By angels and archangels feared,
Ordained by God ere world began,
Revealed by angels unto man,
Proclaimed by men, believed, adored,
By hearts in prayer and praise outpoured,
The theme of prophet, priest and king,
The word of which sweet psalmists sing,
By pilgrims blessed, by suff'rers sung,
The last word breathed by martyr's tongue,
The name most precious and sublime,
Supreme in space, supreme in time,
Destined to live and conquer all
Till all knees everywhere shall fall
And tongues confess — what God proclaims —
This name to be the Name of names,
The name which in high heaven will be
The One Name of eternity;
Then, O my soul, its praise forthtell,
Jesus — the Name ineffable!

— *Henry W. Frost*

I Thank Thee (*A Prayer*)

I thank Thee, Lord, for beauty in the little things of life —
  For dewdrops on a budding rose, bejeweled in the sun,
For wildflow'rs shyly hiding in a recess of the wood,
  For sweet repose that's mine at last when busy day is done.

I thank Thee for the sky of blue, and for the sky of gray,
  For golden sunshine following the silver of the rain,
For Springtime's glad awakening from winter's dreaming sleep.
  For Seedtime's rich fulfillment in wide fields of ripened grain.

I thank Thee for the warm handclasp of friends who've long proved true,
  I thank Thee for a baby's smile and earnest, lisping prayer;
For all these do I thank Thee, God of Beauty, God of Love —
  These things I see, and O, I know that Thou art everywhere!

                                        — *Dorothy Conant Stroud*

Worship

O holy God, undone by guilt depressing,
We come to Thee, our every sin confessing;
Grant us, we pray, Thy cleansing and Thy blessing;
        We worship Thee, O God!

Look down on us as low we bend before Thee;
Hear Thou our prayer, we fervently implore Thee;
Accept our praise, as our fond hearts adore Thee;
        We worship Thee, O God!

Keep Thou our souls entirely true and holy;
Preserve our spirits deeply pure and lowly;
Add strength to strength that we may serve Thee wholly;
        We worship Thee, O God!

Bind us to Thee that naught from Thee may sever;
Protect our lives that we may grieve Thee never;
Enshrine our hearts that we may love Thee ever;
        We worship Thee, O God!

Give us, at last, the house of Thy preparing,
That face to face, Thy heavenly glory sharing,
We may praise Thee, our love for e'er declaring;
        We worship Thee, O God!

                                        — *Henry W. Frost*

HARVEST-HOME

Come, ye thankful people, come,
Raise the song of Harvest-home!
All is safely gathered in,
Ere the winter-storms begin;
God, our Maker, doth provide
For our wants to be supplied;
Come to God's own temple, come;
Raise the song of Harvest-home!

What is earth but God's own field,
Fruit unto his praise to yield?
Wheat and tares therein are sown,
Unto joy or sorrow grown;
Ripening with a wondrous power,
Till the final Harvest-hour:
Grant, O Lord of life, that we
Holy grain and pure may be.

For we know that thou wilt come,
And wilt take thy people home;
From thy field wilt purge away
All that doth offend, that day;
And thine angels charge at last
In the fire the tares to cast,
But the fruitful ears to store
In thy garner evermore.

Come, then, Lord of mercy, come,
Bid us sing thy Harvest-home!
Let thy saints be gathered in,
Free from sorrow, free from sin;
All upon the golden floor
Praising thee forevermore;
Come, with thousand angels, come;
Bid us sing thy Harvest-home!

— *Henry Alford*

ϭⱳ

I THANK THEE, LORD

All the beauty and the grandeur
  Of the universe is mine!
All the treasures of the ocean
  And the mountain heights sublime!

All the diamond-flashing dewdrops,
  All the sunset's purest gold,
All the sunshine on the meadows
  Mine to have and mine to hold!

I've a friend or two to love me;
  I have all the world to love;
I've the solid earth beneath me
  And the bright blue sky above.
I am heir to barns o'erflowing,
  Cattle on a thousand hills,
While a vested choir of songbirds
  For my pleasure sings and trills.

Should I pine for folds of satin
  I may stoop and pluck a rose;
Or for velvet, seek the woodland
  Where the purple violet grows.
Though my steps be slow and halting,
  Yet I mount on eagle's wing;
I've a royal daughter's birthright
  For my Father is a King.

Some may think my lot is common,
  Mine a life of toil and pain,
If so be their eyes are "holden"—
  For I'm counting all things gain.
I've a heart to sing God's praises
  For the best life does afford;
Words are small and inexpressive
  But for all, I thank thee, Lord.

— *Myra Brooks Welch*

ϭⱳ

PRAISE

What do they know of penitence
  Who never wrought Him wrong?
How can the sinless lift to Him
  Redemption's triumph-song?

There lies an eloquence of praise
  Imprisoned in a tear
And crushed within a broken heart
  That God bends low to hear.

— *Edith Daley*

THOU ART MY VICTORY

I prayed for help, I prayed for strength,
  I prayed for victory;
I prayed for patience and for love,
  For true humility.
But as I prayed, my dying Christ
  By faith I seemed to see,
And as I gazed my glad heart cried,
  "All things are mine, thro' Thee!"

If He doth dwell within my heart,
  Why need I strength implore?
The Giver of all grace is mine,
  And shall I ask for more?
And need I pray for victory,
  When He who conquered death
Dwells in my very inmost soul,
  Nearer indeed than breath?

Oh help me, Lord, to realize
  That Thou art all in all;
That I am more than conqueror
  In great things and in small.
No need have I but Thou hast met
  Upon the cruel tree.
Oh precious, dying, risen Lord,
  Thou art my victory!

— *Avis B. Christiansen*

A HYMN FOR FAMILY WORSHIP

Saviour of them that trust in thee,
Once more, with supplicating cries,
We lift the heart and bend the knee,
And bid devotion's incense rise.

For mercies past we praise thee, Lord,
The fruits of earth, the hopes of
    heaven;
Thy helping arm, thy guiding Word,
And answered prayers, and sins for-
    given.

Whene'er we tread on danger's height
Or walk temptation's slippery way,
Be still, to steer our steps aright,
Thy Word our guide, thine arm our
    stay.

Be ours thy fear and favor still,
United hearts, unchanging love;
No scheme that contradicts thy will,
No wish that centres not above.

And since we must be parted here,
Support us when the hour shall come;
Wipe gently off the mourner's tear,
Rejoin us in our heavenly home.

— *Henry Alford*

∽

THANKFULNESS

I'm thankful for the hills from whence comes help from Thee,
The gracious hills of Olivet and Calvary.

I'm thankful for the streams where living waters flow
The streams of grace that make seeds, sown in deserts, grow.

I'm thankful for the light of stars and moon and sun,
The lights of love and truth from Thee, Most Holy One.

I'm thankful for the paths where I may follow Thee,
The paths of righteousness where walk the faithful free.

I'm thankful Father for Thy greatest gift to me,
The gift of Jesus Christ who brought me back to Thee.

— *Albert Leonard Murray*

SOVEREIGNTY

A ship set forth on a tranquil sea
    With its sails full-spread on the bending mast;
It sailed o'er the deep like a bird set free,
    And it reached its haven, all safe, at last;
Its voyage was ended in peace and calm
And the anchor was dropped with a praiseful psalm.

A ship set forth on a storm-tossed tide,
    And soon, the sails were all rent and torn;
One night the breakers were heard at the side
    And the rocks loomed out of the opening morn;
There was sudden shock, there were cries of pain,
And the great ship sank in the seething main.

There was One who sat on the heav'ly throne,
    With His eyes firm-fixt where the seas expand,
The winds were His servants and His alone,
    And the waters were held in His sovereign hand;
And He did what He pleased on the wide, wide sea;
And His name is — Infinite Mystery!

— Henry W. Frost

A VISION

O Son of God and Son of Man,
Who art enthroned in glory now,
Thou art the true and strong, who can
Make my proud heart before Thee bow;—
    I pray Thee bend me more and more
    Till Thee I worship and adore!

Thy throne is fixed on sea of glass
With emerald rainbow circling round;
Thy feet are like to burnished brass,
Thy voice is like to waters' sound;—
    Oh, speak Thy searching word to me
    And cleanse me from iniquity!

Thou art the One whose head is like
The whitened wool, the whiter snow,
And Thou the One whose eyes can strike
Deep terror, till the heart-tears flow;—
    O Christ, look down and let Thy fire
    Burn from my soul all low desire!

Thy face is like the mid-day sun,
And Thou dost bear the two-edged sword,
And Thou canst smite till life's undone,
And Thou canst shine till life's restored;—
O Christ, turn darkness into light
And change my wrong to conquering right!

So may I see Thee, Mighty Lord,
E'en though I fall before Thee dead,
Thee, only Thee, my Lord adored,
Who loved and pitied, died and bled;—
And may the vision never pass
Till I too stand on sea of glass!

— *Henry W. Frost*

THE LORD JEHOVAH REIGNS

The Lord Jehovah reigns,
  His throne is built on high;
The garments He assumes
  Are light and majesty:
His glories shine with beams so bright,
No mortal eye can bear the sight.

The thunders of His hand
  Keep the wide world in awe;
His wrath and justice stand
  To guard His holy law;
And where His love resolves to bless,
His truth confirms and seals the grace.

Through all His mighty works
  Amazing wisdom shines;
Confounds the powers of hell,
  And all their dark designs;
Strong is His arm, and shall fulfill
His great decrees and sovereign will.

And will this sovereign King
  Of glory condescend,
And will He write His name,
  My Father and my Friend?
I love His name, I love His Word;
Join all my powers to praise the Lord!

— *Isaac Watts*

TEACH ME, MY GOD AND KING

Teach me, my God and King,
  In all things thee to see;
And what I do in anything
  To do it as for thee!

A man that looks on glass,
  On it may stay his eye;
Or if he pleaseth, through it pass,
  And then the heavens espy.

All may of Thee partake;
  Nothing can be so mean,
Which with this tincture, "for thy
      sake,"
  Will not grow bright and clean.

A servant with this clause
  Makes drudgery divine;
Who sweeps a room, as for thy laws,
  Makes that and the action fine.

This is the famous stone
  That turneth all to gold;
For that which God doth touch and
      own
  Cannot for less be told.

— *George Herbert*

Amazing, Beauteous Change!

Amazing, beauteous change!
A world created new!
My thoughts with transport range,
The lovely scene to view;
    In all I trace,
    Saviour divine,
    The work is thine,—
    Be thine the praise!

See crystal fountains play
Amidst the burning sands;
The river's winding way
Shines through the thirsty lands;
    New grass is seen,
    And o'er the meads
    Its carpet spreads
    Of living green.

Where pointed brambles grew,
Intwined with horrid thorn,
Gay flowers, forever new,
The painted fields adorn,—
    The blushing rose
    And lily there,
    In union fair
    Their sweets disclose.

Where the bleak mountain stood,
All bare and disarrayed,
See the wide-branching wood
Diffuse its grateful shade;
    Tall cedars nod,
    And oaks and pines,
    And elms and vines
    Confess thee God.

The tyrants of the plain
Their savage chase give o'er,—
No more they rend the slain,
And thirst for blood no more;
    But infant hands
    Fierce tigers stroke,
    And lions yoke
    In flowery bands.

Oh, when, almighty Lord!
Shall these glad scenes arise,
To verify thy word,
And bless our wondering eyes?
    That earth may raise,
    With all its tongues,
    United songs
    Of ardent praise.

— Philip Doddridge

Giving to God

O Lord of heaven, and earth, and sea!
To thee all praise and glory be;
How shall we show our love to thee,
    Who givest all — who givest all?

The golden sunshine, vernal air,
Sweet flowers and fruit thy love declare;
When harvests ripen, thou art there,
    Who givest all — who givest all.

For peaceful homes and healthful days,
For all the blessings earth displays,
We owe thee thankfulness and praise,
    Who givest all — who givest all.

For souls redeemed, for sins forgiven,
For means of grace and hopes of heaven,
What can to thee, O Lord! be given,
    Who givest all — who givest all?

We lose what on ourselves we spend,
We have, as treasures without end,
Whatever, Lord, to thee we lend,
    Who givest all — who givest all.

Whatever, Lord, we lend to thee,
Repaid a thousand-fold will be;
Then gladly will we give to thee,
    Who givest all — who givest all.

— Christopher Wordsworth

FROM ALL THAT DWELL BELOW THE SKIES

From all that dwell below the skies
  Let the Creator's praise arise!
Let the Redeemer's name be sung
  Thro' every land, by every tongue!

Eternal are Thy mercies, Lord,
  Eternal truth attends Thy Word:
Thy praise shall sound from shore to
    shore
  Till suns shall rise and set no more.

  — *Isaac Watts*

ᘯ

EVENING HYMN OF THE ALPINE SHEPHERDS

Brothers, the day declines;
  Above, the glacier brightens;
Through hills of waving pines
  The "vesper halo" lightens!
Now wake the welcome chorus
  To him our sires adored;
To him who watcheth o'er us,—
  Ye shepherds, praise the Lord!

From each tower's embattled crest,
  The vesper-bell has tolled;
'Tis the hour that bringeth rest
  To the shepherd and his fold:
From hamlet, rock, and chalet
  Let our evening song be poured;
Till mountain, rock, and valley
  Re-echo, — Praise the Lord!

Praise the Lord, who made and gave us
  Our glorious mountain-land!
Who deigned to shield, and save us
  From the despot's iron hand:
With the bread of life he feeds us;
  Enlightened by his word,
Through pastures green he leads us,—
  Ye shepherds, praise the Lord!

And hark! below, aloft,
  From cliffs that pierce the cloud,
From blue lakes, calm and soft
  As a virgin in her shroud;
New strength our anthem gathers,
  From Alp to Alp 'tis poured;
So sang our sainted fathers,—
  Ye shepherds, praise the Lord!

Praise the Lord! from flood and fell
  Let the voice of old and young—
All the strength of Appenzel,
  True of heart, and sweet of tongue—
The grateful theme prolong
  With souls in soft accord,
Till yon stars take up our song,—
  Hallelujah to the Lord!

  — *William Beattie*

ᘯ

FILL ALL MY VISION

Fill all my vision, Saviour, I pray,
Let me see only Jesus today;
Tho' through the valley, Thou leadest
    me,
Thy fadeless glory encompasseth me.

Fill all my vision, every desire
Keep for Thy glory; my soul inspire
With Thy perfection, Thy holy love
Flooding my pathway with light from
    above.

Fill all my vision, let naught of sin
Shadow the brightness shining within.
Let me see only Thy blessed face,
Feasting my soul on Thy infinite grace.

Fill all my vision, Saviour divine,
Till with Thy glory my spirit shall
    shine.
Fill all my vision, that all may see
Thy Holy Image reflected in me.

  — *Avis B. Christiansen*

YE SERVANTS OF GOD

Ye servants of God, your Master proclaim,
And publish abroad His wonderful Name;
The Name all-victorious of Jesus extol;
His kingdom is glorious, and rules over all.

God ruleth on high, almighty to save;
And still He is nigh; His presence we have:
The great congregation His triumph shall sing,
Ascribing salvation to Jesus, our King.

"Salvation to God, who sits on the throne,"
Let all cry aloud, and honor the Son:
The praises of Jesus the angels proclaim,
Fall down on their faces, and worship the Lamb.

Then let us adore, and give Him His right,
All glory and power, all wisdom and might,
All honor and blessing, with angels above,
And thanks never ceasing for infinite love.

— Charles Wesley

WORK MOTIVE

Give me work to do, Dear Lord,
And strength that I may do it;
Grant the joy of honest toil,
And bless Thy people through it.

Some would toil for gold, or fame,
Or praise that they might hear it;
Grant that I may serve Thee, Lord,
Enabled by Thy Spirit.

If there is something hard, Dear Lord,
Give me the grace to try it.
I would give my best for Thee,
And offer worship by it.

To work for duty or for gold
Alone, could be work's treason;
But labor prompted by Thy love
Gives it its highest reason.

— Carlton Buck

THY MERCIES

When all Thy mercies, O my God,
My rising soul surveys,
Transported with the view, I'm lost
In wonder, love and praise.

Unnumbered comforts to my soul
Thy tender care bestowed,
Before my infant heart conceived
From whom those comforts flowed.

When worn with sickness, oft hast Thou
With health renewed my face,
And, when in sins and sorrows sunk,
Revived my soul with grace.

Ten thousand, thousand precious gifts
My daily thanks employ,
Nor is the least a cheerful heart
That tastes those gifts with joy.

— Joseph Addison

A Thanksgiving to God for His House

Lord, Thou hast given me a cell
 Wherein to dwell,
A little house, whose humble roof
 Is weather-proof,
Under the spars of which I lie
 Both soft and dry;
Where Thou, my chamber for to
  ward,
 Hast set a guard
Of harmless thoughts, to watch and
  keep
 Me while I sleep.
Low is my porch, as is my fate,
 Both void of state;
And yet the threshold of my door
 Is worn by th' poor,
Who thither come and freely get
 Good words or meat.
Like as my parlor so my hall
 And kitchen's small;
A little buttery, and therein
 A little bin,
Which keeps my little loaf of bread
 Unchipped, unflead;
Some little sticks of thorn or briar
 Make me a fire,
Close by whose living coal I sit,
 And glow like it.
Lord, I confess too, when I dine,
 The pulse is Thine,
And all those other bits that be
 There plac'd by Thee;
The worts, the purslain, and the mess
 Of water-cress,
Which of Thy kindness Thou hast
  sent;
 And my content
Makes those, and my beloved beet,
 To be more sweet.
'Tis Thou that crown'st my glittering
  hearth
 With guiltless mirth,

And giv'st me wassail bowls to drink,
 Spiced to the brink.
Lord, 'tis Thy plenty-dropping hand
 That soils my land,
And giv'st me, for my bushel sown,
 Twice ten for one;
Thou mak'st my teeming hen to lay
 Her egg each day;
Besides my healthful ewes to bear
 Me twins each year;
The while the conduits of my kine
 Run cream, for wine.
All these, and better Thou dost send
 Me, to this end,
That I should render for my part,
 A thankful heart,
Which, fir'd with incense, I resign,
 As wholly Thine;
But the acceptance, that must be,
 My Christ, by Thee.

      — *Robert Herrick*

Majesty of God

The Lord descended from above,
 And bowed the heavens most high,
And underneath his feet he cast
 The darkness of the sky.

On cherubim and seraphim
 Full royally he rode,
And on the wings of mighty winds
 Came flying all abroad.

He sat serene upon the floods,
 Their fury to restrain;
And he, as sovereign Lord and King,
 For evermore shall reign.

Give glory to his awful name,
 And honor him alone;
Give worship to his majesty,
 Upon his holy throne.

      — *T. Sternhold*

PRAISE

I hear ten thousand voices singing
   Their praises to the Lord on high;
Far distant shores and hills are ringing
   With anthems of their nation's joy:

Praise ye the Lord! for He hath given
   To lands in darkness hid, His light,
As morning rays light up the heaven,
   His word has chased away our night.

Hark! Hark! a louder sound is booming
   O'er heaven and earth, o'er land and sea;
The angel's trump proclaims His coming —
   Our day of endless Jubilee.

Hail to Thee, Lord! Thy people praise Thee;
   In every land Thy Name we sing;
On heaven's eternal throne upraise Thee,
   Take Thou Thy power, Thou glorious King!

                       — Author Unknown

THE ONE THOUSANDTH PSALM

O God, we thank Thee for everything.
For the sea and its waves, blue, green and gray and always wonderful;
For the beach and the breakers and the spray and the white foam on the rocks;
For the blue arch of heaven; for the clouds in the sky, white and gray and
     purple;
For the green of the grass; for the forests in their spring beauty; for the wheat
     and corn and rye and barley.
We thank Thee for all Thou hast made and that Thou hast called it good;
For all the glory and beauty and wonder of the world.
We thank Thee that Thou hast placed us in the world to subdue all things
     to Thy glory,
And to use all things for the good of Thy children.

                       — Edward Everett Hale

HIDDEN IN LIGHT

When first the sun dispels the cloudy night,
The glad hills catch the radiance from afar,
And smile for joy. We say, "How fair they are,
Tree, rock, and heather-bloom, so clear and bright!"
But when the sun draws near in westering might,
   Infolding all in one transcendent blaze
   Of sunset glow, we trace them not, but gaze
And wonder at the glorious, holy light.

Come nearer, Sun of Righteousness! that we,
  Whose swift short hours of day so swiftly run,
So overflowed with love and light may be,
  So lost in glory of the nearing Sun,
That not our light, but thine, the world may see,
  New praise to thee through our poor lives be won.
       — *Frances Ridley Havergal*

ADORATION

Joyful, joyful, we adore Thee,
  God of glory, Lord of love;
Hearts unfold like flowers before Thee,
  Opening to the sun above.
Melt the clouds of sin and sadness,
  Drive the dark of doubt away;
Giver of immortal gladness,
  Fill us with the light of day.

All Thy works with joy surround Thee,
  Earth and heaven reflect Thy rays,
Stars and angels sing around Thee,
  Center of unbroken praise.
Field and forest, vale and mountain,
  Flowery meadow, flashing sea,
Chanting bird and flowing fountain,
  Call us to rejoice in Thee.

Thou art giving and forgiving,
  Ever blessing, ever blest,
Wellspring of the joy of living,
  Ocean depth of happy rest!
Thou our Father, Christ our Brother,
  All who live in love are Thine;
Teach us how to love each other,
  Lift us to the Joy divine.

Mortals, join the happy chorus
  Which the morning stars began;
Father-love is reigning o'er us,
  Brother-love binds man to man.
Ever singing, march we onward,
  Victors in the midst of strife,
Joyful music leads us Sunward
  In the triumph song of life.
       — *Henry van Dyke*

FRAGRANCE

She brought her gift of worship to adorn
  The One she loved, and poured it on His brow —
That brow so soon to feel the platted thorn,
  The mockery of those who came to bow.

She brought her gift of service freely there
  And poured it out upon the Saviour's feet —
Those feet that had the piercing nails to bear,
  The journey to the cross — God's Mercy Seat.

And when the women came with burial token
  That dawn, she was not there among the rest . . .
The alabaster box already broken
  She had anointed Him and given her best:
The fragrance of her gift that filled the room
Had reached beyond the cross, beyond the tomb.
       — *Ruth Gibbs Zwall*

THE YOUTH OF JESUS

Shepherd of tender youth,
Guiding in love and truth,
  Through devious ways;
Christ, our triumphant King,
We come Thy name to sing;
Hither our children bring
  To sound Thy praise.

Thou art our holy Lord,
The all-subduing Word,
  Healer of strife;
Thou didst Thyself abase,
That from sin's deep disgrace
Thou mightest save our race,
  And give us life.

Ever be Thou our guide,
Our shepherd and our pride,
  Our staff and song;
Jesus, Thou Christ of God,
By Thy perennial word,
Lead us where Thou hast trod,
  Make our faith strong.

So now, and till we die,
Sound we Thy praises high,
  And joyful sing;
Let all the holy throng
Who to Thy church belong,
Unite and swell the song
  To Christ, our King.

— *Clement of Alexandria*

༄

ADORATION

Holy, holy, holy, Lord;
Mighty God, in glory living,
Sins and wanderings forgiving,
Love to needy men e'er giving;
Three in One and One in Three,
Holy, blessed Trinity.

Holy, holy, holy, Lord;
Father of the life supernal,
Source of all our pleasures vernal,
Author of our hope eternal;
Giver of all good art Thou,
At Thy feet we lowly bow.

Holy, holy, holy, Lord;
Son of God, heaven's splendor wearing,
Yet, as Man, our weakness sharing,
For our sakes the hard cross bearing;
Thou art Prophet, Priest and King;
To Thy throne our praise we bring.

Holy, holy, holy, Lord;
Gracious Spirit, true and tender,
Day by day our sweet befriender
And in need our strong defender,
Thee we fervently adore;
Oh, to love Thee more and more!

Holy, holy, holy, Lord;
Father, Son and Holy Spirit,
Thine the grace and Thine the merit,
We would all Thy gifts inherit,
Till in heaven we worship Thee,
Holy, blessed Trinity!

— *Henry W. Frost*

༄

THANKSGIVING

God of men of gentle grace,
God of men of radiant face.
God of men of valiant race,
We thank Thee!

God of men who do and dare,
God of men who burdens bear,
God of men who freely share,
We thank Thee!

God of men who truth proclaim,
God of men of selfless aim,
God of men who know Thy name,
We thank Thee!

— *Grenville Kleiser*

The Life of the Blessed

Region of life and light!
Land of the good whose earthly toils are o'er!
    Nor frost nor heat may blight
    Thy vernal beauty, fertile shore
Yielding thy blessed fruits for evermore!

    Might but a little part,
A wandering breath, of that high melody
    Descend into my heart,
    And change it till it be
Transformed and swallowed up, O Love! in thee:

    Ah! then my soul should know,
Beloved! where thou liest at noon of day;
    And from this place of woe
    Released, should take its way
To mingle with thy flock, and never stray.

— *Luis Ponce de Leon*

Orazione

One general song of praise arise
To him whose goodness ceaseless flows;
Who dwells enthroned beyond the skies,
And life and breath on all bestows!
Great Source of intellect, his ear,
Benign receives our vows sincere:
Rise then, my active powers, your task fulfill,
And give to him your praise, responsive to my will!

Eternal Spirit, whose command
Light, life, and being gave to all,
Oh, hear the creature of thy hand,
Man, constant on thy goodness call!
By fire, by water, air, and earth,
That soul to thee that owes its birth —
By these he supplicates thy blest repose:
Absent from thee, no rest his wandering spirit knows!

— *Verses selected from "Orazione" by Lorenzo de' Medici*
(Translated by William Roscoe)

THY KINGDOM COME

Thou hope of all the lowly!
    To thirsting souls how kind!
Gracious to all who seek Thee,
    Oh, what to those who find!

My tongue but lisps Thy praises,
    Yet praise be my employ;
Love makes me bold to praise Thee,
    For Thou art all my joy.

In Thee my soul delighting,
    Findeth her only rest;
And so in Thee confiding,
    May all the world be blest!

Dwell with us, and our darkness
    Will flee before Thy light;
Scatter the world's deep midnight,
    And fill it with delight.

O all mankind! behold Him,
    And seek His love to know;
And let your hearts, in seeking,
    Be fired with love and glow!

O come, O come, great Monarch!
    Eternal glory Thine;
The longing world waits for Thee:
    Arise, arise and shine!

— *St. Bernard of Clairvaux*

ᴄᴧᴐ

HOW TEDIOUS AND TASTELESS THE
HOURS

How tedious and tasteless the hours
    When Jesus no longer I see;
Sweet prospects, sweet birds, and sweet
        flowers
    Have all lost their sweetness to me;
The midsummer sun shines but dim,
    The fields strive in vain to look gay;
But when I am happy in Him,
    December's as pleasant as May.

His Name yields the richest perfume,
    And sweeter than music His voice;
His presence disperses my gloom,
    And makes all within me rejoice;
I should, were He always thus nigh,
    Have nothing to wish or to fear;
No mortal so happy as I,
    My summer would last all the year.

Content with beholding His face,
    My all to His pleasure resigned,
No changes of season or place
    Would make any change in my
        mind:
While blest with a sense of His love,
    A palace a toy would appear;
And prisons would palaces prove,
    If Jesus would dwell with me there.

— *John Newton*

ᴄᴧᴐ

From THE EVERLASTING MERCY

I did not think, I did not strive,
The deep peace burnt my me alive;
The bolted door had broken in,
I knew that I had done with sin.
I knew that Christ had given me birth
To brother all the souls on earth,
And every bird and every beast
Should share the crumbs broke at the
    feast.

O glory of the lighted mind.
How dead I'd been, how dumb, how
    blind.
The station brook, to my new eyes,
Was babbling out of Paradise,
The waters rushing from the rain
Were singing Christ has risen again.
I thought all earthly creatures knelt
From rapture of the joy I felt.

— *John Masefield*

THOU DEAR REDEEMER

Thou dear Redeemer, dying Lamb,
  I love to hear of Thee;
No music's like Thy charming Name,
  Nor half so sweet can be.

My Jesus shall be still my theme,
  While in this world I stay;
I'll sing my Jesus' lovely Name
  When all things else decay.

When I appear in yonder cloud,
  With all Thy favored throng,
Then will sing more sweet, more loud,
  And Christ shall be my song.

            — *John Cennick*

LUTHER'S HYMN

A safe stronghold our God is still,
  A trusty shield and weapon;
He'll help us clear from all the ill
  That hath us now o'ertaken.
    The ancient Prince of hell
    Hath risen with purpose fell;
  Strong mail of craft and power
  He weareth in this hour;
On earth is not his fellow.

With force of arms we nothing can,
  Full soon were we down-ridden;
But for us fights the proper Man,
  Whom God himself hath bidden.
    Ask ye, who is this same?
    Christ Jesus is his name,
  The Lord Zebaoth's Son,
  He and no other one
Shall conquer in the battle.

And were this world all devils o'er,
  And watching to devour us,
We lay it not to heart so sore,
  Not they can overpower us.
    And let the Prince of ill
    Look grim as e'er he will,

He harms us not a whit:
  For why? His doom is writ,
One little word shall slay him.

That word, for all their craft and force,
  One moment will not linger,
But, spite of hell, shall have its course,
  'Tis written by his finger.
    And though they take our life,
    Goods, honor, children, wife,
  Yet is their profit small;
  These things shall vanish all,
The city of God remaineth.

            — *Martin Luther*

WORSHIP AND THANKS TO HIM BELONG

Come, let us tune our loftiest song,
  And raise to Christ our joyful strain;
Worship and thanks to Him belong,
  Who reigns, and shall forever reign.

His sovereign power our bodies made;
  Our soul are His immortal breath;
And when His creatures sinned, He
    bled,
  To save us from eternal death.

Extol the Lamb with loftiest song,
  Ascend for Him our cheerful strain;
Worship and thanks to Him belong,
  Who reigns, and shall forever reign.

            — *Robert A. West*

SUNRISE

Though the midnight found us weary,
  The morning brings us cheer;
Thank God for every sunrise
  In the circuit of the year.

            — *Margaret E. Sangster*

PRAISE

Do you hear the angels singing
  Up on high?
Do you hear their voices ringing
  Through the sky?
  Oh, the fulness of their songs
  As their praises they prolong,
  Yea, the voices of that choir
  Never tire!

Do you hear the saints all praising
  Round the throne?
Do you hear them hymns upraising,
  One by one?
  Praising is their glad delight,
  So they rest not day nor night,
  Crying, "Holy!" o'er and o'er,
  Evermore!

Do you hear the saints adoring
  Here below?
Do you hear them praise outpouring
  Midst earth's woe?
  Hark, they sing their sweet refrain
  Thro' their joy and thro' their pain,
  Praising, ever, in their love,
  God above!

Oh, then, add your note, rejoicing,
  To the praise,
Thanks to God for all things voicing,
  Through the days;
  Till the earthly singing's done,
  Till the heavenly is begun,
  Till the anthem, round Christ's feet,
  Swells complete!
          — *Henry W. Frost*

ᕠᕫ

THE CELL

When from the hush of this cool wood
  I go, Lord, to the noisy mart,
Give me among the multitude,
  I pray, a lonely heart.

Yes, build in me a secret cell
  Where quietness shall be a song:
In that green solitude I'll dwell,
  And praise Thee all day long.

          — *George Rostrevor Hamilton*

ᕠᕫ

COMMUNION HYMN

O my soul, do thou keep silence,
  Here thou meetest with thy God,
Come and feast, in sweet reliance,
  But with spirit bowed and awed;
Hush the voice and still the mind,
Here thou wilt thy Saviour find.

O my soul, do thou remember
  This is sacred, holy ground,
Sign of when Christ's every member
  On the cruel cross was found,
There He died in agony;—
Come, then, humbly, gratefully.

O my soul, be thou preparing,
  It is Christ who welcomes thee,
Richest blessing with thee sharing,
  Foretaste of eternity;
He doth grant thee heavenly food,
Giving thee His flesh and blood.

O my soul, thy sins forsaking
  In remembrance of Christ's love,
From this food new vigor taking,
  Set thy face toward things above;
Christ is here thy life to win,
And to free thee from all sin.

O my soul, feast on, believing,
  Eat the bread and drink the wine,
In these tokens Christ perceiving,
  Worship Him, and make Him
    thine;—
Then arise with grateful song
Since thou dost to Christ belong!

          — *Henry W. Frost*

JESUS CHRIST THE LORD

Saviour, blessed Saviour,
　Listen while we sing,
Hearts and voices raising
　Praises to our King.
All we hope we offer,
　All we hope to be,
Body, soul, and spirit,
　All we yield to Thee.

Nearer, ever nearer,
　Christ, we draw to Thee,
Deep in adoration
　Bending low the knee:
Thou for our redemption
　Cam'st on earth to die;
Thou, that we might follow,
　Hast gone up on high.

Clearer still, and clearer,
　Dawns the light from heaven,
In our sadness bringing
　News of sins forgiven;
Life has lost its shadows;
　Pure the light within;
Thou hast shed Thy radiance
　On a world of sin.

Great, and ever greater,
　Are Thy mercies here;
True and everlasting
　Are the glories there,
Where no pain or sorrow,
　Toil or care, is known,
Where the angel legions
　Circle round Thy throne.

　　　　— Godfrey Thring

THE HOMEMAKER

Dear Master, I would tarry long
　In worship at Thy feet,
As Mary, at Thy footstool sit
　And hold communion sweet;
But Lord, I have a house to keep —
　I may not longer stay;
For who would lay the breakfast out,
　Or clear the things away?

I meet Thee in the morning hour
　After the fires are lit,
And precious are the moments then
　As at Thy feet I sit;
But I must haste away so soon
　To make the toast and tea —
Since I can sit no longer, Lord,
　Wilt Thou not walk with me?

For I have but a Martha's task —
　My busy days slip by
Washing and ironing, getting meals,
　Making the cobwebs fly;
But while I go about my work
　Hustling to and fro,
May I not keep my tryst with Thee
　And worship as I go?

So as I scour the pots and pans
　And make the kitchen shine,
I may commune with Thee, dear Lord,
　And know Thy presence mine.
I fellowship with her of old
　Who chose the better part,
For tho' I must have Martha's hands,
　I may have Mary's heart.

　　　　— E. Margaret Clarkson

INDEX OF SUBJECTS

INDEX OF AUTHORS

INDEX OF TITLES AND FIRST LINES